AUTOBIOGRAPHY

OF A PEOPLE

AUTOBIOGRAPHY

OF A PEOPLE

Three Centuries of African American History

Told by Those Who Lived It

Herb Boyd

DOUBLEDAY

New York   London   Toronto   Sydney   Auckland

PUBLISHED BY DOUBLEDAY

a division of Random House, Inc.

1540 Broadway, New York, New York 10036

DOUBLEDAY and the portrayal of an anchor with a dolphin are
trademarks of Doubleday, a division of Random House, Inc.

Book design by Richard Oriolo

Grateful acknowledgment is made for permission to reprint copyrighted material.
Every reasonable effort has been made to trace the ownership of all copyrighted
material included in this volume. Any errors that may have occurred are inadvertent
and will be corrected in subsequent editions, provided notification is sent
to the publisher.

Acknowledgments for individual pieces appear on pages 546–49.

LIBRARY OF CONGRESS CATALOGING-IN-PUBLICATION DATA

Autobiography of a people: three centuries of African American
history told by those who lived it / Herb Boyd. — 1st ed.

p.   cm.

Includes bibliographical references.

1. Afro-Americans—History Sources. 2. Afro-Americans Biography.

I. Boyd, Herb, 1938–

E185.A97   2000

973'.0496073—dc21   99-16576

CIP

ISBN 0-385-49278-2
February 2000
First Edition

1   3   5   7   9   10   8   6   4   2

To my mother.

And to Dr. John Henrik Clarke, Gordon Parks, and Dr. Charshee McIntyre,

whose lives taught me how to live.

ACKNOWLEDGMENTS

It is not possible to acknowledge all those who have helped in this project, but the first on the list, like charity, begins at home. For most of her life, my mother has been a hardworking domestic who sacrificed everything to raise her children. No matter how sick or tired, she rarely ever missed a day of work and was nearly always on time. Along with the lessons she gave us through books, there were the more important lessons of her life—her commitment, her word, her determination to complete any task she started. My wife, Elza, possesses some of these same attributes, and so the discipline my mother instilled continues, as my companion makes sure assignments are kept, each project polished and refined.

Then comes a parade of thoughtful and productive associates—my agent, Marie Brown, who has dutifully shepherded this book and others to contract and completion; to my editors, Stephanie Rosenfeld and Roger Scholl, who believed in this pursuit right from the start and have been unflagging in their devotion. Toward the end of the project when the dauntless task of gathering permissions loomed, Marci Bell was indispensable, tracking down hard-to-find authors and publishers. Also thanks to Allison Warner.

Early on, I benefited from a number of librarians, particularly Sharon Howard and the staff at the Schomburg Research Center in Harlem. Each query I presented was diligently pursued and without them many of the obscure titles would have never been found.

Several friends warrant praise for just being a part of my daily life, keeping me on point, and delivering the incidental bits and pieces of advice, information, and spiritual nourishment we all need to get by. Among these treasured "partners" are Don Rojas, Robert Van Lierop, Robert Allen, Malik Chaka, Playthell Benjamin, David Ritz, Ron Lockett, Ron Williams, Elinor Tatum, Tonya Bolden, Clarence Atkins, Quincy Troupe, Richard Davis, Charles Moore, Akiba Solomon, Bill Katz, Akinshiju Ola, Aziz Adetimirin, Chris Griffith, Kenny Meeks, Richard Muhammad, Hilly Saunders, Conrad Muhammad, Eugene Redmond, Steve Chennault, Cleophus Roseboro, J. P. Lutcher, Alton Maddox, and Louis DeSalle.

But after all is said and done, only I am responsible for whatever miscues make it to print, though I would gladly welcome any of my partners to help shoulder the blame.

CONTENTS

Foreword   xvii

Introduction   1

Part I.

PRE-REVOLUTIONARY VOICES

James Albert Ukawsaw Gronniosaw (1710–?)   17

Olaudah Equiano (1745–1797)   22

Phillis Wheatley (1753–1784)   29

Lemuel Haynes (1753–1833)   31

John Cuffe (c. 1755–?)   34

Part II.

THE LORD WILL PROVIDE

Richard Allen (1760–1831)   41

Old Elizabeth (1766–?)   44

Jupiter Hammon (c.1711–1806)   48

Belinda (c. 1717–?)   50

Benjamin Banneker (1731–1806)   52

Prince Hall (1748–1797)   56

Part III.

FROM THE COTTON PATCH TO THE BIG HOUSE

Jenny Proctor (c. 1845–?)   61

Peter Williams (?–1849)   65

Abd ar-Rahman (c. 1790–?)   68

Austin Steward (1793–1860)   70

Part IV.

LET YOUR MOTTO BE RESISTANCE!

Nat Turner (1800–1831)   81

Henry Highland Garnet (1815–1882)   86

Harriet Jacobs (1815?–1897)   90

Frederick Douglass (1818–1895)   93

John Parker (1827–1900)   97

Osborne Anderson (1830–1872)   103

Part V.

CAUGHT BETWEEN THE BLUE AND THE GRAY

Mattie J. Jackson (1800–?)   113

William Wells Brown (1814–1884)   118

Robert Purvis (1810–1898)   120

Harriet Tubman (1820–1913)   121

Elizabeth Keckley (1824–1907)   122

John Boston (c. 1842–?)   126

Charlotte Forten (1837–1914)   127

Ann (c. 1835–?)   132

Octave Johnson (1840–?)   133

Patsey Leach (1843–?)   134

Part VI.

NO LAND, NO MULES, AND FOR MILLIONS, NO VOTE

John Mercer Langston (1829–1879)   139

Sojourner Truth (c.1797–1883)   144

Samuel Larkin (c. 1840–?) 146

John R. Lynch (1847–1939) 148

Part VII.

DAWN OF A NEW CENTURY

Booker T. Washington (1857?–1915) 155

Lewis Latimer (1848–1928) 161

Henry McNeal Turner (1834–1915) 164

Anna Julia Cooper (1858/9–1964) 168

Mary Church Terrell (1863–1954) 171

Paul Laurence Dunbar (1872–1906) 175

Alice Moore Dunbar-Nelson (1875–1935) 177

Part VIII.

AND SOME OF US ARE BOLD

James Weldon Johnson (1871–1938) 185

W. E. B. Du Bois (1868–1963) 191

Ida B. Wells Barnett (1862–1931) 198

Matthew Henson (1866–1955) 204

Ferdinand "Jelly Roll" Morton (1890–1941) 207

Jack Johnson (1878–1946) 211

Ethel Waters (1896–1977) 215

Part IX.

SEEKING A WIDER WORLD

Addie Hunton (1875–1943) 223

Harry Haywood (1898–1985) 226

Era Bell Thompson (1906–1986) 229

Dorothy West (1909–1998) 234

Richard Wright (1908–1960) 237

Marcus Garvey (1887–1940) 244

Part X.

THE HARLEM RENAISSANCE AND BEYOND

Langston Hughes (1898–1967) 251

Howard "Stretch" Johnson (1915–) 257

Zora Neale Hurston (1891–1960) 262

Paulí Murray (1910–1985) 266

Nate Shaw (c. 1900–) 272

Haywood Patterson (1913–1952) 276

James Cameron (1914–) 280

Adam Clayton Powell, Jr. (1908–1972) 285

Part XI.

ON THE HOME FRONT

Conrad Lynn (1908–1995) 295

Marian Anderson (1900–1993) 298

Nelson Peery (1923–) 301

Althea Gibson (1927–) 305

A. Philip Randolph (1889–1979) 309

Clarence Atkins (1922–) 313

Charles Denby (1907–1983) 317

Maya Angelou (1928–) 323

Coleman Young (1918–1998) 326

Part XII.

THE CALM BEFORE THE STORM

Curtis Morrow (1933–   )   335

Jane (1914–   )   340

Paul Robeson (1898–1976)   343

Sunnie Wilson (1908–1999)   350

Coretta Scott King (1927–   )   355

Constance Baker Motley (1921–   )   360

Part XIII.

AIN'T GONNA LET NOBODY TURN US AROUND

Rosa Parks (1913–   )   369

Ella Baker (1903–1986)   371

James Forman (1928–   )   375

Melba Pattillo Beals (1942–   )   379

Part XIV.

BREAKTHROUGHS AND PERSONAL INTIMACIES

Ossie Davis (1917–   ) and Ruby Dee (1924–   )   389

Anne Moody (1940–   )   394

Sharon Robinson (1950–   )   398

Malcolm X (1925–1965)   401

General Gordon Baker (1942–   )   407

Gordon Parks (1912–   )   409

David Parks (1944–   )   414

Part XV.

TO DIE FOR THE PEOPLE

Kwame Ture (1941–1998)   421

Martin Luther King, Jr. (1929–1968)   427

H. Rap Brown (1943–)   434

Angela Davis (1944–)   438

George Jackson (1941–1971)   441

Elaine Brown (1943–)   445

Randall Robinson (1941–)   448

Part XVI.

A WAY WITH WORDS

LL Cool J (1968–)   455

Johnnie Cochran (1938–)   459

Margaret Walker (1915–)   462

Lee Stringer (1950–)   468

Sam Fulwood (1956–)   471

Tyrone Powers (1961–)   474

Part XVII.

BITTER THE CHASTENING ROD

Audre Lorde (1934–1993)   481

Jill Nelson (1953–)   486

Johnnetta B. Cole (1936–)   490

Max Roach (1924–)   494

Alvin Ailey (1931–1989)   497

Colin L. Powell (1937–)   500

Part XVIII.

''NO JUSTICE, NO PEACE!''

Al Sharpton (1954–   )   507

Bari-Ellen Roberts (1953–   )   511

Anita Hill (1950–   )   516

Gary Franks (1953–   )   522

James McBride (1957–   )   527

Mumia Abu-Jamal (1956–   )   531

Kevin Powell (1966–   )   533

Rev. Bernice King (1963–   )   538

Selected Bibliography   544

Permissions   546

FOREWORD

For centuries the clock has moved on, and relentlessly the Black struggle against racism has moved with it. There have been times however when the ferocity of that struggle seemed to be fading. But history assures us that hope will keep turning up in our diaries. Neither hatred, bigotry, nor lynching trees have been able to halt its flowing. Inexhaustible, it is still running through time, refusing to be rubbed off the pages of African American history.

Autobiography of a People sends me wandering backward to a past that, at times, amounted to a Black man and woman's prison. But it also acquaints me with an eloquent gathering of powerful voices that emerge as one to help the disadvantaged to keep their lives moving. Strangers to weeping, the authors here are involved with turning out our dreams. Having knocked on so many doors that refused to open, they realized what they had to do, then did it. Drawing from the deep wells of their own lives, they ensnare you then suck you into the shadows of their most disgruntled years—while asking for no more than the justice of equality. A talk with their dark past sheds light upon our future. And after questioning a good number of them I find their answers are uncompromising and a formidable truth to power. To rise is to suffer, and outdistancing those born with white skin is still a problem for Black survival. With a delicate blend of suspicion and hostility, we watch closely as history hands out its shrouds and medals with feeble uncertainty.

Of this corpus of authors and personalities, Herb Boyd admits to a dilemma of choice, and possibly to sins of omissions. But this "broad arbitrary cloth" he stitched together doesn't ask for apologies. It generously served its intention—to produce a powerful anthology of a beleaguered race as it struggles through three centuries of inequality. He explains that there is a clear rationale for each choice. But just about everybody who deserved to be there is there. Olaudah Equiano and Ukkasaw Groniossaw introduce us to the African past. Linda Brent (Harriet Jacobs) takes us on a precipitous journey from slavery to freedom. Then along with many others, Maya Angelou and Richard Wright confront the shadowy miscellany of those who wish all Black faces ill. Beyond these and several who have died, others are still climbing those consequential hills—climbing, climbing endlessly over those who conspire to hold them back.

In the full light of so many excruciating years, these voices should pull our tired bones even closer together. So close that it becomes a unified chorus, a seamless cry of hope and fulfillment from Equiano to Bernice King, from the dark African past to the bright African American future.

—GORDON PARKS,
New York, 1999

AUTOBIOGRAPHY

OF A PEOPLE

INTRODUCTION

"My race needs no special defense, for the past history of them in this country proves them to be equal of any people anywhere. All they need is an equal chance in the battle of life."
—Inscribed on a monument to Robert Smalls in Beaufort, South Carolina

THERE IS PROBABLY NO BETTER TIME TO reflect on the past than at the dawn of a new millennium. On this propitious occasion we should remember the long and "stony road we trod," the unwavering determination to survive—and to prevail—no matter the pain or obstacles. The story of African American people is a glorious one, replete with a pantheon of mighty voices and courageous souls who in their combined strength have overcome inestimable odds and carved a special niche in the gallery of world culture.

A sterling testimony to some of those momentous events is gathered between these covers. Though these eyewitnesses have been recorded before, it's never been with the purpose of meshing their firsthand accounts and their precious memories in a seamless way as if they were a single voice. From the heartfelt laments for their homeland of Olaudah Equiano and the slave Belinda at the end of the eighteenth century, to Bernice King's recent exhortation to reclaim our splendid heritage, this book offers a veritable cornucopia of remembrances. Taken from slave narratives, autobiographies, diaries, memoirs, letters, and speeches, these excerpts often address a common theme—the struggle for freedom and self-determination. They passionately denounce racism and white supremacy, their authors expressing their frustration in varying degrees of eloquence and opprobrium.

When Thomas Jefferson asserted African Americans were incapable of "tracing and comprehending the investigations of Euclid," he aroused an emerging black intelligentsia led by such thinkers as Benjamin Banneker, who amassed an impressive collection of documents and projects—including his

Almanacs, which could not have been completed without a thorough background in spherical trigonometry—to refute the founding father's pronouncements. And Banneker was just one of several black intellectuals of the eighteenth century whose achievements stand in marked contrast to the racist dogma that ridiculed and condemned them as inferior human beings. Even as the cornerstone of the republic was being laid, black Americans knew it was imperative to counter the stigma of inferiority, to challenge the widespread notion that they were "brutish, stupid, ignorant, idle, crafty, and libidinous." Early examples of black genius extend from the medicinal research of Dr. James Derham, whose work was commended by the esteemed Dr. Benjamin Rush, to the astounding mathematical calculations of the slave Thomas Fuller. The story goes that Fuller's abilities were so phenomenal that when challenged to calculate the number of seconds a man has lived when age seventy years, seventeen days, and twelve seconds, he responded after only a few minutes of thought. When his examiners smugly dismissed his answer as incorrect, Fuller pointed out that they had failed to account for leap years.[1]

Richard Allen, Absolom Jones, Paul Cuffe, Prince Hall, James Forten, and David Walker were others who vigorously opposed the pseudoscientific premise that "Negroes" should be consigned to the lower rungs of the Great Chain of Being, just a peg above the monkeys and orangutans. The self-taught Walker expressed his rage against racism and slavery in a searing *Appeal,* which was so explosive that even the most militant abolitionists rejected the violence it advocated. "I will stand my ground," Walker wrote. "Somebody must die in this cause. I may be doomed to the stake and the fire or to the scaffold tree, but it is not in me to falter if I can promote the work of emancipation." Whether with Banneker's moral suasion and indignation or Walker's fiery rhetoric, African Americans began to voice their protest. In these selections, the outrage against racism and discrimination usually vacillates between these two polarities, given the era or geographic location in which the person lived.

Even more distressing to black Americans during the embryonic phase of the nation's development was the formation of an immoral legal process and an unfair system of justice. In South Carolina, Virginia, Massachusetts, New York, and Pennsylvania the social and political foundation of slavery emerged, leading to a legal system that would entrench the "peculiar institution" for more than 250 years. And this legal process, writes A. Leon Higginbotham, Jr., "has never been devoid of values, preferences, or policy position. By the very nature of its pronouncements, when the legal process establishes a right for one particular person, group, or institution, it simultaneously imposes a restraint on those whose preferences impinge on the right established. Ultimately, the legal process has always acted as an expression of social control."[2] It was the imposition of such an oppressive system with its draconian edicts that compelled Bishop Henry McNeal Turner and other black nationalists to seek alternatives beyond these shores. Having lost all faith in the creed so central to the Declaration of Independence and the Constitution, they revived the "back to Africa" movement proposed in the early years of the eighteenth century by the American Colonization Society and Paul Cuffe, who in 1815 at his own expense took thirty-eight black Americans to settle in West Africa. These emigrationists were deeply dismayed by a system of justice that gave them no recourse under the law and provided them no relief in the country's highest court. "The Supreme Court," Turner asserted, "is an organized mob against the negro, and every subordinate court in the land has caught its spirit."

Racial humiliation, of course, was not limited to the courts; it was part and parcel of governmental policy of varying degrees of hostility against its sable citizens, expressed most harshly in the Southern states that gradually evolved from a brutal slavocracy to a more benign but no less restrictive Jim Crowism. The "grandfather clause," poll taxes, and literacy tests were just some of the means used to keep African Americans from the voting booths, and if these "black codes" failed there was always outright terrorism from the Ku Klux Klan and other night riders to challenge even the boldest of those who would defy the rules of disenfranchisement.

An option for many black Americans unwilling to endure America's apartheid was migration, first from one part of the South to another, and then westward. But this resulted in little more success than the folly of emigrationism. Hitching your fortune and fate to a wagon train bound for Oklahoma and Kansas was hardly any better than chancing the turbulent waters of the Atlantic and then attempting to hack out an existence in the often inhospitable environment of West Africa. "The debate over migration waned as the movement suddenly lost momentum," Professor Benjamin Quarles concludes in *The Negro in the Making of America,* "for word was seeping back that the migrants were faring badly. Those who went to Kansas found the weather was cold and that jobs were few. White workers voiced their fears that the black migrants would bring about a lowering of wages. The mayor of St. Louis issued a proclamation advising Negroes without money to avoid the city."[3]

Despite countless reasons to pack up and go, most African Americans held their ground, determined to struggle where they were against racism, no matter how pernicious. As you read these excerpts you will discover the inexhaustible tact and ingenuity black men and women have used to deflect or nullify this social disease.

Among the most gallant warriors for freedom and equality have been black women; their powerful and inspiring stories abound in this collection. Sojourner Truth, Ida B. Wells, Anna Julia Cooper, Ella Baker, Angela Davis, Coretta Scott King, Audre Lorde, Anita Hill, and Johnnetta Cole are a few of the better-known voices who join in a righteous chorus of indignation. But there are others, too, such as Jenny Proctor, whose reminiscences of slavery are as poignant as they are uplifting.

Ms. Proctor is one of many strong black women who were at the core of the plantation system, and across the years she and her sisters in the struggle were prominent fixtures in practically every historical watershed. From the Revolutionary era we gather a bit of the complexity and ambiguity of the gifted Phillis Wheatley. Harriet Jacobs provides authentic and startling images of slave life at the edge; Mattie Jackson observes with telling detail events of the Civil War; and Elizabeth Keckley affords us an insider's view of the White House during the Lincoln administration. From Charlotte Forten's diary we have a brief impression of "Jubilee," when the Emancipation Proclamation was made official on January 1, 1863. "The most glorious day this nation has yet seen, I think." Other memorable moments in the nation's later history are recorded by Addie Hunton, Mary Church Terrell, Maya Angelou, Rosa Parks, Constance Baker Motley, and Elaine Brown.

The voices of black women are given added resonance when joined with their male counterparts. Letters between Alice Dunbar-Nelson and Paul Laurence Dunbar are a harbinger to the intimacy, later shared by Angela Davis and George Jackson, and Coretta Scott King and Martin Luther King, Jr. Particularly warm and insightful are the exchanges between Ossie Davis and Ruby Dee; for more than fifty years their love has forged a productive partnership. In the excerpt here, however, they do not discuss the source of their longevity together but rather their involvement in a major breakthrough in the theater— Lorraine Hansberry's A Raisin in the Sun.

But with each major breakthrough there was often a terrible setback. For every step gained on the civil rights battlefield, black Americans were forced to take two steps back in the terror-filled South and parts of the North. At about the same time Charles Mitchell, a certified public accountant and banker, was named minister to Liberia, James Cameron was watching his friends being lynched and worrying about his own neck in Marion, Indiana. His excerpt is among more harrowing incidents in Autobiography of a People.

Cameron miraculously survived this ordeal, but so many others, unlawfully jailed and hounded by the Ku Klux Klan, were not so fortunate. Then there were those who were able to fight back, like the late Coleman Young, former mayor of Detroit, who encountered hostility when he called for a demonstration and a plan for black homeowners to buy and fix up the houses in a white neighborhood. Rather than back down when threatened by their new neighbors, these families led by Young moved into their new homes with shotguns, prepared to defend their right to live where they pleased. Young may have gotten the inspiration for his act from Dr. Ossian Sweet. In 1925, Dr. Sweet and his wife moved into an all-white neighborhood on Detroit's eastside.

Anticipating trouble, several of Dr. Sweet's friends spent the night with the couple. No police officers were stationed in the vicinity. According to news accounts, Sweet and his guests opened fire on a mob of whites who had gathered around the house. Sweet asserted they fired only when rocks crashed through the windows. When the disturbance subsided, one white man was dead and another injured.[4] Sweet, his wife, and their ten friends were taken to police headquarters. After a memorable trial with the famed attorney Clarence Darrow leading their defense team, the Sweet family and the others were acquitted in one of those rare instances in American jurisprudence where African Americans' right to self-defense was upheld.

Such audacity as demonstrated by the actions of Young and Sweet is not uncommon in the odyssey of black Americans. In *Autobiography of a People* there are a number of such dramatic encounters. James Carney, Nelson Peery, Curtis Murrow, David Parks, and Colin Powell are among the uniformed heroes who recall the dangers of war, when black soldiers distinguished themselves beyond the call of duty. Nat Turner and Matthew Henson record spine-tingling, bloodcurdling tales that rarely appear in our history books. Although every school kid knows that Admiral Peary "discovered" the North Pole, they know nothing of the black man who accompanied him and played such a vital role in this success. Nor are many Americans aware of York, the black slave who traveled with Lewis and Clark during their explorations of the West. York's hunting and linguistic skills—which he used to assist Sacagewea, the Shoshone woman, in translations—and his role as an "ambassador" were indispensable for the success of the expedition.[5] Henson and York personify the loyal sidekicks for famous explorers, much in the same way Estevanico (Little Stephen) was for Cortez and Pedro Alonso Nino for Columbus. And even if Nino was not an African as has been claimed, "there were many Negroes who accompanied other European explorers to the New World," John Hope Franklin summarizes in *From Slavery to Freedom*. "As early as 1501, Spain relinquished her earlier ban and permitted Negroes to go into the Spanish lands in the New World. Thirty Negroes, including Nuflo de Olano, were with Balboa when he discovered the Pacific Ocean."[6] The fact that Africans accompanied the plundering conquistadors, however, does not make them heroes in most historical accounts. Like the famed "Buffalo Soldiers," the black cavalrymen assigned to pacify the indigenous people out West, these adventurers are unworthy of glorification.

In *Autobiography of a People,* I have rounded up the usual suspects; the majority of the excerpts are from people who have scratched their names in the sands of time—Frederick Douglass, Booker T. Washington, W. E. B. Du Bois, Marcus Garvey, James Weldon Johnson, Richard Wright, Zora Neale Hurston, Langston Hughes, Gordon Parks, Malcolm X, Adam Clayton Powell, Jr., and Martin Luther King, Jr. It should come as no surprise that it is usually the famous who have the time and wherewithal to write an autobiography. But it is the coterie of unknown informants who are the most essential to the completion of this tapestry of black autobiography.

I have tried to include enough "drylongso," or ordinary folks, and their memories assembled here to project some semblance of black America's wide diversity of experience and recollection. Certainly, Nate Shaw, Charles Denby, Octave Cooper, Clarence Atkins, and Howard Johnson are ordinary people with extraordinary achievements and wonderful stories to tell.

Several themes are repeated throughout the testimonies. In many, religion and work are pivotal. African captives brought to the so-called New World for their labor often depended upon their religions, or their adaptation of the oppressors' forms of worship, for succor and possible salvation. Nary an excerpt is without some mention of labor or God, and this is particularly true of the early narratives where spiritual themes are so prevalent. In this regard we might ask, as John Henrik Clarke does in "Africans at the Crossroads—Notes for an African World Revolution," "What kind of religion did African people have before Judaism, Christianity, and Islam? How did African people determine right from wrong before these religions appeared in Africa? These religions, all made from elements of our own spirituality—dressed up, garnished and brought back to us and sold to us as something original—when there's nothing original in any of the three. . . . Religion or spirituality (the more correct term) was part of the totality of our life. It wasn't a Sunday occurrence; it was a total occurrence."[7] Certainly, a minority of African captives struggled devoutly to hold on to their traditional spirituality, but it was apparently much easier to accept the oppressors' Christianity, although not without modification. The African captives resorted to an array of tactics to retain their gods and spirituality while worshipping the master's imposed religion. Sometimes to retain *orishas* (deities) it was necessary to equate them with a Christian saint, that is, merge the essence of Dumballah, the snake god, with St. Patrick who rid Ireland of snakes. A similar syncretism might occur with St. Anthony, the keeper of the keys and the Yoruba deity, Legba. Thus, during the worship, it was hard for the master to know exactly which god or saint was being supplicated.

"The Negro has not been Christianized as extensively as is generally believed," Zora Neale Hurston observed. "The great masses are still standing before their pagan altars and calling old gods by a new name . . . so the congregation is restored to its primitive altars under a new name of Christ. Then there is the expression known as 'shouting' which is nothing more than a continuation of the African 'possession' by the gods. The gods possess the body of the worshipper and he or she is supposed to know nothing of their actions until the god decamps. This is still prevalent in most Negro Protestant churches and is universal in Sanctified churches."[8] In *Autobiography of a People* you won't find much discussion about the rituals or the liturgy of Christianity, but each author has her or his way of invoking God, of asking the Supreme Being to intercede or to grant the strength to carry on. God for these authors is a living God, a God of possibility, whether propitiated by Ukawsaw Gronnisaw (James Albert), Henry Highland Garnet, Sojourner Truth, Marcus Garvey, or Pauli Murray.

Many prayers for God's intervention came from Southern sharecroppers such as Nate Shaw. Sharecropping was nothing more than an extension of slavery, but, in too many cases, it was a black man's only alternative. The master may have no longer owned the slaves, but he still possessed the land, and at the end of the year he also possessed much of the profit from the sharecropper's labor. The poor tenant farmers owed more than their souls to the company store; they were perpetually in debt, behind in payments for feed, seed, and the leasing of tools and mules. On the farm or off, blacks were relegated to the lowest paying and most arduous forms of employment. According to Carole Marks, black workers "were employed in tanneries, cotton seed oil companies and in rolling mills throughout the South. They were in demand as day laborers for hazardous occupations in the railroad yards, on the docks, and in well digging and sewer building. They did the dirty work of southern society, and lived on the edge of poverty."[9] Even the skilled jobs they held in the urban centers of the South before the Civil War as barbers, wheelwrights, tinsmiths, metal workers, and coopers were stripped from them between 1870 and the first decade of the twentieth century. These were a few of the factors that forced many of them back to the farms and the inevitable debt peonage. A popular sharecropper's prayer or lament summarizes their condition: "Our father who art in heaven. White man owe me eleven, pay me seven. Thy kingdom come, thy will be done. If I hadn't tuck that I wouldn't got none."

Working conditions for blacks in the North were only relatively better at the turn of the century. Here they, like the immigrant workers with whom they competed, were reduced to wage slavery, becoming a reserve of cheap labor and often marginalized in the unions. Worse still, industrialists used them regularly as scabs and strikebreakers. The advent of World War I brought some improvement, but these opportunities were short-lived. For the most part, "black workers (in the North) entered a game where all the rules had changed. They entered factories no longer controlled by labor. They entered a manufacturing economy shifting from industrial to monopolistic concentrations. They were excluded from employment by political as well as economic pressure. They were despised by the very society that profited from them . . . this was freedom in the promised land."[10] This pattern of exploiting unskilled workers with impunity was expected by African American laborers until the eruption of the civil rights movement, though A. Philip Randolph and his threat of a march on Washington in the 1940s had already cracked a fault in the dam of segregation.

During the Great Depression work was scarce. Young Americans, white and black, hopped freight trains traveling from one end of the country to the other seeking some kind of employment. Such was the fate of the famed Scottsboro Boys, just nine of thousands of young hoboes stealing rides on trains. After they were accused of raping two white women, their case highlighted the nation's labor crisis, the troubling race relations, and the antagonisms between the government and the Communist Party. It also created sharp disagreements between the Communist-backed International Labor Defense and the National Association for the Advancement of Colored People, who charged the Communists with using the young men as political pawns and for propaganda purposes. Soon the case was a flash point, galvanizing protest groups all over the world. They were the poster boys of a revived Left movement. "After failing to win the defendants' release in a 1936 trial," Robin Kelley explains in *The Encyclopedia of the American Left*, "the Scottsboro Defense Committee agreed to a strange plea bargain in 1936 whereby four of the defendants were released and the remaining five endured lengthy prison sentences—the last defendant was not freed until 1950."[11] The SDC failed to secure unconditional release for the Scottsboro Boys, but the trial had legal and political implications through a number of appeals that brought about the introduction of blacks onto the jury rolls. The movement to free the defendants also demonstrated the power and effectiveness of mass protest, or even the threat of it. The excerpt from the autobiography of Haywood Patterson, one of the Scottsboro Boys, is one of the most gripping and terrifying examples of racially motivated accusation ever recorded.

Resistance and the search for identity, the quest for self, are also recurring themes in these extracts. "Let your motto be resistance, resistance, resistance," blasted Henry Highland Garnet, one of the more radical abolitionists. "No oppressed people have ever secured their liberty without resistance." The story of black resistance began on the African continent and the slave ships, and the countless mutinies and the costly insurance premium for the slavers indicate that these upheavals occurred quite frequently. During the slave era, resistance varied from subtle to armed revolt. Malingering, running away, injuring or killing the mule, or burning down the barn were ways in which slaves expressed their hatred of bondage. "In all societies, in all stages of history, where there is oppression there is resistance. Black people were not completely docile; they found many ways to resist and rebel. Throughout the Black Belt South individuals and families have resisted attacks, in some cases courageously fought off lynch mobs. However, more significant than this is the pattern of collective resistance."[12] Even the conspiracies to revolt that were discovered and smothered before they could happen—Denmark Vesey, Gabriel

Prosser, and Pompey in New York City—are testimonies of discontent, and the extent to which the enslaved would go to get their freedom. And for hundreds of these rebels and potential rebels, freedom was inextricably bound with identity. The great Frederick Douglass spoke for the voiceless multitude after he had overcome a skirmish with a notorious slave breaker: "This battle with Mr. Covey was the turning point in my career as a slave. It rekindled the few expiring embers of freedom, and revived within me a sense of my own manhood."

From the moment they were snatched from their homeland in Africa, the sense of manhood—or womanhood, for that matter—has always been a significant mission for African Americans. That elusive "I" is a primary quest for the authors of these testimonies. Whether they were Africans or African Americans was an early question that has been answered in countless ways. The great scholar W. E. B. Du Bois talked about several strains of ethnicity in his blood, but "thank God, no Anglo Saxon." Later, while teaching in the South, he would be more specific about his identity, an identity that millions of black Americans would embrace now. "I was thrilled to be for the first time among so many people of my own color or rather of such extraordinary colors, which I had only glimpsed before, but who it seemed were bound to me by new and exciting and eternal ties . . . Into this world I leapt with enthusiasm. A new loyalty and allegiance replaced my Americanism: henceforward I was a Negro."[13] African, Negro, Colored, Afro-American, black, African American—at one time or another all have been accepted nomenclatures for America's darker race.

Still, as James Baldwin noted, "nobody knows my name." From John Williams's novel *The Man Who Cried I Am* to the call and response chant "I Am Somebody," often intoned by the Rev. Jesse Jackson, black Americans have been struggling to assert their presence in a nation that shuns them. Are there ways to transcend race and the need to know who you are, to "eclipse the racial gaze altogether," as Toni Morrison attempts to do in her most recent novel? "I want to inhabit, walk around, a site clear of racist detritus; a place where race both matters and is rendered impotent," Morrison writes.[14] James McBride asked the same question years ago during his search for himself, inextricably bound with the mission to discover his white mother's identity. "It took me many years to find out who she was, partly because I never knew who I was."

Sometimes it was necessary to disguise one's reality, as Frederick Douglass and Linda Brent did in their daring escapes from slavery. But these were momentary masks, soon discarded once the runaways were out of the bloodhounds' reach. There is no way to fathom all the means and devices of concealment, of just "fooling ol' massa." In Ralph Ellison's acclaimed novel *Invisible Man,* identity and dissimulation often converge, but this masking, Ellison explains in his collection of essays, *Shadow and Act,* "is motivated not so much by fear as by profound rejection of the image created to usurp his identity. Sometimes it is for the sheer joy of the joke; sometimes to challenge those who presume, across the psychological distance created by race manners, to know his identity."[15] Some have conjectured that untruths pervade the slave narratives, since full disclosure would have put those left behind at risk. To what extent someone is telling the whole truth cannot be guaranteed with any of these entries, though in most cases questionable facts have been cross-checked. In the end, however, we must wrap our faith in a quote from Mark Twain, who in a letter to William Dean Howells said, "An autobiography is the truest of all books. For while it inevitably consists mainly of extinctions of the truth, shirkings of truth, partial revealments of the truth, with hardly an instance of plain straight truth, the remorseless truth *is* still there, between the lines."

While *Autobiography of a People: Three Centuries of African American History Told by Those Who Lived It* unfolds chronologically and touches some of the highpoints of African American history—those common historical watersheds such as the slave trade, the plantation era, the Civil War, Reconstruction, etc.—it would be impossible to cover every significant episode in this endless drama. That would require a voluminous tome, if not a series of books. And a few of the entries are certain to arouse discussion—perhaps, even consternation. Why is Jelly Roll Morton selected and not Louis "Satchmo" Armstrong, Duke Ellington, Miles Davis, Sidney Bechet, or Charlie Mingus, all of whom wrote compelling autobiographies? Why Jack Johnson and not Muhammad Ali or Joe Louis? Althea Gibson and not Jackie Joyner-Kersee? LL Cool J and not Chuck D? The Rev. Al Sharpton and not Rev. Gardner C. Taylor? Sharon Robinson and not Jackie Robinson? Ossie and Ruby and not Ellen Holly or Sammy Davis, Jr.? There is a clear rationale for each choice, although one could still make a good argument for each alternative above—and others. It boils down to how they fit within the overall purposes of the book, the power of the narrative, its execution, and literary merit. Moreover, I hoped to introduce new names and stories to the reader of this book—many of these well-known personalities have already been widely anthologized.

When I completed the proposal for this project, I knew there would be the dilemma of choice. Inevitably, too, there would be sins of omission. Given the abundance of material available on this subject, volumes are possible. What I've stitched together here is but one broad, arbitrary cloth, one piece in an endless quilt of firsthand accounts. My only wish is that in some small way I have narrowed the scope for future endeavors of this sort. *Autobiography of a People* is just a short leg of a trip that reaches well beyond this and the next millennium.

NOTES

1. Winthrop D. Jordan, *White Over Black—American Attitudes Toward the Negro, 1550–1812*. Baltimore: Penguin Books, 1968, p. 449.
2. A. Leon Higginbotham, Jr., *In the Matter of Color—Race & The American Legal Process: The Colonial Period*. New York: Oxford University Press, 1978, p. 13.
3. Benjamin Quarles, *The Negro in the Making of America*. New York: Collier Books, 1987, p. 159.
4. Wilma Henrickson, *Detroit Perspectives—Crossroads and Turning Points*. Detroit: Wayne State University Press, 1991, p. 316.
5. William Loren Katz, *Black Indians—A Hidden Heritage*. New York: Aladdin Paperbacks, 1986, pp. 96–99.
6. John Hope Franklin, *From Slavery to Freedom: A History of Negro Americans*. New York: Alfred Knopf, 1980, p.33.
7. John Henrik Clarke, *Africans at the Crossroads—Notes for An African World Revolution*. Trenton: Africa World Press, 1991, pp. 8–9.
8. Sterling Stuckey, *Slave Culture—Nationalist Theory & The Foundations of Black America*. New York: Oxford University Press, 1987, p. 97.
9. Carole Marks, *Farewell—We're Good and Gone, The Great Black Migration*. Bloomington: Indiana University Press, 1989, p. 61.
10. Marks, p. 136.
11. Robin Kelley, *The Encyclopedia of the American Left,* edited by Mari Jo Buhle, Paul Buhle, and Dan Georgakas. New York: Garland Press, 1990, p. 686.
12. *Introduction to African American Studies,* edited by Abdul Alkalimat. Chicago: Twenty First Century Books, 1984, p. 91.
13. Arnold Rampersad, *The Art and Imagination of W. E. B. Du Bois,* New York: Schocken Books, 1976, p. 12.
14. Toni Morrison, *The House That Race Built—Black Americans, U.S. Terrain,* edited by Wahneema Lubiano. New York: Pantheon Books, 1997, p. 9.
15. Ralph Ellison, *Shadow and Act*. New York: Vintage Books, 1953, p. 55.

Part I

PRE-REVOLUTIONARY

VOICES

African captives, ruthlessly torn from their homeland, registered their complaint in a number of ways, most violently in countless mutinies aboard the slave ships that plied the Atlantic during the brutal Middle Passage. Much of what we know of these bloody episodes has been distilled from the logs and journals of the slave captains, particularly such notorious slavers as Captain Canot, John Hawkins, and John Newton.

These records, however, provide scarcely any information about African tribal life or the circumstances of the captives before they were marched off to the coastal fortresses and subsequently crammed into the fetid holds of the ships. It is from a few priceless slave narratives that we gather some notion of what village life was like in certain regions of West Africa in the latter part of the eighteenth century. James Albert (Ukawsaw Gronniosaw) was the rambunctious grandson of the King of Bornu. From his narrative we are afforded a brief glimpse of African life and the events that led to his captivity. A restless and inquisitive young man, Gronniosaw's preoccupation with the existence of a Supreme Being will follow and sustain him throughout his ordeal. As we will see in many of the selections in this book, God and religion are common topics for an oppressed people seeking liberation.

Olaudah Equiano also credits the Creator for helping him survive the hellish experience of being sold into slavery. Equiano, who also went by the name Gustavus Vassa, has written perhaps the most anthologized slave narrative. His vivid reminiscence of village life in his native Guinea is hardly exhaustive but does give the reader an excellent idea of the African life so many were forced to leave behind. Among his most remarkable and painful stories is the one included here, which tells of the horrors he witnessed aboard the slave ship that carried him from his homeland.

Although Phillis Wheatley was also born in Africa, she never wrote a slave narrative. Her two most famous poems signify a complex but con-flicted writer who was ambiguous about her African heritage. While it is not certain why she began to write poetry, it may have been to emulate Alexander Pope and other favorites from the neoclassical tradition. Her critics contend she failed to express a stronger concern for the plight of her people; her supporters that it is necessary to read between the lines to detect her subversive intentions. Whatever the case, we cannot ignore the role she played as a literary pioneer.

Noted for being America's first black preacher to an all-white con-gregation, Lemuel Haynes wrote the ''ballad'' that follows in a burst of patriotic pride. Though he did not participate in the Battle of Lexington, he hurried to the scene shortly after it occurred. Unwavering in his critique of slavery, he often noted the hypocrisy of slaveholders pro-testing British oppression. Even now, 225 years later, the defiant message of Haynes's poem (shortened for this book) still resonates with power and conviction.

More than five thousand African Americans fought in the Revolutionary War, and a good number of them—Peter Salem, Salem Poor, Barzil-
lai Lew, and Pomp Blackman—did so with great honor. Unfortunately,
distinguishing themselves on the battlefield did not automatically confer
citizenship to the veterans and their families. Many petitions were
launched by African Americans such as John and Paul Cuffe and others
in 1780, asserting ''no taxation without representation.'' By 1815, the
latter Cuffe, a prosperous ship owner, had given up on the States and
become an ardent colonizationist and at his own expense transported
thirty-eight African Americans to Sierra Leone, many of whom worked
as missionaries.

JAMES ALBERT
UKAWSAW GRONNIOSAW

From *A Narrative of the Most Remarkable Particulars in the
Life of James Albert Ukawsaw Gronniosaw, An African Prince, Written by Himself*

AFRICA AND NEW YORK, 1720-1730

I WAS BORN IN THE CITY OF *BAURNOU*, my mother was the eldest
daughter of the reigning King there. I was the youngest of six children, and
particularly loved by my mother, and my grand-father almost doated on me.

I had, from my infancy, a curious turn of mind; was more grave and
reserved, in my disposition, than either of my brothers and sisters, I often
teazed them with questions they could not answer; for which reason they
disliked me, as they supposed that I was either foolish or insane. 'Twas certain
that I was, at times, very unhappy in myself: It being strongly impressed on my
mind that there was some GREAT MAN of power which resided above the sun,
moon and stars, the objects of our worship.——My dear, indulgent mother
would bear more with me than any of my friends beside.——I often raised my
hand to heaven, and asked her who lived there? Was much dissatisfied when she
told me the sun, moon and stars, being persuaded, in my own mind, that there
must be some SUPERIOR POWER.——I was frequently lost in wonder at the works
of the creation: Was afraid, and uneasy, and restless, but could not tell for
what. I wanted to be informed of things that no person could tell me; and was
always dissatisfied.——These wonderful impressions began in my childhood, and
followed me continuously till I left my parents, which affords me matter of
admiration and thankfulness.

To this moment I grew more and more uneasy every day, insomuch that
one Saturday (which is the day on which we kept our sabbath) I laboured under
anxieties and fears that cannot be expressed; and, what is more extraordinary, I
could not give a reason for it.——I rose, as our custom is, about three o'clock
(as we are obliged to be at our place of worship an hour before the sun rise) we

say nothing in our worship, but continue on our knees with our hands held up, observing a strict silence till the sun is at a certain height, which I suppose to be about 10 or 11 o'clock in *England:* When, at a certain sign made by the Priest, we get up (our duty being over) and disperse to our different houses.—— Our place of meeting is under a large palm tree; we divide ourselves into many congregations; as it is impossible for the same tree to cover the inhabitants of the whole city, though they are extremely large, high and majestic; the beauty and usefulness of them are not to be described; they supply the inhabitants of the country with meat, drink and clothes; the body of the palm tree is very large; at a certain season of the year they tap it, and bring vessels to receive the wine, of which they draw great quantities, the quality of which is very delicious: The leaves of this tree are of a silky nature; they are large and soft; when they are dried and pulled to pieces, it has much the same appearance as the English flax, and the inhabitants of Bournou manufacture it for clothing, &c. This tree likewise produces a plant, or substance, which has the appearance of a cabbage, and very like it, in taste almost the same: It grows between the branches. Also the palm tree produces a nut, something like a cocoa, which contains a kernel, in which is a large quantity of milk, very pleasant to the taste: The shell is of a hard substance, and of a very beautiful appearance, and serves for basons, bowls, &c. . . .

About this time there came a merchant from the *Gold Coast* (the third city in Guinea) he traded with the inhabitants of our country in ivory, &c. he took great notice of my unhappy situation, and inquired into the cause; he expressed vast concern for me, and said, if my parents would part with me for a little while, and let him take me home with him, it would be of more service to me than any thing they could do for me.——He told me that if I would go with him I should see houses with wings to them walk upon the water, and should also see the white folks; and that he had many sons of my age, which should be my companions; and he added to all this that he would bring me safe back again soon.——I was highly pleased with the account of this strange place, and was very desirous of going. . . .

I was now more than a thousand miles from home, without a friend or any means to procure one. Soon after I came to the merchant's house I heard the drums beat remarkably loud, and the trumpets blow—the persons accustom'd to this employ, are oblig'd to go upon a very high structure appointed for that purpose, that the sound might be heard at a great distance: They are higher than the steeples are in *England.* I was mightily pleased with sounds so entirely new to me, and was very inquisitive to know the cause of this rejoicing, and asked many questions concerning it; I was answered that it was meant as a compliment to me, because I was grandson to the King of *Bournou.* . . .

A few days after a *Dutch* ship came into the harbour, and they carried me on board, in hopes that the Captain would purchase me.——As they went, I heard them agree, that, if they could not sell me *then,* they would throw me overboard.—I was in extreme agonies when I heard this; and as soon as ever I saw the *Dutch* Captain, I ran to him, and put my arms round him, and said, "Father save me." (for I knew that if he did not buy me I should be treated very ill, or, possibly murdered) And though he did not understand my language, yet it pleased the Almighty to influence him in my behalf, and he bought me *for two yards of check,* which is of more value *there,* than in *England. . . .*

I was now washed, & clothed in the *Dutch* or *English* manner.—My master grew very fond of me, and I loved him exceedingly. I watched every look, was always ready when he wanted me, and endeavoured to convince him, by every action, that my only pleasure was to serve him well.—I have since thought that he must have been a serious man. His actions corresponded very well with such a character.—He used to read prayers in public to the ship's crew every sabbath day; and when first I saw him read, I was never so surprised in my whole life as when I saw the book talk to my master; for I thought it did, as I observed him to look upon it, and move his lips.—I wished it would do so to me. As soon as my master had done reading I follow'd him to the place where he put the book, being mightily delighted with it, and when nobody saw me, I open'd it and put my ear down close upon it, in great hope that it would say something to me; but was very sorry and greatly disappointed when I found it would not speak, this thought immediately presented itself to me, that every body and every thing despised me because I was black.

I was exceedingly sea-sick at first; but when I became more accustom'd to the sea, it wore off.—My master's ship was bound for *Barbados.* When we came there, he thought fit to speak of me to several gentlemen of his acquaintance, and one of them exprest a particular desire to see me.—He had a great mind to buy me; but the Captain could not immediately be prevail'd on to part with me; but however, as the gentleman seemed very solicitous, he at length let me go, and I was sold for fifty dollars *(four and six penny pieces in English.)* My new master's name was *Vanhorn,* a young gentleman; his home was in *New-England,* in the city of *New-York;* to which place he took me with him. He dress'd me in his livery, & was very good to me. My chief business was to wait at table, and tea, & clean knives, & I had a very easy place; but the servants used to curse & swear surprizingly; which I learnt faster than any thing, 'twas almost the first English I could speak. If any of them affronted me, I was sure to call upon God to damn them immediately; but I was broke of it all at once, occasioned by the correction of an old black servant that lived in the family.— One day I had just clean'd the knives for dinner, when one of the maids took one to cut bread and butter with; I was very angry with her, and called upon God to damn her; when this old black man told me I must not say so: I ask'd him why? He replied there was a wicked man, call'd the Devil, that liv'd in hell, and would take all that said these words and put them in the fire and burn them.——This terrified me greatly, and I was entirely broke of swearing. Soon after this, as I was placing the china for tea, my mistress came into the room just as the maid had been cleaning it; the girl had unfortunately sprinkled the wainscot with the mop; at which my mistress was angry; the girl very foolishly answered her again, which made her worse, and she called upon God to damn her.——I was vastly concern'd to hear this, as she was a fine young lady, and very good to me, insomuch that I could not help speaking to her: Madam, says I, you must not say so: Why, says she? Because there is a black man, call'd the Devil, that lives in hell, and he will put you in the fire and burn you, and I shall be very sorry for that. Who told you this, replied my lady? Old Ned, says I. Very well was all her answer; but she told my master of it, who ordered that old Ned should be tied up and whipp'd, and was never suffered to come into the kitchen, with the rest of the servants, afterwards.——My mistress was not angry with me, but rather diverted at my simplicity, and, by way of talk, she repeated what I had said to many of her acquaintance that visited her; among the rest, *Freelandhouse,* a very gracious, good minister, heard it, and he took a great deal of notice of me, and desired my master to part with me to him. He would not hear of it at first, but, being greatly persuaded, he let me go; and Mr. *Freelandhouse* gave £.50 for me.——He took me home with him, and made me kneel down, and put my two hands together, and prayed for me, and every night and morning he did the same.——I could not make out what it was for, nor the meaning of it, nor what they spoke to when they talked——I thought it comical, but I liked it very well.——After I had been a little while with my new master I grew more familiar, and asked him the meaning of prayer: (I could hardly speak *English* to be understood) he took great pains with me, and made me understand that he pray'd to God, who liv'd in Heaven; that he was my father and *best* friend.——I told him that this must be a mistake; that *my* father lived at *Bournou,* and I wanted very much to see him, and likewise my dear mother, and sister, and I wished he would be so good as to send me home to them; and I added, all I could think of to induce him to convey me back, I appeared in great trouble, and my good master was so much affected that the tears run down his face. He told me that God was a great and good Spirit, that he created all the world, and every person and thing in it, *Ethiopia, Africa* and *America,* and every where. I was delighted when I heard this: There, says I, I always thought so when I lived at home! Now, if I had wings like an eagle, I would fly to tell my dear mother that God is greater than the sun, moon and stars; and that they were made by him.

I was exceedingly pleas'd with this information of my master's, because it corresponded so well with my own opinion; I thought now if I could but get home, I should be wiser than all my country-folks, my grandfather, or father, or mother, or any of them.——But though I was somewhat enlightened, by this information of my master's, yet I had no other knowledge of God than that he was a good Spirit, and created every body, and every thing.—I never was sensible, in myself, nor had any one ever told me, that he would punish the wicked, and love the just. I was only glad that I had been told there was a God, because I had always thought so.

OLAUDAH EQUIANO

From *The Interesting Narrative of the Life of*
Olaudah Equiano, or Gustavus Vassa, the African. Written by Himself

AFRICA AND VIRGINIA, 1750–1760

I WAS BORN, IN THE YEAR 1745. THE distance of this prov-
. . . ince from the capital of Benin and the sea coast must be very considerable: for I had never heard of white men or Europeans, nor of the sea; and
our subjection to the king of Benin was little more than nominal. Every trans-
action of the government, as far as my slender observation extended, was
conducted by the chiefs or elders of the place. The manners and government of
a people who have little commerce with other countries, are generally very
simple; and the history of what passes in one family or village, may serve as a
specimen of the whole nation. My father was one of those elders or chiefs of
whom I have spoken, and was stiled Embrenche; a term, as I remember,
importing the highest distinction, and signifying in our language "a mark of
grandeur." This mark is conferred on the person entitled to it by cutting the
skin across at the top of the forehead, and drawing it down to the eyebrows;
and applying a warm hand to it, while in this situation, and rubbing it until it
shrinks up into a thick wale across the lower part of the forehead. Most of the
judges and senators were thus marked; my father had long borne this badge: I
had seen it conferred on one of my brothers, and I also was destined to receive
it by my parents. Those Embrenche, or chief men, decided disputes, and
punished crimes; for which purpose they always assembled together. The proceedings were generally short; and in most cases the law of retaliation prevailed
. . . Adultery was sometimes punished by slavery or death; a punishment
which, I believe, is inflicted on it throughout most of the nations of Africa; so
sacred among them is the honour of the marriage bed, and so jealous are they
of the fidelity of their wives. . . . The men, however, do not preserve the

same constancy to their wives, which they expect from them; for they indulge in a plurality, though seldom in more than two. Their mode of marriage is this:—Both parties are usually betrothed when young by their parents, though I have known the males betroth themselves. On this occasion a feast is prepared, and the bride and bridegroom stand up in the midst of all their friends, who are assembled for the purpose, while he declares she is henceforth to be looked upon as his wife, and that no person is to pay any addresses to her. This is also immediately proclaimed in the vicinity, on which the bride retires from the assembly. Some time after she is brought home to her husband, and then another feast is made, to which the relations of both parties are invited. Her parents then deliver her to the bridegroom, accompanied with a number of blessings, and at the same time they tie round her waist a cotton string of the thickness of a goose-quill, which none but married women are permitted to wear. She is now considered as completely his wife; and at this time the dowry is given to the new-married pair, which generally consists of *portions of land, slaves and cattle, household goods, and implements of husbandry*. These are offered by the friends of both parties: besides which the parents of the bridegroom present gifts to those of the bride, whose property she is looked upon before marriage; but after it she is esteemed the sole property of the husband. The ceremony being now ended, the festival begins, which is celebrated with bonfires, and loud acclamations of joy, accompanied with music and dancing.

We are almost a nation of dancers, musicians, and poets. Every great event, such as a triumphant return from battle, or other cause of public rejoicing, is celebrated in public dances, which are accompanied with songs and music suited to the occasion. The assembly is separated into four divisions, which dance either apart or in succession, and each with a character peculiar to itself. The first division contains the married men, who in their dances frequently exhibit feats of arms, and the representation of a battle. To these succeed the married women, who dance in the second division. The young men occupy the third; and the maidens the fourth. Each represents some interesting scene of real life, such as a great achievement, domestic employment, a pathetic story, or some rural sport. And as the subject is generally founded on some recent event, it is therefore ever new. This gives our dances a spirit and variety which I have scarcely seen elsewhere. We have many musical instruments, particularly drums of different kinds, a piece of music which resembles a guitar, and another much like a sticcado. These last are chiefly used by betrothed virgins, who play on them on all grand festivals.

As our manners are simple, our luxuries are few. The dress of both sexes is nearly the same. It generally consists of a long piece of calico or muslin, wrapped loosely round the body, somewhat in the form of a Highland plaid. This is usually dyed blue, which is our favourite colour. It is extracted from a berry, and is brighter and richer than any I have seen in Europe. Besides this, our women of distinction wear golden ornaments, which they dispose with some profusion on their arms and legs. When our women are not employed with the men in tillage, their usual occupation is spinning and weaving cotton, which they afterwards dye, and make into garments. They also manufacture earthen vessels, of which we have many kinds; among the rest, tobacco pipes, made after the same fashion, and used in the same manner, as those in Turkey.

Our manner of living is entirely plain; for as yet the natives are unacquainted with those refinements in cookery which debauch the taste. Bullocks, goats, and poultry, supply the greatest part of their food. These constitute likewise the principal wealth of the country, and the chief articles of its commerce. The flesh is usually stewed in a pan; to make it savory we sometimes use also pepper, and other spices, and we have salt made of wood ashes. Our vegetables are mostly plantains, eadas, yams, beans, and Indian corn. The head of the family usually eats alone; his wives and slaves have also their separate tables. Before we taste food we always wash our hands: indeed our cleanliness on all occasions is extreme; but on this it is an indispensable ceremony. After washing, libation is made, by pouring out a small portion of the drink on the floor, and by tossing a small quantity of the food in a certain place, for the spirits of departed relations, which the natives suppose to preside over their conduct, and to guard them from evil. . . .

The first object that saluted my eyes when I arrived on the coast was the sea, and a slave ship, which was then riding at anchor, and waiting for its cargo. These filled me with astonishment, that was soon converted into terror, which I am yet at a loss to describe, and much more the then feelings of my mind when I was carried on board. I was immediately handled and tossed up to see if I was sound, by some of the crew; and I was now persuaded that I had got into a world of bad spirits, and that they were going to kill me. Their complexions too, differing so much from ours, their long hair, and the language they spoke, which was very different from any I had ever heard, united to confirm me in this belief. Indeed such were the horrors of my views and fears at the moment, that if ten thousand worlds had been my own, I would have freely parted with them all to have exchanged my condition with the meanest slave in my own country. When I looked round the ship too, and saw a large furnace or copper boiling, and a multitude of black people, of every description, chained together, every one of their countenances expressing dejection and sorrow, I no longer doubted of my fate; and, quite overpowered with horror and anguish, I fell motionless on the deck, and fainted. When I recovered a little, I found some black people about me, who I believed were some of those who brought me on board, and had been receiving their pay: they talked to me in order to cheer me, but all in vain. I asked them if we were not to be eaten by those white men with horrible looks, red faces, and long hair. They told me I was not: and one of the crew brought me a small portion of spirituous liquor in a wine glass; but, being afraid of him, I would not take it out of his hand. One of the blacks therefore took it from him and gave it to me, and I took a little down my palate, which, instead of reviving me, as they thought it would, threw me into the greatest consternation at the strange feeling it produced, having never tasted any such liquor before.

Soon after this the blacks who brought me on board went off, and left me abandoned to despair. I now saw myself deprived of all chance of returning to my native country, or even the least glimpse of gaining the shore, which I now considered as friendly; and I even wished for my former slavery, in preference to my present situation, which was filled with horrors of every kind, still heightened by my ignorance of what I was to undergo. I was not long suffered to indulge my grief. I was soon put down under the decks, and there I received such a salutation in my nostrils as I had never experienced in my life: so that, with the loathsomeness of the stench, and with my crying together, I became so sick and low that I was not able to eat, nor had I the least desire to taste any thing. I now wished for the last friend, death, to relieve me; but soon, to my grief, two of the white men offered me eatables; and, on my refusing to eat, one of them held me fast by the hands, and laid me across, I think, the windlass, and tied my feet, while the other flogged me severely. I had never experienced any thing of this kind before, and although, not being used to the water, I naturally feared that element the first time I saw it, yet nevertheless, could I have got over the nettings, I would have jumped over the side, but I could not; and besides the crew used to watch us very closely, who were not chained down to the decks, lest we should leap into the water. I have seen some of these poor African prisoners most severely cut for attempting to do so, and hourly whipped for not eating. This indeed was often the case with myself. In a little time after, amongst the poor chained men, I found some of my own nation, which in a small degree gave ease to my mind. I inquired of these what was to be done with us. They gave me to understand we were to be carried to these white people's country to work for them. I was then a little revived, and thought if it were no worse than working, my situation was not so desperate. But still I feared I should be put to death, the white people looked and acted, as I thought, in so savage a manner; for I had never seen among any people such instances of brutal cruelty: and this is not only shewn towards us blacks, but also to some of the whites themselves. One white man in particular I saw, when we were permitted to be on deck, flogged so unmercifully with a large rope near the foremast, that he died in consequence of it; and they tossed him over the side as they would have done a brute. This made me fear these people the more; and I expected nothing less than to be treated in the same manner. I could not help expressing my fearful apprehensions to some of my countrymen; I asked them if these people had no country, but lived in this hollow place, the ship. They told me they did not, but came from a distant one. 'Then,' said I, 'how comes it, that in all our country we never heard of them?' They told me, because they lived so very far off. I then asked, where their women were: had they any like themselves. I was told they had. 'And why,' said I, 'do we not see them?' They answered, because they were left behind. I asked how the vessel could go. They told me they could not tell; but that there was cloth put upon the masts by the help of the ropes I saw, and then the vessel went on; and the white men had some spell or magic they put in the water, when they liked, in order to stop the vessel. I was exceedingly amazed at this account, and really thought they were spirits. I therefore wished much to be from amongst them, for I expected they would sacrifice me; but my wishes were in vain, for we were so quartered that it was impossible for any of us to make our escape.

While we stayed on the coast I was mostly on deck; and one day, to my great astonishment, I saw one of these vessels coming in with the sails up. As soon as the whites saw it, they gave a great shout, at which we were amazed; and the more so as the vessel appeared larger by approaching nearer. At last she came to an anchor in my sight, and when the anchor was let go, I and my countrymen who saw it, were lost in astonishment to observe the vessel stop, and were now convinced it was done by magic. Soon after this the other ship got her boats out, and they came on board of us, and the people of both ships seemed very glad to see each other. Several of the strangers also shook hands with us black people, and made motions with their hands, signifying, I suppose, we were to go to their country; but we did not understand them. At last, when the ship, in which we were, had got in all her cargo, they made ready with many fearful noises, and we were all put under deck, so that we could not see how they managed the vessel.

But this disappointment was the least of my grief. The stench of the hold, while we were on the coast, was so intolerably loathsome, that it was danger-ous to remain there for any time, and some of us had been permitted to stay on the deck for the fresh air; but now that the whole ship's cargo were confined together, it became absolutely pestilential. The closeness of the place, and the heat of the climate, added to the number in the ship, being so crowded that each had scarcely room to turn himself, almost suffocated us. This produced copious perspirations, so that the air soon became unfit for respiration, from a variety of loathsome smells, and brought on a sickness among the slaves, of which many died, thus falling victims to the improvident avarice, as I may call it, of their purchasers. This deplorable situation was again aggravated by the galling of the chains, now become insupportable; and the filth of necessary tubs, into which the children often fell, and were almost suffocated. The shrieks of the women, and the groans of the dying, rendered it a scene of horror almost inconceivable. Happily, perhaps, for myself, I was soon reduced so low here that it was thought necessary to keep me almost continually on deck; and from my extreme youth, I was not put in fetters. In this situation I expected every hour to share the fate of my companions, some of whom were almost daily brought upon deck at the point of death, and I began to hope that death would soon put an end to my miseries. Often did I think many of the inhabitans of the deep much more happy than myself; I envied them the freedom they enjoyed, and as often wished I could change my condition for theirs. Every circumstance I met with served only to render my state more painful, and heighten my apprehensions and my opinion of the cruelty of the whites. One day they had taken a number of fishes; and when they had killed and satisfied themselves with as many as they thought fit, to our astonishment who were on the deck, rather than give any of them to us to eat, as we expected, they tossed the remaining fish into the sea again, although we begged and prayed for some as well as we could, but in vain; and some of my country-men, being pressed by hunger, took an opportunity, when they thought no one saw them, of trying to get a little privately; but were discovered, and the attempt procured for them some very severe floggings.

One day, when we had a smooth sea and moderate wind, two of my wearied countrymen, who were chained together, (I was near them at the time) preferring death to such a life of misery, somehow made through the nettings and jumped into the sea: immediately another quite dejected fellow, who on account of his illness was suffered to be out of irons, also followed their example; and I believe many more would very soon have done the same, if they had not been prevented by the ship's crew, who were instantly alarmed. Those of us who were the most active were in a moment put down under the deck; and there was such a noise and confusion amongst the people of the ship as I never heard before, to stop her and get the boat out to go after the slaves. However, two of the wretches were drowned; but they got the other, and afterwards flogged him unmercifully, for thus attempting to prefer death to slavery. In this manner we continued to undergo more hardships than I can now relate; hardships which are inseparable from this accursed trade. Many a time we were near suffocation from the want of fresh air, being deprived thereof for days together. This, and the stench of the necessary tubs, carried off many. . . .

On the Passage we were better treated than when coming from Africa, and we had plenty of rice and fat pork. We were landed up a river a good way from the sea, about Virginia county, where we saw few of our native Africans, and not one soul who could talk to me. I was a few weeks weeding grass and gathering stones in a plantation; and at last all my companions were distributed different ways, and only myself was left. I was now exceedingly miserable, and thought myself worse off than any of the rest of my companions; for they could talk to each other, but I had no person to speak to that I could understand. In this state I was constantly grieving and pining, and wishing for death rather than any thing else. While I was in this plantation the gentleman to whom I supposed the estate belonged being unwell, I was one day sent for to his dwelling-house to fan him. When I came into the room where he was, I was very much affrighted at some things I saw, and the more so, as I had seen a black woman slave as I came through the house, who was cooking the dinner, and the poor creature was cruelly loaded with various kinds of iron machines; she had one particularly on her head, which locked her mouth so fast that she could scarcely speak, and could not eat nor drink. I much astonished and shocked at this contrivance, which I afterwards learned was called the iron muzzle. Soon after I had a fan put into my hand, to fan the gentleman while he slept; and so I did indeed with great fear. While he was fast asleep I indulged myself a great deal in looking about the room, which to me appeared very fine and curious. The first object that engaged my attention was a watch, which hung on the chimney, and was going. I was quite surprised at the noise it made, and was afraid it would tell the gentleman any thing I might do amiss: and when I immediately after observed a picture hanging in the room, which appeared constantly to look at me, I was still more affrighted, having never seen such things as these before. At one time I thought it was something relative to magic; and not seeing it move, I thought it might be some way the whites had to keep their great men when they died, and offer them libations, as we used to do to our friendly spirits. In this state of anxiety I remained till my master awoke, when I was dismissed out of the room, to my no small satisfaction and relief; for I thought that these people were all made up of wonders. In this place I was called JACOB; but on board the African Snow I was called MICHAEL.

PHILLIS WHEATLEY

From *The Poems of Phillis Wheatley*

BOSTON, 1770S

ON BEING BROUGHT FROM AFRICA TO AMERICA.

'Twas mercy brought me from my Pagan
    land,
Taught my benighted soul to understand
That there's a God, that there's a Saviour too:
Once I redemption neither sought nor knew.
Some view our sable race with scornful eye,
"Their colour is a diabolic die."
Remember, Christians, Negroes, black as Cain,
May be refin'd, and join th' angelic train.

TO THE RIGHT HONOURABLE WILLIAM, EARL OF DARTMOUTH, HIS MAJESTY'S PRINCIPAL SECRETARY OF STATE FOR NORTH-AMERICA, &C.

Hail, happy day, when, smiling like the morn,
Fair Freedom rose New-England to adorn:
The northern clime beneath her genial ray,
Dartmouth, congratulates thy blissful sway:
Elate with hope her race no longer mourns,
Each soul expands, each grateful bosom burns,

While in thine hand with pleasure we behold
The silken reins, and Freedom's charms unfold.
Long lost to realms beneath the northern skies

She shines supreme, while hated faction dies:
Soon as appear'd the Goddess long desir'd,
Sick at the view, she lanquish'd and expir'd;
Thus from the splendors of the morning light
The owl in sadness seeks the caves of night.

No more, America, in mournful strain
Of wrongs, and grievance unredress'd complain,
No longer shalt thou dread the iron chain,
Which wanton Tyranny with lawless hand
Had made, and with it meant t' enslave the land.

Should you, my lord, while you peruse my song,
Wonder from whence my love of Freedom sprung,
Whence flow these wishes for the common good,
By feeling hearts alone best understood,
I, young in life, by seeming cruel fate
Was snatch'd from Afric's fancy'd happy seat:
What pangs excruciating must molest,
What sorrows labour in my parent's breast?
Steel'd was that soul and by no misery mov'd
That from a father seiz'd his babe belov'd:
Such, such my case. And can I then but pray
Others may never feel tyrannic sway?

For favours past, great Sir, our thanks are due,
And thee we ask thy favours to renew,
Since in thy pow'r, as in thy will before,
To sooth the griefs, which thou did'st once deplore.

May heav'nly grace the sacred sanction give
To all thy works, and thou for ever live
Not only on the wings of fleeting Fame,
Though praise immortal crowns the patriot's name,
But to conduct to heav'ns refulgent fane,
May fiery coursers sweep th' ethereal plain,
And bear thee upwards to that blest abode,
Where, like the prophet, thou shalt find thy God.

LEMUEL HAYNES

From *Black Preacher to White America*

LEXINGTON, MASSACHUSETTS, 1775

POEM ON THE INHUMAN TRAGEDY PERPETRATED ON the 19th of April 1775 by a Number of the British Troops under the Command of Thomas Gage, which Parricides and Ravages are shocking Displays of ministerial & tyrannic Vengeance composed by Lemuel a young Mollato who obtained what little knowledge he possesses, by his own Application to Letters.

1

Some Seraph now my Breast inspire
whilst my Urania *sings*
while She would try her solemn Lyre
Upon poetic Strings.

2

Some gloomy Vale or gloomy Seat
where Sable veils the sky
Become that Tongue that w^d repeat
The dreadfull Tragedy

3

The Nineteenth Day of April last
We ever shall retain
As monumental of the past
most bloody shocking Scene

4

Then *Tyrants fill'd wth horrid Rage*
A fatal Journey went
& Unmolested to engage
And slay the innocent

5

Then *did we see old* Bonner *rise*
And, borrowing Spite from Hell
They stride along with magic Eyes
where Sons of Freedom dwell

6

At Lexington *they did appear*
Array'd in hostile Form
And tho our Friends were peacefull there
Yet on them fell the Storm

7

Eight most unhappy Victims fell
Into the Arms of Death
unpitied by those Tribes of Hell
who curs'd them wth their Breath

8

The Savage Band still march along
For Concord *they were bound*
while Oaths & Curses from their Tongue
Accent with hellish Sound

9

To prosecute their fell Desire
At Concord *they unite*
Two Sons of Freedom there expire
By their tyrannic Spite

10

Thus did our Friends endure their Rage
without a murm'ring Word
Till die they must or else engage
and join with one Accord

11

Such Pity did their Breath inspire
That long they bore the Rod
And with Reluctance they conspire
to shed the human Blood

12

But Pity could no longer sway
Tho' 't is a pow'rfull Band
For Liberty now bleeding lay
And calld them to withstand

13

The Awfull Conflict now begun
To rage with furious Pride
And Blood in great Effusion run
From many a wounded Side

14

For Liberty, each Freeman Strives
As its a Gift of God
And for it willing yield their Lives
And Seal it with their Blood

15

Thrice happy they who thus resign
Into the peacefull Grave
Much better there, in Death Confin'd
Than a Surviving Slave

16

This Motto may adorn their Tombs,
(Let tyrants come and view)
"We rather seek these silent Rooms
"Than live as Slaves to You. . . .

JOHN CUFFE

From *Colored Patriots of the American Revolution*

DARTMOUTH, MASSACHUSETTS, 1780

To the Honorable Council and House of Representatives, in General Court assembled, for the State of the Massachusetts Bay, in New England:

The petition of several poor negroes and mulattoes, who are inhabitants of the town of Dartmouth, humbly showeth,—

That we being chiefly of the African extract, and by reason of long bondage and hard slavery, we have been deprived of enjoying the profits of our labor or the advantage of inheriting estates from our parents, as our neighbors the white people do, having some of us not long enjoyed our own freedom; yet of late, contrary to the invariable custom and practice of the country, we have been, and now are, taxed both in our polls and that small pittance of estate which, through much hard labor and industry, we have got together to sustain ourselves and families withall. We apprehend it, therefore, to be hard usage, and will doubtless (if continued) reduce us to a state of beggary, whereby we shall become a burthen to others, if not timely prevented by the interposition of your justice and power.

Your petitioners further show, that we apprehend ourselves to be aggrieved, in that, while we are not allowed the privilege of freemen of the State, having no vote or influence in the election of those that tax us, yet many of our colour (as is well known) have cheerfully entered the field of battle in the defence of the common cause, and that (as we conceive) against a similar exertion of power (in regard to taxation), too well known to need a recital in this place.

We most humbly request, therefore, that you would take our unhappy case into your serious consideration, and, in your wisdom and power, grant us relief from taxation, while under our present depressed circumstances; and your poor petitioners, as in duty bound, shall ever pray, &c.

JOHN CUFFE, ADVENTUR CHILD, PAUL CUFFE,
SAMUEL X GRAY, PERO X HOWLAND, PERO X RUSSELL,
   his mark.   his mark.   his mark.
PERO COGGESHALL.

❧

Part II

THE LORD WILL

PROVIDE

Although large contingents of African Americans were seduced by Lord
John Murray Dunmore's promise of freedom from slavery during the
Revolutionary War and sided with the British, the great majority, having
invested so much sweat and blood in this new country, staked their claim
and renewed their struggle for independence. Richard Allen was among
the single-minded former slaves who held on to the American dream,
even as he challenged the racism endemic in the Methodist Church.
When blacks were regulated to the so-called "nigger pews" at St.
George's Church in Philadelphia, Allen and his associates rose from their
knees, walked out, and founded their own church, African Methodist
Episcopal, where they could worship without insult.

Elizabeth, born a slave in Maryland, was as blessed as Allen in her
mission to bring the Lord's spirit and mercies to her brethren, though
Allen would have been reluctant to have her preach in his Methodist
church. Elizabeth kept her religious fervor to herself until she turned

forty-two, when she had a divine revelation that she was meant to preach the word of God. Through the power of prayer and divine intervention, she learned of her chosen path and traveled widely preaching the Lord's word, despite the rebuke from her male counterparts who doubted her abilities. As an itinerant minister she made up for her long silence over the remainder of her long life by bringing her sermons against slavery to black and white communities. She may not have been the first woman evangelist, but she paved the way for Jarena Lee and many of today's women preachers.

Clearly not a petition of her own hand, Belinda's dictated plea for freedom is a singular utterance endowed with all the same fervent memory of Africa as Gronniosaw and Equiano. For fifty years Belinda toiled faithfully for her master and now with her face "marked with the furrows of time," she brings her petition before the Massachusetts legislature. More often than not, slaves lived and died without ever enjoying even a small portion of the fruits of their backbreaking labor.

Jupiter Hammon, arguably the first published African American writer, whose message as we can see in the following extract from his famous address to the Negroes in the state of New York in 1787 in many respects is as ambivalent as Phillis Wheatley's. His ambivalence may have been a result of his trusted status as a house servant, which gave him a comparatively easier enslavement than others in the fields. Most of Hammon's work expresses a subtle protest against slavery, and he is viewed as a harbinger to the abolitionist movement that arose shortly after his death in 1806.

Mathematician, astronomer, and writer Benjamin Banneker had bigger fish to fry, choosing to assail Thomas Jefferson with accusations of hypocrisy. Although he acquired a wide reputation for his annual almanacs and for assisting Andrew Ellicott in surveying the land that would be Washington, D.C., the self-taught Banneker is perhaps best known for his letter to President Jefferson in which he pleads with him to live up to the high-sounding rhetoric Jefferson had composed for the Declaration of Independence. Along with the letter, Banneker enclosed a manuscript copy of his almanac. It is not known if Jefferson responded to the query, but he did forward the manuscript to the Marquis de Condorcet with a note commending Banneker's mathematical deductions. Banneker's innovations flew in the face of Jefferson's assertions that African Americans were an inferior race and incapable of "comprehending the investigations of Euclid." Banneker and other emerging black thinkers such as Dr. James Derham and Prince Hall were living refutations of the "founding father's" allegations. Another interesting fact: Banneker also devised a clock of wooden works before Eli Terry secured the first U.S. clock patent in 1797.

It was neither to an assembly of elected officials nor to the framer of the Declaration of Independence that Prince Hall directed his speech, but to his "brethren" and members of the African Masonic Lodge, which he founded after being turned away from the white lodge. Beyond his deep interest in lodge activities, Hall was involved in a number of civil affairs, including support for the cause of emancipation. In 1797, he was part of a successful movement to provide schools for free African American children. Hall is exemplary of the African Americans who would make their mark in science, politics, and culture.

RICHARD ALLEN

From *The Life Experience and Gospel Labors of the Rt. Rev. Richard Allen*

🎗

PHILADELPHIA, 1786

I WAS BORN IN THE YEAR OF OUR Lord 1760, on February 14th, a slave to Benjamin Chew, of Philadelphia. My mother and father and four children of us were sold into Delaware state, near Dover; and I was a child and lived with him until I was upwards of twenty years of age, during which time I was awakened and brought to see myself, poor, wretched and undone, and without the mercy of God must be lost. Shortly after, I obtained mercy through the blood of Christ, and was constrained to exhort my old companions to seek the Lord. I went rejoicing for several days and was happy in the Lord, in conversing with many old, experienced Christians. I was brought under doubts, and was tempted to believe I was deceived, and was constrained to seek the Lord afresh. I went with my head bowed down for many days. My sins were a heavy burden. I was tempted to believe there was no mercy for me. I cried to the Lord both night and day. One night I thought hell would be my portion. I cried unto Him who delighteth to hear the prayers of a poor sinner, and all of a sudden my dungeon shook, my chains flew off, and, glory to God, I cried. My soul was filled. I cried, enough for me—the Saviour died. Now my confidence was strengthened that the Lord, for Christ's sake, had heard my prayers and pardoned all my sins. I was constrained to go from house to house, exhorting my old companions, and telling to all around what a dear Saviour I had found. I joined the Methodist Society and met in class at Benjamin Wells's, in the forest, Delaware state. John Gray was the class leader. I met in his class for several years.

My master was an unconverted man, and all the family, but he was what the world called a good master. He was more like a father to his slaves than anything else. He was a very tender, humane man. My mother and father lived with him for many years. He was brought into difficulty, not being able to pay for us, and mother having several children after he had bought us, he sold my mother and three children. My mother sought the Lord and found favor with him, and became a very pious woman. There were three children of us remained with our old master. My oldest brother embraced religion and my sister. Our neighbors, seeing that our master indulged us with the privilege of attending meeting once in two weeks, said that Stokeley's Negroes would soon ruin him; and so my brother and myself held a council together, that we would attend more faithfully to our master's business, so that it should not be said that religion made us worse servants; we would work night and day to get our crops forward, so that they should be disappointed. We frequently went to meeting on every other Thursday; but if we were likely to be backward with our crops we would refrain from going to meeting. When our master found we were making no provision to go to meeting, he would frequently ask us if it was not our meeting day, and if we were not going. We would frequently tell him: "No, sir, we would rather stay at home and get our work done." He would tell us: "Boys, I would rather you would go to your meeting; if I am not good myself, I like to see you striving yourselves to be good." Our reply would be: "Thank you, sir, but we would rather stay and get our crops forward." So we always continued to keep our crops more forward than our neighbors, and we would attend public preaching once in two weeks, and class meeting once a week. At length, our master said he was convinced that religion made slaves better and not worse, and often boasted of his slaves for their honesty and industry. . . .

I had it often impressed upon my mind that I should one day enjoy my freedom; for slavery is a bitter pill, notwithstanding we had a good master. But when we would think that our day's work was never done, we often thought that after our master's death we were liable to be sold to the highest bidder, as he was much in debt; and thus my troubles were increased, and I was often brought to weep between the porch and the altar. But I have had reason to bless my dear Lord that a door was opened unexpectedly for me to buy my time and enjoy my liberty. When I left my master's house I knew not what to do, not being used to hard work, what business I should follow to pay my master and get my living. I went to cutting of cord wood. The first day my hands were so blistered and sore, that it was with difficulty I could open or shut them. I kneeled down upon my knees and prayed that the Lord would open some way for me to get my living. In a few days, my hands recovered and became accustomed to cutting of wood and other hardships; so I soon became able to cut my cord and a half and two cords a day. After I was done cutting I was employed in a brickyard by one Robert Register, at $50 a month, Continental money. After I was done with the brickyard I went to days' work, but

did not forget to serve my dear Lord. . . . February, 1786, I came to Philadelphia. Preaching was given out for me at five o'clock in the morning at St.
George church. I strove to preach as well as I could, but it was a great cross to
me; but the Lord was with me. We had a good time, and several souls were
awakened, and were earnestly seeking redemption in the blood of Christ. I
thought I would stop in Philadelphia a week or two. I preached at different
places in the city. My labor was much blessed. I soon saw a large field open in
seeking and instructing my African brethren, who had been a long forgotten
people and few of them attended public worship. I preached in the commons,
in Southwark, Northern Liberties, and wherever I could find an opening. I
frequently preached twice a day, at 5 o'clock in the morning and in the
evening, and it was not uncommon for me to preach from four to five times a
day. I established prayer meetings; I raised a society in 1786 for forty-two
members. I saw the necessity of erecting a place of worship for the colored
people. I proposed it to the most respectable people of color in this city; but
here I met with opposition. I had but three colored brethren that united with
me in erecting a place of worship—the Rev. Absalom Jones, William White
and Dorus Ginnings. . . . A number of us usually attended St. George's
church in Fourth street; and when the colored people began to get numerous
in attending the church, they moved us from the seats we usually sat on, and
placed us around the wall, and on Sabbath morning we went to church and the
sexton stood at the door, and told us to go in the gallery. He told us to go, and
we would see where to sit. We expected to take the seats over the ones we
formerly occupied below, not knowing any better. We took those seats. Meeting had begun, and they were nearly done singing, and just as we got to the
seats, the elder said, "Let us pray." We had not been long upon our knees
before I heard considerable scuffling and low talking. I raised my head up and
saw one of the trustees, H—— M——, having hold of the Rev. Absalom
Jones, pulling him up off of his knees, and saying, "You must get up—you
must not kneel here." Mr. Jones replied, "Wait until prayer is over." Mr.
H—— M—— said "No, you must get up now, or I will call for aid and force
you away." Mr. Jones said, "Wait until prayer is over, and I will get up and
trouble you no more." With that he beckoned to one of the other trustees,
Mr. L—— S—— to come to his assistance. He came, and went to William
White to pull him up. By this time prayer was over, and we all went out of the
church in a body, and they were no more plagued with us in the church.

OLD ELIZABETH

From *Six Women's Slave Narratives*

I WAS BORN IN MARYLAND IN THE YEAR 1766. My parents were slaves. Both my father and mother were religious people, and belonged to the Methodist Society. It was my father's practice to read in the Bible aloud to his children every sabbath morning. At these seasons, when I was but five years old, I often felt the overshadowing of the Lord's Spirit, without at all understanding what it meant; and these incomes and influences continued to attend me until I was eleven years old, particularly when I was alone, by which I was preserved from doing anything that I thought was wrong.

In the eleventh year of my age, my master sent me to another farm, several miles from my parents, brothers, and sisters, which was a great trouble to me. At last I grew so lonely and sad I thought I should die, if I did not see my mother. I asked the overseer if I might go, but being positively denied, I concluded to go without his knowledge. When I reached home my mother was away. I set off and walked twenty miles before I found her. I staid with her for several days, and we returned together. Next day I was sent back to my new place, which renewed my sorrow. At parting, my mother told me that I had "nobody in the wide world to look to but God." These words fell upon my heart with pondrous weight, and seemed to add to my grief. I went back repeating as I went, "none but God in the wide world." On reaching the farm, I found the overseer was displeased at me for going without his liberty. He tied me with a rope, and gave me some stripes of which I carried the marks for weeks.

After this time, finding as my mother said, I had none in the world to look to but God, I betook myself to prayer, and in every lonely place I found an altar. I mourned sore like a dove and chattered forth my sorrow, moaning in the corners of the field, and under the fences.

I continued in this state for about six months, feeling as though my head were waters, and I could do nothing but weep. I lost my appetite, and not being able to take enough food to sustain nature, I became so weak I had but little strength to work; still I was required to do all my duty. One evening, after the duties of the day were ended, I thought I could not live over the night, so threw myself on a bench, expecting to die, and without being prepared to meet my Maker; and my spirit cried within me, must I die in this state, and be banished from Thy presence forever? I own I am a sinner in Thy sight, and not fit to live where thou art. Still it was my fervent desire that the Lord would pardon me. Just at this season, I saw with my spiritual eye, an awful gulf of misery. As I thought I was about to plunge into it, I heard a voice saying, "rise up and pray," which strengthened me. I fell on my knees and prayed the best I could the Lord's prayer. Knowing no more to say, I halted, but continued on my knees. My spirit was then *taught* to pray, "Lord, have mercy on me— Christ save me." Immediately there appeared a director, clothed in white raiment. . . .

I did not speak much till I had reached my forty-second year, when it was revealed to me that the message which had been given to me I had not yet delivered, and the time had come. As I could read but little, I questioned within myself how it would be possible for me to deliver the message, when I did not understand the Scriptures. Whereupon I was moved to open a Bible that was near me, which I did, and my eyes fell upon this passage, "Gird up thy loins now like a man, and answer thou me. Obey God rather than man," &c. Here I fell into a great exercise of spirit, and was plunged very low. I went from one religious professor to another, enquiring of them what ailed me; but of all these I could find none who could throw any light upon such impressions. They all told me there was nothing in Scripture that would sanction such exercises. It was hard for men to travel, and what would women do? These things greatly discouraged me, and shut up my way, and caused me to resist the Spirit. After going to all that were accounted pious, and receiving no help, I returned to the Lord, feeling that I was nothing, and knew nothing, and wrestled and prayed to the Lord that He would fully reveal His will, and make the way plain. . . .

I felt very unworthy and small, notwithstanding the Lord had shown himself with great power, insomuch that conjecturers and critics were constrained to join in praise to his great name; for truly, we had times of refreshing from the presence of the Lord. At one of the meetings, a vast number of the white inhabitants of the place, and many coloured people, attended—many no doubt from curiosity to hear what the old coloured woman had to say. One, a great scripturian, fixed himself behind the door with pen and ink, in order to take down the discourse in short-hand; but the Almighty Being anointed me with such a portion of his Spirit, that he cast away his paper and pen, and heard the discourse with patience, and was much affected, for the Lord wrought powerfully on his heart. After meeting, he came forward and offered me his hand with solemnity on his countenance, and handed me something to pay for my conveyance home.

I returned, much strengthened by the Lord's power, to go on to the fulfilment of His work, although I was again pressed by the authorities of the church to which I belonged, for imprudency; and so much condemned, that I was sorely tempted by the enemy to turn aside into the wilderness. I was so embarrassed and encompassed, I wondered within myself whether all that were called to be mouth piece for the Lord, suffered such deep wadings as I experienced. . . .

I also held meetings in Virginia. The people there would not believe that a coloured woman could preach. And moreover, as she had no learning, they strove to imprison me because I spoke against slavery: and being brought up, they asked by what authority I spake? and if I had been ordained? I answered, not by the commission of men's hands: if the Lord had ordained me, I needed nothing better.

As I travelled along through the land, I was led at different times to converse with white men who were by profession ministers of the gospel. Many of them, up and down, confessed they did not believe in revelation, which gave me to see that men were sent forth as ministers without Christ's authority. In a conversation with one of these, he said, "You think you have these things by revelation, but there has been no such thing as revelation since Christ's ascension." I asked him where the apostle John got his revelation while he was in the Isle of Patmos. With this, he rose up and left me, and I said in my spirit, get thee behind me Satan.

I visited many remote places, where there were no meeting houses, and held many glorious meetings, for the Lord poured out his Spirit in sweet effusions. I also travelled in Canada, and visited several settlements of coloured people, and felt an open door amongst them.

I may here remark, that while journeying through the different states of the Union, I met with many of the Quaker Friends, and visited them in their families. I received much kindness and sympathy, and no opposition from them, in the prosecution of my labours.

On one occasion, in a thinly settled part of the country, seeing a Friend's meeting house open, I went in; at the same time a Friend and his little daughter followed me. We three composed the meeting. As we sat there in silence, I felt a remarkable overshadowing of the Divine presence, as much so as I ever experienced any where. Toward the close, a few words seemed to be given me, which I expressed, and left the place greatly refreshed in Spirit. From thence I went to Michigan, where I found a wide field of labour amongst my own colour. Here I remained four years. I established a school for coloured orphans, having always felt the great importance of the religious and moral *agri*culture of children, and the great need of it, especially amongst the coloured people. Having white teachers, I met with much encouragement.

My eighty-seventh year had now arrived, when suffering from disease, and feeling released from travelling further in my good Master's cause, I came on to Philadelphia, where I have remained until this time, which brings me to my ninety-seventh year. When I went forth, it was without purse or scrip,—and I have come through great tribulation and temptation—not by any might of my own, for I feel that I am but as dust and ashes before my almighty Helper, who has, according to His promise, been with me and sustained me through all, and gives me now firm faith that he will be with me to the end, and, in his own good time, receive me into His everlasting rest.

JUPITER HAMMON

From *An Address to the Negroes in the State of New York*

NEW YORK, 1787

M Y BRETHREN, WHEN I THINK OF YOU, which is very often, and of the poor, despised, and miserable state you are in, as to the things of this world; and when I think of your ignorance and stupidity, and the great wickedness of most of you, I am pained to the heart. It is at times, almost too much for human nature to bear; and I am obliged to turn my thoughts from the subject. . . . I have wanted exceedingly to say something to you, to call upon you with the tenderness of a father and friend, and to give you the last, and I may say, dying advice of an old man, who wishes your best good in this world, and in the world to come. But while I have had such desires, a sense of my own ignorance, and unfitness to teach others, has frequently discouraged me from attempting to say anything to you; yet, when I thought of your situation, I could not rest easy. . . . I think you will be more likely to listen to what is said, when you know it comes from a Negro, one of your own Nation and colour; and therefore can have no interest in deceiving you, or saying anything to you, but what he really thinks is your interest and duty to comply with. My age, I think, gives me some right to speak to you, and reason to expect you will hearken to my advice. I am now upwards of seventy years old, and cannot expect, though I am well and able to do almost any kind of business, to live much longer. I have passed the common bounds set for man, and must soon go the way of all the earth. I have had more experience in the world than most of you, and I have seen a great deal of the vanity and wickedness of it. I have had great reason to be thankful that my lot has been so much better than most slaves have had. I suppose I have had more advantages and privileges than most of you, who are slaves, have ever known and I believe more than many white people have enjoyed. . . . I do not, my dear friends, say these things about myself to make you think that I am wiser and better than others; but that you might hearken, without prejudice, to what I have to say to you on the following particulars.

"1st. Respecting obedience to masters. Now, whether it is right and lawful, in the sight of God, for them to make slaves of us or not, I am certain that while we are slaves, it is our duty to obey our masters in all their lawful commands, and mind them, unless we are bid to do that which we know to be sin, or forbidden in God's word. . . . It may seem hard for us, if we think our masters wrong in holding us slaves, to obey in all things! . . . As we depend upon our masters for what we eat, and drink, and wear, . . . we cannot be happy unless we obey them. Good servants frequently make good masters.

"Now I acknowledge that liberty is a great thing, and worth seeking for, if we can get it honestly; and by our good conduct, prevail on our masters to set us free: though for my own part I do not wish to be free, yet I should be glad if others, especially the young Negroes, were to be free; for many of us who are grown up slaves, and have always had masters to take care of us, should hardly know how to take care of themselves; and it may be more for our own comfort to remain as we are. That liberty is a great thing we may know from our own feelings, and we may likewise judge so from the conduct of the white people in the late war. How much money has been spent, and how many lives have been lost to defend their liberty. I must say that I have hoped that God would open their eyes, when they were so much engaged for liberty, to think of the state of the poor blacks, and to pity us. . . . Let me beg of you, my dear African brethren, to think very little of your bondage in this life; for your thinking of it will do you no good. If God designs to set us free, he will do it in his own time and way; but think of your bondage to sin and Satan, and do not rest until you are delivered from it. . . ."

BELINDA

From *Unchained Voices*

§

To the honourable the senate and house of representatives, in general court assembled:

The petition of Belinda, an African, Humbly shews,

THAT seventy years have rolled away, since she, on the banks of the Rio de Valta, received her existence. The mountains, covered with spicy forests—vallies, loaded with the richest fruits spontaneously produced—joined to that happy temperature of air, which excludes excess, would have yielded her the most complete felicity, had not her mind received early impressions of the cruelty of men, whose faces were like the moon, and whose bows and arrows were like the thunder and the lightning of the clouds. The idea of these, the most dreadful of all enemies, filled her infant slumbers with horror, and her noon-tide moments with cruel apprehensions! But her affrighted imagination, in its most alarming extension, never represented distresses equal to what she has since really experienced: for before she had twelve years enjoyed the fragrance of her native groves, and ere she had realized that Europeans placed their happiness in the yellow dust, which she carelessly marked with her infant foot-steps—even when she, in a sacred grove, with each hand in that of a tender parent, was paying her devotion to the great Orisa, who made all things, an armed band of white men, driving many of her countrymen in chains, rushed into the hallowed shades! Could the tears, the sighs, the supplications, bursting from the tortured parental affection, have blunted the keen edge of avarice, she might have been rescued from agony, which many of her country's children have felt, but which none have ever described. In vain she lifted her supplicating voice to an insulted father, and her guiltless hands to a dishonoured deity! She was ravished from the bosom of her country, from the arms of her friends, while the advanced age of her parents rendering them unfit for servitude, cruelly separated them from her for ever.

Scenes which her imagination had never conceived of, a floating world, the sporting monsters of the deep, and the familiar meeting of billows and clouds, strove, but in vain, to divert her attention from three hundred Africans in chains, suffering the most excruciating torment; and some of them rejoicing that the pangs of death came like a balm to their wounds.

Once more her eyes were blessed with a continent: but alas! how unlike the land where she received her being! Here all things appeared unpropitious. She learned to catch the ideas, marked by the sounds of language, only to know that her doom was slavery, from which death alone was to emancipate her. What did it avail her, that the walls of her lord were hung with splendor, and that the dust trodden under foot in her native country, crouded his gates with sordid worshippers! The laws rendered her incapable of receiving property: and though she was a free moral agent, accountable for her own actions, yet never had she a moment at her own disposal! Fifty years her faithful hands have been compelled to ignoble servitude for the benefit of an Isaac Royall, until, as if nations must be agitated, and the world convulsed, for the preservation of that freedom, which the Almighty Father intended for all the human race, the present war commenced. The terrors of men, armed in the cause of freedom, compelled her master to fly, and to breathe away his life in a land, where lawless dominion sits enthroned, pouring blood and vengeance on all who dare to be free.

The face of your petitioner is now marked with the furrows of time, and her frame feebly bending under the oppression of years, while she, by the laws of the land, is denied the enjoyment of one morsel of that immense wealth, a part whereof hath been accumulated by her own industry, and the whole augmented by her servitude.

Wherefore, casting herself at the feet of your honours, as to a body of men, formed for the extirpation of vassalage, for the reward of virtue, and the just returns of honest industry—she prays that such allowance may be made her, out of the estate of colonel Royall, as will prevent her, and her more infirm daughter, from misery in the greatest extreme, and scatter comfort over the short and downward path of their lives: and she will ever pray.

BELINDA.
Boston, February, 1782. (538–540).

BENJAMIN BANNEKER

From *The Mind of the Negro as Reflected in Letters*
Written During the Crisis 1800–1860

❧

BALTIMORE, 1791

MARYLAND, BALTIMORE COUNTY,
NEAR ELLICOTTS' LOWER MILLS, AUGUST 19TH, 1791.
THOMAS JEFFERSON, *Secretary of State.*

Sir:—I am fully sensible of the greatness of that freedom, which I take with you on the present occasion, a liberty which seemed to me scarcely allowable, when I reflected on that distinguished and dignified station in which you stand, and the almost general prejudice and prepossession which is so prevalent in the world against those of my complexion.

I suppose it is a truth too well attested to you, to need a proof here, that we are a race of beings who have long laboured under the abuse and censure of the world, that we have long been considered rather as brutish than human, and scarcely capable of mental endowments.

Sir, I hope I may safely admit, in consequence of that report which hath reached me, that you are a man far less inflexible in sentiments of this nature than many others, that you are measureably friendly and well disposed towards us, and that you are ready and willing to lend your aid and assistance to our relief, from those many distressed and numerous calamities, to which we are reduced.

Now, sir, if this is founded in truth, I apprehend you will readily embrace every opportunity to eradicate that train of absurd and false ideas and opinions, which so generally prevails with respect to us, and that your sentiments are concurrent with mine, which are that one universal father hath given being to us all, and that he hath not only made us all of one flesh, but that he hath also without partiality afforded us all the same sensations, and endued us all with the same faculties, and that however variable we may be in society or religion, however diversified in situation or colour, we are all of the same family, and stand in the same relation to him.

Sir, if these are sentiments of which you are fully persuaded, I hope you cannot but acknowledge, that it is the indispensable duty of those who maintain for themselves the rights of human nature, and who profess the obligations of Christianity, to extend their power and influence to the relief of every part of the human race, from whatever burthen or oppression they may unjustly labour under, and this I apprehend a full conviction of the truth and obligation of these principles should lead all to.

Sir, I have long been convinced, that if your love for yourselves and for those inestimable laws, which preserve to you the rights of human nature, was founded on sincerity, you could not but be solicitous that every individual of whatever rank or distinction, might with you equally enjoy the blessings thereof, neither could you rest satisfied, short of the most active diffusion of your exertions, in order, to their promotion from any state of degradation, to which the unjustifiable cruelty and barbarism of men may have reduced them.

Sir, I freely and cheerfully acknowledge that I am of the African race, and in that colour which is natural to them of the deepest dye, and it is under a sense of the most profound gratitude to the supreme ruler of the Universe, that I now confess to you, that I am not under that state of tyrannical thraldom, and inhuman captivity, to which too many of my brethren are doomed, but that I have abundantly tasted of the fruition of those blessings, which proceed from that free and unequalled liberty, with which you are favored, and which, I hope you will willingly allow, you have received from the immediate hand of that being, from whom proceedeth every good and perfect gift.

Sir, suffer me to recall to your mind that time in which the arms and tyranny of the British crown were exerted with every powerful effort in order to reduce you to a state of servitude; look back, I entreat you, on the variety of dangers to which you were exposed; reflect on that time in which every human aid appeared unavailable, and in which even hope and fortitude wore the aspect of inability to the conflict, and you cannot but be led to a serious and grateful sense of your miraculous and providential preservation; you cannot but acknowledge, that the present freedom and tranquility which you enjoy, you have mercifully received, and that is the peculiar blessing of heaven.

This, sir, was a time in which you clearly saw into the injustice of a state of slavery, and in which you had just apprehension of the horrors of its condition, it was now, sir, that your abhorrence thereof was so excited, that you publicly held forth this true and invaluable doctrine, which is worthy to be recorded and remembered in all succeeding ages. ''We hold these truths to be self-evident, that all men are created equal, and that they are endowed by their creator with certain inalienable rights, that among these are life, liberty and the pursuit of happiness.''

Here, sir, was a time in which your tender feelings for yourselves had engaged you thus to declare, you were then impressed with proper ideas of the great valuation of liberty, and the free possession of those blessings to which you were entitled by nature; but, sir, how pitiable is it to reflect that although you were so fully convinced of the benevolence of the Father of mankind, and of his equal and impartial distribution of those rights and privileges which he had conferred upon them, that you should at the same time counteract his mercies, in detaining by fraud and violence so numerous a part of my brethren, under groaning captivity and cruel oppression, that you should at the same time be found guilty of that most criminal act, which you professedly detested in others with respect to yourselves.

Sir, I suppose that your knowledge of the situation of my brethren, is too extensive to need recital here; neither shall I presume to prescribe methods by which they may be relieved, otherwise than by recommending to you and all others, to wean yourselves from those narrow prejudices which you have imbibed with respect to them, and as Job proposed to his friends, ''put your souls in their souls stead,'' thus shall your hearts be enlarged with kindness and benevolence towards them, and thus shall you need neither the direction of myself nor others, in what manner to proceed herein.

And now, sir, although my sympathy and affection for my brethren hath cause my enlargement thus far, I ardently hope that your candour and generosity, will plead with you in my behalf, when I make known to you, that it was not originally my design; but that having taken up my pen, in order to direct to you as a present, a copy of an almanac, which I have calculated for the succeeding year, I was unexpectedly and unavoidably led thereto.

This calculation, sir, is the production of my arduous study in this my advanced stage of life; for having long had unbounded desires to become acquainted with the secrets of nature, I have had to gratify my curiosity herein through my own assiduous application to astronomical study, in which I need not to recount to you the many difficulties and disadvantages which I have had to encounter.

And although I had almost declined to make my calculation for the ensuing year, in consequence of that time which I had allotted therefor, being taken up at the Federal Territory, by the request of Mr. Andrew Ellicott, yet finding myself under several engagements to printers of this State, to whom I had communicated my design, on my return to my place of residence, I industriously applied myself thereto, which I hope I have accomplished with correctness and accuracy, a copy of which I have taken the liberty to direct to you, and which I humbly request you will favorably receive, and although you may have the opportunity of perusing it after its publication, yet I chose to send it to you in manuscript previous thereto, that thereby you might not only have an earlier inspection, but that you might also view it in my own hand-writing.

And now, sir, I shall conclude and subscribe myself, with the most profound respect, your most obedient humble servant,

B. BANNEKER.

PRINCE HALL

From *The Colored Patriots of the American Revolution*

MASSACHUSETTS, 1797

"Beloved Brethren of the African Lodge:

"It is now five years since I delivered a charge to you on some parts and points of masonry. As one branch or superstructure of the foundation, I endeavored to show you the duty of a mason to a mason, and of charity and love to all mankind, as the work and image of the great God and the Father of the human race. I shall now attempt to show you that it is our duty to sympathise with our fellow-men under their troubles, and with the families of our brethren who are gone, we hope, to the Grand Lodge above.

"We are to have sympathy," said he, "but this, after all, is not to be confined to parties or colors, nor to towns or states, nor to a kingdom, but to the kingdoms of the whole earth, over whom Christ the King is head and grand master for all in distress.

"Among these numerous sons and daughters of distress, let us see our friends and brethren; and first let us see *them* dragged from their native country, by the iron hand of tyranny and oppression, from their dear friends and connections, with weeping eyes and aching hearts, to a strange land, and among a strange people, whose tender mercies are cruel,—and there to bear the iron yoke of slavery and cruelty, till death, as a friend, shall relieve them. And must not the unhappy condition of these, our fellow-men, draw forth our hearty prayers and wishes for their deliverance from those merchants and traders, whose characters you have described in Revelations xviii. 11–13? And who knows but these same sort of traders may, in a short time, in like manner bewail the loss of the African traffic, to their shame and confusion? The day dawns now in some of the West India Islands. God can and will change their condition and their hearts, too, and let Boston and the world know that He hath no respect of persons, and that that bulwark of envy, pride, scorn and contempt, which is so visible in some, shall fall.

"Jethro, an Ethiopian, gave instructions to his son-in-law, Moses, in establishing government. Exodus xviii. 22–24. Thus, Moses was not ashamed to be instructed by a black man. Philip was not ashamed to take a seat beside the Ethiopian Eunuch, and to instruct him in the gospel. The Grand Master Solomon was not ashamed to hold conference with the Queen of Sheba. Our Grand Master Solomon did not divide the living child, whatever he might do with the dead one; neither did he pretend to make a law to forbid the parties from having free intercourse with one another, without the fear of censure, or be turned out of the synagogue.

"Now, my brethren, nothing is stable; all things are changeable. Let us seek those things which are sure and steadfast, and let us pray God that, while we remain here, he would give us the grace of patience, and strength to bear up under all our troubles, which, at this day, God knows, we have our share of. Patience, I say; for were we not possessed of a great measure of it, we could not bear up under the daily insults we meet with in the streets of Boston, much more on public days of recreation. How, at such times, are we shamefully abused, and that to such a degree, that we may truly be said to carry our lives in our hands, and the arrows of death are flying about our heads. Helpless women have their clothes torn from their backs. . . . And by whom are these disgraceful and abusive actions committed? Not by the men born and bred in Boston,—they are better bred; but by a mob or horde of shameless, low-lived, envious, spiteful persons—some of them, not long since, servants in gentlemen's kitchens, scouring knives, horse-tenders, chaise-drivers. I was told by a gentleman who saw the filthy behavior in the Common, that, in all places he had been in, he never saw so cruel behavior in all his life; and that a slave in the West Indies, on Sundays, or holidays, enjoys himself and friends without molestation. Not only this man, but many in town, who have seen their behavior to us, and that, without provocation, twenty or thirty cowards have fallen upon one man. (O, the patience of the blacks!) 'T is not for want of courage in you, for they know that they do not face you man for man; but in a mob, which we despise, and would rather suffer wrong than to do wrong, to the disturbance of the community, and the disgrace of our reputation; for every good citizen doth honor to the laws of the State where he resides.

"My brethren, let us not be cast down under these and many other abuses we at present are laboring under,—for the darkest hour is just before the break of day. My brethren, let us remember what a dark day it was with our African brethren, six years ago, in the French West Indies. Nothing but the snap of the whip was heard, from morning to evening. Hanging, breaking on the wheel, burning, and all manner of tortures, were inflicted on those unhappy people. But, blessed be God, the scene is changed. They now confess that God hath no respect of persons, and, therefore, receive them as their friends, and treat them as brothers. Thus doth Ethiopia stretch forth her hand from slavery, to freedom and equality.''

Part III.

§

FROM THE COTTON PATCH

TO THE BIG HOUSE

In the opening line of Jenny Proctor's narrative she disputes the rumor of any ''good days'' of slavery, and the grueling testimony of her experiences in Alabama confirms the fact. If Proctor's piece is typical of the bondage the captives endured, then their housing, nourishment, and clothing were terribly inadequate, the auction block and the possibility of being sold away from the family was a daily concern, learning to read and to write were prohibited, and punishment could be expected for the smallest act of insubordination or disobedience.

While Proctor and her ilk in the deep South were the primary victims of bondage, shuttling them from one farm to another at the height of the domestic slave trade, there were thousands of abolitionists in the North who were untiring in their efforts to end the Atlantic slave trade. Peter Williams of New York City was one of the more outspoken proponents of this cause. At the time of this speech, January 1, 1808, the prohibition against the heinous slave traffic was a moment of joy for black Americans. Williams, a fine orator and rector of St. Phillips Episcopal Church, was mindful of the event's historical significance. And yet, with unnerving prescience, he admonishes his people that it may always be a struggle to earn the respect of the larger society. In addition to providing advice and encouragement to his congregation, Williams also induced such budding intellectuals as Alexander Crummell to study for the Episcopalian ministry, which Crummell did to great success at Oneida Institute and later at Queen's College in England.

Williams's proselytizing would probably not have had any effect on a devout Muslim such as Abd ar-Rahman. Slave owners were often puzzled when some of their captives would suddenly cease activity, drop to their knees, and pray to the East. Only later would they learn that these Africans were Muslims who were merely fulfilling their daily prayers. Though it is estimated that one fifth of the slaves brought to the Americas from West Africa were Muslims, there was no collective worship or mosques where they could openly express their beliefs. Rahman, like other Muslims, was forced to practice his religion surreptitiously and in isolation.

Social scientists, speculating today on the racial and class dimensions that formed this society, would be deeply rewarded studying Austin Steward's insightful analysis of life on a large Virginia plantation. Few historians have given such thorough, specific discussion of social relations and class structure on the plantation as Steward. His perspective from the "Big House" covers in great detail the duties and responsibilities of all the slaves, be they yardboys, fiddlers, cooks, or field hands. Toward the end of his entry he speculates on the demeanor and the apprehensive outlook of the slave master, and the nightmare of rebellion that troubles his sleep.

JENNY PROCTOR

From *Lay My Burden Down*

ALABAMA, 1800S

I'S HEAR TELL OF THEM GOOD SLAVE days, but I ain't never seen no good times then. My mother's name was Lisa, and when I was a very small child I hear that driver going from cabin to cabin as early as 3 o'clock in the morning, and when he comes to our cabin he say, "Lisa, Lisa, git up from there and git that breakfast." My mother, she was cook, and I don't recollect nothing 'bout my father. If I had any brothers and sisters I didn't know it. We had old ragged huts made out of poles and some of the cracks chinked up with mud and moss and some of them wasn't. We didn't have no good beds, just scaffolds nailed up to the wall out of poles and the old ragged bedding throwed on them. That sure was hard sleeping, but even that feel good to our weary bones after them long hard day's work in the field. I tended to the children when I was a little gal and tried to clean the house just like Old Miss tells me to. Then soon as I was ten years old, Old Master, he say, "Git this here nigger to that cotton patch."

I recollects once when I was trying to clean the house like Old Miss tell me, I finds a biscuit, and I's so hungry I et it, 'cause we never see such a thing as a biscuit only sometimes on Sunday morning. We just have corn bread and syrup and sometimes fat bacon, but when I et that biscuit and she comes in and say, "Where that biscuit?" I say, "Miss, I et it 'cause I's so hungry." Then she grab that broom and start to beating me over the head with it and calling me low-down nigger, and I guess I just clean lost my head 'cause I knowed better than to fight her if I knowed anything 't all, but I start to fight her, and the driver, he comes in and he grabs me and starts beating me with that cat-o'-nine-tails, and he beats me till I fall to the floor nearly dead. He cut my back all to pieces, then they rubs salt in the cuts for more punishment. Lord, Lord, honey! Them was awful days. When Old Master come to the house, he say, "What you beat that nigger like that for?" And the driver tells him why, and he say, "She can't work now for a week. She pay for several biscuits in that time." He sure was mad, and he tell Old Miss she start the whole mess. I still got them scars on my old back right now, just like my grandmother have when she die, and I's a-carrying mine right on to the grave just like she did.

Our master, he wouldn't 'low us to go fishing—he say that too easy on a nigger and wouldn't 'low us to hunt none either—but sometime we slips off at night and catch possums. And when Old Master smells them possums cooking 'way in the night, he wraps up in a white sheet and gits in the chimney corner and scratch on the wall, and when the man in the cabin goes to the door and say, "Who's that?" he say, "It's me, what's ye cooking in there?" and the man say, "I's cooking possum." He say, "Cook him and bring me the hindquarters and you and the wife and the children eat the rest." We never had no chance to git any rabbits 'cept when we was a-clearing and grubbing the new ground. Then we catch some rabbits, and if they looks good to the white folks they takes them and if they no good the niggers git them. We never had no gardens. Sometimes the slaves git vegetables from the white folks' garden and some-times they didn't.

Money? Uh-uh! We never seen no money. Guess we'd-a bought something to eat with it if we ever seen any. Fact is, we wouldn't-a knowed hardly how to bought anything, 'cause we didn't know nothing 'bout going to town.

They spinned the cloth what our clothes was made of, and we had straight dresses or slips made of lowell. Sometimes they dye 'em with sumac berries or sweet-gum bark, and sometimes they didn't. On Sunday they make all the children change, and what we wears till we gits our clothes washed was gunny sacks with holes cut for our head and arms. We didn't have no shoes 'cepting some homemade moccasins, and we didn't have them till we was big children. The little children they goes naked till they was big enough to work. They was soon big enough though, 'cording to our master. We had red flannel for winter underclothes. Old Miss she say a sick nigger cost more than the flannel.

Weddings? Uh-uh! We just steps over the broom and we's married. Ha! Ha! Ha!

Old Master he had a good house. The logs was all hewed off smooth-like, and the cracks all fixed with nice chinking, plumb 'spectable-looking even to the plank floors. That was something. He didn't have no big plantation, but he keeps 'bout three hundred slaves in them little huts with dirt floors. I thinks he calls it four farms what he had.

Sometimes he would sell some of the slaves off of that big auction block to the highest bidder when he could git enough for one.

When he go to sell a slave, he feed that one good for a few days, then when he goes to put 'em up on the auction block he takes a meat skin and greases all round that nigger's mouth and makes 'em look like they been eating plenty meat and such like and was good and strong and able to work. Sometimes he sell the babes from the breast, and then again he sell the mothers from the babes and the husbands and the wives, and so on. He wouldn't let 'em holler much when the folks be sold away. He say, "I have you whupped if you don't hush." They sure loved their six children though. They wouldn't want nobody buying them.

We might-a done very well if the old driver hadn't been so mean, but the least little thing we do he beat us for it and put big chains round our ankles and make us work with them on till the blood be cut out all around our ankles. Some of the masters have what they call stockades and puts their heads and feet and arms through holes in a big board out in the hot sun, but our old driver he had a bull pen. That's only thing like a jail he had. When a slave do anything he didn't like, he takes 'em in that bull pen and chains 'em down, face up to the sun, and leaves 'em there till they nearly dies.

None of us was 'lowed to see a book or try to learn. They say we git smarter than they was if we learn anything, but we slips around and gits hold of that Webster's old blue-back speller and we hides it till 'way in the night and then we lights a little pine torch, and studies that spelling book. We learn it too. I can read some now and write a little too.

They wasn't no church for the slaves, but we goes to the white folks' arbor on Sunday evening, and a white man he gits up there to preach to the niggers. He say, "Now I takes my text, which is, Nigger obey your master and your mistress, 'cause what you git from them here in this world am all you ever going to git, 'cause you just like the hogs and the other animals—when you dies you ain't no more, after you been throwed in that hole." I guess we believed that for a while 'cause we didn't have no way finding out different. We didn't see no Bibles.

Sometimes a slave would run away and just live wild in the woods, but most times they catch 'em and beats 'em, then chains 'em down in the sun till they nearly die. The only way any slaves on our farm ever goes anywhere was when the boss sends him to carry some news to another plantation or when we slips off way in the night. Sometimes after all the work was done a bunch would have it made up to slip out down to the creek and dance. We sure have fun when we do that, most times on Saturday night.

All the Christmas we had was Old Master would kill a hog and give us a piece of pork. We thought that was something, and the way Christmas lasted was 'cording to the big sweet-gum backlog what the slaves would cut and put in the fireplace. When that burned out, the Christmas was over. So you know we all keeps a-looking the whole year round for the biggest sweet gum we could find. When we just couldn't find the sweet gum, we git oak, but it wouldn't last long enough, 'bout three days on average, when we didn't have to work. Old Master he sure pile on them pine knots, gitting that Christmas over so we could git back to work. . . .

When Old Master comes down in the cotton patch to tell us 'bout being free, he say, "I hates to tell you, but I knows I's got to—you is free, just as free as me or anybody else what's white." We didn't hardly know what he means. We just sort of huddle round together like scared rabbits, but after we knowed what he mean, didn't many of us go, 'cause we didn't know where to of went. Old Master he say he give us the woods land and half of what we make on it, and we could clear it and work it or starve. Well, we didn't know hardly what to do 'cause he just gives us some old dull hoes and axes to work with; but we all went to work, and as we cut down the trees and the poles he tells us to build the fence round the field and we did, and when we plants the corn and the cotton we just plant all the fence corners full too, and I never seen so much stuff grow in all my born days. Several ears of corn to the stalk, and them big cotton stalks was a-laying over on the ground. Some of the old slaves they say they believe the Lord knew something 'bout niggers after all. He lets us put corn in his crib, and then we builds cribs and didn't take long 'fore we could buy some hosses and some mules and some good hogs. Them mangy hogs what our master give us the first year was plumb good hogs after we grease them and scrub them with lye soap. He just give us the ones he thought was sure to die, but we was a-gitting going now, and 'fore long we was a-building better houses and feeling kind of happy-like. After Old Master dies, we keeps hearing talk of Texas, and me and my old man—I's done been married several years then and had one little boy—well, we gits in our covered wagon with our little mules hitched to it, and we comes to Texas. We worked as sharecroppers around Buffalo, Texas, till my old man he died. My boy was nearly grown then, so he wants to come to San Angelo and work, so here we is. He done been married long time now and git six children. Some of them work at hotels and cafés and filling stations and in homes.

PETER WILLIAMS

From *Negro Orators and Their Orations*

§

NEW YORK, 1808

FATHERS, BRETHREN, AND FELLOW CITIZENS: AT THIS auspicious moment I felicitate you on the abolition of the Slave Trade. This inhuman branch of commerce which, for some centuries past, has been carried on to a considerable extent, is, by the singular interposition of Divine Providence, this day extinguished. An event so important, so pregnant with happy consequences, must be extremely consonant to every philanthropic heart.

But to us, Africans and descendants of Africans, this period is deeply interesting. We have felt, sensibly felt, the sad effects of this abominable traffic. It has made, if not ourselves, our forefathers and kinsmen its unhappy victims; and pronounced on them, and their posterity, the sentence of perpetual slavery. But benevolent men have voluntarily stepped forward to obviate the consequences of this injustice and barbarity. They have striven, assiduously to restore our natural rights; to guaranty them from fresh innovations; to furnish us with necessary information; and to stop the source from whence our evils have flowed.

The fruits of these laudable endeavors have long been visible; each moment they appear more conspicuous; and this day has produced an event which shall ever be memorable and glorious in the annals of history. We are now assembled to celebrate this momentous era; to recognize the beneficial influences of humane exertions; and by suitable demonstrations of joy, thanksgiving, and gratitude, to return to our heavenly Father, and to our earthly benefactors, our sincere acknowledgments.

Review, for a moment, my brethren, the history of the Slave Trade. Engendered in the foul recesses of the sordid mind, the unnatural monster inflicted gross evils on the human race. Its baneful footsteps are marked with blood; its infectious breath spreads war and desolation; and its train is composed of the complicated miseries of cruel and unceasing bondage.

Before the enterprising spirit of European genius explored the western coast of Africa, the state of our forefathers was a state of simplicity, innocence, and contentment. Unskilled in the arts of dissimulation, their bosoms were the seats of confidence; and their lips were the organs of truth. Strangers to the refinements of civilized society, they followed with implicit obedience the (simple) dictates of nature. Peculiarly observant of hospitality, they offered a place of refreshment to the weary, and an asylum to the unfortunate. Ardent in their affections, their minds were susceptible of the warmest emotions of love, friendship, and gratitude.

Although unacquainted with the diversified luxuries and amusements of civilized nations, they enjoyed some singular advantages from the bountiful hand of nature and from their own innocent and amiable manners, which rendered them a happy people. But, alas! this delightful picture has long since vanished; the angel of bliss has deserted their dwelling; and the demon of indescribable misery has rioted, uncontrolled, on the fair fields of our ancestors. After Columbus unfolded to civilized man the vast treasures of this western world, the desire of gain, which had chiefly induced the first colonists of America to cross the waters of the Atlantic, surpassing the bounds of reasonable acquisition, violated the sacred injunctions of the gospel, frustrated the designs of the pious and humane, and, enslaving the harmless aborigines, compelled them to drudge in the mines. . . .

I need not, my brethren, take a further view of our present circumstances, to convince you of the providential benefits which we have derived from our patrons; for if you take a retrospect of the past situation of Africans, and descendants of Africans, in this and other countries, to your observation our advancements must be obvious. From these considerations, added to the happy event which we now celebrate, let us ever entertain the profoundest veneration for our munificent benefactors, and return to them from the altars of our hearts the fragrant incense of incessant gratitude. But let not, my brethren, our demonstrations of gratitude be confined to the mere expressions of our lips.

The active part which the friends of humanity have taken to ameliorate our sufferings has rendered them, in a measure, the pledges of our integrity. You must be well aware that notwithstanding their endeavors, they have yet remaining, from interest and prejudice, a number of opposers. These, carefully watching for every opportunity to injure the cause, will not fail to augment the smallest defects in our lives and conversation; and reproach our benefactors with them as the fruits of their actions.

Let us, therefore, by a steady and upright deportment, by a strict obedience and respect to the laws of the land, form an invulnerable bulwark against the shafts of malice. Thus, evincing to the world that our garments are unpolluted by the stains of ingratitude, we shall reap increasing advantages from the favors conferred; the spirits of our departed ancestors shall smile with complacency on the change of our state; and posterity shall exult in the pleasing remembrance.

May the time speedily commence when Ethiopia shall stretch forth her hands; when the sum of liberty shall beam resplendent on the whole African race; and its genial influences promote the luxuriant growth of knowledge and virtue.

ABD AR-RAHMAN

From *African Muslims in Antebellum America*

AFRICA, 1828

I WAS BORN IN THE CITY OF TOMBUCTOO. My Father had been living in Tombuctoo, but removed to be King in Teembo, in Foota Jallo. His name was Almam Abrahim. I was five years old when my father carried me from Tombuctoo. I lived in Teembo, mostly, until I was twenty-one, and followed the horsemen. I was made Captain when I was twenty-one—after they put me to that, and found that I had a very good head, at twenty-four they made me Colonel. At the age of twenty-six, they sent me to fight the Hebohs, because they destroyed the vessels that came to the coast, and prevented our trade. When we fought, I defeated them. But they went back one hundred miles into the country, and hid themselves in the mountain.—We could not see them, and did not expect there was any enemy. When we got there, we dismounted and led our horses, until we were half way up the mountain. Then they fired upon us. We saw the smoke, we heard the guns, we saw the people drop down. I told every one to run until we reached the top of the hill, then to wait for each other until all came there, and we would fight them. After I had arrived at the summit, I could see no one except my guard. They followed us, and we ran and fought. I saw this would not do. I told every one to run who wished to do so. Every one who wished to run, fled. I said I will not run for an African [Kufr?]. I got down from my horse and sat down. One came behind and shot me in the shoulder. One came before and pointed his gun to shoot me, but seeing my clothes, (ornamented with gold,) he cried out, that! the King. Then every one turned down their guns, and came and took me. When they came to take me, I had a sword under me, but they did not see it. The first one that came, I sprang forward and killed. Then one came behind and knocked me down with a gun, and I fainted. They carried me to a pond of water, and dipped me in; after I came to myself they bound me. They pulled off my shoes, and made me go barefoot one hundred miles, and led my horse before me. After they took me to their own country, they kept me one week. As soon as my people got home, my father missed me. He raised a troop, and came after me; and as soon as the Hebohs knew he was coming, they carried me into the wilderness. After my father came and burnt the country, they carried me to the Mandingo country, on the Gambia. They sold me directly, with fifty others, to an English ship. They took me to the Island of Dominica. After that I was taken to New Orleans. Then they took me to Natchez, and Colonel F[oster] bought me. I have lived with Colonel F. 40 years. Thirty years I laboured hard. The last ten years I have been indulged a good deal. I have left five children behind, and eight grand children. I feel sad, to think of leaving my children behind me. I desire to go back to my own country again; but when I think of my children, it hurts my feelings. If I go to my own country, I cannot feel happy, if my children are left. I hope, by God's assistance, to recover them. Since I have been in Washington, I have found a good many friends. I hope they will treat me in other cities as they have treated me in the city of Washington, and then I shall get my children. I want to go to Baltimore, Philadelphia, and N. York, and then I shall return hither again.

AUSTIN STEWARD

From *Austin Steward: Twenty-two Years a Slave and Forty Years a Freeman*

VIRGINIA, 1828–1829

WHEN EIGHT YEARS OF AGE, I WAS taken to the "great house," or the family mansion of my master, to serve as an errand boy, where I had to stand in the presence of my master's family all the day, and a part of the night, ready to do any thing which they commanded me to perform.

My master's family consisted of himself and wife, and seven children. His overseer, whose name was Barsly Taylor, had also a wife and five children. These constituted the white population on the plantation. Capt. Helm was the owner of about one hundred slaves, which made the residents on the plantation number about one hundred and sixteen persons in all. One hundred and seven of them, were required to labor for the benefit of the remaining nine, who possessed that vast domain; and one hundred of the number doomed to unrequited toil, under the lash of a cruel task-master during life, with no hope of release this side of the grave, and as far as the cruel oppressor is concerned, shut out from hope beyond it.

And here let me ask, why is this practice of working slaves half clad, poorly fed, with nothing or nearly so, to stimulate them to exertion, but fear of the lash? Do the best interests of our common country require it? I think not. Did the true interest of Capt. Helm demand it? Whatever may have been his opinion, I cannot think it did. Can it be for the best interest or good of the enslaved? Certainly not; for there is no real inducement for the slaveholder to make beasts of burden of his fellow men, but that which was frankly acknowledged by Gibbs and other pirates: "we have the power,"—the power to rob and murder on the high seas!—which they will undoubtedly continue to hold, until overtaken by justice; which will certainly come some time, just as sure as that a righteous God reigns over the earth or rules in heaven.

Some have attempted to apologize for the enslaving of the Negro, by saying that they are inferior to the Anglo-saxon race in every respect. This charge I deny; it is utterly false. Does not the Bible inform us that "God hath created of one blood all the nations of the earth?" And certainly in stature and physical force the colored man is quite equal to his white brother, and in many instances his superior; but were it otherwise, I can not see why the more favored class should enslave the other. True, God has given to the African a darker complexion than to his white brother; still, each have the same desires and aspirations. The food required for the sustenance of one is equally necessary for the other. Naturally or physically, they alike require to be warmed by the cheerful fire, when chilled by our northern winter's breath; and alike they welcome the cool spring and the delightful shade of summer. Hence, I have come to the conclusion that God created all men free and equal, and placed them upon this earth to do good and benefit each other, and that war and slavery should be banished from the face of the earth.

My dear reader will not understand me to say, that all nations are alike intelligent, enterprising and industrious, for we all know that it is far otherwise; but to man, and not to our Creator, should the fault be charged. But, to resume our narrative.

Capt. Helm was not a very hard master; but generally was kind and pleasant. Indulgent when in good humor, but like many of the southerners, terrible when in a passion. He was a great sportsman, and very fond of company. He generally kept one or two race horses, and a pack of hounds for fox-hunting, which at that time, was a very common and fashionable diversion in that section of country. He was not only a sportsman, but a gamester, and was in the habit of playing cards, and sometimes betting very high and losing accordingly. . . .

Mrs. Helm was a very industrious woman, and generally busy in her household affairs—sewing, knitting, and looking after the servants; but she was a great scold,—continually finding fault with some of the servants, and frequently punishing the young slaves herself, by striking them over the head with a heavy iron key, until the blood ran; or else whipping them with a cowhide, which she always kept by her side when sitting in her room. The older servants she would cause to be punished by having them severely whipped by a man, which she never failed to do for every trifling fault. I have felt the weight of some of her heaviest keys on my own head, and for the slightest offences. No slave could possibly escape being punished—I care not how attentive they might be, nor how industrious—punished they must be, and punished they certainly were. Mrs. Helm appeared to be uneasy unless some of the servants were under the lash. She came into the kitchen one morning and my mother, who was cook, had just put on the dinner. Mrs. Helm took out her white cambric handkerchief, and rubbed it on the inside of the pot, and it crocked it! That was enough to invoke the wrath of my master, who came forth immediately with his horse-whip, with which he whipped my poor mother most unmercifully—far more severely than I ever knew him to whip a horse.

I once had the misfortune to break the lock of master's shot gun, and when it came to his knowledge, he came to me in a towering passion, and charged me with what he considered the *crime* of carelessness. I denied it, and told him I knew nothing about it; but I was so terribly frightened that he saw I was guilty, and told me so, foaming with rage; and then I confessed the truth. But oh, there was no escaping the lash. Its recollection is still bitter, and ever will be. I was commanded to take off my clothes, which I did, and then master put me on the back of another slave, my arms hanging down before him and my hands clasped in his, where he was obliged to hold me with a vise-like grasp. Then master gave me the most severe flogging that I ever received, and I pray God that I may never again experience such torture. And yet Capt. Helm was not the worst of masters.

These cruelties are daily occurrences, and so degrading is the whole practice of Slavery, that it not only crushes and brutalizes the wretched slave, but it hardens the heart, benumbs all the fine feelings of humanity, and deteriorates from the character of the slaveholders themselves,—whether man or woman. Otherwise, how could a gentle, and in other respects, amiable woman, look on such scenes of cruelty, without a shudder of utter abhorrence? But slaveholding ladies, can not only look on quietly, but with approbation; and what is worse, though very common, they can and do use the lash and cowhide themselves, on the backs of their own slaves, and that too on those of their own sex! Far rather would I spend my life in a State's Prison, than be the slave of the best slaveholder on the earth!

When I was not employed as an errand-boy, it was my duty to stand behind my master's chair, which was sometimes the whole day, never being allowed to sit in his presence. Indeed, no slave is ever allowed to sit down in the presence of their master or mistress. If a slave is addressed when sitting, he is required to spring to his feet, and instantly remove his hat, if he has one, and answer in the most humble manner, or lay the foundation for a flogging, which will not be long delayed.

I slept in the same room with my master and mistress. This room was elegantly furnished with damask curtains, mahogany bedstead of the most expensive kind, and every thing else about it was of the most costly kind. And while Mr. and Mrs. Helm reposed on their bed of down, with a cloud of lace floating over them, like some Eastern Prince, with their slaves to fan them while they slept, and to tremble when they awoke, I always slept upon the floor, without a pillow or even a blanket, but, like a dog, lay down anywhere I could find a place.

Slaves are never allowed to leave the plantation to which they belong, without a written pass. Should any one venture to disobey this law, he will most likely be caught by the *patrol* and given thirty-nine lashes. This patrol is always on duty every Sunday, going to each plantation under their supervision, entering every slave cabin, and examining closely the conduct of the slaves; and if they find one slave from another plantation without a pass, he is immediately punished with a severe flogging.

I recollect going one Sunday with my mother, to visit my grand-mother; and while there, two or three of the patrol came and looked into the cabin, and seeing my mother, demanded her pass. She told them that she had one, but had left it in another cabin, from whence she soon brought it, which saved her a whipping but we were terribly frightened.

The reader will obtain a better knowledge of the character of a Virginia patrol, by the relation of an affair, which came off on the neighboring plantation of Col. Alexander, in which some forty of Capt. Helm's slaves were engaged, and which proved rather destructive of human life in the end.

But I must first say that it is not true, that slave owners are respected for kindness to their slaves. The more tyrannical a master is, the more will he be favorably regarded by his neighboring planters; and from the day that he acquires the reputation of a kind and indulgent master, he is looked upon with suspicion, and sometimes hatred, and his slaves are watched more closely than before.

Col. Alexander was a very wealthy planter and owned a great number of slaves, but he was very justly suspected of being a kind, humane, and indulgent master. His slaves were always better fed, better clad, and had greater privileges than any I knew in the Old Dominion; and of course, the patrol had long had an eye on them, anxious to flog some of "those pampered niggers, who were spoiled by the indulgence of a weak, inefficient, but well-meaning owner."

Col. A. gave his slaves the liberty to get up a grand dance. Invitations were sent and accepted, to a large number of slaves on other plantations, and so, for miles around, all or many of the slaves were in high anticipation of joining in the great dance, which was to come off on Easter night. In the mean time, the patrol was closely watching their movements, and evinced rather a joyful expectancy of the many they should find there without a pass, and the flogging they would give them for that, if not guilty of any other offence, and perhaps they might catch some of the Colonel's slaves doing something for which they could be taught "to know their place," by the application of the cowhide.

The slaves on Col. A.'s plantation had to provide and prepare the supper for the expected vast "turn out," which was no light matter; and as slaves like on such occasions to pattern as much as possible after their master's family, the result was, to meet the emergency of the case, they *took,* without saying, "by your leave, Sir," some property belonging to their master, reasoning among themselves, as slaves often do, that it can not be *stealing,* because "it belongs to massa, and so do *we,* and we only use one part of his property to benefit another. Sure, 'tis all massa's." And if they do not get detected in this removal of "massa's property" from one location to another, they think no more of it.

Col. Alexander's slaves were hurrying on with their great preparations for the dance and feast; and as the time drew near, the old and knowing ones might be seen in groups, discussing the matter, with many a wink and nod; but it was in the valleys and by-places where the younger portion were to be found, rather secretly preparing food for the great time coming. This consisted of hogs, sheep, calves; and as to master's *poultry,* that suffered daily. Sometimes it was missed, but the disappearance was always easily accounted for, by informing "massa" that a great number of hawks had been around of late; and their preparation went on, night after night, undetected. They who repaired to a swamp or other by-place to cook by night, carefully destroyed everything likely to detect them, before they returned to their cabins in the morning.

The night for the dance *came* at last, and long before the time, the road leading to Col. Alexander's plantation presented a gay spectacle. The females were seen flocking to the place of resort, with heads adorned with gaudy bandanna turbans and new calico dresses, of the gayest colors,—their whole attire decked over with bits of gauze ribbon and other fantastic finery. The shades of night soon closed over the plantation, and then could be heard the rude music and loud laugh of the unpolished slave. It was about ten o'clock when the *aristocratic slaves* began to assemble, dressed in the cast-off finery of their master and mistress, swelling out and putting on airs in imitation of those they were forced to obey from day to day.

When they were all assembled, the dance commenced; the old fiddler struck up some favorite tune, and over the floor they went; the flying feet of the dancers were heard, pat, pat, over the apartment till the clock warned them it was twelve at midnight, or what some call "low twelve," to distinguish it from twelve o'clock at noon; then the violin ceased its discordant sounds, and the merry dancers paused to take breath.

Supper was then announced, and all began to prepare for the sumptuous feast. It being the pride of slaves to imitate the manners of their master and mistress, especially in the ceremonies of the table, all was conducted with great propriety and good order. The food was well cooked, and in a very plentiful supply. They had also managed in some way, to get a good quantity of excellent wine, which was sipped in the most approved and modern style. Every dusky face was lighted up, and every eye sparkled with joy. However ill fed they might have been, here, for once, there was plenty. Suffering and toil was forgotten, and they all seemed with one accord to give themselves up to the intoxication of pleasurable amusement.

House servants were of course, "the stars" of the party; all eyes were turned to them to see how they conducted, for they, among slaves, are what a military man would call "fugle-men." The field hands, and such of them as have generally been excluded from the dwelling of their owners, look to the house servant as a pattern of politeness and gentility. And indeed, it is often the only method of obtaining any knowledge of the manners of what is called "genteel society;" hence, they are ever regarded as a privileged class; and are sometimes greatly envied, while others are bitterly hated. And too often justly, for many of them are the most despicable tale-bearers and mischief-makers, who will, for the sake of the favor of his master or mistress, frequently betray his fellow-slave, and by tattling, get him severely whipped; and for these acts of perfidy, and sometimes downright falsehood, he is often rewarded by his master, who knows it is for his interest to keep such ones about him; though he is sometimes obliged, in addition to a reward, to send him away, for fear of the vengeance of the betrayed slaves. In the family of his master, the example of bribery and treachery is ever set before him, hence it is, that insurrections and stampedes are so generally detected. Such slaves are always treated with more affability than others, for the slaveholder is well aware that he stands over a volcano, that may at any moment rock his foundation to the center, and with one mighty burst of its long suppressed fire, sweep him and his family to destruction. When he lies down at night, he knows not but that ere another morning shall dawn, he may be left mangled and bleeding, and at the mercy of those maddened slaves whom he has so long ruled with a rod of iron.

Part IV.

LET YOUR MOTTO

BE RESISTANCE!

Nat Turner troubled many a slaveholder's sleep. In fact, he was their worst nightmare. Of the more than 250 slave insurrections recorded by noted historian Herbert Aptheker, Turner's was by far the bloodiest. His uprising left almost a permanent dread among those who would stifle the freedom of human souls. Ever since his youth, Turner told attorney Thomas Gray, who coaxed this confession from him, that he believed himself divinely blessed with special powers and the gift of prophecy. He interpreted certain marks on his head and breast as proof that he was intended for some great purpose. Given the destiny he imagined for himself and his rebellious, passionate nature, it was an easy task to induce others to follow him and begin the slaughter that would terrify white slave-owning communities all across the South. The revolt, which left some sixty whites dead, would precipitate the enactment of stringent Black Codes to stifle any further insurrections and to keep blacks ''in their place.'' Even a hundred years after his capture and execution, Turner was the source of children's games in parts of the South whereby his name was invoked as an ogre that would abduct them if they misbehaved.

It's clear from Henry Highland Garnet's fiery rhetoric that he was as violently opposed to enslavement as Nat Turner. Nowhere in the annals of African American history is there a more militant address to the slaves of the United States than Garnet's speech before the Convention of Colored Citizens in Buffalo in 1843. To rally the slaves to massive revolt, he cites the bold actions of Turner, Toussaint L'Ouverture, Denmark Vesey, Madison Washington, and Joseph Cinque. "Rather die freemen than live to be slaves," Garnet exhorts his brothers and sisters in chains. "Let your motto be resistance!"

But resistance to slavery did not always result in clamor or violence; sometimes it was expressed in more subtle ways, like quietly stealing away in the night. Before she slipped away, Linda Brent (Harriet Jacobs) was chattel her entire life, including seven years in which she spent hiding from her master and mistress in a small attic, where only a peephole allowed her to see the family and friends she had left behind. Not until she reached free soil in Philadelphia was she able to set aside the trepidation that at any moment the white men who helped her escape would sell her back into slavery.

Like so many slaves who managed to escape from bondage, Frederick Douglass was elated upon reaching the shores of freedom, and he was even more astounded to discover that the nonslaveholding population in New Bedford, Massachusetts, could be as richly endowed as the slaveholders in Maryland. No slave narrative has been as widely read and discussed as Douglass's breathtaking memoirs. The excerpt that follows marks his transition from the South to his early days in the North, his encounter with William Lloyd Garrison's *Liberator,* a prominent antislavery newspaper, and his gradual emergence as the foremost black abolitionist of his day.

Unlike Brent and Douglass, thousands of runaway slaves came from deeper regions of the South, many of them spirited along via the fabled Underground Railroad. John Parker was a "conductor" who knew the intricacies of the route and its hazards as well as anyone. Picking the right season, the right trails, was crucial for a successful escape, and even the most experienced of the conductors were not without harrowing moments of near-capture by patrols—the dreaded "patterollers"—and bounty hunters.

John Brown had no fear of patterollers or slaveholders when he stormed the arsenal at Harper's Ferry. Brown chose this site because of its strategic location on the Potomac River, which was to provide his men an escape route should things go awry. Also in his band of eighteen were five African Americans. Only one of them, Osborne Anderson, survived the counterattack. Brown's plan was to take the arsenal and distribute the weapons there to slaves from the surrounding plantations. In the end Brown was captured, and before he was hanged he declared in his last words that only through the shedding of blood would the nation be purged of the sin of slavery. While Brown's assault was deemed the actions of a "madman," it was among the events many historians believe precipitated the Civil War. Anderson's narrative also corrects several long-standing misconceptions about the raid. They killed more than the papers reported and the slaves in the vicinity of the arsenal were more than passive onlookers.

NAT TURNER

From *Confessions of Nat Turner*

§

VIRGINIA, 1831

SIR,—YOU HAVE ASKED ME TO GIVE a history of the motives which induced me to undertake the late insurrection, as you call it—To do so I must go back to the days of my infancy, and even before I was born. I was thirty-one years of age the 2nd of October last, and born the property of Benj. Turner, of this county. In my childhood a circumstance occurred which made an indelible impression on my mind, and laid the ground work of that enthusiasm, which has terminated so fatally to many, both white and black, and for which I am about to atone at the gallows. It is here necessary to relate this circumstance—trifling as it may seem, it was the commencement of that belief which has grown with time, and even now, sir, in this dungeon, helpless and forsaken as I am, I cannot divest myself of. Being at play with other children, when three or four years old, I was telling them something, which my mother overhearing, said it had happened before I was born—I stuck to my story, however, and related somethings which went, in her opinion, to confirm it—others being called on were greatly astonished, knowing that these things had happened, and caused them to say in my hearing, I surely would be a prophet, as the Lord had shewn me things that had happened before my birth. . . . My grandmother, who was very religious, and to whom I was much attached—my master, who belonged to the church, and other religious persons who visited the house, and whom I often saw at prayers, noticing the singularity of my manners, I suppose, and my uncommon intelligence for a child, remarked I had too much sense to be raised, and if I was, I would never be of any service to any one as a slave—To a mind like mine, restless, inquisitive and observant of every thing that was passing, it is easy to suppose that religion was the subject to which it would be directed, and although this subject principally occupied my thoughts—there was nothing that I saw or heard of to which my attention was not directed—The manner in which I learned to read and write, not only had great influence on my own mind, as I acquired it with the most perfect ease, so much so, that I have no recollection whatever of learning the alphabet—but to the astonishment of the family, one day, when a book was shewn to me to keep me from crying, I began spelling the names of different objects—this was a source of wonder to all in the neighborhood, particularly the blacks—and this learning was constantly improved at all opportunities—when I got large enough to go to work, while employed, I was reflecting on many things that would present themselves to my imagination, and whenever an opportunity occurred of looking at a book, when the school children were getting their lessons, I would find many things that the fertility of my own imagination had depicted to me before; all my time, not devoted to my master's service, was spent either in prayer, or in making experiments in casting different things in moulds made of earth, in attempting to make paper, gunpowder, and many other experiments, that although I could not perfect, yet convinced me of its practicability if I had the means.* I was not addicted to stealing in my youth, nor have ever been—Yet such was the confidence of the negroes in the neighborhood, even at this early period of my life, in my superior judgment, that they would often carry me with them when they were going on any roguery, to plan for them. Growing up among them, with this confidence in my superior judgment, and when this, in their opinions, was perfected by Divine inspiration, from the circumstances already alluded to in my infancy, and which belief was ever afterwards zealously inculcated by the austerity of my life and manners, which became the subject of remark by white and black.——Having soon discovered to be great, I must appear so, and therefore studiously avoided mixing in society, and wrapped myself in mystery, devoting my time to fasting and prayer—By this time, having arrived to man's estate, and hearing the scriptures commented on at meetings, I was struck with that particular passage which says: "Seek ye the kingdom of Heaven and all things shall be added unto you." I reflected much on this passage, and prayed daily for light on this subject—As I was praying one day at my plough, the spirit spoke to me, saying "Seek ye the kingdom of Heaven and all things shall be added unto you." *Question*—what do you mean by the Spirit. *Ans.* The Spirit that spoke to the prophets in former days—and I was greatly astonished, and for two years prayed continually, whenever my duty would permit—and then again I had the same revelation, which fully confirmed me in the impression that I was ordained for some great purpose in the hands of the Almighty.

* When questioned as to the manner of manufacturing those different articles, he was found well informed on the subject.

Several years rolled round, in which many events occurred to strengthen me in this my belief. At this time I reverted in my mind to the remarks made of me in my childhood, and the things that had been shewn me—and as it had been said of me in my childhood by those by whom I had been taught to pray, both white and black, and in whom I had the greatest confidence, that I had too much sense to be raised, and if I was, I would never be of any use to any one as a slave. Now finding I had arrived to man's estate, and was a slave, and these revelations being made known to me, I began to direct my attention to this great object, to fulfil the purpose for which, by this time, I felt assured I was intended. Knowing the influence I had obtained over the minds of my fellow servants, (not by the means of conjuring and such like tricks—for to them I always spoke of such things with contempt) but by the communion of the Spirit whose revelations I often communicated to them, and they believed and said my wisdom came from God. I now began to prepare them for my purpose, by telling them something was about to happen that would terminate in fulfilling the great promise that had been made to me—About this time I was placed under an overseer, from whom I ranaway—and after remaining in the woods thirty days, I returned, to the astonishment of the negroes on the plantation, who thought I had made my escape to some other part of the country, as my father had done before. But the reason of my return was, that the Spirit appeared to me and said I had my wishes directed to the things of this world, and not to the kingdom of Heaven, and that I should return to the service of my earthly master—"For he who knoweth his Master's will, and doeth it not, shall be beaten with many stripes, and thus have I chastened you." And the negroes found fault, and murmured against me, saying that if they had my sense they would not serve any master in the world. And about this time I had a vision—and I saw white spirits and black spirits engaged in battle, and the sun was darkened—the thunder rolled in the Heavens, and blood flowed in streams—and I heard a voice saying, "Such is your luck, such you are called to see, and let it come rough or smooth, you must surely bare it." I now withdrew myself as much as my situation would permit, from the intercourse of my fellow servants, for the avowed purpose of serving the Spirit more fully—and it appeared to me, and reminded me of the things it had already shown me, and that it would then reveal to me the knowledge of the elements, the revolution of the planets, the operation of tides, and changes of the seasons. After this revelation in the year of 1825, and the knowledge of the elements being made known to me, I sought more than ever to obtain true holiness before the great day of judgment should appear, and then I began to receive the true knowledge of faith. And from the first steps of righteousness until the last, was I made perfect; and the Holy Ghost was with me, and said, "Behold me as I stand in the Heavens"—and I looked and saw the forms of men in different attitudes—and there were lights in the sky to which the children of darkness gave other names than what they really were—for they were the lights of the Savior's hands, stretched forth from east to west, even as they were extended on the cross on Calvary for the redemption of sinners. And I wondered greatly at these miracles, and prayed to be informed of a certainty of the meaning thereof—and shortly afterwards, while laboring in the field, I discovered drops of blood on the corn as though it were dew from heaven—and I communicated it to many, both white and black, in the neighborhood—and I then found on the leaves in the woods hieroglyphic characters, and numbers, with the forms of men in different attitudes, portrayed in blood, and representing the figures I had seen before in the heavens. And now the Holy Ghost had revealed itself to me, and made plain the miracles it had shown me—For as the blood of Christ had been shed on this earth, and had ascended to heaven for the salvation of sinners, and was now returning to earth again in the form of dew—and as the leaves on the trees bore the impression of the figures I had seen in the heavens, it was plain to me that the Savior was about to lay down the yoke he had borne for the sins of men, and the great day of judgment was at hand. About this time I told these things to a white man, (Etheldred T. Brantley) on whom it had a wonderful effect—and he ceased from his wickedness, and was attacked immediately with a cutaneous eruption, and blood oozed from the pores of his skin, and after praying and fasting nine days, he was healed, and the Spirit appeared to me again, and said, as the Savior had been baptised so should we be also— and when the white people would not let us be baptised by the church, we went down into the water together, in the sight of many who reviled us, and were baptised by the Spirit—After this I rejoiced greatly, and gave thanks to God. And on the 12th of May, 1828, I heard a loud noise in the heavens, and the Spirit instantly appeared to me and said the Serpent was loosened, and Christ had laid down the yoke he had borne for the sins of men, and that I should take it on and fight against the Serpent, for the time was fast approaching when the first should be last and the last should be first. *Ques.* Do you not find yourself mistaken now? *Ans.* Was not Christ crucified? And by signs in the heavens that it would make known to me when I should commence the great work—and until the first sign appeared, I should conceal it from the knowledge of men—And on the appearance of the sign, (the eclipse of the sun last February) I should arise and prepare myself, and slay my enemies with their own weapons. And immediately on the sign appearing in the heavens, the seal was removed from my lips, and I communicated the great work laid out for me to do, to four in whom I had the greatest confidence, (Henry, Hark, Nelson, and Sam)—It was intended by us to have begun the work of death on the 4th July last—Many were the plans formed and rejected by us, and it affected my mind to such a degree, that I fell sick, and the time passed without our coming to any determination how to commence—Still forming new schemes and rejecting them, when the sign appeared again, which determined me not to wait longer.

Since the commencement of 1830, I had been living with Mr. Joseph Travis, who was to me a kind master, and placed the greatest confidence in me; in fact, I had no cause to complain of his treatment to me. On Saturday evening, the 20th of August, it was agreed between Henry, Hark and myself, to prepare a dinner the next day for the men we expected, and then to concert a plan, as we had not yet determined on any. Hark, on the following morning, brought a pig, and Henry brandy, and being joined by Sam, Nelson, Will and Jack, they prepared in the woods a dinner, where, about three o'clock, I joined them. . . .

I saluted them on coming up, and asked Will how came he there, he answered, his life was worth no more than others, and his liberty as dear to him. I asked him if he thought to obtain it? He said he would, or lose his life. This was enough to put him in full confidence. Jack, I knew, was only a tool in the hands of Hark, it was quickly agreed we should commence at home (Mr. J. Travis') on that night, and until we had armed and equipped ourselves, and gathered sufficient force, neither age nor sex was to be spared, (which was invariably adhered to). We remained at the feast, until about two hours in the night, when we went to the house and found Austin; they all went to the cider press and drank, except myself. On returning to the house, Hark went to the door with an axe, for the purpose of breaking it open, as we knew we were strong enough to murder the family, if they were awaked by the noise; but reflecting that it might create an alarm in the neighborhood, we determined to enter the house secretly, and murder them whilst sleeping. Hark got a ladder and set it against the chimney, on which I ascended, and hoisting a window, entered and came down stairs, unbarred the door, and removed the guns from their places. It was then observed that I must spill the first blood. On which, armed with a hatchet, and accompanied by Will, I entered my master's chamber, it being dark, I could not give a death blow, the hatchet glanced from his head, he sprang from the bed and called his wife, it was his last word, Will laid him dead, with a blow of his axe, and Mrs. Travis shared the same fate, as she lay in bed.

HENRY HIGHLAND GARNET

From *Negro Orators and Their Orations*

BUFFALO, NEW YORK, 1843

BRETHREN AND FELLOW CITIZENS: YOUR BRETHREN OF the North, East, and West have been accustomed to meet together in National Conventions, to sympathize with each other, and to weep over your unhappy condition. In these meetings we have addressed all classes of the free, but we have never, until this time, sent a word of consolation and advice to you. We have been contented in sitting still and mourning over your sorrows, earnestly hoping that before this day your sacred liberties would have been restored. But, we have hoped in vain. Years have rolled on, and tens of thousands have been borne on streams of blood and tears to the shores of eternity. While you have been oppressed, we have also been partakers with you; nor can we be free while you are enslaved. We, therefore, write to you as being bound with you.

Many of you are bound to us, not only by the ties of a common humanity, but we are connected by the more tender relations of parents, wives, husbands, and sisters, and friends. As such we most affectionately address you.

Slavery has fixed a deep gulf between you and us, and while it shuts out from you the relief and consolation which your friends would willingly render, it afflicts and persecutes you with a fierceness which we might not expect to see in the fiends of hell. But still the Almighty Father of mercies has left to us a glimmering ray of hope, which shines out like a lone star in a cloudy sky. Mankind are becoming wiser, and better—the oppressor's power is fading, and you, every day, are becoming better informed, and more numerous. Your grievances, brethren, are many. We shall not attempt, in this short address, to present to the world all the dark catalogue of the nation's sins, which have been committed upon an innocent people. Nor is it indeed necessary, for you feel them from day to day, and all the civilized world looks upon them with amazement.

Two hundred and twenty-seven years ago the first of our injured race were brought to the shores of America. They came not with glad spirits to select their homes in the New World. They came not with their own consent, to find an unmolested enjoyment of the blessings of this fruitful soil. The first dealings they had with men calling themselves Christians exhibited to them the worst features of corrupt and sordid hearts: and convinced them that no cruelty is too great, no villainy and no robbery too abhorrent for even enlightened men to perform, when influenced by avarice and lust. Neither did they come flying upon the wings of Liberty to a land of freedom. But they came with broken hearts, from their beloved native land, and were doomed to unrequited toil and deep degradation. Nor did the evil of their bondage end at their emancipation by death. Succeeding generations inherited their chains, and millions have come from eternity into time, and have returned again to the world of spirits, cursed and ruined by American slavery.

The propagators of the system, or their immediate successors, very soon discovered its growing evil, and its tremendous wickedness, and secret promises were made to destroy it. The gross inconsistency of a people holding slaves, who had themselves ''ferried o'er the wave'' for freedom's sake, was too apparent to be entirely overlooked. The voice of Freedom cried, ''Emancipate your slaves.'' . . .

Fellowmen! patient sufferers! behold your dearest rights crushed to the earth! See your sons murdered, and your wives, mothers and sisters doomed to prostitution. In the name of the merciful God, and by all that life is worth, let it no longer be a debatable question, whether it is better to choose *liberty* or *death*.

In 1822, Denmark Veazie, of South Carolina, formed a plan for the liberation of his fellowmen. In the whole history of human efforts to overthrow slavery, a more complicated and tremendous plan was never formed. He was betrayed by the treachery of his own people, and died a martyr to freedom. Many a brave hero fell, but history, faithful to her high trust, will transcribe his name on the same monument with Moses, Hampden, Tell, Bruce, and Wallace, Toussaint L'Ouverture, Lafayette, and Washington. That tremendous movement shook the whole empire of slavery. The guilty soul-thieves were overwhelmed with fear. It is a matter of fact that at this time, and in consequence of the threatened revolution, the slave States talked strongly of emancipation. But they blew but one blast of the trumpet of freedom, and then laid it aside. As these men became quiet, the slaveholders ceased to talk about emancipation: and now behold your condition to-day! Angels sigh over it, and humanity has long since exhausted her tears in weeping on your account!

The patriotic Nathaniel Turner followed Denmark Veazie. He was goaded to desperation by wrong and injustice. By despotism, his name has been recorded on the list of infamy, and future generations will remember him among the noble and brave.

Next arose the immortal Joseph Cinque, the hero of the Amistad. He was a native African, and by the help of God he emancipated a whole ship-load of his fellowmen on the high seas. And he now sings of liberty on the sunny hills of Africa and beneath his native palm-trees, where he hears the lion roar and feels himself as free as the king of the forest.

Next arose Madison Washington, that bright star of freedom, and took his station in the constellation of true heroism. He was a slave on board the brig *Creole,* of Richmond, bound to New Orleans, that great slave mart, with a hundred and four others. Nineteen struck for liberty or death. But one life was taken, and the whole were emancipated, and the vessel was carried into Nassau, New Providence.

Noble men! Those who have fallen in freedom's conflict, their memories will be cherished by the true-hearted and the God-fearing in all future generations; those who are living, their names are surrounded by a halo of glory.

Brethren, arise, arise! Strike for your lives and liberties. Now is the day and the hour. Let every slave throughout the land do this, and the days of slavery are numbered. You cannot be more oppressed than you have been—you cannot suffer greater cruelties than you have already. *Rather die freemen than live to be slaves.* Remember that you are FOUR MILLIONS!

It is in your power so to torment the God-cursed slaveholders that they will be glad to let you go free. If the scale was turned, and black men were the masters and white men the slaves, every destructive agent and element would be employed to lay the oppressor low. Danger and death would hang over their heads day and night. Yes, the tyrants would meet with plagues more terrible than those of Pharaoh. But you are a patient people. You act as though you were made for the special use of these devils. You act as though your daughters were born to pamper the lusts of your masters and overseers. And worse than all, you tamely submit while your lords tear your wives from your embraces and defile them before your eyes. In the name of God, we ask, are you men? Where is the blood of your fathers? Has it all run out of your veins? Awake, awake; millions of voices are calling you! Your dead fathers speak to you from their graves. Heaven, as with a voice of thunder, calls on you to arise from the dust.

Let your motto be resistance! *resistance!* RESISTANCE! No oppressed people have ever secured their liberty without resistance. What kind of resistance you had better make you must decide by the circumstances that surround you, and according to the suggestion of expediency. Brethren, adieu! Trust in the living God. Labor for the peace of the human race, and remember that you are FOUR MILLIONS!

HARRIET JACOBS

From *Incidents in the Life of a Slave Girl*

VIRGINIA, 1843

I NEVER COULD TELL HOW WE REACHED THE wharf. My brain was all of a whirl, and my limbs tottered under me. At an appointed place we met my uncle Phillip, who had started before us on a different route, that he might reach the wharf first, and give us timely warning if there was any danger. A rowboat was in readiness. As I was about to step in, I felt something pull me gently, and turning round I saw Benny, looking pale and anxious. He whispered in my ear, "I've been peeping into the doctor's window, and he's at home. Good by, mother. Don't cry; I'll come." He hastened away. I clasped the hand of my good uncle, to whom I owed so much, and of Peter, the brave, generous friend who had volunteered to run such terrible risks to secure my safety. To this day I remember how his bright face beamed with joy, when he told me he had discovered a safe method for me to escape. Yet that intelligent, enterprising, noble-hearted man was a chattel! liable, by the laws of a country that calls itself civilized, to be sold with horses and pigs! We parted in silence. Our hearts were all too full for words!

Swiftly the boat glided over the water. After a while, one of the sailors said, "Don't be down-hearted madam. We will take you safely to your husband, in ———." At first I could not imagine what he meant; but I had presence of mind to think that it probably referred to something the captain had told him; so I thanked him, and said I hoped we should have pleasant weather.

When I entered the vessel the captain came forward to meet me. He was an elderly man, with a pleasant countenance. He showed me to a little box of a cabin, where sat my friend Fanny. She started as if she had seen a spectre.

She gazed on me in utter astonishment, and exclaimed, "Linda, can this be *you?* or is it your ghost?" When we were locked in each other's arms, my overwrought feelings could no longer be restrained. My sobs reached the ears of the captain, who came and very kindly reminded us, that for his safety, as well as our own, it would be prudent for us not to attract any attention. He said that when there was a sail in sight he wished us to keep below; but at other times, he had no objection to our being on deck. He assured us that he would keep a good lookout, and if we acted prudently, he thought we should be in no danger. He had represented us as women going to meet our husbands in ———. We thanked him, and promised to observe carefully all the directions he gave us.

Fanny and I now talked by ourselves, low and quietly, in our little cabin. She told me of the sufferings she had gone through in making her escape, and of her terrors while she was concealed in her mother's house. Above all, she dwelt on the agony of separation from all her children on that dreadful auction day. She could scarcely credit me, when I told her of the place where I had passed nearly seven years. "We have the same sorrows," said I. "No," replied she, "you are going to see your children soon, and there is no hope that I shall ever even hear from mine."

The vessel was soon under way, but we made slow progress. The wind was against us. I should not have cared for this, if we had been out of sight of the town; but until there were miles of water between us and our enemies, we were filled with constant apprehensions that the constables would come on board. Neither could I feel quite at ease with the captain and his men. I was an entire stranger to that class of people, and I had heard that sailors were rough, and sometimes cruel. We were so completely in their power, that if they were bad men, our situation would be dreadful. Now that the captain was paid for our passage, might he not be tempted to make more money by giving us up to those who claimed us as property? I was naturally of a confiding disposition, but slavery had made me suspicious of every body. Fanny did not share my distrust of the captain or his men. She said she was afraid at first, but she had been on board three days while the vessel lay in the dock, and nobody had betrayed her, or treated her otherwise than kindly.

The captain soon came to advise us to go on deck for fresh air. His friendly and respectful manner, combined with Fanny's testimony, reassured me, and we went with him. He placed us in a comfortable seat, and occasionally entered into conversation. He told us he was a Southerner by birth, and had spent the greater part of his life in the Slave States, and that he had recently lost a brother who traded in slaves. "But," said he, "it is a pitiable and degrading business, and I always felt ashamed to acknowledge my brother in connection with it." As we passed Snaky Swamp, he pointed to it, and said "There is a slave territory that defies all the laws." I thought of the terrible days I had spent there, and though it was not called Dismal Swamp, it made me feel very dismal as I looked at it.

I shall never forget that night. The balmy air of spring was so refreshing! And how shall I describe my sensations when we were fairly sailing on Chesapeake Bay? O, the beautiful sunshine! the exhilarating breeze! and I could enjoy them without fear or restraint. I had never realized what grand things air and sunlight are till I had been deprived of them.

Ten days after we left land we were approaching Philadelphia. The captain said we should arrive there in the night, but he thought we had better wait till morning, and go on shore in broad daylight, as the best way to avoid suspicion.

I replied, "You know best. But will you stay on board and protect us?"

He saw that I was suspicious, and he said he was sorry, now that he had brought us to the end of our voyage, to find I had so little confidence in him. Ah, if he had ever been a slave he would have known how difficult it was to trust a white man. He assured us that we might sleep through the night without fear; that he would take care we were not left unprotected. Be it said to the honor of this captain, Southerner as he was, that if Fanny and I had been white ladies, and our passage lawfully engaged, he could not have treated us more respectfully. My intelligent friend, Peter, had rightly estimated the character of the man to whose honor he had intrusted us.

The next morning I was on deck as soon as the day dawned. I called Fanny to see the sun rise, for the first time in our lives, on free soil; for such I *then* believed it to be. We watched the reddening sky, and saw the great orb come up slowly out of the water, as it seemed. Soon the waves began to sparkle, and every thing caught the beautiful glow. Before us lay the city of strangers. We looked at each other, and the eyes of both were moistened with tears. We had escaped from slavery, and we supposed ourselves to be safe from the hunters. But we were alone in the world, and we had left dear ties behind us; ties cruelly sundered by the demon Slavery.

FREDERICK DOUGLASS

From *Narrative of the Life of Frederick Douglass, An American Slave*

NEW BEDFORD, MASSACHUSETTS, 1840S

THE IMPRESSION WHICH I HAD RECEIVED respecting the
. . . character and condition of the people of the north, I found to be
singularly erroneous. I had very strangely supposed, while in slavery, that few
of the comforts, and scarcely any of the luxuries, of life were enjoyed at the
north, compared with what were enjoyed by the slaveholders of the south. I
probably came to this conclusion from the fact that northern people owned no
slaves. I supposed that they were about upon a level with the non-slaveholding
population of the south. I knew *they* were exceedingly poor, and I had been
accustomed to regard their poverty as the necessary consequence of their being
non-slaveholders. I had somehow imbibed the opinion that, in the absence of
slaves, there could be no wealth, and very little refinement. And upon coming
to the north, I expected to meet with a rough, hard-handed, and uncultivated
population, living in the most Spartan-like simplicity, knowing nothing of the
ease, luxury, pomp, and grandeur of southern slaveholders. Such being my
conjectures, any one acquainted with the appearance of New Bedford may very
readily infer how palpably I must have seen my mistake.

In the afternoon of the day when I reached New Bedford, I visited the
wharves, to take a view of the shipping. Here I found myself surrounded with
the strongest proofs of wealth. Lying at the wharves, and riding in the stream, I
saw many ships of the finest model, in the best order, and of the largest size.
Upon the right and left, I was walled in by granite warehouses of the widest
dimensions, stowed to their utmost capacity with the necessaries and comforts
of life. Added to this, almost every body seemed to be at work, but noiselessly
so, compared with what I had been accustomed to in Baltimore. There were no

loud songs heard from those engaged in loading and unloading ships. I heard no deep oaths or horrid curses on the laborer. I saw no whipping of men; but all seemed to go smoothly on. Every man appeared to understand his work, and went at it with a sober, yet cheerful earnestness, which betokened the deep interest which he felt in what he was doing, as well as a sense of his own dignity as a man. To me this looked exceedingly strange. From the wharves I strolled around and over the town, gazing with wonder and admiration at the splendid churches, beautiful dwellings, and finely-cultivated gardens; evincing an amount of wealth, comfort, taste, and refinement, such as I had never seen in any part of slaveholding Maryland.

Every thing looked clean, new, and beautiful. I saw few or no dilapidated houses, with poverty-stricken inmates; no half-naked children and bare-footed women, such as I had been accustomed to see in Hillsborough, Easton, St. Michael's, and Baltimore. The people looked more able, stronger, healthier, and happier, than those of Maryland. I was for once made glad by a view of extreme wealth, without being saddened by seeing extreme poverty. But the most astonishing as well as the most interesting thing to me was the condition of the colored people, a great many of whom, like myself, had escaped thither as a refuge from the hunters of men. I found many, who had not been seven years out of their chains, living in finer houses, and evidently enjoying more of the comforts of life, than the average of slaveholders in Maryland. I will venture to assert, that my friend Mr. Nathan Johnson (of whom I can say with a grateful heart, "I was hungry, and he gave me meat; I was thirsty, and he gave me drink; I was a stranger, and he took me in") lived in a neater house; dined at a better table; took, paid for, and read, more newspapers; better understood the moral, religious, and political character of the nation,—than nine tenths of the slaveholders in Talbot county Maryland. Yet Mr. Johnson was a working man. His hands were hardened by toil, and not his alone, but those also of Mrs. Johnson. I found the colored people much more spirited than I had supposed they would be. I found among them a determination to protect each other from the blood-thirsty kidnapper, at all hazards. Soon after my arrival, I was told of a circumstance which illustrated their spirit. A colored man and a fugitive slave were on unfriendly terms. The former was heard to threaten the latter with informing his master of his whereabouts. Straightway a meeting was called among the colored people, under the stereotyped notice, "Business of importance!" The betrayer was invited to attend. The people came at the appointed hour, and organized the meeting by appointing a very religious old gentleman as president, who, I believe, made a prayer, after which he addressed the meeting as follows: *"Friends, we have got him here, and I would recommend that you young men just take him outside the door, and kill him!"* With this, a number of them bolted at him; but they were intercepted by some more timid than themselves, and the betrayer escaped their vengeance, and has not been seen in New Bedford since. I believe there have been no more such threats, and should there be hereafter, I doubt not that death would be the consequence.

I found employment, the third day after my arrival, in stowing a sloop with a load of oil. It was new, dirty, and hard work for me; but I went at it with a glad heart and a willing hand. I was now my own master. It was a happy moment, the rapture of which can be understood only by those who have been slaves. It was the first work, the reward of which was to be entirely my own. There was no Master Hugh standing ready, the moment I earned the money, to rob me of it. I worked that day with a pleasure I had never before experienced. I was at work for myself and newly-married wife. It was to me the starting-point of a new existence. When I got through with that job, I went in pursuit of a job of calking; but such was the strength of prejudice against color, among the white calkers, that they refused to work with me, and of course I could get no employment.* Finding my trade of no immediate benefit, I threw off my calking habiliments, and prepared myself to do any kind of work I could get to do. Mr. Johnson kindly let me have his wood-horse and saw, and I very soon found myself a plenty of work. There was no work too hard—none too dirty. I was ready to saw wood, shovel coal, carry wood, sweep the chimney, or roll oil casks,—all of which I did for nearly three years in New Bedford, before I became known to the anti-slavery world.

In about four months after I went to New Bedford, there came a young man to me, and inquired if I did not wish to take the "Liberator." I told him I did; but, just having made my escape from slavery, I remarked that I was unable to pay for it then. I, however, finally became a subscriber to it. The paper came, and I read it from week to week with such feelings as it would be quite idle for me to attempt to describe. The paper became my meat and my drink. My soul was set all on fire. Its sympathy for my brethren in bonds—its scathing denunciations of slaveholders—its faithful exposures of slavery—and its power-ful attacks upon the upholders of the institution—sent a thrill of joy through my soul, such as I had never felt before!

I had not long been a reader of the "Liberator," before I got a pretty correct idea of the principles, measures and spirit of the anti-slavery reform. I took right hold of the cause. I could do but little; but what I could, I did with a joyful heart, and never felt happier than when in an anti-slavery meeting. I seldom had much to say at the meetings, because what I wanted to say was said so much better by others. But, while attending an anti-slavery convention at Nantucket, on the 11th of August, 1841, I felt strongly moved to speak, and was at the same time much urged to do so by Mr. William C. Coffin, a

* I am told that colored persons can now get employment at calking in New Bedford—a result of anti-slavery effort.

gentleman who had heard me speak in the colored people's meeting at New Bedford. It was a severe cross, and I took it up reluctantly. The truth was, I felt myself a slave, and the idea of speaking to white people weighed me down. I spoke but a few moments, when I felt a degree of freedom, and said what I desired with considerable ease. From that time until now, I have been engaged in pleading the cause of my brethren—with what success, and with what devotion, I leave those acquainted with my labors to decide.

JOHN PARKER

From *His Promised Land*

OHIO, 1846–1847

WHEN I FIRST BEGAN MY WORK AMONG the slaves, all northern Kentucky was still covered with virgin forest, broken here and there by clearings, with many trails and few roads. But the prime bluegrass regions were thickly settled and rich in money and slaves. As the settlers began to build their cabins and make their clearings, the forest gradually disappeared. The increased population made it more difficult for the fugitives to pass through the country successfully, since there were many eyes to watch and few hiding places to conceal.

Another disadvantage was the gradual reduction in the number of slaves in the Borderland. This was due to two causes; so many slaves ran away, their owners, fearful of loss, sold the slaves down the river. As the fugitive depended entirely on his own race for assistance, this removal of his own people increased his difficulties of getting food and directions.

But these obstacles did not deter those slaves who were intelligent and determined to break away from their bondage. The early fall was the time that most of them selected to strike out for themselves. Though the warm summer nights were preferable for comfort, sad experiences had taught him that it was the cornfield on which he must depend for food. Besides, the ground was hard and difficult to track in the autumn.

Frequently they told me that they would wait weeks, after they had decided to run away, waiting for the corn to ripen. As soon as this food supply [was available] they were off. They always started with a bag of provisions and a load of unnecessary things. These were thrown away, until he got down to his knapsack of food.

Men and women whom I helped on their way came from Tennessee, requiring weeks to make the journey, sleeping under the trees in the daytime and slowly picking their dangerous way at night. How they crossed the numerous creeks that lay waiting for them like a trap was unbelievable to me. As a matter of fact, they became backwoodsmen, following the north star, or even mountains, to reach their destination, the Ohio River. Once there they felt they were in view of their promised land, even if they had no way to cross into it. Few had shoes, and these were so worn out by the time they reached me, the soles were held together by twine—making loose-fitting sandals.

These long-distance travelers were usually people strong physically, as well as people of character, and were resourceful when confronted with trouble, otherwise they could have never escaped. The riffraff runaways came from the Borderland, where it was comparatively easy to get away and they were not tested by repeated risks. Some of them were difficult to control.

I had an experience with one of these uncontrollable groups which made me very chary about my fugitives ever after. To begin with, they were stranded on the Kentucky shore, when I appeared rowing slowly along the shore with no object in view. My attention was attracted to them by their talking loud enough for me to know they were colored folks, and their position indicated they were runaways. Landing, I found them with ease and offered my services to get them across the river.

They were suspicious of me, and hesitated until I told them frankly they could go or stay and be captured, before they would go with me. I took them to the home of Tom McCague and concealed them in the hay. They became so noisy before I left them I decided to take them to the house and hide them in his garret.

There they became so noisy Tom McCague sent for me to quiet the lot. It was dark in the garret; [that] was what they were complaining about. I was so mad at their stupidity, one of the men making some slighting remark. I gave him a sound thrashing, and after that the crowd were meek and mild. I never had anything to do with such a rowdy crowd, and was glad to get rid of them as soon as it was dark.

In strong contrast to this shiftlessness and ingratitude of the group of rowdy fugitives, which I have just narrated, was the courage and resourcefulness of a couple of slaves who came to me from southern Kentucky. For some reason these slaves, failing to secure proper directions, had fallen into the hands of a paid spy who was en route to the town marshal's office when the party was overtaken by colored freemen, who forcibly rescued the two fugitives and brought them to my house, which was not only thoughtless, but dangerous to me.

As it was too late to get them away before daylight, I did the second wrong thing by hiding them in my own house, something which I had always refused to do before. So I took them up to my attic, hoping that there was no one [who had] followed the fugitives to my house. Then the rumpus began and I had the fright of my whole life.

For it seems that after the rescue, the Ripley spy met an armed crowd from across the river in pursuit of their own runaways. While the two slaves in my attic were not their property, the party thought this was their one chance to get even if not completely rid of me as a menace to their own slaves. They evidently knew I had received the two men, for I had hardly settled myself down for a nap when there came a hard knocking at my front door. I made the third mistake this night by going directly to my door instead of making my first observations out of the front window. As I unlocked and opened the door the crowd rushed me, seizing me violently.

They were quite forward in their telling me that I had finally been caught in their own trap. They furthermore informed me that two slaves had been seen entering my house, and that they were still concealed somewhere within its four walls, and they proposed to search the house until they found them.

Being helpless in their hands, I made a great bluff of innocence, asking them to search the house, if they wished to do so. They would have done it without my consent, so I made the best of a bad situation, trusting to my resourcefulness to get me out of the trouble. As you will see, it was wise tactics on my part.

First they examined every nook and corner downstairs, placing guards around the house to see that no one got away. Not having formulated a plan, I delayed the search as much as I could, still looking for a loophole. Having finished the first floor, they started up the stairs, when I brought them back to examine a closet which had been overlooked, thus working every conceivable delay to gain time.

At the top of the stairs I shouted in a loud voice to my captors that they could look the house over and even on the roof, [but] they would find no one. This I did for the benefit of the two slaves in the attic, not only to notify them of their danger, but to give them a clue to take refuge on the roof, which was my only chance of getting out of the jam. After this loud talk I conducted the party into my bedroom, kept them busy looking into closets, slamming the doors, and making all the confusion I could, to muffle any row the slaves might make in their efforts to escape capture.

My captors were in no mood to delay matters, feeling sure of finding their prey, then, not finding them as they went from room to room, they became angry and abusive. They also interpreted all my forwardness in helping their search was in an effort to divert them from the real place of concealment.

They then took matters into their own hands and brooked no further interference. I made no complaint, because I knew my men had ample time to do what they were able to in carrying out their plans of concealment or escape, neither of which I was exceedingly doubtful could be done.

All the while I was fairly quaking inwardly with fear, from the discovery of the two slaves that would surely follow when the garret was searched. I put off swallowing this bitter pill as long as I could, as I could see the confiscation of all my land and seized property, and the wreckage of my whole life's work. I had a fleeting hope that in some way the stairs to the attic would be overlooked, as the whole party had passed by them in their search.

It was only a fleeting hope, however, for as we crowded out into the hall one of the searchers exclaimed: "There's the attic stairs." If the man had pronounced the judgment of death upon me, I could not have felt the shock more than I did at this announcement of his discovery.

As we climbed the stairs one at a time I thought it would be best for the slaves as well as myself to confess my guilt, call on the two men to surrender, and thus put an end to my manhunt. Then I calmed down, stood fast on my section of landing on to the last minute and beyond, and held my breath.

I knew the room permitted no hiding place for one man, let alone two, as it was a plain attic with rafters showing overhead and clear floor beneath. The detection of the two men was only a question of a few moments. The man ahead of me carried a lighted lantern, the feeble rays dimly dispelling the darkness of the attic. Looking through the gloom, I saw the shadowy outline of the two . . . figures in the farthest corner.

I faltered and my heart went sick as I waited for the exultant shout of the men about me. If the leader was blind, surely the men who crowded up the stairs would see, but they too stared and said nothing. Could my eyes deceive me? Not at all, because there in front of them I could see the two fugitives, so that it was only a question of time for my captors to be accustomed to the surrounding darkness, to see the slaves as I saw them.

I turned my eyes away, for fear my staring would give the position of the two slaves away. Still I could not conceive how two men could be in plain sight as these were to me, and not be seen by the rest of the party. I suggested that we go back downstairs. Instead, the man with a lantern advanced further into the attic, while the outline of the two fugitives faded away, leaving only an empty space.

A diligent search throughout the garret proved that the men had escaped, [a surprise] to me and a complete puzzle to the searchers. I was really puzzled myself until I discovered the ladder leading to the roof was missing. Then it was that I knew that my two men were hugging the roof, but they had [taken] the precaution to haul up the ladder with them. I had a bad moment when the man with the lantern held it high over his head; it was only the last act of his futile search of the disappointed crowd.

Before leaving they swore unless they found the men, they would return the next night and burn my home. While it was an idle threat, it did indicate to me that they were not satisfied I did not have the two men hid away someplace in my home. It also warned me I must be careful in getting my men away the following night. It was well that I took heed, as you will soon see.

After due allowance of time and also examination, I succeeded in getting the two men down from their precarious position on a slanting roof and hid them in my cellar during the following day. Expecting a visit from my captors of the previous night, I decided to get them out of my house as soon as it was dark, and furthermore I would not guide them out of town, but would assign this task to Tom Collins, who would not be watched.

Without waiting for the people of the town to quiet down, I led the two fugitives along Front Street to the home of Collins. As we entered I saw a man in a shadow, whom I knew was on watch, and we had been discovered. There was no time to lose. In the hurried conference with Collins, we decided his house was not safe and the only available space was in his workshop in his back yard.

We had hardly reached the shop when there was hard knocking at the front door. Then a second and a third impatient and threatening pounding which threatened to force the door from its hinges. Finally Collins, having hurriedly reentered his house, opened the door, dreading the cause of so much violence.

He was faced by the same crowd that had visited my house the night before, and greeted by the statement that he was harboring runaways, who had been seen to enter his house a short time before. Without arguing the point he invited them to enter and search his house, depending on me to take care of the fugitives.

Suspecting that the house was watched on all sides, I slid out the back way through a vacant lot, only to find a man on guard. Fortunately he did not see me. Returning to the shop, I advised the men it was a case of fighting our way through the group of slave owners or overcoming the guard, which I had made up my mind to do, when I was startled to hear voices in the yard headed towards the shop, completely blocking my way out to the alley. Hastily looking around the shop, all I could see was a carpenter's bench and old cupboard, both of which were out of the question as places of concealment.

Lying along the floor in a row were a number of coffins, ready for use. Fortunately, the tops lay on the caskets loosely. Picking up one lid, I motioned a man to get in. He hesitated until I pushed him and placed [the] lid on top of him. The second man I concealed in the same manner. The third casket I selected for myself.

While it has taken time to tell of our actions, I assure you it only took a breath or two to execute them. I let the silence of the shop bear out its grim prospects. We did not have long to wait in our places of self-internment until the crowd trooped into the shop. Though they examined the shop, and cupboard particularly, they did not in that gloom care to touch the row of coffins, feeling assured that no colored man would ever consign his living body to such a place of concealment.

Fortunately, this superstition prevailed. I almost coughed, and I was afraid one of the other men might not be able to control himself as well as I had done. However, the fortunes of war were with us, and the searchers, standing around for a few minutes discussing our disappearance, left the shop apparently to go away.

I stayed in my coffin until my nerves began to jump, then I pushed aside the lid and stepped out of my gruesome hiding place. The two fugitives were as much affected by the coffins as I was, in fact they were more fearful of them than they were of the presence of their enemies. I assure you that if the pursuers had returned, I do not believe I could have persuaded them to return to their caskets.

After waiting until I thought the excitement was all over, I gradually opened the door, only to look into the face of a man who was standing by for us to come back. Leaping back, I drew my pistol and waited.

While I was standing there fearful and expectant of trouble, there was a gentle tap. Then it came to me that my man was Tom Collins with a message. Opening the door slightly, he told me that the house was guarded in front and the alley as well. He did not tarry, but left me with the two charges on my hands. What was I to do? It was evident I could not stop there.

As the front and rear of the Collins house was watched, the only way out was over the side fence through the neighboring yards. Fortunately, my friend and colleague Tom McCague lived a few yards away, so it was only a matter of care and caution to go cross yards to find a safe refuge with him.

This I did, leading the way with my two men following me like two moving shadows. Making my way into the house, I soon had him up, my story told, and the two men left in his care while the would-be watchers kept their silent but hapless vigil.

After carefully surveying the field, I went over more back fences and more lots until I came to another alley, which I followed down to Front Street, thence back home, having finally gotten rid of the two most perplexing fugitives I ever had anything to do with. They went to Canada the next night, with someone else as guide. . . .

OSBORNE ANDERSON

From *A Voice from Harper's Ferry*

§

HARPER'S FERRY, 1859

IT WAS ABOUT TWELVE O'CLOCK IN THE day when we were first attacked by the troops. Prior to that, Capt. Brown, in anticipation of further trouble, had girded to his side the famous sword taken from Col. Lewis Washington the night before, and with that memorable weapon, he commanded his men against General Washington's own State.

When the Captain received the news that the troops had entered the bridge from the Maryland side, he, with some of his men, went into the street, and sent a message to the Arsenal for us to come forth also. We hastened to the street as ordered, when he said—"The troops are on the bridge, coming into town; we will give them a warm reception." He then walks around amongst us, giving us words of encouragement, in this wise:—"Men! be cool! Take aim, and make every last shot count!" "The troops will look for us to retreat on their first appearance; be careful to shoot first." Our men were well supplied with firearms, but Capt. Brown had no rifle at that time; his only weapon was the sword before mentioned.

The troops soon came out of the bridge, and up the street facing us, we occupying an irregular position. When they got within sixty or seventy yards, Capt. Brown said, "Let go upon them!" which we did, when several of them fell. Again and again the dose was repeated.

There was now consternation among the troops. From marching in solid martial columns, they became scattered. Some hastened to seize upon and bear up the wounded and dying,—several lay dead upon the ground. They seemed not to realize, at first, that we would fire upon them, but evidently expected we would be driven out by them without firing. Capt. Brown seemed fully to

understand the matter, and hence, very properly and in our defence, undertook to forestall their movements. The consequence of their unexpected reception was, after leaving several of their dead on the field, they beat a confused
retreat into the bridge, and there stayed under cover until reinforcements came
to the Ferry.

On the retreat of the troops, we were ordered back to our former post.
While going, Dangerfield Newby, one of our colored men, was shot through
the head by a person who took aim at him from a brick store window, on the
opposite side of the street, and who was there for the purpose of firing upon
us. Newby was a brave fellow. He was one of my comrades at the Arsenal. He
fell at my side, and his death was promptly avenged by Shields Green, the
Zouave of the band, who afterwards met his fate calmly on the gallows, with
John Copeland. Newby was shot twice; at the first fire, he fell on his side and
returned it; as he lay, a second shot was fired, and the ball entered his head.
Green raised his rifle in an instant, and brought down the cowardly murdered,
before the latter could get his gun back through the sash.

There was comparative quiet for a time, except that the citizens seemed to
be wild with terror. Men, women and children forsook the place in great
haste, climbing up hillsides and scaling the mountains. The latter seemed to be
alive with white fugitives, fleeing from their doomed city. During this time,
Wm. Thompson, who was returning from his errand to the Kennedy Farm,
was surrounded on the bridge by the railroad men, who next came up, taken a
prisoner to the Wager House, tied hand and foot, and, at a late hour of the
afternoon, cruelly murdered by being riddled with balls, and thrown headlong
on the rocks.

Late in the morning, some of his prisoners told Capt. Brown that they
would like to have breakfast, when he sent word forthwith to the Wager House
to that effect, and they were supplied. He did not order breakfast for himself
and men, as was currently but falsely stated at the time, as he suspected foul
play; on the contrary, when solicited to have breakfast so provided for him, he
refused.

Between two and three o'clock in the afternoon, armed men could be seen
coming from every direction; soldiers were marching and counter-marching;
and on the mountains, a host of blood-thirsty ruffians swarmed, waiting for the
their [sic] opportunity to pounce on the little band. The fighting commenced in
earnest after the arrival of fresh troops. Volley upon volley was discharged, and
the echoes from the hills, the shrieks of the townspeople, and the groans of
their wounded and dying, all of which filled the air, were truly frightful. The
Virginians may well conceal their losses, and Southern chivalry may hide its
brazen head, for their boasted bravery was well tested that day, and in no way
to their advantage. It is remarkable, that except that one foolhardy colored man
was reported buried, no other funeral is mentioned, although the Mayor and

other citizens are known to have fallen. Had they reported the true number, their disgrace would have been more apparent; so they wisely (?) concluded to be silent.

The fight at Harper's Ferry also disproved the current idea that slaveholders will lay down their lives for their property. Col. Washington, the representative of the old hero, stood "blubbering" like a great calf at supposed danger; while the laboring white classes and non-slaveholders, with the marines, (mostly gentlemen from "furrin" parts,) were the men who faced the bullets of John Brown and his men. Hardly the skin of a slaveholder could be scratched in open fight; the cowards kept out of the way until danger was passed, sending the poor whites into the pitfalls, while they were reserved for the bragging, and to do the safe but cowardly judicial murdering afterwards.

As strangers poured in the enemy took positions round about, so as to prevent any escape, within shooting distance of the engine house and Arsenal. Capt. Brown, seeing their manoeuvres, said: "We will hold on to our three positions, if they are unwilling to come to terms, and die like men."

All this time, the fight was progressing; no powder and ball were wasted. We shot from under cover, and took deadly aim. For an hour before the flag of truce was sent out, the firing was uninterrupted, and one and another of the enemy were constantly dropping to the earth.

One of the Captain's plans was to keep up communication between his three points. In carrying out this idea, Jerry Anderson went to the rifle factory, to see Kagi and his men. Kagi, fearing that we would be overpowered by numbers if the Captain delayed leaving, sent word by Anderson to advise him to leave the town at once. This word Anderson communicated to the Captain, and told us also at the Arsenal. The message sent back to Kagi was, to hold out for a few minutes longer, when we would all evacuate the place. Those few minutes proved disastrous, for then it was that the troops before spoken of came pouring in, increased by crowds of men from the surrounding country. After an hour's hard fighting, and when the enemy were blocking up the avenues of escape, Capt. Brown sent out his son Watson with a flag of truce, but no respect was paid to it; he was fired upon, and wounded severely. He returned to the engine house, and fought bravely after that for fully an hour and a half, when he received a mortal wound, which he struggled under until the next day. The contemptible and savage manner in which the flag of truce had been received, induced severe measures in our defence, in the hour and a half before the next one was sent out. The effect of our work was, that the troops ceased to fire at the buildings, as we clearly had the advantage of position.

Capt. A. D. Stevens was next sent out with a flag, with what success I will presently show. Meantime, Jeremiah Anderson, who had brought the message from Kagi previously, was sent by Capt. Brown with another message to John

Henrie, but before he got far on the street, he was fired upon and wounded. He returned at once to the engine house, where he survived but a short time. The ball, it was found, had entered the right side in such manner that death necessarily ensued rapidly. . . .

Of the six men assigned a position in the Arsenal by Captain Brown, four were either slain or captured; and Hazlett and myself, the only ones remaining, never left our position until we saw, with feelings of intense sadness, that we could be of no further avail to our commander, he being a prisoner in the hands of the Virginians. We therefore, upon consultation, as our work for the day was clearly finished, and gain a position where in the future we could work with better success, than to recklessly invite capture and brutality at the hands of our enemies. The charge of deserting our brave old leader and fleeing from danger has been circulated to our detriment, but I have the consolation of known that, reckless as were the half-civilized hordes against whom we contended the entire day, and much as they might wish to disparage his men, they would never have thus charged us. They know better. John Brown's men at Harper's Ferry were and are a unit in their devotion to John Brown and the cause he espoused. To have deserted him would have been to belie every manly characteristic for which Albert Hazlett, at least, was known by the party to be distinguished, at the same time that it would have endangered the future safety of such deserter or deserters. John Brown gave orders; those orders must be obeyed, so long as Captain Brown was in a position to enforce them; once unable to command, from death, being a prisoner, or otherwise, the command devolved upon John Henry Kagi. Before Captain Brown was made prisoner, Captain Kagi had ceased to live, though had he been living, all communication between our post and him had been long cut off. We could not aid Captain Brown by remaining. We might, by joining the men at the Farm, devise plans for his succor; or our experience might become available on some future occasion.

The charge of running away from danger could only find form in the mind of some one unwilling to encounter the difficulties of a Harper's Ferry campaign, as no one acquainted with the out-of-door and in-door encounters of that day will charge any one with wishing to escape danger, merely. It is well enough for men out of danger, and who could not be induced to run the risk of a scratching, to talk flippantly about cowardice, and to sit in judgment upon the men who went with John Brown, and who did not fall into the hands of the Virginians; but to have been there, fought there, and to understand what *did* transpire there, are quite different. As Capt. Brown had all the prisoners with him, the whole force of the enemy was concentrated there, for a time, after the capture of the rifle factory. Having captured our commander, we knew that it was but little two of us could against so many, and that our turn to be taken must come; so Hazlett and I went out at the back part of the building, climbed up the wall, and went upon the railway. Behind us, in the Arsenal, were thousands of dollars, we knew full well, but that wealth had no charms for us, and he hastened to communicate with the men sent to the Kennedy Farm. We travelled up the Shenandoah along the railroad, and overtook one of the citizens. He was armed, and had been in the fight in the afternoon. We took him prisoner, in order to facilitate our escape. He submitted without resistance, and quietly gave up his gun. From him, we learned substantially of the final struggle at the rifle factory, where the noble Kagi commanded. The number of citizens killed was, according to his opinion, much larger than either Hazlett or I had supposed, although we knew there were a great many killed and wounded together. He said there must be at least seventy killed, besides wounded. Hazlett had said there must be fifty, taking into account the defence of the three strong positions. I do not know positively, but would not put the figure below thirty killed, seeing many fall as I did, and knowing the "dead aim" principle upon which we defended ourselves. One of the Southern published accounts, it will be remembered, said twenty citizens were killed, another said fifteen. At last it got narrowed down to five, which was simply absurd, after so long an engagement. We had forty rounds apiece when we went to the Ferry, and when Hazlett and I left, we had not more than twenty rounds between us. The rest of the party were as free with their ammunition as we were, if not more so. We had further evidence that the number of dead was larger than published, from the many that we saw lying dead around.

When we had gone as far as the foot of the mountains, our prisoner begged us not to take his life, but to let him go at liberty. He said we might keep his gun; he would not inform on us. Feeling compassion for him, and trusting to his honor, we suffered him to go, when he went directly into town, and finding every thing there in the hands of our enemies, he informed on us, and we were pursued. After he had left us, we crawled or climbed up among the rocks in the mountains, some hundred yards or more from the spot where we left him, and hid ourselves, as we feared treachery on second thought. A few minutes before dark, the troops came in search of us. They came to the foot of the mountains, marched and counter-marched, but never attempted to search the mountains; we supposed from their movements that they feared a host of armed enemies in concealment. Their air was so defiant, and their errand so distasteful to us, that we concluded to apply a little ammunition to their case, and having a few cartridges on hand, we poured from our excellent position in the rocky wilds some well-directed shots. It was not so dark but that we could see one bite the dust now and then, when others would run to aid them instantly, particularly the wounded. Some lay where they fell, undisturbed, which satisfied us that they were dead. The troops returned our fire, but it was random shooting, as we were concealed from their sight by the rocks and bushes. Interchanging of shots continued for some minutes, with much spirit, when it became quite dark, and they went down into the town. After their return to the Ferry, we could hear the drum beating for a long time; an indication of their triumph, we supposed. Hazlett and I remained in our position three hours, before we dared venture down.

As stated in a previous chapter, the command of the rifle factory was given to Captain Kagi. Under him were John Copeland, Sherrard Lewis Leary, and three colored men from the neighborhood. At an early hour, Kagi saw from his position the danger in remaining, with our small company, until assistance could come to the inhabitants. Hence his suggestion to Captain Brown, through Jeremiah Anderson, to leave. His position being more isolated than the others, was the first to invite an organized attack with success; the Virginians first investing the factory with their hordes, before the final success at the engine house. From the prisoner taken by us who had participated in the assault upon Kagi's position, we received the sad details of the slaughter of our brave companions. Seven different times during the day they were fired upon, while they occupied the interior part of the building, the insurgents defending themselves with great courage, killing and wounding with fatal precision. At last, overwhelming numbers, as many as five hundred, our informant told us, blocked up the front of the building, battered the doors down, and forced their way into the interior. The insurgents were then forced to retreat the back way, fighting, however, all the time. They were pursued, when they took to the river, and it being so shallow, they waded out to a rock, mid-way, and there made a stand, being completely hemmed in, front and rear. Some four or five hundred shots, said our prisoner, were fired at them before they were conquered. They would not surrender into the hands of the enemy, but kept on fighting until every one was killed, except John Copeland. Seeing he could do no more, and that all his associates were murdered, he suffered himself to be captured. The party at the rifle factory fought desperately till the last, from the perch on the rock. Slave and free, black and white, carried out the special injunction of the brave old Captain, to make sure work of it. The unfortunate targets for so many bullets of the enemy, some of them received two or three balls. There fell poor Kagi, the friend and adviser of Captain Brown in his most trying positions, and the cleverest man in the party; and there also fell Sherrard Lewis Leary, generous-hearted and companionable as he was, and in that and other difficult positions, brave to desperation. There fought John Copeland, who met his fate like a man. But they were all "honorable men," noble, noble fellows, who fought and died for the most holy principles. John Copeland was taken to the guard-house, where the other prisoners afterwards were, and thence to Charlestown jail. His subsequent mockery of a trial, sentence and execution, with his companion Shields Green, on the 16th of December—are they not part of the dark deeds of this era, which will assign their perpetrators to infamy, and cause after generations to blush at the remembrance?

Part V

᪐

CAUGHT BETWEEN THE

BLUE AND THE GRAY

For every slave who made a successful escape, there were hundreds of thousands who did not. Even when the Civil War was raging, slaves plotted to get to the "Promised Land," to get beyond the Ohio River. After her family was cruelly separated and sold to different owners, Mattie Jackson bided her time and eventually found the right moment to maneuver her way to freedom, ably assisted by members of the Underground Railroad.

Even before the Civil War temporarily became everyone's biggest problem, a number of political issues and debates faced black Americans. The dispute over the virtues of returning to Africa or some other territory outside the United States, current since the Revolutionary era, remained unresolved. In the early 1860s, emigration to Haiti was another alternative that fueled discussions among African Americans. Famed author William Wells Brown believed emigration to Haiti was as good as any other antislavery tactic. Brown, like many advocates of emigration to

Haiti, felt that the island's environment was conducive to black health and prosperity. Moreover, the government promised to pay fifteen dollars toward the passengers' expenses and sell them land at low prices and long-term credits when they arrived. In the end, the movement was short-lived and convinced only a few black Americans to risk relocation.

Another plan to send African Americans abroad was proposed by President Abraham Lincoln, who on several occasions expressed the sentiment that blacks and whites could not live in harmony in the United States. Under Lincoln's orders, Senator S. C. Pomeroy issued a pamphlet to recruit black Americans to consider relocating to Panama, with its pleasant climate and where opportunities abounded. Robert Purvis, one of the wealthiest black men in America and a devout abolitionist, vigorously opposed the plan.

Harriet Tubman took matters into her own hands. An escaped slave herself, she led nineteen trips into the very bowels of the South to conduct some three hundred slaves to freedom in the score of years before the Civil War. "I freed thousands of slaves," she once boasted, "and I could have freed thousands more, if they had known they were slaves." To get her "passengers" safely from the plantations to freedom, Tubman used all sorts of tactics. Babies were given paregoric to keep them from crying and revealing their location; and she was known to put a pistol to the head of a wavering escapee. "It's either freedom or death," she would announce. From these bold acts she earned the title "Moses of her People," though she self-effacingly brushed aside such accolades. "I had reasoned this out in my mind," she ruminated. "There was one or two things I had a *right* to, liberty or death; if I could not have one, I would have the other; for no man should take me alive; I should fight for my liberty as long as my strength lasted, and when the time come for me to go, the Lord would let them take me." Her heroic feats during the Civil War as a spy, scout, and nurse for the

Union forces have been well documented. When she died in 1913, she was buried with full military honors.

While Tubman was appealing to the president from afar, Elizabeth Keckley was inside the White House. Through her unique perspective we get a glimpse of the president's state of mind during the tumultuous war and some of the dramatic events leading to his assassination. Keckley was not only a fine reporter but also a talented seamstress, having made Mary Todd Lincoln's inaugural gown.

Countless slaves gained their freedom from the disruptions of the war. Classified as "contrabands of war," these recently freed slaves were often at the whim and caprice of the individual Union commanders. Many of the runaways—their masters' farms and plantations under siege—found safety with Union regiments, sometimes working as team-sters, spies, and laborers. We'll never know if John Boston had a partic-ular assignment with the New York Regiment based in Virginia or if this letter ever reached his wife. But one thing is certain: He was free from the "slaver's lash."

Charlotte Forten never knew the feel of the whip on her back because she was born to an illustrious Northern family, but she identified so strongly with the charges who sought her teaching that she must have winced each time they were flogged. One of Forten's major contribu-tions to African American literature was the extensive diary she kept while living in South Carolina at the peak of the Civil War. Her precise rendering of activities on New Year's Day, January 1, 1863, was indeed propitious. It was Emancipation Proclamation Day and the slaves of states in rebellion were set free. What a glorious day, she remarked.

As jubilant as the Emancipation Proclamation made some four million bondsmen and women, many who lived in areas where it was supposedly in effect remained untouched by the executive order, and much had to be done to make the writ meaningful. It certainly did not mean much to the wives of slave men who waited vainly to hear from their husbands off in battle. Ann's letter to her husband serving in Missouri regiment advises him how to post his letters, lest they fall in the hands of her master.

Corporal Octave Johnson was a runaway who lived in a swamp near New Orleans for more than a year before seeking refuge at Camp Parapet and then joining the regiment. How he and others existed as fugitives within four miles of their former plantation is an awe-inspiring study in survival. Unfortunately, many brave men never made it back home. The painful deposition by Patsy Leach is indicative of what many widows of black soldiers suffered. Her master, a Confederate sympathizer, beat her unmercifully each time he thought about her husband fighting against the rebels. No longer willing to endure his savage treatment, she took her youngest child and fled, leaving four of her children behind.

MATTIE J. JACKSON

From *The Story of Mattie J. Jackson*

❧

MEMPHIS AND INDIANAPOLIS, 1850S, 1860S

WHEN ABOUT SIXTEEN YEARS OF AGE, WHILE residing
. . . with her original master, my mother became acquainted with a
young man, Mr. Adams, residing in a neighboring family, whom she much
respected; but he was soon sold, and she lost trace of him entirely, as was the
common occurrence with friends and companions though united by the nearest
ties. When my mother arrived at Captain Tirrell's, after leaving the boat, in
her excitement she scarce observed anything except her little group so miraculously saved from perhaps a final separation in this world. She at length observed that the servant who was waiting to take her to the Captain's residence
in the country was the same man with whom she formed the acquaintance
when sixteen years old, and they again renewed their acquaintance. He had
been married and buried his wife. It appeared that his wife had been in Captain
Tirrell's family many years, and he also, for some time. They had a number of
children, and Capt. Tirrell had sold them down South. This cruel blow, assisted by severe flogging and other ill treatment, rendered the mother insane,
and finally caused her death. . . . .

After my mother had left the Captain to take care of herself and child,
according to agreement with the Captain, she became engaged to Mr. Adams.
He had bought himself previously for a large price. After they became acquainted, the Captain had an excellent opportunity of carrying out his stratagem. He commenced bestowing charity upon Mr. Adams. As he had purchased
himself, and Capt. T. had agreed not to sell my mother, they had decided to

marry at an early day. They hired a house in the city and were to commence housekeeping immediately. The Captain made him a number of presents and seemed much pleased with the arrangement. The day previous to the one set for the marriage, while they were setting their house in order, a man called and enquired for a nurse, pretending he wanted one of us. Mother was absent; he said he would call again, but he never came. On Wednesday evening we attended a protracted meeting. After we had returned home and retired, a loud rap was heard at the door. My Aunt enquired who was there. The reply was, "Open the door or I will break it down." In a moment in rushed seven men, four watchmen and three traders, and ordered mother to take my brother and me and follow them, which she hastened to do as fast as possible, but we were not allowed time to put on our usual attire. They thrust us into a close carriage. For fear of my mother alarming the citizens they threw her to the ground and choked her until she was nearly strangled, then pushed her into a coach. The night was dark and dreary; the stars refused to shine, the moon to shed her light. . . .

We were hurried along the streets. The inhabitants heard our cries and rushed to their doors, but our carriage being perfectly tight, and the alarm so sudden, that we were at the jail before they could give us any relief. There were strong Union men and officers in the city, and if they could have been informed of the human smuggling they would have released us. But oh, that horrid, dilapidated prison, with its dim lights and dingy walls, again presented itself to our view. My sister was there first, and we were thrust in and remained there until three o'clock the following afternoon. Could we have notified the police we should have been released, but no opportunity was given us. It appears that this kidnapping had been in contemplation from the time we were before taken and returned; and Captain Tirrell's kindness to mother,— his benevolence towards Mr. Adams in assisting him to furnish his house,—his generosity in letting us work for ourselves,—his approbation in regard to the contemplated marriage was only a trap. Thus instead of a wedding Thursday evening, we were hurled across the ferry to Albany Court House and to Kentucky through the rain and without our outer garments. My mother had lost her bonnet and shawl in the struggle while being thrust in the coach, consequently she had no protection from the storm, and the rest of us were in similar circumstances. I believe we passed through Springfield. I think it was the first stopping place after we left East St. Louis, and we were put on board the cars and secreted in the gentlemen's smoking car, in which there were only a few rebels. We arrived in Springfield about twelve o'clock at night. When we took the cars it was dark, bleak and cold. It was the 18th of March, and as we were without bonnets and clothing to shield us from the sleet and wind, we suffered intensely. The old trader, for fear that mother might make her escape, carried my brother, nine years of age, from one train to the other. We then took the cars for Albany, and arrived at eight o'clock in the morning. We were then carried on the ferry in a wagon. There was another family in the wagon, in the same condition. We landed at Portland, from thence to Louisville, and were put into John Clark's trader's yard, and sold out separately, except my mother and little brother, who were sold together. Mother remained in the trader's yard two weeks, my sister six, myself four.

Mother was sold to Captain Plasio. My sister to Benj. Board, and myself to Capt. Ephraim Frisbee. The man who bought my mother was a Spaniard. After she had been there a short time he tried to have my mother let my brother stop at his saloon, a very dissipated place, to wait upon his miserable crew, but my mother objected. In spite of her objections he took him down to try him, but some Union soldiers called at the saloon, and noticing that he was very small, they questioned him, and my brother, child like, divulged the whole matter. The Captain, fearful of being betrayed and losing his property, let him continue with my mother. The Captain paid eight hundred dollars for my mother and brother. We were all sold for extravagant prices. My sister, aged sixteen, was sold for eight hundred and fifty dollars; I was sold for nine hundred dollars. This was in 1863. My mother was cook and fared very well. My sister was sold to a single gentleman, whose intended took charge of her until they were married, after which they took her to her home. She was her waiter, and fared as well as could be expected. I fared worse than either of the family. I was not allowed enough to eat, exposed to the cold, and not allowed through the cold winter to thoroughly warm myself once a month. The house was very large, and I could gain no access to the fire. I was kept constantly at work of the heaviest kind,—compelled to move heavy trunks and boxes,—many times to wash till ten and twelve o'clock at night. There were three deaths in the family while I remained there, and the entire burden was put upon me. I often felt to exclaim as the Children of Israel did: "O Lord, my burden is greater than I can bear." I was then seventeen years of age. My health has been impaired from that time to the present. I have a severe pain in my side by the slightest over exertion. In the Winter I suffer intensely with cold, and cannot get warm unless in a room heated to eighty degrees. I am infirm and burdened with the influence of slavery, whose impress will ever remain on my mind and body. For six months I tried to make my escape. I used to rise at four o'clock in the morning to find some one to assist me, and at last I succeeded. I was allowed two hours once in two weeks to go and return three miles. I could contrive no other way than to improve one of these opportunities, in which I was finally successful. I became acquainted with some persons who assisted slaves to escape by the underground railroad. They were colored people. I was to pretend going to church, and the man who was to assist and introduce me to the proper parties was to linger on the street opposite the house, and I was to follow at a short distance. On Sunday evening I begged leave to attend church, which was reluctantly granted if I completed all my work, which was no easy task. It appeared as if my mistress used every possible exertion to delay me from church, and I concluded that her old cloven-footed companion had impressed his intentions on her mind. Finally, when I was ready to start, my mistress took a notion to go out to ride, and desired me to dress her little boy, and then get ready for church. Extensive hoops were then worn, and as I had attached my whole wardrobe under mine by a cord around my waist, it required considerable dexterity and no small amount of maneuvering to hide the fact from my mistress. While attending to the child I had managed to stand in one corner of the room, for fear she might come in contact with me and thus discover that my hoops were not so elastic as they usually are. I endeavored to conceal my excitement by backing and edging very genteelly out of the door. I had nine pieces of clothing thus concealed on my person, and as the string which fastened them was small it caused me considerable discomfort. To my great satisfaction I at last passed into the street, and my master and mistress drove down the street in great haste and were soon out of sight. I saw my guide patiently awaiting me. I followed him at a distance until we arrived at the church, and there met two young ladies, one of whom handed me a pass and told me to follow them at a square's distance. It was now twilight. There was a company of soldiers about to take passage across the ferry, and I followed. I showed my pass, and proceeded up the stairs on the boat. While thus ascending the stairs, the cord which held my bundle of clothing broke, and my feet became entangled in my wardrobe, but by proceeding, the first step released one foot and the next the other. This was observed only by a few soldiers, who were too deeply engaged in their own affairs to interfere with mine. I seated myself in a remote corner of the boat, and in a few moments I landed on free soil for the first time in my life, except when hurled through Albany and Springfield at the time of our capture. I was now under my own control. The cars were waiting in Jefferson City for the passengers for Indianapolis, where we arrived about nine o'clock. My first business, after my arrival at Indianapolis was to find a boarding place in which I at once succeeded, and in a few hours thereafter was at a place of service of my own choice. I had always been under the yoke of oppression, compelled to submit to its laws, and not allowed to advance a rod from the house, or even out of call, without a severe punishment. Now this constant fear and restless yearning was over. It appeared as though I had emerged into a new world, or had never lived in the old one before. The people I lived with were Unionists, and became immediately interested in teaching and encouraging me in my literary advancement and all other important improvements, which precisely met the natural desires for which my soul had ever yearned since my earliest recollection. I could read a little, but was not allowed to learn in slavery. I was obliged to pay twenty-five cents for every letter written for me. I now began to feel that as I was free I could learn to write, as well as others; consequently Mrs. Harris, the lady with whom I lived, volunteered to assist me. I was soon enabled to write quite a legible hand, which I find a great convenience. I would advise all, young, middle aged or old, in a free country to learn to read and write. . . .

WILLIAM WELLS BROWN

From *The Negro's Civil War*

ALL THE OBJECTIONS TO EMIGRATION APPEAR TO centre in the feeling that we ought not to quit the land of our birth, and leave the slave in his chains. This view of the case comes at the first glance with some force, but on a closer examination, it will be found to have but little weight. If it could be shown that our presence here was actually needed, and that we could exert an influence, no matter what position we occupied in the community, then I agree that duty would require us to remain.

But let us look at facts. It must be confessed that we, the colored people of this country, are a race of cooks, waiters, barbers, whitewashers, bootblacks, and chimney sweeps. How much influence has such a class upon a community? . . .

I hold that the descendants of Africa, in this country, will never be respected until they shall leave the cook shop and barber's chair and the whitewash brush. "They who would be free, themselves must strike the blow," means something more than appearing in a military attitude. To emigrate to Hayti, and to develop the resources of the Island, and to build up a powerful and influential government there, which shall demonstrate the genius and capabilities of the Negro, is as good an Anti-Slavery work as can be done in the Northern States of this Union.

Our opponents do not meet the subject fairly and honestly. To attempt to connect the Haytian emigration movement with the old and hateful colonization scheme, is only to create a prejudice in the minds of the people. Originated by a colored nation, in the interests of the colored race, conducted and sustained exclusively by the friends or members of that nation and that race, it is essentially and diametrically opposed to the colonization project, which was originated by slaveholders, in the interests of slavery, and conducted and sustained exclusively by the friends of bondage, and the haters of the Negro.

ROBERT PURVIS

From *The Negro's Civil War*

§

R*OBERT PURVIS, THE WEALTHY NEGRO ABOLITIONIST OF Philadelphia, was not impressed by the pamphlet. He assured Pomeroy in a public letter that few Negroes wished to be colonized:*

Sir, for more than twenty years the question of colonization agitated and divided this country. The "colored" people stamped it with the seal of their reprobation; the whites acquiesced in the justice of their decision, and the vexed and vexing question was put to rest. Now it is revived; the apple of discord is again thrown into the community, and as though you had not already enough to divide and distract you, a new scheme is hit upon, and deliberately sent upon its errand of mischief. . . .

But it is said this is a question of prejudice—of national antipathy and not to be reasoned about. The President has said, "Whether it is right or wrong, I need not now discuss it." Great God! is justice nothing? Is honor nothing? Is even pecuniary interest to be sacrificed to this insane and vulgar hate? . . .

Sir, we were born here and here we choose to remain. . . .

HARRIET TUBMAN

From *The Negro's Civil War*

UNDERGROUND RAILROAD, 1861

GOD WON'T LET MASSA LINKUM BEAT DE South till he do de right ting. Massa Linkum he great man, and I'se poor nigger; but dis nigger can tell Massa Linkum how to save de money and de young men. He do it by setting de niggers free. S'pose dar was awfu' big snake down dar, on de floor. He bite you. Folks all skeered, cause you die. You send for doctor to cut de bite; but snake he rolled up dar, and while doctor dwine it, he bite you agin. De doctor cut out dat bite; but while he dwine it, de snake he spring up and bite you agin, and so he keep dwine, till you kill him. Dat's what Massa Linkum orter know.

ELIZABETH KECKLEY

*From Behind the Scenes, or, Thirty Years
a Slave, and Four Years in the White House*

WASHINGTON, NEW YORK, AND
BOSTON, 1862

IN THE SUMMER OF 1862, FREEDMEN BEGAN to flock into Washington from Maryland and Virginia. They came with a great hope in their hearts, and with all their worldly goods on their backs. Fresh from the bonds of slavery, fresh from the benighted regions of the plantation, they came to the Capital looking for liberty, and many of them not knowing it when they found it. Many good friends reached forth kind hands, but the North is not warm and impulsive. For one kind word spoken, two harsh ones were uttered; there was something repelling in the atmosphere, and the bright joyous dreams of freedom to the slave faded—were sadly altered, in the presence of that stern, practical mother, reality. Instead of flowery paths, days of perpetual sunshine, and bowers hanging with golden fruit, the road was rugged and full of thorns, the sunshine was eclipsed by shadows, and the mute appeals for help too often were answered by cold neglect. Poor dusky children of slavery, men and women of my own race—the transition from slavery to freedom was too sudden for you! The bright dreams were too rudely dispelled; you were not prepared for the new life that opened before you, and the great masses of the North learned to look upon your helplessness with indifference—learned to speak of you as an idle, dependent race. Reason should have prompted kinder thoughts. Charity is ever kind.

One fair summer evening I was walking the streets of Washington, accompanied by a friend, when a band of music was heard in the distance. We wondered what it could mean, and curiosity prompted us to find out its meaning. We quickened our steps, and discovered that it came from the house of Mrs. Farnham. The yard was brilliantly lighted, ladies and gentlemen were moving about, and the band was playing some of its sweetest airs. We approached the sentinel on duty at the gate, and asked what was going on. He told us that it was a festival given for the benefit of the sick and wounded soldiers in the city. This suggested an idea to me. If the white people can give festivals to raise funds for the relief of suffering soldiers, why should not the well-to-do colored people go to work to do something for the benefit of the suffering blacks? I could not rest. The thought was ever present with me, and the next Sunday I made a suggestion in the colored church, that a society of colored people be formed to labor for the benefit of the unfortunate freedmen. The idea proved popular, and in two weeks "the Contraband Relief Association" was organized, with forty working members.

In September of 1862, Mrs. Lincoln left Washington for New York, and requested me to follow her in a few days, and join her at the Metropolitan Hotel. I was glad of the opportunity to do so, for I thought that in New York I would be able to do something in the interests of our society. Armed with credentials, I took the train for New York, and went to the Metropolitan, where Mrs. Lincoln had secured accommodations for me. The next morning I told Mrs. Lincoln of my project; and she immediately headed my list with a subscription of $200. I circulated among the colored people, and got them thoroughly interested in the subject, when I was called to Boston by Mrs. Lincoln, who wished to visit her son Robert, attending college in that city. I met Mr. Wendell Phillips, and other Boston philanthropists, who gave me all the assistance in their power. We held a mass meeting at the Colored Baptist Church, Rev. Mr. Grimes, in Boston, raised a sum of money, and organized there a branch society. The society was organized by Mrs. Grimes, wife of the pastor, assisted by Mrs. Martin, wife of Rev. Stella Martin. This branch of the main society, during the war, was able to send us over eighty large boxes of goods, contributed exclusively by the colored people of Boston. Returning to New York, we held a successful meeting at the Shiloh Church, Rev. Henry Highland Garnet, pastor. The Metropolitan Hotel, at that time as now, employed colored help. I suggested the object of my mission to Robert Thompson, Steward of the Hotel, who immediately raised quite a sum of money among the dining-room waiters. Mr. Frederick Douglass contributed $200, besides lecturing for us. Other prominent colored men sent in liberal contributions. From England a large quantity of stores was received. Mrs. Lincoln made frequent contributions, as also did the President. In 1863 I was re-elected President of the Association, which office I continue to hold.

The war progressed, fair fields had been stained with blood, thousands of brave men had fallen, and thousands of eyes were weeping for the fallen at home. There were desolate hearthstones in the South as well as in the North, and as the people of my race watched the sanguinary struggle, the ebb and flow of the tide of battle, they lifted their faces Zionward, as if they hoped to catch a glimpse of the Promised Land beyond the sulphureous clouds of smoke which shifted now and then but to reveal ghastly rows of new-made graves. Sometimes the very life of the nation seemed to tremble with the fierce shock of arms. In 1863 the Confederates were flushed with victory, and sometimes it looked as if the proud flag of the Union, the glorious old Stars and Stripes, must yield half its nationality to the tri-barred flag that floated grandly over long columns of gray. These were sad, anxious days to Mr. Lincoln, and those who saw the man in privacy only could tell how much he suffered. One day he came into the room where I was fitting a dress on Mrs. Lincoln. His step was slow and heavy, and his face sad. Like a tired child he threw himself upon a sofa, and shaded his eyes with his hands. He was a complete picture of dejection. Mrs. Lincoln, observing his troubled look, asked:

"Where have you been, father?"

"To the War Department," was the brief, almost sullen answer.

"Any news?"

"Yes, plenty of news, but no good news. It is dark, dark everywhere."

He reached forth one of his long arms, and took a small Bible from a stand near the head of the sofa, opened the pages of the holy book, and soon was absorbed in reading them. A quarter of an hour passed, and on glancing at the sofa the face of the President seemed more cheerful. The dejected look was gone, and the countenance was lighted up with new resolution and hope. The change was so marked that I could not but wonder at it, and wonder led to the desire to know what book of the Bible afforded so much comfort to the reader. Making the search for a missing article an excuse, I walked gently around the sofa, and looking into the open book, I discovered that Mr. Lincoln was reading that divine comforter, Job. He read with Christian eagerness, and the courage and hope that he derived from the inspired pages made him a new man. I almost imagined that I could hear the Lord speaking to him from out the whirlwind of battle: "Gird up thy loins now like a man: I will demand of thee, and declare thou unto me." What a sublime picture was this! A ruler of a mighty nation going to the pages of the Bible with simple Christian earnestness for comfort and courage, and finding both in the darkest hours of a nation's calamity. Ponder it, O ye scoffers at God's Holy Word, and then hang your heads for very shame!

Frequent letters were received warning Mr. Lincoln of assassination, but he never gave a second thought to the mysterious warnings. The letters, however, sorely troubled his wife. She seemed to read impending danger in every rustling leaf, in every whisper of the wind.

"Where are you going now, father?" she would say to him, as she observed him putting on his overshoes and shawl.

"I am going over to the War Department, mother, to try and learn some news."

"But, father, you should not go out alone. You know you are surrounded with danger."

"All imagination. What does any one want to harm me for? Don't worry about me, mother, as if I were a little child, for no one is going to molest me;" and with a confident, unsuspecting air he would close the door behind him, descend the stairs, and pass out to his lonely walk.

For weeks, when trouble was anticipated, friends of the President would sleep in the White House to guard him from danger.

Robert would come home every few months, bringing new joy to the family circle. He was very anxious to quit school and enter the army, but the move was sternly opposed by his mother.

"We have lost one son, and his loss is as much as I can bear, without being called upon to make another sacrifice," she would say, when the subject was under discussion.

"But many a poor mother has given up all her sons," mildly suggested Mr. Lincoln, "and our son is not more dear to us than the sons of other people are to their mothers."

"That may be; but I cannot bear to have Robert exposed to danger. His services are not required in the field, and the sacrifice would be a needless one."

"The services of every man who loves his country are required in this war. You should take a liberal instead of a selfish view of the question, mother."

Argument at last prevailed, and permission was granted Robert to enter the army. With the rank of Captain and A. D. C. he went to the field, and remained in the army till the close of the war. . . .

JOHN BOSTON

From *Free at Last*

◊

Upton Hill [*Va.*] January ^{the} 12 1862

My Dear Wife   it is with grate joy I take this time to let you know Whare I am   i am now in Safety in the 14th Regiment of Brooklyn   this Day i can Adress you thank god as a free man   I had a little truble in giting away But as the lord led the Children of Isrel to the land of Canon So he led me to a land Whare fredom Will rain in spite Of earth and hell Dear you must make your Self content i am free from al the Slavers Lash   and as you have chose the Wise plan Of Serving the lord i hope you Will pray Much and i Will try by the help of god To Serv him With all my hart   I am With a very nice man and have All that hart Can Wish But My Dear I Cant express my grate desire that i Have to See you   i trust the time Will Come When We Shal meet again   And if We dont met on earth We Will Meet in heven Whare Jesas ranes   Dear Elizabeth tell Mrs Own[ees] That i trust that She Will Continue Her kindness to you and that god Will Bless her on earth and Save her In grate eternity   My Acomplements To Mrs Owens and her Children   may They Prosper through life   I never Shall forgit her kindness to me   Dear Wife i must Close   rest yourself Contented i am free   i Want you to rite To me Soon as you Can Without Delay   Direct your letter to the 14th Reigment New york State malitia Uptons Hill Virginea In Care of Mr Cranford Comary   Write my Dear Soon As you C   Your Affectionate Husban   Kiss Daniel For me

John Boston

Give my love to Father and Mother

CHARLOTTE FORTEN

From *The Journal of Charlotte Forten*

SOUTH CAROLINA, 1863

THURSDAY, NEW YEAR'S DAY, 1863. THE MOST glorious
. . . day this nation has yet seen, *I* think. I rose early—an event here—
and early we started, with an old borrowed carriage and a remarkably slow
horse. Whither were we going? thou wilt ask, dearest A. To the ferry; thence
to Camp Saxton, to the Celebration. From the Ferry to the camp the "Flora"
took us.

How pleasant it was on board! A crowd of people, whites and blacks, and a
band of music—to the great delight of the negroes. Met on board Dr. and
Mrs. Peck and their daughters, who greeted me most kindly. Also Gen.
S[axton]'s father whom I like much, and several other acquaintances whom I
was glad to see. We stopped at Beaufort, and then proceeded to Camp Saxton,
the camp of the 1st Reg[iment] S[outh] C[arolina] Vol[unteer]s. The "Flora"
c[ou]ld not get up to the landing, so we were rowed ashore in a row boat.

Just as my foot touched the plank, on landing, a hand grasped mine and
well known voice spoke my name. It was my dear and noble friend, Dr.
Rogers. I cannot tell you, dear A., how delighted I was to see him; how *good* it
was to see the face of a friend from the North, and *such* a friend. I think myself
particularly blessed to have him for a friend. Walking on a little distance I
found myself being presented to Col. Higginson, whereat I was so much
overwhelmed, that I had no reply to make to the very kind and courteous little
speech with which he met me. I believe I mumbled something, and grinned
like a simpleton, that was all. Provoking, isn't it? that when one is most in need
of sensible words, one finds them not.

I *cannot* give a regular chronicle of the day. It is impossible. I was in such a state of excitement. It all seemed, and seems still, like a brilliant dream. Dr. R[ogers] and I talked all the time, I know, while he showed me the camp and all the arrangements. . . .

The meeting was held in a beautiful grove, a live-oak grove, adjoining the camp. It is the largest one I have yet seen; but I don't think the moss pendants are quite as beautiful as they are on St. Helena. As I sat on the stand and looked around on the various groups, I thought I had never seen a sight so beautiful. There were the black soldiers, in their blue coats and scarlet pants, the officers of this and other regiments in their handsome uniforms, and crowds of lookers-on, men, women and children, grouped in various attitudes, under the trees. The faces of all wore a happy, eager, expectant look.

The exercises commenced by a prayer from Rev. Mr. Fowler, Chaplain of the reg[iment]. An ode written for the occasion by Prof. Zachos, originally a Greek, now Sup[erintendent] of Paris island—was read by himself, and then sung by the whites. Col. H[igginson] introduced Dr. Brisbane in a few elegant and graceful words. He (Dr. B.) read the President's [Emancipation] Proclamation, which was warmly cheered. Then the beautiful flags presented by Dr. Cheever's Church [in New York] were presented to Col. H[igginson] for the Reg[iment] in an excellent and enthusiastic speech, by Rev. Mr. [Mansfield] French. Immediately at the conclusion, some of the colored people—of their own accord sang "My Country Tis of Thee." It was a touching and beautiful incident, and Col. Higginson, in accepting the flags made it the occasion of some happy remarks. He said *that* tribute was far more effective than any speech he c'ld make. He spoke for some time, and all that he said was grand, glorious. He seemed inspired. Nothing c'ld have been better, more perfect. And Dr. R[ogers] told me afterward that the Col. was much affected. That tears were in his eyes. He is as Whittier says, truly a "sure man." The men all admire and love him. There is a great deal of personal magnetism about him, and his kindness is proverbial. After he had done speaking he delivered the flags to the color-bearers with a few very impressive remarks to them. They each then, Sgt. Prince Rivers and [Cpl.] Robert Sutton, made very good speeches indeed, and were loudly cheered. Gen. Saxton and Mrs. Gage spoke very well. The good Gen. was received with great enthusiasm, and throughout the morning—every little while it seemed to me three cheers were given for him. A Hymn written I believe, by Mr. Judd, was sung, and then all the people united with the Reg[iment] in singing "John Brown." It was grand. During the exercises, it was announced that Fremont was appointed Commander-in-chief of the Army, and this was received with enthusiastic and prolonged cheering. But as it is picket news, I greatly fear that is not true.

We dined with good Dr. R[ogers] at the Col's [T. W. Higginson] table, though, greatly to my regret he, (the Col.) was not there. He partook of some of the oxen, (of which ten had been roasted) with his men. I like his doing that.

We had quite a sumptuous dinner. Our party consisted of Dr. R[ogers], Adjutant D[ewhurst], Capt. R[ogers], Mr. and Miss Ware (Mrs. Winsor's brother and sister), Mr. Hall, their cousin, whom I like much, and Mr. and Miss H[unn] and me. We had a merry, delightful dinner. The only part that I did not enjoy was being obliged to read Whittier's Hymn aloud at the table. I wanted Dr. R[ogers] to do it. But he w'ld insist on my doing it. So of course it was murdered. I believe the older I grow the more averse I get to doing anything in public. I have no courage to do such things.

Col. H[igginson] invited us into his tent—a very nice, almost *homelike* one. I noticed a nice secretary, with writing utensils and "Les Miserables" on it. A *wreath* of beautiful oranges hung against the wall, fronting the door. I wanted to have a good look at this tent; but we were hardly seated when the Dr. and Col. were called away for a moment, and Lieut. Col. Billings coming in w'ld insist upon our going into his tent. I did not want to go at all, but he was so *persistent* we had to. I fear he is a somewhat vain person. His tent was very comfortable too, and I noticed quite a large piece of "Secesh" furniture, something between a secretary and a bureau, and quite a collection of photographs and daguerres. But I did not examine them, for my attention was occupied by Col. H[igginson] to whom I showed Whittier's poem, letter and photo. "He looks old," he said to me sadly, as he handed back the picture.

Dr. R[ogers] introduced me to Dr. H[awks] and his wife—pleasant people, and *good* anti-slavery. They mentioned having Liberators with my letters in them. I am sorry they have come down here.

Col. H[igginson] asked me to go out and hear the band play, which I very gladly did. But it stopped just as we stepped outside of the tent. Just then one of the soldiers came up to the Col. and said "Do Cunnel, do ask 'em to play Dixie, just for me, for my lone self." The Col. made the request, but the leader of the band said he feared they w'ld not be able to play the whole tune as they had not the necessary pieces. "Nebber mind," said the man "jus' half a tune will do." It was found impossible to play even that but the leader promised that the next time they came they would be fully prepared to play Dixie for him.

The Dress Parade—the first I had ever seen—delighted me. It was a brilliant sight—the long line of men in their brilliant uniform, with bayonets gleaming in the sunlight. The Col. looked splendid. The Dr. said the men went through with the drill remarkably well. It seemed to me nothing c'ld be more perfect. To me it was a grand triumph—that black regiment doing itself honor in the sight of the white officers, many of whom, doubtless "came to scoff." It was typical of what the race, so long downtrodden and degraded will yet achieve on this Continent.

After the Parade, we went to the Landing, intending to take a boat for Beaufort. But the boat was too crowded, and we decided to wait for another. It was the softest, loveliest moonlight. We sat down among the ruins of the old fort. Just [as soon] as the boat had reached a favorable distance from the shore the band in it commenced playing Home, sweet Home. It was exquisitely beautiful. The lovely moonlight on the water, the perfect stillness around seemed to give new beauty to that ever beautiful old song. And then as my dear friend, Dr. R[ogers] said, "It came *very near* to us all."

Finding the night air damp we went to the tent of Mr. Fowler, the chaplain, whom I like much better in private conversation than as an orator. He is a thoroughly good, earnest man. Thither came Col. H[igginson] and Dr. H[awks]. We sat around the nice fire—the tent has *chimney* and fire place, made by Mr. F[owler]'s own skilful hands. Col. H[igginson] is a perfectly delightful person in private.—So genial, so witty, so kind. But I noticed when he was silent, a careworn almost sad expression on his earnest, noble face. My heart was full when I looked at him. I longed to say "I thank you, I thank you, for that noble glorious speech." And yet I *c'ld not*. It is always so. I do not know how to talk. Words always fail me when I want them most. The more I feel the more impossible it is for me to speak. It is very provoking. Among other things, Col. H[igginson] said how amusing it was to him—their plan of housekeeping down here. "This morning I was asked "Well, Colonel, how many oxen shall we roast today." And I said, just as calmly as I w'ld have ordered a pound or two of beef, at home.—well I think *ten* will do. And then to be consulted as to how many gallons of molasses, and of vinegar, and how many pounds of ginger w'ld be wanted seemed very odd." I wish I c'ld reproduce for you the dry humorous tones in which this was said. We had a pleasant chat, sitting there in the firelight, and I was most unwilling to go, for besides the happiness of being in the society of the Col. and the Dr. we wanted dreadfully to see the "shout" and grand jubilee which the soldiers were going to have that night. But it was already late, and hearing that the "Flora" was coming we had to hasten to the Landing. I was sorry to say good-bye to Dr. R[ogers]. What an *unspeakable* happiness it was to see him. But I fear for his health. I fear the exposure of a camp life. Am glad to see that he has warm robes and blankets, to keep him comfortable. I wish I c'ld do something for him. He has done so much for me.

Ah, what a grand, glorious day this has been. The dawn of freedom which it heralds may not break upon us at once; but it will surely come, and sooner, I believe, than we have ever dared hope before. My soul is glad with an exceeding great gladness. But before I close, dear A., I must bring our little party safe home to Oaklands. We had a good time on the Flora. L[izzie Hunn] and I promenaded the deck, and sang John Brown, and Whittier's Hymn and "My Country Tis of Thee." And the moon shone bright above us, and the waves beneath, smooth and clear, glistened in the soft moonlight. At Beaufort we took the row boat, and the boatmen sang as they rowed us across. Mr. Hall was with us, and seemed really to appreciate and enjoy everything. I like him. Arrived at St. Helena's we separated, he to go to "Coffin's Point" (a dreadful name, as Dr. R[ogers] says) and we to come hither [Oaklands]. Can't say that I enjoyed the homeward drive very much. T'was so intensely cold, yes *intensely,* for these regions. I fear some of the hot enthusiasm with which my soul was filled got chilled a little but it was only for a short time.

Old friend, my good and dear A. a very, very happy New Year to you! Dear friends in both my Northern homes a happy, happy New Year to you, too! And to us all a year of such freedom as we have never yet known in this boasted but hitherto wicked land. The hymn, or rather one of the hymns that those boat[men] sung [*sic*] is singing itself to me now. The refrain "Religion so . . . sweet" was so sweet and touching in its solemnity. . . .

ANN

From *Free at Last*

❧

MISSOURI, 1864

Paris Mo Jany 19, 1864

My Dear Husband I r'ecd your letter dated Jan'y 9th also one dated Jany 1st but have got no one till now to write for me. You do not know how bad I am treated. They are treating me worse and worse every day. Our child cries for you. Send me some money as soon as you can for me and my child are almost naked. My cloth is yet in the loom and there is no telling when it will be out. Do not send any of your letters to Hogsett especially those having money in them as Hogsett will keep the money. George Combs went to Hannibal soon after you did so I did not get that money from him. Do the best you can and do not fret too much for me for it wont be long before I will be free and then all we make will be ours. Your affectionate wife

Ann

P.S. Sind our little girl a string of beads in your next letter to remember you by. Ann

OCTAVE JOHNSON

From *Free at Last*

[*New Orleans, La. February? 1864*]

Deposition of Octave Johnson, Corporal Co. C, 15th Regt. Corps d'Afrique.

I was born in New Orleans; I am 23 years of age; I was raised by Arthur Thiboux of New Orleans; I am by trade a cooper; I was treated pretty well at home; in 1855 master sold my mother, and in 1861 he sold me to S. Contrell of St. James Parish for $2,400; here I worked by task at my trade; one morning the bell was rung for us to go to work so early that I could not see, and I lay still, because I was working by task; for this the overseer was going to have me whipped, and I ran away to the woods, where I remained for a year and a half; I had to steal my food; took turkeys, chickens and pigs; before I left our number had increased to thirty, of whom ten were women; we were four miles in the rear of the plantation house; sometimes we would rope beef cattle and drag them out to our hiding place; we obtained matches from our friends on the plantation; we slept on logs and burned cypress leaves to make a smoke and keep away mosquitoes; Eugene Jardeau, master of hounds, hunted for us for three months; often those at work would betray those in the swamp, for fear of being implicated in their escape; we furnished meat to our fellow-servants in the field, who would return corn meal; one day twenty hounds came after me; I called the party to my assistance and we killed eight of the bloodhounds; then we all jumped into Bayou Faupron; the dogs followed us and the alligators caught six of them; "the alligators preferred dog flesh to personal flesh;" we escaped and came to Camp Parapet, where I was first employed in the Commissary's office, then as a servant to Col. Hanks; then I joined his regiment.

PATSEY LEACH

From *Free at Last*

§

KENTUCKY, 1865

Camp Nelson Ky 25″ March 1865
I am a widow and belonged to Warren Wiley of Woodford County Ky. My husband Julius Leach was a member of Co. D. 5″ U.S. C[*olored*]. Cavalry and was killed at the Salt Works Va. about six months ago. When he enlisted sometime in the fall of 1864 he belonged to Sarah Martin Scott County Ky. He had only been about a month in the service when he was killed. I was living with aforesaid Wiley when he died. He knew of my husbands enlisting before I did but never said any thing to me about it. From that time he treated me more cruelly than ever whipping me frequently without any cause and insulting me on every occasion. About three weeks after my husband enlisted a Company of Colored Soldiers passed our house and I was there in the garden and looked at them as they passed. My master had been watching me and when the soldiers had gone I went into the kitchen. My master followed me and Knocked me to the floor senseless saying as he did so, "You have been looking at them darned Nigger Soldiers" When I recovered my senses he beat me with a cowhide When my husband was Killed my master whipped me severely saying my husband had gone into the army to fight against white folks and he my master would let me know that I was foolish to let my husband go he would "take it out of my back," he would "Kill me by picemeal" and he hoped "that the last one of the nigger soldiers would be Killed" He whipped me twice after that using similar expressions The last whipping he gave me he took me into the Kitchen tied my hands tore all my clothes off until I was entirely naked, bent me down, placed my head between his Knees, then whipped me most unmercifully until my back was lacerated all over, the blood oozing out in several places

so that I could not wear my underclothes without their becoming saturated with blood. The marks are still visible on my back. On this and other occasions my master whipped me for no other cause than my husband having enlisted. When he had whipped me he said "never mind God dam you when I am done with you tomorrow you never will live no more." I knew he would carry out his threats so that night about 10 o'clock I took my babe and travelled to Arnolds Depot where I took the Cars to Lexington I have five children, I left them all with my master except the youngest and I want to get them but I dare not go near my master knowing he would whip me again. My master is a Rebel Sympathizer and often sends Boxes of Goods to Rebel prisoners. And further Deponent saith not.

Her
Signed Patsey Leach
mark

❧

Part VI

NO LAND, NO MULES, AND

FOR MILLIONS, NO VOTE

With the Civil War over and slavery on the wane, black Americans were optimistic as the Reconstruction period began to unfold. Radical Republicans were mainly responsible for promulgating gossip that former slaves could expect forty acres and a mule as part of a reparations program. Moreover, the government was in the process of developing a Freedmen's Bureau to oversee the needs of the recently emancipated who were without jobs, homes, and security from the vengeful rebels. The forty acres and a mule were nothing but a vicious rumor, but the Freedmen's Bureau became a reality, though it fell far short of its overall promise.

The bureau's greatest accomplishment was in the realm of education and elective office, according to John Mercer Langston's memories, which he relates in the third person. As a representative of the bureau, Langston traveled throughout the former slaveholding states attending events and witnessing a variety of programs of improvement, mostly within the realm of education. Langston himself is testament to this country's slow but meaningful advances in politics, as the first black elected to public office in the United States. He is an ancestor of the poet and writer Langston Hughes.

An issue often ignored in the past, but held dear by Sojourner Truth, was the equal rights of women, especially black women. While black men were given the franchise with the enactment of the Fifteenth Amendment—and their vote would be decisive in the presidential election of 1868 when the nearly half million black votes turned the tide for Ulysses Grant—black women and other women were not allowed the suffrage. In her inimical style, Truth hammers away at this disparity with a zeal unmatched by women of any color, demanding equal pay and equal justice.

Black men may have had the right to vote, yet Reconstruction, on the whole, brought them little improvement. Black veterans felt particularly slighted and they made their displeasure known loud and clear. They wanted to know: Would they be compensated for their services during the war? And if their property was confiscated by the government, were they entitled to any remuneration? Samuel Larkin, who served several months in a Union regiment, is an example of the countless veterans who only received partial—if any—recompense for their bravery.

As noted earlier, blacks made substantial gains in the electoral arena, although to suggest black officeholders constituted a "domination," the position of many apologists for slavery, is to greatly exaggerate their power. (Several years later, director D. W. Griffith would glorify this misconception in his film *Birth of a Nation.*) Among the prominent black politicians of the day was John R. Lynch, a congressman from Mississippi. How the state of Mississippi adjusted to political reform is at the core of Lynch's entry.

JOHN MERCER LANGSTON

From *From the Virginia Plantation to the National Capitol*

VIRGINIA, 1867

Mr. LANGSTON, AFTER AN EXTENDED AND successful trip through Mississippi and Alabama, on his journey northward learned through the newspapers that President Johnson had in contemplation a change in the commissionership of the Bureau of Refugees, Freedmen and Abandoned Lands, and that his own name had been mentioned in connection with the place. After his arrival at the national capital, he visited the Executive Mansion, and there had a full and free talk with the president on the subject. President Johnson was outspoken and positive in his opposition to General Howard, and did not hesitate to declare his purpose to relieve him of his position. His expressions with regard to him and his management of the Bureau were extremely severe, sometimes blasphemous. Throughout his conversation he indulged in most harsh and offensive criticism of him, insisting that he should be relieved. He stated that he would be exceedingly glad if the colored people could agree upon some able and efficient man of their own number for that position. He declared his readiness to appoint him, and intimated his willingness to give the place to Mr. Langston. Finally, he went so far as to give him time to consider the matter. However, Mr. Langston insisted that the highest interests of the colored people and the efficiency of this service instituted in their behalf, seemed to him to require the continuance of General Howard at the head of the Bureau. From his observation of the service, with close inspection of the results already accomplished, Mr. Langston claimed that President Lincoln had made no mistake in calling General Howard to the commissionership, for he appeared to be in every way sagacious, wise and efficient. Besides, he had already won the confidence of the liberal people of the country, whose great church, missionary and charitable organizations were supplementing in outlays and labor the enterprises so much needed to further the work of the Bureau among the emancipated and impoverished classes of the South.

In this same interview with the president, as he discovered that Mr. Langston did not incline to accept the commissionership of the Bureau, he suggested to him that he would appoint him, if he preferred, as United States Minister to Hayti. But Mr. Langston showed no disposition whatever to accept this foreign place.

On leaving the president however, Mr. Langston did promise to call upon him again at an early day, to give him his conclusions fully and decidedly in regard to these matters. Upon consultation with friends well advised and in whom he had special confidence, he took another course entirely. He called upon General Howard, his chief, and made bold as he conceived it to be his duty, to make known to him the purposes of President Johnson, as stated. He advised General Howard also that he had no doubt that General Grant, who was then acting as secretary of war *ad interim,* standing firmly for his continuance in his position, would succeed even as against the president, in keeping him there. He further stated what he had said to the president on the subject and that he would be glad to say even more in the same direction to the secretary of war. Accordingly a call was arranged, and Mr. Langston accompanied by Col. L. Edwin Dudley, a white friend of his and a special admirer and friend of General Howard, and Mr. John T. Johnson, a prominent colored citizen of Washington city, a friend also of General Howard, fully alive to his great services to his race and deeply conscious of his worth, visited General Grant for the purposes indicated. . . . He said he had no influence with the president, and would only be able to sustain General Howard, as he did so in his official capacity. Besides, he added that he did not know that he would be kept in his place for the next twenty-four hours. He did not hesitate to speak in severe and earnest terms against the policy which seemed to be actuating the president generally, nor did he hesitate to express his views in emphatic and eloquent manner with regard to what the negro had a right to expect of the government in the way of protection and support, even to the extent of the bestowal of full citizenship, including the ballot. It was when he had completed these utterances that Mr. Langston, in the presence of his friends, full of excitement, moved by the sentiments of the great secretary and matchless general, rushing to him and thanking him for what he had said, declared that such words and such opinions would make him the next president of the United States, and that in the name of the negroes of the country, their friends and the loyal masses, he would then and there nominate him. His friends not only bore intelligent and emphatic testimonies in favor of General Howard and his retention as chief of the Bureau, but being moved as Mr. Langston himself was by the words of General Grant, expressed their enthusiastic approval of his suggestion to make the secretary president of the United States.

For the entire two years and a half of his service in the Bureau, Mr. Langston made repeated visits to the former slaveholding States, in labors connected with the general advancement of the freed people. . . .

On the twenty-sixth day of October, 1867, he made his first visit to Raleigh, North Carolina. He had heard much of the colored people of the Old North State, both free and slave; how that the former down to 1835, had enjoyed, measurably, the advantages of public schools and the elective franchise; and that the older persons of that class exhibited in conduct and life, mentally and morally, the good effects implied in that social condition. He had also heard that in that State special pains had been taken by slaveholders for a long time, with respect to their slaves, to put many of them to trades; and that in that Commonwealth more than any other of the South, it would be found that colored persons were in large numbers master-workmen in the different mechanical callings. In his early life, he had made the acquaintance of a young black man of North Carolina, who, having mastered in that State all that was merely mechanical in the trade of the gunsmith, so that he manipulated in the most skillful manner, every material used in his art, even from its crudest condition to its most improved and polished state, but had however, been given no real knowledge of the science of his calling. His case was, indeed, characteristic; the use of the hands simply was improved, with adequate exercise of the memory; and there the negro mechanic, as the young man claimed, was left to struggle as best he might. And yet, so much of merely mechanical instruction had its beneficial results in moral and material advantage.

Going into North Carolina with such impressions as to the more improved condition of the colored people, and to the capital of the State of which he had heard also many pleasant things, he expected to find not only a large colored population, but one of unusual improvement, advanced in material circumstances. He expected to find schools and churches among them, well-ordered, of large membership and attendance. He expected to find among them too leading men of their own color, prepared really to direct and encourage them in the cultivation of the useful things of freedom. In all these respects he found no evidences of unworthy life and thriftlessness calculated to disappoint him. Far otherwise. For the homes of the people indicated on their part the possession of industrial wisdom and prosperity. The large attendance of orderly, comparatively well-dressed children in the schools, indicated the popular estimate put upon education; and the several large churches of varying denominational character discovered the general appreciation of morality and religion prevailing among the people. The leading man at that time found among these people, residing in Raleigh, enjoying the respect and confidence of all classes, prominent in politics and influential in the work of education and general improvement, was the Hon. James H. Harris. . . . This gentleman, with others of like prominence, white and colored, including the governor of the State, composed the committee which received and entertained Mr. Langston on his first visit to Raleigh; and it was he who introduced him when he made his first speech there in the African Methodist Episcopal church on "The education and elevation of the colored people." . . .

Going subsequently into South Carolina, Mr. Langston visited Columbia, the capital, and Charleston, the principal cities of the State. In the Palmetto State he was received and treated with marked consideration and kindness. His principal meeting was held at Charleston on the Battery, in sight of Fort Sumter, upon which the first gun of the Rebellion was fired. No one shall ever describe the beauty of the city, the sea and the sky, as they appeared on the evening on which the whole city seemed to turn out to hear the colored orator from the North; and no pen can record in sufficiently just and truthful manner, the sober and considerate behavior with which the vast concourse of white and colored people of this Southern city heard him. He discoursed of those means of education, property and character, with loyal devotion to the government, which were essential to the elevation of the colored American, formerly enslaved, and the reconciliation and happiness of the white American, formerly the owner and master of the slaves. As he closed his speech in the prediction of a future to South Carolina and the nation in which all shall forget past differences of condition and nationality in the consciousness of their unity and happiness in being simply American citizens, the applause which greeted that utterance was full, cheering, enthusiastic and deafening.

He left the city of Charleston feeling that the work of education and improvement of the black and white races would go rapidly on, resulting not more in the complete renovation and exaltation of the former than the happiness and prosperity of the latter. . . .

At the meeting held at Mechanic's Institute, Capt. P. B. S. Pinchback was made president, assisted by a large number of vice-presidents. The audience was an immense one, bright and brilliant by reason of the presence of so large number of beautifully dressed ladies, and distinguished by the attendance of many persons of note and character. Perhaps no meeting held in any one of the great cities of the Union among the colored citizens, was ever honored by the presence of so many men of their own class noted for their wealth, intelligence and social position. . . .

Among the most agreeable things connected with his tours, his labors and his experiences under the Freedmen's Bureau in the South, was the cordial welcome which he received everywhere from the devoted, laborious, self-sacrificing workers, mostly white persons, who having left pleasant Northern homes and families, had gone among the emancipated classes, where they gave their services generally upon the most limited remuneration, sometimes without pay, to the education and elevation of the ex-slaves. But the consideration above all others which renders him satisfaction in largest measure in connection with his labors is found in the fact that so many of the young boys and young girls whom he found in the schools of the freed people of the Southern States, have since by diligence, perseverance, industry and good conduct, won for themselves respectability, influence, usefulness and name in the community. One of this class of representative young colored men, having reached exalted useful position and won national name for himself as an educator and orator, has recently died and been buried, amid universal regret and sorrow, in the soil of his own native State of North Carolina. Dr. John C. Price, the president of Livingstone College, so active, energetic and useful in life, shall not be forgotten nor lose his influence in death!

SOJOURNER TRUTH

From *Daughters of Africa*

§

MY FRIENDS, I AM REJOICED THAT YOU are glad, but I don't know how you will feel when I get through. I come from another field—the country of the slave. They have got their liberty—so much good luck to have slavery partly destroyed; not entirely. I want it root and branch destroyed. Then we will all be free indeed. I feel that if I have to answer for the deeds done in my body just as much as a man, I have a right to have just as much as a man. There is a great stir about colored men getting their rights, but not a word about the colored women; and if colored men get their rights, and not colored women theirs, you see the colored men will be masters over the women, and it will be just as bad as it was before. So I am for keeping the thing going while things are stirring; because if we wait till it is still, it will take a great while to get it going again. White women are a great deal smarter, and know more than colored women, while colored women do not know scarcely anything. They go out washing, which is about as high as a colored woman gets, and their men go about idle, strutting up and down; and when the women come home, they ask for their money and take it all, and then scold because there is no food. I want you to consider on that, chil'n. I call you chil'n; you are somebody's chil'n, and I am old enough to be mother of all that is here. I want women to have their rights. In the courts women have no rights, no voice; nobody speaks for them. I wish woman to have her voice there among the pettifoggers. If it is not a fit place for women, it is unfit for men to be there.

I am above eighty years old; it is about time for me to be going. I have been forty years a slave and forty years free, and would be here forty years more to have equal rights for all. I suppose I am kept here because something remains for me to do; I suppose I am yet to help to break the chain. I have done a great deal of work; as much as a man, but did not get so much pay. I used to work in the field and bind grain, keeping up with the cradler; but men doing no more, got twice as much pay. . . . We do as much, we eat as much, we want as much. I suppose I am about the only colored woman that goes about to speak for the rights of the colored women. I want to keep the thing stirring, now that the ice is cracked. What we want is a little money. You men know that you get as much again as women, when you write, or for what you do. When we get our rights, we shall not have to come to you for money, for then we shall have money enough in our own pockets; and maybe you will ask us for money. But help us now until we get it. It is a good consolation to know that when we have got this battle once fought we shall not be coming to you any more. . . .

I am glad to see that men are getting their rights, but I want women to get theirs, and while the water is stirring I will step into the pool. Now that there is a great stir about colored men's getting their rights is the time for women to step in and have theirs.

SAMUEL LARKIN

From *Free at Last*

§

[*Nashville, Tenn. February 9, 1872*]

Am a colored man. I live in Davidson County. Ten miles from Nashville on the Lebanon Turnpike—have lived there, and about two miles from there since 1864— Before the War I lived in Huntsville Ala. and came to Nashville Tenn. with Col. Chapins Regiment (Union) in 1862. and remained with the Regiment several months. I then settled in Nashville. and had with me about five hundred Dollars. that I had made by working. which money I invested in horses. I bought three horses one mule. and a blind horse. which animals I worked in teams hauling different stores &c. for merchants and others in Nashville Tenn. and did an express business. I kept my stock in a stable on Vine St. near Church. Sometime in the month of August 1863, my three horses, mule and blind horse—were working as usual. two of the horses in one wagon. two in another. and the mule in a dray. when a squad of Soldiers under charge of an Officer took them all. wagons and dray included. drove them to a Government Wagon yard on corner of Broad and Spruce Sts. Nashville Tenn. when one of my drivers came to me. (I was then working on Cedar St. Nashville) and told me the Government Troops had taken all my stock. I immediately went to the Wagon yard on corner of Broad & Spruce Sts. and found my wagons. and the Blind horse—they had taken the other three horses and the mule on toward the Camps on Franklin Turnpike. I followed on out, and met the Officer and Soldiers who had my stock with others. and I asked the Officer to return me my Stock. he asked if I could point them out. I said yes. and did so— He then said he could not return them. that he had orders to press all serviceable stock he could find. for the use of the Government, but that I would be paid in full for all my Stock. Upon finding that I could not get my Stock, I returned to the aforesaid Wagon Yard and my blind horse. with the two Wagons was returned to me. but I never got back the three horses and mule. nor did I ever get pay for the same— I saw my three horses and mule. many times afterward. being driven in Government teams. and used by the Government.

his

Samuel X Larkin

mark

JOHN R. LYNCH

From *The Autobiography of John Roy Lynch*

MISSISSIPPI, 1872

EIGHTEEN SEVENTY-TWO WAS AN IMPORTANT YEAR IN the
political history of the state and nation. It was the year of the presidential
and congressional elections. President Grant was a candidate for renomination.
A strong opposition to him, however, had developed in the ranks of the Republicans. This opposition was under the able and aggressive leadership of such
strong and influential men as Horace Greeley of New York, Charles Sumner of
Massachusetts, Carl Schurz and B. Gratz Brown of Missouri, and many others.
The rupture between the president and Senator Charles Sumner grew out of
the movement to bring about the annexation of Santo Domingo, which was
strongly supported by the president and bitterly opposed by Senator Sumner,
who was at that time chairman of the Senate Committee on Foreign Relations.
In this fight the administration had the support of a large majority of the
Republican senators, which resulted in having Senator Sumner deposed from
the chairmanship of the important Committee on Foreign Relations and the
selection of Senator Cameron of Pennsylvania to succeed him. This step increased the bitterness growing out of differences in the party upon this matter.
Public sentiment in the party throughout the country, however, was on the side
of the administration. This sentiment was so strong even in Senator Sumner's
own state of Massachusetts that it resulted in the passage of a resolution by the
state legislature censuring the senator for his attitude towards, and opposition
to, the national administration of his own party. But this resolution was re-
scinded at a subsequent session of the legislature. This, however, was not an
indication of a change of sentiment among the Republicans of that state, but it
was evidence of the very high esteem in which this great and grand man was

held by the people of his state and which was so strong that they were willing to overlook and forgive what in their opinion was nothing more than a mistaken judgment on his part.

The opposition within the party to the national administration took tangible shape which resulted in the call for an Independent-Republican convention at Cincinnati, which nominated Horace Greeley of New York for president and B. Gratz Brown of Missouri for vice-president. An understanding had evidently been reached by which the Democrats would endorse and support this ticket instead of nominating and supporting one of their own. This was the course that was adopted by the National Democratic Convention which was subsequently held at Baltimore. The Republican convention was held at Philadelphia in June and renominated President Grant without opposition, but substituted Senator Henry Wilson of Massachusetts for ex-Speaker Colfax of Indiana for vice-president. The issue was thus joined between the two parties, but it soon developed that the result would be determined more upon the personality of the opposing candidates than upon the issues of the campaign. It looked for a while as if the contest would not only be an animated and exciting one, but that the result of the election would be close and doubtful.

This was the first national election that Mississippi was to take part in since the readmission of the state into the Union. The National Republican Convention at Philadelphia that year was the first one to which I had been elected as a delegate. The delegation from my state conferred upon me the distinguished honor of making me a member of the Committee on Platform and Resolutions. The chairman of that committee made me a member of the subcommitee that prepared the platform. . . .

Part VII.

❧

DAWN OF A

NEW CENTURY

Plagued by increasing unemployment, disenfranchisement, and the scourge of terrorism led by the Ku Klux Klan, black Americans' predicament in the decades following Reconstruction only got worse. Except for general advancements in higher education, marked by the founding of such institutions as Howard, Fisk, and Atlanta Universities, blacks could point to little with lasting, unequivocal pride. But Tuskegee Institute, with Booker T. Washington at the helm, was among black America's cherished landmarks, and here the formidable founder recounts the steps taken to bring the school into existence. Students at Tuskegee were taught to be self-sufficient and exemplars of strong character. From this campus—which students built of bricks they made—came a coterie of cooks, plumbers, nurses, coopers, cobblers, millwrights, carpenters, blacksmiths, and young men and women who perfected their skills in agriculture. And Washington, who was out of bed before the break of day to feed his prized hogs, regularly visited every class, checking on the progress of the students and the faculty of Tuskegee. The institute would be the rock from which he would launch his claim for national recognition.

At the same time Washington was meeting with Andrew Carnegie and other financial investors in his educational enterprise, Lewis Latimer was honing his skills as a draftsman with Hiram Maxim of gun fame. This apprenticeship would be extremely useful in his next critical and little-known endeavor—working with Thomas Edison to perfect the electric lightbulb.

Latimer and his cohorts were actively trying to advance the condition of the human race while white Mississippians were doing all they could to bring back the days when they had exclusive power and blacks could not vote. By 1890 they had effectively achieved this end with a revision of the state constitution. Meanwhile, in South Carolina, a senator had drafted a proposal asking the federal government to provide financial aid to help blacks emigrate from the South back to Africa. Former U.S. Senator Blanche K. Bruce of Mississippi, along with most African American spokesmen, rejected this "back to Africa" plan, believing it was not in the best interest of an emerging leadership class that would be robbed of its prominent thinkers. One highly vocal exception was Bishop Henry McNeal Turner, a prominent nationalist, who endorsed the plan in a letter to Bruce. Despite his supportive argument, the bill never made it through Congress.

Anna Julia Cooper's aspirations were far from conventional. Her aim, much like her predecessor Sojourner Truth, was to ensure a place for women in all endeavors. Her excerpt is a fine, insightful appeal to women's self-respect, insisting that women be given the same chance to excel, intellectually and professionally, as men. Cooper certainly made her mark, attaining a reputation and status unparalleled for black women at the end of the nineteenth century. Not only was she one of the few

African American women to speak at the Chicago World's Fair in 1893, she was invited to participate in the virtually all–black men's first Pan-African Conference in London in 1900. In 1925, at the age of sixty-seven, Cooper was awarded her doctorate from the University of Paris.

Mary Church Terrell may not have been as outspoken on the gender question as Cooper, but as an active member of several black women's organizations her clout and prestige were strongly felt. She was also an intimate associate of numerous black notables, including Frederick Douglass and Paul Laurence Dunbar, whose accomplishments and friend-ship she fondly recalls. These famous friends were also subjects in the hundreds of essays and articles she published in magazines, journals, and newspapers. Her articles were often criticized for failing to capture the complexity of the black experience, but they were more than effective as introductions to white readers unfamiliar with black life.

The love story between the magnificently gifted literary giant Paul Laurence Dunbar and his wife-to-be, Alice, has been rarely told. Inter-spersed through all of their letters are details from their developing love affair, notes to each other about their book projects, and priceless tidbits of information about friends and African American history. Paul is by far the more famous of the two, having published his first book of poetry, *Oak and Ivy,* in 1893 to great acclaim. Several notable black literary critiques assailed Dunbar for his dialect poetry, thereby connecting him with the racist plantation literature of Joel Chandler Harris. Still, others believed he captured the speech patterns of the recently emancipated slaves and they emulated his style in their own works. No such contro-versy surrounded the poetry and fiction written by his wife, though hardly any of it achieved wide review. If she lacked her husband's fame, she was equally versatile as a teacher, journalist, speaker, and activist in the women's movement.

BOOKER T. WASHINGTON

From *Up from Slavery*

§

ALABAMA, 1870–1880

IN MAY, 1881, NEAR THE CLOSE OF my first year in teaching
. . . the night-school, in a way that I had not dared expect, the opportunity
opened for me to begin my life-work. One night in the chapel, after the usual
chapel exercises were over, General Armstrong referred to the fact that he had
received a letter from some gentlemen in Alabama asking him to recommend
some one to take charge of what was to be a normal school for the coloured
people in the little town of Tuskegee in that state. These gentlemen seemed to
take it for granted that no coloured man suitable for the position could be
secured, and they were expecting the General to recommend a white man for
the place. The next day General Armstrong sent for me to come to his office,
and, much to my surprise, asked me if I thought I could fill the position in
Alabama. I told him that I would be willing to try. Accordingly, he wrote to
the people who had applied to him for the information, that he did not know of
any white man to suggest, but if they would be willing to take a coloured man,
he had one whom he could recommend. In this letter he gave them my name.

Several days passed before anything more was heard about the matter.
Some time afterward, one Sunday evening during the chapel exercises, a messenger came in and handed the general a telegram. At the end of the exercises
he read the telegram to the school. In substance, these were its words:
"Booker T. Washington will suit us. Send him at once."

There was a great deal of joy expressed among the students and teachers,
and I received very hearty congratulations. I began to get ready at once to go to
Tuskegee. I went by way of my old home in West Virginia, where I remained
for several days, after which I proceeded to Tuskegee. I found Tuskegee to be a

town of about two thousand inhabitants, nearly one-half of whom were coloured. It was in what was known as the Black Belt of the South. In the county
in which Tuskegee is situated the coloured people outnumbered the whites by
about three to one. In some of the adjoining and near-by counties the proportion was not far from six coloured persons to one white.

I have often been asked to define the term "Black Belt." So far as I can
learn, the term was first used to designate a part of the country which was
distinguished by the colour of the soil. The part of the country possessing this
thick, dark, and naturally rich soil was, of course, the part of the South where
the slaves were most profitable, and consequently they were taken there in the
largest numbers. Later and especially since the war, the term seems to be used
wholly in a political sense—that is, to designate the counties where the black
people outnumbered the white.

Before going to Tuskegee I had expected to find there a building and all the
necessary apparatus ready for me to begin teaching. To my disappointment, I
found nothing of the kind. I did find, though, that which no costly building and
apparatus can supply,—hundreds of hungry, earnest souls who wanted to
secure knowledge.

Tuskegee seemed an ideal place for the school. It was in the midst of the
great bulk of the Negro population, and was rather secluded, being five miles
from the main line of railroad, with which it was connected by a short line.
During the days of slavery, and since, the town had been a centre for the
education of the white people. This was an added advantage, for the reason that
I found the white people possessing a degree of culture and education that is
not surpassed by many localities. While the coloured people were ignorant,
they had not, as a rule degraded and weakened their bodies by vices such as are
common to the lower class of people in the large cities. In general, I found the
relations between the two races pleasant. For example, the largest, and I think
at that time the only hardware store in the town was owned and operated
jointly by a coloured man and a white man. This copartnership continued until
the death of the white partner.

I found that about a year previous to my going to Tuskegee some of the
coloured people who had heard something of the work of education being done
at Hampton had applied to the state Legislature, through their representatives,
for a small appropriation to be used in starting a normal school in Tuskegee.
This request the Legislature had complied with to the extent of granting an
annual appropriation of two thousand dollars. I soon learned, however, that
this money could be used only for the payment of the salaries of the instruc-
tors, and that there was no provision for securing land, buildings, or apparatus.
The task before me did not seem a very encouraging one. It seemed much like
making bricks without straw. The coloured people were overjoyed, and were

constantly offering their services in any way in which they could be of assistance in getting the school started.

My first task was to find a place in which to open the school. After looking the town over with some care, the most suitable place that could be secured seemed to be a rather dilapidated shanty near the coloured Methodist church, together with the church itself as a sort of assembly-room. Both the church and the shanty were in about as bad condition as was possible. I recall that during the first months of school that I taught in this building it was in such poor repair that, whenever it rained, one of the older students would very kindly leave his lessons to hold an umbrella over me while I heard the recitations of the others. I remember, also, that on more than one occasion my landlady held an umbrella over me while I ate breakfast.

At the time I went to Alabama the coloured people were taking considerable interest in politics, and they were very anxious that I should become one of them politically, in every respect. They seemed to have a little distrust of strangers in this regard. I recall that one man, who seemed to have been designated by the others to look after my political destiny, came to me on several occasions and said, with a good deal of earnestness: "We wants you to be sure to vote jes' like we votes. We can't read de newspapers very much, but we knows how to vote, an' we wants you to vote jes' like we votes." He added: "We watches de white man, and we keeps watching de white man till we finds out which way de white man's gwine to vote; an' when we finds out which way de white man's gwine to vote, den we votes 'xactly de other way. Den we know we's right."

I am glad to add, however, that at the present time the disposition to vote against the white man merely because he is white is largely disappearing, and the race is learning to vote from principle, for what the voter considers to be for the best interests of both races.

I reached Tuskegee, as I have said, early in June, 1881. The first month I spent in finding accommodations for the school, and in travelling through Alabama, examining into the actual life of the people, especially in the country districts, and in getting the school advertised among the class of people that I wanted to have attend it. The most of my travelling was done over the country roads, with a mule and a cart or a mule and a buggy wagon for conveyance. I ate and slept with the people, in their little cabins. I saw their farms, their schools, their churches. Since, in the case of the most of these visits, there had been no notice given in advance that a stranger was expected, I had the advantage of seeing the real, everyday life of the people.

In the plantation districts I found that, as a rule the whole family slept in one room, and that in addition to the immediate family there sometimes were relatives, or others not related to the family, who slept in the same room. On more than one occasion I went outside the house to get ready for bed, or to wait until the family had gone to bed. They usually contrived some kind of place for me to sleep, either on the floor or in a special part of another's bed. Rarely was there any place provided in the cabin where one could bathe even the face and hands, but usually some provision was made for this outside the house, in the yard.

The common diet of the people was fat pork and corn bread. At times I have eaten in cabins where they had only corn bread and "black-eye peas" cooked in plain water. The people seemed to have no other idea than to live on this fat meat and corn bread,—the meat, and the meal of which the bread was made, having been bought at a high price at a store in town, notwithstanding the fact that the land all about the cabin homes could easily have been made to produce nearly every kind of garden vegetable that is raised anywhere in the country. Their one object seemed to be to plant nothing but cotton; and in many cases cotton was planted up to the very door of the cabin.

In these cabin homes I often found sewing-machines which had been bought, or were being bought, on instalments, frequently at a cost of as much as sixty dollars, or showy clocks for which the occupants of the cabins had paid twelve or fourteen dollars. I remember that on one occasion when I went into one of these cabins for dinner, when I sat down to the table for a meal with the four members of the family, I noticed that, while there were five of us at the table, there was but one fork for the five of us to use. Naturally there was an awkward pause on my part. In the opposite corner of that same cabin was an organ for which the people told me they were paying sixty dollars in monthly instalments. One fork, and a sixty-dollar organ!

In most cases the sewing-machine was not used, the clocks were so worthless that they did not keep correct time—and if they had, in nine cases out of ten there would have been no one in the family who could have told the time of day—while the organ, of course, was rarely used for want of a person who could play upon it.

In the case to which I have referred, where the family sat down to the table for the meal at which I was their guest, I could plainly see that this was an awkward and unusual proceeding, and was done in my honour. In most cases, when the family got up in the morning, for example, the wife would put a piece of meat in a frying-pan and put a lump of dough in a "skillet," as they called it. These utensils would be placed on the fire, and in ten or fifteen minutes breakfast would be ready. Frequently the husband would take his bread and meat in his hand and start for the field, eating as he walked. The mother would sit down in a corner and eat her breakfast, perhaps from a plate and perhaps directly from the "skillet" or frying-pan, while the children would eat their portion of the bread and meat while running about the yard. At certain seasons of the year, when meat was scarce, it was rarely that the children who were not old enough or strong enough to work in the fields would have the luxury of meat.

The breakfast over, and with practically no attention given to the house, the whole family would, as a general thing, proceed to the cotton-field. Every child that was large enough to carry a hoe was put to work, and the baby—for usually there was at least one baby—would be laid down at the end of the cotton row, so that its mother could give it a certain amount of attention when she had finished chopping her row. The noon meal and the supper were taken in much the same way as the breakfast.

All the days of the family would be spent after much this same routine, except Saturday and Sunday. On Saturday the whole family would spend at least half a day, and often a whole day, in town. The idea in going to town was, I suppose, to do shopping, but all the shopping that the whole family had money for could have been attended to in ten minutes by one person. Still, the whole family remained in town for most of the day, spending the greater part of the time in standing on the streets, the women, too often, sitting about somewhere smoking or dipping snuff. Sunday was usually spent in going to some big meeting. With few exceptions, I found that the crops were mortgaged in the counties where I went, and that the most of the coloured farmers were in debt. The state had not been able to build schoolhouses in the country districts, and, as a rule, the schools were taught in churches or in log cabins. More than once, while on my journeys, I found that there was no provision made in the house used for school purposes for heating the building during the winter, and consequently a fire had to be built in the yard, and teacher and pupils passed in and out of the house as they got cold or warm. With few exceptions, I found the teachers in these country schools to be miserably poor in preparation for their work, and poor in moral character. The schools were in session from three to five months. There was practically no apparatus in the schoolhouses, except that occasionally there was a rough blackboard. I recall that one day I went into a schoolhouse—or rather into an abandoned log cabin that was being used as a schoolhouse—and found five pupils who were studying a lesson from one book. Two of these, on the front seat, were using the book between them; behind these were two others peeping over the shoulders of the first two, and behind the four was a fifth little fellow who was peeping over the shoulders of all four.

What I have said concerning the character of the schoolhouses and teachers will also apply quite accurately as a description of the church buildings and the ministers.

I met some very interesting characters during my travels. As illustrating the peculiar mental processes of the country people, I remember that I asked one coloured man, who was about sixty years old, to tell me something of his history. He said that he had been born in Virginia, and sold into Alabama in

1845. I asked him how many were sold at the same time. He said, "There were five of us; myself and brother and three mules."

In giving all these descriptions of what I saw during my month of travel in the country around Tuskegee, I wish my readers to keep in mind the fact that there were many encouraging exceptions to the conditions which I have described. I have stated in such plain words what I saw, mainly for the reason that later I want to emphasize the encouraging changes that have taken place in the communities, not wholly by the work of the Tuskegee school but by that of other institutions as well.

LEWIS LATIMER

From the Schomburg Center for Research in Black Culture

❧

PHILADELPHIA, 1882

SCHOOL ST. IN BOSTON IS PRACTICALLY AN eastern continua-
tion of Beacon St., and it was in the building of the five cent savings bank,
in the middle of the south side of the block, that I was employed when in 1876
Alexander Graham Bell made his application for United States patent on his
telephone.

The father of Mr. Bell an English Subject, had invented a system of "visible
speech" by means of which deaf mutes could talk to each other, and at the
time of which I write Alexander Graham Bell was teaching this method in the
college of Liberal arts, located on Beacon Street. Here he had day and night
classes and I was obliged to stay at the office until after 9 P.M. when he was
free from his night classes, to get my instructions from him as to how I was to
make the drawings for the application for a patent upon the telephone.

In 1879 I had moved to Bridgeport Conneticutt and was at work in a
machine shop doing a short job of mechanical drawing, when a stranger came
in and expressed himself as delighted to find a draughtsman, as he had for
weeks been looking for one to make some Patent Office drawings for him; this
stranger proved to be Sir Hiram Maxim of Gun fame, altho he was up to that
time plain Hiram Maxim. He was at this time chief engineer and inventor of
the U.S. Electric Lighting Co., and he engaged me there and then to become
his draughtsman and private secretary. Within a week from the time we first
met I was installed in Mr. Maxim's office busily following my vocation of
mechanical draughtsman, and acquainting myself with every branch of electric
incandescent light construction and operation.

This was in the fall; in the early spring of the following year, the factory was moved to New York, and I went with it. I had qualified myself to take charge of producing the carbons for the lamps, when I was not drawing, and worked through the day helping to make lamps and at night locating them in stores and offices.

Electrical measurement had not then been invented and all our work was by guess. Office bell wire was the only kind on the market, and our method of figuring was that it was a good guess that that size wire would carry a certain number of lamps without dangerous heating. A number of mysterious fires about this time were probably the fruit of our ignorance.

The Equitable Building, Fisk and Hatch, the Union Club, and a number of other places were supplied with lamps and the man to run them.

These were strenuous times, and we made long hours each day.

At the factory by seven in the morning, and after the days work some where running lamps until twelve o'clock or later at night. When we had the first Ave factory in New York fairly in running order we began to extend our business and I went with Mr. Maxim to Philadelphia to assist him in putting in a plant in the Philadelphia Ledger office, after fitting up this plant I was dispatched to Montreal Canada to fit up the railroad station and yards of Hochelage with incandescent and arc lamps. As all of our assistants were french speaking natives I had to write out a list of such orders as I must use to make clear to my work men what I wanted them to do, and these orders I had to have the clerk teach me to express in French. This was my nightly lesson. My day was spent climbing telegraph poles and locating arc lamps on them with the assistance of my laborers who seemed much impressed with my effort to speak their language.

When this job was done I returned to New York to find a demand for a man to go to London, England and establish a factory there. As I was the only man there who understood every branch of the manufacture I was chosen to do the work and in the Spring of 1882 my wife and I embarked on the Anconia for London.

To a man who had chummy relations with Hiram Maxim and other great inventors the relations of English bosses and employees were to say the least peculiar. The prevailing motif seemed to be humility of the workman and the attitude that nothing that I can do can repay you for permitting me to earn an honest living.

My assistant and myself were in hot water from the first moment to the end of our engagement, and as we were incapable of assuming a humility we could not feel there was a continual effort to discount us and to that end the leading men would ask us about some process and failing to perform it would write to the U.S. saying that we did not understand our business. The people in the U.S. having tested us in many cases simply wrote to us repeating the charge and we would see the leading men and explain and demonstrate the process to them so obscure.

In nine months time we had the factory in running order with every man familiar with the particular branch of the manufacture which fell to him, and as our easy independence was setting a bad example to the other work men, we were released from our contract and permitted to return to the U.S.

Here we found the ranks closed up and every place filled.

After a few months in the Olmstead Company the Edison People sent for me and I became one of the faces at 65 Fifth Avenue. A few months later I went into the engineering department as draughtsman and after several years here became draughtsman in the legal department of the Edison Company later the General Electric Co. Here I remained for thirty years until I was retired. Thus was I one of the pioneers in the electric lighting industry from its creation intil [sic] it had become world wide in its influence.

HENRY McNEAL TURNER

From *Respect Black—The Writings and Teachings of H. M. Turner*

WASHINGTON, D.C., 1890

I AM SURE YOU ARE TOO GENEROUS TO regard a dissimilarity of views as an affront, though the writer be less distinguished than yourself. Nevertheless, you may remember telling me some years ago that Senators and bishops are equals. Therefore, presuming upon your own postulations, I venture upon the quicksands of some meager adverse criticisms of a few of your assertions as were reported by the representative of the *Evening Star.* . . .

You say, "What nonsense all this talk about sending all the blacks back to Africa is." True, you are right, if such a nefarious scheme is in contemplation, for thousands and hundreds of thousands of us are no more fit to go back to Africa than we are fit to go to Paradise. Thousands of us would be a curse to the continent, especially that portion of us who have no faith in the negro, or his possibilities or even his future probabilities, who worship white gods, who would rather be a white dog on earth than a black cherub in heaven, who are fools enough to believe the devil is black, and therefore that all who are black are consanguinely related to him; ignorant black preachers who will stand up in the pulpit and represent this and that species of crime and vice as being black as sin; and still another portion of us, who will study for years in college and even graduate, to follow the high calling of a waiter or a boot black, as though classic lore was a prerequisite to such an exalted occupation; who had rather be a white man's scullion than a black man's prince, who regard Africa as next door to hades, while it is the richest continent under heaven. And still another class of us, who, while professing to be Christians, will work as hard to dissuade young ministers from going with the Gospel to the land of our progenitors as if they were going to leap over a fatal precipice; who pretend to be serving God, and have no aim higher than to get to heaven to be white; who profess faith in a bodily resurrection from the dead, and yet expect that resurrected and glorified body to be white; that class of us who would rather go forty miles to hear a white ass bray than a hundred yards to hear a black seraph sing; that portion of our race who will sit in the presence of their beautiful daughters and babble about the solution of the negro problem being the admixture and intermixture of the races, while Senator Ingalls thunders from the Senate of the nation that there can never be any assimilation and proclaims it blood poison, a term never dreamed of by the pro-slavery advocates, but which, coming from that source, clinches every law now existing which forbids intermarriage between the two races, and will be the product of others not yet enacted. I take no issue with Mr. Ingalls, however; he simply voices the white sentiment of the nation, be they Democrats, Republicans, Prohibitionists, or any other party. The issue I am taking is against the folly of too many of our own race.

Now sir, if [these] are the kind of negroes you refer to, I say with double emphasis, it would be "nonsense" to talk of their returning to Africa. Such prattle would be but the jargon of folly. Every colored man in this country who is not proud of himself, his color, his hair, and his general make-up is a monstrosity. He is a curse to himself and will be to his children. He is no lower than a brute, and does not deserve the breath he breathes, much less the bread he eats. Any man, though he be as black as midnight, who regards himself inferior to any other man that God ever made, is simply a walking ghoul and ought to join his invisible companions at the first opportunity, unless he does it to the extent of his natural or acquired ability.

But who is "a Senator" that has been nonsensical enough to talk about all the colored people returning to Africa? I had not heard of anyone worth notice speaking about it prior to your interview. The man who is guilty of setting afloat such senseless pratings should be arrested, adjudged insane, and sent to the asylum.

Senator Butler indicates nothing of the kind in his $5,000,000 bill, which should have been five hundred million or five billion as a start, for billions will have to come sooner or later. It will take billions of dollars to solve that problem, which the Supreme Court of the United States imposed when it decitizened the negro in the latter part of 1883, for civil rights and citizenship are one and inseparable, as you told me out of your own mouth. Nor does the bill of Senator Butler say one word about going to Africa. True, other Senators, such as Morgan, Vance, Hampton, and other individuals have brought Africa before the country in their speeches, but not as a part of any definite programme. The gist of every speech that has been delivered upon the Butler bill has been upon the theory that if the negro went anywhere it must be at his own option.

Possibly no negro in the nation has spoken more vociferousaly in favor of the Butler bill than myself, but I have kept in harmony with the spirit of the bill. Let the negro go if he desires or remain here if he prefers. Let him exercise his own intellect, and these would-be censors of his manhood—hands off, unless they are asked for advice. The country is full of toadstool or fungus leaders, giving free advice to the Southern negro, who know no more about his real condition than they do about Liberia.

The colored men in Charleston, Columbia, Savannah, Chattanooga, Mobile, Natchez, Vicksburg, and Montgomery do not fully realize the condition of the Southern negro—I mean in the aggregate. How much less those at a greater distance. The Southern negro is in the country, not in the cities, and to know their wants, wishes, desires, and needs, you must go among them, mingle with them, and hear and see for yourself. And when you say they have no desire to go to Africa, I say, who know the real condition of our race as well as any man who lives, a million at least of them desire to go somewhere. They want freedom, manhood, liberty, patriotism, or the right to protect themselves. At least a million of us have found out that this nation is a failure, that it either cannot or has no disposition to protect the rights of a man who is not white. Not a court in the nation has given a decision in favor of the black man in twelve years. The Supreme Court is an organized mob against the negro, and every subordinate court in the land has caught its spirit. Buy a railroad ticket in Washington for the Rio Grande, and I will give you a hundred dollars for every meal of victuals you purchase, unless you go round the back way and enter the kitchen and eat amid filth and smoke, and then pay as much for it as the Queen of England would have to pay. Take your own State, Mississippi. A few weeks ago, I walked up to the ticket window to purchase a ticket for Atlanta, and the agent told me to go out and come around to the back window and I could buy a ticket. I remonstrated against such proscription, and he replied by saying, "We make Senator Bruce go round there and you will have to do the same, and all other niggers." This occurred in Jackson, Miss. As for the railroad cars, I will say nothing. You know too well. I happen to be used to them, however, and did not get frightened when I saw them.

Much has been said about the politics of Senator Butler, and how, for his Democratic proclivities, his bill of five millions should be odious to every black man. I grant that the presumption is that Senator Butler has no special love for the negro; I shall therefore join in with the presumption and suppose him to be a negro hater, for argument's sake, at all events. And who cares if he is? I have the same right to hate him he has to hate me; the same civil and divine right. I do not seek or want his love. I ask no white man's love the odds of a finger snap, nor black man's either, but if I am hungry or thirsty and my enemy brings me bread or water I shall satisfy my anxiety. If I knew that heaven was so full of Democrats that only one seat remained, I should seek that seat. If I knew that John Brown, Lincoln, Sumner, Stevens, Chase, Grant, and all the heroes of freedom were in perdition, it would be no temptation for me to go there.

I care not what animus prompted Senator Butler. Immortality enthroned his brow from the moment he offered that bill. He will now go down in history as the pioneer of a movement that heaven and earth will indorse in less than fifty years. Heaven indorses it now. Not a bill has been offered in Congress in fifteen years that even contemplated any relief for the negro as a race. Mobs have broken open jails by scores and by hundreds, and the lynch-law victims could be counted by thousands, and other things too numerous to mention; but beyond a little thunder during Presidential campaigns, nothing has been said or done about it. But Senator Butler comes forth with a bill, which, if it passes—and grant, O my God, that it may—will enable at least a hundred thousand self-reliant black men to go where they can work out their own destiny, and lay the foundation of a future arena for useful activity; for unless we can find a field for our educated sons and daughters, we may burn our colleges in a few years to the ground, for higher education in a short time will be a nuisance unless we can put it to work, and we cannot do it here, shut out, as we are, from every educated business employment by reason of our color. And a race who cannot hew out conditions and manufacture possibilities is a failure. If our inadequacy to such a result is too self-evident even to make the experiment, then the doom of the negro race is sealed, and slavery is his normal sphere.

But while I accept the doctrine of the unity of the human race, I believe the negro division of it is the junior race of the world, and that this boy race has a long and mighty future before it, and that an enslavement here, while actuated by the cupidity of the whites, is intended to be in the order of Providence, the culmination of glorious results. What we will be, no earthly creature can divine; but one thing is sure, we must be put in full possession of every right and privilege here, or this nation must pay us $40,000,000,000 for our 200 years' service, and let us go where we can have unconditional manhood. I have calculated how much this nation owes the negro, and it figures out just $40,000,000,000. We must have it and will have it, or full manhood here, and we are not going to receive full manhood recognition here. The whites will not concede it. Therefore, as soon as these old slave dwarfs, slave mannikins, and slave fools die out, our children and their children will play a new deal in the programme of the future. . . .

ANNA JULIA COOPER

From A Voice from the South

WASHINGTON, D.C., 1891

IT SEEMS HARDLY A GRACIOUS THING TO say, but it
. . . strikes me as true, that while our men seem thoroughly abreast of the
times on almost every other subject, when they strike the woman question they
drop back into sixteenth century logic. They leave nothing to be desired generally in regard to gallantry and chivalry, but they actually do not seem sometimes to have outgrown that old contemporary of chivalry—the idea that
women may stand on pedestals or live in doll houses, (if they happen to have
them) but they must not furrow their brows with thought or attempt to help
men tug at the great questions of the world. I fear the majority of colored men
do not yet think it worth while that women aspire to higher education. Not
many will subscribe to the "advanced" ideas of Grant Allen already quoted.
The three R's, a little music and a good deal of dancing, a first rate dress-maker
and a bottle of magnolia balm, are quite enough generally to render charming
any woman possessed of tact and the capacity for worshipping masculinity.

My readers will pardon my illustrating my point and also giving a reason
for the fear that is in me, by a little bit of personal experience. When a child I
was put into a school near home that professed to be normal and collegiate,
i. e. to prepare teachers for colored youth, furnish candidates for the ministry,
and offer collegiate training for those who should be ready for it. Well, I found
after a while that I had a good deal of time on my hands. I had devoured what
was put before me, and, like Oliver Twist, was looking around to ask for more.
I constantly felt (as I suppose many an ambitious girl has felt) a thumping from
within unanswered by any beckoning from without. Class after class was organized for these ministerial candidates (many of them men who had been

preaching before I was born). Into every one of these classes I was expected to go, with the sole intent, I thought at the time, of enabling the dear old principal, as he looked from the vacant countenances of his sleepy old class over to where I sat, to get off his solitary pun—his never-failing pleasantry, especially in hot weather—which was, as he called out "Any one!" to the effect that *"any* one" then meant *"Annie* one."

Finally a Greek class was to be formed. My inspiring preceptor informed me that Greek had never been taught in the school, but that he was going to form a class *for the candidates for the ministry,* and if I liked I might join it. I replied—humbly I hope, as became a female of the human species—that I would like very much to study Greek, and that I was thankful for the opportunity, and so it went on. A boy, however meager his equipment and shallow his pretentions, had only to declare a floating intention to study theology and he could get all the support, encouragement and stimulus he needed, be absolved from work and invested beforehand with all the dignity of his far away office. While a self-supporting girl had to struggle on by teaching in the summer and working after school hours to keep up with her board bills, and actually to fight her way against positive discouragements to the higher education; till one such girl one day flared out and told the principal "the only mission opening before a girl in his school was to marry one of those candidates." He said he didn't know but it was. And when at last that same girl announced her desire and intention to go to college it was received with about the same incredulity and dismay as if a brass button on one of those candidate's coats had propounded a new method for squaring the circle or trisecting the arc.

Now this is not fancy. It is a simple unvarnished photograph, and what I believe was not in those days exceptional in colored schools, and I ask the men and women who are teachers and co-workers for the highest interests of the race, that they give the girls a chance! We might as well expect to grow trees from leaves as hope to build up a civilization or a manhood without taking into consideration our women and the home life made by them, which must be the root and ground of the whole matter. Let us insist then on special encouragement for the education of our women and special care in their training. Let our girls feel that we expect something more of them than that they merely look pretty and appear well in society. Teach them that there is a race with special needs which they and only they can help; that the world needs and is already asking for their trained, efficient forces. Finally, if there is an ambitious girl with pluck and brain to take the higher education, encourage her to make the most of it. Let there be the same flourish of trumpets and clapping of hands as when a boy announces his determination to enter the lists; and then, as you know that she is physically the weaker of the two, don't stand from under and leave her to buffet the waves alone. Let her know that your heart is following her, that your hand, though she sees it not, is ready to support her. To be plain, I mean let money be raised and scholarships be founded in our colleges and universities for self-supporting, worthy young women, to offset and balance the aid that can always be found for boys who will take theology.

The earnest well trained Christian young woman, as a teacher, as a home-maker, as wife, mother, or silent influence even, is as potent a missionary agency among our people as is the theologian; and I claim that at the present stage of our development in the South she is even more important and necessary.

Let us then, here and now, recognize this force and resolve to make the most of it—not the boys less, but the girls more.

MARY CHURCH TERRELL

From *A Black Woman in a White World*

§

CHICAGO, 1891

THE YEAR FOLLOWING THE CRITICAL ILLNESS during which I lost my first baby and came near losing my life, my father invited me to visit the World's Fair while he and his family were there, and generously paid the expense of the trip. The Midway Plaisance with all its original denizens and dancers was something new under the sun, and many perfect ladies who went there to see them perform came away shocked. Compared with what one commonly sees on the stage today, however, and what one beheld at the second World's Fair, those exotic ladies knew nothing but the A B C of sending thrills down the spines of American sightseers by their terpsichorean stunts.

The first World's Fair was held in 1893 to celebrate the four hundredth anniversary of the discovery of America by Columbus, a year later than it should have been, when Chicago was only an overgrown village and was not the stirring, milling, mammoth metropolis of the West that it now is. . . .

But there are two impressions of the World's Fair which have left a more delightful flavor in my memory than anything else. One was the great honor paid to Frederick Douglass by people of the dominant race as well as by those in his own group. The other was meeting Paul Dunbar just as he was starting his career as a poet.

Mr. Douglass was the commissioner in charge of the exhibit from Haiti at the Fair, and he employed Paul Dunbar to assist him. Mr. Douglass was accustomed to entertain his friends there by taking them to see the exhibits which he especially liked. Following this custom, he invited me to go with him one afternoon to take in some of the sights. As we walked along, either through the grounds or in the buildings, Mr. Douglass was continually halted by admiring people who begged the privilege of shaking hands with him. A mother would stop him and say, "You are Frederick Douglass, aren't you? Please shake hands with my little son [or maybe a little daughter], because when he grows up I want him to say that he has shaken hands with the great Frederick Douglass."

"Let's get on the scenic railway," suggested Mr. Douglass, "so that we may have a chance to talk a little. Nobody can get us there." But he had reckoned without his host, for we had no sooner settled ourselves on that little railroad than a man reached over two seats to touch him on the shoulder and greet him. "Well, we'll go up on the Eiffel Tower," chuckled Mr. Douglass. "I know nobody can interrupt us when we are in one of those cages." But just as we started to ascend, a man in another cage shouted, "Hello, Mr. Douglass, the last time I saw you was in Rochester."

The great man had become deeply interested in Paul Dunbar, because his struggle for existence and recognition had been so desperate. The fact that Mr. Douglass was the first person I ever heard mention Paul Dunbar's name is a recollection that I cherish. By appointment I had gone to see him in his home in Anacostia, across the Potomac River from Washington. After we had finished the business I had gone to transact, the "Sage of Anacostia" inquired, "Have you ever heard of Paul Dunbar?" I told him I had not. Then Mr. Douglass rehearsed the facts in the young man's life.

"He is very young, but there is no doubt that he is a poet," he said. "He is working under the most discouraging circumstances in his home, Dayton, Ohio. He is an elevator boy, and on his meager wage of four dollars a week he is trying to support himself and mother. Let me read you one of his poems," said Mr. Douglass. And then he arose to get it. I can see his fine face and his majestic form now, as he left the room. He soon returned with a newspaper clipping and began to read "The Drowsy Day." When Mr. Douglass had read several stanzas, his voice faltered a bit and his eyes grew moist. "What a tragedy it is," he said, "that a young man with such talent as he undoubtedly possesses should be so terribly handicapped as he is."

Fate decreed that I should be with both these renowned men shortly before they passed away. I was with Mr. Douglass just a few hours before he died suddenly at his home. A little before noon he had attended a meeting of the National Council of Women. As soon as one of the officers spied him entering the door, she announced from the platform that Frederick Douglass was in the house. A committee was immediately appointed to escort him to the platform, and when he reached it the audience gave him the Chautauqua salute.

When the meeting adjourned and the admiring women had ceased paying homage to Mr. Douglass, which I enjoyed at a distance, I came forward and greeted him. He and I left what is now called the Columbia Theatre and walked together to the corner. There he stopped and asked me to have lunch with him. But I was not feeling very well and declined the invitation, alas! Lifting the large, light sombrero which he often wore, he bade me good-bye. About seven o'clock that evening a friend came by our house to tell us that Frederick Douglass had just died suddenly, while he was at the table describing to his wife the ovation tendered him in the forenoon by the members and officers of the National Council of Women. How deeply I regretted then that I had been unable to spend another hour in the company of that great man whom I would never see again!

When Paul Dunbar married he brought his wife and his mother to live in my father's house, which was next door to ours. Precious memories rush over me like a flood every time I pass that house. I can see Paul Dunbar beckoning me, as I walked by, when he wanted to read me a poem which he had just written or when he wished to discuss a word or a subject on which he had not fully decided. Paul often came to see me to read his poems or his prose articles before he sent them to magazines. Sometimes he would tauntingly wave back and forth a check which he had just received and say, "Wouldn't you like to see that?" Then, after he thought he had aroused my curiosity sufficiently, he would show it me and say, "Now, look quick. Don't keep it long. Give it back to me right away."

The Ohio State Federation of Colored Women's Clubs invited me to deliver an address when it met in Dayton, Ohio. Paul had been critically ill for a long time, but when he heard I was coming he wrote me a letter inviting me to stop with him. Knowing that his mother had the burden of the house resting on her shoulders in addition to the mental and physical strain of nursing her son, whose life had been despaired of even then, I declined. Almost by return mail Paul wrote again, urging me to stop with his mother and himself, saying it would do him so much good to talk over the good old times. I could not resist that and I went to his house.

When I saw him then, he was wasted and worn by disease and he was coughing his precious young life away. He was cheerful, however, when not actually racked with pain. And he was perfectly resigned to his fate.

Some beautiful young girls of the dominant race once called, while I was with Paul, to chat with him a while and pay their respects. When they had gone, in a nervous effort to relieve the tension of my own feelings, I turned to him and said, "Sometimes I am tempted to believe you are not half so ill as you pretend to be. I believe you are just playing the role of interesting invalid, so as to receive the sympathy and homage of those beautiful girls."

"Sometimes I think I'm just loafing myself," he laughingly replied. How well he remembered this was shown a short while after I returned home, not long before he passed away. He sent me a copy of his *Lyrics of Sunshine and*

Shadow, which at that time was his latest book. On the flyleaf he had written with his own hand (a feat which, during the last year of his illness, was often difficult for him to perform) the following lines:

> *"Look hyeah, Molly,*
> *Ain't it jolly*
> *Jes a loafin round?*
> *Tell the Jedge*
> *Not to hedge,*
> *For I am still in town."*

PAUL LAURENCE DUNBAR

From the Schomburg Center for Research in Black Culture

❧

WASHINGTON, D.C., 1898

Washington, D.C. 1/12 '98

My Darling:—I have just had a letter from my English publisher saying that the reviews of my book are many and *favorable*. He sends them, and if they are what he calls favorable I don't know where the *un* would come in. I went through them like wagon over a rutty road, first up and then down. Half the time I am so discouraged I feel like throwing down the pen with a good sound "damn." Everything I do falls so far below what I conceive. I am only a mediocre wretch I knew and all I asked was to be allowed to work along quietly, making a living and no noise, but here I must be pulled out into the glare of public gaze and stand where I never intended to stand on a level with criticism of men whose advantages and antecedents have been so much greater than mine. I am sick of it. I'll send you the reviews a little later.

I shall decline Mrs. Ruffin's offer with a great deal of pleasure. She shall not say I asked her for anything or received anything at her hands.

I have had your letter only a short time, but I've read it over four or five times. It is a dear little scrawl. "Sass" Miss Lyons and come to me by all means anytime evermore. I know I shall be happier and feel more settled in mind when you are here.

This morning I have had a perfect fit of almost hysterical nervousness. It seemed that I could not stay at my work. But I have stuck it out and it is now 10 minutes to twelve, maybe the walk at noon will do me good.

I have the plot in my head for a new short novel. It is a wee bit racy, but striking, I think. If I do anything with it, I shall attempt to publish it anonymously. I thought perhaps you might collaborate with me on it. But, really,

I've so many irons in the fire that the consideration of any other serious literary work ought to be put off until far into the future. Doesn't my change of tone remind you of Aldrich's "Farewell to the Muse?" I simply can't let the pen alone. What would a Medford wedding cost us and when does Lent begin? Oh those d--d Lippincotts.

Your Devoted Husband
Paul
With love and kisses

ALICE MOORE DUNBAR-NELSON

From the Schomburg Center for Research in Black Culture

BROOKLYN, NEW YORK, 1898

33 Poplar St.

Saturday night

My darling.—Sleeping as a dog and thoroughly disgusted with my own lazi-
ness, for I've simply frittered the whole day away. I have made up my mind to
write you as an inspiration for ability to correct a lot of exam papers.

It is strange, dear, how I find myself unconsciously loving you more and
more, and looking forward to the days of the far future—not the immediate—
time when we shall simply marry, but the days away ahead. I find myself
studying about mothers of famous men, about lovely homes, about wifehood
and all that it means, about the best way to keep you in your life work.

I do not agree with you in saying that your ability is mediocre and that you
are content to merely make a living. You are not mediocre, and I will not let
you be content. I shall spur you on like a whirl-wind whip until you work or
quiver with exhaustion. Your field is your own, no one can deny you that. Did I
ever tell you what Gilder of the Century said about you in a private conversation? He said "Mr. Dunbar is a *literary* man, not a *colored literary* man, but one
about whom there is no question." Well, I've often thought of that and I want
you to live up to it. To be content with a little would be mediocre and vain—
to aspire ever higher, to study as you work, to read and be restless until you
can survey the world from the top of the latter, this is what I want my Paul to
do.

Whatever ambition I may have had for myself, I have lost in you. To stand
by your side, urging, helping, strengthening, encouraging you is now my

prayer. To be an inspiration to you, a comforter and a real helpmate, this is what I want.

Some time ago I heard a sermon, a peculiar one. It was written by a young curate and poorly delivered, but there were some excellent sentiments therein, though crudely expressed. "The law of compensation is not nearly so cruel as the laws of heredity," he said. "If a man drinks and is immoral the law of compensation punishes him with disease and ill-health, but the law of heredity does more than this—it punishes him by inflicting upon the innocent one whom he brings into the world his torments and warped nature. He is forced to see reflected before him daily his past deeds even in his child's weak moral nature in its actual physical or mental deformity."

Is not that a terrible thought? "Reflect," he continued, "every time you do a wrong or abuse your own nature, you hurt not yourself alone, it is like a ripple in the water, ever widening, ever increasing, touching infinitude as it were. You hurt the whole human race, for you weaken your children, and through them humanity. You have no *right* to drag down the standard of humanity. You have a right to do as you wish to yourself if you intend to die at once and childless, but otherwise you do a wrong against nature and humanity and they will be revenged!"

Those were his thoughts—my words, of course. Paul, won't you keep all that in mind, dear? Some day when we can look with pride upon our children, who must be better, nobler, purer, farther advanced in every way than either of us, it will be pleasant to know that we thought of their future now, won't it?

I find myself unconsciously reverting to you in every moment, spare or otherwise. Not an hour passes that I do not kiss you in spirit or dream some tender little day-dream. Sometimes I only have time to touch your hands when I am spoken to, and start to find myself in the midst of a conversation. I look forward to moments when I can be alone and with you, even as poor Peter Ibbetson in his prison looked forward to nightfall when he could see and kiss his Mary in his fantastic dreams. My long suffering of those last two months, dear, was a veritable Godsend. My love came out of it like a Phoenix from the flames, strengthened, purified, beautified. Tempestuous passion, mad desire impatient for pleasures have gone and I am as a wife to you now, true-hearted, constant, a little more prudent, ambitious for you and desirious that we both get and maintain the proper position before the eyes of the world.

Oh my darling, be true to me, love me and do not disappoint me. Do not be impatient because I ask you to wait. Your longing is not keener than mine, for my lips long, and ache and quiver almost with pain for the touch and thrill of yours. But let us be brave, we have the future to think of.

Sometimes a thought comes to me like the chill of a winter night. Suppose he will tire of you and marry another instead?—Paul, Paul, you would not desert me, would you? It is weak to cry out thus isn't it? But I love you so, life of my life, soul of my soul, heart of my heart, I love you so, I cannot imagine an existence apart from you, or a life wherein you were not the chief element—I cannot even imagine Heaven without you. I wouldn't go there— better a Hell with you, than a Paradise without you.

Am I extravagant? It is all true.

There—I will stop.

Send me Azalia's letter back. How does the enclosed card strike you.

Your own Wife—

N.B. I forgot to congratulate you upon the adjudication of the differences between Dodd & Mead and Lippincott. It is very good and I am proud and happy therefor. How fortunate for us both is your great, good luck.

Can I "collaborate" with you? What can I do? Whatever little ability I may possess I will be only too proud to place at your disposal.

What do you think of a book of plantation nursery rhymes and folk tales? The idea fermented in my cranium about eighteen months—no two years ago. I wrote Harper Bros. about it and they advised me to go ahead. Well, for a year I let the matter drop, and finally last Nov. 9th I put up some tales, Rhymes and a few sheets of music I had written out and sent them. They promptly returned saying it was too incomplete and advised me to work on it again. I as promptly threw the stuff in a drawer and there it lies. It would be a good idea if it had your touch, your dialect and your name with some good illustrations. Some day suppose you try your hand at my crudity and evolve something from it.

Why publish the new novel anonymously? You can't afford to. Boil down the raciness and use your own name. Again I shall try to stop.

With heart and love attuned to yours,

I am,
Your devoted wife,
Alice

Part VIII

AND SOME OF

US ARE BOLD

If there was a corona of optimism in black America as the twentieth century dawned, a few of those hopeful rays emanated from Broadway, where such creative forces as James Weldon Johnson and his brother, J. Rosamond, Will Marion Cook, Harry T. Burleigh, and Bob Cole were infusing a taste of soul to the moribund musicals. The eminently versatile James Weldon Johnson invokes this period as he recalls the prominence of the Marshall Hotel, which was such a radiant point in the emergence of blacks on the New York stage. The Johnsons and Cole were extremely productive artistic pioneers, and their shows presented ample opportunity to display the wealth of musical, dance, and theatrical skills of the black community.

Keeping pace with the promising developments in the cultural realm was the increased activity on the political front, highlighted by the ideological tension and debate between Booker T. Washington and W. E. B. Du Bois. Du Bois offers a reasonably balanced account of their dispute. Of deeper pertinence is the widespread rise of the black intelligentsia, the so-called "Talented Tenth," and the role they would ultimately play in such organizations as the Afro-American Council, the Niagara Movement, and the NAACP. Du Bois would have a key role in most of these organizational and institutional developments, sometimes with his essays and articles but mostly with his tireless commitment to social change. Over the course of his lifetime, which stretched nearly a century, Du Bois was involved in practically every critical event and issue affecting black Americans. He was the first African American to earn a Ph.D. from Harvard University; his book *The Philadelphia Negro* is viewed by many scholars as a seminal text in sociology; and as the founder and editor of *The Crisis* magazine, a monthly published by the NAACP, he had a platform from which to comment on social, political, and cultural affairs. And he accomplished this task with unrivaled passion and brilliance.

Acclaimed for her relentless crusade against lynching, Ida B. Wells Barnett was an obvious choice to be among the founders of the NAACP, but when her name was left from a committee designated to oversee the initial proceedings, she gradually withdrew from the organization. In her narrative not only are we given privy to the early inner workings of the NAACP, we see some aspects of Ms. Barnett's combative and principled stands when faced with exclusion and an incipient form of sexism.

While black and white activists were breaking ground on the civil rights front, Matthew Henson was forging a trail across uncharted terrain in his journey with Admiral Robert Peary to the North Pole. There is still much controversy about whether Henson actually placed the U.S. flag at the North Pole, though in this account Peary is given the credit. Like York with Lewis and Clark during their explorations of the West, Henson was a loyal and resourceful companion to Peary; his skills were indispensable to the success of this historic quest. In 1945 Henson, who worked for many years as a messenger in the New York Customs House, received a medal for "outstanding service to the government of the United States in the field of science."

While the frigid climate of the North Pole is in direct contrast to the often red-hot streets of New Orleans, Henson's boldness was matched by Jelly Roll Morton's audacity. This pianist and composer claimed he invented jazz, and given the reputation he accrued among musicians and critics from Chicago to San Francisco, he might have. Morton was an extremely confident pianist who could imitate and surpass every stylist of his day. He composed a number of fascinating tunes, some of which became important for the early jazz ensembles who were among the first to record.

But the epitome of boldness was Jack Johnson. Like Morton in the concert hall, he took on all comers in the boxing ring, overcoming his opponents with an artful defense and a powerful combination of punches. In 1908, he became the first black heavyweight champion. His victory sparked a movement to bring back a former champ, a "great white hope" to put the uppity Johnson in his place. When Johnson handily defeated Jim Jeffries, race riots broke out all over the country. His classic showdown with Jess Willard, yet another "white hope" dispatched to dethrone him, is still a source of debate among those who believe he took a dive and those who insist he was out of shape and lost the match to a superior fighter. Johnson gives us his version of that controversial match and the thinking behind his strategy. Even outside the ring, where racism was more impregnable, Johnson was a battler, but with less success. He was unfazed by the social customs of the day, twice marrying white women. In 1912 he was charged with violating the Mann Act when he allegedly took a white woman across state lines for immoral purposes. A charade of circumstances followed, with Johnson fleeing the country and living abroad for seven years. The Willard fight was his ticket back to the states.

Ethel Waters was no less daring than Henson, Morton, and Johnson. No amount of Jim Crow and racial prejudice could stop her from asserting that defiant "Northern attitude." She even stood up to Bessie Smith and her coterie in the heart of Dixie, challenging the blues diva despite the threat of bodily harm. Sweet Mama String Bean, as Ms. Waters was once called, was fearless, whether the adversary was the Klan or a robust Ms. Smith. Her greatest claim was still on the horizon in Hollywood, where she would be among the highest paid black actresses in the 1940s. After a series of situation comedies on radio and television, Waters devoted the latter part of her life to Christian Crusades, often appearing with the Rev. Billy Graham.

JAMES WELDON JOHNSON

From *Along This Way*

❧

NEW YORK CITY, 1 9 0 0 – 1 9 0 5

SHORTLY AFTER THE HAPPENINGS JUST RELATED, Rosamond and I decided to get away from Jacksonville as quickly as possible and go to New York. . . .

We found that some marked changes had taken place in West 53rd Street. Two hotels that had been opened by Negro proprietors the previous fall were now running in full blast. It is true they were hotels more in name than in fact—in each case the building was an adapted private house—but they fulfilled their main purpose, providing good food, quite adequately. The Marshall, located between Sixth and Seventh Avenues, occupied a brownstone, four-story and basement house which in the years before had been a fashionable dwelling. Both hotels served very good meals. On Sunday nights there was a special dinner with music. The Sunday night dinners had become so popular that tables were booked days in advance. The music was good also. At the Marshall there was a four-piece orchestra that was excellent. . . .

These hotels brought about a sudden social change. They introduced or made possible a fashionable sort of life that hitherto had not existed. Prior to their opening there was scarcely a decent restaurant in New York in which Negroes could eat; I knew of only one place with excellent food and a social air where they were welcome. The sight offered at these hotels, of crowds of well-dressed colored men and women lounging and chatting in the parlors, loitering over their coffee and cigarettes while they talked or listened to the music, was unprecedented. The sight had an immediate effect on me and my brother; we decided to give up our lodgings with our old landlady at No. 260, and move to the Marshall. We took the large backroom on the second floor, put in a piano, and started to work. This move had consequences we did not dream of.

Bob Cole lived two doors from the Marshall, and that made it convenient for the trio to work together. We worked according to a schedule. We rose between nine and ten o'clock, breakfasted at about eleven, and began work not later than twelve. When we didn't go to the theater, our working period approximated ten hours a day. We spent the time in actual writing or in planning future work. In our room and without stopping work, we snatched a bite to eat at the fag-end of the afternoon. Always, we went downstairs for a midnight supper. And this was by no means a light supper; it was our main and most enjoyed meal. Sometimes it consisted of planked steak or broiled lobster. This supper generally cost us more than we were justified in spending; but, if we had done a good day's work, the money spent seemed a minor matter; if we hadn't made much progress, the gay air of the dining room, gayer around midnight than at any other hour, stimulated us. Looking back at those days, the elation and zest with which we usually worked seem prodigious. We laid down a strict rule against interruptions; but there were several intimates who were not included under the rule: Harry T. Burleigh who sometimes brought along the manuscript of an ''art song'' he had just finished and played it over; Will Marion Cook, despite his animosity against Bob Cole; Theodore Drury, who had begun his productions of grand opera at the Lexington Opera House; and Paul Dunbar, who, however, had lost his interest in things theatrical. Another intimate whom we were always glad to see was young Jack Nail, then the most popular young colored man in New York, an exceedingly handsome boy. He belonged because of his real appreciation of the things the members of this group were trying to do. He came in frequently of evenings. If we were busy, he took a chair and sat quietly smoking his pipe while we, after a grunt of greeting, went on working. There was in him a quality that made his presence more helpful than distracting.

Our room, particularly of nights, was the scene of many discussions; the main question talked and wrangled over being always that of the manner and means of raising the status of the Negro as a writer, composer, and performer in the New York theater and world of music. The opinions advanced and maintained, often with more force than considerateness, were as diversified as the personalities in the group. However, the only really bitter clashes were those occurring between Cole and Cook. Seldom did they meet and part without a clash. Cole was the most versatile man in the group and a true artist. In everything he did he strove for the fine artistic effect, regardless of whether it had any direct relation to the Negro or not. Nevertheless, there was an element of pro-Negro propaganda in all his efforts and it showed, I think, most plainly when he was engaged in matching the white artist on the latter's own field. Cook was the most original genius among all the Negro musicians—

probably that statement is still true. He had received excellent training in music, both in this country and in Berlin at the Hochschule; he had studied the violin under Joachim. But he had thrown all these standards over; he believed that the Negro in music and on the stage ought to be a Negro, a genuine Negro; he declared that the Negro should eschew "white" patterns, and not employ his efforts in doing what "the white artist could always do as well, generally better." Both these men tended toward eccentricity, both were hot-tempered, and the argument did not always oscillate between their divergent points of view; it did not always keep itself above personalities. Cook never hesitated to make belittling comments on Cole's limitations in musical and general education; he would even sneer at him on a fault in pronunciation. Cole was particularly sensitive on this side, and Cook's taunts both humiliated and maddened him.

Burleigh's position was unique. He had been a student at the National Conservatory while Dvorák was the director. He had studied harmony with Rubin Goldmark and counterpoint with Max Spicker. Not only had he studied with Dvorák but he had spent considerable time with him at his home. It was he who called the attention of the great Bohemian composer to the Negro spirituals. He had been the baritone soloist at St. George's Church for seven years—a position he still holds. His reputation as a composer was already well in the making, based on a number of "art songs" written in the best modern manner. Among us, however, it was as a master that he was held. On all questions in the theory and science of music he was the final authority. In this acceptance, both Cook and my brother, with their own very good musical training, always joined. Some years later Kurt Schindler said to me that on a question in the theory of music he would accept Mr. Burleigh's decision as quickly as that of any other musician in New York. Drury was the picturesque one. He was light bronze in color and quite good-looking, especially when he flashed his teeth in a smile. He cultivated a foreign air, in fact, a foreign appearance; he might easily have been taken for a member of one of the African nationalities of the Mediterranean border. He was a singer, and had forced his voice up to enable him to sing certain grand opera rôles; the result being the making of a straining tenor out of an excellent baritone. He was at the beginning of his enterprise which annually, for four or five years, gave Negro New York a one-night season of grand opera. Whatever may have been said of these productions artistically, they were, as popular social events, huge successes. They were for the first two or three seasons huge successes financially.

In all of our discussions and wrangles we were unanimous on one point; namely, that the managers, none of whom at that time could conceive of a Negro company playing anything but second and third-class theaters, had to be convinced. It is true that Cook's operetta, *Clorindy,* had been produced at the Casino Theater Roof Garden, and the following summer, his operetta, *Jes Lak*

White Folks, had been produced at the New York Theater Roof Garden, also that many top-notch Negro performers had appeared in the best vaudeville houses; but as yet, no professional Negro company had played a regular engagement on the stage proper of any first-class, legitimate "Broadway" house.

About this time Cook persuaded me to use my good offices to have Dunbar collaborate with him on another piece, a full-length opera to be called *The Cannibal King. Clorindy,* for which Dunbar was the librettist, had been a big success. For *Jes Lak White Folks* Cook was his own librettist, and the piece did not go over so well as its predecessor; so Cook wanted Dunbar's touch and, still more, his name again. But the great success of the first piece was not due alone to Dunbar, nor was the partial failure of the second piece due alone to Cook. In *Clorindy,* New York had been given its first demonstration of the possibilities of Negro syncopated music, of what could be done with it in the hands of a competent and original composer. Cook's music, especially his choruses and finales, made Broadway catch its breath. In *Jes Lak White Folks,* the book and lyrics were not so good, nor was the cast; and, naturally, the music was not such a startling novelty. I did my best to persuade Paul to do the book and lyrics for *The Cannibal King,* but he was obdurate. He told me with emphasis, "No, I won't do it. I just can't work with Cook; he irritates me beyond endurance." Finally, I undertook the work of writing the lyrics, and actually got Cook to agree to have Bob Cole do the book. We began work on neutral ground, four or five blocks over, at Harry Burleigh's apartment on Park Avenue. We celebrated the end of the first day's work with a beefsteak dinner, deliciously cooked by Harry's brother, Reginald. But despite the inaugural love feast, discord entered and prevailed, and *The Cannibal King* was never wholly completed. Enough was finished, however, to enable Cook to negotiate a sale to a producer for a flat cash price that gave us several hundred dollars apiece. This was my first work with Cook; later, through the years, we wrote a number of songs in collaboration.

The Marshall gradually became New York's center for Negro artists. For a generation that center had been in Negro Bohemia, down in the Tenderloin. There, in various clubs, Negro theatrical and musical talent foregathered. The clubs of Negro Bohemia were of diverse sorts. There were gambling clubs and poker clubs—a fine distinction between the two being involved; there were clubs frequented particularly by the followers of the ring and turf, where one got a close-up of the noted Negro prize fighters and jockeys; there were "professional" clubs, that served as meeting places and exchanges for Negro theatrical performers. Among the clubs of Negro Bohemia were some that bore a social aspect corresponding to that of the modern night club. These had their regular habitués, but they also enjoyed a large patronage of white sightseers and slummers and of white theatrical performers on the lookout for "Negro stuff," and, moreover, a considerable clientele of white women who had or sought to have colored lovers. The most popular of the "professional" clubs was Ike Hine's. It was principally a club for Negroes connected with the theater, but it drew the best elements from the various circles of Bohemia— except the gamblers. No gambling was allowed, and the conduct of the place was in every respect surprisingly orderly. This club occupied what formerly was a three-story and basement dwelling. In the basement was a chop suey restaurant. The parlor, on the main floor, was carpeted and furnished with chairs and tables. The walls of this room were entirely covered with photographs and lithographs of Negro "celebrities." The back parlor contained a few chairs and tables, a piano, and also a buffet. The floor of the room was bare and provided space for the entertainers and for dancing. On the floor above one or two of the rooms were given over to "acts" for rehearsals. The top floor was used as living quarters by the proprietor and his wife.

As the Marshall gained in popularity, the more noted theatrical stars and the better-paid vaudevillians deserted the down-town clubs and made the hotel their professional and social rendezvous. Up to 53rd Street came Bert Williams; tall and broad-shouldered; on the whole, a rather handsome figure, and entirely unrecognizable as the shambling, shuffling "darky" he impersonated on the stage; luxury-loving and indolent, but highly intelligent and with a certain reserve which at times exhibited itself as downright snobbishness; talking with a very slow drawl and getting more satisfaction, it seemed, out of being considered a great raconteur than out of being a great comedian; extremely funny in his imitations in the West Indian dialect. (He was himself a West Indian; born in Nassau.) Bert was a good story teller, but not a better one, we thought, than his very pretty wife, Lottie. All of Lottie's stories centered around one character, and that character was Bert. She recited very comically—the comicality heightened by her prettiness—her trials and tribulations with Bert on the "road," the chief of them being the many devices to which she had to resort to get him out of bed in time to catch early trains, Bert the while listening meekly and grinning good-naturedly. Up, too, came George Walker, very black, very vigorous, and very dapper, being dressed always a point or two above the height of fashion. George, the hail-fellow-well-met, the mixer, the diplomat; frequently flashing that celebrated row of gleaming teeth in making his way to his objective; but serious withal and the driving force of the famous team; working tirelessly to convince New York managers that Negro companies should be booked in first-class houses, and, finally, succeeding. And Aida Overton, George Walker's wife; not as good-looking as Lottie Williams, but more than making up for what she lacked in looks by her remarkable talent; a wonderful dancer, and the possessor of a low-pitched voice with a natural sob to it, which she knew how to use with telling effect in "putting over" a song; beyond comparison, the brightest star among women on the Negro stage of the period, and hardly a lesser attraction of the Williams and Walker company than the two comedians. And up came Ernest Hogan, not an Irishman, but a natural-black-face comedian; ranked by some critics, erroneously, I think, as a greater comedian than Bert Williams; expansive, jolly, radiating infectious good humor; provoking laughter merely by the changing expressions of his mobile face—a face that never, even on the stage, required cork or paint to produce comical effects. Behind these well-known performers came others less noted, and also a crowd of those who love to follow the clouds of glory trailed by the great. In time, the Marshall came to be one of the sights of New York. But it was more than a "sight"; its importance as the radiant point of the forces that cleared the way for the Negro on the New York stage cannot be overestimated.

W . E . B . D U B O I S

From *The Autobiography of W. E. B. Du Bois*

❧

ATLANTA, 1900–1910

I N 1905 I WAS STILL A TEACHER at Atlanta University and was in my imagination a scientist, and neither a leader nor an agitator; I had much admiration for Mr. Washington and Tuskegee, and I had in 1894 applied at both Tuskegee and Hampton for work. If Mr. Washington's telegram had reached me before the Wilberforce bid, I should have doubtless gone to Tuskegee. Certainly I knew no less about mathematics than I did about Latin and Greek.

Since the controversy between me and Washington has become historic, it deserves more careful statement than it has had hitherto, both as to the matters and the motives involved. There was first of all the ideological controversy. I believed in the higher education of a Talented Tenth who through their knowledge of modern culture could guide the American Negro into a higher civilization. I knew that without this the Negro would have to accept white leadership, and that such leadership could not always be trusted to guide this group into self-realization and to its highest cultural possibilities. Mr. Washington, on the other hand, believed that the Negro as an efficient worker could gain wealth and that eventually through his ownership of capital he would be able to achieve a recognized place in American culture and could then educate his children as he might wish and develop their possibilities. For this reason he proposed to put the emphasis at present upon training in the skilled trades and encouragement in industry and common labor.

These two theories of Negro progress were not absolutely contradictory. Neither I nor Booker Washington understood the nature of capitalistic exploitation of labor, and the necessity of a direct attack on the principle of exploitation as the beginning of labor uplift. I recognized the importance of the Negro gaining a foothold in trades and his encouragement in industry and common labor. Mr. Washington was not absolutely opposed to college training and sent his own children to college. But he did minimize its importance, and discouraged the philanthropic support of higher education. He thought employers "gave" laborers work, thus opening the door to acquiring wealth. I openly and repeatedly criticized what seemed to me the poor work and small accomplishment of the Negro industrial school, but did not attack the fundamental wrong of giving the laborer less than he earned. It was characteristic of the Washington statesmanship that whatever he or anybody believed or wanted must be subordinated to dominant public opinion and that opinion deferred to and cajoled until it allowed a deviation toward better ways. It was my theory to guide and force public opinion by leadership. While my leadership was a matter of writing and teaching, the Washington leadership became a matter of organization and money. It was what I may call the Tuskegee Machine.

The years from 1899 to 1905 marked the culmination of the career of Booker T. Washington. In 1899 Mr. Washington, Paul Laurence Dunbar, and myself spoke on the same platform at the Hollis Street Theater, Boston, before a distinguished audience. Mr. Washington was not at his best and friends immediately raised a fund which sent him to Europe for a three months' rest. He was received with extraordinary honors: he had tea with the aged Queen Victoria, but two years before her death; he was entertained by two dukes and members of the aristocracy; he met James Bryce and Henry M. Stanley; he was received at the Peace Conference at The Hague and was greeted by many distinguished Americans, like ex-President Harrison, Archbishop Ireland and two justices of the Supreme Court. Only a few years before he had received an honorary A.M. from Harvard; in 1901, he received a LL.D. from Dartmouth; and that same year he dined with President Roosevelt to the consternation of the white South.

Returning to America he became during the administrations of Theodore Roosevelt and William Taft, from 1901 to 1912, the political referee in all Federal appointments or action taken with reference to the Negro and in many regarding the white South. In 1903 Andrew Carnegie made the future of Tuskegee certain by a gift of $600,000. There was no question of Booker T. Washington's undisputed leadership of the ten million Negroes in America, a leadership recognized gladly by the whites and conceded by most of the Negroes.

But there were discrepancies and paradoxes in this leadership. It did not seem fair, for instance, that on the one hand Mr. Washington should decry political activities among Negroes, and on the other hand dictate Negro political objectives from Tuskegee. At a time when Negro civil rights called for organized and aggressive defense, he broke down that defense by advising acquiescence or at least no open agitation. During the period when laws disfranchising the Negro were being passed in all the Southern states, between 1890 and 1909, and when these were being supplemented by "jim-crow" travel laws and other enactments making color caste legal, his public speeches, while they did not entirely ignore this development, tended continually to excuse it, to emphasize the shortcomings of the Negro, and were interpreted widely as putting the chief onus for his condition upon the Negro himself.

All this naturally aroused increasing opposition among Negroes and especially among the younger class of educated Negroes, who were beginning to emerge here and there, particularly from Northern institutions. This opposition began to become vocal in 1901 when two men, Monroe Trotter, Harvard 1895, and George Forbes, Amherst 1895, began the publication of the Boston *Guardian.* The *Guardian,* a weekly periodical, was bitter, satirical, and personal; but it was well edited, it was earnest, and it published facts. It attracted wide attention among colored people; it circulated among them all over the country; it was quoted and discussed. I did not wholly agree with the *Guardian,* and indeed only a few Negroes did, but nearly all read it or were influenced by it.

This beginning of organized opposition, together with other events, led to the growth at Tuskegee of what I have called the Tuskegee Machine. It arose first quite naturally. Not only did presidents of the United States consult Booker T. Washington, but governors and congressmen; philanthropists conferred with him, scholars wrote to him. Tuskegee became a vast information bureau and center of advice. It was not merely passive in these matters but, guided by Emmett Scott, a young secretary who was intelligent, suave and farseeing, active efforts were made to concentrate influence at Tuskegee. After a time almost no Negro institution could collect funds without the recommendation or acquiescence of Mr. Washington. Few political appointments of Negroes were made anywhere in the United States without his consent. Even the careers of rising young colored men were very often determined by his advice and certainly his opposition was fatal. How much Mr. Washington knew of this work of the Tuskegee Machine and was directly responsible, one cannot say, but of its general activity and scope he must have been aware.

Moreover, it must not be forgotten that this Tuskegee Machine was not solely the idea and activity of black folk at Tuskegee. It was largely encouraged and given financial aid through certain white groups and individuals in the North. This Northern group had clear objectives. They were capitalists and employers of labor and yet in most cases sons, relatives, or friends of the Abolitionists who had sent teachers into the new Negro South after the war. These younger men believed that the Negro problem could not remain a matter of philanthropy. It must be a matter of business. These Negroes were not to be encouraged as voters in the new democracy, nor were they to be left at the mercy of the reactionary South. They were good laborers and they could be made of tremendous profit to the North. They could become a strong labor force and properly guided they would restrain the unbridled demands of white labor, born of the Northern labor unions and now spreading to the South and encouraged by European socialism.

One danger must be avoided and that was to allow the silly idealism of Negroes, half-trained in missionary "colleges," to mislead the mass of laborers and keep them stirred-up by ambitions incapable of realization. To this school of thought, the philosophy of Booker T. Washington came as a godsend and it proposed by building up his prestige and power, to control the Negro group. The control was to be drastic. The Negro intelligentsia was to be suppressed and hammered into conformity. The process involved some cruelty and disappointment, but that was inevitable. This was the real force back of the Tuskegee Machine. It had money and it had opportunity, and it found in Tuskegee tools to do its bidding.

There were some rather pitiful results in thwarted ambition and curtailed opportunity. I remember one case which always stands in my memory as typical. There was a young colored man, one of the most beautiful human beings I have ever seen, with smooth brown skin, velvet eyes of intelligence, and raven hair. He was educated and well-to-do. He proposed to use his father's Alabama farm and fortune to build a Negro town as an independent economic unit in the South. He furnished a part of the capital but soon needed more and he came North to get it. He struggled for more than a decade; philanthropists and capitalists were fascinated by his personality and story; and when, according to current custom, they appealed to Tuskegee for confirmation, there was silence. Mr. Washington would not say a word in favor of the project. He simply kept still. Will Benson struggled on with ups and downs, but always balked by a whispering galley of suspicion, because his plan was never endorsed by Tuskegee. In the midst of what seemed to us who looked on the beginnings of certain success, Benson died of overwork, worry, and a broken heart.

From facts like this, one may gauge the bitterness of the fight of young Negroes against Mr. Washington and Tuskegee. The controversy as it developed was not entirely against Mr. Washington's ideas, but became the insistence upon the right of other Negroes to have and express their ideas. Things came to such a pass that when any Negro complained or advocated a course of action, he was silenced with the remark that Mr. Washington did not agree with this. Naturally the bumptious, irritated, young black intelligentsia of the day declared: "I don't care a damn what Booker Washington thinks. This is what I think, and *I have a right to think.*"

It was this point, and not merely disagreement with Mr. Washington's plans, that brought eventually violent outbreak. It was more than opposition to a program of education. It was opposition to a system and that system was part of the economic development of the United States at that time. The fight cut deep: it went into social relations; it divided friends; it made bitter enemies. I can remember that years later, when I went to live in New York and was once invited to a social gathering among Brooklyn colored people, one of the most prominent Negroes of the city refused to be present because of my attitude toward Mr. Washington.

When the *Guardian* began to increase in influence, determined effort was made to build up a Negro press for Tuskegee. Already Tuskegee filled the horizon so far as national magazines and the great newspapers were concerned. In 1901 the *Outlook,* then the leading weekly, chose two distinguished Americans for autobiographies. Mr. Washington's *Up From Slavery* was so popular that it was soon published and circulated all over the earth. Thereafter, every magazine editor sought articles with Washington's signature and publishing houses continued to ask for books. A number of talented "ghost writers," black and white, took service under Tuskegee, and books and articles poured out of the institution. An annual letter "To My People" went out from Tuskegee to the press. Tuskegee became the capital of the Negro nation. Negro newspapers were influenced and finally the oldest and largest was bought by white friends of Tuskegee. Most of the other papers found it to their advantage certainly not to oppose Mr. Washington, even if they did not wholly agree with him.

I was greatly disturbed at this time, not because I was in absolute opposition to the things that Mr. Washington was advocating, but because I was strongly in favor of more open agitation against wrongs and above all I resented the practical buying up of the Negro press and choking off even mild and reasonable opposition to Mr. Washington in both the Negro press and the white.

Then, too, during these years there came a series of influences that were brought to bear upon me personally, which increased my discomfort and resentment. I had tried to keep in touch with Hampton and Tuskegee, for I regarded them as great institutions. I attended the conferences which for a long time were held at Hampton, and at one of them I was approached by a committee. It consisted of Walter Hines Page, editor of the *Atlantic Monthly;* William McVickar, Episcopal bishop of Rhode Island; and Dr. H. B. Frissell, principal of Hampton and brother of a leading New York banker. They asked me about the possibilities of my editing a periodical to be published at Hampton. I told them of my dreams and plans, and afterwards wrote them in detail. But one query came by mail: that was concerning the editorial direction. I replied firmly that editorial decisions were to be in my hands, if I edited the magazine. This was undiplomatic and too dogmatic; and yet, it brought to head the one real matter in controversy: would such a magazine be dominated by and subservient to the Tuskegee philosophy, or would it have freedom of thought and discussion? Perhaps if I had been more experienced, the question could have been discussed and some reasonable outcome obtained; but I doubt it. I think any such magazine launched at the time would have been seriously curtailed in its freedom of speech. At any rate, the project was dropped.

Beginning in 1902 pressure was put upon me to give up my work at Atlanta University and go to Tuskegee. There again I was not at first adverse in principle to Tuskegee, except that I wanted to continue the studies which I had begun and if my work was worth support, it was worth support at Atlanta University. I was unable to obtain assurance that my studies would be continued at Tuskegee, and that I would not sink to the level of a "ghost writer." I remember a letter came from Wallace Buttrick late in 1902, asking that I attend a private conference in New York with Felix Adler, William H. Baldwin, Jr., George Foster Peabody, and Robert Ogden. The object of the conference was ostensibly the condition of the Negro in New York City. I went to the conference and did not like it. Most of the more distinguished persons named were not present. The conference itself amounted to little, but after adjournment I was whisked over to William H. Baldwin's beautiful Long Island home and there what seemed to me to be the real object of my coming was disclosed. Mr. Baldwin was at that time president of the Long Island Railroad and slated to be president of the Southern. He was a rising industrial leader of America; also he was a prime mover on the Tuskegee board of trustees. Both he and his wife insisted that my place was at Tuskegee; that Tuskegee was not yet a good school, and needed the kind of development that I had been trained to promote.

This was followed by two interviews with Mr. Washington himself. I was elated at the opportunity and we met twice in New York City. The results to me were disappointing. Booker T. Washington was not an easy person to know. He was wary and silent. He never expressed himself frankly or clearly until he knew exactly to whom he was talking and just what their wishes and desires were. He did not know me, and I think he was suspicious. On the other hand, I was quick, fast-speaking and voluble. I had nothing to conceal. I found at the end of the first interview that I had done practically all the talking and that no clear and definite offer or explanation of my proposed work at Tuskegee had been made. In fact, Mr. Washington had said about as near nothing as was possible.

The next interview did not go so well because I myself said little. Finally, we resorted to correspondence. Even then I could get no clear understanding of just what I was going to do at Tuskegee if I went. I was given to understand that the salary and accommodations would be satisfactory. In fact, I was invited to name my price. Later in the year I went to Bar Harbor for a series of speeches in behalf of Atlanta University, and while there met Jacob Schiff, the [William J.] Schieffelins and Merriam of Webster's dictionary. I had dinner with the Schieffelins and their mother-in-law, whose father [Melville W.

Fuller] was once Chief Justice of the United States. Again I was urged to go to Tuskegee.

Early in the next year I received an invitation to join Mr. Washington and certain prominent white and colored friends in a conference to be held in New York. The conference was designed to talk over a common program for the American Negro and evidently it was hoped that the growing division of opinion and opposition to Mr. Washington within the ranks of Negroes would thus be overcome. I was enthusiastic over the idea. It seemed to me just what was needed to clear the air.

There was difficulty, however, in deciding what persons ought to be invited to the conference; how far it should include Mr. Washington's extreme opponents, or how far it should be composed principally of his friends. There ensued a long delay and during this time it seemed to me that I ought to make my own position clearer than I had hitherto. I was increasingly uncomfortable under the statements of Mr. Washington's position: his depreciation of the value of the vote; his evident dislike of Negro colleges; and his general attitude which seemed to place the onus of blame for the status of Negroes upon the Negroes themselves rather than upon the whites. And above all I resented the Tuskegee Machine. . . .

IDA B. WELLS BARNETT

From *Crusade for Justice*

§

THE YEAR BEFORE THIS OCCURRENCE, 1909, WAS the one hundredth anniversary of the birth of Abraham Lincoln. Just before his birthday, a round robin had been sent through the country for signatures and was then given to the press. It called attention to the fact that while the country was preparing to celebrate Lincoln's one hundredth anniversary, the Negro race, whose history was inseparably linked with that of Lincoln, was still far from emancipation. It spoke of lynchings, peonage, convict lease systems, disfranchisement, and the jim crow cars of the South.

It suggested that the finest celebration of Lincoln's one hundredth anniversary would be one which put forth some concrete effort to abolish these conditions. That appeal was signed by Jane Addams and myself, representing Chicago, and by many representative thinkers in other parts of the country.

The immediate celebration of this centenary which took place in Chicago was held in Orchestra Hall on the night of 12 February, at which time an address was delivered by Dr. Du Bois, and a chorus of one hundred voices sang Negro spirituals. It was the first presentation of Negro music in the Loop and was led by Mr. James A. Munday of the Negro Fellowship League. That presentation made such a profound impression that Mr. Munday was encouraged and almost every year since there has been such a chorus presentation in the Loop.

Miss Jane Addams headed a committee of citizens who arranged this celebration and raised the money with which to pay the necessary expenses. There were only two colored members of this committee, one of which was myself, and I was very proud of the fact that the Negro chorus of one hundred voices singing the spirituals was my idea and was carried so splendidly by the members of our league.

Not long after that came a summons from New York, asking a conference of those who had signed the round robin which had been sent out in January. Following this a group of representative Negroes met in New York City in a three-day conference, deliberating on the form which our activities ought to take. It was called the National Negro Committee, although many white persons were present. There was an uneasy feeling that Mr. Booker T. Washington and his theories, which seemed for the moment to dominate the country, would prevail in the discussion as to what ought to be done.

Dr. Du Bois had written his *The Souls of Black Folk* the year following the fiasco of the Afro-American Council in Saint Paul.* Although the country at large seemed to be accepting and adopting Mr. Washington's theories of industrial education, a large number agreed with Dr. Du Bois that it was impossible to limit the aspirations and endeavors of an entire race within the confines of the industrial education program.

Mr. Washington had a short time before held a conference of representative Negro men from all sections of the country, whose expenses had all been paid by some unknown person, and the feeling prevailed at our conference that an effort would be made to tie us to the chariot wheels of the industrial education program. Mr. Oswald Garrison Villard, the grandson of William Lloyd Garrison, was very active in promoting our meeting. He had been an outspoken admirer of Mr. Washington, and the feeling seemed general that an endorsement of his industrial education would be the result.

Mr. Washington himself did not appear. But this feeling, like Banquo's ghost, would not down. I was among those who tried to allay this feeling by asserting that most of those present were believers in Dr. Du Bois's ideas. It was finally decided that a committee of forty should be appointed to spend a year in devising ways and means for the establishment of an organization, and that we should come together the following year to hear its report. It was to be known as the National Negro Committee.

The subcommittee which had been appointed to recommend the names of persons to be on that committee included Dr. Du Bois, who was the only Negro on it. It was also decided that the reading of that list should be the last thing done at the last session of our conference. Excitement bubbled over and warm speeches were made by William Monroe Trotter, editor of the *Guardian*, Boston, Massachusetts, Rev. R. C. Ransom, pastor of Bethel A.M.E. Church,

---

* Mrs. Barnett regarded the Saint Paul meeting as a fiasco because it was dominated by Booker T. Washington, who succeeded in having the council elect a slate of officers friendly to him. Emma Lou Thornbrough, "The National Afro-American League, 1887–1908," *Journal of Southern History* 27 (Feb. 1961):504.

New York City, Dr. J. W. Waldrom, pastor of the big Baptist church in Washington, D.C., and Dr. J. W. Mossell of Philadelphia and his good wife, Mrs. Gertrude Mossell.

Last but not least came T. Thomas Fortune and many others. They were all my personal friends, and I went from one to the other trying to allay the excitement, assuring them that their fears were groundless; that I had seen the list of names; that I had been elected as one, and that Mr. Washington's name was not only not on the list, but that mine was, along with others who were known to be opposed to the inclusiveness of Mr. Washington's industrial ideas.

When at last the moment arrived at which the committee was to make its report, Dr. Du Bois had been selected to read it. This was a compliment paid him by the white men who had been associated with him in the work, and I thought it gave notice of their approval of his plan and their disposition to stand by the program of those who believed that the Negro should be untrammeled in his efforts to secure higher education. Dr. Du Bois read the forty names chosen, and immediately after a motion to adopt was carried and the meeting adjourned.

Then bedlam broke loose; for although I had assured my friends that my name had been among those chosen, when Dr. Du Bois finished his list my name had not been called. I confess I was surprised, but I put the best face possible on the matter and turned to leave.

Mr. John Milholland, a warm friend of the Negro, was the man who had led the fight against President Roosevelt for his discharge of the Negro soldiers who wouldn't tell on their comrades when Brownsville, Texas, was shot up. President Roosevelt called it "a conspiracy of silence" and had all that company dishonorably discharged. Senator Foraker of Ohio, who fought that action in Congress and was afterward politically destroyed because he dared to oppose President Roosevelt's action, was ably supported by John Milholland, of the organization which he founded for that purpose. Mr. Milholland met me in the aisle as I was leaving the building and said, "Mrs. Barnett, I want to tell you that when that list of names left our hands and was given to Dr. Du Bois to read, your name led all the rest. It is unthinkable that you, who have fought the battle against lynching for nearly twenty years single-handed and alone when the rest of us were following our own selfish pursuits, should be left off such a committee."

I merely replied that it was very evident that someone did not want my presence on it, and that so far as I was concerned I would carry on just as I had done; that I was very glad that there was going to be a committee which would try to do something in a united and systematic way, because the work was far too large for any one person. As I reached the sidewalk on my way home, Miss

May Nerney, the secretary, came running out and said, "Mrs. Barnett, they want you to come back."

The friend who was escorting me objected to my doing so, but finally consented to go back himself and see what was wanted. As I stood on the sidewalk waiting for his return, Miss Mary Ovington, who had taken active part in the deliberations, swept by me with an air of triumph and a very pleased look on her face. Mr. Harvey Thompson came back for me, and I returned to the building, where a great number of the friends were still discussing the personnel of that committee.

There were Mr. Milholland, Mr. William English Walling, Mr. Charles Edward Russell, and the other members of the committee who selected the names, all standing and awaiting my return. Dr. Du Bois was with them. He walked up to me and said, "Mrs. Barnett, I knew that you and Mr. Barnett were with Mrs. Wooley in the Douglass Center and that you would be represented through her. And I took the liberty of substituting the name of Dr. Charles E. Bentley for yours, Dr. Bentley to represent the Niagara Movement." "But," I said, "Dr. Bentley did not think enough of your movement to be present." "Well," he said, "nobody excepting those who were present in this room tonight knows that any change was made, and if you will consent I will go at once to the Associated Press office and have your name reinstated." I refused to permit him to do so. I told him that as he had done this purposely I was opposed to making any change.

Of course, I did a foolish thing. My anger at having been treated in such fashion outweighed my judgment and I again left the building. Those white men had done all they could to rectify the deliberate intention of Dr. Du Bois to ignore me and my work. I was too furiously indignant at him to recognize my obligation to try to hold up their hands. Mr. Milholland did not stop there. He went to the office of Mr. Villard next day and told him that a great mistake had been made and that it would not do to let the public know that I had been left off this committee. Mr. Villard told him that the conference had adopted the forty names presented; it had now adjourned and he had no power to add to the number.

Mr. Milholland called me up and said that he had offered to resign himself in order that my name should appear; that he had told Mr. Villard it would be a calamity to the work if I were not named and asked my consent to his doing this. I refused to permit him to do so, this time not out of a spirit of resentment, but because I knew that the new movement would need men of Mr. Milholland's type to initiate the work that we had planned to do. And so I definitely refused to accept his offer.

I learned afterward that Mrs. Celia Parker Wooley, who was present and had been named on the committee, had also gone to Mr. Villard and told him that a mistake had been made. She said that she had made the same mistake herself and she did not want him to do the same. I came away from New York steadfast in my refusal to permit any change, but somehow before the committee sent out its letterhead they added my name to the list.*

The following fall the incident concerning the sheriff occurred. Mr. Milholland said that the committee regarded that as the most outstanding thing that had been done for the race during the year. I wrote back promptly to say that I was sorry that I would be financially unable to make the trip. Back came his reply assuring me that the committee was prepared to pay all expenses in connection with my coming, thus leaving me no choice but to accept.

I went back to that next meeting, had one of the leading places on their program at Cooper Union, was domiciled at the Henry Street Settlement House and was shown every courtesy and attention possible. It was at this time that the name National Association for the Advancement of Colored People was chosen. Dr. Du Bois was taken from Atlanta University and put in charge of publicity and research.

At the meeting of the executive committee the discussion came up as to whether we should try to have articles representing our cause appear in periodicals already established, since to attempt a publication would be expensive, to say the least. Miss Addams was very much in favor of the opinion that the former was the better plan. When asked for my views I said that by all means I favored establishing our own organ, for then we could publish whatever we chose whenever we wished; whereas if we sent articles to other magazines we would have to depend upon their good will to say nothing of the disposition to change our views to suit their own ideas. This view prevailed, and the *Crisis* was born almost immediately.

Thus was launched the movement which now has the national reputation as the NAACP. This movement, which has lasted longer than almost any other movement of its kind in our country, has fallen far short of the expectations of its founders. The reason is not far to seek. It has kept Miss Mary White Ovington as chairman of the executive committee. Miss Ovington's heart is in this work, but her experience has been confined solely to New York City and Brooklyn, and a few minor incidents along the color line.

It is impossible for her to visualize the situation in its entirety and to have the executive ability to seize any of the given situations which have occurred in a truly big way. She has basked in the sunlight of the adoration of the few college-bred Negroes who have surrounded her, but has made little effort to know the soul of the black woman; and to that extent she has fallen far short of

* For a detailed account of the founding of the NAACP, see Charles Flint Kellogg, *NAACP: A History of the National Association for the Advancement of Colored People, Volume 1 (1909–1920)* (Baltimore: Johns Hopkins Press, 1967).

helping a race which has suffered as no white woman has ever been called upon to suffer or to understand.

I cannot resist the conclusion that, had I not been so hurt over the treatment I had received at the hands of the men of my own race and thus blinded to the realization that I should have taken the place which the white men of the committee felt I should have, the NAACP would now be a live, active force in the lives of our people all over this country.

MATTHEW HENSON

From *A Black Explorer at the North Pole*

§

NORTH POLE, 1909

IT WAS DURING THE MARCH OF THE 3d of April that I
. . . I endured an instant of hideous horror. We were crossing a lane of
moving ice. Commander Peary was in the lead setting the pace, and a half hour
later the four boys and myself followed in single file. They had all gone before,
and I was standing and pushing at the upstanders of my sledge, when the block
of ice I was using as a support slipped from underneath my feet, and before I
knew it the sledge was out of my grasp, and I was floundering in the water of
the lead. I did the best I could. I tore my hood from off my head and struggled
frantically. My hands were gloved and I could not take hold of the ice, but
before I could give the "Grand Hailing Sigh of Distress," faithful old Ootah
had grabbed me by the nape of the neck, the same as he would have grabbed a
dog, and with one hand he pulled me out of the water, and with the other
hurried the team across.

He had saved my life, but I did not tell him so, for such occurrences are
taken as part of the day's work, and the sledge he safeguarded was of much
more importance, for it held, as part of its load, the Commander's sextant, the
mercury, and the coils of piano-wire that were the essential portion of the
scientific part of the expedition. My kamiks (boots of sealskin) were stripped
off, and the congealed water was beaten out of my bearskin trousers, and with
a dry pair of kamiks, we hurried on to overtake the column. When we caught
up, we found the boys gathered around the Commander, doing their best to
relieve him of his discomfort, for he had fallen into the water also, and while
he was not complaining, I was sure that his bath had not been any more
voluntary than mine had been.

When we halted on April 6, 1909, and started to build the igloos, the dogs and sledges having been secured, I noticed Commander Peary at work unloading his sledge and unpacking several bundles of equipment. He pulled out from under his *kooletah* (thick, fur outer-garment) a small folded package and unfolded it. I recognized his old silk flag, and realized that this was to be a camp of importance. Our different camps had been known as Camp Number One, Number Two, etc., but after the turning back of Captain Bartlett, the camps had been given names such as Camp Nansen, Camp Cagni, etc., and I asked what the name of this camp was to be—"Camp Peary"? "This, my boy, is to be Camp Morris K. Jesup, the last and most northerly camp on the earth." He fastened the flag to a staff and planted it firmly on the top of his igloo. For a few minutes it hung limp and lifeless in the dead calm of the haze, and then a slight breeze, increasing in strength, caused the folds to straighten out, and soon it was rippling out in sparkling color. The stars and stripes were "nailed to the Pole."

A thrill of patriotism ran through me and I raised my voice to cheer the starry emblem of my native land. The Esquimos gathered around and, taking the time from Commander Peary, three hearty cheers rang out on the still, frosty air, our dumb dogs looking on in puzzled surprise. As prospects for getting a sight of the sun were not good, we turned in and slept, leaving the flag proudly floating above us.

This was a thin silk flag that Commander Peary had carried on all of his Arctic journeys, and he had always flown it at his last camps. It was as glorious and as inspiring a banner as any battle-scarred, blood-stained standard of the world—and this badge of honor and courage was also blood-stained and battle-scarred, for at several places there were blank squares marking the spots where pieces had been cut out at each of the "Farthests" of its brave bearer, and left with the records in the cairns, as mute but eloquent witnesses of his achievements. At the North Pole a diagonal strip running from the upper left to the lower right corner was cut and this precious strip, together with a brief record, was placed in an empty tin, sealed up and buried in the ice, as a record for all time.

Commander Peary also had another American flag, sewn on a white ground, and it was the emblem of the "Daughters of the Revolution Peace Society"; he also had and flew the emblem of the Navy League, and the emblems of a couple of college fraternities of which he was a member.

It was about ten or ten-thirty A.M., on the 7th of April, 1909, that the Commander gave the order to build a snow-shield to protect him from the flying drift of the surface-snow. I knew that he was about to take an observation, and while we worked I was nervously apprehensive, for I felt that the end of our journey had come. When we handed him the pan of mercury the hour was within a very few minutes of noon. Laying flat on his stomach, he took the elevation and made the notes on a piece of tissue-paper at his head. With sun-blinded eyes, he snapped shut the *vernier* (a graduated scale that subdivides the smallest divisions on the sector of the circular scale of the sextant) and with the resolute squaring of his jaws, I was sure that he was satisfied, and I was confident that the journey had ended. Feeling that the time had come, I ungloved my right hand and went forward to congratulate him on the success of our eighteen years of effort, but a gust of wind blew something into his eye, or else the burning pain caused by his prolonged look at the reflection of the limb of the sun forced him to turn aside; and with both hands covering his eyes, he gave us orders to not let him sleep for more than four hours, for six hours later he purposed to take another sight about four miles beyond, and that he wanted at least two hours to make the trip and get everything in readiness.

I unloaded a sledge, and reloaded it with a couple of skins, the instruments, and a cooker with enough alcohol and food for one meal for three, and then I turned in to the igloo where my boys were already sound asleep. The thermometer registered 29° below zero. I fell into a dreamless sleep and slept for about a minute, so I thought, when I was awakened by the clatter and noise made by the return of Peary and his boys.

The Commander gave the word, "We will plant the stars and stripes—*at the North Pole!*" and it was done; on the peak of a huge paleocrystic floeberg the glorious banner was unfurled to the breeze, and as it snapped and crackled with the wind, I felt a savage joy and exultation. Another world's accomplishment was done and finished, and as in the past, from the beginning of history, wherever the world's work was done by a white man, he had been accompanied by a colored man. From the building of the pyramids and the journey to the Cross, to the discovery of the new world and the discovery of the North Pole, the Negro had been the faithful and constant companion of the Caucasian, and I felt all that it was possible for me to feel, that it was I, a lowly member of my race, who had been chosen by fate to represent it, at this, almost the last of the world's great *work.* . . .

FERDINAND
''JELLY ROLL'' MORTON

From *Mister Jelly Roll*

❧

ST. LOUIS, 1912

IT WAS ALONG ABOUT THAT TIME THAT the first hot ar-
. . . rangements came into existence. Up until then, everything had been
in the heads of the men who played jazz out of New Orleans. Nowadays they
talk about these jam sessions. Well, that is something I never permitted. Most
guys, they improvise and they'll go wrong. Most of the so-called jazz musicians
still don't know how to play jazz until this day; they don't understand the
principles of jazz music. In all my recording sessions and in all my band work, I
always wrote out the arrangements in advance. When it was a New Orleans
man, that wasn't so much trouble, because those boys knew a lot of my breaks;
but in traveling from place to place I found other musicians had to be taught.
So around 1912 I began to write down this peculiar form of mathematics and
harmonics that was strange to all the world.

For a time I had been working with McCabe's Minstrel Show and, when
that folded in St. Louis, I began looking around for a job. My goodness, the
snow was piled up till you couldn't see the streetcars. I was afraid that I'd meet
some piano player that could top me a whole lot, so I wouldn't admit that I
could play. I claimed that I was a singer. At that time I kinda figured I was a
pretty good singer, which was way out of the way, but I figured it anyhow.
Well, I was hired at the Democratic Club where they had a piano player named
George Reynolds. He was a bricklayer trying to play piano. He couldn't even
read music. In fact, none of the boys couldn't read much and so it was very
tough for them to get those tough tunes. They bought sheet music just to learn
the words of the songs.

This George Reynolds, that couldn't read, played for me while I sang. Of course, George was a little bit chesty, because all the girls around were making eyes at him (he was a fairly nice-looking fellow); but I thought, if this guy's the best, the other piano players must be very, very terrible. So I asked George to play me one of the numbers I was going to sing. He played it, although he didn't seem very particular about doing it. I told him, "One of these parts here you don't play right. I'd like a little more pep in it." I forget what tune it was, some popular number of that time.

"Well," he said, not knowing I could play, "if you don't like the way I'm playing, you do better."

"Okay," I said, "if you don't play my tunes right, I can play them myself." So I sat down and showed him his mistakes.

Immediately he had a great big broad smile on his face. Seeing that I was superior to him, he wanted to make friends with me. I didn't object and we gotten to be friends right away. He asked me did I read music. I told him a little bit. So he put different difficult numbers on the piano—he thought they were difficult, but they were all simple to me. I knew them all. By that time he started getting in touch with the different musicians around town that was supposed to be good and they started bringing me different tunes. They brought me all Scott Joplin's tunes—he was the great St. Louis ragtime composer—and I knew them all by heart and played them right off. They brought me James Scott's tunes and Louis Chauvin's and I knew them all. Then Audie Mathews (the best reader in the whole bunch) brought me his *Pastimes* and I played it. So he decided to find out whether I could really read and play piano and he brought me different light operas like *Humoresque,* the *Overture* from *Martha,* the *Miserery* from *Ill Travadore* and, of course, I knowed them all.

Finally they brought me *The Poet and the Peasant.* It seems like in St. Louis, if you was able to play this piece correctly, you was really considered the tops. The man that brought it was the best musician in town and he hadn't been able to master this piece. Well, I had played this thing in recitals for years, but I started looking at it like I hadn't ever seen it before. Then I started in. I got to a very fast passage where I also had to turn the page over. I couldn't turn the page, due to the fact I had to manipulate this passage so fast. I went right on. Audie Mathews grabbed the tune from in front of me and said, "Hell, don't be messing with this guy. This guy is a shark!" I told them, "Boys, I been kidding you all along. I knew all these tunes anyhow. Just listen." Then I swung the *Miserery* and combined it with the *Anvil Chorus.*

You find, though, that people act very savage in this world. From then on it was George Reynolds' object to try to crush me. He couldn't do this, but he made things so unpleasant that I finally took a job out in the German section of town. The manager wanted a band, so I got some men together, although there wasn't many to pick from—clarinet, trumpet, mandolin, drums, and myself. These were not hot men, but they were Negroes and they could read. They didn't play to suit me, but I told them if they played what I put down on paper, they would be playing exactly as I wanted. Then I arranged all the popular tunes of that time—I even made a jazz arrangement of *Schnitzelbank*—and we made some pretty fair jazz for St. Louis in 1912.

St. Louis had been a great town for ragtime for years because Stark and Company specialized in publishing Negro music. Among the composers the Starks published were: Scott Joplin (the greatest ragtime writer who ever lived and composer of *Maple Leaf Rag),* Tom Turpin, Louis Chauvin, Audie Mathews, and James Scott. But St. Louis wasn't like New Orleans; it was prejudiced. I moved on to Kansas City and found it was like St. Louis, except it did not have one decent pianist and didn't want any. That was why I went on to Chicago. In Chicago at that time you could go anywhere you wanted regardless of creed or color. So Chicago came to be one of the earliest places that jazz arrived, because of nice treatment—and we folks from New Orleans were used to nice treatment.

Up to this time the published arrangements of hot music were simply a matter of writing down the ragtime tunes played by some theatre band. Then *Jelly Roll Blues* became so popular with the people of Chicago that I decided to name it in honor of the Windy City. I was the only one at the time that could play this tune, *The Chicago Blues.* In fact, I had a hard time trying to find anyone who could take it down. I went to Henri Klickman (author of the *Hysterics Rag* and arranger for the Will Rossiter publishing house), but he didn't know enough. So, finally, I wrote the score out myself. Dave Payton and several more said what I had put down was "wrong," but, when I said, "Correct me then," they couldn't do it. We argued for days and days, but they couldn't find no holes in my tune. Finally, Klickman made an arrangement from my score and the song was published.

Immediately brass bands all over the country took it over and it was considered the hottest band arrangement anywhere. Here's the way we used to sing it at the old Elite Café . . .

> In New Orleans, in New Orleans, Louisiana town,
> There's the finest boy for miles around.
> Lord, Mister Jelly Roll, your affection he has stole.
> What? No! I sho must say, babe,
> You certainly can't abuse.
> Isn't that a shame?
> Don't you know that strain?

That's the Jelly Roll Blues.
He's so tall and chancey,
He's the ladies' fancy.
Everybody know him,
Certainly do adore him.

When you see him strolling, everybody opens up,
He's red-hot stuff,
Friends, you can't get enough.
Play it soft—don't abuse.
Play them Jelly Roll Blues . . .

JACK JOHNSON

From *In the Ring—and Out*

DEFINITE ARRANGEMENTS FOR MY FIGHT WITH Willard began when Jack Curley came to London to talk it over with me. The selection of Willard came about in the process of hunting the "white hope." The result of the fight ended that search, which had been carried on so intensely and bitterly that it had caused me much trouble and sorrow, because of the persecution to which I was subjected. On his arrival in London, Curley asked me if I meant business in meeting Willard. I told him I certainly did and that he would not find it difficult to make terms with me. The first night of Curley's stay in London, we visited the Coliseum where Oscar Ash and Lillie Braton were appearing. We did not talk shop that night. The next day we went to lunch and the preliminaries began, and in the evening at dinner we began to talk more freely. I told Curley to put all the cards on the table and to deal from the top of the deck. I had known him a long time. We had been close friends and had met in previous mutually satisfactory business deals. At one time in my life, when I was in serious trouble, he had stood loyally by me. As a result of this, I had the utmost confidence in him.

He frankly told me that if I lost the fight to Willard I could return to the United States without being molested. He said that I would be able to engage in a prosperous occupation and would gain new friends and please old acquaintances who were anxious to see me comfortably and peacefully settled down at home. These hints were inducements of course, but the greatest inducement of all was the opportunity it offered me to see my mother, for all who know me and who have read about me, know that whatever other failings I may have had, the love I had for my mother was so deep and sincere that I would have done anything to end the separation between us. After Curley had talked a while, explaining the chances I would have and mentioning my mother several times, I became more anxious than ever to get back home. After that first conversation with him, I did not care any more for the title of world's champion than a child does for the stick from which the lollypop has vanished. In fact, I despised it.

Curley explained that Frazee and Webber, amusement promoters, were associated with him in arranging with me to meet Willard. The fight, he said, would be held in Juarez, Mexico, and Villa, the revolutionary bandit leader who then controlled northern Mexico would finance the fight. Curley remained in London a week or so, and when he departed we had reached an agreement, as far as I was concerned, which would give Willard the championship and permit me to return home. He gave me sufficient money to defray transportation expenses to Mexico and I set about making preparations for going to the scene of the proposed fight. I did not tell my wife nor Gus, my nephew, that I had agreed to lose the fight, but pretended that I had entered into the deal with the hope and expectation of winning.

Taking our leave of London, we embarked for Rio de Janeiro early in 1914. We made a brief stay on our arrival at the South American port, and then departed for Buenos Aires, where we remained for six weeks and where I put on several boxing exhibitions . . .

It was our intention to go from Barbados to Vera Cruz or Tampico, Mexico, but owners of vessels and crews were dubious about venturing far out to sea because of the submarine danger which they believed existed, because of Germany's threats to carry on "ruthless sea warfare." We finally persuaded the owner of a small sailing vessel to attempt a trip to Havana, Cuba, a port which we reached after a hazardous trip during which we were driven by a gale and nearly wrecked. After I reached Havana, I learned from the newspapers that it was the intention of Carranza, president of Mexico, to capture me if I sought to land either at Vera Cruz or Tampico, and turn me over to the United States authorities, whereupon I got into communication with Curley, who had gone to Juarez to arrange for the fight. After several cable messages, I induced him to come to Havana. Upon his arrival, I explained my predicament and sought to have the scene of the Willard fight changed to Havana, because I was eager to go through with my part of the bargain. Then I intended to surrender to the United States, but I did not wish to risk capture by Carranza, because I foresaw that such a circumstance would involve me in official red tape and delays which I was in no mind to contend with.

On his arrival in Havana, Curley said that Frazee, Webber and himself had made arrangements for me to return to the United States if I lost to Willard, but first I was to take the films of the fight and exhibit them in South America and Europe, which sections of the globe were to be my exclusive territory. I collected the fight percentage due me just before the fight, but an additional percentage, which Willard's managers owed me if I lived up to my agreement to lie down, was not paid until the fight was almost over. They tried hard to renege on payments to me and even went so far as to try and deprive me of the films which were to be given me, according to contract. Pictures of the fight were made by Mace, and when I learned that the situation was not ripe for my return to the United States, I immediately left Havana for London. I was told when my boat was ready to leave that the films were not in readiness but that they would be sent to me in London as soon as they were finished. I waited for the pictures several weeks and when they did not arrive, I cabled to Curley asking why they had not been sent. He replied that they were on the way. I watched eagerly for their arrival, and when they did arrive, I was astounded to find that they were blank—that they never had been on a spool. I cabled demanding an explanation and in reply was told that the deception or mistake was due to Mace, the maker of the films.

This turn of affairs enraged me and I started other inquiries by cable, the result of which, among other things, brought me the information that Curley and his associates had made no move whatever to provide for my return to the United States. The failure of the films to arrive had not caused me to lose faith in my supposed friends. I tried to believe in them and to charge the delay in the films to other causes, but when I found that they had not kept their word in paving the way for me to return home I became not only cognizant of the fact that I had been flim-flammed but that I was up against a pretty raw deal. Therefore, I kept silent, but was not inactive. Inquiring at the office of the American Express Company, I learned that a film of the Willard-Johnson fight was being shipped to London from the United States. I knew that some plot was under way and I hired detectives to trace and watch the shipment. When it arrived I stayed close around the express company's office, knowing that some one would call for it.

I was not mistaken in this. A young man named A. Weil, who now lives in Chicago, appeared on the scene to claim the films. When they were transferred to him, I snatched them from him and obtained possession, though not until after a heated argument and various attempts to get them from me had taken place. I contracted with Barker & Company, one of the largest film firms in England to make prints of the films, and these I put on exhibition throughout England. I also sold the rights to the pictures to a South American company and with the proceeds from this sale and the display of the pictures in the United Kingdom was able to realize very satisfactory returns—returns which were ample enough to make me feel somewhat repaid for the manner in which Curley and his partners had bilked me. I also sold the Australian rights to the pictures to Rufe Nailor.

Preceding the fight with Willard, I did no serious training. I engaged in a few boxing exhibitions and did a few "strong man" stunts, such as pulling against horses and permitting a horse to stand on my stomach. This was about the extent of my training. I had no wish to undergo the ordeal of strict training knowing as I did how the fight was to terminate. Mrs. Johnson, my nephew Gus, my sparring partners and friends were curious and alarmed over my failure to train properly and several times demanded to know what my object was in being so indifferent. I boxed occasionally with Bob Armstrong, Sam McVey and some other American boxers whom I had previously fought in America, but as I always had been able to box rings around all of them, they never knew whether or not I was in shape.

On one occasion Mahoney, an American contractor who had played a big part in the Spanish-American War, and who then was living in Havana overheard me talking to Willard and repeating "Hit me! Come on, hit me!" I was then a big favorite in the betting. What Mahoney heard caused him to take quick leave of the arena and re-enter by another way, when he laid a big bet on Willard. He won a big sum of money, of course. . . .

I did not tell Mrs. Johnson I was going to lose the fight until a few moments before I entered the ring. Curley had paid me my fight percentage before I left my home. No one knew that the money was there, and I employed four policemen to guard the home, though they did not know that it was because of the money, and with the understanding that they merely were to watch the premises. I instructed Mrs. Johnson to sit at the ringside and watch the fight; that there was more money due me, and until this money was paid to me, I would not let the fight take the course agreed upon. Delay in paying this money was due to the incomplete count of gate receipts, which was under way when the fight started. Mrs. Johnson was to signal me when she had received the additional money, and I was to signal her so that she might leave the ringside. The fight was originally intended to end in the tenth round, but when that round arrived the money had not been paid. It was nearing the twenty-sixth round when the money was turned over to Mrs. Johnson. I had specified that it should be in $500 bills in order that the package should be small and the amount quickly counted. After examining it she gave me the signal. I replied that everything was O.K. by a pre-arranged sign and she departed. In the twenty-sixth round I let the fight end as it did. I felt very sorry for Mrs. Johnson, to have to relinquish the belt, but I was not sorry that I had lost the championship—or rather permitted another to attain it. On the contrary, I was happy, because I hopefully looked forward to my speedy return to the United States, where I would again be with my old friends and above all, with my mother. It was this expectation of my return to my native land, my friends and my mother that determined my part in the historic Johnson-Willard fight and explains why and how I lost it.

ETHEL WATERS

From *His Eye Is on the Sparrow*

ATLANTA, 1917

TWO VAUDEVILLE THEATERS SQUATTED SIDE BY SIDE on Decatur Street in the blowzy, noisy heart of Atlanta's Negro section. As a two-girl team, Jo Hill and I were booked into the showhouse at No. 81 Decatur. This was run by Charles P. Bailey, a Georgia cracker and a sort of self-appointed czar. You did what Mr. Bailey said—if you wanted to work for him. He even made all the performers on his bill live at Lonnie Reed's boardinghouse. . . .

Bailey's theater always drew big crowds. A Jewish fellow who ran the place right next door to it, at 91 Decatur Street, had to bring in big-name players to attract business.

One of these big names he booked while I was there was Stringbeans, one of the highest-paid acts in the Negro theatrical world at that time. Mr. Bailey, too, booked important names, turns like Speedy Smith, Buddy Austin, Joe Bright, and Billy Higgins, who later wrote "There'll Be Some Changes Made." Eddie Heywood's father played the piano at No. 81, and Ben Bow was a partner in the management of the stock company.

So the original Stringbeans was playing at 91 Decatur Street while I, Sweet Mama Stringbean, the feminine version of that long, thin green vegetable, was working just next door.

Stringbeans, whose real name was Butler May, was a fine man and a good buddy. He never resented my taking over his professional name. He and his wife, Sweetie May, became good friends of mine. His wife worked with him on the stage, and their act was billed as Stringbeans and Sweetie. Stringbeans accentuated his thinness by wearing very tight clothes. When he walked out on the stage he wore a thick chain across his vest with a padlock on it. The chain was just slack enough for the padlock to hang in front of his pants fly. This always got a guffaw from his admirers out front.

I stopped working for Mr. Charles P. Bailey for a grotesque and comical reason, with love being the cause of my dismissal. It seems to me, sometimes, that having a sense of humor always interferes with enjoying a love life on any large and satiating scale.

Anyway, one of the actors in Mr. Bailey's stock company fell for me. His wife, he, and I were all working at the time in an afterpiece. There were no rehearsals for these, and you gave your own cues. I liked being in these olios because you could die sitting down, standing up, or any other way you found convenient. If you forgot your lines you just made up other lines as you went along. The whole thing was so informal it bordered sometimes on chaos.

In this particular afterpiece the action called for my admirer's wife to stab me in the back. One night a pal buzzed me that she was going to use a real knife on me instead of the paper one supplied by the management.

Where I come from it ain't ethical to blow the whistle even on people who are planning to stab you. The situation required fast strategy, but the only out I could think of was to report sick to Mr. Bailey, hoping to be excused from the slicing party.

Mr. Bailey glanced at me and said I never looked healthier, and fired me. Jo Hill and I lost no time in going to work for his opposition next door. . . .

Bessie Smith was booked into 91 Decatur Street while I was working there. Bessie was a heavy-set, dark woman and very nice-looking. Along with Ma Rainey, she was undisputed tops as a blues singer. When she came to Atlanta she'd heard a good deal about my low, sweet, and then new way of singing blues.

Bessie's shouting brought worship wherever she worked. She was getting fifty to seventy-five dollars a week, big money for our kind of vaudeville. The money thrown to her brought this to a couple of hundred dollars a week. Bessie, like an opera singer, carried her own claque with her. These plants in the audience were paid to throw up coins and bills to get the appreciation money going without delay the moment she finished her first number. And if Bessie ordered it, her followers would put the finger on you and run you right off the stage and out of sight, maybe forever.

Bessie was in a pretty good position to dictate to the managers. She had me put on my act for her and said I was a long goody. But she also told the men who ran No. 91 that she didn't want anyone else on the bill to sing the blues.

I agreed to this. I could depend a lot on my shaking, though I never shimmied vulgarly and only to express myself. And when I went on I sang "I Want to Be Somebody's Baby Doll so I Can Get My Lovin' All the Time."

But before I could finish this number the people out front started howling, "Blues! Blues! Come on, Stringbean, we want your blues!"

The two-man orchestra struck up Bessie's music and kept it up through three refrains while the audience, feeling cheated, kept yelling, "We want Stringbeans and her blues!"

Before the second show the manager went to Bessie's dressing room and told her he was going to revoke the order forbidding me to sing any blues. He said he couldn't have another such rumpus. There was quite a stormy discussion about this, and you could hear Bessie yelling things about "these Northern bitches." Now nobody could have taken the place of Bessie Smith. People everywhere loved her shouting with all their hearts and were loyal to her. But they wanted me too.

There had been such a tumult at that first show that Bessie agreed that after I took two or three bows for my first song I should, if the crowd still insisted, sing "St. Louis Blues."

And each audience did insist. I remained courteous and deferential to her, always addressing her as "Miss Bessie." I was as crazy about her shouting as everyone else, even though hers was not my style, but I didn't enjoy the conflict. It was just more of the contentiousness I'd known all my life. Besides, I sensed this was the beginning of the uncrowning of her, the great and original Bessie Smith. I've never enjoyed seeing a champ go down, and Bessie was all champ.

When I closed my engagement in that theater Miss Bessie called me to her. "Come here, long goody," she said. "You ain't so bad. It's only that I never dreamed that anyone would be able to do this to me in my own territory and with my own people. And you know damn well that you can't sing worth a—"

Bessie was an earthy, robust woman, and after that we always understood each other. I liked her and I hope she came to like me.

I'd encountered Jim Crow all over the South and in many Northern towns as well. But it was in Atlanta that I learned how racial discrimination can hedge in a colored person and make him feel boxed up. There was a strict curfew law for Negroes in Atlanta which said we all had to be off the streets by midnight. Being a tall, high-spirited kid from the North, accustomed to keeping any hours I chose, I didn't like this.

The white people I encountered in the South never overlooked a chance to put me in my place, as it is called. They could tell I was from the North by my accent and possibly my manner, which has never been that of a downtrodden untouchable.

If I went to buy something in an Atlanta store, the white clerk would give me one look and say:

"I see you're one of those fresh Yankee niggers."

What disturbed me much more than this was the usual reaction of the

Southern colored girl with me. "Don't answer," she'd whisper nervously. "Don't say *anything*."

Now when I was called a nigger in Philadelphia it never meant a thing. But I was beginning to find out it did mean something in the South. Young as I was, I felt the acceptance of inferiority by the Southern Negro was a big, important factor. I regarded the whites, showering their scorn and contempt on other people because of their color, as odd and possibly feeble-minded and the tip-off that they were scared to death of us.

But that three fourths of the Southern Negroes should complacently accept all that contempt upset me. I was also shocked to find out that Southern Negroes were prejudiced against those of their own people like me who lived in the North.

I keep learning more about racial prejudice all the time. My biggest surprise of all has been the reaction of white people who wear their tolerance like a plume when I tell them I've never minded even slightly being a Negro.

They are stunned. It's difficult to convince them that I mean that and am not just keeping a stiff upper lip and being brave and gallant.

Keeping a stiff upper lip, hell!

I have the soundest of reasons for being proud of my people. We Negroes have always had such a tough time that our very survival in this white world with the dice always loaded against us is the greatest possible testimonial to our strength, our courage, and our immunity to adversity.

We are close to this earth and to God. Shut up in ghettos, sneered at, beaten, enslaved, we always have answered our oppressors with brave singing, dancing, and laughing. Our greatest eloquence, the pith of the joy and sorrow in our unbreakable hearts, comes when we lift up our faces and talk to God, person to person. Ours is the truest dignity of man, the dignity of the undefeated.

I write all this to explain why I am not bitter and angry at white people. I say in all sincerity that I am sorry for them. What could be more pitiful than to live in such nightmarish terror of another race that you have to lynch them, push them off sidewalks, and never be able to relax your venomous hatred for one moment? As I see it, it is these people, the Ku-Kluxers, the White Supremacists, and the other fire-spitting neurotics who are in the deep trouble.

Dictys and the others among my own people who despise Negroes who are poor and ignorant and condemned to live like animals arouse my fury as no white people ever can. We Negroes have lived through so much together—centuries of slavery, terror, segregation, and unending concentrated abuse—that I'll never understand how some of us who have one way or another been able to lift ourselves a little above the mass of colored people can be so insanely brutal as to try to knock the hell out of our own blood brothers and sisters. . . .

Part IX.

❧

SEEKING A WIDER WORLD

For black Americans, World War I was another opportunity to demonstrate their worth, to display again the extent of their patriotism and bravery in the face of danger on the battlefield. Despite the scarcity of food, living accommodations, and raging discrimination, the soldiers carried out their duties promptly and with great precision. Black women contributed to the war effort, too. The women in the units were there to prepare and to serve the food, and to treat the soldiers' wounds. Though a witness to the valor of the 369th Regiment, the legendary "Hellfighters," who withstood enemy fire for 191 consecutive days without losing an inch of territory, Addie Hunton seems more affected by the unenviable task of burying the dead, a detail left mainly for the black units. After the war Hunton returned home to Atlanta and devoted the rest of her life to the fight for racial and gender equality. She became a vice president and field secretary of the NAACP, and in 1927 was a principal organizer of the fourth Pan-African Congress held in New York City.

Harry Haywood returned from fighting the "Huns" only to reen-
counter the age-old racism problem at home. From the battlefields of
Europe, he literally stepped right into the middle of one of the worst
race riots in the nation's history. The survival instincts he learned from
the war were quickly applied to the growing menace of the mob, and
Haywood moved with the stealth and assurance that would serve him
well during his long years of daring activism as a key member of the
Communist Party. During the late 1920s he was instrumental in devising
the Black Belt Theory, a plan to establish an autonomous black republic
in the South. Subsequently, the concept of self-determination would become the official position of the Communist Party in its attempt to
organize African Americans. By 1943, the plan was abandoned by the
party, though Haywood continued to support it until his ouster from the
party in 1959.

In contrast to the conflict abroad and the turmoil in Chicago, Era
Bell Thompson experienced a relative calm coming of age on the Western plains. Even so, she found excitement in her youth through encounters with the numerous hoboes and tramps who passed through, and
from participating in Native American rituals and ceremonies around her
hometown in North Dakota. This interest in her surroundings may have
laid the foundation for the wanderlust that would later find her traveling
the world, writing about the strange and exotic for a number of publications, including *Ebony* magazine, where she was international editor from
1964 to 1986.

If Ms. Thompson was inspired to learn of the world's cultures,
Dorothy West was satisfied investigating the human drama right under
her nose in her hometown of Boston and later in Martha's Vineyard. It
is the latter environment with its prosperous denizens that she meticu-
lously examines here, including fleeting cameos of the renowned composer Harry T. Burleigh and Adam Clayton Powell, Jr. From this sketch

we gather some indication of West's fine sense of character development that made her novels so engrossing. With her cousin, poet Helene Johnson, West was among the youngest writers associated with the Harlem Renaissance. In 1932, she was part of a group of intellectuals led by Langston Hughes and Louise Thompson who were invited to the Soviet Union to make a film about race relations in the South. Hughes and his crew soured on the project when their Soviet sponsors presumed to know more about the black experience than they did. The film was never made. West was also the editor and founder of two magazines that promoted a social realist point of view. One of her contributing editors, Richard Wright, provided the publications with a radical orientation.

The incomparable power of Richard Wright's prose has been thoroughly discussed by leading literary critics for years, and the finest example of his remarkable insight is found in his autobiographical work. He was practically alone among African American authors in making his fear and distress come alive on the page. In one brief scene with a white store owner, Wright manages to pack a full discourse on race relations. Searing, psychologically troubling moments like this one are grist for Wright's fevered imagination and the root of intensity for his novels. When he published *Native Son* in 1940 the book was an immediate best seller and Wright became the most famous black writer in the world. The increasing fame, however, jeopardized his relationship with the Communist Party, of which he had been a member since 1932. In 1944 he quit the party and three years later quit the United States, taking up residence in France. A few critics contend that the separation from America—and the social milieu that fueled his imagination—lessened the impact of his fiction. That may be true, but it did not affect his nonfiction, and *Pagan Spain, Black Power,* and a collection of essays, *White Man, Listen!* are compelling accounts of a mature artist at work.

No black leader before or after Marcus Garvey possessed his infinite magnetism, his mesmerizing oratory skills, or his astonishing vision. At one time it was reported that he had more than two million card-carrying members in his Universal Negro Improvement Association. He purchased ships, bought land, published newspapers, built stores and factories, and stood at the center of an organization that unnerved the federal government; he also infuriated prominent figures such as W. E. B. Du Bois, who felt Garvey was a "demagogue" and was misleading black Americans. In the long run, the dispute between them would be mutually debilitating. For a leader who harbored such grand notions of accomplishment, it is perhaps not surprising that his fall from grace would be so heartbreaking for thousands of his followers. The bigger the dream, the harder the fall. Some historians believe Garvey was guilty of mail fraud while others contend that he lost control of an unwieldy organization and a few corrupt lieutenants. Garvey may not have achieved his great dreams, but his legacy of nationalism remains an enduring emblem of pride.

ADDIE HUNTON

From *Two Colored Women with the American Expeditionary Forces*

$

FRANCE, 1918

SPRINGTIME HAD COME AGAIN, BUT SO DIFFERENT from the spring of that other year. Then the voices of spring had been deadened by the thunderous guns around Verdun, Soissons, and Chateau Thierry. Then those guns with their deep and ominous challenge were holding the whole world in tense and fearful waiting. Women of every land were listening with tender yearning and burning anxiety for a word from their heroes on the fields of France. Men of mature years who had been a part of the conflicts of other days could scarce conceal their eagerness for the fray as they gently encouraged those anguished women and commended their wonderful spirit of endurance and patriotism. It was springtime, but the Crown Prince still hammered on Verdun, the Hindenburg line was still unbroken and the foe was not yet hurled back from the Marne in sure defeat. It was the springtime when late, but with grim determination to win or die, the American Forces had at last taken their place in the World Conflict.

But all that was now a part of the past and springtime had come once again in France. Meantime a spirit of change had crept over all the land. After one tremendous shout for victory the world had fallen into the silence that follows a supreme struggle—the silence of exhaustion, the silence of death. Many of the thousands who had pressed forward in those terrific battles crying "Victory!" had fallen and lain together under the bleak, dark winter skies of France. It was a period, too, of reckoning and realization of the price paid. But springtime had come again in France with its song-birds and blood-red poppies, and with it the quick consciousness that the dead lying en-masse on the battle-fields must be given resting places befitting heroes.

Here was a tremendous task for the surviving American soldiers, but far more sacred than tremendous. Whose would be the hands to gather as best they could and place beneath the white crosses of honor the remains of those who had sanctified their spirits through the gift of their lifeblood? It would be a gruesome, repulsive and unhealthful task, requiring weeks of incessant toil during the long heavy days of summer. It also meant isolation, for these cemeteries for the American dead would be erected on or near the battlefields where the men had fallen. But it would be a wonderful privilege the beauty and glory of which would reveal itself more and more as the facts of the war should become crystallized into history.

Strange that the value of such a task did not gather full significance in the minds of all American soldiers. Strange that when other hands refused it, swarthy hands received it! Yet, perhaps, not so strange, for Providence hath its own way, and in those American cemeteries in France we have strong and indisputable evidence of the wonderful devotion and loyalty and the matchless patience and endurance of the colored soldier. The placing of this task—the most sacred of the whole war—in his hands may have been providentially planned. It may have been just another means, as against the force of arms, to hasten here at home the recognition and enforcement of those fundamental principles that for four long years had held the world in deadly struggle.

We looked upon these soldiers of ours—the splendid 813th, 815th and 816th Pioneer Regiments and the numerous fine labor battalions—as they constructed the cemeteries at Romagne, Beaumont, Thiencourt, Belleau Woods, Fere-en-Tardenois and Soissons. We watched them as they toiled day and night, week after week, through drenching rain and parching heat. And yet these physical ills were as naught compared with the trials of discriminations and injustices that seared their souls like hot iron, inflicted as they were at a time when these soldiers were rendering the American army and nation a sacred service. Always in those days there was fear of mutiny or rumors of mutiny. We felt most of the time that we were living close to the edge of a smoldering crater. At Belleau Woods the soldiers *en-masse* banished some who mistreated them. We recall an incident at Romagne. Even though it was May the nights were winter cold, so that when one snuggled between army blankets in the tent, it required a bit of heroism to crawl out. This particular night we had just retired when shots were heard, fired in rapid succession. Without thought of the cold we began dressing and were sitting wrapped in cloak thinking rapidly about what was happening when someone called, "It is only a fire!" What a relief it was! What did it matter if the whole camp burned in comparison with our boys being goaded by prejudice beyond reason! Rations were often scarce and poor at Romagne because we were so far from supplies, hence we prepared and served food for the soldiers all day long. But this was but a small task compared with that of keeping the men in good spirits and reminding them again and again of the glory of the work they had in hand. Always, whether in the little corner set aside in the Y barracks as our reception room, or among the books they liked so well to read, whether by the side of the piano or over the canteen, we were trying to love them as a mother or a dear one would into a fuller knowledge and appreciation of themselves, their task and the value of forbearance.

We had gone from Romagne—women of fine spirit had taken our place and were lovingly ministering to the needs of these soldiers, when things happened too grievous to be calmly borne. At one stroke down came tents of discrimination and injustice, but the work there went on and the soldiers completed the difficult task assigned them.

For weeks at Romagne we watched these men fare forth with the dawn to find the dead on the 480 square miles of battlefield of the Meuse-Argonne. At eventide we would see them return and reverently remove the boxes from the long lines of trucks and place them on the hillside beside the waiting trenches that other soldiers had been digging all the long busy day. Far into the night we would sit in our darkened tent looking out on the electric-lighted cemetery, watching the men as they lowered the boxes into the trenches. Sometimes we could hear only a low murmur of voices, and sometimes again there would come to us a plaintive melody in keeping with the night hour and its peculiar task. . . .

HARRY HAYWOOD

From *Black Bolshevik*

CHICAGO, 1919

ON JULY 28, 1919, I LITERALLY STEPPED into a battle that was to last the rest of my life. Exactly three months after mustering out of the Army, I found myself in the midst of one of the bloodiest race riots in U.S. history. It was certainly a most dramatic return to the realities of American democracy.

It came to me then that I had been fighting the wrong war. The Germans weren't the enemy—the enemy was right here at home. These ideas had been developing ever since I landed home in April, and a lot of other Black veterans were having the same thoughts.

I had a job as a waiter on the Michigan Central Railroad at the time. In July, I was working the Wolverine, the crack Michigan Central train between Chicago and New York. We would serve lunch and dinner on the run out of Chicago to St. Thomas, Canada, where the dining car was cut off the train. The next morning our cars would be attached to the Chicago-bound train and we would serve breakfast and lunch into Chicago.

On July 27, the Wolverine left on a regular run to St. Thomas. Passing through Detroit, we heard news that a race riot had broken out in Chicago. The situation had been tense for some time. Several members of the crew, all of them Black, had bought revolvers and ammunition the previous week when on a special to Battle Creek, Michigan. Thus, when we returned to Chicago at about 2:00 P.M. the next day (July 28), we were apprehensive about what awaited us.

The whole dining car crew, six waiters and four cooks, got off at the Twelfth Street Station in Chicago. Usually we would stay on the car while it backed out to the yards, but the station seemed a better route now. We were all tense as we passed through the station on the way to the elevated which would take us to the Southside and home. Suddenly a white trainman accosted us.

"Hey, you guys going out to the Southside?"

"Yeah, so what?" I said, immediately on the alert, thinking he might start something.

"If I were you I wouldn't go by the avenue." He meant Michigan Avenue which was right in front of the station.

"Why?"

"There's a big race riot going on out there, and already this morning a couple of colored soldiers were killed coming in unsuspectingly. If I were you I'd keep off the street, and go right out those tracks by the lake."

We took the trainman's advice, thanked him, and turned toward the tracks. It would be much slower walking home, but if he were right, it would be safer. As we turned down the tracks toward the Southside of the city, towards the Black ghetto, I thought of what I had just been through in Europe and what now lay before me in America.

On one side of us lay the summer warmness of Lake Michigan. On the other was Chicago, a huge and still growing industrial center of the nation, bursting at its seams; brawling, sprawling Chicago, "hog butcher for the nation" as Carl Sandburg had called it.

As we walked, I remembered the war. On returning from Europe, I had felt good to be alive. I was glad to be back with my family—Mom, Pop and my sister. At twenty-one, my life lay before me. What should I do? The only trade I had learned was waiting tables. I hadn't even finished the eighth grade. Perhaps I should go back to France, live there and become a French citizen? After all, I hadn't seen any Jim Crow there.

Had race prejudice in the U.S. lessened? I knew better. Conditions in the States had not changed, but we Blacks had. We were determined not to take it anymore. But what was I walking into?

Southside Chicago, the Black ghetto, was like a besieged city. Whole sections of it were in ruins. Buildings burned and the air was heavy with smoke, reminiscent of the holocaust from which I had recently returned.

Our small band, huddled like a bunch of raw recruits under machine gun fire, turned up Twenty-sixth Street and then into the heart of the ghetto. At Thirty-fifth and Indiana, we split up to go our various ways; I headed for home at Forty-second Place and Bowen. None of us returned to work until the riot was over, more than a week later.

The battle at home was just as real as the battle in France had been. As I recall, there was full-scale street fighting between Black and white. Blacks were snatched from streetcars and beaten or killed; pitched battles were fought in ghetto streets; hoodlums roamed the neighborhood, shooting at random. Blacks fought back.

As I saw it at the time, Chicago was two cities. The one was the Chamber of Commerce's city of the "American Miracle," the Chicago of the 1893 World Columbian Exposition. It was the new industrial city which had grown in fifty years from a frontier town to become the second largest city in the country.

The other, the Black community, had been part of Chicago almost from the time the city was founded. Jean Baptiste Pointe DuSable, a Black trapper from French Canada, was the first settler. Later came fugitive slaves, and after the Civil War—more Blacks, fleeing from post-Reconstruction terror, taking jobs as domestics and personal servants.

The large increase was in the late 1880s through World War I, as industry in the city expanded and as Blacks streamed north following the promise of jobs, housing and an end to Jim Crow lynching. The Illinois Central tracks ran straight through the deep South from Chicago to New Orleans, and the Panama Limited made the run every day.

Those that took the train north didn't find a promised land. They found jobs and housing, all right, but they had to compete with the thousands of recent immigrants from Europe who were also drawn to the jobs in the packing houses, stockyards and steel mills.

The promise of an end to Jim Crow was nowhere fulfilled. In those days, the beaches on Lake Michigan were segregated. Most were reserved for whites only. The Twenty-sixth Street Beach, close to the Black community, was open to Blacks—but only as long as they stayed on their own side.

The riot had started at this beach, which was then jammed with a late July crowd. Eugene Williams, a seventeen-year-old Black youth, was killed while swimming off the white side of the beach. The Black community was immediately alive with accounts of what had happened—that he had been murdered while swimming, that a group of whites had thrown rocks at him and killed him, and that the policeman on duty at the beach had refused to make any arrests.

This incident was the spark that ignited the flames of racial animosity which had been smoldering for months. Fighting between Blacks and whites broke out on the Twenty-sixth Street beach after Williams's death. It soon spread beyond the beach and lasted over six days. Before it was over, thirty-eight people—Black and white—were dead, 537 injured and over 1,000 homeless.

The memory of this mass rebellion is still very sharp in my mind. It was the great turning point in my life, and I have dedicated myself to the struggle against capitalism ever since. . . .

ERA BELL THOMPSON

From *American Daughter*

NORTH DAKOTA, 1920S

MANDAN MARKS THE BEGINNING OF THE REAL west. It is here Mountain Time begins, here the Indians come from the reservations to greet the tourist trains and dance at the big rodeo; here, on this side of the river, live the rattlers; and farther to the west, in the famed Bad Lands, is the town of Medora, once the ranch home of Teddy Roosevelt and his fabulous friend, the French nobleman, Marquis de Mores.

The town was proud of its historical significance, worked hard to maintain it. Few Negroes had ever lived in Mandan, never more than two or three at a time. Most of its seven thousand people were Russian-German, living in Dutch and Russian hollows, bits of the Old Country, complete in their quaintness, transplanted deep between the sharp hills at the north end of town. Scrubbed wooden benches leaned against light-blue and pale-green houses, earthenware jugs stood by the doors. English was seldom spoken.

Here Pop opened his secondhand store in a little four-room house on Main Street between Wagner's Hotel and the Morton Construction Company. For a long time the store smelled. Its former tenant made and sold moonshine, and the tenants before him had babies, so many babies they were said to have slept sideways of the bed. Pop scrubbed the store, drenched it with creosote, and burned sulphur, but it retained the sour odor of bad liquor and something else—customers. All night long men tapped on the back doors and windows calling softly for a bootlegger named Joe. They thought Deacon Thompson was running a speakeasy. . . .

In all Mandan there was not one Baptist church, so, with many apologies to his past faith, Pop succumbed to Mr. Wagner's urging and went to Mass.

"They all right," he commented dryly when we got home, "but I'm too old for that religion." He rubbed his knees. "Them hard prayer benches and all that gettin' up and gettin' down—and with my rheumatism, too—Lord to day, I wouldn't last out the week!" He looked at me. "You join if you want to, one religion just as good as another with you 'cause you ain't goin' to do no different no way."

"They wear hats to church," I replied. "I hate hats."

So Pop and I went over to the pretty Methodist church, where they stayed put in their pews and sang doleful hymns and took Deacon Thompson on probation and accepted me and my sins in full.

As the rodeo time drew near, Pop's excitement grew with that of the town's, and the call of the kitchen was strong upon him. "Lots of money to be made out there at that thing," he reasoned. "Now I could sell some of my chicken sandwiches an' make a killin'." So, when the rodeo opened, Pop, like the Indians, pitched his tent at the fairgrounds and began to hawk his wares. Afternoons and evenings I sold sandwiches over the oilcloth counter, while Pop mysteriously converted each wizened, over-aged hen into sixteen golden-brown, highly inflated morsels at a quarter a sandwich. Business got so good I went to Bismarck and got Gwyn to help us. Carnival people, fed up on the traditional American hot dog and hamburger, flocked to our stand, and even the Indians deserted their tents and tepees—after I found Priscilla. She was living with the other Indians at the far end of the race track, where spotted ponies grazed on wild grass, dried meat hung in long strips on ropes between the trees, and dogs snapped at the flies and scratched their mangy sides. When Priscilla came to visit me, she asked for a hot dog.

"Try chicken," I urged. "You've got dogs at home."

"How much?" she asked.

"Ten cents to you." I looked at the old woman beside her. "Is that your mother?"

"Yes." She said something in Sioux. The woman pulled her shawl around her thin shoulders and smiled at me. She said nothing. "My mother don't speak American," said the girl.

Old Country, I thought. Only it wasn't Old Country; it was this country. Nearly all my friends were second generation; their parents spoke the mother-tongue, wore the native clothes, had the ways of the fatherland, even the Indians. In a sense I was second generation, too, only Pop had no other language and, in the ways of the world, was far ahead of me. My Latin and geometry didn't make any more sense to my father than they did to their fathers. They didn't make too much sense to me.

"Both of you try chicken," I offered, giving them the biggest pieces I could find.

The next morning the old lady returned. Gwyn and Pop tried to wait on her, but she stood at the counter, silent and unmoved. When I came at noon, she was still there. "Chick-on," she said, holding out a dime.

"So that's why she waited for you! Tell her chicken's a quarter, and we don't pick out no more big pieces," Pop said peevishly.

"More," I said, picking up a quarter from the cash box. "Like this."

She shook her head and smiled. "Chick-on."

"Pop," I pleaded. "You know I can't talk Indian. This is Priscilla's mother, Priscilla is my friend from the School. Can't we let her have it this time? She likes your cooking; she'll tell her friends, and you'll get lots of trade."

Pop had visions of the whole tribe descending upon him with dimes. "Give her somethin' an' git her away from here. She been takin' up cash-customer room all day. Then you go find that friend of yours an' stop them folks, hear? I got no time to interrupt my cookin' to go fightin' Indians!"

I slipped off to the stables every chance I got and rode the white trick horse that belonged to the boss of the rodeo. "You like horses, don't you, girlie?" he asked one afternoon when I brought the mare back.

"Crazy about them."

"Ever do much ridin', hard ridin'?"

"Are you kidding? I come from a bronco-busting family, wild Montana broncs, real horses!" I neglected to mention Bessie.

"Yeah? How'd you like to ride for me, travel along with my outfit? I'd teach you some tricks—you've got a way with horses—and you'd be a good drawin' card."

Some of the bravado went out of me. "I don't know," I backed down, "you'll have to ask my father." And that ended that career.

I loved the Indian war dances. Every evening they gathered in front of the grandstand in the twilight, dressed in all their fine feathers and elk's teeth and beaded moccasins, the chiefs and warriors wearing long head-dresses and carrying fierce hatchets in their fringed buffalo pants. Beneath the war paint was gentleness and a quiet joy in their make-believe. The dance was a picturesque thing, weird and exotic. A tall brave would step out into the center of the chanting circle, head bent low, knees pumping high, dancing to the throb of the tom-toms; a strenuous dance it was, punctuated by blood-curdling yells, a dance that raised beads of sweat on his naked, brown back, made his makeup run down his high cheeks. While the bucks danced, I often joined the squaws in a smooth little side step around the edge of the circle until some brash individual asked what tribe I belonged to: the Crows or the Blackfeet.

I hated to see the roundup close, see the carnival people and the Indians move on. The money Gwyn earned was to help pay her tuition to the state university in September. I wondered which would be nicer, going with the rodeo as a trick rider or with Gwyn as a freshman, so I went home to Thompson's Secondhand Store with Pop. . . .

I wanted to attend the local business college, but there was no money except the thousand-dollar note the elevator man still owed us on the farm. Crops failed miserably after we left Sterling, and land values decreased until the note was worthless.

"Maybe I could get something out of it," I told Father.

"How you goin' to collect when the lawyers couldn't?"

"If I get anything, can I have it?"

"Yes, Lord, if you get it!"

I sat down and wrote the elevator man a letter about the business college, and he sent me a check for seventy-five dollars. Pop never quite got over it, but he let me keep the money. In October I went up to the high school and talked to the principal. It was a little irregular, he said, but if I thought I could make up the work, why, yes, I could take a postgraduate commercial course; so I went back to school and kept the seventy-five dollars.

My first day wasn't too happy. As the principal and I started down the hall for the commercial room, classes began to pass down the long, dark corridor, and the students were upon us before they noticed me. Some stopped stock-still and stared the way people did on Main Street, some shied away, and one big, husky boy even made with a scream. I hurried along, trying to keep up with the long strides of the principal, ignoring the confusion that followed in my wake.

The blonde shorthand teacher was wholly unprepared for my coming. As she talked, her big gray eyes never moved from my face. She was seeing her first colored girl. "She'll work hard and catch up," the principal was saying; "I'm sure she will."

"Catch up! Why, we're a month ahead of her now. A whole month, and I already have one backward class!"

"I know, I know," he soothed. "She'll take her work home, she'll practice hard. Won't you?" He stopped short with sudden apprehension; but I was so busy returning the stare I nearly missed my cue.

"Well," she said peevishly, "I'll try it. But if she can't keep up, she can't stay!"

I stayed and had a wonderful time. The first few days the little class was divided between those bent upon being nice to me and the others. By the end of the second week they were all bent on being nice to me, vying to walk home with me. Teacher changed, too. With nothing else to do except shorthand, I caught up so rapidly she urged me to join her bookkeeping class and she let me practice typing when there was an extra machine. And, when there wasn't, I used the principal's portable. Soon I was writing for the school paper, taking part in all their activities and creating a few of my own.

I couldn't resist the gymnasium long. I played basketball with all four teams and stayed after school to practice acrobatics, because right then my sole desire was to become a lady contortionist. There being only one shower in the girls' dressing room, several of us went in together. At first my new friends watched me undress, watched to see if the color went all the way up and if any washed off in the water, and I think they were glad when it didn't because they knew then I wasn't a phony.

That winter I found another interest—the *Chicago Defender.* By enlarging upon and fictionalizing the commonplace events of the Evans and Thompson households, I created enough news to become a correspondent. My first feature, an attack upon Mr. Garvey's "Back to Africa" movement, brought my first fan mail, a letter from one of his followers who even scorched the outside of the letter; so I gave up social reform, assumed the pseudonym of "Dakota Dick," and began writing in the "Lights and Shadows" column as a bad, bad cowboy from the wild and woolly West. The Mandan Chamber of Commerce could not have done better. Came friendly letters from colored pen pals beyond the hills. When an article to *Physical Culture* magazine netted me three dollars, I traded contortionism for journalism and hooked my wagon to a literary star.

DOROTHY WEST

From *The Richer, The Poorer*

§

MARTHA'S VINEYARD, 1920S

WE WERE AMONG THE FIRST BLACKS TO vacation on
. . . Martha's Vineyard. It is not unlikely that the Island, in particular
Oak Bluffs, had a larger number of vacationing blacks than any other section of
the country.

There were probably twelve cottage owners. To us it was an agreeable
number. There were enough of us to put down roots, to stake our claim to a
summer place, so that the children who came after us would take for granted a
style of living that we were learning in stages.

The early blacks were all Bostonians, which is to say they were neither
arrogant nor obsequious, they neither overacted nor played ostrich. Though the
word was unknown then, in today's connotation they were "cool." It was a
common condition of black Bostonians. They were taught very young to take
the white man in stride or drown in their own despair. Their survival was
proved by their presence on the Island in pursuit of the same goal of happiness.

Every day, the young mothers took their children to a lovely stretch of
beach and scattered along it in little pools. They made a point of not bunching
together. They did not want the whites to think they knew their place.

There was not much exchange except smiles between the new and the old,
no more was needed. Bostonians do not rush into relationships. Sometimes the
children took their shovels and pails and built castles together. It was a pretty
scene. The blacks in all their beautiful colors, pink and gold and brown and
ebony. The whites in summer's bronze.

The days were full. There were berries to pick, a morning's adventure.
There were band concerts for an evening's stroll. There were invitations to

lemonade and cookies and whist. There was always an afternoon boat to meet, not so much to see who was getting off, but to see and talk to whatever friends had come for that same purpose.

For some years, the black Bostonians, growing in modest numbers, had this idyll to themselves. The flaws were put in perspective because no place is perfection.

And then came the black New Yorkers. They had found a fair land where equality was a working phrase. They joyously tested it. They behaved like New Yorkers because they were not Bostonians. There is nobody like a Bostonian except a man who is one.

The New Yorkers did not talk in low voices. They talked in happy voices. They carried baskets of food to the beach to make the day last. They carried liquor of the best brands. They grouped together in an ever increasing circle because what was the sense of sitting apart?

Their women wore diamonds when the few Bostonians who owned any had left theirs at home. They wore paint and powder when in Boston only a sporting woman bedecked her face in such bold attire. Their dresses were cut low. They wore high heels on sandy roads.

I had a young aunt who would duck behind a hedge and put us children on watch while she rubbed her nose with a chamois when we told her it was shiny. We did not think her performance was unusual. It was the New Yorkers who seemed bizarre, who always seemed to be showing off wherever they gathered together.

The New Yorkers were moving with the times. They had come from a city where they had to shout to be heard. It was a city that offered much, judgeships, professorships, appointments to boards, stardom on stage and more. Whoever wanted them had to push. The New Yorkers wanted them. They were achievers. They worked hard and they played hard.

They would unwind in another generation. They would come to the Island to relax not to posture. They would come to acknowledge that the Bostonians had a certain excellence that was as solid an achievement as money.

But in the meantime they lost the beach for the Bostonians. That beach like no other, that tranquil spot at that tranquil end of the Island. All one summer the Bostonians saw it coming like a wave they could not roll back. It came the next summer. The beach became a private club, with a gate that only dogs could crawl under, and a sign that said, "For members only."

You lose some, and by the same token, you win some. The world was not lost, just a piece of it. And in the intervening years more has been gained than was ever forfeited, more has been fought for and won, more doors have opened as fewer have closed.

Harry T. Burleigh, the composer, who left a priceless legacy in his long research of Negro spirituals—those shouts of grace and suffering and redemption that might have perished forever if he had not given his gifts to preserving them—he was the first to bring back glad tidings of the Island's fair land to his New York friends, who had always thought of Massachusetts as a nice place to come from, but not to go to unless bound and gagged.

Mr. Burleigh had come to stay at Shearer Cottage in the Highlands, a quiet boardinghouse operated by Boston friends, who had recommended the seclusion of the lovely wooded area, where New York's busy lights seemed as remote as the Island stars seemed near.

He was very good to the children of his friends. There were seven or eight of us who were his special favorites. He gave us money every time he saw us. We did not know any better than to spend it in one place. With abundant indulgence he would give us some more to spend in another. He rented cars and took us on tours of the Island. He told us about his trips abroad. To be with him was a learning experience.

There is a snapshot of him in a family album. Under the snapshot, in the handwriting of that aunt who could take us or leave us, there is the caption: "H.T.B., the children's friend." He was rich and well known in important circles at the time. There were a dozen glowing captions that would have applied. I think it is a tribute to him—and perhaps to my aunt—that she chose this simple inscription.

Mr. Burleigh's summers were spent working as well as sunning. Every weekday morning he went to a church in Vineyard Haven where he had use of the piano. Many of the spirituals sung around the world were given arrangements within God's hearing in an Island church.

In the course of time Mr. Burleigh grew to regret the increasing number of New Yorkers who brought their joyous living to his corner of the Highlands. He had extolled this sacred spot, and they were taking over. Who can say they did not share his vision? They simply expressed it in a different way.

Adam Clayton Powell came to summer at Shearer Cottage when he was a boy. He came with his father. His mother stayed home. Adam came to our house to play every day, and every day Adam's father came to ask my mother if his son was somewhere around. We were sorry for Adam that a boy as big as he was had a father who was always following him around. I can see that great tall man, who looked so like Adam was to grow up to look, striding up the road to ask my mother in his mellifluous preacher's voice if she had seen his boy. He would hold her in conversation, and she would turn as pink as a rose. He seemed to make her nervous, and we didn't know why. Sometimes he would come twice a day to see if Adam had lost his way between our house and Shearer Cottage. He never did, but all that summer his father couldn't rest until he had seen for himself. . . .

RICHARD WRIGHT

From *American Hunger*

CHICAGO, 1920S

MY FIRST GLIMPSE OF THE FLAT BLACK stretches of Chicago depressed and dismayed me, mocked all my fantasies. Chicago seemed an unreal city whose mythical houses were built of slabs of black coal wreathed in palls of gray smoke, houses whose foundations were sinking slowly into the dank prairie. Flashes of steam showed intermittently on the horizon, gleaming translucently in the winter sun. The din of the city entered my consciousness, entered to remain for years to come. The year was 1927.

What would happen to me here? Would I survive? My expectations were modest. I wanted only a job. Hunger had long been my daily companion. Diversion and recreation, with the exception of reading, were unknown. In all my life—though surrounded by many people—I had not had a single satisfying, sustained relationship with another human being and, not having had any, I did not miss it. I made no demands whatever upon others.

The train rolled into the depot. Aunt Maggie and I got off and walked slowly through the crowds into the station. I looked about to see if there were signs saying: FOR WHITE—FOR COLORED. I saw none. Black people and white people moved about, each seemingly intent upon his private mission. There was no racial fear. Indeed, each person acted as though no one existed but himself. It was strange to pause before a crowded newsstand and buy a newspaper without having to wait until a white man was served. And yet, because everything was so new, I began to grow tense again, although it was a different sort of tension than I had known before. I knew that this machine-city was governed by strange laws and I wondered if I would ever learn them.

As we waited for a streetcar to take us to Aunt Cleo's home for temporary lodging, I looked northward at towering buildings of steel and stone. There were no curves here, no trees; only angles, lines, squares, bricks and copper wires. Occasionally the ground beneath my feet shook from some faraway pounding and I felt that this world, despite its massiveness, was somehow dangerously fragile. Streetcars screeched past over steel tracks. Cars honked their horns. Clipped speech sounded about me. As I stood in the icy wind, I wanted to talk to Aunt Maggie, to ask her questions, but her tight face made me hold my tongue. I was learning already from the frantic light in her eyes the strain that the city imposed upon its people. I was seized by doubt. Should I have come here? But going back was impossible. I had fled a known terror, and perhaps I could cope with this unknown terror that lay ahead.

The streetcar came. Aunt Maggie motioned for me to get on and pushed me toward a seat in which a white man sat looking blankly out the window. I sat down beside the man and looked straight ahead of me. After a moment I stole a glance at the white man out of the corners of my eyes; he was still staring out the window, his mind fastened upon some inward thought. I did not exist for him; I was as far from his mind as the stone buildings that swept past in the street. It would have been illegal for me to sit beside him in the part of the South that I had come from.

The car swept past soot-blackened buildings, stopping at each block, jerking again into motion. The conductor called street names in a tone that I could not understand. People got on and off the car, but they never glanced at one another. Each person seemed to regard the other as a part of the city landscape. The white man who sat beside me rose and I turned my knees aside to let him pass, and another white man sat beside me and buried his face in a newspaper. How could that possibly be? Was he conscious of my blackness?

We went to Aunt Cleo's address and found that she was living in a rented room. I had imagined that she lived in an apartment and I was disappointed. I rented a room from Aunt Cleo's landlady and decided to keep it until I got a job. I was baffled. Everything seemed makeshift, temporary. I caught an abiding sense of insecurity in the personalities of the people around me. I found Aunt Cleo aged beyond her years. Her husband, a product of a southern plantation, had, like my father, gone off and left her. Why had he left? My aunt could not answer. She was beaten by the life of the city, just as my mother had been beaten. Wherever my eyes turned they saw stricken, frightened black faces trying vainly to cope with a civilization that they did not understand. I felt lonely. I had fled one insecurity and had embraced another.

When I rose the next morning the temperature had dropped below zero. The house was as cold to me as the southern streets had been in winter. I dressed, doubling my clothing. I ate in a restaurant, caught a streetcar and rode south, rode until I could see no more black faces on the sidewalks. I had now crossed the boundary line of the Black Belt and had entered that territory where jobs were perhaps to be had from white folks. I walked the streets and looked into shop windows until I saw a sign in a delicatessen: PORTER WANTED.

I went in and a stout white woman came to me.

"Vat do you vant?" she asked.

The voice jarred me. She's Jewish, I thought, remembering with shame the obscenities I used to shout at Jewish storekeepers in Arkansas.

"I thought maybe you needed a porter," I said.

"Meester 'Offman, he eesn't here yet," she said. "Vill you vait?"

"Yes, ma'am."

"Seet down."

"No, ma'am. I'll wait outside."

"But eet's cold out zhere," she said.

"That's all right," I said.

She shrugged. I went to the sidewalk. I waited for half an hour in the bitter cold, regretting that I had not remained in the warm store, but unable to go back inside. A bald, stoutish white man went into the store and pulled off his coat. Yes, he was the boss man . . . I went in.

"Zo you vant a job?" he asked.

"Yes, sir," I answered, guessing at the meaning of his words.

"Vhere you vork before?"

"In Memphis, Tennessee."

"My brudder-in-law vorked in Tennessee vonce," he said.

I was hired. The work was easy, but I found to my dismay that I could not understand a third of what was said to me. My slow southern ears were baffled by their clouded, thick accents. One morning Mrs. Hoffman asked me to go to a neighboring store—it was owned by a cousin of hers—and get a can of chicken à la king. I had never heard the phrase before and I asked her to repeat it.

"Don't you know nosing?" she demanded of me.

"If you would write it down for me, I'd know what to get," I ventured timidly.

"I can't vite!" she shouted in a sudden fury. "Vat kinda boy ees you?"

I memorized the separate sounds that she had uttered and went to the neighboring store.

"Mrs. Hoffman wants a can of Cheek Keeng Awr Lar Keeng," I said slowly, hoping that he would not think I was being offensive.

"All vite," he said, after staring at me a moment.

He put a can into a paper bag and gave it to me; outside in the street I opened the bag and read the label: Chicken à La King. I cursed, disgusted with myself. I knew those words. It had been her thick accent that had thrown me off. Yet I was not angry with her for speaking broken English; my English, too, was broken. But why could she not have taken more patience? Only one answer came to my mind. I was black and she did not care. Or so I thought . . . I was persisting in reading my present environment in the light of my old one. I reasoned thus: Though English was my native tongue and America my native land, she, an alien, could operate a store and earn a living in a neighborhood where I could not even live. I reasoned further that she was aware of this and was trying to protect her position against me.

(It was not until I had left the delicatessen job that I saw how grossly I had misread the motives and attitudes of Mr. Hoffman and his wife. I had not yet learned anything that would have helped me to thread my way through these perplexing racial relations. Accepting my environment at its face value, trapped by my own emotions, I kept asking myself what had black people done to bring this crazy world upon them?

(The fact of the separation of white and black was clear to me; it was its effect upon the personalities of people that stumped and dismayed me. I did not feel that I was a threat to anybody; yet, as soon as I had grown old enough to think I had learned that my entire personality, my aspirations had long ago been discounted; that, in a measure, the very meaning of the words I spoke could not be fully understood.

(And when I contemplated the area of No Man's Land into which the Negro mind in America had been shunted I wondered if there had ever existed in all human history a more corroding and devastating attack upon the person-alities of men than the idea of racial discrimination. In order to escape the racial attack that went to the roots of my life, I would have gladly accepted any way of life but the one in which I found myself. I would have agreed to live under a system of feudal oppression, not because I preferred feudalism but because I felt that feudalism made use of a limited part of a man, defined him, his rank, his function in society. I would have consented to live under the most rigid type of dictatorship, for I felt that dictatorships, too, defined the use of men, however degrading that use might be.

(While working in Memphis I had stood aghast as Shorty had offered himself to be kicked by the white men; but now, while working in Chicago, I was learning that perhaps even a kick was better than uncertainty . . . I had elected, in my fevered search for honorable adjustment to the American scene, not to submit and in doing so I had embraced the daily horror of anxiety, of tension, of eternal disquiet. I could now sympathize with—though I could never bring myself to approve—those tortured blacks who had given up and had gone to their white tormentors and had said: "Kick me, if that's all there is for me; kick me and let me feel at home, let me have peace!"

(Color hate defined the place of black life as below that of white life; and the black man, responding to the same dreams as the white man, strove to bury within his heart his awareness of this difference because it made him lonely and afraid. Hated by whites and being an organic part of the culture that hated him, the black man grew in turn to hate in himself that which others hated in him. But pride would make him hide his self-hate, for he would not want whites to know that he was so thoroughly conquered by them that his total life was conditioned by their attitude; but in the act of hiding his self-hate, he could not help but hate those who evoked his self-hate in him. So each part of his day would be consumed in a war with himself, a good part of his energy would be spent in keeping control of his unruly emotions, emotions which he had not wished to have, but could not help having. Held at bay by the hate of others, preoccupied with his own feelings, he was continuously at war with reality. He became inefficient, less able to see and judge the objective world. And when he reached that state, the white people looked at him and laughed and said:

("Look, didn't I tell you niggers were that way?"

(To solve this tangle of balked emotion, I loaded the empty part of the ship of my personality with fantasies of ambition to keep it from toppling over into the sea of senselessness. Like any other American, I dreamed of going into business and making money; I dreamed of working for a firm that would allow me to advance until I reached an important position; I even dreamed of or-ganizing secret groups of blacks to fight all whites. . . . And if the blacks would not agree to organize, then they would have to be fought. I would end up again with self-hate, but it was now a self-hate that was projected outward upon other blacks. Yet I knew—with that part of my mind that the whites had given me—that none of my dreams was possible. Then I would hate myself for allowing my mind to dwell upon the unattainable. Thus the circle would com-plete itself.

(Slowly I began to forge in the depths of my mind a mechanism that repressed all the dreams and desires that the Chicago streets, the newspapers, the movies were evoking in me. I was going through a second childhood; a new sense of the limit of the possible was being born in me. What could I dream of that had the barest possibility of coming true? I could think of nothing. And, slowly, it was upon exactly that nothingness that my mind began to dwell, that constant sense of wanting without having, of being hated without reason. A dim notion of what life meant to a Negro in America was coming to conscious-ness in me, not in terms of external events, lynchings, Jim Crowism, and the endless brutalities, but in terms of crossed-up feeling, of psyche pain. I sensed that Negro life was a sprawling land of unconscious suffering, and there were but few Negroes who knew the meaning of their lives, who could tell their story.)

Word reached me that an examination for postal clerk was impending and at once I filed an application and waited. As the date for the examination drew near, I was faced with another problem. How could I get a free day without losing my job? In the South it would have been an unwise policy for a Negro to have gone to his white boss and asked for time to take an examination for another job. It would have implied that the Negro did not like to work for the white boss, that he felt he was not receiving just consideration and, inasmuch as most jobs that Negroes held in the South involved a personal, paternalistic relationship, he would have been risking an argument that might have led to violence.

I now began to speculate about what kind of man Mr. Hoffman was, and I found that I did not know him; that is, I did not know his basic attitude toward Negroes. If I asked him, would he be sympathetic enough to allow me time off with pay? I needed the money. Perhaps he would say: "Go home and stay home if you don't like this job"? I was not sure of him. I decided, therefore, that I had better not risk it. I would forfeit the money and stay away without telling him.

The examination was scheduled to take place on a Monday; I had been working steadily and I would be too tired to do my best if I took the examination without the benefit of rest. I decided to stay away from the shop Saturday, Sunday, and Monday. But what could I tell Mr. Hoffman? Yes, I would tell him that I had been ill. No, that was too thin. I would tell him that my mother had died in Memphis and that I had gone down to bury her. That lie might work.

I took the examination and when I came to the store on Tuesday Mr. Hoffman was astonished, of course.

"I didn't sink you vould ever come back," he said.

"I'm awfully sorry, Mr. Hoffman."

"Vat happened?"

"My mother died in Memphis and I had to go down and bury her," I lied. He looked at me, then shook his head.

"Rich, you lie," he said.

"I'm not lying," I lied stoutly.

"You vanted to do somesink, zo you zayed ervay," he said, shrugging.

"No, sir. I'm telling you the truth." I piled another lie upon the first one.

"No. You lie. You disappoint me," he said.

"Well, all I can do is tell you the truth," I lied indignantly.

"Vy didn't you use the phone?"

"I didn't think of it." I told a fresh lie.

"Rich, if your mudder die, you vould tell me," he said.

"I didn't have time. Had to catch the train." I lied yet again.

"Vhere did you get the money?"

"My aunt gave it to me," I said, disgusted that I had to lie and lie again.

"I don't vant a boy vat tells lies," he said.

"I don't lie," I lied passionately to protect my lies.

Mrs. Hoffman joined in and both of them hammered at me.

"Ve know. You come from ze Zouth. You feel you can't tell us ze truth.

But ve don't bother you. Ve don't feel like people in ze Zouth. Ve treat you nice, don't ve?'' they asked.

"Yes, ma'am," I mumbled.

"Zen vy lie?"

"I'm not lying," I lied with all my strength.

I became angry because I knew that they knew that I was lying. I had lied to protect myself, and then I had to lie to protect my lie. I had met so many white faces that would have violently disapproved of my taking the examination that I could not have risked telling Mr. Hoffman the truth. But how could I now tell him that I had lied because I was so unsure of myself? Lying was bad, but revealing my own sense of insecurity would have been worse. It would have been shameful, and I did not like to feel ashamed.

Their attitudes had proved utterly amazing. They were taking time out from their duties in the store to talk to me, and I had never encountered anything like that from whites before. A southern white man would have said: "Get to hell out of here!" or "All right, nigger. Get to work." But no white people had ever stood their ground and probed at me, questioned me at such length. It dawned upon me that they were trying to treat me as an equal, which made it even more impossible for me ever to tell them that I had lied, why I had lied. I felt that if I confessed I would give them a moral advantage over me that would be unbearable.

"All vight, zay and vork," Mr. Hoffman said. "I know you're lying, but I don't care, Rich."

I wanted to quit. He had insulted me. But I liked him in spite of myself. Yes, I had done wrong, but how on earth could I have known the kind of people I was working for? Perhaps Mr. Hoffman would have gladly consented for me to take the examination, but my hopes had been far weaker than my powerful fears.

Working with them from day to day and knowing that they knew I had lied from fear crushed me. I knew that they pitied me and pitied the fear in me. I resolved to quit and risk hunger rather than stay with them. I left the job that following Saturday, not telling them that I would not be back, not possessing the heart to say good-bye. I just wanted to go quickly and have them forget that I had ever worked for them. . . .

MARCUS GARVEY

From *The Philosophy and Opinions of Marcus Garvey*

NEW ORLEANS, 1920S

MY WORK IS JUST BEGUN, AND WHEN the history of my suffer-ing is complete, then future generations of Negroes will have in their hands the guide by which they shall know the "sins" of the twentieth century. I, and I know you, too, believe in time, and we shall wait patiently for two hundred years, if need be, to face our enemies through our posterity.

After my enemies are satisfied, in life or death I shall come back to you to serve even as I have served before. In life I shall be the same: in death I shall be a terror to the foes of Negro liberty. If death has power, then count on me in death to be the real Marcus Garvey I would like to be. If I may come in an earthquake, or a cyclone, or plague, or pestilence, or as God would have me, then be assured that I shall never desert you and make your enemies triumph over you. Would I not go to hell a million times for you?

If I die in Atlanta my work shall then only begin, but I shall live, in the physical or spiritual [sense] to see the day of Africa's glory. When I am dead wrap the mantle of the Red, Black and Green around me, for in the new life I shall rise with God's grace and blessing to lead the millions up the heights of triumph with the colors that you well know. Look for me in the whirlwind or the storm, look for me all around you, for, with God's grace, I shall come and bring with me countless millions of black slaves who have died in America and the West Indies and the millions in Africa to aid you in the fight for Liberty, Freedom and Life.

The civilization of today is gone drunk and crazy with its power and by such it seeks through injustice, fraud and lies to crush the unfortunate. But if I am apparently crushed by the system of influence and misdirected power, my cause shall rise again to plague the conscience of the corrupt. For this I am satisfied, and for you, I repeat, I am glad to suffer and even die. Again, I say, cheer up, for better days are ahead. I shall write the history that will inspire the millions that are coming and leave the posterity of our enemies to reckon with the hosts for the deeds of their fathers.

With God's dearest blessings, I leave you for a while.

. . . Two months after I was confined at Atlanta, they [my enemies] succeeded in taking away the new ship from the unfaithful men who represented me. The same group of men in Wall Street who . . . had used the old officers to destroy the Black Star Line maneuvered to get the officers of the Black Cross Navigation and Trading Company to sign up with them to accept a cargo to Miami through a Negro broker. This Negro broker influenced the men to allow him to accept the freight. . . . The result was, in working out the scheme to get the ship, they got one or two shippers to place aboard the boat a small tonnage of cargo and then they went around to prospective shippers and influenced them not to ship any freight on the boat to Miami. The ship could not sail with the small amount of cargo; these men in turn libeled the boat for non-performance of contract with a demand to the extent of $25,000 . . . so the boat that was purchased and equipped for $200,000 was taken away while I was in prison for $25,000. Efforts were also made to get the $22,250 lodged with the Shipping Board for the Black Star Line.

When I was sent to Atlanta my enemies made sure that would have been the last of me. From what I could gather it seemed that they had reached even the Deputy Warden of the prison with their influence, with the suggestion of making it hard for me whilst there. The Deputy Warden of the institution made every effort to carry out the wishes of my enemies. When I was drafted for work he gave me the hardest and dirtiest tasks in the prison, thinking that would have ruffled my spirits to cause further punishment. But I philosophically accepted the duties and executed them to the best of my ability. After being so engaged for a short while, the Warden (a high-typed man of character and consideration), Mr. J. W. Snooks, called me into his office and had me transferred to the best position that a colored man could have in prison; this I also executed to the best of my ability during the entire time that I remained there. I have absolutely no complaint to make during the time I spent at Atlanta under Warden Snooks.

Whilst I was confined efforts were made to secure for me a pardon or communication [commutation?]. I was informed that President Coolidge would have acted immediately upon the application for pardon a few months after I was in Atlanta but [for] the pressure brought to bear upon him by my enemies.

Instead of signing the papers for my release he returned them with a statement of "Premature." It was not until two years after he finally granted me commutation.

I had hoped that on my release from Atlanta I would have had the opportunity of returning to New York to straighten out the affairs of the Universal Negro Improvement Association, the Black Star Line and the Black Cross Navigation and Trading Company, but my enemies made sure of their game in not allowing me to return to New York. They had already swallowed up all the assets of the companies, which could be removed only by my presence in New York. So they skillfully influenced the Department of Labor and the Department of State to deport me to Jamaica. On the order of President Coolidge I was shunted to New Orleans, and from there to my homeland—Jamaica.

Part X .

§

THE HARLEM RENAISSANCE

AND BEYOND

Apart from slavery and Reconstruction, the Harlem Renaissance of the 1920s is the most widely discussed chapter in African American history. Because it followed such dismal years the actual achievements of this brief period may be exaggerated, but regardless it remains an intriguing era with a host of colorful characters and luminaries. Langston Hughes stands at the pinnacle of the hundreds who ventured to America's black capital, endowing it with his matchless array of literary gifts. As Hughes relates "it was a period when the Negro was in vogue," and, since he was in the vortex of the era, he is probably the best witness to the events of that day (and nights), especially the storied adventures and achievements of the "literati."

Howard "Stretch" Johnson was a unique personality during the Harlem Renaissance. Not only was he a talented hoofer who often performed with his dancing siblings in front of Duke Ellington's Band at the Cotton Club in the late 1920s, he was also a political activist and a member of the Communist Party. Whether in the realm of culture or politics, Johnson has been an endless source of information for researchers seeking to know more about the last five decades of American history, particularly from a leftist perspective.

When it comes to telling a story, Zora Neale Hurston may have been the best of her era. So good were her stories that she was finally convinced to attempt a novel. She excelled in this idiom and she reveals here some of the circumstances surrounding her works, including her most famous book, *Their Eyes Were Watching God.* Hurston is considered a fixture in the Harlem Renaissance, though her real literary triumphs did not occur until after those halcyon days were over. At the core of her diverse literary output is her background in African and African American folklore, a pursuit she embarked on in her hometown of Eatonville, Florida, after encouragement from Franz Boas, her anthropology professor while she was a student at Columbia. Colorful and rambunctious, Hurston cut a memorable swath through a period suffused with glamorous personalities.

Hurston was an inveterate traveler and by 1941 was in California. Pauli Murray also made it to the West Coast, but under comparatively more difficult conditions. Murray, who is best known as a feminist, a lawyer, and a priest, hopped freight cars from New York to Vallejo at a time when thousands of American youth traveled by train searching for jobs. To endure such a venture required a great amount of fortitude, which Murray inherited from her family, who established the first schools for free blacks in North Carolina and Virginia. Like her forebears, she would also devote herself to education. She was a law professor at Yale and Brandeis, and she taught in Ghana. Murray was a founding member of the NOW and the National Association of Women, and was the first African American woman ever ordained by the Episcopal Church.

The Great Depression, however, did not send everybody scurrying from one town to another to find employment. Nate Shaw roamed a bit, but never too far from the farmland of Tukabahchee County, Alabama. What little we know about the relationship between black farmers and unions has come from people such as Shaw who vividly recalls his experiences with the Sharecroppers' Union, which like the larger Southern Tenant Farmers' Union never had the impact it promised. During the 1930s the Socialist Party took an active role in organizing poor white and black sharecroppers who were battered by the Depression and New Deal crop reduction programs. Facing eviction from their farms, the farmers forged a union to halt the diminishing prospects of the plantation system. What began on a promising note ended with rancor with internal and external pressures exacerbating the conflict between Socialist and Communist organizers.

Young black men in the South had a number of good reasons to pack up and head for the North. With the ravage of floods washing away topsoil and the boll weevil menacing the crops, decent jobs on the farms were scarce. Haywood Patterson, like Paulí Murray, climbed aboard a train in Alabama hoping to find a way to make a living somewhere else. What he found, along with eight other young black men, was a mob of white farmers ready to lynch them. They were falsely accused of raping two white women on the train. These nine youths became known as the Scottsboro Boys, so named because of the location where the incident occurred. Their case became the cause celebre of the 1930s.

The perils of racism were, of course, by no means limited to the deep South. In Indiana, James Cameron and two friends conspired to commit a robbery. When the time came, Cameron balked. Nevertheless, his two friends went ahead with the plan and in the course of the robbery allegedly raped a woman and killed her husband. Though Cameron did not participate in the crime, he was arrested along with his friends. Taking the law into their own hands, a mob dragged Cameron's friends from their cell and lynched them. Another noose was prepared for Cameron. But his life was miraculously spared. Cameron swears he heard a woman's voice asking that the noose be removed from his neck, but he learned later it was a voice only he heard. Never before has there been such a gripping account from someone so close to the hot breath of vigilantes, but Cameron recalls the incident without melodrama.

Adam Clayton Powell, Jr.'s enemies were far more subtle and sophisticated than the rabid throng who threatened Cameron's life. To fight them, Powell took his protest to the streets of Harlem, rousing his army of demonstrators with the slogan, "Don't Buy Where You Can't Work." Many scholars contend these tactics were pivotal in the rise of the civil rights movement a score of years later. It is certainly true that the success of these boycotts was instrumental in Powell's political ascendance. Suave and debonair, Powell beguiled political activists with the same charisma that brought worshipers to Abyssinian Baptist Church. He moved almost effortlessly from the pulpit to New York City's council, becoming the body's first black member. Three years later he was in Washington, D.C., as a congressman representing Harlem, a position he held for eleven successive terms. As chairman of the House Committee on Education and Labor, he was extremely effective and introduced a number of progressive legislative bills in Congress.

LANGSTON HUGHES

From *The Big Sea*

❧

NEW YORK, 1926

IT WAS A PERIOD WHEN LOCAL AND visiting royalty were
. . . not at all uncommon in Harlem. And when the parties of A'Lelia
Walker, the Negro heiress, were filled with guests whose names would turn
any Nordic social climber green with envy. It was a period when Harold
Jackman, a handsome young Harlem school teacher of modest means, calmly
announced one day that he was sailing for the Riviera for a fortnight, to attend
Princess Murat's yachting party. It was a period when Charleston preachers
opened up shouting churches as sideshows for white tourists. It was a period
when at least one charming colored chorus girl, amber enough to pass for a
Latin American, was living in a pent house, with all her bills paid by a gentleman whose name was banker's magic on Wall Street. It was a period when
every season there was at least one hit play on Broadway acted by a Negro cast.
And when books by Negro authors were being published with much greater
frequency and much more publicity than ever before or since in history. It was
a period when white writers wrote about Negroes more successfully (commer-
cially speaking) than Negroes did about themselves. It was the period (God
help us!) when Ethel Barrymore appeared in blackface in *Scarlet Sister Mary!* It
was the period when the Negro was in vogue.

I was there. I had a swell time while it lasted. But I thought it wouldn't last
long. (I remember the vogue for things Russian, the season the Chauve-Souris
first came to town.) For how could a large and enthusiastic number of people
be crazy about Negroes forever? But some Harlemites thought the millennium
had come. They thought the race problem had at last been solved through Art
plus Gladys Bentley. They were sure the New Negro would lead a new life

from then on in green pastures of tolerance created by Countee Cullen, Ethel Waters, Claude McKay, Duke Ellington, Bojangles, and Alain Locke.

I don't know what made any Negroes think that—except that they were mostly intellectuals doing the thinking. The ordinary Negroes hadn't heard of the Negro Renaissance. And if they had, it hadn't raised their wages any. As for all those white folks in the speakeasies and night clubs of Harlem—well, maybe a colored man could find *some* place to have a drink that the tourists hadn't yet discovered.

HARLEM LITERATI

The summer of 1926, I lived in a rooming house on 137th Street, where Wallace Thurman and Harcourt Tynes also lived. Thurman was then managing editor of the *Messenger,* a Negro magazine that had a curious career. It began by being very radical, racial, and socialistic, just after the war. I believe it received a grant from the Garland Fund in its early days. Then it later became a kind of Negro society magazine and a plugger for Negro business, with photographs of prominent colored ladies and their nice homes in it. A. Phillip Randolph, now President of the Brotherhood of Sleeping Car Porters, Chandler Owen, and George S. Schuyler were connected with it. Schuyler's editorials, à la Mencken, were the most interesting things in the magazine, verbal brickbats that said sometimes one thing, sometimes another, but always vigorously. I asked Thurman what kind of magazine the *Messenger* was, and he said it reflected the policy of whoever paid off best at the time.

Anyway, the *Messenger* bought my first short stories. They paid me ten dollars a story. Wallace Thurman wrote me that they were very bad stories, but better than any others they could find, so he published them.

Thurman had recently come from California to New York. He was a strangely brilliant black boy, who had read everything, and whose critical mind could find something wrong with everything he read. I have no critical mind, so I usually either like a book or don't. But I am not capable of liking a book and then finding a million things wrong with it, too—as Thurman was capable of doing. . . .

During the summer of 1926, Wallace Thurman, Zora Neale Hurston, Aaron Douglas, John P. Davis, Bruce Nugent, Gwendolyn Bennett, and I decided to publish "a Negro quarterly of the arts" to be called *Fire*—the idea being that it would burn up a lot of the old, dead conventional Negro-white ideas of the past, *épater le bourgeois* into a realization of the existence of the younger Negro writers and artists, and provide us with an outlet for publication not available in the limited pages of the small Negro magazines then existing, the *Crisis, Opportunity,* and the *Messenger*—the first two being house organs of inter-racial organizations, and the latter being God knows what.

Sweltering summer evenings we met to plan *Fire*. Each of the seven of us agreed to give fifty dollars to finance the first issue. Thurman was to edit it, John P. Davis to handle the business end, and Bruce Nugent to take charge of distribution. The rest of us were to serve as an editorial board to collect material, contribute our own work, and act in any useful way that we could. For artists and writers, we got along fine and there were no quarrels. But October came before we were ready to go to press. I had to return to Lincoln, John Davis to Law School at Harvard, Zora Hurston to her studies at Barnard, from whence she went about Harlem with an anthropologist's ruler, measuring heads for Franz Boas.

Only three of the seven had contributed their fifty dollars, but the others faithfully promised to send theirs out of tuition checks, wages, or begging. Thurman went on with the work of preparing the magazine. He got a printer. He planned the layout. It had to be on good paper, he said, worthy of the drawings of Aaron Douglas. It had to have beautiful type, worthy of the first Negro art quarterly. It had to be what we seven young Negroes dreamed our magazine would be—so in the end it cost almost a thousand dollars, and nobody could pay the bills.

I don't know how Thurman persuaded the printer to let us have all the copies to distribute, but he did. I think Alain Locke, among others, signed notes guaranteeing payments. But since Thurman was the only one of the seven of us with a regular job, for the next three or four years his checks were constantly being attached and his income seized to pay for *Fire*. And whenever I sold a poem, mine went there, too—to *Fire*.

None of the older Negro intellectuals would have anything to do with *Fire*. Dr. Du Bois in the *Crisis* roasted it. The Negro press called it all sorts of bad names, largely because of a green and purple story by Bruce Nugent, in the Oscar Wilde tradition, which we had included. Rean Graves, the critic for the *Baltimore Afro-American,* began his review by saying: "I have just tossed the first issue of *Fire* into the fire." Commenting upon various of our contributors, he said: "Aaron Douglas who, in spite of himself and the meaningless grotesqueness of his creations, has gained a reputation as an artist, is permitted to spoil three perfectly good pages and a cover with his pen and ink hudge pudge. Countee Cullen has written a beautiful poem in his 'From a Dark Tower,' but tries his best to obscure the thought in superfluous sentences. Langston Hughes displays his usual ability to say nothing in many words."

So *Fire* had plenty of cold water thrown on it by the colored critics. The white critics (except for an excellent editorial in the *Bookman* for November, 1926) scarcely noticed it at all. We had no way of getting it distributed to bookstands or news stands. Bruce Nugent took it around New York on foot and some of the Greenwich Village bookshops put it on display, and sold it for us. But then Bruce, who had no job, would collect the money and, on account of salary, eat it up before he got back to Harlem.

Finally, irony of ironies, several hundred copies of *Fire* were stored in the basement of an apartment where an actual fire occurred and the bulk of the whole issue was burned up. Even after that Thurman had to go on paying the printer.

Now *Fire* is a collector's item, and very difficult to get, being mostly ashes.

That taught me a lesson about little magazines. But since white folks had them, we Negroes thought we could have one, too. But we didn't have the money.

Wallace Thurman laughed a long bitter laugh. He was a strange kind of fellow, who liked to drink gin, but *didn't* like to drink gin; who liked being a Negro, but felt it a great handicap; who adored bohemianism, but thought it wrong to be a bohemian. He liked to waste a lot of time, but he always felt guilty wasting time. He loathed crowds, yet he hated to be alone. He almost always felt bad, yet he didn't write poetry.

Once I told him if I could feel as bad as he did *all* the time, I would surely produce wonderful books. But he said you had to know how to *write*, as well as how to feel bad. I said I didn't have to know how to feel bad, because, every so often, the blues just naturally overtook me, like a blind beggar with an old guitar:

> *You don't know,*
> *You don't know my mind—*
> *When you see me laughin',*
> *I'm laughin' to keep from cryin'.*

About the future of Negro literature Thurman was very pessimistic. He thought the Negro vogue had made us all too conscious of ourselves, had flattered and spoiled us, and had provided too many easy opportunities for some of us to drink gin and more gin, on which he thought we would always be drunk. With his bitter sense of humor, he called the Harlem literati, the "niggerati."

Of this "niggerati," Zora Neale Hurston was certainly the most amusing. Only to reach a wider audience, need she ever write books—because she is a perfect book of entertainment in herself. In her youth she was always getting scholarships and things from wealthy white people, some of whom simply paid her just to sit around and represent the Negro race for them, she did it in such a racy fashion. She was full of side-splitting anecdotes, humorous tales, and tragicomic stories, remembered out of her life in the South as a daughter of a travelling minister of God. She could make you laugh one minute and cry the next. To many of her white friends, no doubt, she was a perfect "darkie," in the nice meaning they give the term—that is a naïve, childlike, sweet, humorous, and highly colored Negro.

But Miss Hurston was clever, too—a student who didn't let college give her a broad *a* and who had great scorn for all pretensions, academic or otherwise. That is why she was such a fine folklore collector, able to go among the people and never act as if she had been to school at all. Almost nobody else could stop the average Harlemite on Lenox Avenue and measure his head with a strange-looking, anthropological device and not get bawled out for the attempt, except Zora, who used to stop anyone whose head looked interesting, and measure it.

When Miss Hurston graduated from Barnard she took an apartment in West 66th Street near the park, in that row of Negro houses there. She moved in with no furniture at all and no money, but in a few days friends had given her everything, from decorative silver birds, perched atop the linen cabinet, down to a footstool. And on Saturday night, to christen the place, she had a *hand*-chicken dinner, since she had forgotten to say she needed forks.

She seemed to know almost everybody in New York. She had been a secretary to Fannie Hurst, and had met dozens of celebrities whose friendship she retained. Yet she was always having terrific ups-and-downs about money. She tells this story on herself, about needing a nickel to go downtown one day and wondering where on earth she would get it. As she approached the subway, she was stopped by a blind beggar holding out his cup.

"Please help the blind! Help the blind! A nickel for the blind!"

"I need money worse than you today," said Miss Hurston, taking five cents out of his cup. "Lend me this! Next time, I'll give it back." And she went on downtown.

Harlem was like a great magnet for the Negro intellectual, pulling him from everywhere. Or perhaps the magnet was New York—but once in New York, he had to live in Harlem, for rooms were hardly to be found elsewhere unless one could pass for white or Mexican or Eurasian and perhaps live in the Village—which always seemed to me a very arty locale, in spite of the many real artists and writers who lived there. Only a few of the New Negroes lived in the Village, Harlem being their real stamping ground.

The wittiest of these New Negroes of Harlem, whose tongue was flavored with the sharpest and saltiest humor, was Rudolph Fisher, whose stories appeared in the *Atlantic Monthly*. His novel, *Walls of Jericho,* captures but slightly the raciness of his own conversation. He was a young medical doctor and X-ray specialist, who always frightened me a little, because he could think of the most incisively clever things to say—and I could never think of anything to answer. He and Alain Locke together were great for intellectual wise-cracking. The two would fling big and witty words about with such swift and punning innuendo that an ordinary mortal just sat and looked wary for fear of being caught in a net of witticisms beyond his cultural ken. I used to wish I could talk like Rudolph Fisher. Besides being a good writer, he was an excellent singer, and had sung with Paul Robeson during their college days. But I guess Fisher was too brilliant and too talented to stay long on this earth. During the same week, in December, 1934, he and Wallace Thurman both died.

Thurman died of tuberculosis in the charity ward at Bellevue Hospital, having just flown back to New York from Hollywood.

HOWARD ''STRETCH'' JOHNSON

From His Unpublished Memoirs

NEW YORK CITY, 1928

THE FIRST TIME I HEARD OF THE Cotton Club was in 1928 when
the Duke Ellington Orchestra broadcast on a nationwide evening hook-up
on WABC, the CBS affiliate. We couldn't wait to hear the strains of *East St.
Louis Toodle-Oo,* the Ellington theme song of that time, gradually swelling as the
voice-over of Ted Husing, in an impeccable accent and mellifluous baritone
announced, ''. . . and now from the Cotton Club . . . the aristocrat of
Harlem, where Park Avenue, Broadway, and Hollywood rub elbows . . . the
Jungle Band of Duke Ellington!''

We didn't know at the time that the splendid sound of the Ellington
organization was not jungle music. At the age of 13, I didn't know jungle music
from juke box or jazz! In fact, the only live music I had experienced was the
concert band that used to play at Orange Park on Sunday afternoons, the
exciting Jenkins Orphanage Band from Charleston, South Carolina, and a tacky
pickup band that played at Kinney's Hall on Broome Street in Newark when
my father took me on one of his mysterious expeditions to that area in what I
guess was a kind of male bonding. I later felt Ellington's sound was a creative
form of irony which masked the commercial pandering to an upper-class white
audience thrilled at the opportunity to witness and hear what it thought was
genuine black exotica. So, in our innocence, Irving Overby, Robby Benjamin,
and I with four hastily-recruited sidemen, formed our version of the Ellington
Orchestra, playing kazoos for brass, tissue paper folded over combs for reeds,
and washboards and pots and pans with thimbles for rhythm and percussion.
Inspired by Ellington, we played in the Overby's cellar where our ''jungle''
music would not bring the neighborhood down on us. When we thought we

had hit the proper Ellingtonian chord or a carbon copy of the guttural level of a Bubber Miley growl, we stopped playing and burst out laughing from the sheer joy of it.

My next connection with the Cotton Club came through my sister, Winnie, who danced at local affairs sponsored by social clubs that wanted a floor show, and "something more" than just the usual dance routine. Bill "Bojangles" Robinson, one of the Cotton Club's stars, had heard about Winnie's talent and offered her a week at the Alhambra Theatre with him, if she could learn his "Doin' The New Lowdown" routine from the Broadway show "Blackbirds of 1928." Winnie learned the routine in no time. She had what might be called a photographic memory in her muscles, and could reproduce a step within two or three tries, if they were complicated, and once was enough for the simpler combinations. She got her week with the great Bojangles. We sat in the orchestra as Winnie came out, watching in awe as Bojangles introduced her as his protege. Winnie looked as pretty as a picture and danced alongside "Bo" as if she had been in his act for years. The audience loved her and demonstrated it with cheers and whistles. Winnie became the celebrity of our family, and the talk of the neighborhood.

Her performance with Bojangles came to the attention of Elida Webb, a choreographer and talent scout for the Cotton Club. She sought out Winnie and tapped her for the chorus of the revue "Flying Colors." The plan was that she would go to the Cotton Club for more permanent employment, given that most Broadway productions had limited runs. But with Clifton Webb, Tamara Geva, Charles Butterworth, and Patsy Kelly as principals, and a young team, Vilma and Buddy Ebsen, later of "Beverly Hillbillies" fame, doing a captivating eccentric dance, "Flying Colors" went over big. Agnes DeMille did the choreography, her first shot at Broadway, and one of her innovations was the production of a major number "Smoking Reefers," the first time black and white girls were to perform on stage as equals. I should say the first admissible time, because black girls light enough to pass for white had made the Ziegfeld Follies, and white girls bold enough to say they were black had worked the Cotton Club. I was thrilled with Winnie's success, but more than that I relished the occasional times I was invited to go to New York as her part-time escort. At 17 and quite bashful, I was overwhelmed with the beauty of the chorus girls like Jackie Godfrey, who became my secret passion. But Muriel Cooke, who was married to a Wall Street executive on the sly, later to marry Lee Gaines of the Delta Rhythm Boys, Wilhelmina Gray, later to become Tondelayo of Hollywood fame, had their own magnetism for me. It was as if I were permitted to view the inside of a sultan's harem, being backstage and sometimes in the dressing room where the girls casually changed costumes between numbers, revealing curves of thigh, breast and calf with a nonchalance that made it all the more sensual and alluring. I stayed in a constant state of heat. Furthermore, I was permanently spoiled for the less glamorous girls of the neighborhood. After "Flying Colors" closed, Winnie was hired for the Cotton Club chorus. . . .

Elida Webb informed us there was an apartment available next door to the Cotton Club at 646 Lenox Avenue—the club was at 642. We joked about the location, saying "They want to make sure Winnie gets to work on time!" In fact, we could hear the band playing the dance music before the show started— and during these first days at our new home the band was Cab Calloway's. It was the "Minnie the Moocher" show. Cab had a stentorian voice. We could hear him singing "Hi-de-hi-de-hi-de-ho!" as if he were in the next room. It was a constant thrill to us being right on top of the most famous night club in the world. Cab also could sing a ballad like no one else I had ever heard. When Cab was addressing a ballad, I felt as though it was the real Cab without the ridiculous tom-foolery that he put on for the white folks. His voice took on a different timbre. My special favorites were his versions of Harold Arlen's "World On A String" and "That's What I Hate About Love." Benny Paine, the pianist, often accompanied Cab in duets on some of the ballads, and they were a royal treat in close harmony.

During this period I received a postgraduate course in the complexities of class relationships in American society—with the Cotton Club as the laboratory. The owners of the club were mobsters who had grown wealthy on prohibition. They represented a band of the most vicious thugs and racketeers that has ever been produced in New York. Until he was killed in 1928, Arnold Rothstein, a bona fide gambler whose biggest achievement was the rigging of the 1919 World Series, was a major figure in the Cotton Club management. . . .

The arrogance of the mob toward society in general was exponentially multiplied when it was mixed with white racist attitudes toward the performers. They had no respect for women in the show, except in the few instances where family members escorted chorines back and forth to work. Apparently among the denizens of the underworld, there was a kind of respect for the *family* as an institution. Usually, the mobsters or their visiting friends from out of town, would point out a chorine, as if at a slave market for after-the-show drinks or hijinks.

At the club, the bosses had red velvet curtains that could be drawn, and when that happened, we knew that the party was going to be no-holds-barred. Lena Horne's stepfather, a Cuban refugee who had been chased into exile by the Batista regime for his radical political activities in Havana, once took issue when the mobsters refused to raise Lena's pay. He was beaten unmercifully, further contributing to the ubiquitous atmosphere of iron fist in a velvet glove dictatorship that pertained at the club. Ironically, Lena's stepfather had escaped the brutality of Batista, only to encounter it indirectly through the mob, which had a tacit alliance with the Cuban tyrant who had made Havana "the whore-house of the Western Hemisphere."

Despite a seemingly uninspiring setting, Duke Ellington's creativity thrived. Other artists had made the most of less than ideal circumstances, creating masterpieces—Van Gogh (Absinthe Drinkers), Toulouse Lautrec (Moulin Rouge), Picasso (Guernica), and Gorky (Lower Depths). In a similar mode, African-American artists extracted vitality, emotional strength, and universal truths from the material conditions of life in the ghetto, and the myriad ways in which they dealt with their oppression. The relationship was often vividly expressed in Ellington's music at the club. The sensitivity, lyricism and beauty of the maestro's sound when the band was "growling" made it clear that the jungle did not necessarily have to be African. Harlem was one of the feeding grounds for the mob—and the mob was only an illegitimate shadow of the larger predators who exploited the community.

The savages were not the stereotyped blacks in loincloths with bones through their noses, as depicted in the Tarzan movies from the back lots of Hollywood. For us, they were the upper class elites who sought vicarious "kicks" out of hobnobbing with their underworld counterparts, while projecting their libidinous urges on the black performers. The mob controlled most of the entertainment in Harlem and the rest of New York, except for a few night spots. These black entrepreneurs did not have the capital to invest in the kind of spectacular shows mounted at the Cotton Club, but after the performers finished their chores for the white audiences, they still had enough spirit and energy to put on dazzling, impromptu shows at the black-owned spots for black audiences.

Most of these clubs began their activities at two or three in the morning when the white-owned clubs were through with the black entertainers. Among the more notable ones were Jeff Blount's Lenox Club, Happy Rhones' Radium Club, the 101 Ranch on 138th Street (named after the famous New Orleans club) with its bizarre transvestite and homosexual chorus line, and Pod's and Jerry's or, more formally, The Patagonia on 133rd Street, where Billie Holiday furthered her fledgling career as a vocalist after her dance act flopped. After the repeal of Prohibition in 1933, the club was renamed The Log Cabin.

One of the most popular after-hours clubs was Dickey Wells's Shim-Sham Club, which also catered to white customers. Today, in keeping with the parlance of the recording industry, the Shim-Sham would be called a crossover club. The Shim-Sham or Shimmy was a dance invented by homosexuals from the chorus line at the 101 Ranch. "Shim" was a contraction of the term *she-him*, and the "sham" was a word serving the dual purpose of denoting the female role played by males, as well as the shambling nature of the steps, particularly the first eight bars. The Shimmy combined a hip and shoulder wiggle that was part of the opening movements.

Dickey Wells was a former Cotton Club dancer who later became a pimp and entrepreneur. He ran his club as economically as possible, employing a "jug" band called the Shim-Shammers or Kenny Watts and his Kilowatts, instead of regular musicians. Watts played the piano, Eddie Dougherty drums, Fletch Jahon, Eddie "Hawk" Johnson, Heywood Jackson, and Milton Lane played kazoos, with Carol Walrond, the brother of Harlem Renaissance poet and author, Eric Walrond, on bass. The sound they created was somewhere between Red McKenzie's Mound City Blue Blowers and Duke Ellington, if you can imagine that. Fletch and Sammy Page did vocals and whistled, and the group was fronted by an extraordinary "hoofer" whose percussive rhythms afforded an unusually inspirational jazz motif. His name was Baby Lawrence, a master of technique, rhythmic flow, and continuous innovation. Later, during the bebop phase he was recognized as the preeminent jazz hoofer.

"Virgie" was also a stellar attraction, doing a fast, "dirty" song like "I Want to Be Your Yale Man," followed by an exceedingly sensuous "shake" dance during which she would simulate copulation with folded dollar bills stuck out by customers on the edge of the tables. Her act climaxed—no pun intended—with a vigorous snatching of the bill with her genitals. When really challenged Virgie was reputed to be able to pick up a dime with her labia. Despite many visits to Dickie's, I never saw that degree of expertise exhibited.

Breakfast dances were held all over Harlem in the thirties, and Small's Paradise was the epitome. Next to being in the show at the Cotton Club, Small's paradise Breakfast Dance was the most exciting thing that happened to me. Later, the legendary joint would be purchased by basketball great Wilt Chamberlain, and whimsically renamed "Big Wilt's Small's." At Small's, the breakfast dance started at 4 a.m. Monday and continued until noon or 1 p.m. Hardly an entertainer, musician, sportsman, gambler, prostitute or pimp functioning in Harlem missed the breakfast dance—it was the crossroads of Harlem's vibrant nightlife. Yet, it connected with the everyday life as well, because the entertainment, gambling, and tourism industry in Harlem in the thirties employed more people in the various services and related businesses than any other trade in the community. Otherwise, the gainfully employed worked outside Harlem—domestic work was available in the "slave markets" of the Bronx and Brooklyn for the women, while black men had to rely on hard, unskilled labor, when it was available. Oddly, Blumstein's, the leading department store on 125th Street, did not employ African Americans. It was only after Reverend Adam Clayton Powell, Jr. formed the Coordinating Committee for Employment that Jim Crow was beaten down at Blumstein's. The Hotel Theresa, standing like a twelve story monument to racism at the corner of 125th Street and Seventh Avenue, did not admit black guests until after the second World War. . . .

ZORA NEALE HURSTON

From Dust Tracks on a Road

❧

CALIFORNIA, 1929

WHILE I WAS IN THE RESEARCH FIELD in 1929, the idea of "Jonah's Gourd Vine" came to me. I had written a few short stories, but the idea of attempting a book seemed so big, that I gazed at it in the quiet of the night, but hid it away from even myself in daylight.

For one thing, it seemed off-key. What I wanted to tell was a story about a man, and from what I had read and heard, Negroes were supposed to write about the Race Problem. I was and am thoroughly sick of the subject. My interest lies in what makes a man or a woman do such-and-so, regardless of his color. It seemed to me that the human beings I met reacted pretty much the same to the same stimuli. Different idioms, yes. Circumstances and conditions having power to influence, yes. Inherent difference, no. But I said to myself that that was not what was expected of me, so I was afraid to tell a story the way I wanted, or rather the way the story told itself to me. So I went on that way for three years. . . .

In May, 1932, the depression did away with money for research so far as I was concerned. So I took my nerve in my hand and decided to try to write the story I had been carrying around in me. Back in my native village, I wrote first "Mules and Men." That is, I edited the huge mass of material I had, arranged it in some sequence and laid it aside. It was published after my first novel. Mr. Robert Wunsch and Dr. John Rice were both on the faculty at Rollins College, at Winter Park, which is three miles from Eatonville. Dr. Edwin Osgood Grover, Dr. Hamilton Holt, President of Rollins, together with Rice and Wunsch, were interested in me. I gave three folk concerts at the college under their urging.

Then I wrote a short story, "The Gilded Six-Bits," which Bob Wunsch read to his class in creative writing before he sent it off to *Story Magazine*. Thus I came to know Martha Foley and her husband, Whit Burnett, the editors of *Story*. They bought the story and it was published in the August issue, 1933. They never told me, but it is my belief that they did some missionary work among publishers in my behalf, because four publishers wrote me and asked if I had anything of book-length. One of the editors of the J. B. Lippincott Company, was among these. He wrote a gentle-like letter and so I was not afraid of him. Exposing my efforts did not seem so rash to me after reading his letter. I wrote him and said that I was writing a book. Mind you, not the first word was on paper when I wrote him that letter. But the very next week I moved up to Sanford where I was not so much at home as at Eatonville, and could concentrate more and sat down to write "Jonah's Gourd Vine."

I rented a house with a bed and stove in it for $1.50 a week. I paid two weeks and then my money ran out. My cousin, Willie Lee Hurston, was working and making $3.50 per week, and she always gave me the fifty cents to buy groceries with. In about three months, I finished the book. The problem of getting it typed was then upon me. Municipal Judge S. A. B. Wilkinson asked his secretary, Mildred Knight, if she would not do it for me and wait on the money. I explained to her that the book might not even be taken by Lippincott. I had been working on a hope. She took the manuscript home with her and read it. Then she offered to type it for me. She said, "It is going to be accepted, all right. I'll type it. Even if the first publisher does not take it, somebody will." So between them, they bought the paper and carbon and the book was typed.

I took it down to the American Express office to mail it and found that it cost $1.83 cents to mail, and I did not have it. So I went to see Mrs. John Leonardi, a most capable woman lawyer, and wife of the County Prosecutor. She did not have the money at the moment, but she was the treasurer of the local Daughter Elks. She "borrowed" $2.00 from the treasury and gave it to me to mail my book. That was on October 3, 1933. On October 16th, I had an acceptance by wire.

But it did not come so simply as that. I had been hired by the Seminole County Chamber of Commerce to entertain the business district of Sanford with my concert group for that day. I was very glad to get the work, because my landlord was pressing me for the back rent. I now owed $18. I was to receive $25 for the day, so I saw my way clear to pay up my rent, and have a little over. It was not to be that way, however. At eight o'clock of October 16th, my landlady came and told me to get out. I told her that I could pay her that day, but she said she didn't believe that I would ever have that much money. No, she preferred the house. So I took

my card table and my clothes up to my Uncle Isaiah's house and went off
to entertain the city at eleven o'clock. The sound truck went up and down
the streets and my boys sang. That afternoon while I was still on the sound
truck, a Western Union messenger handed me a wire. Naturally I did not
open it there. We were through at three o'clock. The Chamber of Commerce not only paid us, we were all given an order which we could take to
any store we wanted and get what we chose. I needed shoes, so I took
mine to a shoe store. My heart was weighing as much as cord-wood, and
so I forgot the wire until I was having the shoes fitted. When I opened it
and read that "Jonah's Gourd Vine" was accepted and that Lippincott was
offering me $200 advance, I tore out of that place with one old shoe and
one new one on and ran to the Western Union office. Lippincott had asked
for an answer by wire and they got it! Terms accepted. I never expect to
have a greater thrill than that wire gave me. You know the feeling when
you found your first pubic hair. Greater than that. When Producer Arthur
Hornblow took me to lunch at Lucey's and hired me at Paramount, it was
nice—very nice. I was most elated. But I had had five books accepted then,
been a Guggenheim Fellow twice, spoken at three book fairs with all the
literary greats of America and some from abroad, and so I was a little more
used to things. So you see why that editor is *Colonel* to me. When the Negroes in the South name a white man a colonel, it means CLASS. Something like a monarch, only bigger and better. And when the colored
population in the South confer a title, the white people recognize it because
the Negroes are never wrong. They may flatter an ordinary bossman by
calling him "Cap'n" but when they say "Colonel," "General" and "Governor" they are recognizing something internal. It is there, and it is accepted because it can be seen.

I wrote "Their Eyes Were Watching God" in Haiti. It was dammed up
in me, and I wrote it under internal pressure in seven weeks. I wish that I
could write it again. In fact, I regret all of my books. It is one of the trag-
edies of life that one cannot have all the wisdom one is ever to possess in
the beginning. Perhaps, it is just as well to be rash and foolish for a while.
If writers were too wise, perhaps no books would be written at all. It
might be better to ask yourself "Why?" afterwards than before. Anyway,
the force from somewhere in Space which commands you to write in the
first place, gives you no choice. You take up the pen when you are told,
and write what is commanded. There is no agony like bearing an untold
story inside you. You have all heard of the Spartan youth with the fox under his cloak.

"Dust Tracks on a Road" is being written in California where I did not
expect to be at this time.

I did not come out here to California to write about the state. I did not come to get into the movies. I came because my good friend, Katharane Edson Mershon, invited me out here to rest and have a good time. However, I have written a book here, and gone to work in the movies. This surprises me because I did not think that I would live long enough to do anything out here but die. . . .

PAULÍ MURRAY

From *Pauli Murray: The Autobiography of a*
Black Activist, Feminist, Lawyer, Priest, & Poet

NEW YORK AND CALIFORNIA, 1929

WHEN I BEGAN MY SOPHOMORE YEAR IN September
. . . 1929 at the Thirty-second Street Annex of Hunter College, I was
working after school on West Forty-sixth Street as a dinner waitress in one of
the Alice Foote MacDougall restaurants. They were famous for their colorful
Italian or Spanish decor, their coffee, and their broiled half chicken or filet
mignon dinners. We worked a five-hour shift six nights a week for a weekly
wage of four dollars exclusive of tips. Except for its executives and its hostesses
and cashiers, the chain was entirely staffed by Negroes, and like other downtown restaurants in those days it drew the color line. Once when a Negro
couple was refused service the entire kitchen crew and waitress staff walked
out in a spontaneous protest, but the policy did not change. The color line
extended to our own meals. White hostesses and cashiers were served in the
dining room from the regular menu; we ate on bare tables in the basement and
were given leftovers so tasteless we invariably threw them into the garbage can.
If we ate at all on the job, it was because of our skill in ordering an extra
chicken dinner and stealing it from the tray between kitchen and dining room
without getting caught. . . .

. . . By the end of my sophomore year I had lost fifteen pounds and was
suffering from malnutrition, and things continued to grow worse. That fall I
was laid off from the restaurant and had to stop school to look for work. With
so many thousands of people unemployed in New York City alone, finding a job
that would even cover bare living expenses was almost impossible. Downtown
along Sixth Avenue (now the Avenue of the Americas), storefront employment
offices were besieged by hundreds of men scrambling for a half-dozen jobs

posted in hastily scrawled handwriting on a bulletin board out front, only to be erased seconds later. Seldom were any jobs posted for women. For a short time I worked as a typist for fifty cents an hour at the headquarters of the Congregational and Christian Churches, but this source of income soon dried up. Although I had no experience in household work, I was so desperate I tried a position as part-time housekeeper for a professional woman who lived in a studio apartment in Greenwich Village. My major responsibility was to prepare and serve her dinner, for which she supplied the menu. After she tasted my first meal, she paid me for the day and let me go.

Until that fall I had given no thought to marriage. Then I met Billy, a young man who was also a stranger in New York trying to work and go to school. He earned a pittance as caretaker of a women's residence and slept in the basement where he worked. We were drawn together by our mutual loneliness and rootlessness, sharing whatever small pleasures we could find that did not cost money. When matters began to get serious and my straitlaced upbringing was a barrier to premarital sex, we got married secretly, fearing I would lose my room at the Y if our marriage became known. We were both twenty at the time, and Billy lied about his age in order to get the marriage license, saying he was twenty-four.

It was a dreadful mistake. We were so poor that we spent our honeymoon weekend in a cheap West Side hotel. Both of us were sexually inexperienced, and the bleak atmosphere aggravated our discomfiture. We had no money to begin housekeeping and no place where we could meet in privacy. After several months of mounting frustration, we gave up in despair. Billy left the city, and some years later we had the marriage annulled.

Around that time a job suddenly materialized in a downtown office through a peculiar circumstance. The Y employment bureau received a telephone call from The Open Road, Inc., a travel agency at 11 West Forty-second Street. The agency would like to hire "an intelligent colored girl" as switchboard operator and stenographer, but wanted to hear her voice over the telephone before interviewing her. The salary was twenty dollars a week, five dollars more than I had ever earned. The agency was apparently satisfied with my telephone voice and employed me without interviewing anyone else. Such hiring was unique in the early thirties; clerical jobs for Negro women in downtown white business firms were virtually nonexistent.

The experiment lasted only a few months. In an economy move, The Open Road merged with World Tourist Agency, a group that arranged tours to the Soviet Union, and when the merger was completed I was out of work again. Those few months on my employment record were sufficient, however, to create difficulties for me years later in a federal security clearance check. Although I knew almost nothing about the agency beyond answering the telephone and taking occasional correspondence, the FBI apparently suspected it of

Communist leanings and raised insinuating questions about my association with it.

Losing the job at The Open Road was the last straw in a series of disappointments. My goal to save money and return to school seemed further away than ever. I needed a change of luck and began thinking of hitchhiking to California to make a fresh start. Since I had already done some hitchhiking in New England with a friend, Dorothy Hayden, the potential dangers of traveling alone across the continent did not occur to me.

Fortunately, I got to California that spring without having to hitchhike. A friend of Dorothy Hayden's who had driven to New York was returning home to Vallejo and was glad to take me along to help with the driving. Leaving my few belongings in Dorothy's care, I started out blithely with only a few dollars and no idea what I would do when I reached the Coast. We crossed the country on U.S. Route 30, and although the trip was recklessly conceived, my discovery of the changing face of the vast United States soon dwarfed the troubles I had left behind. Each hour was filled with wonderment over the miles of flatland with their oceans of waving green wheat, the breathtaking mountain passes in the Rockies, the thousands of sheep clogging the highway in Utah as herdsmen drove them to their spring feeding grounds, and the silence of the Great Salt Lake Desert. Before we reached California I had scribbled what became my first published poem, "Song of the Highway."

The attempt to begin a new life in California did not survive my arrival in Vallejo, where I was to stay a few days with my friend's family. A letter from Aunt Pauline, forwarded from New York, was waiting for me and brought me back to reality. She had written that she was ill, and since I was not in school she wanted me to come home to Durham as soon as possible. I had not told her of my plan to go to California for fear she would veto it, and now I had to wire her revealing my financial predicament. Aunt Pauline wired back that she had no money for my return fare. It was typical of her to let me take the consequences of my choices even though she was worried almost out of her mind, as she told me later. I realized I would have to extricate myself from this scrape through my own efforts and that cross-country traveling, which at first had seemed a lark, was now an awesome necessity: awesome because the immense expanse of the continent I had seen was no longer an appealing prospect for hitchhiking. As I recalled those long stretches of deserted highway where farms were miles apart and we seldom saw another car, the thought of being stranded alone was unnerving. At best, hitchhiking was unpredictable and I had no idea how long it would take to get back to New York.

My hosts finally suggested that if I had the guts to try it, I could ride fast freights going east and make the trip in about two weeks. Hopping freights was a more terrifying thought than thumbing rides on a lonely road. I had never forgotten a gruesome experience in Durham when I was a sixth grader. We schoolchildren had sneaked into the freight yards and were walking along the tracks looking for lumps of tar to chew, when we came upon a burlap sack covering the decapitated body of a man who had just been killed by a moving train. His brains were strewn along the roadbed.

The urgency of getting home finally overruled my dread, and less than a week after arriving in Vallejo I set out for the Southern Pacific Railroad freight yards in Oakland. I did not know in that spring of 1931 that I was about to join an estimated 200,000 to 300,000 homeless boys—and a smattering of girls— between the ages of twelve and twenty, products of the Depression, who rode freights or hitchhiked from town to town in search of work. Thousands lived in "jungles" near railroad tracks, constituting the "tragic army" which aroused the alarm of the Children's Bureau, U.S. Department of Labor, and created a national problem which eventually led to the establishment of the Civilian Conservation Corps. These young people were part of a larger army of nearly three million homeless unemployed men who also rode the rails and lived in jungles. One railroad official reported that some ten thousand transients per month were traveling through the Southern Pacific freight yards in 1931. In the same year, 831 were killed on the arterial highways and dozens met their deaths under freight trains.

It was well for me that I was ignorant of these conditions and also that my sex was not immediately apparent to the hundreds of rough men and boys I encountered during the trip. I carried a small knapsack containing minimum camping equipment, and my attire—scout pants and shirt, knee-length socks, walking shoes, and a short leather jacket—together with my slight figure and bobbed hair made me appear to be a small teenage boy like thousands of others on the road. No one questioned me about my gender and I soon discovered that my boyish appearance was a protection. Also, a single-mindedness that has often led me to overlook obvious difficulties and make costly mistakes was in this case beneficial. The imperative of getting home made me ignore hazards which upon sober reflection would have forced me to abandon the journey.

Hoboes faced the ever-present risk of being shot by armed railroad guards in the big railroad divisions where the freight trains were assembled. When the long trains pulled out of the yards, we had to choose between two dangers. If we ignored the guards who shouted warnings to stay off the train as they ran along the walkways on top of the cars, we became targets for their bullets. If we waited for them to get off, the train had picked up such speed that we risked being thrown under the wheels trying to swing onto a fast-moving boxcar. Another hazard was the fierce cold of windy nights, which forced us to try to keep warm by riding too close to the engine, in the path of hot cinders that blew back upon us. One night the only shelter from the wind I could find was on a flatcar loaded with bridge timber. I crawled into a crevice covered by long wooden beams and went to sleep. Next morning I discovered that the heavy beams shifted every time the train lurched and this shifting had provided my crevice; a strong enough lurch would have dislodged some of the heaviest beams and crushed me to death.

Crossing the country, I learned to ride cattle trains, fruit-butter-and-egg trains, "hot shots" (fast express freights), and "manifestos" (nonstop express freight trains). When refrigerator cars carried citrus fruit, the narrow ice chests, or "reefers," at each end of the car were left empty. The hobo's haven was an open reefer which could be entered through the small trapdoor at the top of the empty ice chamber. The upraised door was held by a jack, and if one was small enough to wriggle through the opening one could slither down inside the steel-plated cell floored with wooden slats and ride in comfort out of sight of railroad "bulls."

Along with a thin migrant worker called "Oklahoma," I managed to scramble down into one of these empty cells, and we rode across the desert and through the mountains for eighteen hours. We had no food or water with us, but the car was carrying crates of oranges, and our hunger and thirst drove us to explore every inch of our cell for an opening to the fruit. We loosened the slats on the floor of our compartment, worked our fingers underneath the partition and through to the crates on the other side. Oklahoma succeeded in ripping open the end of a crate, I stuck my hand through, and after much scraping and bruising reached the oranges. We collected fifteen apiece, quartered them with our knives, and gobbled them down. When we finished, we covered our theft by wrapping the peelings in the tissue covers and throwing them out the trapdoor over the side of the car. I did not know until later that if the steel jack had collapsed and the trapdoor fallen, we would have been sealed inside. People were known to starve to death in sealed ice chests because no one knew they were there and they could not make themselves heard.

The one time my sex proved to be an advantage was near the end of the trip, two days away from New York. I had caught a train alone, spent the night inside an open reefer, and awakened next morning to find the train standing still. I climbed out, right into the arms of a yard policeman who had taken his position on top of the car I was riding in without knowing I was there. I told him my hard-luck story about getting home, which he seemed to believe. But he did not believe I was female and sent for a woman officer to examine me. When he was finally satisfied, he escorted me back to the reefer and cautioned me to stay hidden until the train reached its termination point in the Jersey City yards.

Incredibly, aside from being banged against the sides of boxcars a few times when hopping onto moving freights, I made the trip without a single unpleasant experience and in only ten days. Later I shuddered when reading news accounts of a girl who had lost her legs under the wheels of a freight and of a man who survived six days in a refrigerator car without food or water and within sight of crates of fruit he could not reach. I learned also that around the same time I was riding freights, nine Negro boys were taken off a freight in Scottsboro, Alabama, and charged with raping two white female hoboes who were riding on the same train. I believed that Aunt Pauline's prayers helped to bring me through safely, just as years later I believed her prayers helped me through my bar examinations.

Twenty-four days after leaving New York, I arrived back at Dorothy Hayden's apartment, so cinder-blackened that I resembled a chimney sweep. It took three successive soakings in a hot bath to get me clean.

NATE SHAW

From *All God's Dangers*

ALABAMA, 1931

A HEAP OF FAMILIES, WHILE I WAS LIVIN on the Tucker place down on Sitimachas, was leavin goin north. Some of my neighbors even picked up and left. The boll weevil was sendin a lot of em out, no doubt. I knowed several men went north, some with their families and some without; they sent for their families when they got to where they was goin. More went besides what I knowed of, from all parts of this southern country. They was dissatisfied with the way of life here in the south—and when I was livin on the Pollard place it come pretty wide open to me and touched the hem of my garment. But my family was prosperin right here, I didn't pay no attention to leavin. I wanted to stay and work for better conditions. I knowed I was in a bad way of life here but I didn't intend to get out—*that* never come in my mind. I thought somehow, some way, I'd overcome it. I was a farmin man at that time and I knowed more about this country than I knowed about the northern states. I've always been man enough to stick up for my family, and love them, and try to support em, and I just thought definitely I could keep it up. In other words, I was determined to try.

And durin of the pressure years, a union begin to operate in this country, called it the Sharecroppers Union—that was a nice name, I thought—and my first knowin about this union, this organization, that riot come off at Crane's Ford in '31. I looked deep in that thing, too—I heard more than I seed and I taken that in consideration. And I knowed what was goin on was a turnabout on the southern man, white and colored; it was somethin unusual. And I heard about it bein a organization for the poor class of people—that's just what I wanted to get into, too; I wanted to know the secrets of it enough that I could become in the knowledge of it. Now I heard talk about trucks comin into this country deliverin guns to the colored people but I decided all that was talk, tryin to accuse the niggers of gettin into somethin here that maybe they weren't—and maybe they were. But didn't no trucks haul no guns to nobody. Colored people hadn't been armed up for nothin; it was told like that just to agitate the thing further. Of course, some of these colored folks in here had some good guns—you know a Winchester rifle is a pretty good gun itself. But they didn't have nothin above that. It weren't nothin that nobody sent in here for em to use, just their own stuff.

Well, they killed a man up there, colored fellow; his name was Adam Cole. And they tell me—I didn't see it but I heard lots about it and I never did hear nothin about it that backed me off—Kurt Beall, the High Sheriff for Tukabahchee County, got shot in the stomach. He run up there to break up this meetin business amongst the colored people and someone in that crowd shot him. That kind of broke him up from runnin in places like that.

And these white folks woke up and stretched themselves and commenced a runnin around meddlin with niggers about this organization. And it's a close thing today. One old man—and he was as big a skunk as ever sneaked in the woods—old man Mac Sloane, come up to me one day—he didn't come to my home, he met me on the outside—old man Mac Sloane come to me hot as a stove iron, "Nate, do you belong to that mess they carryin on in this country?"

I just cut him off short. I didn't belong to it at that time, but I was eager to join and I was aimin to join, just hadn't got the right opportunity.

"No, I don't belong to nothin."

Mac Sloane, white man, said, "You stay out of it. That damn thing will get you killed. You stay out of it. These niggers runnin around here carryin on some kind of meetin—you better stay out of it."

I said to myself, 'You a fool if you think you can keep me from joinin.' I went right on and joined it, just as quick as the next meetin come. Runnin around and givin me orders—he suspected I might be the kind of man to belong to such a organization; put the finger on me before I ever joined. And he done just the thing to push me into it—gived me orders not to join.

The teachers of this organization begin to drive through this country—they couldn't let what they was doin be known. One of em was a colored fella; I disremember his name but he did tell us his name. He wanted us to organize and he was with us a whole lot of time, holdin meetins with us—that was part of his job. We colored farmers would meet and the first thing we had to do was join the organization. And it was said, we didn't want no bad men in it at all, no weak-hearted fellows that would be liable to give the thing away. It was secret with them all that joined it; they knowed to keep their mouths shut and meet the meetins. And this teacher said—don't know where his home was; he had a different way of talkin than we did—"I call em stool pigeons if they broadcast the news about what's happenin.'' And said, if a nigger, like myself, went and let out any secrets to the white folks about the organization, the word was, "Do away with him.''

Had the meetins at our houses or anywhere we could have em where we could keep a look and a watch-out that nobody was comin in on us. Small meetins, sometimes there'd be a dozen, sometimes there'd be more, sometimes there'd be less—niggers was scared, niggers was scared, that's tellin the truth. White folks in this country didn't allow niggers to have no organization, no secret meetins. They kept up with you and watched you, didn't allow you to associate in a crowd, unless it was your family or your church. It just worked in a way that the nigger wasn't allowed to have nothin but church services and, O, they liked to see you goin to church, too. . . .

First thing the organization wanted for the colored people was the privilege to have a organization. That's one of the best things they ever could fight for and get on foot. From my boy days comin along, ever since I been in God's world, I've never had no rights, no voice in nothin that the white man didn't want me to have—even been cut out of education, book learnin, been deprived of that. How could I favor such rulins as have been the past?

The teacher would send out literatures and these literatures would get around in colored folks' boxes and they got so bold they went to puttin em in white folks' boxes. I couldn't definitely say what them literatures said—I aint a readin man—but they said enough that the big white men didn't like it at all. Malcolm Todd, who married my wife's oldest sister, he heard a white man say, "The Lord is bringin down the world, the Lord is bringin down the world.''

Well, it was many conditions that called for such a organization as *that*. Niggers had to get back and get back quick when the white man spoke. Had to be humble and submissive under em. My color needed a protection so long, so long. You couldn't get a nigger to poke his head out in them days for nothin—scared, and—I looked at it from another angle and that was the worst thing that could ever hit my attention. We had too many colored people that if they knowed anything was goin on amongst their own color, any sort of plot at all, they'd turn it in to the white people. No use to try gettin together to do somethin bout the conditions we was livin under because somebody would run and stick his head under the white man's shirttail, and that was that. I call em Uncle Toms. They'll prowl into the niggers' business to get the dope and carry it to the white folks. Uncle Tom's a devil of a man; he's a enemy to his race.

Niggers was scared to run their business together, buy their fertilize together, sell their cotton together, because the white man—the average colored man was workin on the white man's place, and if he weren't on the white man's place he had to cooperate with the white man to get furnished and so on. And the white man held the final rule over the Negro—"Bring the cotton to me." I heard it; it was told to others and it was told to me.

Conditions has been outrageous every way that you can think against the colored race of people. Didn't allow em to do this, didn't allow em to do that, didn't allow em to do the other. Knowin and comin into the knowledge of what was goin on and how it was goin on in the United States as far as I knowed, which was the state of Alabama as far as I knowed, Tukabahchee County—I knew that it was a weak time amongst the colored people. They couldn't demand nothin; they was subject to lose what they had if they demanded any more.

Good God, there wasn't but few privileges that we was allowed. If you was flesh and blood and human and you tended to want to help and support your friends in the community, and make somethin of yourself—white folks didn't allow you that privilege. But we had the privilege of workin for the white man—he who had the chance had better do it; get yourself together and get over yonder in Mr. So-and-so's field or anywhere else he told you and do what he tell you to do. And when pay time come he'd pay you what he wanted to, and in many cases it'd be less than what he'd pay a white man. And some work, like pickin cotton in the fields, white folks didn't fill a basket—most of em. That was niggers' work. And if a poor white man got out there and picked cotton, he was pickin cotton like a nigger. Colored man just been a dog for this country for years and years. White man didn't ask you how you felt about what he wanted to do; he'd just go ahead and do it and you had to fall under his rulins. And bein in his home country, he been allowed to do as he please by the capital of the United States.

HAYWOOD PATTERSON

From *Scottsboro Boy*

ALABAMA, 1931

THE FREIGHT TRAIN LEAVING OUT OF CHATTANOOGA, go-
ing around the mountain curves and hills of Tennessee into Alabama, it
went so slow anyone could get off and back on.

That gave the white boys the idea they could jump off the train and pick up
rocks, carry them back on, and chunk them at us Negro boys.

The trouble began when three or four white boys crossed over the oil
tanker that four of us colored fellows from Chattanooga were in. One of the
white boys, he stepped on my hand and liked to have knocked me off the train.
I didn't say anything then, but the same guy, he brushed by me again and liked
to have pushed me off the car. I caught hold of the side of the tanker to keep
from falling off.

I made a complaint about it and the white boy talked back—mean, serious,
white folks Southern talk.

That is how the Scottsboro case began . . . with a white foot on my
black hand.

"The next time you want by," I said, "just tell me you want by and I let you
by."

"Nigger, I don't ask you when I want by. What you doing on this train
anyway?"

"Look, I just tell you the next time you want by you just tell me you want
by and I let you by."

"Nigger bastard, this a white man's train. You better get off. All you black
bastards better get off!"

I felt we had as much business stealing a ride on this train as those white boys hoboing from one place to another looking for work like us. But it happens in the South most poor whites feel they are better than Negroes and a black man has few rights. It was wrong talk from the white fellow and I felt I should sense it into him and his friends we were human beings with rights too. I didn't want that my companions, Roy and Andy Wright, Eugene Williams and myself, should get off that train for anybody unless it was a fireman or engineer or railroad dick who told us to get off.

"You white sonsofbitches, we got as much right here as you!"

"Why, you goddamn nigger, I think we better just put you off!"

"Okay, you just try. You just try to put us off!"

Three or four white boys, they were facing us four black boys now, and all cussing each other on both sides. But no fighting yet.

The white boys went on up the train further.

We had just come out of a tunnel underneath Lookout Mountain when the argument started. The train, the name of it was the Alabama Great Southern, it was going uphill now, slow. A couple of the white boys, they hopped off, picked up rocks, threw them at us. The stones landed around us and some hit us. Then the white fellows, they hopped back on the train two or three cars below us. We were going toward Stevenson, Alabama, when the rocks came at us. We got very mad.

When the train stopped at Stevenson, I think maybe to get water or fuel, we got out of the car and walked along the tracks. We met up with some other young Negroes from another car. We told them what happened. They agreed to come in with us when the train started again.

Soon as the train started the four of us Chattanooga boys that was in the oil tanker got back in there—and the white boys started throwing more rocks. The other colored guys, they came over the top of the train and met us four guys. We decided we would go and settle with these white boys. We went toward their car to fight it out. There must have been ten or twelve or thirteen of us colored when we came on a gang of six or seven white boys.

I don't argue with people. I show them. And I started to show those white boys. The other colored guys, they pitched in on these rock throwers too. Pretty quick the white boys began to lose in the fist fighting. We outmanned them in hand-to-hand scuffling. Some of them jumped off and some we put off. The train, picking up a little speed, that helped us do the job. A few wanted to put up a fight but they didn't have a chance. We had color anger on our side.

The train was picking up speed and I could see a few Negro boys trying to put off one white guy. I went down by them and told them not to throw this boy off because the train was going too fast. This fellow, his name was Orville Gilley. Me and one of the Wright boys pulled him back up.

After the Gilley boy was back on the train the fight was over. The four of us, Andy and Roy Wright, Eugene Williams and myself, we went back to the tanker and sat the same way we were riding when the train left Chattanooga.

The white fellows got plenty sore at the whupping we gave them. They ran back to Stevenson to complain that they were jumped on and thrown off—and to have us pulled off the train.

The Stevenson depot man, he called up ahead to Paint Rock and told the folks in that little through-road place to turn out in a posse and snatch us off the train.

It was two or three o'clock in the afternoon, Wednesday, March 25, 1931, when we were taken off at Paint Rock. . . .

A mob of white farmers was waiting when the train rolled in. They closed in on the boxcars. Their pistols and shotguns pointed at us. They took everything black off the train. They even threw off some lumps of coal, could be because of its color. Us nine black ones they took off from different cars. Some of these Negroes I had not seen before the fight and a couple I was looking at now for the first time. They were rounding up the whites too, about a half dozen of them. I noticed among them two girls dressed in men's overalls and looking about like the white fellows.

I asked a guy who had hold of me, "What's it all about?"

"Assault and attempt to murder."

I didn't know then there was going to be a different kind of a charge after we got to the Jackson County seat, Scottsboro.

They marched us up a short road. We stopped in front of a little general store and post office. They took our names. They roped us up, all us Negroes together. The rope stretched from one to another of us. The white folks, they looked mighty serious. Everybody had guns. The guy who ran the store spoke up for us:

"Don't let those boys go to jail. Don't anybody harm them."

But that passed quick, because we were being put into trucks. I kind of remember this man's face, him moving around there in the storm of mad white folks, talking for us. There are some good white people down South but you don't find them very fast, them that will get up in arms for a Negro. If they come up for a Negro accused of something, the white people go against him and his business goes bad.

After we were shoved into the truck I saw for the first time all us to become known as "The Scottsboro Boys." There were nine of us. Some had not even been in the fight on the train. A few in the fight got away so the posse never picked them up.

There were the four from Chattanooga, Roy Wright, about fourteen; his brother, Andy Wright, nineteen; Eugene Williams, who was only thirteen; and myself. I was eighteen. I knew the Wright boys very well. I had spent many nights at their home and Mrs. Wright treated me as if I were her own son. The other five boys, they were Olen Montgomery, he was half blind; Willie Roberson, he was so sick with the venereal he could barely move around; a fellow from Atlanta named Clarence Norris, nineteen years old; Charlie Weems, the oldest one among us, he was twenty; and a fourteen-year-old boy from Georgia, Ozie Powell. I was one of the tallest, but Norris was taller than me.

All nine of us were riding the freight for the same reason, to go somewhere and find work. It was 1931. Depression was all over the country. Our families were hard pushed. The only ones here I knew were the other three from Chattanooga. Our fathers couldn't hardly support us, and we wanted to help out, or at least put food in our own bellies by ourselves. We were freight-hiking to Memphis when the fight happened.

Looking over this crowd, I figured that the white boys got sore at the whupping we gave them, and were out to make us see it the bad way.

We got to Scottsboro in a half hour. Right away we were huddled into a cage, all of us together. It was a little two-story jimcrow jail. There were flat bars, checkerboard style, around the windows, and a little hallway outside our cell.

We got panicky and some of the kids cried. The deputies were rough. They kept coming in and out of our cells. They kept asking questions, kept pushing us and shoving, trying to make us talk. Kept cussing, saying we tried to kill off the white boys on the train. Stomped and raved at us and flashed their guns and badges.

We could look out the window and see a mob of folks gathering. They were excited and noisy. We were hot and sweaty, all of us, and pretty scared. I laughed at a couple of the guys who were crying. I didn't feel like crying. I couldn't figure what exactly, but didn't have no weak feeling.

After a while a guy walked into our cell, with him a couple of young women.

"Do you know these girls?"

They were the two gals dressed like men rounded up at Paint Rock along with the rest of us brought off the train. We had seen them being hauled in. They looked like the others, like the white hobo fellows, to me. I paid them no mind. I didn't know them. None of us from Chattanooga, the Wrights, Williams, and myself, ever saw them before Paint Rock. Far as I knew none of the nine of us pulled off different gondolas and tankers ever saw them.

"No," everybody said.

"No," I said.

"No? You damn-liar niggers! You raped these girls!" . . .

JAMES CAMERON

From *A Time of Terror*

❧

MARION, INDIANA, 1930S

I COULD HEAR THE MOB TRAMPING UP THE jail stairs. In another moment, they would be at the door of my cell block. They would open the door, walk inside, and all hell would break out. Time was running out for me. Outside the door, the corridor was fast becoming jammed with violent men, ruthless men, black-people-hating white men. The leaders held back until they quieted down. The men carried ropes, shotguns, knives, clubs, swords, and rifles. One of the men held a submachine gun in the cradle of his arm. He acted like he knew how to use it. He was a big, burly, bushy-haired man with coldlooking gray eyes, glassy-looking, like he was high on some kind of a "fix." It was frightening to look at him.

The men gathered around the door of my cellblock. They were the elite group of black intimidators. Their act now was to complete the path of destruction, death, and tyranny. While they were deciding on the kill, I closed my eyes for a moment to will my disappearance. I opened them again when I heard the eerie jangling of keys on the key ring. I was still in the cell block. There was no time to hide. There was no place to hide. Events happened so fast there was not even time to pray.

At the sight of the mobsters, the black prisoners began jumping around, apparently searching for cover in their miserable mental agony. Even the white prisoners were nervous. All of them were just plain scared.

I was standing in a corner with seven or eight other black prisoners. Big John was among them. Somehow, I felt a small measure of security with them so near. I believed with all my heart, perhaps, because I wanted to believe it, that they would have fought the mob to their deaths had they anything with which to fight.

The man with the submachine gun entered the cell block first. Oddly, a young white girl, very pretty, still in her teens, followed closely behind. Her eyes were wide, like a frightened and startled doe. They seemed to me to be full of question marks and uncertainty. While the machine gunner held us inmates in our tracks, several other men dressed in the deadgear of the Ku Klux Klan flooded the cell block with the others. The corridor inside the cell block was jammed tight with mobsters. They stood around awhile peering at the cowering knot of prisoners.

Sheriff Campbell shouldered his way through the crowd. One of his pearl-handled revolvers dangled limply from his right hand. He was breathing hard and perspiring profusely. He paused, uncertain of his next move. There was a harried look about him.

Meanwhile, two men with drawn pistols had separated me and Charles, the other sixteen year old, from the rest of the prisoners.

"What's your name?" Charles was asked.

"Charles Haynes," he answered, shakily.

"Mine's Henry Burton," I lied to them.

Sheriff Campbell made his way over to the small group surrounding me and Charles.

"Come on," he said to the men, impatiently. "Let's get out of here! These are nothing but boys. Cameron isn't in here, anyway. You've already hung two of them. That should satisfy you!"

Then he turned around and walked out of the cell block.

The mob leaders shuffled about restlessly. They paced up and down in the cell block, pondering their next move. Every reference they made to me was preface with an angry epithet:

"That black-assed son-of-a-bitch! He thinks he's a smart nigger! We'll find him."

Reluctantly, they withdrew from the cell block and returned to the gay crowd down in the streets. I began to hope for the first time. Now I had time to say a few prayers. I prayed for deliverance.

One of the first mobsters to reach the street called out to the crowd:

"Cameron ain't in there!"

"That's a damn lie," came the angry response from the crowd. "He's in there and we aim to get him! We want him!"

The whole multitude seemed to yell its approval. They stomped their feet, they began chanting, the way crowds do at a football game for their favorite action hero-star:

"We want Cameron!"

"We want Cameron!"

"We want Cameron!"

I thought I would die during that chant. To think they wanted me that bad! I could have sworn my heart stopped beating with every chant. Again, I prayed wondering if any kind of prayer would do any good. I wondered if Abe and Tommy believed in prayers and had they prayed to God, too, before their deaths.

The noise being made in the streets by the crowd made it clearly understood that they were not going to accept anything less than the three of us. Repeated shouts, chants, demanding that I be dragged out of the jail, fell upon the ears of the leaders of the mob. I was the one person they wanted more than anything else in the world.

The ring leaders huddled together and talked briefly among themselves. Then they turned and reentered the jail. The crowd thundered its approval. A point had been made. The cheers were wild in enthusiasm.

I was it again!

The mobsters marched back upstairs to my cell block. Again, the machine gunner led the way inside. No one dared to breathe.

Inside the cell block, the machine gunner barked in a deadly tone:

"Aw right, all you niggers get over to this side of the cell block."

He pointed with the barrel of his infernal gun just where he meant for us blacks to assemble and line up.

We moved slowly, painfully, and formed a ragged, nervous, broken line along the north wall of the cellblock. I tried to hold back the tears. They kept rolling down my cheeks. My own whimperings, though, were soon lost in a jungle of pitiful bleats from the black prisoners all around me. The mob might take one of them—or all of them. Who was there to stop them? Who was going to stop them? Law and order for the black man was a national farce, a complete mockery. It had always been so. The black man was not an equal. The mob made its own law and order.

"James Cameron is in here and we mean to git him! NOW, where in the hell is he?" members of the mob wanted to know.

An old black man in tattered plaid shirt and baggy pants dropped to his knees. He held out his hands in supplication, as if in prayer to God:

"Please, Mister White Folks," he sobbed, "Dat boy ain't in heah. Honest he ain't."

They didn't believe him. One of the mobsters kicked the old in the face. The toe of the man's shoe went into the old man's mouth, knocking him back against the steel bars of the cells. The old man spit out seven or eight bloody, rotten teeth. His face immediately took on a frightening swelling that resembled some grotesque mask used by makeup men in some way-out horror movie.

"Don't you black-assed sons-of-bitches lie to us," one of the leaders shouted at the rest of the black men. "If you don't tell us who he is, we'll hang every god damn nigger in this jail!"

I waited, afraid to move a muscle. Now the chips were really down. Now was the time for me to present myself as a living sacrifice. But nobody in the line moved. Heavy, labored breathing was the only sound. Impulsively, I acted like I was going to give myself up when Big John and another black man grabbed hold of me. I got the message.

And outside, the crowd had become very impatient. They took up their chant again:

"We want Cameron!"

"We want Cameron!"

"We want Cameron!"

Tension was racing to a climax. Human endurance was fast approaching its capacity. Seven or eight of the black men glared their defiance at the mobsters. They had become too angry to remember their own fear. But they were helpless and powerless to fight. They stood with me.

One of the mobsters stepped forward and smacked one of the defiant ones across the mouth with his fist, knocking the man to his knees. Then, all but the prisoners standing with me, broke ranks and fell down on their hands and knees. They crawled and groveled to members of the mob nearest them, like dogs to their masters. They made obeisance to representatives of the god of white supremacy. They hugged the mobsters knees, kissed their hands, and begged them to spare their lives. Several of the men began to bawl like little children lost in a frightened world. They begged with tongues thickened with fear. Tears rolled down their faces and into their gaping mouths.

"Lawdy, Mister Bossman, we ain't done nuttin. We's jist a bunch ob pooh ol' niggers in heah fer train riding!"

"Lawd, ham mercy!"

"Please, please, don't hurt us, Mister White Folks!"

It was sickening and unbelievable sight. I am sure I would not have believed it had it been something told to me. But I saw the scene. I heard the words. I felt all the anguish and anxiety. But, at the same time, I knew in my heart I would have never acted like that as the price of my life. I would much rather be dead as a man than alive as a whimpering coward.

One of the black prisoners standing nearby, sprayed one of the groveling prisoners with vomit. The latter ignored it and kept right on begging for mercy. The standee kept right on puking.

"Lawd, ham mercy!"

"Tell us where Cameron is or we are going to hang every god-damn one of you niggers!" the mobsters repeated.

Still nobody pointed me out. The crawlers renewed their sobs and their pleas with increased fervor:

"Please, don't hang us, Mister White Folks!"

"Aw right," a man with a shotgun called out. "Let's take all of these black bastards out and string up every god-damn one of them!"

"No! No! No!" It was Charlie's father speaking. "Please! Please! Please!"

He hugged the shotgun man's knees and tried to kiss his hands, to caress him, to plead with him. A huge fist crashed down on the old man's head, knocking him flat on the floor.

"God dammit, nigger. Tell us where Cameron is! This if your last chance, you damn fool!" the mobster shouted at the prisoner in a fit of anger.

The old man was a pitiful sight, as were the seventeen or eighteen other black men down on their hands and knees, crawling around like a bunch of trained animals. Above their weeping and wailing and pleadings, sounded the hysterical guffaws of the members of the mob. Most of them had doubled over with laughter as tears of complete enjoyment ran out of their eyes. To them, this was a sight that every white person in the world should be able to see. What a spectacle!

Still whimpering and pleading, Charlie's father looked up at the mobsters around him. He looked at his son standing near me. He was a completely broken man in mind, body and spirit. He lowered his head for a moment, as if in prayer. Then, slowly, painfully, it seemed, he turned eyes full of fear, and anguish, and surrender to the corner where I stood. His voice quavered. His whole body shook with the emotion of naked fear. Uncontrolled tears ran down from his bruised and bloodshot eyes. The index finger on his gnarled hand was unsteady, shaking like a leaf in the wind, as he pointed to me!

"Dere he is!" he said, finally, and slumped to the floor.

The other black men down on the floor on their hands and knees, now that the ice had been broken, sobbed out their agreement:

"Dat's him, Mister White Folks! Dat's him! It ain't none ob us! Dat's him!" All of them seemed to babbling at once.

For a brief second no one moved. But every eye was on me. Then the mob came close and took me. The nightmare I had often heard happened to other helpless victims now became my reality. Brutally and dehumanizingly faced with death, I understood what it meant to be a black man in America. With the noose around my neck and death in my brains, I waited for the end. . . .

ADAM CLAYTON POWELL, JR.

From *Adam by Adam*

❧

HARLEM, 1930S

. . . D URING THE EARLY 1930S THERE WAS NO Department of Public Welfare in the City of New York. Not a single agency of any type—city or state—even indirectly, much less directly, existed or had been set up to cope with the problem of the Depression. Then financiers Seward Prosser and Harvey Gibson organized a citizens' committee. These deans of industry and finance had been impressed by my control of the masses in the Harlem Hospital fight, and in the spring of 1932 they called me to meet with them in the board room of one of the important banking houses of Wall Street. I was not yet twenty-four.

The room where we met breathed opulence and understated elegance. The portraits of men who had made America and who had in turn become legends looked down upon us. After we had been seated, Prosser and Gibson asked me what I thought they should do to relieve the suffering in Harlem. "Get together all the available money you can for Harlem," I told them. "We will not give one penny of it away but will make people work for the money. Even if I have to put them in one spot and have them scrub that same spot all day long, they will work for the money."

They believed in my proposal and we set up the committee headquarters in the Abyssinian Baptist Church. It was the first relief program, private or otherwise, in New York City. Every Saturday an armored truck would arrive and give me $2000, sometimes $3000, in cash. I had from one hundred and fifty to two hundred men and women working. They were scrubbing, painting, and conducting adult education classes. No one loafed. But it was not enough to meet the need. Even though men who had gone to college jumped in and gave their time and formed the first staff, it was still not enough. Thousands would line up every day, asking for just "something" to do for a few dollars.

My father gave me a $1000 gift and we set up a free food kitchen in the gymnasium of the church. It was staffed by volunteer workers, led by Albert Jordan who years before had been the maintenance superintendent of the Knickerbocker Theatre. With contributions from meat markets and grocery stores, we were able to feed a thousand people a day. I was reminded of an incident during my childhood, when one day a panhandler came by to ask for a handout. Mother had no money but gave him a hot loaf of freshly baked bread she made every Saturday morning. He threw it into our trash can as he walked away cursing us. But in 1932 men and women, black and white, a thousand a day, stood in line for a slice of bread and a bowl of soup.

I learned something in those days that I will never forget: there is such a thing as gratitude. People have often said to me through the years, "Why do you work so hard for the masses? The masses are never grateful for what you do. When you need them, they will forget what you have done."

This is totally untrue. The bread that we literally cast upon the waters in 1932 returned, and every man and woman to whom I was able to give even a small sum on Saturdays, and every man and woman who was able to get a little something to eat each day, has remembered—to this day.

For every one person I helped over the years, a score rose up to stand by me. The sons and daughters of the parents we helped in the 1930s have gone on to high places, but they have been taught the story of what happened back in those days, when all their parents wanted was someone who cared . . . and I did care. And there is a reward when one gives of oneself wholeheartedly and without stint. Deep within there comes an inner glow that nothing can purchase and no one can steal.

The Great Depression continued to increase in intensity. People were being evicted by the thousands in the dead of winter with snow on the ground. Morning after morning the curbstones of Harlem were lined with the miserable, battered, broken remnants of what was called furniture. What could I do? What should I do? An average of a hundred and fifty people a day would stand in line in my office with eviction notices. My heart was sick from the suffering of these people.

By this time the city had set up its first Department of Public Welfare, but it was ill equipped and poorly staffed. Public relief was a new thing, and even though we sent delegations to the relief bureau to demand money to cover rents for those in need, it was unobtainable. Dr. W. Adrian Freeman, brilliant Western Reserve University traumatic surgeon and member of the Abyssinian Baptist Church, who maintained his offices adjacent to the community center, suggested a new idea to me: "Why not organize a rent strike?"

I then developed the following technique. I would walk the streets looking for an evicted family, and when I found one, I immediately sent a protest committee to the owner of the building, saying "Put that family back in their home or we will have every family in the building refuse to pay their rent."

No one paid any attention to our threats, so we carefully organized our first house. When we had finished organizing the building, all the tenants in the house went on a rent strike. A treasury was set up into which they paid their rent as it became due. The landlord dared not evict the entire house because the expenses to the City Marshal, the loss of rent, and the cost of painting and fixing required for new tenants would have been prohibitive. Before long the landlord gave in. So we moved our first family back into the very apartment from which it had been evicted. The rent strike idea spread and Donnellan Phillips, one of my co-workers, organized the Consolidated Tenants League. The day of the avaricious landlord had started to come to a close.

On March 19, 1937, Harlem burst into flames of riot. The winds of the ghetto had fanned resentment and an igniting spark was all that was needed. On that afternoon the rumor spread that a Puerto Rican boy, allegedly caught stealing in Kress's five-and-ten-cent store located on Harlem's major thorough-fare, West 125th Street, had been beaten by the store manager. Mobs poured into the streets. Groups collected that ranged from three to ten thousand persons each. The first race riot started by Negroes in the history of America was under way. It lasted for only one night, but when it was over there were dead and wounded and property losses worth millions of dollars. The damage to plate glass alone amounted to $200,000.

Why? Harlem was a community that had been built to house about eighty thousand whites, mostly German and Irish. Within one decade it became the world's largest racial ghetto because three hundred thousand Negro people from the South and the Caribbean had poured into it. Despite the fact that Harlem had quadrupled its population, not a single new school or hospital had been built in the district; and to aggravate matters, the private hospitals in the Harlem area refused to accept Negro patients. At the same time, not more than twenty new apartment houses had been built. And so, in this compact area, three hundred thousand Negro people were forced to live, serviced by institutions created for only eighty thousand.

Naturally, with the ancient law of supply and demand working, Harlemites had to pay a tax on being black. Rents were 20 percent higher than for similar accommodations elsewhere in New York City. Foodstuffs were 17 percent above the general level. Life insurance rates were doubled. Credit clothing stores thrived on usury rates of 100 percent.

Resentment in Harlem was also fanned by the fact that into the community each morning came shopkeepers whose coffers flowed with the black man's money, and who left in the evening taking all that money with them, because not a single store in Harlem owned by a white would employ a Negro except as a porter or maid. I made a survey in 1936 and found that out of five thousand people who worked on 125th Street, from river to river, only ninety-three were Negroes, and they were all menials.

This, then, was Harlem in the Great Depression. It had no real leadership and no mass organization. It was exploited by politicans, victimized by merchants, and hampered by woefully inadequate educational and health facilities. The important Negro mass organizations—the National Urban League and the National Association for the Advancement of Colored People—were living in their downtown ivory towers, totally insulated from the sufferings of their people.

On March 20, 1937, the morning following the riot, a group came to me and asked, "Why should we allow these 125th Street merchants to take our money and not give us employment? Look at what the Negro people have done in the Negro section of Chicago."

As a result of this meeting I organized the Coordinating Committee for Employment. This was the first time a mass organization had been created on the basis of group rather than individual memberships. By this time masses of people had already been organized by me and had been marching with me for seven years. Now, I felt, the time had come to stretch out and bring in other organizations. They came: the Garvey Black Nationalists joined us because I had always preached that Negroes must have self-respect before they can demand respect from others; the West Indians came because I had worked hard to abolish the artificial barrier between them and the native-born Negro people; the left-wing organizations stepped into line because I had cooperated with them in the fight for the freedom of the Scottsboro Boys. And, naturally, our first meeting was held in the Abyssinian Baptist Church, the great foundation upon which so many people's movements have been built.

The Abyssinian Baptist Church, then as now, gave us office space free, and therefore no money was necessary to underwrite the expenses of our mass movements. The vast membership of the church, over ten thousand, always stood as the united primary task force to give the initial backing to my mass meetings and to spearhead the initiation of any worthwhile cause.

The Coordinating Committee for Employment was shunned by the national Negro leaders—leaders who wouldn't be recognized by five people if they walked down Lenox Avenue on a crowded August night.

The co-chairman of our committee was the brilliant Reverend Dr. William Lloyd Imes, minister of St. James Presbyterian Church and president of the Alumni Association of Union Theological Seminary, later to be president of Knoxville College in Tennessee. I was young and Dr. Imes was mature. I acted before I thought and he thought before he moved. I was impetuous and impatient, but Dr. Imes always paused to reason. He was a great man, with the mind of a scholar, the soul of a saint, the heart of a brother, the tongue of a prophet, and the hand of a militant.

Then there was Arnold Johnson, executive secretary of the committee, a black Cuban, suave, handsome, young, radical, and always dressed impeccably. Arnold at heart was a revolutionary, against everything and everyone he felt was wrong.

The treasurer of the committee was Mrs. Genevieve Chinn, a West Virginia socialite, wife of Harlem's leading eye, ear, nose, and throat specialist—a handsome young woman who presided over her luxurious Whitestone Landing mansion with all the dignity of a person to the manner born. Yet in her heart Mrs. Chinn was a passionate fighter, side by side with us, for the uplifting of the masses.

It was a strange group. James W. Ford, the perennial Vice Presidential candidate of the Communist Party, was working side by side with Capt. A. L. King, head of the remnants of the nationalist Garvey movement. And because the police were watching our every move and rumors had come to us that the Department of Justice had assigned agents to infiltrate, we never again met in Harlem. Instead we gathered in the Greenwich Village apartment of a Wall Street broker, Sascha Iskander Hourwich. Though we dreamed different dreams, we all had but one objective: the full emancipation and equality of all peoples. Because we were operating in the period of the Great Depression, we took as our first goal economic equality.

We began to picket 125th Street stores from river to river. We made it a disgrace for anyone in Harlem to cross a picket line. One Saturday we closed down Chock Full O'Nuts, a New York restaurant chain, thus forcing them to employ their first Negro salesgirl. Today the vast majority of their employees are Negroes and Jackie Robinson, a Negro, served for sometime as a vice-president of the company.

I developed a technique for hitting similar types of stores that were in competition with each other. We would pick off only one, leaving the other free to do business, even though its policy was just as bad. For example, we picketed Grant's and let Woolworth's go unpicketed; in two weeks Grant's capitulated. Then we hit Woolworth's . . . and it was all over in one weekend.

Our slogan, as proclaimed from picket signs, sound trucks, and picketers, was "Don't Buy Where You Can't Work!" Our campaign increased in power. One Saturday alone we closed ten stores that later signed contracts with us overnight. . . .

❧

Part XI

ON THE HOME FRONT

One enduring consequence of the Great Depression was World War II. Another was the heightened political consciousness of the black community. Of course, there was nothing new about philosophical and ideological differences among black thinkers, but the intensity of the debates among the various members on the Left was never as widespread, and never as serious and contentious. Conrad Lynn was right in the maelstrom of these exchanges, arguing vociferously for the Communist Party. Defending and advancing the party line was attractive for a number of reasons to African Americans during this era, given the deplorable economic and racial situation. The Communist Party devoted considerable time and attention developing programs that might appeal to African Americans, and none was more seductive than the demand for racial equality. When Lynn wasn't on the ramparts for his party, he was an active campaigner against fascism in Spain. In the succeeding decades, Lynn would express similar energy and conviction during the struggle for civil rights and black liberation.

Contralto Marian Anderson may not have been as politically active as Lynn, but her principles and integrity were just as unassailable. When informed the Daughters of the American Revolution had turned down her concert date appearance at Constitution Hall, Anderson fumed. (The denial prompted Eleanor Roosevelt to resign from the DAR.) But Anderson agreed to perform the following month, Easter Sunday, at the Lincoln Memorial, an event she poignantly recalls. Later it was learned that the apparent snub was not an act of discrimination on the part of the DAR but a conflict in scheduling.

Unlike Conrad Lynn, Nelson Peery earned his military stripes before establishing a reputation in radical political circles. Granting us a glimpse of the troubled race relations in the army, Peery also places black soldiers within a broader context of economic and political ramifications. Like the sharp analysis that fueled his revolutionary articles and essays, his writing here deftly excoriates U.S. governmental policies and discloses why it was necessary for the Roosevelt administration to acquiesce to the militancy advocated by A. Philip Randolph and others.

Althea Gibson could have used some of Randolph's clout in the realm of tennis. Practically everything in tennis, including the uniforms and balls, was white. But this was not going to derail the relentless desire of the skinny girl from Harlem with the powerful serve and the gazelle-like speed and leaps across the court. World War II was in full tilt when Gibson took up the sport in earnest and soon she was earning recognition on the restricted lawns and at the top tournaments. Within a few years Gibson was completely in control of her devastating athletic ability and on her way to defeating opponents who once took advantage of her inexperience. She was leaping the racial nets in tennis before Jackie Robinson was stealing home for the Brooklyn Dodgers.

A. Philip Randolph, an astute labor organizer and founder of the Brotherhood of Sleeping Car Porters Union, proposed a massive March on Washington in 1940 if the government did not end its discrimination in the defense industries and the armed forces. Before Randolph could activate his threat, President Franklin Roosevelt issued an executive order forbidding discrimination in war industries and government training programs, and establishing a President's Committee on Fair Employment Practices. Despite gaining this concession, Randolph felt a need to keep the pressure on, as he explains in this speech in Detroit in 1942.

Clarence Atkins was a teenager when Randolph was waging his campaign for equal rights. As a youth Atkins was a frequent visitor at the home of Mary McLeod Bethune, who at one time was a key adviser to President Franklin D. Roosevelt. He also attended Bethune-Cookman College founded by Ms. Bethune, where he honed his skills in music and current affairs, particularly the works of James Weldon Johnson and Zora Neale Hurston, both natives of Florida. His love of music led him inexorably to jazz and his preparation as an eyewitness to the bebop explosion. Since those early years at the turntable and nightclubs, Atkins has become an authoritative chronicler of the music, becoming an intimate acquaintance of such stalwarts as Betty Carter, Art Taylor and Jackie McLean.

In Detroit, Charles Denby was listening to another kind of rhythm as a riveter in the production of airplane parts, a rare job for African Americans. From this excerpt, it seems Denby spent as much time riveting as trying to make things better for other workers. His efforts were consistent with the emerging radicalism of the union movement in Detroit. Black workers were among the rank and file, even if they were denied leadership positions in the United Automobile Workers or the Teamsters. To some degree they were a union within a union, demanding their rights from an organization of workers who in many respects were no less racist than the company that employed them all.

Noted poet and author Maya Angelou takes us back to her high school days in the Fillmore District of San Francisco, recounting the telling effects the war had on the Japanese-American population. The irony of the Japanese being dislodged by African Americans newcomers from the South was a circumstance that did not escape Angelou's keen awareness. The mass internment of Japanese Americans following the bombing of Pearl Harbor was a deep concern to many African Americans, particularly those who saw them as another people of color being unfairly detained in concentration camps. Blacks on the Left like Peery and Denby were even more alarmed when their comrades, especially the American Communist Party, suspended all Japanese-American members and their spouses and endorsed their internment. Meanwhile, German prisoners of war were receiving preferential treatments at various camps in Michigan.

In several ways Coleman Young's entry is a summary of Lynn's and Denby's accounts. The radical Left was approaching its last hurrah in the late 1940s, and it is not surprising that its final death knell would resonate most dramatically within the union movement in the automobile plants of Detroit. The "Arsenal of Democracy," as the city was called during the war, was now the mausoleum of activism, though, as Young notes, that spirit did not fade without leaving a legacy that would later propel him into the mayoral office. That radical legacy would also resurface in the 1960s with such black militant worker organizations as the Dodge Revolutionary Union Movement and the League of Revolutionary Black Workers.

CONRAD LYNN

From *There Is a Fountain*

NEW YORK CITY, 1936

COMMUNIST PARTY MEMBERS, DEVOTED STUDENTS OF R. Palme Dutt's *Fascism* and *Social Revolution,* were preoccupied with the onward march of Mussolini and Hitler. In the Harlem unit, we watched with horrified fascination as Ciano led the Italian fascist airmen in blowing up women and children in Ethiopia. Ciano did not hesitate to write poetry about the glory of the spectacle of huge bursts of blood and limbs erupting from the earth. We did not know at the time that Stalin had a contract with the Italian dictator to supply oil for his planes.

Hirohito's minions were decimating China. Hitler was preparing to march into the Rhineland. But no place held a more passionate concern for us than the dark Spanish terrain. There a government pledged to socialist change had been elected, but the fascists, with the connivance of international capitalism, were determined to overthrow it. Even before Franco had begun his uprising, Italian airmen had received orders to bomb Republican strongholds.

In France, we had seen how in 1934 the united front had temporarily forestalled the bid for power of the croix de feu. At the beginning of 1936 the united front tactic had been expanded into the Popular Front policy. At first, the significance of this policy was unclear to me.

The Harlem branch of the Party designated me as one of the delegates to the city committee in January 1936. At the first meeting I attended, I was struck by the lack of discussion about the ominous international events that were bringing a new world war ineluctably closer. When I asked if Russia was really selling oil to Mussolini, Weiss, the Harlem leader, mumbled something about the Soviet Union needing currency to secure strategic materials to prepare for its inevitable showdown with Hitler. The colonial sufferings, said Weiss, were regrettable, but the fate of the world depended on what happened in the advanced industrial nations. He said that this was where my major attention should be directed.

I soon had the opportunity to test this advice. That month I secured an assignment to the Workers' Education Project, which was devoted to teaching union workers, in order to enable them to function intelligently in their own self-interest, with one another as well as with their employers. During my free time I handled a few legal cases. Experience with the Party had convinced me that I had better obtain as much practice as possible.

The organizing drives of the Committee of Industrial Organizations in 1934 and 1935 had demonstrated the potential for militancy of the American working class, but Roosevelt and his New Deal cabinet rode with the punches and won over such key leaders as Walter Reuther and Philip Murray. It seemed clear to me that an American revolution was not imminent. Only the rush to World War II could provide another opportunity comparable to 1914–1918.

On the Workers' Education Project I met some of the best political minds ever collected under one roof. They were men and women dedicated to the cause of labor, and they represented every party and tendency on the left. For the first time, Trotskyists, Lovestoneites, Stammites, Socialists, Anarchists, and Henry Georgeites mingled with orthodox Communists.

My local reputation as a polemicist preceded me. Eddie Welch, Ella Baker, Paulí Murray, and Hezekiah Riley—all black intellectuals—shoved reading matter under my nose, critical of the Communist party. But the tactic boomeranged. A Communist is as much of an emotional being as he or she is a rational animal, and from 1928 on—with varying ups and downs—my basic loyalty had been to the Communist party. And I read only in the Party's press about its clashes with other elements of the left.

When the leadership noticed my spirited defense of the official line, it decided to use me in factional disputes. My most persistent opponent was an Italian-American schoolteacher, Agnes Martocci. She was a Socialist and the most articulate and truthful debater I had ever met. It was not unusual at a public meeting for the Party to assign three speakers to contain her.

I had one natural advantage. As a black, I represented the most oppressed masses anywhere in the world, whether we were speaking of the United States, the Caribbean, or Africa. The Socialists were hampered by the Norman Thomas line, tirelessly repeated, that no special bid needed to be made to blacks to win them to socialism. Black people, Norman Thomas pointed out, were part of the working class, and when the working class achieved power, blacks would share it.

World events were making a shambles of that thesis. It was true that in France the workers had beaten back the fascists, and Leon Blum, the able

Socialist leader, had been elected by a popular front in which the Communists functioned. When Blum ordered the massacre of the Algerian revolutionaries in air raids at Setif, I insisted in a stormy meeting that the Socialists and their allies had to bear full responsibility for that terrible crime.

By now it was becoming clear to the Trotskyists and Lovestoneites that my commitment to the violent revolution was too deep for me ever to become a member of the Socialist Party. The former two groups redoubled their efforts to win me over.

I particularly admired Eddie Welch, a big, brown-skinned, hot-tempered man with a vitriolic tongue, which he used with the resonance of Paul Robeson. (It was not until forty years later that I learned in Harry Haywood's *Black Bolshevik* that Eddie had been a Communist youth delegate to the Sixth Congress of the International in Moscow in the twenties.) One evening at a political meeting in Harlem of the American League Against War and Fascism, he noticed a picture of Stalin on the wall. Eddie strode down the center aisle, pushed aside the chairman of the evening, and ripped down Stalin's picture.

He turned to the astonished audience and said, "Black revolutionaries should not stand for homage to the bloody collaborator of Mussolini in Ethiopia and the French in Algeria."

I was surprised to find myself standing and cheering. Party members gaped, and the Socialists looked at me in bewilderment. It was obvious to everyone that my position in the Communist party was becoming untenable. My loyalty to the colored people of the world was far greater than my loyalty to a political party. I had used the Communist party as an instrument; the goal was the liberation of the nonwhite peoples of the earth.

Just about this time the Spanish civil war began, and deep differences on the left were put aside for a while. The Communist party busied itself selecting comrades to enter the International Brigade. I sensed that the Party regarded me as too unreliable for such an assignment. But my early childhood friend, Tom Page, was picked to go, and many of my acquaintances in other parties volunteered.

Spain proved to be the last test of the classic tactics of revolution. Marx and Engels had been fascinated by the barricades of the French Revolution; but they had been forced to learn by the tragic end of the Paris Commune that romantic illusions about the efficacy of masses in the streets needed revision.

MARIAN ANDERSON

From *My Lord, What a Morning*

WASHINGTON, D.C., 1939

EASTER SUNDAY IN 1939 WAS APRIL 9, and I had other
. . . concert dates to fill before it came. Wherever we went I was met by
reporters and photographers. The inevitable question was, "What about Washington?" My answer was that I knew too little to tell an intelligent story about
it. There were occasions, of course, when I knew more than I said. I did not
want to talk, and I particularly did not want to say anything about the D. A. R.
As I have made clear, I did not feel that I was designed for hand-to-hand
combat, and I did not wish to make statements that I would later regret. The
management was taking action. That was enough.

It was comforting to have concrete expressions of support for an essential
principle. It was touching to hear from a local manager in a Texas city that a
block of two hundred tickets had been purchased by the community's D. A. R.
people. It was also heartening; it confirmed my conviction that a whole group
should not be condemned because an individual or section of the group does a
thing that is not right.

I was informed of the plan for the outdoor concert before the news was
published. Indeed, I was asked whether I approved. I said yes, but the yes did
not come easily or quickly. I don't like a lot of show, and one could not tell in
advance what direction the affair would take. I studied my conscience. In
principle the idea was sound, but it could not be comfortable to me as an
individual. As I thought further, I could see that my significance as an individual
was small in this affair. I had become, whether I liked it or not, a symbol,
representing my people. I had to appear.

I discussed the problem with Mother, of course. Her comment was characteristic: "It is an important decision to make. You are in this work. You intend to stay in it. You know what your aspirations are. I think you should make your own decision."

Mother knew what the decision would be. In my heart I also knew. I could not run away from this situation. If I had anything to offer, I would have to do so now. It would be misleading, however, to say that once the decision was made I was without doubts.

We reached Washington early that Easter morning and went to the home of Gifford Pinchot, who had been Governor of Pennsylvania. The Pinchots had been kind enough to offer their hospitality, and it was needed because the hotels would not take us. Then we drove over to the Lincoln Memorial. Kosti was well enough to play, and we tried out the piano and examined the public-address system, which had six microphones, meant not only for the people who were present but also for a radio audience.

When we returned that afternoon I had sensations unlike any I had experienced before. The only comparable emotion I could recall was the feeling I had had when Maestro Toscanini had appeared in the artist's room in Salzburg. My heart leaped wildly, and I could not talk. I even wondered whether I would be able to sing.

The murmur of the vast assemblage quickened my pulse beat. There were policemen waiting at the car, and they led us through a passageway that other officers kept open in the throng. We entered the monument and were taken to a small room. We were introduced to Mr. Ickes, whom we had not met before. He outlined the program. Then came the signal to go out before the public.

If I did not consult contemporary reports I could not recall who was there. My head and heart were in such turmoil that I looked and hardly saw, I listened and hardly heard. I was led to the platform by Representative Caroline O'Day of New York, who had been born in Georgia, and Oscar Chapman, Assistant Secretary of the Interior, who was a Virginian. On the platform behind me sat Secretary Ickes, Secretary of the Treasury Morgenthau, Supreme Court Justice Black, Senators Wagner, Mead, Barkley, Clark, Guffey, and Capper, and many Representatives, including Representative Arthur W. Mitchell of Illinois, a Negro. Mother was there, as were people from Howard University and from churches in Washington and other cities. So was Walter White, then secretary of the National Association for the Advancement of Colored People. It was Mr. White who at one point stepped to the microphone and appealed to the crowd, probably averting serious accidents when my own people tried to reach me.

I report these things now because I have looked them up. All I knew then as I stepped forward was the overwhelming impact of that vast multitude. There seemed to be people as far as the eye could see. The crowd stretched in a great semicircle from the Lincoln Memorial around the reflecting pool on to the shaft of the Washington Monument. I had a feeling that a great wave of good will poured out from these people, almost engulfing me. And when I stood up to sing our National Anthem I felt for a moment as though I were choking. For a desperate second I thought that the words, well as I know them, would not come.

I sang, I don't know how. There must have been the help of professionalism I had accumulated over the years. Without it I could not have gone through the program. I sang—and again I know because I consulted a newspaper clipping—"America," the aria "O mio Fernando," Schubert's "Ave Maria," and three spirituals—"Gospel Train," "Trampin'," and "My Soul Is Anchored in the Lord."

. . . There were many in the gathering who were stirred by their own emotions. Perhaps I did not grasp all that was happening, but at the end great numbers of people bore down on me. They were friendly; all they wished to do was to offer their congratulations and good wishes. The police felt that such a concentration of people was a danger, and they escorted me back into the Memorial. Finally we returned to the Pinchot home.

I cannot forget that demonstration of public emotion or my own strong feelings. In the years that have passed I have had constant reminders of that Easter Sunday. It is not at all uncommon to have people come backstage after a concert even now and remark, "You know, I was at that Easter concert." In my travels abroad I have met countless people who heard and remembered about that Easter Sunday.

In time the policy at Constitution Hall changed. I appeared there first in a concert for the benefit of China Relief. The second appearance in the hall, I believe, was also under charitable auspices. Then, at last, I appeared in the hall as does any other musical performer, presented by a concert manager, and I have been appearing in it regularly. The hall is open to other performers of my group. There is no longer an issue, and that is good. . . . .

NELSON PEERY

From *Black Fire*

FORT HUACHUCA, ARIZONA, 1940S

THE MORE THE GOVERNMENT SPOKE OF DEMOCRATIC war aims, the greater became the Fascist terror against the blacks. The cops in Alexandria, Louisiana, shot down twelve black soldiers. The sadistic lynching of Cleo Wright in Sikeston, Missouri, was a carnival of horror. After the torture and burning was over, scores of cars filled with white men, women, and children dragged the broken body of the black youth through his neighborhood. They stopped a few times to challenge the blacks to fight. With their men bottled up in Fort Huachuca, there was no response from the women and children.

The sullen demoralization of the soldiers ripened toward violence. Army G-2—military intelligence, something akin to a military FBI—fearing the explosion, warned the black newspapers that they would draft their personnel if they became inflammatory. If necessary they would (and on occasion they did) confiscate their papers. When the small local press, the *Southwest Georgian,* exposed a lynching in Newton, Georgia, in 1943, the editor was immediately drafted and his paper folded. Half the staff of the militant *California Eagle* was drafted. Finally, the G-2 warned that although the seizure of individual issues of papers was permissible, banning the black press would "only serve to supply ammunition for agitation to colored papers." The issue of freedom of the press wasn't even involved. The black press's response was to militantly declare its patriotism.

Shaken by the low morale of the Negro people for the war, *Time* magazine ran a special edition exposing the wretched, segregated conditions of the Negro soldier. Its aim was to force the government to do something about it. The

Negro press attacked *Time,* stating that such information would make slackers out of the Negro soldier.

Most of us understood that Hitler was worse than Senator Bilbo or Rankin or Talmage or Thurmond. We understood that his concentration camps were worse than the chain gangs and prison farms. The historical base of our consciousness was firmer than this understanding. The chain gang and lynch mob preceded Hitler and would be here after he was gone. There was no room for illusions. Somewhere along the line we would have to fight it out here.

The battle began at Gurdon, Arkansas. The black Ninety-forth Engineer Battalion from Fort Custer, Michigan, was on maneuvers. A few isolated fights between the troops and the police and MPs escalated to an attack by police and the town's mob against the unarmed soldiers. Northern white officers were beaten and called "nigger lovers" while the MPs stood by. The unarmed black troops scattered into the woods. Some of them caught freight trains back to Michigan, where the Army court-martialed them for desertion. We began to secure and hide ammunition.

When the United States entered World War I, the economy was almost at full employment for white workers. The rapid expansion of war production created an immediate and severe labor shortage. The employers sent agents into the black labor reserve of the South. They pulled millions of sharecroppers and service workers into well-paying jobs in the factories at the very beginning of the war. That war had something in it for everyone.

World War II began during the Depression. Millions of unemployed white workers had preference in hiring. In the spring of 1942, blacks constituted fewer than 3 percent of the war workers. The labor shortage began late in the year. Then the doors opened a crack to the black workers. The head of the Brotherhood of Sleeping Car Porters, A. Philip Randolph, organized the march on Washington to force a fair employment policy in the war against fascism. [The government had no intention of giving in until Secretary of War Stimson, an open white supremacist, convinced Roosevelt that Randolph's real aim was to prevent the Communists from taking over the civil rights movement.] Mark Eldridge, appointed chair of the Fair Employment Practices Committee (FEPC), immediately went on a speaking tour that spring to assure whites they had nothing to fear from the FEPC. He received a standing ovation from a Southern white audience when he stated, ". . . not even all the mechanized armies of the earth, Allied and Axis . . . could force the Southern white people to abandonment of the principle of social segregation."

By February 1942 the war was in full swing. The whites of Detroit rioted and attacked blacks moving into a federal housing project at the edge of "their" community. Thirty-five thousand white workers laid down their tools and walked out of the huge Douglas Aircraft plant when one black was hired.

In the summer of 1942, poll takers in Harlem found that only 11 percent of the blacks believed they would be better off after the war.

The Marine Corps had never admitted blacks. The navy stopped accepting them between 1919 and 1930. In 1930 they accepted a few mess men. After World War I, the army had practically stopped recruiting blacks. Congress, under political pressure, developed a quota system and put a lid on the size of the army. The Negro-hating generals got around congressional intent. While keeping the names "infantry," "cavalry," and "artillery," most of the black combat outfits became labor and service organizations. On paper, each black combat soldier became two soldiers, one combat (on paper) and one labor (actually). The trick cut the black slots in half and assigned the other half to the recruitment of whites. The generals were then able to form a lily-white Tank and Air Corps.

Self-appointed black leaders, and those appointed by the white political structure, appeared as if by magic. They began maneuvering to take control of the simmering movement of the working-class black. Forced to fight Hitler, the working-class black deeply believed the fight should start here and now. The army held the greatest concentration of blacks, and the Ninety-third was the pawn to be fought over. The Ninety-third Division plus the post complement numbered close to twenty-five thousand men at Fort Huachuca. The commanders realized the danger of keeping that number of men bottled up in the desert without decent recreation and almost completely cut off from social contact with women. The United Service Organization (USO) never stopped at Huachuca. The commanding generals trembled at the thought of white women dancing and singing before black troops. The USO directors didn't want it to happen, and we didn't expect it.

In June 1942 our pay went from twenty-one to fifty dollars a month. Suddenly we had money to spend and nothing to spend it on. The tension increased.

Fry, the tent and tar paper town near the gate to the fort, became the scene of unending fights as the soldiers turned more and more to the whores and the bootleg whiskey. A few rough bars with names like Yazoo City and Selma Beer Garden sprang up. They made matters worse.

We nicknamed Fry "The Hook." Anyone who went there was going to get caught by something—the clap, a knife blade, or, if he was lucky, a tough black fist. The army built a huge recreation center we called the Green Top. With its hundred-yard-long bar, it was to be an alternative to The Hook. The latest easy-riding blues jelly-rolled from the jukeboxes. Neat young black barmaids imported from Texas and Louisiana served five-cent beer. Everyone flirted with them, and though they were not allowed to dance with the soldiers, for three dollars they would slip away or make an after-hours date.

There was no directive against going to Tucson, Bisbee, or Nogales. Phoenix was off-limits. The black 364th Infantry regiment, ordered to Phoenix from Hawaii, resisted the segregation and police brutality. A hundred of them took up arms and fought it out with the MPs and cops. They killed one officer, one white enlisted man, and a white civilian before being overwhelmed.

Getting out of the fort was almost impossible. As the tension neared the flash point, the decision was made to provide army trucks for transportation.

Trouble began the first weekend. A convoy from the 368th went to Bisbee. A restaurant owner told a soldier, "We don't serve niggers." The soldier knocked him out and his pals trashed the place. In the ensuing melee a black soldier was shot by the cops. The soldiers tried to set the town on fire and retreated toward their trucks. The city cops and military police from the Eighth Air Force surrounded them. The soldiers were savagely beaten and some received long prison sentences. The generals declared Bisbee off-limits. The merchants lost a million dollars in trade and the soldiers lost a place to relax. The convoys were still going to Tucson and Nogales. Our little group in the platoon decided it was better to go to Mexico, even though it was farther away.

ALTHEA GIBSON

From *I Always Wanted to Be Somebody*

NEW YORK CITY, 1940S

I BEGAN TAKING LESSONS FROM FRED JOHNSON IN the
. . . summer of 1941, but it wasn't until a year later that he entered me in
my first tournament. The American Tennis Association, which is almost all
Negro, was putting on a New York State Open Championship at the Cosmo-
politan Club, and Fred put me in the girls' singles. It was the first tournament I
had ever played in, and I won it. I was a little surprised about winning, but not
much. By this time I was accustomed to winning games. I think what mostly
made me feel good was that the girl I beat in the finals, Nina Irwin, was a white
girl. I can't deny that that made the victory all the sweeter to me. It proved to
my own satisfaction that I was not only as good as she was, I was better.

Nina, incidentally, also took lessons from Fred Johnson, but I think he was
pleased when I won. The other members had no choice; they had to like it. I
won, didn't I? Actually, even though almost all the club members were Negro,
a lot of them probably were rooting for Nina because they thought I was too
cocky and they figured it would do me good to get beat. It's always been a fault
of mine that I don't let many people get close to me, and not many of those
people had any way of knowing what I was really like or what made me that
way. I guess they do now. But in those days part of my defense was in being
assertive and a show-off. Just the same, winning softened a lot of opinions
about me. After I showed them the championship material that was in me,
things changed noticeably around the club. I found that I was accepted solely on
my merits, and my attitude toward people didn't seem to matter so much any
more. Not many people, I've found out, find fault with a winner.

Later in the same year—the summer of 1942—the club took up a collection to send me to the A.T.A. national girls' championship at Lincoln University in Pennsylvania. That was my first national tournament, and I lost in the finals. The girl who beat me was Nana Davis, whose name is now Nana Davis Vaughan, and I think it's interesting to read what Nana said about that match to a reporter who talked to her after I won at Wimbledon:

"Althea was a very crude creature. She had the idea she was better than anybody. I can remember her saying, 'Who's this Nana Davis? Let me at her.' And after I beat her, she headed straight for the grandstand without bothering to shake hands. Some kid had been laughing at her and she was going to throw him out."

There wasn't any A.T.A. national championship tournament in 1943 because of the war and the restrictions on travel, but I won the girls' singles in both 1944 and 1945, and then, when I turned eighteen, my life began to change. For one thing, the social workers I had been reporting to no longer had charge of me. I wasn't a minor any more. Of course, I no longer was in line for the allowance I had been getting, either, but that didn't seem so important stacked up against the fact that I was able to run my own life at last. I had made friends with a girl named Gloria Nightingale, and I went to live with her in her family's apartment. I got a job as a waitress and I paid rent to Gloria's grandmother. . . .

It was through Gloria that I met Edna and Sugar Ray Robinson. Ray and Edna were real good friends; I felt that they liked me, and I was crazy about them. When Ray went into the army, I stayed with Edna a lot. I was what you might call her Girl Friday. I did everything I could to make our relationship a lasting one. When Ray was in training, I used to go and live with Edna in a place on the other side of the mountain from his camp at Greenwood Lake, New York. We used to take a long hike from our cottage to Ray's cabin—it must have been about three miles—every morning, and that wonderful mountain air seemed great to a kid from 143rd Street. Not that there was anything the matter with the air in Harlem; it was just that there were an awful lot of people using it.

Both Edna and Ray were kind to me in lots of ways. They seemed to understand that I needed a whole lot of help. I used to love to be with them. They had such nice things. Sometimes they would even let me practice driving one of their fancy cars, even though I didn't have a license. I think it gave Ray a kick to see how much fun I got out of it. . . .

Being eighteen, I was able to play in the A.T.A. national women's singles in 1946; I was out of the girls' class. They played it at Wilberforce College in Ohio, and the A.T.A. paid my expenses out there and saw to it that I was put up in the college dormitory. I got to the finals and lost to Roumania Peters, a Tuskegee Institute teacher who was an experienced player; she had won the title in 1944. It was my inexperience that lost the match for me. Roumania was an old hand at tournament play and she pulled all the tricks in the trade on me. I wasn't ready for it. But I didn't feel too bad. There was no disgrace connected with losing in the finals.

I probably wouldn't have minded much at all if I hadn't felt so strongly that I had let Roumania "psych" me out of the match. I was overconfident, there's no doubt about it, and she really worked on me. She won the first set, 6–4, and after I pulled out the second, 9–7, she began drooping around the court as though she was half dead. She looked for all the world as though she was so exhausted she couldn't stand up. Naturally, I thought I had it made. It was quite a shock to me when Roumania managed to keep running long enough to win the third set, 6–3. It was also a good lesson for me. Unhappily, some of the A.T.A. people who had come out from New York were pretty disappointed in me. Maybe they thought they hadn't got their money's worth out of me because I had lost. I remember one of them saying something to the effect that they were through with me, that they didn't think much of my attitude, and I know I was a pretty dejected kid for a while. But I had played well enough, anyway, to attract the attention of two tennis playing doctors, Dr. Hubert A. Eaton of Wilmington, North Carolina, and Dr. Robert W. Johnson of Lynchburg, Virginia, who were getting ready to change my whole life.

They thought I was a good enough prospect to warrant special handling. I've often wondered if, even then, at that early stage of the game, they were thinking in terms of me someday playing at Forest Hills or Wimbledon. Whether they were or weren't, they certainly were looking to the future. It was their idea that what I ought to do first was go to college, where I could get an education and improve my tennis at the same time. "There are plenty of scholarships available for young people like you," Dr. Eaton told me. "It wouldn't be hard at all to get you fixed up at some place like Tuskegee."

"That would be great," I told him, "except I never even been to high school."

That stopped them for a while, but the two doctors talked it over with some of the other A.T.A. people and decided that I was too good a tennis prospect to let go to waste. I suppose, now that I think hard on it, they already were hoping that I might just possibly turn out to be the Negro player they had been looking for to break into the major league of tennis and play in the white tournaments. Although they never said so to me—not for a long time. The plan they finally came up with was for me to leave New York City and go to Wilmington to live with Dr. Eaton during the school year, go to high school there, and practice with him on his private backyard tennis court. In the summer I would live with Dr. Johnson in Lynchburg and I would travel with him in his car to play the tournament circuit. Each doctor would take me into his family as his own child and take care of whatever expenses came up during the part of the year I was with him. It was an amazingly generous thing for them to want to do, and I know I can never repay them for what they did for me.

Not that it was an easy decision for me to make. I was a city kid and I liked city ways. How did I know what it would be like for me in a small town, especially in the South? I'd heard enough stories to worry me. Up north, the law may not exactly be on your side, but at least it isn't always against you just because of the color of your skin. I would have to go into this strange country, where, according to what I'd heard, terrible things were done to Negroes just because they were Negroes, and nobody was ever punished for them. I wasn't at all sure going into something like that was a good idea. Harlem wasn't heaven but at least I knew I could take care of myself there.

I might have turned down the whole thing if Edna and Sugar Ray hadn't insisted that I should go. "You'll never amount to anything just bangin' around from one job to another like you been doin'," Ray told me. "No matter what you want to do, tennis or music or what, you'll be better at it if you get some education." In the end I decided he was right, and I wrote Dr. Eaton and told him I was coming. That was in August, 1946. He wrote me back and said I should get there by the first week in September. It didn't even leave me time to change my mind.

A . PHILIP RANDOLPH

From The Voice of Black America

DETROIT, 1942

FELLOW MARCHERS AND DELEGATES TO THE POLICY Conference of the March on Washington Movement and friends: We have met at an hour when the sinister shadows of war are lengthening and becoming more threatening. As one of the sections of the oppressed darker races, and representing a part of the exploited millions of the workers of the world, we are deeply concerned that the totalitarian legions of Hitler, Hirohito and Mussolini do not batter the last bastions of democracy. We know that our fate is tied up with the fate of the democratic way of life. And so, out of the depth of our hearts, a cry goes up for the triumph of the United Nations. But we would not be honest with ourselves were we to stop with a call for a victory of arms alone. We know this is not enough. We fight that the democratic faiths, values, heritages and ideals may prevail.

Unless this war sounds the death knell to the old Anglo-American empire systems, the hapless story of which is one of exploitation for the profit and power of a monopoly-capitalist economy, it will have been fought in vain. Our aim, then, must not only be to defeat Nazism, fascism and militarism on the battlefield but to win the peace, for democracy, for freedom and the Brotherhood of Man without regard to his pigmentation, land of his birth or the God of his fathers.

We therefore sharply score the Atlantic Charter as expressing a vile and hateful racism and a manifestation of the tragic and utter collapse of an old, decadent democratic political liberalism which worshiped at the shrine of a world-conquering monopoly capitalism. This system grew fat and waxed powerful off the flesh, blood, sweat and tears of the tireless toilers of the human race and the sons and daughters of color in the underdeveloped lands of the world.

When this war ends, the people want something more than the dispersal of equality and power among individual citizens in a liberal, political, democratic system. They demand with striking comparability the dispersal of equality and power among the citizen-workers in an economic democracy that will make certain the assurance of the good life—the more abundant life—in a warless world.

But, withal this condition of freedom, equality and democracy is not the gift of the Gods. It is the task of men—yes, men—brave men, honest men, determined men. . . .

Thus our feet are set in the path toward equality—economic, political and social and racial. Equality is the heart and essence of democracy, freedom and justice. Without equality of opportunity in industry, in labor unions, schools and colleges, government, politics and before the law, without equality in social relations and in all phases of human endeavor, the Negro is certain to be consigned to an inferior status. There must be no dual standards of justice, no dual rights, privileges, duties or responsibilities of citizenship. No dual forms of freedom. . . .

But our nearer goals include the abolition of discrimination, segregation and Jim Crow in the government, the Army, Navy, Air Corps, U. S. Marine, Coast Guard, Women's Auxiliary Army Corps and the Waves, and defense industries; the elimination of discrimination in hotels, restaurants, on public transportation conveyances, in educational, recreational, cultural, and amusement and entertainment places such as theaters, beaches and so forth.

We want the full works of citizenship with no reservations. We will accept nothing less.

But goals must be achieved. They are not secured because it is just and right that they be possessed by Negro or white people. Slavery was not abolished because it was bad and unjust. It was abolished because men fought, bled and died on the battlefield.

Therefore, if Negroes secure their goals, immediate and remote, they must win them and to win them they must fight, sacrifice, suffer, go to jail and, if need be, die for them. These rights will not be given. They must be taken.

Democracy was fought for and taken from political royalists—the kings. Industrial democracy, the rights of the workers to organize and designate the representatives of their own choosing to bargain collectively is being won and taken from the economic royalists—big business.

Now, the realization of goals and rights by a nation, race or class requires belief in and loyalty to principles and policies. . . . Policies rest upon principles. Concretely, a policy sets forth one's position on vital public questions such as political affiliations, religious alliances. The March on Washington

Movement must be opposed to partisan political commitments, religious or denominational alliances. We cannot sup with the Communists, for they rule or ruin any movement. This is their policy. Our policy must be to shun them. This does not mean that Negro Communists may not join the March on Washington Movement.

As to the composition of our movement. Our policy is that it be all-Negro, and pro-Negro but not anti-white, or anti-Semitic or antilabor, or anti-Catholic. The reason for this policy is that all oppressed people must assume the responsibility and take the initiative to free themselves. Jews must wage their battle to abolish anti-Semitism. Catholics must wage their battle to abolish anti-Catholicism. The workers must wage their battle to advance and protect their interests and rights.

The essential value of an all-Negro movement such as the March on Washington is that it helps to create faith by Negroes in Negroes. It develops a sense of self-reliance with Negroes depending on Negroes in vital matters. It helps to break down the slave psychology and inferiority complex in Negroes which comes and is nourished with Negroes relying on white people for direction and support. . . .

Therefore, our program is in part as follows:

1. A national conference for the integration and expression of the collective mind and will of the Negro masses.

2. The mobilization and proclamation of a nationwide series of mass marches on the city halls and city councils to awaken the Negro masses and center public attention upon the grievances and goals of the Negro people and serve as training and discipline of the Negro masses for the more strenuous struggle of a March on Washington, if, as, and when an affirmative decision is made thereon by the Negro masses of the country through our national conference.

3. A march on Washington as an evidence to white America that black America is on the march for its rights and means business.

4. The picketing of the White House following the March on Washington and maintaining the said picket line until the country and the world recognize the Negro has become of age and will sacrifice his all to be counted as men, free men.

This program is drastic and exacting. It will test our best mettle and stamina and courage. Let me warn you that in these times of storm and stress, this program will be opposed. Our Movement, therefore, must be well knit together. It must have moral and spiritual vision, understanding, and wisdom. . . .

Our day-to-day exercise of our civil rights is a constant challenge. In theaters, hotels, restaurants, amusement places, even in the North, now there is discrimination against Negroes. This is true in every large city. Negroes have the moral obligation to demand the right to enjoy and make use of their civil and political privileges. If we don't, we will lose the will to fight for our citizenship rights, and the public will consider that we don't want them and should not have them. This fight to break down these barriers in every city should be carefully and painstakingly organized. By fighting for these civil rights the Negro masses will be disciplined in struggle. Some of us will be put in jail, and court battles may ensue, but this will give the Negro masses a sense of their importance and value as citizens and as fighters in the Negro liberation movement and the cause for democracy as a whole. It will make white people in high places and the ordinary white man understand that Negroes have rights that they are bound to respect.

The giant public protest meetings must continue. They are educative and give moral strength to our movement and the Negro masses.

For this task we need men and women who will dedicate and consecrate their life, spirit, mind and soul to the great adventure of Negro freedom and justice.

Our divisions must serve as Negro mass parliaments where the entire community may debate the day-to-day issues such as police brutality, high rents, and other questions and make judgments and take action in the interest of the community. These divisions should hold meetings at least twice a month. In them every Negro should be made to feel his importance as a factor in the Negro liberation movement. We must have every Negro realize his leadership ability, the educated and uneducated, the poor and wealthy. In the March on Washington Movement the highest is as low as the lowest and the lowest is as high as the highest. Numbers in mass formation is our key, directed, of course, by the collective intelligence of the people.

Let us put our weight behind the fight to abolish the poll tax. This will give the black and white workers of the South new hope. But the Negro people are not the only oppressed section of mankind. India is now waging a world-shaking, history-making fight for independence. India's fight is the Negro's fight.

Now, let us be unafraid. We are fighting for big stakes. Our stakes are liberty, justice and democracy. Every Negro should hang his head in shame who fails to do his part now for freedom. This is the hour of the Negro. It is the hour of the common man. May we rise to the challenge to struggle for our rights. Come what will or may, let us never falter.

CLARENCE ATKINS

From His Unpublished Memoirs

NEW YORK CITY, 1942

LIKE A. PHILIP RANDOLPH, JAMES WELDON Johnson, Mary McLeod Bethune and Zora Neale Hurston, I am a native of Florida. All of these notable Black Americans left the sunshine state long before I set out for the North. When I departed, I hoped I was leaving the evils of Jim Crow behind me. After a brief layover at Howard University, which I found not to my liking, I packed again and headed for Harlem. It was 1941 and I was 19. With World War II looming larger by the day, I was concerned about being drafted since I was classified as 1A, but after I got a job with the Pennsylvania Railroad my status changed. My job was considered essential to the war and I avoided the military.

But there was no avoiding the jazz scene. When I hit the Apple, Harlem was struggling to overcome the ravages of the Depression, and there was nothing like a lively jazz club to shake the doldrums. One of my favorite haunts was Minton's Playhouse. I spent many a night at this legendary jazz spot, soaking up the new sounds, and exchanging musical ideas with some of the giants of jazz.

Maybe I should tell you something about Minton's before recalling some of my memorable nights in the club. Henry Minton, its founder, was a run-of-the-mill tenor saxophone player who was also one of several managers of the Rhythm Club. That site was a daytime hangout for many musicians and entertainers of the late thirties and the early forties. It also afforded facilities for rehearsals which made it practicable for Minton to become business agent for the Musicians' Union, Local 802, which had only recently begun to accept African Americans as card-carrying members.

Subsequently, Mr. Minton (as he was usually called) bought a bar on 118th Street between Seventh and St. Nicholas Avenues in the Hotel Cecil. This happened about 1939, and he hired a popular bandleader, Teddy Hill, as manager. He had just recently concluded a European tour. Hill had excellent contacts with many prominent musicians such as Roy Eldridge, one of the former stars in his band, and Dizzy Gillespie who had succeeded Eldridge as lead trumpet in the touring band. Considering Hill's contacts and relationships in the industry, it was only natural that his associates come uptown to hang out at his spot after their late-night gigs, particularly on Monday nights which was the night off from their regular jobs.

As the club's performance schedule was more firmly established, the house band included trumpeter Joe Guy as leader, drummer Kenny "Klook" Clark, Thelonious Monk on piano, and Nick Fenton on bass. At various times Coleman Hawkins, Roy Eldridge and guitarist Charlie Christian were regulars in the band.

There is no doubt that the hiring of Teddy Hill as manager for Minton's was a pivotal factor in bringing about the musical mix and creative colloquy which turned out to be the breeding ground and catalyst for the cosmic transition in jazz—Bebop.

On any given night the bandstand for the late-night jam session might include Monk, Coleman Hawkins, Dizzy, bassist Leonard Gaskin, a very young Max Roach, bassist George Duvivier or Wes Montgomery. As further evidence of Minton's fertile influence, it provided an early stage for young guitarist George Benson and a spotlight for the burgeoning talents of the self-accompanied vocalist (destined to be a chart-topping jazz singer) Carmen McRae, who regularly performed between band sets. Simultaneously, Hill brought in a tremendously gifted, self-taught saxophone player Eddie "Lockjaw" Davis. With the advent of Lockjaw, the quality and energy of the music intensified. It was during his stint there that he began his partnership with Johnny Griffin which was a classic pairing.

At this juncture the music at Minton's seemed to move intermittently between subtle but distinct stylings: a hard driving, soul-searching swing mode and an electrifying and push-pull testiness which always seemed to characterize the jam sessions involving Monk, Diz, Bud Powell, Max, Kenny Clark, Charlie Christian, Eldridge, and the Bean, Coleman Hawkins. The "Bird," Charlie Parker, who perfected his innovations at Minton's was not among the original players at the club; his prominence would occur much later. The sets were rife with experimentation and challenge which, in retrospect, we now know were merely the birth pangs of the Bebop revolution.

The early 1940s was a most prolific period in the cultural life of New York City and a golden period in the night life of Harlem. I can still hear the music that filled the joint, still hear the challenging sessions, with the musicians trading fours as they formulated new vistas of sound. Oddly, Mr. Minton was virtually invisible during this nurturing period. I guess he was preoccupied in making sure the bills were paid. Most of the time he was cooped up in his office that was located somewhere upstairs in the hotel.

Meanwhile, downtown on 52nd Street or "Swing Street," between Fifth and Sixth Avenues, the new music was asserting itself. Jazz clubs on the block were opening, door-to-door, while just around the corner on Broadway, "Birdland" was beginning to earn its reputation as the "Jazz Corner of the World." As a budding vocalist myself, the music was my obsession and my path never led to my residence on "Sugar Hill" at 153rd and St. Nicholas until after the last set was over at the Playhouse, as Minton's was popularly known.

Any devotee of the Playhouse can recall that King Pleasure, one of the initiators of Bebop singing or vocalese, often performed his unique style of putting lyrics to popular solos at the club, the same creations he demonstrated for his friends and patrons in nearby Dewey Park. Another recollection is the regular appearance of the youthful pianist Billy Taylor when he first came to the city. . . .

During regular hours, the patrons of the Playhouse at its peak were, for the most part, a fairly integrated group of hustlers, pimps, and prostitutes with a sprinkling of ordinary people and extraordinary people such as author Ralph Ellison. There were some whites in attendance, and John Hammond was among the most notable. It was Hammond who heard Charlie Christian in Oklahoma City and brought him to New York for Benny Goodman to hear him, who subsequently hired him. But at night, the room came alive for me as the "Talented Tenth" of entertainment and night-life gathered to bask and bathe in the glory of jazz at its best. I count myself blessed and privileged to have been there and accepted for what they recognized as my "familiarity with erudition" in the genre.

The Playhouse was the source of many memorable and thrilling experiences, not only for me but for aficionados, followers of the industry, and just average citizens of the era. It was an integral part of my life, and I was a veritable fixture at the club. I knew all the musicians, the bartenders, staff and the "in crowd" who called the joint their second home, and they all knew me. Adele, who presided over the kitchen could "burn" and enjoyed a reputation that extended beyond the Playhouse. The music was piped in the bar where I usually sat, and from where I could exercise my "kitchen privilege" and go directly to Adele to order my meals. The food and the music were an unsurpassable staple for me and other youngsters who had one eye and ear cocked toward the latest news from abroad.

My world changed immeasurably, however, when Minton's closed in 1974, ending one of the most magical periods of my life and one of the most fruitful periods of the history of jazz in New York City. Henry Minton retired and moved to California where he later died and my existence was invaded by the vagaries of the real, the mundane world.

CHARLES DENBY

From *Indignant Heart*

DETROIT, 1943

I CAME BACK TO DETROIT IN APRIL, 1943, and I was never so glad for anything in my life. Wide Modden, my roommate, was working at one of the newer plants. One morning, he said for me to come to the plant because they were hiring Negroes. He hoped I'd get into the department where he was working. They had recently had a stoppage because Negroes were put in that department.

I said, "How come? Isn't there a union now?" I had seen pictures of the union when I was still in the South.

Wide said, "The union doesn't mean everything to Negroes that some people think."

There were only three Negroes in Wide's department. I asked what the jobs paid. I had the feeling all the time that I'd like to get a higher paying job. Christine and little Matthew were down South and I had to send money to them. Wide said that his job paid a dollar nine cents an hour. I asked what the best job paid and he said the best job was riveting and that it paid a dollar sixteen cents an hour. I told him I would try to get riveting. Only a few Negroes were riveting. They had gone to the company riveting school. It took three months to complete the course and they earned only sixty cents an hour while they were learning.

The employment office was practically filled. I met up with a white fellow from Tennessee who had just come to Detroit. We got in a conversation. He asked me what I was going to ask for.

I told him riveting.

He said he didn't know the names of any jobs and would ask for the same thing. He'd never been North before or in a plant. He was in the line behind me.

When I reached the desk I asked the man for riveting. He told me that there weren't any riveting jobs. He asked if I had riveted before.

I said, yes, in Mobile, on bridges and in shipyards. I was lying to him but I wanted to get the job.

He said that was an altogether different kind of riveting and that my experience wouldn't apply. If I wanted to learn he could send me to the school and they would pay me sixty cents an hour. He said he had a laboring job open, it only paid eighty-seven cents an hour but it was in the department with Wide. The man promised I might get on another job in a day or two that paid more. I accepted on that basis.

We had to sit after we were hired, until twenty-five, or so, were ready and then a girl would carry us up to the foreman. I waited for the fellow from Tennessee. When he came up he asked if I got a riveting job.

I told him, no, because I had the wrong experience.

He said they had given him a job, riveting. "And I just come in from the fields."

I asked him if he had said that he had experience or if they mentioned going to school.

He said, no.

I got kinda mad and went back to the man at the desk. He said he was busy and that he had given me the last available job.

On the job the next day, I asked the foreman where the dope room was located. They gave me a job in the dope room with Wide Modden. It was a small room sealed up very tight. The air was pumped in to the workers and then pumped out again. We glued cloth on the airplane's aileron. After several coats of different kinds of glue the aileron would be as hard as any other part of the plane. The glue had a strong, peculiar odor. There were many men and women who didn't last an hour in the dope room. The odor of the glue made the average person sick. The fumes took away our appetite. We ate only because we were supposed to eat.

The foreman was a German named Hans. I could never remember his last name. I was about the fifth Negro hired into the dope room. After that, they came in regularly from three to five each week. When they hired about twenty men they began to bring in Negro women. In two or three months, they had sixty-five Negro women. As the men were drafted to the army they were replaced by older men. As the women came in they transferred the white men out and left only Negroes. After a few months there were only about ten percent of the whites left. Four or five white women came in to repair tears and snags in the cloth covering the aileron. They hung around outside in the sewing room. The sewing room was nice. It had fans and the women had stools to sit on and they wore clothes like the office workers. . . .

In two months the Negro women complained about the dope room. They wanted out. They asked why they couldn't get work in the sewing room. The work was more relaxing and easier. They asked the foreman if they had a chance to get in there. I wasn't acquainted with anything about the principles or program of the union. One thing I had heard was that they didn't allow discrimination if the union had a contract with the company. I didn't think the union knew what was going on in our shop. I saw the steward with his button but I didn't think our discussing was carried to the union office.

I went to the steward to ask him if the Negro women, the first six especially, had any chance to get in the sewing room.

He said he didn't think so. All the women in the sewing room were old-timers at the plant and the union went by seniority.

I told this to the women and the men. Some of them felt the steward had told me a lie. The next day three of us went to the foreman and asked him. We made a mistake, we raised the question of what the chief steward had told us and he said the steward was right. The company was hiring every day.

One night the Negro matron who cleaned up after the sewing women, rode home on the same bus with me. I asked her how long all the women had been in the sewing room. She said they were hiring two and three new women a day.

I told the women the news and they got mad. We called the steward into the dope room. All of us stood around. He said he didn't know anything about it. If we wanted to make an issue we had to get the badge number of one of the new women. He knew when he told us, that no Negro man could do it.

I got one Negro woman to find out where the matron lived. The matron brought us in the names and we made two lists and handed one to the steward. At this time he stretched his eyes. He said if they had just hired these women then the Negro women had a chance.

We went to the foreman but he said it wasn't his affair and that his job was to see that everybody worked. He said for us to take it up with the steward. We didn't know anything about union procedure. But we decided if we didn't get the six oldest women out to the sewing room in a week, all of us would walk out. . . .

We had heard of strikes, but how they were formed, or carried out, we didn't dream. Not one of us knew the difference between an authorized strike and a wildcat strike. The week came around and we started arguing again. We had a vicious argument. We didn't get production out. We collected our pails of dope, brushes and scissors, walked over, and set them down.

The steward came running up and said, "What are you doing? Go back to work."

We told him, "We want the women in the sewing room. We're not going to work."

The steward called the foreman, the foreman said the company had to get transfer slips and it was the same old story they gave us the week before.

We said, "We're not going to work."

As we walked out of the dope room three Negro men and two women yelled, "Let's go!"

All the workers in the other departments saw us walking and stopped work. "Are you going home?" they began to holler.

Work stopped completely on that floor. The plant had a fence around it with three or four guards at the gates. The guards closed the gates to keep us in. They held up their hands and said we had to stay. Other workers began milling around.

Three men came out of the main office and asked, "What's wrong? We want to settle this the right way."

Someone came up and told us that this was the plant manager. Several men came running across the street from the union hall. They went to telling us to go back.

"Wait a minute. You can't do this, it isn't authorized. Go back to work."

We insisted that we would go out, even if we had to wait until they opened the gate at lunchtime.

The plant manager called two of the women, me and Bill into the office. The union officers introduced themselves as president, and vice president and two shop committeemen. We argued for two hours before we agreed to go back to work. We agreed on the basis of time. They would take not more than one week to get the transfers. We had the word of the plant manager, the union president and the vice president. They told us they hadn't known about the situation and would have done something had they known. We didn't know, we thought they were telling the truth. We talked awhile and finally went back in the department.

Shortly after we started work, the white chief steward gave up his button and quit his job. We had put him on the spot. He claimed he had heart trouble and couldn't take the commotion. They selected a white woman. She and the committeeman came in the dope room and pinned a button on me. We had a talk, they said that I had full privilege to talk to the foreman.

"If you can't settle something, call in the chief steward. If the foreman calls the superintendent, then call the chief steward. We always try to negotiate a grievance peacefully."

I asked her about the women and she said it was all taken care of in the office. She told me the union had just signed a no-strike pledge and that we had wildcatted.

"Wearing this button means you have an obligation to the union. You have to obey union procedure."

I told her that I, personally, had no grievance, except that the women in the dope room wanted to be in the sewing room. I told her I hadn't joined the union yet.

She whispered, "Don't tell anyone. You can go over this afternoon and join. Keep the button on."

When she left, one or two Negroes said she gave me the button to stop my pushing for the women. We all said we didn't care what she or the union or the plant said. If the union took sides with the company we'd go to another shop. We weren't thinking of the union or abiding by any procedure. We didn't know what procedure meant.

Monday came, no news. At noon we asked the foreman about the transfer slips. He said they'd be sent down. We said we wouldn't work unless they were sent now. He called the superintendent and the steward. Both of them told us that there were thousands of transfer slips and that ours had gotten mixed up. We said if they weren't unmixed by the next morning, we were leaving.

The steward said, "This is a wildcat."

We said, "We're not asking anybody to come. If they work, okay, if they don't work, okay. We'll leave and go to another plant."

We huddled ourselves together. The chief steward came but we were so mad we didn't listen. She ran out. The steward yelled that I would be fired because I was wearing a union button.

Bill laughed, "That's why they gave you the button, to keep you quiet. We're going out even if you don't go."

I pulled the button off and asked if that was why they'd given it to me. I thumped it up in the air as far as I could thump it. "I'm going out. God damn it. The women should be in the sewing room."

The plant manager and another official came when we were part way up the aisle. They talked for an hour. After a long plea and threats of blackmail we went in the office. They told us there was a war going on and that we had to work. We still said we were leaving. We told them they had gone back on their word. The superintendent said they would make out new slips and within three days the women would be transferred. We accepted, all the women signed and we felt we had won a victory.

A Negro committeeman came to see us the day before the women were supposed to go out of the dope room. We didn't know him but we felt glad when he said he was a committeeman. We thought everything would be solved fairly now, because he was a Negro. The white committeeman stayed but the Negro did all the talking. The white man backed him up. He talked for half an hour telling us the transfers would be ready the next morning. But, he said, the sewing room at the larger sister plant was a better place to work, the women could go there and they would get more money. The large plant would pay fifteen cents more per hour and we had to remember a war was going on. It wouldn't last very long and we would soon be without jobs again. Every worker wanted to make money.

"You decide. It's entirely up to you. The transfers are ready and they'll be here in the morning, but I'd like to know if you wouldn't rather work in the other plant and make more money?"

The women looked at me. He saw them and turned, "Wouldn't you like to make more money, Matthew?"

I answered him, "Well, yes."

He said, "Come on give me an answer. Why not make fifteen cents an hour more?"

None of us were familiar with union politics. We accepted and the transfers came in at once.

The women went to the new plant but they were put on machines. There was no sewing room. The women got mad and drove over at noon for three days in a row. It smelled bad to us. The women drove up another day and told us there had never been a sewing room at that plant. We immediately started a group to discuss what to do. We went to the Negro committeeman and the white committeeman and told them what the women had said. They told us to meet them in the union hall. They said we could ask for transfer back but it would take a month before it went through. A few days later the women came over and said they had gotten accustomed to the work and to the women they worked with and had decided to stay.

The sewing room in that plant is still lily white. It was moved to the main plant and then to smaller plant. But there are still no Negroes in the sewing room today. The Negro committeeman is now international representative of the union. Every one of us said he was the one who caused us to be sold out. He is the one responsible for the lily white department in the plant. All of us hated him; some guys said he ought to be killed.

A week later, we were still organized. The Negro committeeman came to see me. He said, "We noticed that you asked for riveting when you applied for a job."

I said I had, but that I wouldn't go to the riveting school when it meant that I had to work for sixty cents an hour.

He said the company and the union had discussed the situation and had changed their minds. They had found that many workers who had never had training were as good, or better, at riveting as the trained ones.

"If you want that job and ten cents more pay it can be arranged."

They transferred me to riveting and I had never held an airgun in my hand before. At that time I didn't know they changed me to break up the gang we had got together. . . .

MAYA ANGELOU

From *I Know Why the Caged Bird Sings*

❧

SAN FRANCISCO, 1940S

IN THE EARLY MONTHS OF WORLD WAR II, San Francisco's Fillmore district, or the Western Addition, experienced a visible revolution. On the surface it appeared to be totally peaceful and almost a refutation of the term "revolution." The Yakamoto Sea Food Market quietly became Sammy's Shoe Shine Parlor and Smoke Shop. Yashigira's Hardware metamorphosed into La Salon de Beauté owned by Miss Clorinda Jackson. The Japanese shops which sold products to Nisei customers were taken over by enterprising Negro businessmen, and in less than a year became permanent homes away from home for the newly arrived Southern Blacks. Where the odors of tempura, raw fish and *cha* had dominated, the aroma of chitlings, greens and ham hocks now prevailed.

The Asian population dwindled before my eyes. I was unable to tell the Japanese from the Chinese and as yet found no real difference in the national origin of such sounds as Ching and Chan or Moto and Kano.

As the Japanese disappeared, soundlessly and without protest, the Negroes entered with their loud jukeboxes, their just-released animosities and the relief of escape from Southern bonds. The Japanese area became San Francisco's Harlem in a matter of months.

A person unaware of all the factors that make up oppression might have expected sympathy or even support from the Negro newcomers for the dislodged Japanese. Especially in view of the fact that they (the Blacks) had themselves undergone concentration-camp living for centuries in slavery's plantations and later in sharecroppers' cabins. But the sensations of common relationship were missing.

The Black newcomer had been recruited on the desiccated farm lands of Georgia and Mississippi by war-plant labor scouts. The chance to live in two- or three-story apartment buildings (which became instant slums), and to earn two- and even three-figured weekly checks, was blinding. For the first time he could think of himself as a Boss, a Spender. He was able to pay other people to work for him, i.e. the dry cleaners, taxi drivers, waitresses, etc. The shipyards and ammunition plants brought to booming life by the war let him know that he was needed and even appreciated. A completely alien yet very pleasant position for him to experience. Who could expect this man to share his new and dizzying importance with concern for a race that he had never known to exist?

Another reason for his indifference to the Japanese removal was more subtle but was more profoundly felt. The Japanese were not whitefolks. Their eyes, language and customs belied the white skin and proved to their dark successors that since they didn't have to be feared, neither did they have to be considered. All this was decided unconsciously.

No member of my family and none of the family friends ever mentioned the absent Japanese. It was as if they had never owned or lived in the houses we inhabited. On Post Street, where our house was, the hill skidded slowly down to Fillmore, the market heart of our district. In the two short blocks before it reached its destination, the street housed two day-and-night restaurants, two pool halls, four Chinese restaurants, two gambling houses, plus diners, shoeshine shops, beauty salons, barber shops and at least four churches. To fully grasp the never-ending activity in San Francisco's Negro neighborhood during the war, one need only know that the two blocks described were side streets that were duplicated many times over in the eight- to ten-square-block area.

The air of collective displacement, the impermanence of life in wartime and the gauche personalities of the more recent arrivals tended to dissipate my own sense of not belonging. In San Francisco, for the first time, I perceived myself as part of something. Not that I identified with the newcomers, nor with the rare Black descendants of native San Franciscans, nor with the whites or even the Asians, but rather with the times and the city. I understood the arrogance of the young sailors who marched the streets in marauding gangs, approaching every girl as if she were at best a prostitute and at worst an Axis agent bent on making the U.S.A. lose the war. The undertone of fear that San Francisco would be bombed which was abetted by weekly air raid warnings, and civil defense drills in school, heightened my sense of belonging. Hadn't I, always, but ever and ever, thought that life was just one great risk for the living?

Then the city acted in wartime like an intelligent woman under siege. She gave what she couldn't with safety withhold, and secured those things which lay in her reach. The city became for me the ideal of what I wanted to be as a grownup. Friendly but never gushing, cool but not frigid or distant, distinguished without the awful stiffness.

To San Franciscans "the City That Knows How" was the Bay, the fog, Sir Francis Drake Hotel, Top o' the Mark, Chinatown, the Sunset District and so on and so forth and so white. To me, a thirteen-year-old Black girl, stalled by the South and Southern Black life style, the city was a state of beauty and a state of freedom. The fog wasn't simply the steamy vapors off the bay caught and penned in by hills, but a soft breath of anonymity that shrouded and cushioned the bashful traveler. I became dauntless and free of fears, intoxicated by the physical fact of San Francisco. Safe in my protecting arrogance, I was certain that no one loved her as impartially as I. . . . .

Pride and Prejudice stalked in tandem the beautiful hills. Native San Franciscans, possessive of the city, had to cope with an influx, not of awed respectful tourists but of raucous unsophisticated provincials. They were also forced to live with skin-deep guilt brought on by the treatment of their former Nisei schoolmates.

Southern white illiterates brought their biases intact to the West from the hills of Arkansas and the swamps of Georgia. The Black ex-farmers had not left their distrust and fear of whites which history had taught them in distressful lessons. These two groups were obliged to work side by side in the war plants, and their animosities festered and opened like boils on the face of the city.

San Franciscans would have sworn on the Golden Gate Bridge that racism was missing from the heart of their air-conditioned city. But they would have been sadly mistaken.

A story went the rounds about a San Franciscan white matron who refused to sit beside a Negro civilian on the streetcar, even after he made room for her on the seat. Her explanation was that she would not sit beside a draft dodger who was a Negro as well. She added that the least he could do was fight for his country the way her son was fighting on Iwo Jima. The story said that the man pulled his body away from the window to show an armless sleeve. He said quietly and with great dignity, "Then ask your son to look around for my arm, which I left over there."

COLEMAN YOUNG

From *Hard Stuff*

❧

DETROIT, 1947–1948

THE INTERLUDE OF 1947 AND 1948 MIGHT have been the most volatile, stimulating, highly charged moment of twentieth-century American politics, as well as, in my estimation, the last hurrah for the radical left. The electricity, as usual, was generated by the Communist presence in the labor movement. The Communists constituted the most uninhibited political force behind the racial revolution occurring within the major unions, and as a result I had only a few quarrels with them in the abstract.

My more germane reservations about the party had to do with its organizational rigidity, which conflicted with my billet as an outspoken advocate for freedom of expression. But I was in total support of the constitutional right of any citizen to affiliate as he saw fit, about which the same could not be said of the United States government. The federal position was clearly stated by the 1947 Taft-Hartley Act, which required Communist Party members to disavow their memberships in order to remain in labor unions.

Taft-Hartley was a colossal triumph for Walter Reuther, a landmark in his dogged campaign to rid the UAW-CIO of a left-wing element. Michigan handed Reuther and the conservatives a bonus when it took Taft-Hartley a step further with the Callahan Act, which required "subversives" to register as foreign agents and labor unions to make their records public. Unwilling to accept the troubling fact that such un-American legislation could hold forth in America, the Wayne County CIO promptly took aim at Callahan and Taft-Hartley. My first substantial duty in my new county office was to drum up enough signatures to put the repeal of the Callahan Act on the ballot.

The symbolic events of the period seemed to congregate at Detroit's enormous Labor Day parades down Woodward Avenue, and in 1947 the parade was characterized by labor's split over Taft-Hartley. Reuther led the strutting UAW brigade, and farther down the line was a string of Wayne County CIO floats decorated with crepe-paper protests against Taft-Hartley and the Callahan Act. In the 1948 parade, the left wing was led by Progressive Party presidential candidate Henry Wallace, but his presence was overshadowed by that of President Truman, who kicked off his campaign by addressing the huge crowd at Cadillac Square. The breach within the CIO was on public display that afternoon, as the Reuther caucus paraded to the square behind Truman while the leftists and Progressives peeled off in another direction to rally in behalf of Henry Wallace. (I was left to keep order while Sam Sage was busy squabbling over who should get to drive the revolutionary Tucker automobile that was part of our procession.)

Although the Wayne County CIO was not officially associated with the Wallace campaign, our obvious preference for his third-party candidacy was regarded as insubordination and put us at odds with the parent UAW-CIO, which had endorsed Truman and expected its affiliations to do the same. In his confirmed tradition, Reuther had impugned the motives of the Progressive Party by falsely publicizing it as a Communist front, when in fact it had been formed by Wallace when he realized that his New Deal policies would not be accommodated by the Democratic Party. Wallace was a reform-minded liberal who had been secretary of agriculture—like his father and grandfather—and then Vice-President to FDR before falling into disfavor with the administration and being replaced on the 1944 ticket by Harry Truman. Under Truman, Wallace served briefly as secretary of commerce, which proved to be an untenable assignment for a labor-oriented politician entirely unsympathetic to big business. Wallace's vision of economic reform was described in his book *Sixty Million Jobs,* in which he advocated a massive government program to ensure full employment. When he organized the Progressive Party as a vehicle for carrying out his program, he immediately became the presidential favorite of several large unions, including the steelworkers.

I jumped into the Wallace movement as a Progressive Party candidate for the state senate. To this day, it remains the biggest political mistake of my life. I say that not in terms of ideology, to which I owed first consideration, but with grudging respect to the realities of the day. My limb was sawed off, and it took me fifteen years to rehabilitate my position with the Democratic Party.

In retrospect, it's apparent that the Progressive Party was ill-fated from the beginning. I should have realized what we were up against when we set about to finance the Wallace campaign. Our initial fund-raiser was so large and promising that we held it at Olympia Stadium, the home of the Red Wings; but it seemed that for everyone willing to give to Wallace, there was somebody just as willing to take. Being in charge of security at the stadium rally, I had unexpected difficulty collecting the money from the collectors, one of whom escaped with the contributions of an entire row of seats.

Like the Progressive Party and virtually everything else I associated myself with in those days, the Callahan Act repeal campaign was a noble and lost cause. Although we collected more than enough signatures in two weeks, the secretary of state refused to certify our referendum petition, which meant that the repeal was never placed on the ballot. Even so, our efforts were not altogether in vain, because they put the Wayne County Council in motion politically and expanded our horizon.

Because of the activism of our CIO council and the swirl of action around the Progressive Party, it seemed as if Detroit were the center of the radical universe in those days. It was a second home, for instance, to the likes of Paul Robeson, the famous baritone, actor, football player, and activist, who sang at Reverend Hill's church when he came to town and attended evening meetings at many of our houses. One night, when there was a session planned at the Grosse Pointe Park residence of Sid Rosen, the state treasurer for the Progressive Party, Robeson arrived late, only to learn that Sid's six-year-old son had been trying his best to stay awake so that he could meet the great singer. When he heard this, Robeson tiptoed up to the boy's bedroom, and seconds later the Broadway version of "Old Man River" was booming through the house.

Another visitor was Benjamin Davis—not to be confused with my military friends Benjamin O. Davis, Sr. and Jr.—who spoke at the Greater Macedonia Baptist Church about his experience as the first black councilman in New York. As might be expected, Ike and Mike et al. filed the event as a Communist rally because of Davis's political persuasion. The police and the FBI both operated by a simple rule of thumb for that type of affair—incrimination by association. The advocates of change in whose circles I traveled found it curious that the government snoops lumped us all together as Communists/subversives and failed to recognize our individual discrepancies, because, in fact, we represented a myriad of political and social affiliations that had to be superseded if we were to pull together an effectual left-wing coalition. At any of our get-togethers, there were likely to be Progressives and Communists and Trotskyites and Socialists and Jews and Baptists and Catholics and Poles and Italians, for starters—and, of course, varying proportions of blacks and whites.

It was around that period that I began pushing the slogan "Black and White Unite to Fight." If there has been a prevailing theme to all my efforts of the past six decades, it has been the paramount importance of racial unity in addressing the country's socioeconomic problems. My ambitions as a union official were scarcely different from my ambitions as a mayor—to raise the American standard of citizenship, with particular attention given to those who most need it. In unions or cities or nations, that cannot be accomplished without a common willingness to leave behind personal differences for the greater good.

At my urging, the Wayne County Council broadened its scope in an effort to become an all-purpose vehicle for social change in the near and far community. That meant sticking our noses into countless places where others thought we didn't belong, such as the public establishments of downtown Detroit, many of which were still segregated. We protested that the Graystone Ballroom only allowed blacks on Monday nights. We protested that Negro League teams could not play games at Briggs Stadium, where the Tigers played, and that the Tigers had not signed any black players—unlike their rivals the Cleveland Indians, who won the 1948 pennant with Satchel Paige and my favorite player, Larry Doby. We could have picketed any number of restaurants that refused to serve blacks but chose the Barlum Towers (now the Cadillac Towers) coffee shop. After two or three days, the Barlum finally consented to offer us a table for lunch. I went in and ordered with three or four others—a couple of them white—but elected not to eat my food. I'd too often heard my father and his brothers tell tales from their restaurant days about the various misdeeds they had visited upon the food of the white folks who had fucked them over at one time or another, which included spitting on it and dipping in certain of their private parts. Having won the battle of the Barlum, I just paid for my lunch and chatted with my friends while they ate. I didn't even drink the water.

We also took an interest in the perils that black homeowners were encountering when they dared move into white neighborhoods. When two black families bought houses in Corktown, a working-class enclave within the shadow of Briggs Stadium, they were greeted by a mob of about two thousand whites who blockaded the area, stoned the houses, broke windows, dumped garbage, burned crosses, and patrolled the streets in KKK robes. One strange man sat in a hearse wearing a sheet, with a blue light shining on him, whatever the hell that meant. The incident received a lot of attention, and at one of our regular Wayne County CIO meetings, somebody suggested that we pass a resolution to raise some money for these families. Resolution, hell, I said—we ought to go out there and demonstrate. I thought it was important to make a show of solidarity within the labor movement. So under cover of darkness, about a half-dozen of us, black and white, stole into one of the houses, armed with shotguns. We had plenty of muscle available to handle the situation with force, but that would have probably set off another riot like the one less than five years before. Our plan, instead, was to secure the houses, then fix them up. That's the kind of demonstration that demonstrates something. I figured that if black and white union leaders worked together out in the open to paint and repair the houses, it not only would increase their value—which was the antithesis of what was expected when black people moved into a white neighborhood—but would make a statement that if anybody was going to fuck with black home-owners, they would be fucking with the entire trade union membership of Wayne County.

It was a solid plan, the tricky part being what to do if the mob tried to spoil the party. Our anxieties were confirmed at about midnight, when several of them stormed the porch of the house we occupied. It would have been helpful to identify the motherfuckers for our own edification—we weren't so naive as to think that the police would be interested—but we weren't able to get a look at their faces. After we kicked open the door and racked back our shotguns, we saw nothing but asses. The situation cooled off considerably after that. The next day, we put union leaders out there on ladders with paint brushes in their hands, making sure that the white ones were the most visible. We wanted it clear that this wasn't a black program, it was a solidarity program. When those black people settled into their new homes, it was an outstanding example of what could be accomplished by black and white unity. . . .

Part XII.

THE CALM BEFORE

THE STORM

Compared to other wars in which American troops were involved, the conflict in Korea was minor. But for Curtis Morrow and his foxhole buddies, "death just became a way of life" on the battlefield, where a round of fire could often mean the death of a comrade-in-arms. Morrow shows us war from the bottom of foxhole, under a ceaseless barrage of heavy artillery; it seems there was not a moment when this last of the U.S. Army's all-black regiments wasn't on the brink of annihilation. In 1948, President Harry Truman issued an executive order desegregating the armed services. For the first time the units were integrated and by 1951, integration in the Korean forces jumped from 9 percent to 30 percent of troops in the field.

The dissatisfaction that Morrow's comrades express about the States is not evident in the excerpt from Jane, a resident in an all-black town in what is probably Oklahoma. Jane's grandparents were part of the "exodusters" who migrated to the territory in the 1870s. Thousands of

African Americans, fed up with the Black Codes of the South that limited their opportunities, left Mississippi, Louisiana, Arkansas, Alabama, and Georgia and traveled to the North and West. Many of them settled first in Kansas, but when whites in the territory openly attacked them they moved on to Oklahoma.

In the Midwest on the plains, in the urban sprawl of Sandusky, or marching across the endless vistas of Spain, Paul Robeson was a fighter for the dispossessed. A true renaissance man with integrity, Robeson sided with the underprivileged both here and abroad, lending his powerful voice to the voiceless, and championing a number of unpopular causes. To hear him expound on a topic was to witness a full exegesis. Practically all of his endeavors were completed with astounding excellence, whether in sports, music, drama, language, oratory, or politics. His political activism, for such an acclaimed artist, is matchless. Unions, community groups, and cultural institutions all beckoned his presence, and the indefatigable Robeson did his best to answer most of the calls. This speech is but an example of his ability to dissect a subject and to give it both cultural and political relevance.

Detroit in the 1940s, as Coleman Young has related, may have been a city full of hard workers, but when the sun went down and folks wanted to find a place to let it all hang out, all they had to do was to call Sunnie Wilson. And there was a good chance through the mid-1950s that Wilson was the host of the party. Owning or managing a succession of nightclubs, cocktail lounges, and bars, Wilson was the "host with the most" in the city's renowned Paradise Valley. On any given evening at his popular Swamp Room you might catch Duke Ellington, T-Bone Walker, Dizzy Gillespie, or Etta James.

Coretta Scott was a talented vocalist, but her classical aspirations would have hardly been suited for the Swamp Room. They were, however, perfectly in accord with the curriculum at the New England Con-

servatory of Music, where she had enrolled to study. A graduate of
Antioch College and a native of Alabama, she had her mind set on a
long career in music when she met Martin Luther King, Jr., then studying for his divinity degree at Boston University. After earning her degree
in music, Scott's aspirations to perform and to teach music were soon
shelved. Her husband had a date with destiny and she was needed to
make sure he kept this appointment and others.

Educational opportunities for Coretta and Martin in Boston were
comparatively unbridled; such was not the case for thousands of black
children in the nation's segregated public schools. To undermine segregation and the "separate but equal" status, the NAACP had sponsored all
sorts of litigation. The most far-reaching and momentous attack made its
way to the Supreme Court as *Brown v. the Board of Education, Topeka.*
Attorney Constance Baker Motley was an eyewitness to the court proceedings and the ultimate decision that would revolutionize race relations
in America. Although the Supreme Court ruled that separate educational
facilities were inherently unequal, there was still the large question of
how relief would be granted, given the variety of local conditions. A
little more than a year after the historic decision, the court ruled again
that the defendants should make a "reasonable start toward full compli-
ance." Southern states were on the ropes but not defeated, and it would
take several other dramatic civil rights rulings to bring about full equality
for African American citizens.

CURTIS MORROW

From *What's a Commie Ever Done to Black People?*

KOREA, 1951

YES, WE EVEN VOLUNTEERED FOR FRONT-LINE DUTY. We . . . wanted to experience the excitement of fighting in a real war. We wanted to know how it felt to kill an enemy soldier. We also wanted the adventure and opportunities made available in case we decided to make the military our career.

I believe we would have thought differently if we had been aware of the many horrors connected with war. It's not something you go into one day and out the next. It's an everyday thing; you do the same thing every day until you are wounded to the point you are unable to function ever again as a soldier or you are killed. But there was always the possibility that you might survive. And it was that pitiful little ray of hope that kept us pushing on day after day. And one day our friend and squad leader Corporal Elmer Bailey's hopes and prayers ceased to exist. He was killed in a hail of machine-gun fire. All we were supposed to do was make contact with the enemy and get the hell out of there (like we had done together so many times before). The last I remember of him he was standing there firing his carbine and yelling from the pit of his stomach at us (his squad members) to clear the area while he provided cover fire for us.

The brother had saved my life once before. If it hadn't been for him I would have frozen to death the time I fell asleep in sub-zero temperature (35 degrees below). There had been other times too. He had been my first foxhole partner and schooled me and other members of our squad and platoon in the do's and don'ts. He was like a big brother to us all, always looking out for the men in his squad. Now he was gone, dead. I wondered how his poor old grandmother would take it when she got the news. I guess she'll never know how he died—like a real hero, standing his ground on a mountain ridge in a country she probably never heard of before, laying down a field of fire to enable members of his squad a chance to clear an ambush that none of us were supposed to escape. Those of us who did survive that ambush vowed to give no quarter to our enemies thereafter.

After a while I just stopped remembering the names of replacements. Chinese Communists were knocking our guys out of action so fast you really didn't get a chance to learn many replacements' names. I don't mean to imply that it's only the new replacements that had a priority on dying. We were all targets. However, the longer you've been in action, the more alert you become; the faster you react, the sharper your instincts. Even so, with all that and more, nothing is guaranteed to keep anyone alive in war. . . .

It got to where we considered a man who lost a limb or two as being lucky. Sure, they paid a price, but at least they got out of this hell hole alive. Such reasoning never lasted long, however, because maybe it's better to be dead than living the rest of your life with missing arms or legs—or both.

After a while death just became a way of life. There were always so many dead bodies around. One just tended to think, "It's better them than me." Or, if it was some of our guys, I'd think that I too could very easily be lying there among them.

During my tour I had plenty of time to think about the power of prayer. Some of the best prayers on this earth I've been told (and believe), have been said in war. I've seen men who, at every opportunity they had, would take out their Bible and read. Too many times I would learn after the next incoming volley of enemy mortar fire or a fire-fight that these men were no longer with us. It was very confusing to me, a 17-to-18 year-old infantry soldier who had been taught that salvation was through prayer to God. Yet, those who prayed the hardest still died, sometimes even first.

"Well," a soldier once said, "at least they stand the best chance of going to heaven."

We, the old-timers, would tell the newcomers, "It's OK to read your Bible, Soldier, but first clean your weapon, check your ammunition, become familiar with the area in front of your position, make sure your bowel is clear before the night." . . .

All atheists become believers after their first serious engagement with the enemy, after the first time they experience a barrage of enemy artillery or mortar fire. One quickly realizes at such a time that one must call someone's name, and Satan is the last name that comes to mind when calling for help and deliverance. But the most ridiculous person I've ever witnessed was some soldier attempting to preach "his" words of God under such conditions. In the Army, these men are called chaplains. "Really," I would think, "what can they tell me?"

They usually came around just before a major assault. I could see the fear in their faces. Man, they could barely wait to get the hell out of there. And I'd be wishing I could go with them. After a short prayer from their Bible, usually the 27th Psalm, they would proceed to do just that, get the hell out of there. And we, the poor unfortunate combat infantrymen, with the blessings of their version of God, would be sent on our way to kill, maim, suffer, and die. And those of us that were somehow spared would have to live with the horrible memories for the rest of our lives.

Of course, it would be different if you were only required to fight in one battle, just one engagement with a declared enemy, and then be returned to your base for a hot shower and meal. But it's not like that. War is very repetitious. The only difference is the faces. After each fight there would be new faces to replace the ones taken out of action due to wounds or death. Sometimes old faces would return, those that suffered wounds the army felt were not serious enough. Some guys would be hit and returned two, sometimes even three, times.

I was only sent back once, the result of a minor wound, although it could have cost me an eye. We were going through a mine field that had been cleared by members of the 77th Combat Engineers Battalion. Each mine had been dug up and marked, but one of our guys had accidently gotten his rifle tangled in some wires that were connected to a fuse, which set off the fuse, injuring me and a couple of others. Our wounds were superficial, and we removed the splinter-shrapnel with our fingers. But one piece imbedded above my left eye sent me to the battalion aid station.

At the field hospital they quickly removed a piece of shrapnel about one-quarter of an inch long, then assigned me to a bunk, saying they'd keep me for twenty-four hours for observation. Sounded damn good to me. I had thought maybe I'd even get a chance to get deloused and have a shower out of the deal, not to mention a couple of hot meals. Well, I had just finished the meal when in the bunk next to mine they brought in a white soldier from the 27th RCT that had been shot in the head while on a patrol. The other wounded in the tent were waiting to be sent to a general hospital, but this soldier was worse off than anyone else. Half his head was blown away; I could see his brains. They couldn't bandage it up. Morphine did nothing to ease his pain. There was nothing anyone could do for him but watch the poor soldier as he lay there, suffering and pleading for someone to please kill him and end the pain. "Please, somebody stop it. Stop it. I can't stand it. Let me die. Please, let me die. Oh God please"—then a lone mournful wail. . . .

I put cotton in my ears, covered my head with a blanket, and lay there all night listening to the loud moans of the dying soldier and the muttered voice of the Army chaplain as he uttered what I suspected to be prayers throughout the night. Sometimes in between the moans and the prayers I could make out the distant sounds of small arms firing and exploding rounds fired from our long range field artillery, which searched for targets miles away. My right eye, the one not covered with bandages, was wet. God how I wished I could just wake up and find that all this had been a bad nightmare.

At daybreak the soldier was dead. I took the bandage from my eye, asked for a rifle and some C-rations, and hitched a ride on a passing half-track back to the front and my outfit.

"Damn," Private Gadson, a New Yorker, said, "you mean you didn't even wait for some hot chow before leaving?"

Around March 6, 1951, I, along with a couple of other members of my squad, returned from a barbwire stringing detail to find other members of our platoon gathered around two replacements.

"Sarah Vaughn and Nat King Cole still singing jazz and blues, man. And Satchmo, well, he still bowing and scraping."

"Yeah, and black people is getting damned tired of just sitting around watching Whitey fuck us over and doing nothing about it," interjected the second new man.

"Yeah, well we spoke up, and here we is," continued the first one.

I found a spot near and joined the circle. Eight of us were sitting around, chewing the fat, some cleaning weapons, some playing cards, but we were all very interested in what the new men were talking about.

"You mean you didn't volunteer to come here and serve your country, soldier?" asked one of the men, jokingly.

"Well sir," replied one of the replacements. "I had a choice of either getting strung up by a lynch mob, going to jail, or joining the army."

"Yeah, ha ha, that's why he chose to serve our country," said the second replacement.

"OK, I'll ask, what the hell did you do? Look at a white woman?"

"Naa man, I kicked a white hillbilly's ass for trying to screw my woman, and I mean he tried to do it right in front of me." After a momentary pause he continued. "I mean the son of a bitch told me to get out of my house until he finish."

"Wait a minute, man, that's against the law," I said.

"My man, in Georgia, it's an unwritten law that a white man can do anything he damn please to black people, even to the extent of demanding sex with a black man's woman. And there's not a damn thing we can do about it. No white law-enforcement officer will come to our defense."

"Where are you from anyway?" he asked.

"Chicago," I told him, "not that that means anything."

"You damn right," said one of the oldtimers (a soldier with three or more months of combat time). "Whites can do anything they wish to a Negro or any other minority, and the reason is simple. The law is always on their side, no matter what the crime is.''

''Well, if I get out of this shit alive, this is going to be one Negro that's going to send some of them whites to hell ahead of him.'' It was Sergeant Bedgood, our platoon sergeant, joining the conversation. ''Meanwhile we're here in Korea, supposedly fighting the evil forces of communism and defending the cause of freedom, justice, and all that shit—for others.''

There was a moment of silence, as we digested the sergeant's words and waited for him to continue.

''You hear those sounds?'' asked the sergeant, looking at the two replacements. He was referring to the distant sounds of exploding artillery and bombs, sounds always heard up front.

''Yes sir, Sergeant,'' both newcomers answered in unison.

''Well, you'll be hearing it as long as you are here, although you won't hear the one that gets you. Or the bullet that kills you. That's about the only thing you can be sure of here. And the only chance we all have of surviving this motherfuckin' war is sticking together. And that means our joint firepower. In a fight, the more there is, the better our chances of living to see daylight of the following day. That talk about fighting for liberty, justice, and all that bullshit is another fight, one we'll have to fight when and if we survive this one. . . .''

JANE

From *My Soul Is My Own*

OKLAHOMA, 1950S

I WAS BORN IN AN ALL BLACK TOWN. Then I knew what
. . . was what there. I knew why the town was there, why it was named,
and everything about it. And we were very proud of our town. And ah, then I
come here and find that everyone was very, very closed. It was as though, you
were enmeshed in a sort of, ah oh what do you call it? You were enmeshed in a
sort of a closed society that was closed because of what had happened not
because of preference. And, so ah, I wanted to know why. And then as I began
to investigate I found out more and more things that were different. One
person would tell me one thing, one would tell me another. And then I began
to go through the record books to find out actually what happened. And ah, I
went all the way to the state library. I went to the county historical society, the
library here. I went through what I could find in the library in at the university
and what was there from another local university library. And ah, I put all the
facts together. It took me five years of research to put this together. I began
researching this in 1979. And after I had put it together, then I began to write.
So ah, this is how long it had taken, you see.

My home town. O.K. It's a old like town. And it's right at the edge of the
Indian reservation and, Indian reservations for the so called, civilized tribes, the
Creeks, the Cherokees, the Seminoles, the Choctaws. Those are the tribes that
were near my home town. My mother is Creek. My father is a native of Africa.
He went to school in England through the efforts of the missionaries. And then
came to the United States with the missionaries at the time when the, the
Italians took over the government of his country from the English. And ah,

after going through, to a college, which I don't know even exists anymore, he went to Meharry, to a medical school for blacks in Tennessee. He finished there and then went to Wisconsin and ah, he was to do intern work at Wisconsin but, ah it was very cold to him and he came back to Indiana and he practiced there for a while. And then felt like he had to go back and do his internship somewhere ah in order to validate the state's requirements for his license, so he came out west to do an internship with the Indians.

No, I remember the year that he came from, from England to America, that was 1892. And ah, then ah, there was a run for property and that must have been around the year of 18, oh no, 1904, 1905, 1906. Where the people who wanted property ran to cover the land and the land that they covered by this running was theirs. And this was how they apportioned the land that was near the Indians ah for, native Americans and ah, so my mother's brother's ran and that's how they got the, the farms that were between two small towns. Now that's all I know. And that ah, it was somewhere between there and, my mother contracted pneumonia and my father went out to see her and thought that she was the most beautiful woman he had ever seen. That was in September and he went back in, at Christmas time and married her. So, that's how my parents got together.

You see my mother was 19 when they got married and my father I'm sure was near 40, because he, see he, had gone through school in England and when you came from his country you were very grown even there because I don't know what kind of missionary schools that they had there before you went to school in England. See? So, there was a large difference between their ages, I'm sure.

My father became Mayor of the town. One of the beginnings of the town was Mar, Marcus Garvey's ah, interest in taking people back to Africa . . . was the fact that he felt that there, was no way that black people were going to get a good deal in these United States. And he, what was his name, the man for whom the town was named, along with another man who ah, was the son of one of the people that was with John Brown's raid. And ah, they were trying to get water and they discovered that the water was very, very metallic and they kept sounding farther and farther down and they'd spent so much time there, that they decided, well maybe we better start a town here. And they started a town and they made a gin for cotton because cotton was a large crop around the place and ah, the Creek Indians knew a lot, quite a lot because they had been brought there from Florida. They kept them moving farther and farther west until they got them to New Mexico from Florida.

So, they were very, very, experienced cotton growers and ah, with the help of one of their, I don't remember what his name was ah, his English name, they called him . . . , but I don't remember what his real name was. But he, he was ah, over the gin and there was a Mr. Green and Mr. Tate they had the, had the gin and ah, then they went to the capital of the state at that time and got the place incorporated as a black town. And my father was the Mayor at the time. It's still there today! . . .

PAUL ROBESON

From *Paul Robeson Speaks*

NEW YORK CITY, 1951

WE ARE HERE TODAY TO WORK OUT ways and means of finding jobs for colored actors and colored musicians, to see that the pictures and statues made by colored painters and sculptors are sold, to see that the creations of Negro writers are made available to the vast American public. We are here to see that colored scientists and professionals are placed in leading schools and universities, to open up opportunities for Negro technicians, to see that the way is open for colored lawyers to advance to judgeships—yes, to the Supreme Court of these United States, if you please.

It is not just a question of jobs, of positions, of commercial sales. No—the questions at hand cannot be resolved without the resolution of deeper problems involved here. We are dealing with the position in this society of a great people—of fifteen million closely-bound human beings, of whom ten millions in the cotton and agricultural belt of the South form a kind of nation based upon common oppression, upon a magnificent common heritage, upon unified aspiration for full freedom and full equality in the larger democratic society.

The Negro people today are saying all up and down this nation (when you get on the streets, into the churches, into the bars to talk to them): "We will not suffer the genocide that might be visited upon us. We are prepared to fight to the death for our rights."

Yes, we are dealing with a great people. Their mere survival testifies to that. One hundred millions sacrificed and wasted in the slave ships, on the cotton plantations, in order that there might be built the basic wealth of this great land. It must have been a tremendously strong people, a people of tremendous stamina, of the finest character, merely to have survived. Not only have the Negro people survived in this America, they have given to these United States almost a new language, given it ways of speech, given it perhaps the only indigenous music. . . .

So we are dealing with a people who come from great roots. There is no need to quote the names of an Anderson or a Hayes and many more; or of the great scientists—of a Julian, of a Carver. No need today for the Negro people to prove any more that they have a right to full equality. They have proven it again and again.

The roots of this great outpouring we are talking about today in the cultural expression of my people, is a great culture from a vast continent. If these origins are somewhat blurred in this America of ours, they are clear in Brazil where Villa-Lobos joins Bach with African rhythms and melodies; in Cuba and Haiti a whole culture, musical and poetic, is very deep in the Africa of its origins—an African culture quite comparable to the ancient culture of the Chinese—similar in religious concepts, in language, in poetry, in its sculpture, in its whole esthetic—a culture which has deeply influenced the great artists of our time—a Picasso, a Modigliani, a Brancusi, an Epstein, a deFalla, a Milhaud. So we are today discussing the problems of a proud people, rich in tradition, a people torn from its ancient homeland but who in 300 years have built anew, have enriched this new Continent with its physical power, with its intellect, with its deep, inexhaustible spirit and courage.

As I have said, in spite of all these contributions to our culture, the fruits have been taken from us. Think of Handy, one of the creators of the Blues; think of Count Basie, playing to half-filled houses at the Apollo; colored arrangers receiving a pittance while white bands reap harvests. What heartbreak for every Negro composer! Publishing houses taking his songs for nothing and making fortunes. Theatres in the heart of the Negro communities dictating to Negro performers what they shall act . . . arrogantly telling Negro audiences what they shall see.

I went to a whole group of my Negro friends. I wanted them to put down some of the things in which they were interested this morning. What did they want you to know? Here are some things that I will read:

> Negroes have carried on an important struggle in the United States throughout the history of this country, even before there was any significant progressive movement in the U.S.: this is a lesson progressives must learn—and accept it as a privilege and duty to join in the struggle. The progressive movement must understand with crystal clarity that the Negro people of the United States have never retreated or compromised in their aspirations, and progressives must follow a dynamic path with them. For if they do otherwise, they will find themselves conscious or unconscious allies of reactionaries and pseudo-liberals. Progressives must re-orient

themselves to the qualitative change that has come about in the unalienable and rightful demand of the United States Negro. The Negro men and women of the United States want equality for everybody, in everything, everywhere, now.

This is awfully good, I must say.

Whites must come forward and put up a struggle, no matter what the repercussions; struggle must be constant in unions, housing organizations and not only where Negroes are involved—whites must take action every day and not wait for Negroes to raise issues in order to come in on the struggle. . . . Peace is crucial in this question. Its maintenance depends on whether or not democracy is extended to the Negro. Support must be twofold. In order to show support politically, there must be an understanding and appreciation of Negro culture. There must be a willingness to learn. If present U.S. cultural patterns do not permit the utilization of Negro talent, then independent means must be found.

Another comment:

The U.S. theatre must show the totality of Negro life, thereby eliminating stereotypes in their extreme. To off set the so-called objective reporting in the white press, all positive accomplishments by Negro cultural workers should be designated as such. Every Negro artist needs and must now demand free and equal opportunity to develop in fields of his or her endeavor. White progressives must recognize that in joining the Negro struggle, they join on the Negro people's terms.

Mr. Hood, in Cincinnati, put it very sharply: We must work together. We are a unit—certainly we are, but to the trade union leader (we say) we seek your co-operation; we no longer ask your permission.

Let us touch for a moment on radio and television. We all know the difficulties—no major hours with Negro talent, an occasional guest appearance eagerly awaited by the Negro audience. Why this discrimination? Well, these mass media are based on advertising, commercialism at its worst, and the final answer is very simple. It goes to the root of all that has been said. The final answer is: "The South won't take it."

Now, I had a program myself in the '40's, all set up by one of the biggest advertising agencies, a very fine program, a dignified program in which I would have been doing Othello and many other things. One morning they said, "We made some inquiries and the South just won't have it. You can come on once in a while and sing with Mr. Voorhees, and so forth, but no possibility of a Negro artist having his own program." Not *that* dignity. And so we have allowed the South with its patterns to determine for all America how, when and where the Negro will be denied an opportunity.

I think that public opinion could be aroused on this issue. This is a matter of national protest, of national pressure. These media happen to be under the control of Federal Communications. We are dealing here with matters as serious as the passage of an Anti-Lynch Bill, Anti-Poll Tax and Free Voting Legislation, of F.E.P.C., of the whole issue of Federal and States rights. We can demand a change in the public interest in the pursuance of democratic procedures. Added to this, of course, can be pressure on the advertisers who wax fat today from the purchases of Negro customers. These latter, plus their allies, could have very decisive influence.

The films today are of vast significance and influence. Here, too, the South determines the attempts to camouflage, to pass off so-called progressive films, to find new approaches to the treatment of the Negro. They have been very thoroughly analyzed and exposed for what they are by V. J. Jerome in his exhaustive pamphlet on "The Negro in Hollywood Films." Here, too, the mounting of the right kind of campaign could shake Hollywood to its foundations, and help would be forthcoming from all over the world. Their markets everywhere in the world could be seriously affected, if the lead came from here.

The struggle on this front could have been waged with some real measure of success at any time, but today conditions insure the careful heeding of the collective wrath of the Negro people and their allies. For today, in the struggle extending all over the world, all pronouncements of our wonderful democracy ring hollow and clearly false as soon as one points the finger at the oppression of fifteen million second- and third-class citizens of this land.

There is no way to cover that up. One day, Willie McGee; the next, Martinsville; the next, Cicero; the next, Groveland, Florida. Behind these horrors is the mounting anger of a long-suffering people, of a people that has its Denmark Veseys, its Frederick Douglasses, its Sojourner Truths, its Harriet Tubmans, its Du Bois's, its Benjamin Davis's—a people that fought for its freedom in the great Civil War and buried the hated Confederate flags in the dust.

Behind these people and their allies here in the U.S. are the tens and tens of millions of advanced workers through the world, west and east, bulwarked by the overwhelming millions of a fast-emerging colonial world hastening to final and complete control of their destinies, inspired by the events of a November 7th, thirty-four years ago, by the victories of many new People's Democracies, by the world-shattering creation of the new People's Republic of China. This world in change makes possible here new levels of action, insures victories hitherto unsuspected. The millions of India watch and Mr. Bowles will have his hands and his mouth full to convince these people that the civilization extolled by Byrnes of South Carolina, Smith of Georgia, Connally of Texas, is just the thing to bring new vistas of freedom and individual liberty to that ancient continent. I often get letters from India. They seem to be somewhat doubtful.

The Government can be pressured in this time and it certainly can be pressured on this issue. Most important for us here is the recognition of the Negro's rights to all kinds of jobs in the arts, not only the rights of the artists, but technical jobs for engineers, all sorts of opportunities in production, in scenic design, at all levels. I am very much interested in that. I've got a son, Paul, who studied engineering at Cornell, majored in Communications. I'd like to see him get a good job in television.

And so in the case of Actors Equity—we who are members of Equity must fight not only for the rights of Negro actors, we must see that the stage-hands are there. We must fight within the AFL, Equity's parent organization, for the right of Negroes to work in *every* field. And so in the American Guild of Musical Artists and in the American Federation of Radio Artists—they are shouting an awful lot these days about how democratic and American they are: Let them show it!

The final problem concerns new ways, new opportunities based upon a deep sense of responsibility in approaching the problem of the Negro people in its totality. There are despoilers abroad in our land, akin to these who attempted to throttle our Republic at its birth. Despoilers who would have kept my beloved people in unending serfdom, a powerful few who blessed Hitler as he destroyed a large segment of a great people. Today they would recreate the image of Hitler, stifle millions of the hitherto oppressed as they struggle forth for their emancipation, destroy the People's Republics where life has been created anew, where the forces of nature have been turned to man's prosperity and good.

All these millions of the world stand aghast at the sight and the very name of *that* America—but they love *us;* they look to *us* to help create a world where we can all live in peace and friendship, where we can exchange the excellences of our various arts and crafts, the manifold wonders of our mutual scientific creations, a world where we can rejoice at the unleashed powers of our innermost selves, of the potential of great masses of people. To them *we* are the real America. Let us remember that.

And let us learn how to bring to the great masses of the American people *our* culture and *our* art. For in the end, what are we talking about when we talk about American culture today? We are talking about a culture that is restricted to the very, very few. How many workers ever get to the theatre? I was in concerts for 20 years, subscription concerts, the two thousands seats gone before any Negro in the community, any worker, could even hear about a seat.

Even then, the price was $12.00 for six concerts. How could working people ever hear these concerts? Only by my going into the trade unions and singing on the streets and on the picket lines and in the struggles for the freedom of our people—only in this way could the workers of this land hear me.

We are talking about a culture which as yet has no relationship to the great masses of the American people. I remember an experience in England. I sang not only in Albert Hall, the concert halls, but also in the picture theatres, and one night I came out and a young woman was standing there with her mother, an aged lady. "My grandmother wants to thank you very much. She always wanted to hear you in person. She heard you tonight and she's going home. She just had sixpence above her bus fare." So she was able to hear me. Later, that was so in the Unity Theatre in London—now a theatre which has stretched all over England. Here in America, in 1948 in the Deep South, I remember standing singing to white workers in Memphis, workers who had come out on strike that Negro workers might get equal wages.

In the theatre I felt this years ago and it would interest you to know that the opening night of *Othello* in New York, in Chicago, in San Francisco (I never told this to the Guild), I told Langner he could have just one-third of the house for the elite. I played the opening night of *Othello* to the workers from Fur, from Maritime, from Local 65.

Just the other night I sang at the Rockland Palace in the Bronx, to this people's audience. We speak to them every night. To thousands. Somewhere, with the impetus coming from the arts, sciences and professions, there are literally millions of people in America who would come to hear us, the Negro artists. This can be very important. Marian Anderson, Roland Hayes, all of us started in the Baptist Churches. I'm going right back there very soon. If you want to talk about audiences, I defy any opera singer to take those ball parks like Sister Tharpe or Mahalia Jackson. It is so in the Hungarian communities (I was singing to the Hungarian-Americans yesterday), the Russian-Americans, the Czech-Americans . . . all of them have their audiences stretching throughout this land.

The progressive core of these audiences could provide a tremendous base for the future, a tremendous base for our common activity and a necessary base in the struggle for peace. These people must be won. We can win them through our cultural contributions. We could involve millions of people in the struggle for peace and for a decent world.

But the final point. This cannot be done unless we as artists have the deepest respect for these people. When we say that we are people's artists, we must mean that. I mean it very deeply. Because, you know, the people created our art in the first place.

Haydn with his folk songs—the people made it up in the first place. The language of Shakespeare—this was the creation of the English-speaking people;

the language of Pushkin, the creation of the Russian people, of the Russian peasants. That is where it came from—a little dressed up with some big words now and then which can be broken down into very simple images.

So, in the end, the culture with which we deal comes from the people. We have an obligation to take it back to the people, to make them understand that in fighting for their cultural heritage they fight for peace. They fight for their own rights, for the rights of the Negro people, for the rights of all in this great land. All of this is dependent so much upon our understanding the power of this people, the power of the Negro people, the power of the masses of America, of a world where we can all walk in complete dignity.

SUNNIE WILSON

From *Toast of the Town*

DETROIT, 1952

THOUGH THE DEMOCRATS MET DEFEAT AGAINST the
. . . Republican ticket of Eisenhower and Nixon in 1952, I resumed my
entrepreneurial activities by setting out to create a gathering spot for my
patrons at the Mark Twain. I brought my Forest Club B license over to the
hotel and opened a new downstairs cocktail lounge, the Swamp Room. The
Mark Twain's downstairs lounge had one of the prettiest bars in the country. I
had a nice jukebox and adorned the room with potted palm trees. On one wall
I had a mural of a Louisiana swamp with moss-covered trees rising out of the
water. The lounge featured the Chicken Shack's famous white piano and everybody played on it, from Duke Ellington to Nat King Cole. In the early 1950s
pianist Hugh Lawson and bassist Ernie Farrow* performed as a duo for Sunday
sessions in the Swamp Room. Later in the decade, pianist-saxophonist Teddy
Harris led a five-piece band at the Swamp Room.

During the early 1950s, saxophone giant Lester "The Prez" Young
stayed at my place. He often came to town with Norman Granz's Jazz at
the Philharmonic series, which featured a great lineup of talent. The Prez
didn't say much to anyone. He'd go up to his room with his scotch and
horns and lock his door. He'd lay around his room and play his horn until
it was time to go to his gig.

Texas-born blues guitarist T-Bone Walker became another regular at the
Mark Twain. A skinny fella, T-Bone was a lovable guy who could really play the

---

* Hugh Lawson and Ernie Farrow later appeared at the Blue Bird Inn and became members of Yusef Lateef's band,
recording many records for the Savoy label.

guitar. He stayed at my place when he was performing at Raymond "Sportree" Jackson's Sportree Reed's Bar at Hastings and Adams, or the Frolic.

One time T-Bone Walker stayed in the lucky suite and threw a big party. While he was busy drinking and entertaining his guests, someone stole his watch and ring. Enraged, he began cussing everybody out in the room. Later, a fella called and told T-Bone that his girlfriend had picked up the watch and ring. This fella brought the stolen items to T-Bone's room. I humorously reminded T-Bone, who was still very mad, "You should be very thankful. If you'd been staying in another room, you would have never got those things back."

Among the many musicians who checked in at my place was trumpeter Dizzy Gillespie. He stayed, until one day I went to his room and couldn't find him anywhere. He had left without a word. Dizzy was a fine young man, but a little hard to figure out sometimes. Walking down the street a few days later, I passed a restaurant, and in the front window I saw Dizzy having lunch with drummer J. C. Heard. I didn't blame Dizzy for preferring the company of another musician, especially a talent like J. C. Heard. Yet I still felt a little jealous that J. C. had made off with my tenant. So I went into the place and walked up to the table where Dizzy and J. C. were sitting. "Hello, J. C.," I said addressing Mr. Heard without looking at Dizzy. "I need a favor from you."

"What do you need, Mr. Wilson?" asked J. C.

"I'd like to learn to play the drums," I told him.

"What? Sunnie, you're a businessman. You don't really want to play the drums," he said, a little amused at my request.

I repeated resolutely, "I want to learn to play the drums."

"Listen, Sunnie, I don't have the time, and besides you. . . ."

"No, I want you to teach me."

"Why?" asked J. C., who was starting to get annoyed by my prodding.

"Because if I learn to play the drums," I answered, "I can get my old tenant back." Then we all burst out laughing.

Dizzy wasn't the only one to leave my place without paying his bill. Down through the years, musicians must have given me a bushel basket full of bad checks and IOUs. Until this day, singer Etta James and her mother still owe me nine hundred dollars. When comedian Mantan Moreland came to town to play the Flame Show Bar with his partner Bud Harris in the 1950s, he didn't have enough money to get back on the road. Mantan found his fame in the old Charlie Chan films. I put him up at the Mark Twain. One day the desk clerk told me, "Your friend Mantan is racking up an exorbitant bill." I told the clerk, "Don't worry. I'm going to have a talk with my guest." I confronted Mantan and said, "Mantan, they tell me you're running up quite a bill, that you're on that phone all day. I just can't cover your bills."

Instead of showing any sign of apprehension or concern, Mantan gushed with excitement. "Man, I was just thinking about you," he said. Wary of his intentions, I asked, "What do you mean, man?" "Let's get an act together," he answered.

People have tried to buy me off with all sorts of things, but I never had someone attempt to pay his bills by offering me a part in a stage act. By that time in life I had no interest in returning to the stage. Unfortunately, my friend Mantan never showed much interest in paying his tab. Years later I'd see Mantan some place, and he'd say, "I'm still writing that script for us."

Not all of my guests slipped out so easy, however. One day a delivery truck pulled up to the hotel. The drivers saw the rear end and two legs of a big fat man hanging out a first-floor window. The delivery men came in and told me a man was caught in one of my windows and was hollering for help. This man was a blues singer, a big heavy fella. I knew he was trying to skip out on his tab because the drivers had seen his bags lying on the ground outside the window. When I entered the room, I saw the front half of this man with the window resting on top of his huge frame.

"Mr. Wilson, please get me out. The window fell down on me."

I slowly inspected the situation, taking my time as the man hung painfully over the windowsill.

"What are you doing in that window?" I asked. "You weren't trying to leave without paying, were you?"

"Oh no, Mr. Wilson."

"Does it hurt?" I asked.

"Yes, Mr. Wilson. Please get me out of here."

"Well if you're hurt, then maybe I ought to call the police."

"No, no, Mr. Wilson, don't call the police," pleaded the man.

"Give me my money then," I demanded.

"Yes sir, Mr. Wilson, I'll get your money."

I then got a few people together outside, and we pulled the man out of the window. I made him walk around the building and enter the front door. Sensing this fella was getting upset, I said a few humorous words and made him laugh. Then I made him promise to pay me.

But for the most part my guests never made trouble, especially those from the gospel music world, guests like the Five Blind Boys, the Daisy Sisters, the Clouds of Joy, Pearl Bailey, and Sister Rosetta Tharpe. Miss Tharpe was a religious singer, but when times got bad on the road, she would resort to performing in jazz houses and cabarets. During the holidays, these singers would perform live on the radio. One Easter morning Rosetta Tharpe and T-Bone Walker joined a number of the gospel singers in a impromptu session in the second-floor lobby. They brought down guitars and horns. The harmonies were the most beautiful sound I've ever heard.

The Reverend C. L. Franklin, father of singing star Aretha Franklin, used to stay at my place on occasion. In the early days before he became famous, he had the Bethel Baptist Church on Hastings. I used to loan him chairs from the Forest Club. He'd come and get them on Sunday and return them Monday morning. Joe Von Battle, owner of Joe's Record Shop on Hastings Street, recorded Franklin's sermons at Bethel Baptist Church and leased the recordings to Chess records in Chicago. They became million-sellers. Although Franklin had an ego, I got along with him. We used to drink together and jokingly taunt each other. I liked to get him riled up. I would start by saying, "I could make you a big man." He'd respond with, "You can't make me a big man. I'm already a big man."

After his boastful announcement, I would keep up the contest. "I got to make you a big man, because you can't sing and you can't preach." By then he would start to get upset. "God-damn it, I'm a big man and you're just a little man!" Then I would stop him, and calmly say, "See that—that's what I mean. You're always trying to prove you're big. I can help you, fella." We would go on and on with this.

What I liked about Reverend Franklin is that even after he began to make it big, he still took time out to hone his skills as an orator. I respected the fact that the Reverend Franklin believed he had more to learn. He studied under another reverend who taught him how to preach. Reverend Franklin sent for this man and put him up in my hotel. They held regular sessions. Soon Reverend Franklin began to sound just like this man. He adopted the same low inflections and vocal rises.

By the 1950s, many up-and-coming names in the music world were guests at the Mark Twain. When Nat King Cole came back to play a big show on Grand River, he brought a forty-piece orchestra with him and they all stayed at my place. Another guest, singer Bobby Bland, became the hotel's honorary steward. When I stepped out or had business out of town, he damn near ran the place.

B. B. King stayed at the Mark Twain. While performing at a downtown theater, he related that he had no money to put up his band. Learning of his predicament, a shoe-shine man approached B. B. backstage and told him to contact Sunnie Wilson at the Mark Twain Hotel. I put up B. B.'s band and the next morning fed every member. B. B. and I became great friends and he has never forgotten the help I gave him. Whenever he came to town, he'd come by to see me. Years later, in 1976, I promoted a show for him at the Windsor Arena in Canada.

During the 1950s, the most prestigious black-owned hotel was the Gotham at 111 Orchestra Place. Known from coast to coast, the Gotham was designed by renowned architect Albert Kahn, and built by white businessman Albert B. Hartz in 1925 at a cost of $590,000. A nine-story establishment, the Gotham boasted three hundred rooms decorated with plush carpeting and solid mahogany furniture. The hotel's Ebony Dining Room served excellent food. Since the Mark Twain only had a snack bar, my associates and I ate our meals at the Gotham, which was within walking distance of my hotel. The Gotham's chef, Mr. Madison, outclassed the cook at the Book Cadillac Hotel. He made beautiful ice sculptures that adorned the fine cloth-covered tables.

Among the Gotham's noted African American guests were poet Langston Hughes, Congressman Adam Clayton Powell, and singer Billie Holiday. At the Gotham I met a young Sammy Davis Jr. when he stayed at the hotel with his family. Some whites came to the Gotham, but their numbers were limited because they had their own places downtown. . . .

CORETTA SCOTT KING

From *My Life with Martin Luther King, Jr.*

§

BOSTON, 1950S

I FEEL VERY STRONGLY THAT I WAS *SENT* to Boston, di-
. . . rected there, because it was in Boston that I met Martin Luther King,
Jr. Neither Martin nor I believed in destiny, in the sense of predestination that
one cannot change. But we both felt that God guided our lives in the way that
He wanted us to serve, so that we might be the instruments of His creative
will.

I believe that there is a plan and a purpose for each person's life and that
there are forces working in the universe to bring about good and to create a
community of love and brotherhood. Those who can attune themselves to these
forces—to God's purpose—can become special instruments of His will.

From the time I was very young, I had strong hope, not only about success
for myself but also about serving humanity. Now, I feel that I was being led to
Martin Luther King, Jr., to fulfill this hope with him. And even though we
were both very young in Boston and even though our courtship was not too
different from a thousand others, it was all leading us where we were going.

Of course, I had no premonition of this at the time; quite the contrary. I
had not planned to get married for a long time. I was deeply interested in
developing my voice and my potential in music; and by now I had reason to
think that I had enough talent to achieve some success. I wanted to give myself
an opportunity to find out if this was so. At the least I would have the
satisfaction of having developed what talent I had to its full capacity. Whether
or not it was ever used professionally, I knew I would be a happier person for
having done so.

All these years I had waited, and now I was here in Boston in this environment where I was absorbing music. Everything about it seemed so right. I was very happy.

Martin Luther King, who changed all this, came along in my second semester.

We met through a mutual friend at the conservatory named Mary Powell. She was a little older than I was and was married to a nephew of Dr. Benjamin Mays, the president of Morehouse College in Atlanta. I was attracted to her because she was very intelligent and mature and we shared a similar southern background. Most of the students at the conservatory were younger than either of us—and had just graduated from high school.

Of course, another reason we became friendly was that there were very few African Americans at the conservatory. By the time I had left Antioch, there were about thirty black students, but at the conservatory there were only about fifteen or twenty, including part-time students.

Think of the waste that pitifully small figure represents! White people always marvel at the number of African-American performers in jazz and popular music, and then they say, with great surprise in their voices, "Why, I bet so-and-so is almost good enough to play in a symphony orchestra!"

How naive and unsophisticated America has made its white population, and how unconsciously cruel. First-rate black performers, with extraordinary talent, either were not able to get professional training at first-rate institutions or, if they had the training, were not able to find the jobs. How many symphonies, do you imagine, had any blacks playing in them, for example, in 1951, when I was studying?

One of the worst evils of segregation was the waste of this creative force and the ruin of the lives of talented men and women who happened to be black.

The problem was not exclusive to the conservatory. There were only a limited number of black students in the entire Boston area. Though there were no signs posted, as there were in the South, we certainly did not feel completely welcome at many white restaurants and nightclubs in the Boston area. Because of this, most of our social life was conducted at a few "southern-style restaurants" or at parties in private homes. Naturally, for all these reasons, black students were thrown together and, naturally too, there was a lot of matchmaking going on in the group.

Mary Powell was a bit of a matchmaker herself, though, as I later learned, Martin had nudged her into the role. One day late in January 1952 she said to me, "Have you heard of M. L. King, Jr.?" (In those days everyone called him M.L., and in his own family that was always his name.)

When I answered, "No," Mary began to tell me about him. "Dr. Mays tells me that he is a very promising young man," she said. "He is at Boston University taking his doctorate. He is a Baptist minister, ordained in his father's church, the Ebenezer Baptist Church in Atlanta. He has been preaching at churches around Boston and is very brilliant. I want you to meet him."

The moment Mary told me the young man was a minister I lost interest, for I began to think of the stereotypes of ministers I had known—fundamentalists in their thinking, very narrow, and overly pious. Genuine piety is inspiring, but many of the ministers I had met went around wearing a look of sanctity that they seemed to put on like their black suits. The fact that young King was a Baptist also prejudiced me. In the African Methodist Episcopal Zion Church we felt that baptism by sprinkling was adequate. I remember hearing my father and mother discuss with their Baptist friends whether it was necessary to be immersed in order to be saved. I thought I would never want to become a Baptist because I did not think it was necessary to be baptized by immersion.

However, that was not the thing that mattered; it was just one of those minor prejudices that came to the surface. I was really thinking of the Baptist churches—and my own church too—as being overly emotional. Though I was deeply religious, I was moving away from fundamentalism. After I left Antioch I decided that I wanted to identify myself with a church or religious body that was more liberal than the kind I was brought up in. I intended to investigate the Quakers and Unitarianism. I was, in fact, dissatisfied with organized religion as I knew it and sought to find a faith with which I could identify totally.

For this and other reasons, I did not attend church regularly when I first went to Boston. I was the only black living in the Beacon Hill section, and I did not feel comfortable going to the churches in that area. I said to myself, "I can worship in my room."

Mary Powell had known Martin Luther King, Jr., in Atlanta when he was at Morehouse College and she was at Spelman. They met again in Boston. They ate at the same restaurant, the Western Lunch Box, near the conservatory, where black students attending the various institutions of learning often gathered. It specialized in southern cooking—we would call it soul food now. I did not go there much because I lived far away on Beacon Hill.

One day Martin said to her, "Mary, I am about to get cynical. I have met quite a few girls here, but none that I am particularly fond of. Do you know any nice, attractive young ladies?"

She mentioned two girls, one of whom Martin had already met and then he asked, "Who is the other one?"

"Coretta Scott," Mary said, and began to describe me. According to Martin she gave me a good character reference: a very nice girl, intelligent, pretty—all those things. But she warned him that she did not think I was religious enough, that I did not often go to church. Later he told me that this did not bother him, that he did not want for a wife a fundamentalist or anyone too set in her beliefs. He asked Mary for my telephone number, and after some of Martin's powerful persuading, she gave it to him.

When he called me and said, "This is M. L. King, Jr.," I didn't recognize who he was. He quickly said, "A mutual friend of ours told me about you and gave me your telephone number. She said some very wonderful things about you and I'd like very much to meet you and talk to you. . . ."

The next day I waited for him on the steps outside the conservatory, on the Huntington Avenue side, in a cold January drizzle, with a scarf on my head and my coat buttoned up tight. The green car pulled up to the curb, and as I walked down the steps I could see the young man sitting in the car. My first thought was "How short he seems" and the second was "How unimpressive he looks."

I have been quoted as saying that when I first met Martin I thought "he was a typical man—smoothness, jive. Some of it I had never heard of in my life. It was what I call intellectual jive." There was nothing typical about Martin the man, but when we first met that is how he came across to me.

Martin drove me to Sharaf's Restaurant on Massachusetts Avenue, where we had lunch, cafeteria style. I took off my coat and scarf. I still remember everything I was wearing that day. I remember the shoes I had on and the light-blue suit and the black coat. Martin looked at me very carefully. At that time I was wearing bangs that had a natural wave, and my hair was long. He liked that and said so. I was rather self-conscious but tried not to react too much; to remain as poised as I usually was.

It was a little difficult, for in those few minutes I had forgotten about Martin being short and had completely revised my first impression. He radiated charm. When he talked, he grew in stature. Even when he was so young, he drew people to him from the very first moment with his eloquence, his sincerity, and his *moral* stature. I knew immediately that he was very special.

We got our lunch and sat down at a table and began to talk. This young man became increasingly better looking as he talked, so strongly and convincingly. With a very masculine self-possession, he seemed to know exactly where he was going and how he was going to get there. In our discussion, I must have made some reasonably intelligent comments, for he said, "Oh, I see you know about some other things besides music."

Then we had to go back to the conservatory. In the car, Martin suddenly became very quiet, and he said, "Do you know something?"

"What is that?" I asked.

Very quietly but intensely he said, "You have everything I have ever wanted in a wife. There are only four things, and you have them all."

Somewhat flustered, I said, "I don't see how you can say that. You don't even know me."

"Yes, I can tell," he said. "The four things that I look for in a wife are character, intelligence, personality, and beauty. And you have them all. I want to see you again. When can I?"

Still trying to keep my poise, I said, "I don't know. I'll have to check my schedule. You may call me later."

I know it sounds strange that Martin should talk about marriage so soon in our relationship. However, Martin was ready to get married and was quite consciously looking for a wife. He already knew exactly where he was heading in his life and had formed a pretty good idea of the kind of wife who would fit in with that life. I do not mean to say that he was cold and calculating, without any romantic ideas. That is certainly not the case. What is true is that Martin was remarkably mature for his age. He knew the sort of person he himself was, and the sort of woman he needed. It was as if he had no time for mistakes, as if he had to make up his mind quickly and correctly, and then move on with his life. Our courtship had this quality, but so did the rest of Martin's life until the end. Think of all he did by the time he was thirty-nine! . . .

CONSTANCE BAKER MOTLEY

From *Equal Justice Under Law*

❧

TOPEKA, KANSAS, 1954–1955

JUSTICE HARLAN'S DISSENT IN *PLESSY* FORMED THE basis of our legal arguments to end segregation in education. We abandoned his Thirteenth Amendment argument, however, since we had successfully invoked the equal protection clause of the Fourteenth Amendment in other cases involving state action. We consistently argued that the state was powerless, under the Fourteenth Amendment, to make racial distinctions with respect to civil or political rights. But we needed a persuasive argument as to why, even when the facilities provided black children were equal, segregation violated this amendment. After all, Harlan's Fourteenth Amendment argument was rejected by the overwhelming majority of the Court in *Plessy,* a powerful precedent against us. We had to convince the Court that *Plessy* either was wrongly decided or should not be extended to public education. We were fully aware that getting the Supreme Court to reverse long-standing precedent would be virtually impossible without new evidence of the harmful effects of segregation on a state's black citizens.

We needed to prove that segregation, even where facilities are equal, has a harmful psychological effect on the ability of black children to learn. This new evidence was developed at the trial of the *Brown* case. All the lawyers involved in preparing the brief were convinced that it was necessary to allege and prove some injury to black children from the state's segregation policies. But the majority in *Plessy* had found Plessy's argument about the effect of state-decreed segregation on nonwhites fanciful.

Kansas permitted (but did not require) segregation in elementary schools in first-class (large) cities as defined by statute, which applied only to these schools, apparently because few blacks went to high school. There was only one city that met the definition, Topeka. All other public school systems in Kansas were integrated. A large black population had moved to Topeka in connection with railroad construction in the last century, so most blacks in the state lived there.

I sent a draft complaint to our lawyers in the Kansas case as early as 1950, right after the Supreme Court's decision in *Sweatt*, in accordance with our plan to tackle the public schools. Similar model complaints were sent to other local NAACP lawyers who requested LDF assistance.

Robert Carter was lead counsel in the trial court in Kansas and argued the case on direct appeal to the Supreme Court. Jack Greenberg participated in the trial. Psychologist Kenneth Clark's work (along with others) on the psychological effects of segregation on black children, their self-image, and their ability to learn had been introduced at the Kansas trial and was, indeed, new. The trial was held in a three-judge federal district court, because a state statute was under attack on federal constitutional grounds. It found that segregation in public education had a detrimental effect on Negro (as we were called then) children but denied injunctive relief enjoining the Kansas statute, on the ground that the Negro and white schools in Topeka were substantially equal. The federal statute allowed for a direct appeal of the three-judge-court ruling to the Supreme Court. The appeal was taken and consolidated by the Supreme Court with school segregation cases in four other jurisdictions: South Carolina, Virginia, Delaware, and the District of Columbia.

In the cases involving two predominantly black rural counties, Clarendon, in South Carolina, and Prince Edward, in Virginia, the three-judge federal district court panels upheld the constitutionality of the state's laws on compulsory segregation in public education, even though the facilities for Negro children were found unequal to those for white children. In both instances, the local school board was ordered to equalize the facilities for Negro children, and when Thurgood and Spottswood Robinson III proceeded with the oral argument in Supreme Court, the plaintiffs conceded that the facilities had been equalized.

In the Delaware case, involving New Castle County, both elementary and high school students were plaintiffs. Their action was brought in the state court, the Delaware Court of Chancery, to enjoin state statutory and constitutional provisions that required racial segregation in education. The chancellor, Collin Seitz, ruled in favor of the Negro children and ordered their immediate admission to white schools on the ground that the schools provided for them were inferior with respect to teacher training, pupil-teacher ratio, extracurricular activities, physical plant, and time and distance involved in travel. The chancellor also found that segregation itself resulted in an inferior education for Negro children but did not rest his decision on that ground. The Supreme

Court of Delaware, affirming the chancellor's decree, suggested that a modification of the decree might be in order if the schools were equalized later but found the Negro schools unequal under *Plessy v. Ferguson*. The school authorities appealed to the U.S. Supreme Court. The argument there was made by Louis Redding of Wilmington, Delaware, assisted by Jack Greenberg (both had been trial counsel). The Supreme Court also agreed to review a case filed in U.S. District Court for the District of Columbia seeking admission of Negro children to schools attended by white children. The district court dismissed the complaint, and an appeal was taken to the U.S. Court of Appeals for the District of Columbia Circuit. The Supreme Court, in an unprecedented move, issued a writ of certiorari to the court of appeals before judgment, because of the importance of the constitutional question presented as to federal authority, so that it could hear the case along with the four state cases. The case was argued in Supreme Court by trial counsel George E. C. Hayes and Frank Reeves, both of Washington, D.C., and members of Marshall's inner circle.

In its opinion relating to the four state cases, the Court first dealt with the history and intent of the framers of the Fourteenth Amendment and the states in ratifying it and found the issues inconclusive. It then reviewed the status of public education at the time the amendment was proposed and ratified and found it far from comparable to the status of public education in 1954. The Court next reviewed how earlier Courts had construed the amendment from shortly after its adoption until the 1950 decision in *Sweatt,* where it had expressly reserved judgment on whether *Plessy v. Ferguson* should be held inapplicable to public education. The Court then noted that this question was directly presented by the *Brown* cases. It said: "Here, unlike *Sweatt v. Painter,* there are findings below that the Negro and white schools involved have been equalized, or are being equalized, with respect to buildings, curricula, qualifications and salaries of teachers, and other tangible factors. Our decision, therefore, cannot turn on merely a comparison of these tangible factors in the Negro and white schools involved in each of the cases. We must look instead to the effect of segregation itself on public education." The Court first concluded that education today is perhaps the most important function of state government.

It then said: "We come then to the question presented: Does segregation of children in public schools solely on the basis of race, even though the physical facilities and other tangible factors may be equal, deprive the children of the minority group of equal education opportunities? We believe that it does." Its basic holding was: "To separate them from others of similar age and qualifications solely because of their race generates a feeling of inferiority as to their status in the community that may affect their hearts and minds in a way unlikely ever to be undone." In reaching its conclusion, the Supreme Court adopted the findings of the Kansas court: "The effect of this separation on their educational opportunities was well stated by a finding in the Kansas case by a court which nevertheless felt compelled to rule against the Negro plaintiffs: 'Segregation of white and colored children in public schools has a detrimental effect upon the colored children. The impact is greater when it has the sanction of the law; for the policy of separating the races is usually interpreted as denoting the inferiority of the Negro group. A sense of inferiority affects the motivation of a child to learn. Segregation with the sanction of the law, therefore, has a tendency to [retard] the educational and mental development of Negro children and to deprive them of some of the benefits they would receive in a racial[ly] integrated school system.'

"Whatever may have been the extent of psychological knowledge at the time of *Plessy v. Ferguson,* this finding is amply supported by modern authority. Any language in *Plessy v. Ferguson* contrary to this finding is rejected."

In the District of Columbia case, the Court said: "We have this day held that the Equal Protection Clause of the Fourteenth Amendment prohibits the states from maintaining racially segregated public schools. The legal problem in the District of Columbia is somewhat different, however. The Fifth Amendment, which is applicable in the District of Columbia, does not contain an equal protection clause as does the Fourteenth Amendment which applies only to the states. But the concepts of equal protection and due process, both stemming from our American ideal of fairness, are not mutually exclusive. The equal protection of the laws is a more explicit safeguard to prohibited unfairness than due process of law, and, therefore, we do not imply that the two are always interchangeable phrases. But, as this Court has recognized, discrimination may be so unjustifiable as to be violative of due process."

The Supreme Court then set the cases down for re-argument on the two questions addressed in the briefs relating to the relief to be granted in these cases in the event that the plaintiffs should prevail. That is, if segregation was deemed unconstitutional, should Negro students be admitted forthwith or after a reasonable time for adjustment, and how should the courts proceed in determining a reasonable time?

No one associated with us in preparing the briefs or oral arguments called to see if there was going to be a victory party. Those who knew Thurgood knew that "party" was his middle name. Everyone converged on LDF's offices, which were then on West Forty-third Street next to Town Hall and not far from the NAACP national headquarters on Fortieth Street. It was bedlam; the party went on most of the night. I remember being there when the clock struck 3:30 a.m.

Becoming a part of history is a special experience, reserved for only a few. It's like earning a law degree or a Ph.D.; nobody can take it away from you. You may be forgotten, but it's like immortality: You will always be there.

As the night went on, Marshall began to worry about the dawn. It might even be fair to say that, as people left, he sensed the new reality in personal terms—a task ahead even greater than the one he had just accomplished. He kept saying to those assembled, "There is nothing to party about—your task has just begun. . . ."

Part XIII.

❧

AIN'T GONNA LET NOBODY

TURN US AROUND

The long-standing system of American apartheid received devastating blows from a series of Supreme Court decisions; even so, no one expected the knockout punch would come from a mild-mannered seamstress who was not physically tired as the press reported, but politically tired of moving to the back of the bus. This resolve by Rosa Parks in 1955 would lead to a sustained boycott and the creation of the Montgomery Improvement Association. Her bold act would earn Parks the sobriquet "Mother of the Civil Rights Movement." Parks's actions were critical in toppling the long-standing segregation, but it was just one of several initiatives by activists in the community, mostly under the guidance of E. D. Nixon, a member of A. Philip Randolph's Brotherhood of Sleeping Car Porters, who served as director of a housing project recreation program in Montgomery. Nixon, Parks's mentor, was the quiet strategist and organizer behind the successful boycott and retired as president of the Alabama NAACP in 1977.

If Ms. Parks was the "Mother of the Civil Rights Movement," then Ella Baker was the godmother. Of redoubtable conviction and inestimable organizing skills, Baker was a quiet, unassuming tactician who avoided the limelight with the same vigor she gave to molding at least three significant civil rights organizations. She was the moving hand and the wise counsel behind the Southern Christian Leadership Council (SCLC), the Student Nonviolent Coordinating Committee (SNCC), and the Mississippi Freedom Democratic Party (MFDP). Baker came to the civil rights movement with a résumé crammed with political experience. A graduate of Shaw University in North Carolina, Baker was unable to find gainful employment and so forced to take all kinds of menial jobs in restaurants and factories, at the same time writing for local newspapers in New York City. In 1932 she helped organize the Young Negroes' Cooperative League, a consumer collective, before taking a job with the NAACP as a field secretary from 1940 to 1946. Frustrated with the organization's bureaucracy, she returned to New York City and took a job working to desegregate the school system. By 1958, she was executive director of the Southern Christian Leadership Council, and from this position she would oversee the creation of the Student Nonviolent Coordinating Committee.

A number of courageous activists assisted Baker, but none more tireless than James Forman. He was hurrying to the Southern protest scene to file stories for the *Chicago Defender,* but ultimately, the trip was his indoctrination into the civil rights movement. From this beginning, Forman's commitment would be indefatigable, and in subsequent years as an organizer and activist, he was a veritable pimpernel, moving from one center of action to another. The articles he wrote about the struggle for integration at Central High School in Little Rock vividly captured the turmoil and intensity of the event.

Melba Pattillo Beals was one of the Little Rock Nine who eventually integrated all-white Central High. She immerses us in the trauma and terror these young pioneers faced as graduation neared for one of them. What happened at Central High School was an extension of the 1954 *Brown v. Board of Education* decision; it was a legal action with a human face. Now the notion of the Supreme Court's order "with all deliberate speed" was put to the test and seventy-five black students signed up to attend Central High School. Only Pattillo and eight others were chosen for the challenging ordeal.

ROSA PARKS

From *Rosa Parks: My Story*

❧

MONTGOMERY, ALABAMA, 1955

WHEN I GOT OFF FROM WORK THAT evening of December
. . . 1, I went to Court Square as usual to catch the Cleveland Avenue
bus home. I didn't look to see who was driving when I got on, and by the time
I recognized him, I had already paid my fare. It was the same driver who had
put me off the bus back in 1943, twelve years earlier. He was still tall and
heavy, with red, rough-looking skin. And he was still mean-looking. I didn't
know if he had been on that route before—they switched the drivers around
sometimes. I do know that most of the time if I saw him on a bus, I wouldn't
get on it.

I saw a vacant seat in the middle section of the bus and took it. I didn't
even question why there was a vacant seat even though there were quite a few
people standing in the back. If I had thought about it at all, I would probably
have figured maybe someone saw me get on and did not take the seat but left it
vacant for me. There was a man sitting next to the window and two women
across the aisle.

The next stop was the Empire Theater, and some whites got on. They
filled up the white seats, and one man was left standing. The driver looked
back and noticed the man standing. Then he looked back at us. He said, "Let
me have those front seats," because they were the front seats of the black
section. Didn't anybody move. We just sat right where we were, the four of us.
Then he spoke a second time: "Y'all better make it light on yourselves and let
me have those seats."

The man in the window seat next to me stood up, and I moved to let him
pass by me, and then I looked across the aisle and saw that the two women

were also standing. I moved over to the window seat. I could not see how standing up was going to "make it light" for me. The more we gave in and complied, the worse they treated us.

I thought back to the time when I used to sit up all night and didn't sleep, and my grandfather would have his gun right by the fireplace, or if he had his one-horse wagon going anywhere, he always had his gun in the back of the wagon. People always say that I didn't give up my seat because I was tired, but that isn't true. I was not tired physically, or no more tired than I usually was at the end of a working day. I was not old, although some people have an image of me as being old then. I was forty-two. No, the only tired I was, was tired of giving in.

The driver of the bus saw me still sitting there, and he asked was I going to stand up. I said, "No." He said, "Well, I'm going to have you arrested." Then I said, "You may do that." These were the only words we said to each other. I didn't even know his name, which was James Blake, until we were in court together. He got out of the bus and stayed outside for a few minutes, waiting for the police.

As I sat there, I tried not to think about what might happen. I knew that anything was possible. I could be manhandled or beaten. I could be arrested. People have asked me if it occurred to me then that I could be the test case the NAACP had been looking for. I did not think about that at all. In fact if I had let myself think too deeply about what might happen to me, I might have gotten off the bus. But I chose to remain.

ELLA BAKER

From *Black Women in White America*

RALEIGH, NORTH CAROLINA, 1957

IN MY ORGANIZATIONAL WORK, I HAVE NEVER thought in terms of my "making a contribution." I just thought of myself as functioning where there was a need. And if I have made a contribution I think it may be that I had some influence on a large number of people.

As assistant field secretary of the branches of the NAACP, much of my work was in the South. At that time the NAACP was the leader on the cutting edge of social change. I remember when NAACP membership in the South was the basis for getting beaten up or even killed.

I used to leave New York about the 15th of February and travel through the South for four to five months. I would go to, say, Birmingham, Alabama and help to organize membership campaigns. And in the process of helping to organize membership campaigns, there was opportunity for developing community reaction. You would go into areas where people were not yet organized in the NAACP and try to get them more involved. Maybe you would start with some simple thing like the fact that they had no street lights, or the fact that in the given area somebody had been arrested or had been jailed in a manner that was considered illegal and unfair, and the like. You would deal with whatever the local problem was, and on the basis of the needs of the people you would try to organize them in the NAACP.

Black people who were living in the South were constantly living with violence. Part of the job was to help them to understand what that violence was and how they in an organized fashion could help to stem it. The major job was getting people to understand that they had something within their power that they could use, and it could only be used if they understood what was happening and how group action could counter violence even when it was perpetrated by the police or, in some instances, the state. My basic sense of it has always been to get people to understand that in the long run they themselves are the only protection they have against violence or injustice. If they only had ten members in the NAACP at a given point, those ten members could be in touch with twenty-five members in the next little town, with fifty in the next and throughout the state as a result of the organization of state conferences, and they, of course, could be linked up with the national. People have to be made to understand that they cannot look for salvation anywhere but to themselves.

I left the NAACP and then worked at fund-raising with the National Urban League Service Fund and with several national health organizations. However, I continued my work with the NAACP on the local level. I became the advisor for the Youth Council. Then I served as President of the New York branch at a point where it had sunk to a low level in membership and otherwise. And in the process of serving as President we tried to bring the NAACP back, as I called it, to the people. We moved the branch out of an office building and located it where it would be more visible to the Harlem community. We started developing an active branch. It became one of the largest branches. I was President for a couple of years. It was strictly volunteer work which lasted until four o'clock in the morning, sometimes.

When the 1954 Supreme Court decision on school desegregation came, I was serving as chairman of the Educational Committee of the New York branch. We began to deal with the problems of *de facto* segregation, and the results of the *de facto* segregation which were evidenced largely in the achievement levels of black children, going down instead of going up after they entered public school. We had called the first committee meeting and Kenneth Clark became the chairman of that committee. During that period, I served on the Mayor's Commission on School Integration, with the subdivision on zoning. In the summer of 1957, I gave time to organizing what we called Parents in Action for Quality Education.

I've never believed that the people who control things really were willing and able to pay the price of integration. From a practical standpoint, anyone who looked at the Harlem area knew that the potential for integration *per se* was basically impossible unless there were some radically innovative things done. And those innovative things would not be acceptable to those who ran the school system, nor to communities, nor even to the people who call themselves supporters of integration. I did a good deal of speaking, and I went to Queens, I went to the upper West side, and the people very eagerly said they wanted school integration. But when you raised the question of whether they would permit or would welcome Blacks to live in the same houses with them, which was the only practical way at that stage to achieve integration,

they squirmed. Integration certainly had to be pushed concurrently with changing the quality of education that the black children were getting, and changing
the attitudes of the educational establishment toward the black community.

I don't think we achieved too much with the committee except to pinpoint
certain issues and to have survived some very sharp confrontations with the
Superintendent and others on the board of Education. But out of it came
increased fervor on the part of the black communities to make some changes.
One of the gratifying things to me is the fact that even as late as this year I have
met people who were in that group and who have been continuously active in
the struggle for quality education in the black communities ever since.

There certainly has been progress in the direction of the capacity of people
to face this issue. And to me, when people themselves know what they are
looking for and recognize that they can exercise some influence by action,
that's progress. . . .

There are those, some of the young people especially, who have said to me
that if I had not been a woman I would have been well known in certain places,
and perhaps held certain kinds of positions. . . .

For myself, circumstances frequently dictated what had to be done as I saw
it. For example, I had no plans to go down and set up the office of SCLC. But
it seemed unless something were done whatever impetus had been gained
would be lost, and nobody else was available who was willing or able to do it.
So I went because to me it was more important to see what was a potential for
all of us than it was to do what I might have done for myself. I knew from the
beginning that as a woman, an older woman, in a group of ministers who are
accustomed to having women largely as supporters, there was no place for me
to have come into a leadership role. The competition wasn't worth it.

The movement of the '50's and '60's was carried largely by women, since
it came out of church groups. It was sort of second nature to women to play a
supportive role. How many made a conscious decision on the basis of the larger
goals, how many on the basis of habit pattern, I don't know. But it's true that
the number of women who carried the movement is much larger than that of
men. Black women have had to carry this role, and I think the younger women
are insisting on an equal footing.

I don't advocate anybody following the pattern I followed, unless they find
themselves in a situation where they think that the larger goals will be short-
changed if they don't. From the standpoint of the historical pattern of the
society, which seems to assume that this is the best role for women, I think that
certainly the young people who are challenging this ought to be challenging it,
and it ought to be changed. But I also think you have to have a certain sense of
your own value, and a sense of security on your part, to be able to forgo the
glamor of what the leadership role offers. From the standpoint of my work and
my own self-concepts, I don't think I have thought of myself largely as a

woman. I thought of myself as an individual with a certain amount of sense of the need of people to participate in the movement. I have always thought what is needed is the development of people who are interested not in being leaders as much as in developing leadership among other people. Every time I see a young person who has come through the system to a stage where he could profit from the system and identify with it, but who identifies more with the struggle of black people who have not had his chance, every time I find such a person I take new hope. I feel a new life as a result of it.

JAMES FORMAN

From *The Making of Black Revolutionaries*

LITTLE ROCK, ARKANSAS, 1958

THE TRAIN FROM MEMPHIS COULD NOT ROLL fast enough for me. I stood on the platform with the top part of the door open, looking out at the countryside as the train headed for Little Rock.

Going to Little Rock in September of 1958 was something I had to do for the sake of my existence, it seemed. For months, in Boston, I had felt torn about being in a safe, quiet graduate school while black people in Arkansas risked their lives. Now Little Rock was reactivated and I had another chance to go—a better chance, because I was neither in school nor working full time. It was also a test for me; a test of my reactions to a Southern protest scene, a test of my ability to be mobile and go anywhere necessary on short notice with little or no money. Lee Blackwell, managing editor of the *Chicago Defender,* had given me press credentials and promised to pay for stories filed from Little Rock.

The clickity-clack of the train sounded like music to me. The sun was shining brightly. I waved to the brothers and sisters working in the fields picking cotton, to the old people sitting on their porches smoking corncob pipes or just sitting looking at the blue-colored coaches roll by. I just waved and waved. I was at home, I was with my folks, country folks, the people I loved the best.

When I got to Little Rock, I took a cab to the office of the *Arkansas State Press,* the newspaper owned by the Bateses, L. C. and his wife, Daisy Mae, who was the principal black figure in the Little Rock crisis. I did not know her and did not know what type of reception I would receive. When she met me in the office, she began to ask questions. Then she told me, in a polite way, that she did not know me and there was no reason for her to trust me. The White Citizens' Council, an organization of middle-class whites banded together to stop desegregation, had sent black people as paid informers into protest groups to try to discredit them and it was possible that I was an agent of the White Citizens' Council. Her cautious, but forthright position impressed me and I made a mental note of it for future use. I told her that there was no reason why she should trust me; only time would tell if I were trustworthy, and meanwhile I would not push myself on her and her husband or on the movement there. During the next two weeks in Little Rock I became a very close friend of the family and was often invited to their house.

I admired the Bateses very much. Their newspaper had lost all its advertisers except Carnation milk, but even that company was running only a public service ad with no mention of the product. Pressure from the White Citizens' Council had done this. I had been conscious of those councils ever since they began forming after 1954, and could not understand why some influential black organization like the NAACP had not created a public furor and mass protests about them. The Bates's experience was one more example of why this should be done.

When I got to Little Rock, the Supreme Court had just ruled that desegregation of Little Rock schools must proceed. The state then closed down all the public schools in Little Rock. They would stay closed for the entire year; right now the issue was in the courts again. I felt that, for all its greatness, the fight in Little Rock was losing some valuable time. For instance, it seemed to me that the fight should not just be confined to the school issue and, even if it were confined to the school issue, there should be some street confrontation. During my stay in Little Rock, the whites would often take to the streets and demonstrate against "integration." The eyes of the world were upon Little Rock; the United States's image abroad was threatened. There could have been mass rallies in support of the students. Instead, the black community seemed to be passively waiting for court decisions—which was in fact the case. But, although I doubted that the purely legalistic approach was advisable, I did not feel I had the right to make these suggestions to the Bateses since they had decided upon the legal approach and they had to live there, paying the price for their courage. It was an error not to state my feelings.

While in Little Rock I filed several stories with the *Defender*. They were published, but I received no money for them; I would have been stranded in Little Rock if it hadn't been for a lucky night of sociable poker at the Bates's home.

The articles reported on people's reactions for the most part. Several black residents blamed what had happened on Faubus's politicking for a third term by appealing to die-hard segregationists; others brought out an older, deeper racism. In one article, I told how I had gone up to three men and asked them, "What do you think about today's ruling of the Supreme Court?"

"We heard it," the crippled man said. "It had to be. Faubus can't stop the federal government." He was a short dark-skinned man who touched his crutches as he spoke.

"Yes . . . you're right," the brown-skinned man on the grass said. "Old Faubus got a lot of money from those segregationists. He is subject to hide, to run away. You can never tell what that slippery dude will do. . . . What do you think?" he said to me.

After a while, the man on the grass asked me did I see an American flag flying on the State Capitol. "You know every other capitol has a flag they raise in the morning and take down at night. Did you see an American flag up there?"

"No."

"How long you been around here?"

"Not long."

"Well, there hasn't been an American flag up there since they lynched that colored man and drug him down Ninth Street."

"How long ago was that?" I asked.

"Before you were born. It's been a long time."

"It sure has," the crippled man said. "They drug him down this street. They took the benches out of the Methodist church, my church, and they burned the man on Ninth and Broadway."

"When they did that," the man on the grass said, "they took the American flag down and ran up a Confederate flag."

"This is a rough town," the crippled man said. "It's too rough for a capitol. . . . They call it a capitol. But it ain't no capitol. No capitol at all."

"What did he do?" I asked.

"Well," the crippled man said, "they tell me he was trying to catch a runaway buggy that had a white woman in it. I was living around here then. I was on the other side of town but I heard about it. They say he was chasing the buggy and the white men said he was trying to rape the woman."

"And they tell me," the man on my right said (he had been quiet all this time), "that the Negroes left here and went to Hot Springs and Chicago and everywhere. They left the poor man alone. . . . I heard the white woman tried to tell them that the man was trying to help her. . . . But, son, sometimes these white people here don't listen to nobody."

"What was the man's name?"

None of the three men knew.

When I returned to the office of the *Arkansas State Press* I asked the secretary if she knew anything about this murder. She, too, had heard about it. She didn't have any details. However, she called someone and in twenty minutes handed me the following information:

Mr. John Carter of 2000 Monroe Street was mobbed by two hundred white men, shot with 250 bullets, and hung on a telephone on Ninth and Broadway, Wednesday, May 4, 1927. The reason for this action was that he was supposed to have raped Mrs. B. E. Steward and her nineteen-year-old daughter, Glennie, on Twelfth Street Pike, the attack occurring at ten o'clock in the morning. He was found and caught just off Hot Springs Pike at the Sipper Inn at six o'clock in the afternoon, by E. V. McElvain. Carter, about twenty-eight years of age, who was believed to be an escaped convict, was identified by the daughter.

On my last night in Little Rock, I interviewed a student who was supposed to enter Central High. She had been writing on a pad before I came into the room and left it on a chair. I glanced at it later and saw that she had written, "Is it dignity to be able to go into a five-and-ten-cent store and buy a coffee pot, but not be able to buy a cup of coffee?" Her words stuck in my mind because they expressed so clearly the struggle against dehumanization that all black people were engaged in. I thought about the incident in Memphis at the lunch counter when I was a child and realized that my purpose in life at this time came down to something very simple: If my life could make it possible for future black children not to have that experience, then it was worth living. . . .

MELBA PATTILLO BEALS

From *Warriors Don't Cry*

Central High School Negroes Pass: One on Honor Roll
Principal Matthews Says He Will Not Reveal Grades
But Confirms Green Will Graduate
—*Arkansas Gazette*, Wednesday, May 23, 1958

LET'S KEEP THE NIGGER FROM GRADUATING.'' THAT was the rallying cry in the halls of Central High that unleashed unimaginable terror upon us. Pressure was exerted on all eight of us; the goal was to get us out by any means possible. In case that plan failed, our antagonists worked at convincing us that even if Ernie had the grades to graduate, he should not march with the other seniors to receive his Central High diploma.

"We ain't gonna let no nigger wear our cap and gown," one boy shouted at me as I walked the hallway to English class. I pushed my way past him, flashed a smile and a pleasant "Thank you."

At first, some of my late-night telephone callers pleaded with me in a civil tone to ask Ernie to receive his diploma by mail. "We don't want his picture taken with us. My daddy says you'all ain't getting back in our school next year, no how. So this is the only time we'll have that ink spot in the middle of all those pictures the news people take."

Another gruff-voiced man became angrier with each rude call. "We're gonna hang us a nigger at the same time your nigger takes our diploma," he said. On and on those calls came, keeping our phone ringing almost as much as it had at the beginning of the school year. At the same time, I received threatening notes sneaked into my books and in my locker.

I could see more evidence that the principal, vice-principals, and teachers had lost any hopes of corraling belligerent students. Even as school officials observed them, clusters of students threw rocks as we entered or exited the building. The hallways were like a three-ring circus, with hooligans completely ignoring commands to cease their outrageous behavior.

Because the situation was growing more explosive, Mrs. Huckaby called us into her office to double-check on our scheduled exams. While inside school, we were once again closely followed by bodyguards.

I was much more frightened than I had been in recent months because there were no longer islands of sanity within the insanity of that school. Just outside the principal's office, people threw rotten eggs and walked on my heels, whereas before that area had been a comparatively safe place to walk.

During those last days, time seemed to drag on and on as though some divine force were slowing the hands on the clock. I had no choice but to perform one of the most hazardous duties of the day—opening my locker. That meant standing still for several minutes, with my eyes and attention focused inside while my back was exposed to passersby.

I had developed a habit of reaching my hand into my locker to find hidden objects before I poked my face in. On Tuesday afternoon, I was searching my locker for my eyeglass case when I reached my hand down deep inside to see whether or not it had fallen. Suddenly there was the sound of popping guns and the smell of smoke just behind me. I quickly turned to see a flaming object flying toward my face. I put my hand up to deflect it. That's when I felt the pain on my first three fingers. I had shielded my eyes from several sparking hot firecrackers linked together by a wire. My hand hurt, but I could only be grateful it wasn't my eyes that had been burned.

As I was issued bandages from the office to dress the wound, I consoled myself by thinking of the calendar on the kitchen wall. I had marked off almost all the days of the month of May. Ernie would attend baccalaureate services the following Sunday evening, and graduation would be the following Tuesday, one week from this day. I would be an unwelcome Central High student in that building only a few more days.

"What are you staring at, nigger?" I was indeed staring, transfixed and elated at seeing what the boy was carrying. It was the sight I had been waiting for, praying for.

"The graduation gown Ernie's gonna wear," I said loud and clear. I couldn't help responding to his snide remark as I glared back at the boy wearing the flattop haircut and black shirt. In his right hand he was carrying his gown on a hanger, and his left hand was holding his cap. He was attempting to block my way, but he had no free hands. I simply made a wide circle around him. Nothing, not even his foul mouth spewing ugly words, could make me unhappy at that moment. The sight of that gown meant summer and freedom were right around the corner.

At home the phone calls were coming fast and vicious. "We got a way of gettin' you darkies now, for certain. We're offering ten thousand dollars for your head on a platter." I gulped as I replaced the receiver in its cradle. I couldn't help thinking about how that was an awful lot of money. Poor folks might take a notion to collect. They'd get ten thousand dollars for my head. Did that mean they'd have to cut it off to collect? I told Grandma India of my fears.

"Surely you've got something better to do besides speculating about white folks' silliness," she said.

"I can't help worrying about Ernie. One of those students could be an impostor—anybody could wear a robe."

"Impostor?" Grandma looked up from her needlework with a question.

"You know, someone from the KKK who wants to collect that reward money could pretend to be a graduate."

"I don't think Ernie is in any real danger during graduation because he'll be there among six hundred and one white graduates. Besides, God's watching after Ernie just like he's watching over you."

"But . . ." I tried to continue being in my pity pot. She motioned me to shush my mouth and hold my hands out so she could circle the embroidery thread around them to straighten it out. After a long moment she said, "You're fretting a mighty lot this evening. Hard work is always the cure for worry. So busy yourself doing those dishes and getting ready for your final exams."

I had always imagined that my last day of the term at Central High School would be marked by a grand ceremony, with a massive choir singing hallelujah, or perhaps some wonderful award from my community—a parade maybe. I imagined the roar of helicopters overhead towing flying banners of congratulations—something—anything. But it was just the same as any other day. Four of us, Thelma, Elizabeth, Jeff, and I, rode home together early that afternoon. We wouldn't be going back to Central High for at least three months. Long spaces of silence punctuated our talk about how we thought we did on our exams.

"It's over," Conrad said, greeting me as I climbed the steps to our front door. "You don't have to integrate anymore."

"Well, praise the Lord," Grandma India said, her arms wide open to receive me. "You see, you made it." She squeezed me and kissed my cheek.

"Well, well, young lady, welcome to summer." Mother Lois handed me a large box that I rushed to open. "You're very special to have come through all this. I thought you deserved a special summer outfit."

Early on Wednesday morning, I built a fire in the metal trash barrel in the backyard, fueled by my school papers. Grandma had said it would be healing to write and destroy all the names of people I disliked at Central High: teachers, students, anyone who I thought had wronged me. It was against the law to burn anything at that time of the year, but she said a ceremony was important in order to have the official opportunity to give that year to God. Grandma India stood silent by my side as I fed the flame and spoke their names and forgave them.

After a long moment she walked over to water her flowerbed. The four o'clocks were blooming purple and red. We stood together for what must have been half an hour, with only the sound of the crackling fire and the garden hose. Finally she said, "Later, you'll be grateful for the courage it built inside you and for the blessing it will bring."

Grateful, I thought. Never. How could I be grateful for being at Central High? But I knew she was always right. Still I wondered just how long I would have to wait for that feeling of gratitude to come to me.

COVERAGE CURBED TO ASSURE DIGNITY
OF CENTRAL HIGH SCHOOL GRADUATION:
Each Graduating Senior to Receive
8 Admission Tickets;
Press Admitted Only by Ticket.
—*Arkansas Gazette,* Tuesday, May 27, 1958

Even though I had made it through the school year, Ernie still had to survive that one final brave act. I counted on being with him, on applauding for him from our isolated though well-guarded section of the audience.

"None of you will be allowed to attend either the graduation commencement or the baccalaureate service," Mother Lois announced over dinner. "The authorities believe it would not only risk your lives, but also make it more difficult for them to protect Ernie and his family should they have to do so. They've also forbidden any non-white reporters or photographers to attend."

"But, Mom!"

"But nothing. This is no time to satisfy a whim and unravel everything you've accomplished. There'll be enough of a circus, what with the soldiers, FBI, city police, and who knows all."

"The paper says every policeman not on vacation will be on duty from six o'clock on," Grandma said. "They wouldn't go to all that trouble and expense unless they expected something to happen."

"Besides," Mother Lois continued, "their best efforts should be directed to protecting Ernie."

She's right, I thought to myself. It was selfish of me to want to go, I suppose. But what I knew to be practical advice didn't lessen my disappointment at not being able to watch Ernie march triumphantly to the stage to receive that diploma. That night I wrote in my diary:

Dear God,
Please walk with Ernie in the graduation line at Central. Let him be safe.

Quigley Stadium was where the 101st troops set up their headquarters. It was there, on Tuesday evening, May 27, with 4,500 people looking on, that Ernie received his diploma. I held my breath as I listened to the radio broadcast news of the graduation ceremonies. At 8:48 P.M., Ernie became the first of our people to graduate from Central High School in all its forty-nine years. Chills danced up my spine as I sat in the big green living room chair with Mama and Grandma nearby. "It really happened," I whispered. "We made it."

The audience had been applauding those who previously marched, but when Ernie appeared they fell silent.

"What the heck," Mother Lois said. "Lots of people in the rest of the world are applauding for Ernie and for all of you who made it through this year."

"Who cares if they applaud, they didn't shoot him. There was no violence. Everybody is alive and well." Grandma stood and applauded.

Ernie was escorted from the stadium by police to a waiting taxi in which he, his family, and their guest departed. The newspapers said Ernie's diploma cost taxpayers half a million dollars. Of course, we knew it cost all of us much, much more than that. It cost us our innocence and a precious year of our teenage lives.

Part   XIV.

❦

BREAKTHROUGHS AND

PERSONAL INTIMACIES

The breakthrough in the deep South on the educational front in Little Rock was, to some degree, matched in the recording industry by Motown. And on Broadway. Ossie Davis and Ruby Dee were participant observers to the opening of Lorraine Hansberry's play *A Raisin in the Sun,* and Dee was a member of the original cast. Additionally rewarding about this excerpt is the give and take between the longtime couple, their separate ways of recalling the same incidents. *A Raisin in the Sun,* a title taken from a poem by Langston Hughes, was the first play on Broadway written by a black woman and directed by a black man, Lloyd Ricards. The cast alone would have earned the play a place in history with such future black stars as Sidney Poitier, Claudia McNeil, Diana Sands, Ms. Dee, Lonne Elder, III, Lou Gossett, Jr., Glynn Turman, Ivan Dixon, and Douglas Turner Ward. Elder and Ward would later also win acclaim as playwrights. The play ran for thirteen months on Broadway and Hansberry won the New York Drama Critics Circle Award. Most of the original cast starred in the film version in 1961. Four years later, at thirty-four, Hansberry died of cancer.

What Ella Baker and others had theoretically formulated at Shaw College months before was now being applied by a few charter members of SNCC at Tougaloo College in Mississippi. The volunteers in SNCC, including Anne Moody, were the most recent group of young black activists to challenge the South's citadel of racism. These were dangerous times for Moody and her young cohorts. Exploding bombs ripped apart offices where they planned their protests. In 1947, the Congress of Racial Equality sent an interracial team on the first "freedom rides." This was part of their "Journey of Reconciliation," which was the brain-child of James Farmer, who got the idea from his affiliation with the Fellowship of Reconciliation.

The same year members of CORE were sitting nervously on buses riding through the South, Jackie Robinson was signing a contract with the Brooklyn Dodgers, and the color line in baseball was erased. The racial abuse he received may not have been as life-threatening as that encountered by the freedom riders, but it was equally unsettling. There were better ballplayers in the Negro Leagues where Robinson had toiled before this opportunity came, yet it's doubtful if any possessed his desire and fortitude to deal with the pressure on and off the field. Sharon Robinson, Jackie Robinson's daughter, was only ten when the courageous cadres of SNCC sped across the violent countryside of Mississippi. She was waging her own coming-of-age battle with her classmates, some of whom believed her father was an "Uncle Tom" for supporting Nixon in the election of 1960. Not only does she explain the extent of her personal dilemma, she warmly captures the political sniping her father endured, how his independent stance often placed him in a no-man's-land between opposing groups and philosophies.

Like Jackie Robinson, Malcolm X was also a man who thought

for himself, no matter how controversial the issue. But the wrath Malcolm received from his enemies was far more dangerous than anything Robinson ever experienced. In the years previous to the speech Malcolm delivers here, there was much discussion about the gap between the civil rights movement and the black militancy advocated by Malcolm. That gap was beginning to shrink by 1964. An expression of Malcolm's changing attitude is evident by his presence on the dais with Fannie Lou Hamer, whom he showers with praise for her resolute conviction against segregation and white supremacy. Many pundits conclude that Malcolm X (El Hajj Malik El-Shabazz) was beginning to mellow after leaving the Nation of Islam and experiencing the universal brotherhood during a pilgrimage to Mecca. They contend that, had he lived, his ideas would have converged with those of Dr. Martin Luther King, Jr., who was thinking and acting more globally during the last years of his life. Malcolm and King represented an indomitable pair, and surely caused many restless nights for J. Edgar Hoover and the FBI.

With the civil rights movement having reached its apex, things began to heat up in the Caribbean, Latin America, Africa, and other parts of the Third World, most destructively in Vietnam. Across the U.S. young men were getting draft notices asking them to report for physical examination and possible duty in some far away Asian jungle. General Gordon Baker was not about to be anybody's private or grunt, and fired off a formidable epistle which over the years has lost none of its resonance and power.

Gordon Parks's son, David, received one of these draft letters. Unlike Baker, when his number came up, he went willingly. The elder Parks kept mum; it was his son's decision, and he would support whatever the boy chose to do. Along with a little survival advice, Gordon gave his son a camera to take some pictures and told him to keep a diary. Pages of that diary are posted here, where David discloses the ravages of war. The riveting conjunctions between Gordon's excerpt and David's diary entries highlight not only their personal reflections on the war and the civil rights movement, but the broader political arena.

OSSIE DAVIS AND RUBY DEE

From *With Ossie & Ruby*

❧

NEW YORK CITY, 1959

R UBY: I SHOULD HAVE ALREADY READ THE play that had been sent to me a few days earlier, so before getting out of bed, before the demands of the day gobbled up my time and attention, I did. I had to give an answer about whether or not I wanted to be a part of this project sometime before noon. It was not an easy play to read. It had emotional depth, rich dialogue, and a great sense of truth. Here were engaging characters with dimension and distinct personalities. I couldn't remember reading any play like it. I was moved and excited, filled with questions and some reservation as I got up, contemplating the title, *A Raisin in the Sun,* taken from the Langston Hughes poem "Dream Deferred."

Lloyd Richards, whom I had known as a teacher at Paul Mann's studio and as an actor, was to be the director of this new play by a young author, Lorraine Hansberry. Although he didn't specify which part he had in mind for me, I knew it was Beneatha, the restless, ambitious younger sister of Walter Lee. Lloyd called about noon for my reaction to the play. Would I be interested? Oh, yes. I was delighted, ecstatic. When was it to go into rehearsal? . . . And I loved the part of Beneatha—so fresh, challenging, and different from anything I'd done before.

"No, no, Ruby," Lloyd began, "forgive me for not making it clear. I want you to look at Ruth, the wife. You'll be Sidney's wife. He's agreed to do Walter Lee."

My heart flopped over and sank. Ruth? It seemed I'd been playing that same character, more or less, in almost everything I'd done since *Anna:* as Ossie's wife in *No Way Out;* as Jackie's wife in *The Jackie Robinson Story;* twice as

Sidney's wife in *Go, Man, Go* and in *Edge of the City;* and as Nat Cole's betrothed in *The St. Louis Blues.*

I tried to persuade Lloyd to see that I could do Beneatha, but he insisted that he needed a special kind of actor who linked all the characters, who was an engaging person on her own, and who, in a sense, was the tapestry against which all the other characters came to life. It was a flattering appraisal of what I had to offer. Although sorely disappointed, I agreed to play Ruth. No matter what, I very much wanted to be a part of *A Raisin in the Sun.*

Phil Rose was the producer, and the first reading of the play was held at his house. The cast included Sidney Poitier, Claudia McNeil, Diana Sands, Lou Gossett, John Fiedler, Ivan Dixon, Lonne Elder, Glynn Turman, and me. Bob Nemiroff, Lorraine's husband, was also among those present that first day.

Lorraine was so young, I thought. She looked like a teenager, but there was a definite air of maturity about her. Hearing her speak, I quickly forgot about her youth. She spoke with an authority, tinged with wit. I felt I was in the presence of a superior intellect. Clearly, she had written herself in the character of Beneatha—iconoclastic, impatient, and brilliant. I realized, as I listened to Diana Sands read the part, that Lloyd was right. Although I believed I could play the extraordinary Beneatha, I was relieved that the challenge would not be mine. I also realized that I was most comfortable listening to Lorraine as she discussed or argued some point with people I judged to be her intellectual equal.

I shall always remember our meeting after the first preview in New Haven. Lloyd had been rehearsing the play as a straightforward drama. We explored the truths of the characters, and the realities of the circumstances. We actors respected Lloyd's patience, and his persistence both in pursuing Lorraine's vision and in incorporating the distinct talents of the cast. And he was in the process of making history as the first black director of a drama on Broadway.

That first audience, however, let us know that *A Raisin in the Sun* was more than a drama; it was a comedy-drama. Sidney and I opened the play. We had scarcely begun the opening scene when the laughter began—a reaction for which we were not prepared, as I recall.

At the next rehearsal, Lloyd injected a new rationale into the action. I felt flustered. Had I been doing something wrong? What he was saying to me now seemed partly a contradiction of some elements on which we had previously agreed. As I tried to accommodate the new instructions, I began to cry. I recovered quickly, and the unusual rehearsal continued.

When it was over, Lorraine met me on stage, and asked if she could do anything, or explain anything, to make it easier to accept Lloyd's new, altered directions. At that moment, I felt uncomfortable, patronized, and incapable of expressing my dilemma. I soon realized that Lloyd was simply trying to get us to embrace an added facet of Lorraine—her sense of humor.

To accommodate the change, there only needed to be an adjustment in attitude. I think Lloyd could have skipped all the explanation and justification, though, and simply said, "People want to laugh at this particular dramatic reality. Lighten up, Ruby. Let them."

On the other hand, I should have remembered that part of the creative process is arriving at solid conclusions that sometimes must be changed or abandoned in an instant.

That reminds me of the time when we often did staged readings. One night we were reading a piece about a black youth involved in integrating a lunch counter in the South. Ossie had written the piece for District 65, the Retail Workers Union, for Negro History Week.

Frequently in such performances, a few actors played many parts. At one point, early in the drama, Will Geer took the role of a black grandmother, and the audience howled. Now Will Geer, a white actor and a friend, was a folksy, gregarious person with a sense of humor and a distinct cracker drawl. I remember the shock of hearing people, not titter, but guffaw during our serious presentation.

The four of us looked at each other, read the looks, and immediately turned our serious drama into a satire. The reading was an enormous success.

OSSIE: *A Raisin in the Sun* was a hit. Broadway ate it up. I liked it, too, but Ruby and I had a basic bone to pick.

In our opinion, this play was meant to be a warning, as Langston's poem suggested. Walter Lee Younger was a frustrated young black man whose dreams of better things for his family had been too long deferred, and he was on the verge of exploding, either into crime or into revolution. Lorraine didn't say which, but she did imply that if America wanted racial peace, something drastic had to be done about the hundreds of thousands of Walter Lees all over this country. That sentiment, in our opinion, expressed the author's clear intent. But somehow, in the production, that clear intent became subverted.

Sure, Walter, goaded by dreams of what he could not have in America because of racism, was about to explode; but not to worry. Lena, his mother, the strong and domineering head of the household, was totally in charge. America could depend on her to keep Walter under control, no matter what. The people who filled the theater night after night had nothing to worry about.

The play that had started out as a fire alarm ringing in the night, a wake-up call that America desperately needed, had somehow been transmuted into a domestic comedy-drama about a family's urgent need for decent housing. Their solution to the race problem was simply to exercise their right to buy a house in a white neighborhood.

All this being said, *A Raisin in the Sun* was still a most important work, a vital part of the message America needed to hear, and a part of the Struggle. It was a dramatic breakthrough, no matter how you looked at it. We finally accepted it as that.

In August 1959, Sidney left the show and I took over the role.

I owe Lloyd Richards big for a simple piece of instruction. Just as I was about to go on stage one day, he asked me to do something—something I couldn't handle at the time, but it turned out to be the key that finally unlocked the cell, and set me free to become an actor.

"Ossie," he said, "do me a favor. I want you to go out there on that stage; I want you to confront Claudia McNeil. Forget the lines, forget the character, forget how Lorraine has written the scene, forget the rest of the play. Just make her give you the money, you hear me? Don't leave that stage until she gives you that check for ten thousand dollars!"

The money Lloyd was talking about was the proceeds from a life insurance payment, which Walter Lee needed to invest in a liquor store. In the scene, as written, Mama turns him down.

If only I could have done it. If only I could have become enraged—really fought with Claudia—it would have made the scene between us, not only real, but electric. It would have scared the hell out of the audience, and nailed them to their seats. Unfortunately, for me, I had never been enraged in all my life! I could only fake it, imitating Lloyd and Sidney. And the audience can always spot a fake.

Now, of course, thirty years later, I can do it. Now I know exactly how to do it. Rage? I've finally got the hang of it now. And if ever I get another chance to play Walter Lee Younger, I'm going out there and *make* Claudia McNeil give me that damn check for $10,000. That's what acting is all about!

Though rage was not available to me at that time—I could not fly off the handle, like most people—anger, I had, but not enough for an actor. I don't remember ever losing my temper, nor has ambition, jealousy, or revenge pushed me into action. Inaction is the way I prefer to meet a crisis. I am emotionally slow, to the point of being dense. Staid, almost to the point of being stolid. When the role I am playing calls for aggression, I have to squeeze my innards mighty hard, like a rooster trying to lay an egg.

Ruby, on the other hand, is a natural and intuitive defender of the innocent and of the helpless. Ruby, spontaneous, gloriously impulsive; She of the instant reflex—as Claudia McNeil found out one matinee day.

It was vacation time, and Diana Sands had been replaced in the role of Beneatha by Billie Allen, her understudy, for two weeks. There is a scene near the end of the first act that calls for Lena, the mother, played brilliantly by Claudia McNeil, to lash out in anger and slap Beneatha hard across the face. Now, most actors know how to pull a punch and fake a blow, but Claudia— powerful and heavyset—had never bothered to learn.

So every performance, she would haul off and slap with all her might.

Diana knew how to duck and roll with the slap, but Billie didn't. We tried to teach Billie Diana's technique, but she never got the hang of it. That matinee, Claudia, as usual, had almost knocked Billie to her knees when Ruby stepped into Claudia's face, and growled under her breath—right there on stage— "You hit that girl one more time like that and I'll knock you flat on your ass!"

Claudia, almost shocked out of her senses, nearly forgot her lines, but being the trooper that she was, she bravely carried on. Then, when the curtain came down, she crumpled like an accordion and fell to the floor in a faint. And there she lay until the stage manager finally found some smelling salts and revived her just in time for the second act.

Claudia was a heavyweight, flat of foot and solid. Ruby was a bantamweight, at best, but in a fistfight, I'd back Ruby Dee every time. Luckily, it never came to that. Claudia hauled Ruby before Actors Equity, complaining about her "most unprofessional behavior," and at the union's insistence, Ruby apologized; but Billie never had to stumble again.

ANNE MOODY

From *Coming of Age in Mississippi*

❧

MISSISSIPPI, 1964

A FEW WEEKS AFTER I GOT INVOLVED WITH the Tougaloo chapter of the NAACP, they organized a demonstration at the state fair in Jackson. Just before it was to come off, Medgar Evers came to campus and gave a big hearty speech about how "Jackson was gonna move." Tougaloo sent four picketers to the fair, and one of them was Dave Jones. Because he was chosen to be the spokesman for the group, he was the first to be interviewed on TV. That evening when the demonstration was televised on all the news programs, it seemed as though every girl in the dorm was down in the lounge in front of the set. They were all shooting off about how they would take part in the next demonstration. The girl Dave was now seeing was running all around talking about how good he looked.

Dave and the other demonstrators had been arrested and were to be bailed out around eight that night. By eight-thirty a lot of us were sitting outside on the dormitory steps awaiting their arrival, and they still hadn't shown up. One of the girls had just gone inside to call the NAACP headquarters in Jackson, when suddenly two police cars came speeding through the campus. Students came running from every building. Within minutes the police cars were completely surrounded, blocked in from every direction. There were two cops in the front seat of each car. They looked frightened to death of us. When the students got out of the cars, they were hugged, kissed, and congratulated for well over an hour. All during this time the cops remained in their seats behind locked doors. Finally someone started singing "We Shall Overcome," and everyone joined in. When we finished singing, someone suggested we go to the football field and have a big rally. In minutes every student was on the football field singing all kinds of freedom songs, giving testimonies as to what we were going to do, and praying and carrying on something terrible. The rally ended at twelve-thirty and by this time, all the students were ready to tear Jackson to pieces.

The following evening Medgar Evers again came to campus to, as he put it, "get some of Tougaloo's spirit and try and spread it around all over Jackson." He gave us a good pep talk and said we would be called upon from time to time to demonstrate. . . .

During the summer a white student moved into the room across the hall from me. Her name was Joan Trumpauer, and she told me she worked for SNCC as a secretary. In a short time we got to know each other very well, and soon I was going into Jackson with Joan and hanging out at her office. SNCC was starting a voter registration drive in the Delta (Greenwood and Greenville) and was recruiting students at Tougaloo. When they asked me if I wanted to canvass every other weekend, I agreed to go.

The first time I went to the Delta, I was with three other girls. A local family put us up and we slept two to a room. The second time I was there I stayed at the Freedom House—a huge white frame house that SNCC was renting from a widow for sixty dollars a month. This time I was with Bettye Poole, who had been canvassing for SNCC for a couple of months, and Carolyn Quinn, a new recruit like me. We arrived at the Freedom House on a Friday night about twelve-thirty and found fifteen boys all sleeping in one large room on triple-decker beds. They were all sleeping in their clothes. Some of the boys got up and we played cards for a while. A couple of them were from McComb, Mississippi, which was only twenty miles from Centreville. We cracked jokes about how bad the whites were in Wilkinson County. Around 2 A.M. I started to get sleepy and asked where the girls were going to stay. I was told we were going to stay right in the same room with all those boys. I was some shocked. Now I understood why Bettye Poole was wearing jeans; just then she was climbing into one of the empty bunks and settling down for the night. Here I was with only a transparent nylon pajama set to sleep in. Carolyn Quinn wasn't prepared either. The two of us just sat up in chairs until some extra pairs of pants were found for us. The boys explained that they slept in their clothes because they had had bomb threats, and had to be ready to run anytime. They all slept here in this one big room because it was sheltered by another house.

The next morning I woke up to the sounds of someone banging on a skillet and hollering, "Come and get it! Come and get it!" When we walked in the kitchen, the boy who'd made the racket said, "All right, girls, take over. Us boys have been cooking all week." Most of the guys were angry because he had gotten them up in that manner, but they didn't make a big fuss over it. Carolyn and I started cooking. When we announced that the food was ready, the boys ran over each other to get to the kitchen. It seemed they thought the food would disappear. It did. Within five minutes, everything on the table was gone. The food ran out and three boys were left standing in line.

I really got to like all of the SNCC workers. I had never known people so willing and determined to help others. I thought Bob Moses, the director of SNCC in Mississippi, was Jesus Christ in the flesh. A lot of other people thought of him as J.C., too.

The SNCC workers who were employed full-time were paid only ten dollars a week. They could do more with that ten dollars than most people I knew could do with fifty. Sometimes when we were in the Delta, the boys would take us out. We did not finish with our work some Saturdays until ten or eleven, and all the Negro places had a twelve o'clock curfew. But we would have more fun in an hour than most people could have in twenty-four. We would often go to one place where the boys had made friends with the waitresses, and they would sneak us fifths of liquor. Those SNCC boys had friends everywhere, among the Negroes, that is. Most whites were just waiting for the chance to kill them all off.

I guess mostly the SNCC workers were just lucky. Most of them had missed a bullet by an inch or so on many occasions. Threats didn't stop them. They just kept going all the time. One Saturday we got to Greenville and discovered that the office had been bombed Friday night. The office was located up two flights of outside steps in a little broken-down building. It seemed as though a real hard wind would have blown it away. The bomb knocked the steps off, but that didn't stop the rally on Saturday night. Some of the boys made steps. When the new steps began to collapse, we ended up using a ladder. I remember when the rally ended, we found that the ladder was gone. For a few minutes we were real scared. We just knew some whites had moved it. We were all standing up there in the doorway wondering what to do. There was only one exit, and it was too high up to jump from. We figured we were going to be blown up. It seemed as though the whites had finally trapped us. The high school students were about to panic, when suddenly one of the SNCC boys came walking up with the ladder and yelled up to ask if the excitement was over. A lot of the other guys were mad enough to hit him. Those that did only tapped him lightly and smiled as they did it. "The nerve of those guys!" I thought.

Things didn't seem to be coming along too well in the Delta. On Saturdays we would spend all day canvassing and often at night we would have mass rallies. But these were usually poorly attended. Many Negroes were afraid to come. In the beginning some were even afraid to talk to us. Most of these old plantation Negroes had been brainwashed so by the whites, they really thought that only whites were supposed to vote. There were even a few who had never heard of voting. The only thing most of them knew was how to handle a hoe. For years they had demonstrated how well they could do that. Some of them had calluses on their hands so thick they would hide them if they noticed you looking at them.

On Sundays we usually went to Negro churches to speak. We were split into groups according to our religious affiliation. We were supposed to know how to reach those with the same faith as ourselves. In church we hoped to be able to reach many more Negroes. We knew that even those that slammed doors in our faces or said, "I don't want no part of voting" would be there. There would also be the schoolteachers and the middle-class professional Negroes who dared not participate. They knew that once they did, they would lose that $250 a month job. But the people started getting wise to us. Most of them stopped coming to church. They knew if they came, they would have to face us. Then the ministers started asking us not to come because we scared their congregations away. SNCC had to come up with a new strategy.

As the work continued that summer, people began to come around. I guess they saw that our intentions were good. But some began getting fired from their jobs, thrown off plantations and left homeless. They could often find somewhere else to stay, but food and clothing became a problem. SNCC started to send representatives to Northern college campuses. They went begging for food, clothing and money for the people in Mississippi, and the food, clothing and money started coming in. The Delta Negroes still didn't understand the voting, but they knew they had found friends, friends they could trust.

That summer I could feel myself beginning to change. For the first time I began to think something would be done about whites killing, beating, and misusing Negroes. I knew I was going to be a part of whatever happened. . . .

SHARON ROBINSON

From *Stealing Home*

CONNECTICUT, 1964

I WAS BARELY THROUGH MY FIRST SEMESTER OF high school when my cousin Chuckie phoned, feverish with news. "Your father is an Uncle Tom!"

"He is not!" I shouted into the phone. I was fifteen at the time and not sure of all the implications of the term, but I knew it was a put-down and I wasn't about to let my cousin get away with insulting my father even if I didn't completely understand it. Chuckie's words still stung, but pride would not allow me to let him know how much.

It was obvious to me even then that Dad didn't deserve the name-calling; no one did. My father never sold his soul or his people. Even if I was not yet old enough to let it roll off my back as easily as it rolled off other people's tongues, I knew that in those times, we needed to be unified, not attacking each other. And while my father did make mistakes, those armed with rocks like the words "Uncle Tom" were those who neither knew my father nor the glass houses of their own collective history.

Before Chuckie could even respond to my vehement denial, I asked, fearing the answer, "What makes you say that?" Maybe my father had said or done something outrageous. I knew that he was capable of being very outspoken and controversial. I remembered all the loud arguing that would go on after Thanksgiving dinner. It was as much a part of the day's rituals as watching football on television. Chuckie's mother, Brenda, was the loudest and most self-righteous of the group. She and Dad would jump in each other's faces trying to get their opinions heard over the shouting. My cousins and I learned after the first few confrontations not to take their loud words seriously. Their political arguments were part of the day's fun. At the start of the fireside chat, my cousins, brothers, and I would head for the playroom.

Chuckie said that he had overheard his mother talking to his dad, my mother's brother, and anyway, "He's a Republican, isn't he?" This wasn't really a question. This was a charge.

"I'm not sure," I had to admit. Chuckie had me there. "I'll call you back." I hung up quickly realizing that I needed facts.

I thought back to the first time I recognized party affiliation as defining of character, beliefs, personal choice. I was in the fifth grade and my teacher took a vote before the Kennedy/Nixon election of 1960. He divided us according to how our parents were voting. My mother was a faithful Democrat, supporting John F. Kennedy. At the start of the 1960 presidential campaign season my father had been a strong supporter of the liberal Democrat Hubert Humphrey. Humphrey was strong on both labor and civil rights issues. Senator Kennedy, on the other hand, was better financed but had a shaky voting record on civil rights legislation. In 1957, he had voted to weaken the civil rights bill and received strong endorsement from Governor John Patterson of Alabama, an arch-segregationist. Kennedy beat Humphrey in the primaries and became the nominee for the Democratic party.

The Kennedy camp assumed that my father would maintain his Democratic affiliation and automatically support JFK. The two sat down in a private meeting. My father came away still distrustful of Kennedy because the candidate did not look him directly in the eyes. My father ultimately supported Richard Nixon, believing that it was important to have blacks affiliated with both parties so that their vote would not be taken for granted. As a registered Independent, my father was able to work on either side. The decision to support Nixon lost my father his job as a columnist for the New York Post and he was placed on an unpaid leave of absence from Chock Full O'Nuts. While campaigning for the Republican candidate, Richard Nixon, Dad became disenchanted and several times considered dropping out but chose to keep campaigning on his behalf. Ultimately, it was the response of the two candidates to the jailing of Martin Luther King Jr. that swayed the black community in favor of Kennedy. The Kennedy group stepped in and worked on behalf of his release. Nixon refused, in spite of the urging of his black supporters, my father included, to use his influence to get King out of jail. King was released and the black community credited JFK.

At ten, I did not really understand politics. I wanted Kennedy to win because he represented youth, new direction, vitality, hope—not to mention good looks. But my views didn't matter and the teacher insisted that I go on the Republican side, my father's side.

After the class activity, I went home and pleaded with my father to switch sides for my sake. I even tried telling him that he was probably the only black person in American not supporting Kennedy. I didn't know this to be true but it felt that way. This wasn't the first time my father had taken a controversial stance that seemed counter to the mood of black people. During Dad's baseball days he was increasingly asked to comment on things outside of baseball. In 1949, this extended to testimony before the House Un-American Activities Committee in response to a statement made by Paul Robeson that blacks would not fight Russia for America. Dad, caught between his belief that there were in effect two battles raging—one against foreign enemies and the other against domestic foes—felt that the black man must fight both and testified to such. The actual words of his text were lost in the effort by others to pit one black man against another. . . .

MALCOLM X

From *Malcolm X Speaks*

HARLEM, 1964

REV. [JOSEPH] COLES [JR.], MRS. HAMER, HONORED guests, brothers and sisters, friends and enemies; also ABC and CBS and FBI and CIA:

I couldn't help but be very impressed at the outstart when the Freedom Singers were singing the song "Oginga Odinga" because Oginga Odinga is one of the foremost freedom fighters on the African continent. At the time he visited in Atlanta, Georgia, I think he was then the minister of home affairs in Kenya. But since Kenya became a republic last week, and Jomo Kenyatta ceased being the prime minister and became the president, the same person you are singing about, Oginga Odinga, is now Kenyatta's vice president. He's the number-two man in the Kenya government.

The fact that you would be singing about him, to me is quite significant. Two or three years ago, this wouldn't have been done. Two or three years ago, most of our people would choose to sing about someone who was, you know, passive and meek and humble and forgiving. Oginga Odinga is not passive. He's not meek. He's not humble. He's not nonviolent. But he's free.

Oginga Odinga is vice president under Jomo Kenyatta, and Jomo Kenyatta was considered to be the organizer of the Mau Mau; I think you mentioned the Mau Mau in that song. And if you analyze closely those words, I think you'll have the key to how to straighten the situation out in Mississippi. When the nations of Africa are truly independent—and they *will* be truly independent because they're going about it in the right way—the historians will give Prime Minister, or rather, President Kenyatta and the Mau Mau their rightful role in African history. They'll go down as the greatest African patriots and freedom fighters that that continent ever knew, and they will be given credit for bringing about the independence of many of the existing independent states on that continent right now. There was a time when their image was negative, but today they're looked upon with respect and their chief is the president and their next chief is the vice president.

I have to take time to mention that because, in my opinion, not only in Mississippi and Alabama, but right here in New York City, you and I can best learn how to get real freedom by studying how Kenyatta brought it to his people in Kenya, and how Odinga helped him, and the excellent job that was done by the Mau Mau freedom fighters. In fact, that's what we need in Mississippi. In Mississippi we need a Mau Mau. In Alabama we need a Mau Mau. In Georgia we need a Mau Mau. Right here in Harlem, in New York City, we need a Mau Mau.

I say it with no anger; I say it with very careful forethought. The language that you and I have been speaking to this man in the past hasn't reached him. And you can never really get your point across to a person until you learn how to communicate with him. If he speaks French, you can't speak German. You have to know what language he speaks and then speak to him in that language.

When I listen to Mrs. Hamer, a black woman—could be, my mother, my sister, my daughter—describe what they had done to her in Mississippi, I ask myself how in the world can we ever expect to be respected as *men* when we will allow something like that to be done to our women, and we do nothing about it? How can you and I be looked upon as men with black women being beaten and nothing being done about it, black children and black babies being beaten and nothing being done about it? No, we don't deserve to be recognized and respected as men as long as our women can be brutalized in the manner that this woman described, and nothing being done about it, but we sit around singing "We Shall Overcome."

We *need* a Mau Mau. If they don't want to deal with the Mississippi Freedom Democratic Party, then we'll give them something else to deal with. If they don't want to deal with the Student Nonviolent Committee, then we have to give them an alternative. Never stick someone out there without an alternative. [Or] we waste our time. Give them this or give them that. Give them the choice between this or that.

When I was in Africa, I noticed some of the Africans got their freedom faster than others. Some areas of the African continent became independent faster than other areas. I noticed that in the areas where independence had been gotten, someone got angry. And in the areas where independence had not been achieved yet, no one was angry. They were sad—they'd sit around and talk about their plight, but they weren't mad. And usually, when people are sad, they don't do anything. They just cry over their condition.

But when they get angry, they bring about a change. When they get angry, they aren't interested in logic, they aren't interested in odds, they aren't interested in consequences. When they get angry, they realize the condition that they're in—that their suffering is unjust, immoral, illegal, and that anything they do to correct it or eliminate it, they're justified. When you and I develop that type of anger and speak in that voice, then we'll get some kind of respect and recognition, and some changes from these people who have been promising us falsely already for far too long.

So you have to speak their language. The language that they were speaking to Mrs. Hamer was the language of brutality. Beasts, they were, beating her— The two Negroes, they weren't at fault. They were just puppets. You don't blame the puppet, you blame the puppeteer. They were just carrying out someone else's orders. They were under someone else's jurisdiction. They weren't at fault; in a way they were, but I *still* won't blame them. I put the blame on that man who gave the orders. And when you and I begin to look at him and see the language he speaks, the language of a brute, the language of someone who has no sense of morality, who absolutely ignores law—when you and I learn how to speak his language, then we can communicate. But we will never communicate talking one language while he's talking another language. He's talking the language of violence while you and I are running around with this little chicken-picking type of language—and think that he's going to understand.

Let's learn his language. If his language is with a shotgun, get a shotgun. Yes, I said if he only understands the language of a rifle, get a rifle. If he only understands the language of a rope, get a rope. But don't waste time talking the wrong language to a man if you want to really communicate with him. Speak his language—there's nothing wrong with that. If something was wrong with that language, the federal government would have stopped the cracker from speaking it to you and me.

I might say, secondly, some people wonder, well, what has Mississippi got to do with Harlem? It isn't actually Mississippi; it's America. America is Mississippi. There's no such thing as a Mason-Dixon Line—it's America. There's no such thing as the South—it's America. If one room in your house is dirty, you've got a dirty house. If the closet is dirty, you've got a dirty house. Don't say that that room is dirty but the rest of my house is clean. You're over the whole house. You have authority over the whole house; the entire house is under your jurisdiction. And the mistake that you and I make is letting these *Northern* crackers shift the weight to the Southern crackers.

The senator from Mississippi is over the Judiciary Committee. He's in Washington, D.C., as Mrs. Hamer has pointed out, illegally. Every senator from a state where our people are deprived of the right to vote—they're in Washington, D.C., illegally. This country is a country whose governmental system is run by committees—House committees and Senate committees. The committee chairman occupies that position by dint of his seniority. Eastland is over the Judiciary Committee because he has more seniority than any other senator after the same post or on that committee; he's the chairman. Fulbright, another cracker, from Arkansas, is over the Foreign Relations Committee. Ellender, of Louisiana, is over the Agriculture and Forestry Committee. Russell, of Georgia, is over the Armed Services Committee.

And it goes right on down the line. Out of sixteen committees, ten of them are in the hands of Southern racists. Out of twenty congressional committees, thirteen are in the hands, or at least they were before the recent elections, in the hands of Southern racists. Out of forty-six committees that govern the foreign and domestic direction of this country, twenty-three are in the hands of Southern racists. And the reason they're in the hands of Southern racists is because in the areas from which they come, the black man is deprived of his right to vote. If we had the ballot in that area, those racists would not be in Washington, D.C. There'd be some black faces there, there'd be some brown and some yellow and some red faces there. There'd be some faces other than those cracker faces that are there right now.

So, what happens in Mississippi and the South has a direct bearing on what happens to you and me here in Harlem. Likewise, the Democratic Party, which black people supported recently, I think, something like 97 per cent. All of these crackers—and that's what they are, crackers—they belong to the Democratic Party. That's the party they belong to—the same one you belong to, the same one you support, the same one you say is going to get you this and get you that. Why, the base of the Democratic Party is in the South. The *foundation* of its authority is in the South. The head of the Democratic Party is sitting in the White House. He could have gotten Mrs. Hamer into Atlantic City. He could have opened up his mouth and had her seated. Hubert Humphrey could have opened his mouth and had her seated. Wagner, the mayor right here, could have opened up his mouth and used his weight and had her seated. Don't be talking about some crackers down in Mississippi and Alabama and Georgia—all of them are playing the same game. Lyndon B. Johnson is the head of the Cracker Party.

Now, I don't want to be stepping on toes or saying things that you didn't think I was going to say, but don't ever, ever, ever call me up here to talk about Mississippi. It's controlled right up here from the North. Mississippi is controlled from the North. Alabama is controlled from the North. These Northern crackers are in cahoots with the Southern crackers, only these Northern crackers smile in your face and show you their teeth and they stick the knife in your back when you turn around. You at least know what that man down there is doing and you know how to deal with him.

So all I say is this, this is all I say: when you start talking about one, talk about the others. When you start worrying about the part or the piece, worry about the whole. And if this piece is no good, the entire pie is no good, because it all comes out of the same plate. It's made up out of the same ingredients. . . .

So I say, in my conclusion, as Mrs. Hamer pointed out, the brothers and sisters in Mississippi are being beaten and killed for no reason other than they want to be treated as first-class citizens. There's only one way to be a first-class citizen. There's only one way to be independent. There's only one way to be free. It's not something that someone gives to you. It's something that you take. Nobody can give you independence. Nobody can give you freedom. Nobody can give you equality or justice or anything. If you're a man, you take it. If you can't take it, you don't deserve it. Nobody can give it to you. So if you and I want freedom, if we want independence, if we want respect, if we want recognition, we obey the law, we are peaceful—but at the same time, at any moment that you and I are involved in any kind of action that is legal, that is in accord with our civil rights, in accord with the courts of this land, in accord with the Constitution—when all of these things are on our side, and we still can't get it, it's because we aren't on our own side.

We don't yet realize the real price necessary to pay to see that these things are enforced where we're concerned. And until we realize this, they won't be enforced where we're concerned. We have to let the people in Mississippi as well as in Mississippi, New York, and elsewhere know that freedom comes to us either by ballots or by bullets. That's the only way freedom is gotten. Freedom is gotten by ballots or bullets. These are the only two avenues, the only two roads, the only two methods, the only two means—either ballots or bullets. And when you know that, then you are careful how you use the word *freedom*. As long as you think we are going to sing up on some, you come in and sing. I watch you, those of you who are singing—are you also willing to do some swinging?

They've always said that I'm anti-white. I'm for anybody who's for freedom. I'm for anybody who's for justice. I'm for anybody who's for equality. I'm not for anybody who tells me to sit around and wait for mine. I'm not for anybody who tells me to turn the other cheek when a cracker is busting up my jaw. I'm not for anybody who tells black people to be nonviolent while nobody is telling white people to be nonviolent. I know I'm in the church, I probably shouldn't be talking like this—but Jesus himself was ready to turn the synagogue inside out and upside down when things weren't going right. In fact, in the Book of Revelations, they've got Jesus sitting on a horse with a sword in his hand, getting ready to go into action. But they don't tell you or me about that Jesus. They only tell you and me about that peaceful Jesus. They never let you get down to the end of the book. They keep you up there where everything is, you know, nonviolent. No, go and read the whole book, and when you get to Revelations, you'll find that even Jesus' patience ran out. And when his patience ran out, he got the whole situation straightened out. He picked up the sword.

I believe that there are some white people who might be sincere. But I think they should prove it. And you can't prove it to me by singing with me. You can't prove it to me by being nonviolent. No, you can prove it by recognizing the law of justice. And the law of justice is "as ye sow, so shall ye reap." The law of justice is "he who kills by the sword shall be killed by the sword." This is justice. Now if you are with us, all I say is, make the same kind of contribution with us in our struggle for freedom that all white people have always made when they were struggling for their own freedom. You were struggling for your freedom in the Revolutionary War. Your own Patrick Henry said "liberty or death," and George Washington got the cannons out, and all the rest of them that you taught me to worship as my heroes, they were fighters, they were warriors.

But now when the time comes for our freedom, you want to reach back in the bag and grab somebody who's nonviolent and peaceful and forgiving and long-suffering. I don't go for that—no. I say that a black man's freedom is as valuable as a white man's freedom. And I say that a black man has the right to do whatever is necessary to get his freedom that other human beings have done to get their freedom. I say that you and I will never get our freedom nonviolently and patiently and lovingly. We will never get it until we let the world know that as other human beings have laid down their lives for freedom—and also taken life for freedom—that you and I are ready and willing and equipped and qualified to do the same thing. . . .

And if you all don't want to do it, we'll do it. We'll do it. We have brothers who are equipped, and who are qualified, and who are willing to—As Jesus said, "Little children, go thee where I send thee." We have brothers who can do that, and who will do that, and who are ready to do that. And I say that if the government of the United States cannot bring to justice people who murder Negroes, or people who murder those who are at the forefront fighting in behalf of Negroes, then it's time for you and me to retire quietly to our closets and devise means and methods of seeing that justice is executed against murderers where justice has not been forthcoming in the past.

I say in my conclusion that if you and I here in Harlem, who form the habit ofttimes of fighting each other, who sneak around trying to wait for an opportunity to throw some acid or some lye on each other, or sprinkle dust on each other's doorsteps—if you and I were really and truly for the freedom of our people, we wouldn't waste all of that energy thinking how to do harm to each other. Since you have that ingenuity, if you know how to do it, let me know; I'll give you some money and show you where to go, and show you who to do it to. And then you'll go down in history as having done an honorable thing. . . .

GENERAL GORDON BAKER

From *Black Nationalism in America*

DETROIT, 1965

Gentlemen:

This letter is in regards to a notice sent to me, General Gordon Baker, Jr., requesting my appearance before an examining station to determine my fitness for military service.

How could you have the NERVE knowing that I am a black man living under the scope and influence of America's racist, decadent society??? You did not ask me if I had any morals, principles, or basic human values by which to live. Yet, you ask if I am qualified. QUALIFIED FOR WHAT, might I ask? What does being "Qualified" mean: qualified to serve in the U.S. Army? . . . To be further brainwashed into the insidious notion of "defending freedom"?

You stand before me with the dried blood of Patrice Lumumba on your hands, the blood of defenseless Panamanian students, shot down by U.S. marines; the blood of my black brothers in Angola and South Africa who are being tortured by the Portuguese and South African whites (whom you resolutely support) respectively; the dead people of Japan, Korea, and now Vietnam, in Asia; the blood of Medgar Evers, six Birmingham babies, the blood of one million Algerians slaughtered by the French (whom you supported); the *fresh* blood of ten thousand Congolese patriots dead from your ruthless rape and plunder of the Congo—the blood of defenseless women and children burned in villages from Napalm jelly bombs . . . With all of this blood of my non-white brothers dripping from your fangs, you have the damned AUDACITY to ask me if I am "qualified." White man; listen to me for I am talking to you!

I AM A MAN OF PRINCIPLES AND VALUES: principles of justice and national liberation, self-determination, and respect for national sovereignty. Yet, you ask if I am "physically fit" to go to Asia, Africa, and Latin America to fight my oppressed brothers (who are completely and resolutely within their just rights to free their fatherland from foreign domination). You ask me if I am qualified to join an army of FOOLS, ASSASSINS and MORAL DELIN-QUENTS who are not worthy of being called men! You want me to defend the riches reaped from the super-exploitation of the darker races of mankind by a few white, rich, super-monopolists who control the most vast empire that has ever existed in man's one million years of History—all in the name of "Free-dom"!

Why, here in the heart of America, 22 million black people are suffering unsurmounted toil: exploited economically by every form of business—from monopolists to petty hustlers; completely suppressed politically; deprived of their social and cultural heritage.

But, all men of principle are fighting-men! My fight is for Freedom: UHURU, LIBERTAD, HALAUGA, and HARAMBEE! Therefore, when the call is made to free South Africa; when the call is made to liberate Latin America from the United Fruit Co., Kaiser and Alcoa Aluminum Co., and from Standard Oil; when the call is made to jail the exploiting Brahmins in India in order to destroy the Caste System; when the call is made to free the black delta areas of Mississippi, Alabama, South Carolina; when the call is made to FREE 12TH STREET HERE IN DETROIT!: when these calls are made, send for me, for these shall be Historical Struggles in which it shall be an honor to serve!

Venceremos!

General G. Baker, Jr.

GORDON PARKS

From *Voices in the Mirror*

❧

NEW YORK CITY, 1965

BY NOVEMBER 1965 THE BITTER ORDEAL OF Vietnam
. . . had escalated into a large-scale undeclared war, and as we plunged
deeper into the futility of it, David was drafted. Several of his friends gathered
at our house to discuss their draft situations—Morton and Arnold, two Jewish
brothers; Joe and Harold, two blacks; Johnny, an Irishman; Jimi, a West
Indian; and Bruce, a young Swede from Pennsylvania. Measuring the passion in
their voices, it was hard to decide who would go and who would not. The
Jewish brothers seemed hopelessly split on the issue, as were the two blacks.
The Irishman and the West Indian were reluctant, but they vacillated as the
argument took its course. David seldom ventured an opinion, which was so
unlike him, but Bruce was gung ho. "Those Commie bastards need their asses
kicked real good, and I'm one for helping do it!"

David had never talked to me about it; he had simply shown me his papers
and shrugged. I wasn't going to try and influence him one way or the other. It
was his life; his decision to make. But I was prepared to back up whatever he
decided.

He didn't pack any clothes the day before he was scheduled to go, and I
slept very little that night. But at dawn I heard him stumbling about, and I got
up and peered into the hallway, seeing only a pair of ski boots, poles and two
tennis rackets. Was he going to ski, to play tennis, or to the army?

"What's up, David?" I hollered up the stairs.

"My number!" he hollered back. "I'm getting ready to meet the man!"

I was relieved but unhappy. Before he left that morning I gave him a 35-
mm camera and a large supply of film. "Take some pictures in your spare time,

keep a diary and get it off to me whenever you have a chance. Good luck and remember, I'm not anxious to have any heroes in the family.'' Elizabeth and I embraced him for a long moment, then he was gone. We were worried and painfully aware of the odds against his coming back. Considering the mood of the country he was off to help defend, I could only hope that he wouldn't have to return to yet another battleground.

Outwardly, the black revolution seemed to be charging straight ahead, but inwardly its forces, all battling on the road toward liberation, were not joined without defect. Splintered, armed with desperate solutions, they had grudgingly made their own camps. Roy Wilkins of the NAACP, and Whitney Young of the Urban League, both moderates, fought the war over white corporate tables. Young turks, rallying to the Black Power cry of Stokely Carmichael, rejected the moderates and branded the Black Muslims as isolationists. Packing M-1 rifles and draped in bandoliers, the Black Panthers rejected all the others and gathered for a showdown with the police. The Black Muslims, thirsty for the white lawmen's blood, had spilled some of their own. It was no way to run a revolution. Effective leadership was crumbling to ruin.

Suddenly the possibility of assassination was weighing heavily on the minds of those who had been gaveled into the ordeal of command. By contrast, the younger militants seemed to be obsessed with a hunger for danger.

Stokely Carmichael screamed ''Black Power'' until he was hoarse. Eldridge Cleaver, an outspoken Black Panther, told the meanest cops on the beat that they were only fat, gristle and blood. From behind prison walls, Bobby Seale, a Black Panther co-founder, clamored for all-out revolution. Their leader, Huey Newton, the baddest of them all, lifted his M-1 rifle when seven white cops approached him outside the Panther headquarters. One asked him what he intended to do with the gun. With his finger resting firmly on the trigger, he answered, ''I'm gonna unload it on all of you if you try to take it.'' The cops backed down. That same afternoon a dozen young blacks joined up with the Panthers. The brothers on the block had got Huey's message—and so had the cops.

What followed seems to have taken place on some distant, belligerent landscape. But it was here in America where, with its warped sense of democracy, this nation played out a frightful drama. Lawless men advocated law to justify their lawlessness; and an oppressed minority embraced the bloodiest kind of violence to espouse their rights. Young blacks from all walks of life— from the ghettos, cottonfields, barrios, universities and colleges—bowed to their consciences, banded together and prepared for the bloodletting. Seething with anger, they suppressed all fear and made themselves ready to do battle with the iron-sided forces. Throughout the remainder of the 1960s they would flirt with death day and night.

Stokely Carmichael had been propelled to the center of the black revolution by racism. An early admirer of Martin Luther King and nonviolence, he had finally turned, his patience with white society exhausted. It was his strident call for Black Power that set off a chain of reaction hardly to be equaled in our time. At twenty-five, he was now being lionized, damned and discussed more than any other leader in the civil rights movement. Conservative blacks were especially disturbed by him. They found him irresponsible and divisive. But he went on screaming "Black Power" until, for many blacks, it was *the* promise in the air.

He was breathing fury into a gathering of students at Berkeley, California, when I caught up with him. "The white man says, 'Work hard, nigger, and you will overcome.' If that were true, the black man would be the richest man in the world! My dad believed in that hard work and overcome stuff! He worked like a dog, day and night! But only death came to that poor black man!—and in his early forties! My grandfather had to run, run, run. I ain't running no more! And hell no! We ain't going to Vietnam! Ain't no Vietcong ever called me nigger! If I'm to do any fighting it's going to be right here at home! I will not fight in Vietnam and run in Georgia!" The audience sent up a dazzling roar. "Black Power! Black Power! Black Power!"

To Roy Wilkins the term meant anti-white. "Going it alone offers a disadvantaged minority little except the chance to shrivel and die." Said Whitney Young: "There's no dignity in withdrawal from society. It gives too many Negroes a chance to escape responsibility. It's better for a black man to find a dollar in his pocket instead of a hole." But CORE's Floyd McKissick quipped, "Black Power's got to be good if the white man's against it." Martin Luther King found the term confusing but he never denounced it, and he joined Stokely in linking the Vietnam protest to the civil rights issue.

Smiling sardonically, Stokely met Wilkins's charge of inciting violence with a shrug. "I'm just telling the white man he's beat my head enough. I won't take anymore. White power makes the laws, and white power, in the form of white cops with guns, enforces those laws. As for separatism, what are Wilkins and Young talking about? The whites separated us a long time ago. And they intend to keep it that way."

The three months I traveled with him were filled with tension, anxiety and justifiable paranoia. Pieced together, the threats in the South alone would have stretched a respectable distance. He was absolutely sure some "redneck" would put a bullet through his brain before the summer was over. Normally tranquil and unflappable, he seemed like a young man cocky enough to stroll into the Mississippi legislature and demand to have his dirty underwear washed there. And he had a sense of humor that sustained him during those disgruntled days and nights. Once describing an experience that was by no means funny, he managed to make it funny: "We're on a march in my favorite state, Mississippi.

[The white folks love me down there.] Hell was breaking loose. John Lewis, SNCC's chairman, was showing guts—too much guts. You could hear the billy clubs cracking against his head a mile off. He goes down time and time again, moaning, 'I love you. I love you.' And they pick him up again. Bam! Smack! Bam! 'You black son-of-a-bitch!' Bam! And John, a true believer in non-violence, sinks half conscious to the pavement. Now we're retreating, and they're coming after us with cattle prods and dogs. I holler, 'They've come far enough, baby! Open up!' Crack! Bam! Pow! The crackers begin to scatter, running, shooting out streetlights. Bang! Bang! A big army captain's telling them to put on the spotlight. 'Shut that damn light off!' A brother zings a burst past the captain's ankles. The captain hollers, 'Orders changed! *Ree*-treet! *Reetreet*! These niggers have gone loco! Retreet!' " It was impossible not to laugh as Stokely rocked back and forth screaming "*Reetreet! Reetreet*!"

He had tried nonviolence, but a very violent afternoon in Birmingham had shorn him of it. Seeing a pregnant black woman knocked head over heels by the jet from a fire hose; seeing people trampled by horses, lying with bleeding legs and arms, was too much. "Things blurred, and they carried me screaming all the way to the airport. From that day on I knew if I was hit, I would hit back." Somewhere beyond Martin Luther King's pacificist teachings, he turned his back on white society. Suddenly, bigotry and death in Mississippi were no different from bigotry and death in Vietnam. At the midpoint of one anguished day he said, "I'd rather die fighting in Mississippi tomorrow than live twenty years fighting in Saigon."

One night, weary, angry and confused, and aware that his role was growing beyond his youthful experience, he confided, "I don't really know where I'm headed. I'd like to go somewhere and think things over for a while. Perhaps I've gone as far as I can go at this point. I finished A Choice of Weapons this morning. Hell, I don't know. Maybe your way is the way to go." I felt he was groping for advice, but when I offered none he said, "Whatever happens, we've stirred the conscience of black people. We've got the community on the path to complete liberation. I suppose it's pride, more than color, that binds me to my race. Blackness is necessary, but the concern has to go further than that to reach anyone who needs it. Mississippi taught me that one's life isn't too much to give to help rid a nation of fascists. Albert Camus says, 'In a revolutionary period it is always the best who die. The law of sacrifice leaves the last word to the cowards and the timorous, since the others have lost it by giving the best of themselves.' I dig Camus."

"To die in Alabama rather than Saigon." Stokely's words had brought my thoughts back to the ravaged city from where David had written his last letter to me: "I just got out of surgery a few days ago, and my buddy Jeff Greenfield is headed back to the states in a coffin. We were on a search and destroy mission. He was to the left of me behind the track driver. Sniper fire opened up and I heard a cracking sound. I whirled around to see blood gushing from his helmet. I felt his pulse; he was gone. We hit the water firing, flushed out sixteen Charlies and shot them up like fish in a barrel. I got three kills.

"On the way back to base our track hit a mine. I caught shrapnel in the forehead and just above my left eye. No sweat, Dad, I'll be fine; just got something I'd rather have done without—a Purple Heart. Love ya, David."

He had written about taking three lives—and in a manner that was cold and swaggering. And this from a son who had once told me he would never be able to kill. But now he had done it, and with a feeling of triumph.

Stokely. David. Two young men caught up in wars being fought thousands of miles apart. Sudden death was possible for either of them, but facing it, Stokely would have more reason to know why he was about to die. Yet, that mattered little. Both had been placed in death's easy reach by stupidity and human failings. And both would go on fighting in confusion.

DAVID PARKS

From *GI Diary*

VIETNAM, 1967

April 24, 1967

Went to Saigon for three days to see the bean doctor. Damn, what a place. The women are beautiful and the soldiers live high on the hog. Went to a few night clubs and wound up with a fine Vietnamese dish. A fantastic evening. The guys stationed there really have the life. No wonder the war is lasting so long. The officers and noncoms don't want to give up the kind of living they have up there. Saigon is full of young men running around on motorbikes. I wonder why they aren't out here fighting with us.

May 8, 1967

In the hospital again. Same old jazz—the shrapnel wound in the bean department. A big lump keeps forming and they keep lancing it. God, some of the things you see here. One guy came in so badly shot up he tried to kill himself with a knife. I held him down while the medic put him out with a needle. An ARVN came in this morning with a foot blown off, dripping blood all over the floor. He didn't say anything or cry out. Probably just wondering where he would get another foot. Hope I don't have to go through anything like that.

The rains have started. Nothing but rain for the next four months, they say. My company is with the engineers building a temporary base on the Plain of Reeds. Everything out there is under water. After that we'll be on security and patrols.

May 15, 1967

Lot of thinking lately—the people I love, war, sex and what have you. Frankly I'm mixed up. The Stateside news bugs me. On the one hand you have Stokely Carmichael saying Negroes shouldn't be fighting for this country. On the other hand some Negro leaders think just the opposite. I doubt that most of them have ever been to war. One thing's for sure: I have been, and I'm fed up with it. This war is pointing up a lot of my mistakes. It's like the old man kept on telling me, "Champ, it looks like you're going to have to learn the hard way." If I get out of here in one piece, I'm going to be a different man. If you want to get something out of life, you're going to have to grab it and hold on to it. When I was in school before, I didn't realize this. I'm greedy now and don't think anything will step in my way.

Hope to be back with the fellows tomorrow.

May 17, 1967

Back with the company. It's hot and we're moving again toward another operation which starts tomorrow. I don't know where. They will probably deadline our tracks because of the mud. The jeeps can hardly make it on the roads. I never knew rain could be so troublesome.

Guys have been coming and going so fast it's hard to know anyone any more. Some of our guys are being transferred out to other units like the 273rd Infantry, and we get some of their men. The 273rd came over five months after our division, and the exchange will prevent our unit from being depleted when our one-year tour of duty is up. I won't be going since I've been transferred once. Twice is against the rules.

May 18, 1967

Passmore, the CO's RTO, told me that the old man is looking for another RTO—he needs two. So I asked Thomas if I could have the job, and he said he'd try me out. That's great. I'm getting fed up with being an FO. The night and ambush patrols are really hairy. So now I'm on the command track for the whole company. A lot of guys don't like it. A Negro shouldn't be working on top secret stuff from headquarters. I worked hard for it, so screw them. No more details. Those radios are on twenty-four hours a day, and Passmore and I have to stay with them. The noncoms who used to keep their foot in my rectum are being a little nicer now. They're afraid I'll rat on them. Of course I never would, and the CO couldn't care less if I did. Passmore really has two jobs, watching the radio and wiping the old man's behind. We are at Camp Bravo, but not for long. Something is brewing.

May 21, 1967

We just came back off of a real hot one. We stayed on alert for two days while the straight legs made their sweep. They finally caught up with Charlie, but this time he didn't run. He hit back and we went in and really put the hurt on him. The straight legs were having it bad when we got there, but they were fighting their asses off. They were using their M-16s and 45s. It was the largest battle fought to date by division units in the Mekong Delta. We came in with about thirty tracks and our machine guns were chattering all over the place. We went through the slime and up and over the Vietcong bunkers. Before long Charlie took off. Nineteen of our guys were killed and forty-six wounded. But we bagged 195 Charlies.

The men in B Company, 4th Battalion, 48th Infantry, took the brunt of it. But it took the fly-boys, the 415th Artillery, and our APCs to clear the decks. Charlie hit a few of our tracks with recoilless rifles. Nothing serious.

The war is really going full blast now. There is even talk that we might push the ground attack into North Vietnam. That would mean four years' duty over here instead of one. I just couldn't take it. I'd blow my mind.

I haven't heard from that school. Wish they would let me know something—yes, no, or even maybe. I've still got about six months to pull. Where in hell are the letters from home?

May 25, 1967

Rain has brought everything to a standstill, and Bravo is under about ten feet of water. Sometimes I would prefer action to sitting around listening to these officers beat their gums. It's either how many battles they've won or how many broads they've laid. At times they act like children the way they demand attention. And you'd better jump if you don't want your ass out on that firing line. The only way to keep cool with them is to lie quiet. Show the slightest sign of intelligence and you've had it. Especially if you're a Negro. Pratt and Gurney are pretty bright souls. But every time you see them they are pulling a shit detail while the white cats lie in their bunks enjoying life. A couple of the white guys got so ashamed that they came to the old man today and complained about Pratt and Gurney getting all the shit. I hope it does some good, but I doubt it.

Sgt. Paulson is detail boss. Capt. Thomas is a good officer and most of the time he treats me OK, probably because I'm his RTO. But sometimes he forgets himself. I made the mistake of showing him a clipping Deedee sent about Martin Luther King's denouncing the war. "Who the hell does he think he is? Just because he got a Nobel Prize he thinks he can run the fucking world." He went on, ripping King apart. I said that I thought Dr. King was a man who believed in justice for all people. Then I shut my big mouth. I wasn't in the mood for a night patrol.

❧

TO DIE FOR THE

PEOPLE

Both Gordon and David Parks offer commentary on the increasingly strident rhetoric of Stokely Carmichael (Kwame Ture). To Gordon it was a sign of the times; yet it was very disheartening for his son to hear Ture chastise those who would fight to defend U.S. imperialism and praise the Vietcong. For the students at Morgan State it was a speech to cheer, though many of them were somewhat uncertain when Ture railed against the school's traditional conservative outlook. In keeping with one of his mentors, Malcolm X, Ture had internationalized his perspective, gone from the struggle for civil rights, to beyond "Black Power," to a cry for total liberation. Ture's rhetoric moved from campus to the ghetto, where it received an even stronger reception from young militants discontent with the country's rampant racism, lack of jobs, police brutality—and a society that viewed them as dispensable.

Dr. Martin Luther King, Jr., had not moved as far to the left as Ture, but there was more than one sign that he was on his way. His critique of capitalism during this last speech before the Southern Christian Leadership Council was indicative of his expanding perspective. The government's intransigence had pushed King to his nonviolent limits, and as he spoke out against the war in Vietnam and began to plan a poor people's campaign, a new, more radical civil rights leader emerged. To some extent he was being energized by the younger generation of student activists clamoring for black studies. And undoubtedly he was concerned whether his message had any relevance to the militants in the Black Panther Party or in black nationalists organizations whose rhetoric of retaliation was commanding much more attention.

Right to the end of his life Dr. King never stopped talking about his dream, despite his growing militancy. That dream stood in marked contrast to the cataclysm that H. Rap Brown (Jamil Abdullah Al-Amin) proposed for the American government. Following an appearance in Baltimore and a subsequent disturbance, a warrant was issued for Brown's arrest. Rather than surrender to authorities in Maryland, Brown arranged passage to New York to confer with his lawyer. He never made it. While in jail in Alexandria, Virginia, he wrote a series of letters denouncing the U.S. and calling for a massive black revolution. These were the words that prompted the youthful protest and the urban revolts that rocked the nation. From Watts to Newark flames engulfed the cities, and there was a general feeling among activists that the revolution was right around the corner.

Revolution was never far from Angela Davis's world, nor was it a concept alien to Jonathan Jackson, who Davis so lovingly recalls. Jonathan adored his older brother, George, and felt it was his duty to help him escape from prison. He would be killed attempting to free him. George was one of the famed Soledad Brothers, inmates charged with killing a prison guard and at the center of a nationwide movement to liberate them from the penitentiary. His letters to Angela would spark a passionate correspondence between them, ranging over a number of so-cial, political, economic, and romantic themes. The prison letters of George Jackson are some of the most powerful in the English language. They touch on a plethora of issues, but mainly they are political essays, miniature manuals for revolt, treatises on ideology, and last but not least, personal messages to his family and comrades.

One target of Jackson's passion was the Black Panther Party, which honored him with the title of Field Marshal. The Party was in disarray because many of the leaders had either been killed or were in prison when Huey Newton offered Elaine Brown the position of chairwoman. For days, she mulled over the decision, and it took support from her friends and relatives in Philadelphia and her sister comrades in the party to instill the confidence she needed to take on this "awesome responsi-bility of leadership." The Panthers blazed across the national firmament like a streak of lightning, promoting a slogan to "off the pig." The declaration was daring and it scared and aroused law enforcement agen-cies to combat. When the air cleared, the Panthers counted their dead. Fortunately, some of the programs they initiated, such as feeding the children, defending the indigent, and caring for the sick, had a lasting impact and were later adopted by municipal and federal agencies.

Restoring legitimacy and power to an existing organization was Elaine Brown's dilemma. Creating a wholly new organization was Randall Robin-son's burden. To launch TransAfrica, a fundraiser was proposed by Robin-son's brother, Max, then a famous news commentator and the first black national anchor. A hundred people, including Arthur Ashe and the Rev. Benjamin Hooks of the NAACP, attended the event and they succeeded in raising ten thousand dollars. Within a couple of years TransAfrica was on its way to influencing U.S. foreign policy in South Africa. Now the war against apartheid had an unbending adversary on the Western front.

KWAME TURE

From Stokely Speaks

§

BALTIMORE 1967

IT'S GOOD TO BE BACK HERE AT Morgan. I used to party here when I was at school—after we sat-in in Baltimore on Route 40.

I hope some of the people who have been disagreeing with the concept of Black Power are here. I would suggest they read two articles—one that I wrote for the *New York Review of Books* in September [1966] and one that appeared in the *Massachusetts Review* in 1966.

They explain the theoretical concept of Black Power; they criticize the exponents of the coalition theory and those who say that integration is the only route to solving the racial problem in this country.

I would think that at a black university it would be absurd for me to talk about Black Power, that rather I should talk to black students about what their role is to be in the coming struggle. And so my remarks today are addressed to you, black students of Morgan, to give you a chance to hear some of the things that you never hear about, your need to stop being ashamed of being black and come on home. Though there are many members of the press here, you should pay them no mind because they will not be able to understand what we are talking about.

When I was supposed to speak at this university in October, they canceled the speech. Now I understand there were all sorts of bureaucratic tieups for canceling the speech. We know that elections were close at hand in Maryland and there was a feeling—on my part, I am not saying that anyone really said this—that the people were scared, and so they canceled the speech. They were scared that if I spoke here on the "your house is your castle" concept, Mahoney would win.* One of the reasons I want to talk about that is that I think it is important to understand what that means. What I think the country is trying to do is to kill the free speech of the Student Nonviolent Coordinating Committee. . . .

I'd like to read from one of my favorite men, Frederick Douglass—I hope he is yours. You know Baltimore was his home spot, where he spent his early age. It was from Baltimore that he escaped to freedom.

I want to read it because I think it is crystal clear in our minds what we must do in this generation to move for Black Power. Our mothers scrubbed floors. Our fathers were Uncle Toms. They didn't do that so we could scrub floors and be Uncle Toms. They did it so that this generation can fight for Black Power—and that is what we are about to do and that is what you ought to understand.

Mr. Douglass said:

Those who profess to favor freedom, yet deprecate agitation, are men who want crops without plowing up the ground; they want rain without thunder and lightning; they want the ocean without the awful roar of its many waters.

Power concedes nothing without demands—it never did and it never will. Find out just what any people will submit to and you have found out the exact amount of injustice and wrong which will be imposed upon them; and these will continue till they have resisted with either words or blows or with both. The limits of tyrants are prescribed by the endurance of those whom they suppress.

Following in Mr. Douglass's footsteps we intend to strike our first blow for our liberation, and we will let the chips fall where they may. We do not wish to earn the good will of anybody who is oppressing us. They should rather try to earn our good will, since they have been oppressing us.

This country has been able to make us ashamed of being black. One of the first recognitions of a free people is that we must be united as a people; we must understand the concept of peoplehood and not be ashamed of ourselves. We must stop imitating white society and begin to create for ourselves and our own and begin to embody our own cultural patterns so that we will be holding to those things that we have created, and holding them dear.

For example: it is nonsensical for black people to have debutante balls. It is nonsensical because you are imitating that which white society has given to you and that which you know nothing about. Your fathers slaved for one year to

* An avid segregationist, George Mahoney ran against Spiro Agnew for governorship of Maryland. His campaign slogan on the issue of integrated housing was "A Man's Home Is His Castle."

save $500 so that you can walk up in some white dress for one night talking about virginity. Wouldn't it be better to take that $500 and give it to Morgan so that you could begin to develop a good black institution?

Imitation runs deep in the black community in this country. It runs very deep. You know, when we first got people to go to college and they went to the first white university in this country, there were things called fraternities and sororities. Our black brothers and sisters could not get into these fraternities. They were kept out because of the color of their skin. So what did our brothers do? They turned around and formed something called Alphas, and only light-skinned Negroes could get in. Our black sisters, not to be outdone, formed AKA, for bluebloods only. The other dark-skinned brothers, not to be outdone, set up Omega and Kappa. And then, of course, we had the counterparts, the Deltas.

Now, wouldn't it have been far better if those people, instead of imitating a society that had been built on excluding them, had turned around and built a fraternity that included everybody, light-skinned and dark-skinned?

Perhaps that is the greatest problem you, as black students, face: you are never asked to create, only to imitate. . . .

Is that what you are imitating? Is it for you not to reason why at a university, but to do and die? Do you not have the guts to say: Hell, no. Do you not have the guts to say, I will not allow anyone to make me a hired killer.

When I decide to kill, since it is the greatest crime that man can commit, I alone will make that decision, and I will decide whom to kill.

You are now at a vast black university where they have already incorporated violence in your thinking. And here you are marching around every Friday, or Thursday, or Wednesday or whatever it is, with your shoes spit-shined, until three o'clock in the morning—marching with a gun in your hand, learning all about how to shoot.

And somebody talks about violence. No, I am not violent, I don't believe in violence. I don't want no Black Power. I ain't got nothing to do with violence. Over in Vietnam they put you on a front line and you are shooting. But that is not violence because you can't define for yourself. You ought to tell the school that if you wanted to learn how to kill you would have gone to West Point. You came here to learn how to help your people of Baltimore in the ghettos, and then you turn your backs on them as soon as you get a chance.

What can you tell a black man who lives in the ghettos in Baltimore about killing? Hasn't he been subjected to it all of his life? What is your analysis about the rebellions that have been occurring all around the state?

Are you like everybody else? Are you against violence? Do you analyze? Do you recognize what it means?

The reason they say that we preach violence isn't because we preach violence, but because we refuse to condemn black people who throw rocks and bottles at policemen. That is why. And I say that is the only reason why. Look at all the other Negro leaders—so-called leaders—every time there is a riot:

> We deplore violence, we avoid use of violence, it is very, very bad, there is only a small group of vagabonds, they don't represent our community, and violence never accomplishes anything.
>
> Yes, we are training our boys to go to Vietnam. We think it is a good thing to send them to Vietnam, but violence never accomplishes anything at all. . . .

Do you question what they tell you at school? Or do you only accept, carry it back, get over, go out to further stymie black people in the ghetto?

I blame you for the rebellions across the country this summer. And I will blame you again when they increase this summer. It is your obligation to be back in the ghetto helping out black people who are looking, who are acting, begging, and thinking a way to solve their problems. And you are running out of the ghetto as fast as your sports cars and Mustangs can carry you.

What is your responsibility, black students of Morgan? Do you know about Du Bois? Have you read Douglass? Do you know Richard Wright? Can you quote J. A. Rogers? Do you know Claude McKay?

Can you understand, can you understand LeRoi Jones? There is a young man with me now. His name is Eldridge Cleaver. He just spent eight years in jail. He is writing some of the most profound writing that has come out in the country from black men. Do you know him? Have you read his stuff? Why haven't you read his stuff? Is it because you are too busy trying to find out where the Kappas are partying Friday night?

Why is it that you haven't read his stuff? Is it that you are spit-shining your shoes so that you can become a lieutenant colonel to go to Vietnam when you graduate?

Why is it that you haven't read his stuff? Is it that you don't want to read anything about being black because you, too, are ashamed of it and are running from it? So you want to run to your debutante ball. So you want to run to your Kappa fraternity ball and forget all else.

When the ghettos rebel you are going to be the buffer, and you are the ones who are going to be caught in the middle. The gate is swinging open. Brothers and sisters, you had better come home early this summer. You had better take what knowledge you have and use it to benefit black people in the ghetto.

You had better recognize that individualism is a luxury that black students can no longer afford. You had better begin to see yourself as a people and as a group and, therefore, you need to help to advance that group.

Can you be aggressive? Can you say that Baltimore is almost 52 per cent black, and black people should own it, run it, lock stock and barrel? Or are you afraid?

Can you not go out and organize those people to take the political power that they have been denied and by which they've been oppressed and exploited? Can you not help? Are you too busy trying to be a doctor and lawyer so that you can get a big car and a big house and talk about your house in the suburbs. Am I the only one out there? . . .

Can you begin to say that James Brown is us, that he is a musical genius as much as Bach or Beethoven? Can you understand your culture? Can you make them teach it to you here in college, rather than teach you Bach and Beethoven, which is only one-sided? Why can't you also have James Brown so that you can begin to know what culture is all about?

I want to finish with one quote—actually there are two quotes I want to finish with.

I want to read it because I don't want to make a mistake. The quote I want to read before I close is from Bertrand Russell. You know about the war tribunal. You should. Bertrand Russell is calling the war tribunals to judge the leaders of this country for their actions in Vietnam. I have been asked to serve on it and I am greatly honored. I want to read a quote he calls "An Appeal to My Conscience." The war in Vietnam should have interest for you not only personally, but also because it is very political for black people. When McNamara says he is going to draft 30 per cent of the black people out of the ghettos, baby, that is nothing but urban removal. You should realize you are going to be the fellows leading the charges of your black people. Do you have the guts to stand up now and say I will not follow law and order, I will follow my own conscience. That's what they sent Eichmann to jail for, you know, because he followed law and order.

The choices are very clear. You either suffer or you inflict suffering. Either you go to the Leavenworth federal penitentiary in Kansas or you become a killer. I will choose to suffer. I will go to jail. To hell with this country.

Mr. Russell:

Just as in the case of Spain, Vietnam is a barbarous rehearsal. It is our intention that neither the bona fides nor the authenticity of this tribunal will be susceptible to challenge from those who have so much to hide.

President Johnson, Dean Rusk, Robert McNamara, Henry Cabot Lodge, General Westmoreland and their fellow criminals will be brought before a wider justice than they recognize and a more profound condemnation than they are equipped to understand.

That is a profound statement.

The last statement that I want to leave you with is by John Donne. He said the "death of any man diminishes me because I am involved in mankind."

This generation is not involved in mankind. When we began to crawl, they sent six million people to an oven and we blinked our eyes. When we walked, they sent our uncles to Korea. And we grew up in a cold war. We, this generation, must save the world. We must become involved in mankind. We must not allow them the chance to kill everything and anything that gets in their way. We must not become part of the machine.

I want to read my favorite quotation to conclude.

"If I am not for myself, who will be? If I am for myself alone, who am I? If not now, when? And if not you, who?"

MARTIN LUTHER KING, JR.

From *Where Do We Go from Here?*

§

ATLANTA, 1967

NOW, IN ORDER TO ANSWER THE QUESTION, "Where . . . do we go from here?" which is our theme, we must first honestly recognize where we are now. When the Constitution was written, a strange formula to determine taxes and representation declared that the Negro was sixty percent of a person. Today another curious formula seems to declare that he is fifty percent of a person. Of the good things in life, the Negro has approximately one half those of whites. Of the bad things of life, he has twice those of whites. Thus half of all Negroes live in substandard housing. And Negroes have half the income of whites. When we view the negative experiences of life, the Negro has a double share. There are twice as many unemployed. The rate of infant mortality among Negroes is double that of whites and there are twice as many Negroes dying in Vietnam as whites in proportion to their size in the population.

In other spheres, the figures are equally alarming. In elementary schools, Negroes lag one to three years behind whites, and their segregated schools receive substantially less money per student than the white schools. One-twentieth as many Negroes as whites attend college. Of employed Negroes, seventy-five percent hold menial jobs.

This is where we are. Where do we go from here? First, we must massively assert our dignity and worth. We must stand up amidst a system that still oppresses us and develop an unassailable and majestic sense of values. We must no longer be ashamed of being black. The job of arousing manhood within a people that have been taught for so many centuries that they are nobody is not easy.

Even semantics have conspired to make that which is black seem ugly and degrading. In Roget's *Thesaurus* there are 120 synonyms for blackness and at least sixty of them are offensive, as for example, blot, soot, grim, devil, and foul. And there are some 134 synonyms for whiteness and all are favorable, expressed in such words as purity, cleanliness, chastity, and innocence. A white lie is better than a black lie. The most degenerate member of a family is a "black sheep." Ossie Davis has suggested that maybe the English language should be reconstructed so that teachers will not be forced to teach the Negro child sixty ways to despise himself, and thereby perpetuate his false sense of inferiority, and the white child 134 ways to adore himself, and thereby perpetuate his false sense of superiority.

The tendency to ignore the Negro's contribution to American life and to strip him of his personhood is as old as the earliest history books and as contemporary as the morning's newspaper. To upset this cultural homicide, the Negro must rise up with an affirmation of his own Olympian manhood. Any movement for the Negro's freedom that overlooks this necessity is only waiting to be buried. As long as the mind is enslaved, the body can never be free. Psychological freedom, a firm sense of self-esteem, is the most powerful weapon against the long night of physical slavery. No Lincolnian emancipation proclamation or Johnsonian civil rights bill can totally bring this kind of freedom. The Negro will only be free when he reaches down to the inner depths of his own being and signs with the pen and ink of assertive manhood his own emancipation proclamation. And, with a spirit straining toward true self-esteem, the Negro must boldly throw off the manacles of self-abnegation and say to himself and to the world, "I am somebody. I am a person. I am a man with dignity and honor. I have a rich and noble history. How painful and exploited that history has been. Yes, I was a slave through my foreparents and I am not ashamed of that. I'm ashamed of the people who were so sinful to make me a slave." Yes, we must stand up and say, "I'm black and I'm beautiful," and this self-affirmation is the black man's need, made compelling by the white man's crimes against him.

Another basic challenge is to discover how to organize our strength in terms of economic and political power. No one can deny that the Negro is in dire need of this kind of legitimate power. Indeed, one of the great problems that the Negro confronts is his lack of power. From old plantations of the South to newer ghettos of the North, the Negro has been confined to a life of voicelessness and powerlessness. Stripped of the right to make decisions concerning his life and destiny he has been subject to the authoritarian and sometimes whimsical decisions of this white power structure. The plantation and ghetto were created by those who had power, both to confine those who had no power and to perpetuate their powerlessness. The problem of transforming the ghetto, therefore, is a problem of power—confrontation of the forces of power demanding change and the forces of power dedicated to the preserving of the status quo. Now power properly understood is nothing but the ability to achieve purpose. It is the strength required to bring about social, political, and economic change. Walter Reuther defined power one day. He said, "Power is the ability of a labor union like the UAW to make the most powerful corporation in the world, General Motors, say, 'Yes' when it wants to say 'No.' That's power."

Now a lot of us are preachers, and all of us have our moral convictions and concerns, and so often have problems with power. There is nothing wrong with power if power is used correctly. You see, what happened is that some of our philosophers got off base. And one of the great problems of history is that the concepts of love and power have usually been contrasted as opposites— polar opposites—so that love is identified with a resignation of power, and power with a denial of love.

It was this misinterpretation that caused Nietzsche, who was a philosopher of the will to power, to reject the Christian concept of love. It was this same misinterpretation which induced Christian theologians to reject the Nietzschean philosophy of the will to power in the name of the Christian idea of love. Now, we've got to get this thing right. What is needed is a realization that power without love is reckless and abusive, and love without power is sentimental and anemic. Power at its best is love implementing the demands of justice, and justice at its best is power correcting everything that stands against love. And this is what we must see as we move on. What has happened is that we have had it wrong and confused in our own country, and this has led Negro Americans in the past to seek their goals through power devoid of love and conscience.

This is leading a few extremists today to advocate for Negroes the same destructive and conscienceless power that they have justly abhorred in whites. It is precisely this collision of immoral power with powerless morality which constitutes the major crisis of our times.

We must develop a program that will drive the nation to a guaranteed annual income. Now, early in this century this proposal would have been greeted with ridicule and denunciation, as destructive of initiative and responsibility. At that time economic status was considered the measure of the individual's ability and talents. And, in the thinking of that day, the absence of worldly goods indicated a want of industrious habits and moral fiber. We've come a long way in our understanding of human motivation and of the blind operation of our economic system. Now we realize that dislocations in the market operations of our economy and the prevalence of discrimination thrust people into idleness and bind them in constant or frequent unemployment against their will. Today the poor are less often dismissed, I hope, from our consciences by being branded as inferior or incompetent. We also know that no matter how dynamically the economy develops and expands, it does not eliminate all poverty.

The problem indicates that our emphasis must be twofold. We must create full employment or we must create incomes. People must be made consumers by one method or the other. Once they are placed in this position we need to be concerned that the potential of the individual is not wasted. New forms of work that enhance the social good will have to be devised for those for whom traditional jobs are not available. In 1879 Henry George anticipated this state of affairs when he wrote *Progress and Poverty*:

> The fact is that the work which improves the condition of mankind, the work which extends knowledge and increases power and enriches literature and elevates thought, is not done to secure a living. It is not the work of slaves driven to their tasks either by the task, by the taskmaster, or by animal necessity. It is the work of men who somehow find a form of work that brings a security for its own sake and a state of society where want is abolished.
>
> Work of this sort could be enormously increased, and we are likely to find that the problems of housing and education, instead of preceding the elimination of poverty, will themselves be affected if poverty is first abolished. The poor transformed into purchasers will do a great deal on their own to alter housing decay. Negroes who have a double disability will have a greater effect on discrimination when they have the additional weapon of cash to use in their struggle.
>
> Beyond these advantages, a host of positive psychological changes inevitably will result from widespread economic security. The dignity of the individual will flourish when the decisions concerning his life are in his own hands, when he has the means to seek self-improvement. Personal conflicts among husbands, wives, and children will diminish when the unjust measurement of human worth on the scale of dollars is eliminated.

Now our country can do this. John Kenneth Galbraith said that a guaranteed annual income could be done for about twenty billion dollars a year. And I say to you today, that if our nation can spend thirty-five billion dollars a year to fight an unjust, evil war in Vietnam, and twenty billion dollars to put a man on the moon, it can spend billions of dollars to put God's children on their own two feet right here on earth.

Now, let me say briefly that we must reaffirm our commitment to nonviolence. I want to stress this. The futility of violence in the struggle for racial justice has been tragically etched in all the recent Negro riots. Yesterday, I tried to analyze the riots and deal with their causes. Today I want to give the other side. There is certainly something painfully sad about a riot. One sees screaming youngsters and angry adults fighting hopelessly and aimlessly against impossible odds. And deep down within them, you can see a desire for self-destruction, a kind of suicidal longing.

Occasionally Negroes contend that the 1965 Watts riot and the other riots in various cities represented effective civil rights action. But those who express this view always end up with stumbling words when asked what concrete gains have been won as a result. At best, the riots have produced a little additional antipoverty money allotted by frightened government officials, and a few water-sprinklers to cool the children of the ghettos. It is something like improving the food in the prison while the people remain securely incarcerated behind bars. Nowhere have the riots won any concrete improvement such as have the organized protest demonstrations. When one tries to pin down advocates of violence as to what acts would be effective, the answers are blatantly illogical. Sometimes they talk of overthrowing racist state and local governments and they talk about guerrilla warfare. They fail to see that no internal revolution has ever succeeded in overthrowing a government by violence unless the government had already lost the allegiance and effective control of its armed forces. Anyone in his right mind knows that this will not happen in the United States. In a violent racial situation, the power structure has the local police, the state troopers, the National Guard and, finally, the army to call on—all of which are predominantly white. Furthermore, few if any violent revolutions have been successful unless the violent minority had the sympathy and support of the nonresistant majority. Castro may have had only a few Cubans actually fighting with him up in the hills, but he could never have overthrown the Batista regime unless he had the sympathy of the vast majority of Cuban people.

It is perfectly clear that a violent revolution on the part of American blacks would find no sympathy and support from the white population and very little from the majority of the Negroes themselves. This is no time for romantic illusions and empty philosophical debates about freedom. This is a time for action. What is needed is a strategy for change, a tactical program that will bring the Negro into the mainstream of American life as quickly as possible. So far, this has only been offered by the nonviolent movement. Without recognizing this we will end up with solutions that don't solve, answers that don't answer, and explanations that don't explain.

And so I say to you today that I still stand by nonviolence. And I am still convinced that it is the most potent weapon available to the Negro in his struggle for justice in this country. And the other thing is that I am concerned about a better world. I'm concerned about justice. I'm concerned about brotherhood. I'm concerned about truth. And when one is concerned about these, he can never advocate violence. For through violence you may murder a murderer but you can't murder murder. Through violence you may murder a liar but you can't establish truth. Through violence you may murder a hater, but you can't murder hate. Darkness cannot put out darkness. Only light can do that.

And I say to you, I have also decided to stick to love. For I know that love is ultimately the only answer to mankind's problems. And I'm going to talk about it everywhere I go. I know it isn't popular to talk about it in some circles today. I'm not talking about emotional bosh when I talk about love, I'm talking about a strong, demanding love. And I have seen too much hate. I've seen too much hate on the faces of sheriffs in the South. I've seen hate on the faces of too many Klansmen and too many White Citizens Councilors in the South to want to hate myself, because every time I see it, I know that it does something to their faces and their personalities and I say to myself that hate is too great a burden to bear. I have decided to love. If you are seeking the highest good, I think you can find it through love. And the beautiful thing is that we are moving against wrong when we do it, because John was right, God is love. He who hates does not know God, but he who has love has the key that unlocks the door to the meaning of ultimate reality.

I want to say to you as I move to my conclusion, as we talk about "Where do we go from here," that we honestly face the fact that the movement must address itself to the question of restructuring the whole of American society. There are forty million poor people here. And one day we must ask the question, "Why are there forty million poor people in America?" And when you begin to ask that question, you are raising questions about the economic system, about a broader distribution of wealth. When you ask that question, you begin to question the capitalistic economy. And I'm simply saying that more and more, we've got to begin to ask questions about the whole society. We are called upon to help the discouraged beggars in life's marketplace. But one day we must come to see that an edifice which produces beggars needs restructuring. It means that questions must be raised. You see, my friends, when you deal with this, you begin to ask the question, "Who owns the oil?" You begin to ask the question, "Who owns the iron ore?" You begin to ask the question, "Why is it that people have to pay water bills in a world that is two-thirds water?" These are questions that must be asked.

Now, don't think that you have me in a "bind" today. I'm not talking about communism.

What I'm saying to you this morning is that communism forgets that life is individual. Capitalism forgets that life is social, and the kingdom of brotherhood is found neither in the thesis of communism nor the antithesis of capitalism but in a higher synthesis. It is found in a higher synthesis that combines the truths of both. Now, when I say question that whole society, it means ultimately coming to see that the problem of racism, the problem of economic exploitation, and the problem of war are all tied together. These are the triple evils that are interrelated. . . .

H . RAP BROWN

From *Die Nigger, Die*

ALEXANDRIA, VIRGINIA, 1967

IN MAY OF 1967 I WAS ELECTED Chairman of SNCC. It was not a position which I sought, but people seemed to feel that I would be a good one to articulate the positions of the organization. Even though the press began projecting me as a "Black Power leader" and all that kind of mess, I knew that it didn't matter what position a dude had, it didn't mean he was a leader, even if he had the title of Chairman or President. The leader might be a dude in the organization who ain't got no title, no office. When I was head of SNCC, that's all I was. I was not a leader of Black people. I had a public platform because I was Chairman of SNCC and therefore what I said got heard by a lot of people. But I don't think I can articulate the sentiments of Black folks any better than the brothers and sisters did in Detroit. I'm just in a position where maybe I can explain what the brother is talking about, because there're a lot of negroes who don't understand. That does not mean leadership.

It was obvious when I became Chairman that I was in for trouble. For a year, "the man" had let Carmichael travel around the country talking about Black Power and "the man" realized that he had made a serious mistake. He recognized too late that Black people, like the Vietnamese people, were escalating their war of liberation. So it was clear to me that if Black people began to respond by accepting a revolutionary analysis, "the man" was going to try and silence me. But if you're serious you don't worry about things like that. You do your job and you're either carried off the battlefield or you walk off victorious.

The first move that the government made against me came in the last week of July, '67, when I went to speak in Cambridge, Maryland . . . I got to

Cambridge about an hour late and the people were still waiting. Well, the Black community was full of negro cops. And there were white cops and National Guardsmen on Race Street. That's the street which divides the Black community from the white. They were stationed in front of all the stores.

I spoke and afterwards I went up to the local office of the Movement. There wasn't anything going on. People were just standing around talking, both in the office and out on the street and everything was cool. There was this young sister who wanted us to walk her home because she was afraid. She lived near Race Street and she was afraid of all those white cops that were stationed down there. So I was walking down the street with her and I noticed that everybody who was around was walking with us. They were just tagging along behind us, which ain't too cool a thing to do. We got about halfway down the street and somebody opened fire from some bushes which were behind me. So people began to scatter. I got shot—I was hit in the head with some of the shotgun pellets. I dove on the ground and rolled over up against this wooden fence. There were three of us trapped out there—a girl, another brother and myself. The cops who were doing the shooting just kept shooting. For about five minutes they sustained their fire and they were steadily knocking splinters out of that fence. And you talk about getting low. The Vietcong ain't had nothing on me about getting low. The brother was getting kind of nervous and wanted to try and get out of there. I figured the safest thing to do was to stay low because I didn't know whether there were other cops around just waiting for us to try and make a run for it. But he wanted to get on out and he told me to get up and let him by. I told him that I wasn't about to get up. So he crawled around me and went about 15 yards and he found a gate that was open. He yelled back and told us so I crawled on down there. The girl was too scared to move. Just as I got to the gate, he struck a match to light a cigarette. "Put that match out!" I told him but by then the police had seen the match and opened fire on us. By that time, though, I was through the gate.

We got away and I went to somebody's house to try and get myself a little first aid. I was still bleeding. The people stopped the bleeding and got me to a doctor's office. He gave me some kind of shot, which made me dizzy. By this time the brothers had heard what had happened and they were mad and had gone home to get their pieces.

I went back out in the streets to see what was going on. The brothers were out and they were hiding on both sides of the street so that if any crackers came down through there, they had them in a cross fire. The only thing wrong was that the brothers would've ended up shooting each other, because they had their cross fire laid out wrong. So I told 'em. I left after that.

The next day, while in Washington, D.C., I heard that there was a 13-state federal warrant out for my arrest. So I called William Kunstler, SNCC's New York attorney and he told me that the FBI had contacted him and wanted to work out some way for me to surrender. I said, "Surrender!! She-e-it." Kunstler decided that I should come to New York and surrender there. Well, I wasn't in favor of surrendering. Let the muthafuckas come and get me. However, I knew this was not the time, so I said, O.K., and told him that I'd come up the next day. The whole thing was set up for the following noon.

The next day I went to National Airport to catch the plane to New York and surrender. When I left the house that morning I saw this dude standing outside and I knew he was "the man." When I got to the airport, I thought the FBI was having a convention, there were so many of them. I was dressed in my dungarees so it was obvious that I wasn't trying to sneak out of town. Wasn't no way in the world I could disguise myself and I didn't see no point in trying to hide. I hadn't done a damned thing but exercise my right to "Free Speech."

I went on down and got a shuttle pass and the airport police came up to me. "Are you Rap Brown?" I said, "Yeah." "Would you come with us?" I said, "For what?" "There's a warrant out for your arrest." I said, "I know it. I'm going to New York to surrender to the Federal Bureau of Faggots. That's where I'm on my way to now." They said, "Well, we have to notify the authorities." I said, "Good. Call the FBI because the agreement was made with them." Well, they called the muthafuckas and the pigs denied it so they came back with some more pigs. I called Kunstler and explained to him what had happened. It was obvious to me by that time that I had been the victim of a setup. They'd never intended to let me get to New York. They could've arrested me there in Washington because they knew where I was staying. But they wanted to make it appear as if I was trying to run away.

I was arrested and taken to Alexandria, Virginia, and was in the custody of the Virginia authorities. They put me in jail and sent this negro FBI agent to interrogate me. I blew that bootlicker's mind. I told him, "Now, you know why they sent you in here. If I was Bobby Baker, you wouldn't be here. You wouldn't be nowhere around here. Only reason they sent you in here is 'cause they think I'm gon' talk to you because you're cullard." I laughed at him. "I know you got a little tape recorder on you. . . ."

When the federal government released me, I was on federal property and I decided to stay because the Virginia authorities couldn't arrest me as long as I was on federal property. (So the story goes.) Well, the federal government ejected me from the building. When I got out on the steps, a lot of Black folks had come over from Washington, D.C. I told them to bring me some lumber. They could have my 40 acres and a mule, I was setting up camp right there on the steps. Well, that's when a little shoving contest began. The federal marshalls tried to shove me off the steps and I shoved them and they shoved me and eventually they shoved me on out into the street where I was arrested by the Virginia cops. They also arrested my man, Donald Brown, who was then a student at Howard. I guess they didn't want anything brown in their white town.

They put me in the city jail in Alexandria and when the Black community got the word they came down to the jail. I heard a lot of noise and I didn't find out until later that they had come down there and were willing to break me out. And who stopped them? The militants! The so-called revolutionaries! "Don't you see all them guns?" Well, the people saw all the guns. If they could've broken in there and gotten me out, I was for leaving with 'em. But the militants were out there stopping the revolutionary process. That showed me where the militants were at. If the revolution is abortive, it'll be because of them. They're the people who talk the most and when it comes time for action, they won't shut up. They gon' stop the people.

Half of the Black "militants" ain't nothing but a bunch of potheads, bootleg preachers and coffeehouse intellectuals. They are caught up in that whole identity thing. They just discovered that they were Black, because they were working so hard all their lives to be white. They're further away from being revolutionaries than the poor people who are not militantly political. But the coffeehouse intellectual, the Black militant, thinks he's political because he reads Fanon. Books don't make revolutionaries. I contend that the Black people who burned down Watts and Detroit don't have to read. These cats have lived more than the intellectual has read. So they are political by having learned from their existence. Oppression made these cats political. The militants spend all their time trying to program white people into giving them some money. "The man" has created a new type of Tom. They are willing to be anything, as long as they can be Black first. Black capitalists, Black imperialists, Black oppressors—anything, so long as it's Black first. . . .

ANGELA DAVIS

From Angela Davis, an Autobiography

LOS ANGELES, 1960S

GEORGIA AND PENNY JACKSON ASKED ME TO attend a . . . meeting of the Democratic Club in Pasadena, which was headed by Don Wheeldin, a Black man who had a long history of involvement in progressive causes. He wanted to raise the issue of the Soledad Brothers case before this meeting in order to appeal to the membership for financial and political support. A sister named Fannie, who was a student at UCLA and one of the leading activists in the Soledad Committee, had driven us there. Since we had to drop Georgia and Penny off when the meeting was over, they invited us to stop by the house for coffee. . . .

This was the first time I had exchanged more than a few words of greeting with Jonathan. George had mentioned him in the letter, praising him for his intelligence and especially for his unshakable commitment to him. He had said that Jon was somewhat withdrawn and had asked me to try to get him interested in attending the Soledad meetings at Kendra and Franklin's. I decided to talk to him about the committee right then.

Jonathan only wanted to talk about George. All of his interests, all of his activities were bound up in some way with his brother in Soledad. At sixteen, Jonathan was carrying a burden which most adults would refuse. The last time he had seen George on the "free" side of the walls, he was a seven-year-old. From that time to this, there had been the visits overseen by armed guards in Chino, Folsom, San Quentin, Soledad. And the letters. The letters in which they had developed the relationship which should have unfolded at home, in the streets, in the gym, on the baseball field. But because it had been cramped into prison visitors' cubicles, into two-page, censored letters, the whole relationship revolved around a single aim—how to get George out here, on this side of the walls.

Jonathan was extremely proud of the relationship he had with his brother, proud of its maturity and of the trust George had in him. In the course of our conversation, he brought out a thick sheaf of letters he had received from the various prisons his brother had inhabited over the last ten years. He wanted us to read George's descriptions of the brutal treatment he and the other brothers had received at the hands of the prison guards.

Without ever having been involved in mass movements, he instinctively understood the need to get large numbers of people pushing for the freedom of his brother. As he talked about his experiences at Pasadena High School, where he was finishing his third year, he bitterly complained about the apathy of most of his classmates. They didn't know what struggle was all about, he said—particularly the white students, who were in the majority at the school. He showed Fannie and me an article which he had written in the school newspaper, running down the facts of the Soledad Brothers case and criticizing the students for not being involved in issues such as this.

The article was brilliantly written. Like George, he expressed himself in powerful and compelling language. Recalling that George had said in his letter that we should try to attract Jonathan to the work of the defense committee, I told him that we were sorely in need of good writers to get the literature of the committee together. As Fannie and I were leaving, I said we were expecting to see him at the next meeting.

Jon was present at the next meeting on 50th Street and after that he rarely missed a session. He never said much during the meetings, but when it came to producing material and distributing it, he was a dedicated worker.

As the Soledad Committee gained in influence, and as its work became more complicated and demanding, I began to spend a great deal of time with the Jackson family. Frances, Penny or Georgia and I frequently had joint speaking engagements in order to publicize the activities of the committee. More often than not, Jonathan accompanied us. We grew closer, and I came to look upon him not only as a brother in struggle, but as something like a blood brother as well.

My communications with George became more regular. We too grew closer. As we agreed and disagreed with each other on political questions, a personal intimacy also began to develop between us. In his letters, which dealt for the most part with subjects such as the need to popularize communist ideas among the Black masses, the need to develop the prison movement, the role of women in the movement, etc., George also talked about himself, his past life, his own personal desires and aspirations, his fantasies about women, his feelings about me. "I've been thinking about women a lot lately," he once wrote. "Is there anything sentimental or otherwise wrong with that? That couldn't be. It's never bothered me too much before, the sex thing. I would do my exercise and the hundreds of katas, stay busy with something . . ."

I came to know George not only through the letters we exchanged, but also through the people who were close to him—through Jon and the rest of the Jackson family, through John Thorne, who, as his lawyer, saw him regularly. The closer I felt to George, the more I found myself revealing to those who knew George a side of me I usually kept hidden except from the most intimate of friends. In the letters I managed to get to him I responded not only to the political questions he posed; I also told him that my feelings for him had grown deeper than a political commitment to struggle for his freedom; I felt a personal commitment as well.

George knew about the tons of hate mail which poured into my office at UCLA demanding that I be expelled from the university. He knew about the many threats which had been made on my life and was concerned for my safety. . . . He wrote me that he wanted Jon to stay with me as much as possible. Jon also received a message from his brother asking him to make sure that I was secure from the racists and reactionaries who might try to make me a martyr.

When George's book *Soledad Brother* was being prepared for publication, he asked me to read over the manuscript and make suggestions for improvements. The evening I received it, I thought I would skim through a few of the letters, saving the bulk of the book for another time. But once I got started, it was impossible to put the manuscript down until I had seen every word—from the first letter to the last. I was astounded. The formidable magnetism of the letters came not only from their content, not only from the way they traced George's personal and political evolution over the last five years—but even more from the way they articulated so clearly, so vividly, the condition of our people inside prison walls and outside. And in several passages George stated so precisely, so naturally, the reasons our liberation could only be achieved through socialism.

GEORGE JACKSON

From *Soledad Brother*

§

CALIFORNIA, 1970

*Angela,**

I am certain that they plan to hold me incommunicado. All of my letters except for a few to my immediate family have come back to me with silly comments on my choice of terms. The incoming mail is also sent back to the outside sender. The mail which I do receive is sometimes one or two weeks old. So, my sweet sister, when I reach you, it will be in this manner.

. . . I'm going to write on both sides of this paper, and when I make a mistake I'll just scratch over it and continue on. That is my style, completely informal.

Was that your sister with you in court? If so, she favored you. Both very beautiful people. You should have introduced me.

They are going to take your job, I know they are—anything else would be expecting too much. They can't, however, stop you from teaching in public institutions, can they?

They hate us, don't they? I like it that way, that is the way it's supposed to be. If they didn't hate me I would be doing something very wrong, and then I would have to hate myself. I prefer it this way. I get little hate notes in the folds of my newspaper almost every day now. You know, the racist stuff, the traditional "Dear nigger" stuff, and how dead I am going to be one day. They think they're mad at me now, but it's nothing compared to how it will be when I really get mad myself. . . .

* Angela Y. Davis

I have ideas, ten years' worth of them, I'd like all those brothers on Fiftieth Street to be aware of them. Tell Fay Stender to give you a copy of my thoughts on Huey Newton and politics. . . . At the end of these writings, titled "Letter to Huey Newton," there should be a note on revolutionary culture and the form it should take in the black Amerikan colonies. That was the best section. Without that section the power would be lost. Fay and I don't agree altogether on political methods. But that is only because we are viewing things from very different levels of slavery. Mine is an abject slavery.

I think of you all the time. I've been thinking about women a lot lately. Is there anything sentimental or otherwise wrong with that? There couldn't be. It's never bothered me too much before, the sex thing. I would do my exercises and the hundreds of katas, stay busy with something . . . this ten years really has gone pretty quickly. It has destroyed me as a person, a human being that is, but it was sudden, it was a sudden death, it seems like ten days rather than ten years.

Would you like to know a subhuman. I certainly hope you have time. I'm not a very nice person. I'll confess out front, I've been forced to adopt a set of responses, reflexes, attitudes that have made me more kin to the cat than anything else, the big black one. For all of that I am not a selfish person. I don't think so anyway, but I do have myself in mind when I talk about us relating. You would be the generous one, I the recipient of that generosity.

They're killing niggers again down the tier, all day, every day. They are killing niggers and "them protesters" with small workings of mouth. One of them told a pig today that he was going to be awful disappointed with the pig if the pig didn't shoot some niggers or protesters this evening when he got off work. The pig found it very amusing. They went off on a twenty minute political discussion, pig and his convict supporter. There is something very primitive about these people. Something very fearful. In all the time I've been down here on Maximum Row, no brother has ever spoken to one of these people. We never speak about them, you know, across the cells. Every brother down here is under the influence of the party line, and racist terms like "monky" have never been uttered. All of these are beautiful brothers, ones who have stepped across the line into the position from which there can be no retreat. All are fully committed. They are the most desperate and dauntless of our kind. I love them. They are men and they do not fight with their mouths. They've brought them here from prisons all over the state to be warehoused or murdered. Whichever is more expedient. That Brother Edwards who was murdered in that week in January told his lawyer that he would never get out of prison alive. He was at the time of that statement on Maximum Row, Death Row, Soledad, California. He was twenty-one years old. We have made it a point to never exchange words with these people. But they never relent. Angela, there are some people who will never learn new response. They will carry what they incorporated into their characters at early youth to the grave. Some can never be educated. As an historian you know how long and how fervently we've appealed to these people to take some of the murder out of their system, their economics, their propaganda. And as an intelligent observer you must see how our appeals were received. We've wasted many generations and oceans of blood trying to civilize these elements over here. It cannot be done in the manner we have attempted it in the past. Dialectics, understanding, love, passive resistance, they won't work on an activistic, maniacal, gory pig. It's going to grow much worse for the black male than it already is, much, much worse. We are going to have to be the vanguard, the catalyst, in any meaningful change.

When generalizing about black women I could never include *you* in any of it that is not complimentary. But my mother at one time tried to make a coward of me, she did the same with Jon. She is changing fast under crisis situation and apocalyptic circumstance. John and Fleeta's mothers did the same to them, or I should say tried. And so did every brother's mother I've ever drawn out. I am reasonably certain that I can draw from every black male in this country some comments to substantiate that his mother, the black female, attempted to aid his survival by discouraging his violence or by turning it inward. The blacks of slave society, U.S.A., have always been a matriarchal subsociety. The implication is clear, black mama is going to have to put a sword in that brother's hand and stop that "be a good boy" shit. Channel his spirit instead of break it, or to break it I should say. Do you understand? *All* of the sisters I've ever known personally and through other brothers' accounts begged and bullied us to look for *jobs* instead of being satisfied with the candy-stick take. The strongest impetus a man will ever have, in an individual sense, will come from a woman he admires. . . .

As an individual, I am grateful for you. As the black male, I hope that since your inclination is to teach you will give serious consideration to redeeming this very next generation of black males, by reaching for today's black female. I am not too certain about my generation. There are a few, and with these few we will keep something. But we have altogether too many pimps and punks, and black capitalists (who want a piece of the putrescent pie). There's no way to predict. Sometimes people change fast. I've seen it happen to brothers overnight. But then they have to learn a whole new set of responses and attack reflexes which can't be learned overnight. So cats like me who have no tomorrows have to provide examples. I have an ideal regarding tomorrow, but I live an hour at a time, right in the present, looking right over my nose for the trouble I know is coming.

There is so much that could be done, right now. . . . But I won't talk about those things right here. I will say that it should never be easy for them to destroy us. If you start with Malcolm X and count *all* of the brothers who have died or been captured since, you will find that not even one of them was really *prepared* for a fight. No imagination or fighting style was evident in any one of the incidents. But each one that died professed to know the nature of our enemies. It should never be so easy for them. Do you understand what I'm saying? Edward V. Hanrahan, Illinois State Attorney General, sent fifteen pigs to raid the Panther headquarters and murder Hampton and Clark. Do you have any idea what would have happened to those fifteen pigs if they had run into as many Viet Cong as there were Panthers in that building. The VC are all little people with less general education than we have. The argument that they have been doing it longer has no validity at all, because they were doing it just as well when they started as they are now. It's very contradictory for a man to teach about the murder in corporate capitalism, to isolate and expose the murderers behind it, to instruct that these madmen are completely without stops, are licentious, totally depraved—and then not make adquate preparations to defend himself from the madman's attack. Either they don't really believe their own spiel or they harbor some sort of subconscious death wish.

None of this should have happened as it did. I don't know if we'll learn in time or not. I am not well here. I pretend that all is well for the benefit of my family's peace of mind. But I'm going to cry to you, so you can let the people on Fiftieth Street know not to let this happen to them, and that they must resist that cat with *all* of their strength when he starts that jail talk. . . .

Nothing, absolutely nothing comes as a surprise to me. There is much to be said about these places but I must let this go right now or I won't be able to post it until tomorrow. In the event that you missed it, (my writing is terrible, I know), I think a great deal of you. This is one slave that knows how to love. It comes natural and runs deep. Accepting it will never hurt you. Free, open, honest love, that's me.

Should you run into Yvonne* tell her that I love her also and equally. Tell her that I want to see her, up close. Tell her I'm not a possessive cat, never demanding, always cool, never get upset until my (our) face and freedom get involved. But make her understand that I want to hold her (chains and all) and run my tongue in that little gap between her two front teeth. (That should make her smile.)

Power to the People!

George

* Yvonne is Angela Davis's middle name.

ELAINE BROWN

From *A Taste of Power*

❧

OAKLAND, CALIFORNIA, 1974

. . . **D**URING THAT FIRST MONTH OF MY TENURE as chairman of the Black Panther Party, I began to lose the thread that connected me to what I had become.

Whatever I thought about Bobby Seale, it was certainly never that he was an enemy of our people or party. Bobby's condemnation had nothing to do with his competence or commitment. There was no justification for it. It had to do with a cocaine-boosted rage. I had to admit that all of Huey's subsequent heavy-handed acts had the same foundation. I had to reckon with my own role in all of it, and wonder whether I could continue to have a role in any of it. I was not losing the thread as much as the faith.

Faith was all there was. If I did not believe in the ultimate rightness of our goals and our party, then what we did, what Huey was doing, what he was, what *I* was, was horrible. If the party had no humane and lasting value, that would nullify the loss of so many precious lives: of John and Bunchy and George and Jonathan and Fred. It would mean a disastrous mistake had been made in a Faustian bargain.

I had to face the question of whether to go or to bide. I had to accept the consequences of the answer. And I had to face it alone. I could no longer hide behind Huey.

I had remained above the fray of that last month of terror, as I had my whole life in the party. Now I was compelled to confront what my participation in the party really meant. Was my loyalty determined by personal aggrandizement? Was my commitment rooted only in my private dreams? Were the songs and words I wrote simply embellishments of deeds that could be measured more by caprice than by principle? Was I duplicitous—something far worse than anything Bobby had ever really been—ready to foster what was an illusion of revolution?

Alone, thinking, rocking, I began to hear the sounds of the old, repetitive piano scales that had filled my youth. Like the other pieces of my childhood, they were morsels of life scavenged by my mother, trying to drown out the sound of scurrying gutter rats and escape the despair. I began to taste the salt air of Atlantic City, remembering how my mother had squeezed her sweatshop salary to dress up my childhood with vacations there; to pay for a decent hotel room, even if it was not one close to the beach where hotel rooms were for "whites only." I felt the cold of New Year's Day, when we watched Philadelphia's Mummers' Parade, where whites wore blackface and blacks were not allowed to participate. I could smell the soap and talcum powder of summer baths on York Street, throughout which my mother sat with me to keep the roaches from falling into the tub.

It was strange that such little remembrances would shock me into finally recognizing that my mother had carried me on her back all those years. With her coarse lessons and hard ways, she had tried to steal a life for me. Nevertheless, I had felt the weight of our poverty, the indignity of our lives.

I had experienced the pathetic bustling joy of everybody in our neighborhood when somebody "hit the number." I had heard the sorrow in the sound of bongos and "do-waps" on North Philly streets produced by gangs of wine-drinking youngbloods angry at all the wrong people. I had felt the degradation in the impossibility Nita and Barbara and the rest of us girls had known trying to see beauty in our dark skin or our full lips or the texture of our African hair or even in the size and shape of our feet and derrieres.

I had come to know that York Street was as American for black people as baseball at Connie Mack Stadium was for whites. I knew that millions of black mothers had tried, like my own, to gloss over the pain with piano lessons and stolen new dresses, the way they smoothed Vaseline onto patent-leather Easter shoes. I knew that millions of blacks had been forced to find hope in playing numbers and relief in Scotch or heroin. I knew that millions had found comfort in the strength of the Joe Louises and Jackie Robinsons and Marian Andersons and Josephine Bakers who had clawed their way out of our degradation. I knew that millions had found salvation in the name of Jesus.

I had become mad. Huey had surely become mad. Perhaps that was really our bond. Perhaps it was the bond of all of us, really, our rage.

Huey had hated the senseless cycles of life on the streets of West Oakland. He had wanted more for his friends, more for his family, more for his father, even more for his dear Armelia Newton, who had, like my own mother, tried to hold the head of her seventh son high above the stench of being black in America.

Huey had seized a moment in the historical chain to make another bid for our humanity. From the first Africans who had leaped from slave ships in suicidal rejection of slavery, we had struggled for freedom. A thousand slaves had slit the throats and poisoned the food of their masters, living with the singular desire to live free or find freedom in hell. A thousand blacks had run for freedom, dodging bullets and "nigger dogs," riding the third rail of the Underground Railroad to freedom. A million blacks had linked themselves to the Harriet Tubmans and Frederick Douglasses and Sojourner Truths and Marcus Garveys and W. E. B. Du Boises and Martin Luther Kings and El Haj Malik El-Shabazzes. Still, we were not free.

Huey had created his Black Panther Party with both his brilliance and his madness. Now he had made me chairman of that party, calling me out. I was afraid. The question was whether I held a scepter of terror or a sword of freedom. The question was whether to go or to bide.

The answer came in the echoing cries of Mrs. Huggins and Mrs. Carter and Mrs. Jackson and the other hurting mothers who had given their sons to our struggle. It was in seeing the sum of the bits and pieces of my thirty-one years.

The answer was love—the love that was inside the madness. It was about not forgetting. It was about living and about dying for freedom. This was all we could do if the Dorothy Clarks and Armelia Newtons were ever to see the other side of the mountain. I had to hold on.

RANDALL ROBINSON

From *Defending the Spirit*

❧

WASHINGTON, D.C., 1977

MONTHS EARLIER RONALD WALTERS HAD MET with
. . . Herschelle Challenor, the Africa Subcommittee counsel, and me at
the Washington home of C. Payne Lucas, president of Africare, to lay plans for
the new organization. It was Challenor who suggested that we name the organization TransAfrica. All of us thought that Richard Gordon Hatcher, the young
black mayor of Gary, Indiana, would be a good choice to chair the board of
directors.

"Who knows him?" I asked.

"I know him," said Walters. "I'll call him now." He did and Hatcher
agreed to fill the position he would hold for fifteen years.

Robert C. S. Powell was a large man, in girth and style. A black Episcopal
priest, he chaired the Africa Committee of the National Council of Churches at
the New York building known to all who did business with the Interchurch
Center as the God Box. Equipped with an instinctive understanding of ecclesi-
astical politics, an intimidating intellect, and a velvet-cloaked arrogance, Father
Powell, a founding TransAfrica board member, thought the idea of TransAfrica
was seminally important and won for it from his church colleagues a funding
stream that would flow unbroken for several years until his untimely death at
the age of forty-two. He had only just returned home from Kenya the evening
before he died of a heart attack while sitting beside his wife, Bernice, at the
Sunday morning worship service at New York's Cathedral of St. John the
Divine.

Early in 1978 I resigned my position as administrative assistant to Charles
Diggs. Shortly thereafter, in a made-over second-floor one-bedroom apartment

on Eighteenth Street in Northwest Washington, TransAfrica began its work
with a two-person staff—myself as executive director and Dolores Clemons as
my assistant.

High on our agenda was the creation of a fundamentally different U.S.
foreign policy toward the white minority regimes of southern Africa. Since
1948 and the codification of apartheid, the Republic of South Africa had successfully buffered its racialist tyranny with Western corporate investment and
the sympathetic company of neighboring white minority regimes that Pretoria
either ran or influenced in Namibia, Rhodesia, and the Portuguese colonies of
Angola and Mozambique. When Portugal pulled out of Africa in the mid-1970s
and its colonies became independent, South Africa's rulers began sponsoring
armed insurgencies aimed at destabilizing the new black-run nations. Public
declarations notwithstanding, the United States during the Nixon and Reagan
presidencies supported South Africa's policies unreservedly.

The Carter administration, falling between the Republican presidencies,
had a mixed record, demonstrating resolve to Rhodesia's obdurate whites,
political cowardice to Angola's beleaguered government, and, for all quantifi-
able intents and purposes, neutrality to South Africa's white rulers.

TransAfrica's task was to effect a 180-degree turn in American policy
toward South Africa and the general region. How could this be done? We had
no money and no reliable place to find it in large amounts. Virtually none
could be expected from the corporate community. Some three hundred American corporations had invested upwards of two billion dollars in an apartheid
system whose labor inequities produced extraordinary returns on investment.

What constituency could we count on to give money or rally to a call?
While in Cape Town, I had gone to Table Mountain and looked westward
across the South Atlantic toward Robben Island where Nelson Mandela had
been imprisoned for life. But almost no one in the United States knew who
Nelson Mandela was, or anything else about South Africa, much less American
policy toward it.

What could we reasonably expect from approaches to the conventional
establishment forces? The prospects there seemed dim indeed. After all, the
chairman of the House Africa Subcommittee, Charles Diggs, could not coax
the subcommittee to approve even modest sanctions against South Africa. Many
thoughtful African-Americans saw possible value in surmounting the de facto
barriers to black membership in virtually all white old-line foreign policy
ballast organizations like the Council on Foreign Relations. But what had Council members ever done, save bury human suffering abroad in esoteric writings
and pedantic talks? After all, the Council was and remains a citadel of motionless hand-wringing where the parameters for suggested foreign policy adjustment are so close as to touch each other. What could prospective African-
American members hope for, in any case, sharing membership in the Council

with the likes of foreign policy's P. T. Barnum and every tyrant's presumptive sponsor, Henry Kissinger, who seemed to think that a human right was a punch landed by a prizefighter?

We could not hope to win by wiggling the conventional levers, testifying before change-deaf committees, writing futile letters to habit-guided policy-makers, or depending alone on the cogency and decency of our views. It was not nearly enough to be *right*. No group in America was listened to less in Washington than the amiable but fangless liberal church establishment. We could not allow ourselves to be sapped of energy and buried in circular debate with the defenders of the status quo.

We had to find a way to set our own terms and break the longstanding control of the anonymous graybeard policy bullies. With an even firmer conviction, we had to assume that they had not the faintest idea of what they were doing or talking about. Foreign policymaking, as near to a science as phrenology, had to be demystified. Americans had to be made aware of all the needless hurt that had been caused in their name. African-Americans had to be made to understand that this American policy affront to Africa was an insult to them as well.

I arrived at this rudimentary wisdom through painful experience. For the first two years of TransAfrica's existence, I testified before congressmen who talked to their staff members throughout my increasingly spiritless readings. I organized letters from black leaders to the congressmen who hadn't listened to my testimony—or, from what I could see, to anyone else's on the subject. I debated on television, with Senator George McGovern, against Senator James McClure of Idaho and Senator S. I. Hayakawa of California, the former president of San Francisco State who had won his Senate seat on the heels of quelling a much publicized student uprising at his school. Senator Hayakawa, a conservative crusader for continued white minority rule in Rhodesia, regularly slept through hearings and was known to feel that the Panama Canal Zone should forever be a possession of the United States inasmuch as we had "stolen it fair and square." Senator Jesse Helms asked me, in the middle of a hearing on South Africa, how much my suit had cost me and how I could afford it. During another Senate hearing, being questioned by Jacob Javits, of New York, I responded on one occasion with a question of my own. "I ask the questions here," he said in reproof. Why, I thought but didn't say, must that be? Mark Siljander, a Republican on the House Subcommittee on Africa, once argued strongly in a public session that Congress should appropriate millions of dollars in arms to support the destabilizing insurgency in "Angolia." That no such country existed appeared to matter little to the foreign policy "expert" Siljander.

In order to prevail, we had to find a way to focus public pressure on the White House, State Department, and Congress. We had, somehow, to provoke media coverage. The news industry had never evinced much interest in Africa and the Caribbean. When these areas were covered at all, they were usually covered negatively, and without context or linear comprehensiveness. It further appeared that what little interest the American media had in the black world was disproportionately paid to areas with significant concentrations of whites. This gave us a chance to win media, and thus public, attention for proposed and existing policies affecting South Africa, Rhodesia, and Namibia, where whites were tenaciously swimming against the tide of history. From this new attention, we thought, would follow accountability for policymakers, and thus better and more humane American policies. But for the rest of Africa and the Caribbean, where no whites to speak of lived, our chances of building media interest, and our own influence, were significantly smaller.

❧

Part XVI

A WAY WITH WORDS

What was it like to be a youngster during the time when rap was but a fledgling genre? When bebop and doo-wop would gave way to hip-hop? LL Cool J was in the mix, so to speak, and eager to vocalize his nascent scribbling in notebooks to a wide audience, which he would later do with much success. No one would have wagered then that rap and hip-hop culture would be such a phenomenon, and that before the millennium rap records would outsell all the other musical categories, including country-and-western. Moreover, there seems to be no end in sight for the righteous flava of rap.

Another more conventional style of "rapping" occurs in the courtroom from gifted lawyers, and none possessed as golden a tongue as Johnnie Cochran. Today he is best known for his successful defense of O. J. Simpson and Geronimo Pratt, but what about the lesser-known cases long before he was in the public spotlight? As one of the attorneys for Patty Diaz, Cochran resorted to a ploy during his closing argument

that is exemplary of his surprise tactics. It was clearly a harbinger of
future gambits that would include expanding his practice to the East
Coast and providing counsel for Abner Louima, sodomized by the New
York City police in 1997, and Amadou Diallo, an unarmed African
immigrant killed in a barrage of gunfire from four white New York City
plainclothes officers in 1999.

For a black woman, persuading an editor to take stock of her literary
abilities has always taken great effort and lots of luck in the publishing
industry. With exquisite style Margaret Walker explains some of the
pitfalls of being a black female writer in America. From this speech we
can see that she is as talented an orator as she was a gifted scribe. She
was less successful, however, in her suit against Alex Haley in 1977,
whom she charged with plagiarism. Her allegation that the author of
Roots had lifted portions of her novel *Jubilee* was dismissed as an unsub-
stantiated claim. A similar suit brought against Haley by a white author
was settled out of court. Walker was again at the center of literary
storm in 1988 with her tell-all biography of Richard Wright, particularly
her analysis of his obsessions and his demonic genius.

Lee Stringer's demons were a glass pipe, a nugget of crack cocaine,
and a torch. Step by horrifying step he introduces the inner sanctum
where he dwelled, the heavy addiction that eventually left him homeless
and wondering where to find the next puff of crack. It is simply incredible that he was able to rally himself from the incubuslike grip of crack
and live to tell the tale. Thousands of African Americans were destroyed
by the crack epidemic that swept across the country in the early 1980s.
Charges arose that this flow of processed cocaine was part of a government conspiracy to narcotize the black community and curtail the development of political consciousness. An investigative report from the *San
Jose Mercury News* in 1997 confirmed the suspicions, alleging a connection
between drug dealers and the CIA.

There were also allegations of the FBI's involvement in the spread of drugs, but Tyrone Powers's stint with the bureau was waylaid by racism. Indeed, the racism was palpable, but Powers's greatest enemy was his own conscience, his own struggle to rationalize why he had chosen to be a law enforcement agent. Each day he thought of the trouble FBI agents had presented to black people. This questioning of his motives and purposes would plague his first weeks at the academy.

It is often said that a journalist has about five minutes to become an expert on a topic or issue, and Sam Fulwood had only a few more minutes to get ready for his assignment in South Africa. He quickly had to bolster his knowledge of African history and culture, which at that moment consisted of snippets in newspapers about the massacre in Sharpeville and the murder of Steven Biko, which did as much to unsettle him as to inform. In several ways, Fulwood was not unlike the majority of African Americans who were often too busy to stay abreast of the breaking news in South Africa.

LL COOL J

From *I Make My Own Rules*

HARLEM, 1979

IF GETTING EQUIPMENT GAVE ME THE TOOLS to perfect my craft, the Sugar Hill Gang gave me the inspiration. It was 1979 and the Sugar Hill Gang was blowing up the charts with "Rapper's Delight." They had taken Chic's "Good Times," a song that had been out for a while, but was still rocking, and turned it into a rap song. It changed the face of music and it was the Sugar Hill Gang, along with Afrika Bambaataa and the Zulu Nation, who got me into rap. A lot of people look back at Sugar Hill as some corny group, but to me they brought rap to a whole other level. They put rap on the map.

I was 11 when I first saw the Sugar Hill Gang perform. It was at the old Harlem Armory, not too far from the Apollo. They had been promoting this concert for more than a month in my neighborhood. There were flyers on every tree, light post, and brick wall in St. Albans and I wanted to be there. Because for the first time, there was a form of music that literally spoke to me. Sugar Hill had my voice. They rapped about things I could relate to or wanted to relate to. They rapped about women and money, and about money and women. They had checkbooks, credit cards, cars, and clothes.

But I couldn't have cared less about the cars, the clothes, and even the women. What they really had that I wanted most was the power to say whatever they wanted. I mean all of those things were nice, but I never got into rap for the cars, the clothes, or the women. I got into rap for the power. I wanted to be heard. I wanted to make a record and hear it on the radio. It was just that simple.

I begged my mother every day for a good two weeks to take me to that concert. And every day the answer was, "No!" Sometimes, it was even "No, and don't ask me again.'' The night before the concert, though, my mother came into my room and pulled out two tickets. Yo! I couldn't believe it. I loved her for that. I loved her anyway, but I really loved her for that. I was so excited, I could barely sleep.

The next day I got up early and got dressed in the flyest gear I had: jeans, a real tight, tight, tight red T-shirt, and a jean hat. (Of course I wore a hat!) All I could think of was how good the show was going to be. I made Moms take me there two hours early so I could see the groups arrive. We got to the armory early enough to get a spot at the barricade, right out front. It was so early, they hadn't even opened the doors yet. More and more people started showing up, so I hugged that barricade like my life depended on it. I didn't want anyone to get in front of me. I saw the Crash Crew come in with their matching Crash Crew jackets, looking like a real group. I was in awe. I stood around for at least an hour and a half just checking everything out.

When the doors finally opened, I ran in and got right up front next to the stage. My mother went to find a seat. But I wasn't about to sit in a seat. I had to be where the action was. I didn't want to be looking over anybody's head. I wanted a clear shot at hip hop.

Besides the Crash Crew, the Funky Four Plus One also performed. I remember their whole act. It was pure energy, and it was exciting. And the crowd was feeling it. Sometimes, though, it seems that all good things must come to an end. While the Sugar Hill Gang was performing, someone shot off a gun and all hell broke loose. People were running and shoving and pushing. I jumped over the barricade and crawled under the stage, and all I could see were all kinds of feet shuffling and running, trying to get out, and people were screaming and yelling. I don't know how, but somehow my mother found me and grabbed me and dragged me out of there. Nobody was hurt—it turns out someone just fired a gun into the air—but I wasn't really surprised when she told me that was the last time she was taking me to a show. She obviously had not felt the excitement and exhilaration I had experienced. And she was not about to go back to another show where people got wild and rowdy and started shooting off guns and freaking.

Stuff like that happens at rap shows today. That's why insurance is so high and that's why ticket prices are ridiculous. I wish miserable people would stop making everyone else miserable. Then again, you know the cliché: misery loves company.

But then, I wasn't thinking about the consequences of actions like that. Frankly, I didn't even care except for the fact that my moms said she wouldn't take me anymore. I figured she wouldn't have to, though—because I would be up on that stage the next time.

That concert gave me a yearning to go where I am now and to do what I'm doing today. I could see myself up on stage with the mike in my hand, people screaming and rocking, and me just loving it. Sometimes I used to sit in my room and imagine I was a teacher in a classroom with a thousand students. And I'd be teaching in rhymes. Now that it's a reality for me, though, I realize it's much more and much different than I ever imagined. And then some. . . .

For the first time in my life I had power. No one could tell me to shut up. I could say something, anything I wanted, and not be afraid. I could be as powerful as I always wanted to be.

The music and rhymes helped me escape all the pain. It was an opportunity to dream. One thing about a pen and piece of paper—nobody can stop you. You can just go wherever you want to go in the world of lyrics and words:

I'm on the move. It's 1765—no one knows that I escaped the plantation and built a spaceship and flew here. I can write that. Know what I mean? *Psyche! I'm really in Bed-Stuy. Just kidding, I'm on another planet—the mirror image of the Earth. Everything here is the opposite, except there's only one sex and we mate mentally.* Yeah, through words I could go wherever I thought to go.

I would come home from school some days (I had my own keys, and if I forgot my keys I would climb in a back window that I always kept unlocked) and if Roscoe was out I would play some of my mother's record albums on the sneak. My mother didn't know it then, but I was in love with music. I kept this secret so no one (like Roscoe) could spoil it.

Sometimes I would stare at a record and imagine what the world was like inside the vinyl: happy people having parties, having fun, laughing, loving. My reality at the time was that reefer, cocaine, and dirty magazines were all lying around the house. But I was getting high off Harold Melvin and the Blue Notes, Marvin Gaye, and the O'Jays.

When I went to my grandparents' house on the weekends, my grandfather was still cranking up his jazz at high volume. Miles Davis, Wes Montgomery, Richard Groove Holmes, and Freddie Hubbard were in heavy rotation in the Griffith household. It used to bug me out when I was a kid, but by now I was digging all that jazz. I would even listen to the Beatles and the Rolling Stones, and even the Smothers Brothers. You believe that? Well it's true, and I was learning to appreciate all kinds of music. I preferred some genres to others, but I could recognize what was good and what wasn't so good. . . .

Of all the different types of music, R&B was where I discovered what true love, the kind of love that I wasn't getting at home, was all about. One song that stuck out was "Brandy." That guy really missed Brandy, and I could relate. I would lie on the living room floor and be missing my grandmother and my grandfather listening to it. I found out later that it was all fiction and that Brandy was a dog or something. But it didn't matter to me then. I was feeling the soul of that song.

Meanwhile, rap was getting strong, and I was getting hooked. There were a lot of underground rap tapes circulating in my neighborhood in Queens and even some in Long Island, and I listened to them all: Kurtis Blow, Grandmaster Flash and the Furious Five, and, of course, the Sugar Hill Gang. With each new group, I got deeper and deeper into it—and it got deeper and deeper into me. It was an escape into a fantasy world. The images were so vivid and so much better than the real life I was living. I was just hypnotized. There was power in this rap music, and it put me under a spell I've never come out of. Rap spoke to me, and in it I found myself and the power of my voice. Rap music was my escape from a living hell.

I guess I started rapping with kids around my way in Long Island when I was about nine, when Kenny and I began writing rhymes in the McCulloughs' backyard. Before long I was spending more time working on rhymes than I was on homework.

By the time I was 13, I was itching to start my thing on the underground rap circuit where acts like Luvbug Starski before me became famous. And more than anything I knew I wanted to make records. So I spent most of my time in the basement making tapes. I was determined to be heard.

Jay Philpot was one of the most popular DJs in my area. There were others, the Disco Twins, who were known Queenswide, and the Albino Twins, but Jay was Mr. Farmer's. He was like a big brother to me and just about all the other kids in the neighborhood. He had the biggest system around with huge speakers, the best turntables, and the latest mixer. Several up-and-coming DJs in the neighborhood got together, calling themselves Ebony Sounds, and they all chipped in to buy the equipment. But it was stored at Jay's house because there was no disputing it: Jay was the man in charge. When Jay got on the turntables, he did his thing. The scratching, the mixing, and that bass, you could feel it all the way to Ilion Avenue. He drew a crowd wherever he went.

I wanted to grab the mike and rock with his beats so bad I could taste it. All summer I had been begging Jay to let me get on the mike. But he looked at me as a little snot-nosed kid. He kept telling me, "Maybe next year, kid." I couldn't wait until next year. Next year is forever when you're 13. I had been practicing and writing rhymes for almost two years. As far as I was concerned, I was ready. . . .

JOHNNIE COCHRAN

From *Journey to Justice*

❧

LOS ANGELES, 1980S

ONE NIGHT IN HOLLYWOOD, A THIRTEEN-year-old Latina named Patty Díaz was fast asleep in her family's apartment. At 3 A.M., Stanley Tanabe, an LAPD officer in full uniform and wearing his sidearm, knocked at the apartment door and demanded admittance. He claimed he was responding to a report of a woman screaming and he said he would not leave until he had thoroughly searched the Díaz apartment. He went to the back bedroom, where he sexually assaulted little Patty in the presence of her ten-year-old brother and two-year-old sister. He then left the apartment but returned within five minutes carrying what he purported was a composite drawing of a suspect. He then left, telling the terrified, stunned thirteen-year-old girl that he would return.

The very next morning, Patty and her mother went to the Hollywood police station and filed a complaint. However, the sergeant's log of that complaint, which contained an accurate description of Tanabe, was withheld from detectives subsequently assigned to investigate the matter. Moreover, the detectives were instructed by their superiors to keep their probe "hush-hush."

One evening a month later, while Patty's mother was out, Tanabe made good on his threat. Once again in full uniform, he forced his way into the apartment and attempted to assault the girl. At that moment, Patty's mother returned and the girl seized the opportunity to run to a neighbor's apartment and telephone police. Tanabe was arrested as he tried to get in his unmarked police car and flee the scene. He was subsequently tried and convicted of sexual battery and burglary and sentenced to two years in prison, of which he served just a little more than twelve months.

For Patty Díaz, the months that followed were a nightmare. She was diagnosed as suffering from post-traumatic stress disorder with psychotic features. Three times she tried to take her own life by slashing her wrists. The last attempt took place on her *quinceañera,* or fifteenth birthday. Traditional Latino families, such as the Díazes, regard that as their daughter's "coming-out" day and mark it with a celebration in her honor second only to her wedding. Patty's *quinceañera* coincided with the day of Tanabe's release from prison. She spent it alone, sobbing in her room before attempting, once again, to end the life she had come to regard as a source of torment to herself and shame to her family.

Eric Ferrer and I took her case. From the start, it was a cause that engaged every fiber of our moral and legal beings. The police department's conduct had been unconscionably reckless and deceitful, and the city's response had been callous. The injury done to poor Patty Díaz and her mother was so clear. Moreover, as we began to investigate, we discovered that there had been ample warning of Tanabe's problems. He initially had entered the police academy in 1980 but was unable to complete his training. At the time, two of his training officers noted what they believed was mental rigidity on his part and predicted that if Tanabe were ever allowed to become a police officer, he might subject himself and the city to civil and criminal liability. He subsequently applied to three other police departments and was rejected on psychological grounds. Finally, he reapplied to the LAPD and was accepted.

We demanded that the city pay Patty Díaz and her mother $750,000. The city offered them only $150,000. We went to trial. While cross-examining the LAPD captain in charge of the case, I forced him to admit that the sergeant's log had been withheld from the investigating detectives and that the investigation had been flawed and negligent. I can still hear the jury's collective intake of breath when we compelled that admission. I also recall the tears in their eyes when Patty Díaz, a pained but courageous witness on her own behalf, displayed for the jurors the still vivid scars on her wrists.

Eric and I knew that much would ride on my final argument, and we labored over how to make it equal to the demands of the case. The entire trial had been tape-recorded, so we devised a simple but forceful stratagem. I would argue, and, as I returned to each critical piece of testimony, I would signal Eric. He would have the tape keyed to precisely that moment in the trial so that the jurors could hear it once again for themselves. It worked flawlessly.

Then, as I brought my argument to a close, I experienced one of those moments of intuition that veteran trial lawyers learn to trust. I could feel the jury was with me. I needed to hold them there, and I improvised. I turned away from them for a second, then quickly turned back, making eye contact with each of the four Latinos on the panel. Without preamble, I spoke to them in Spanish. *"Sólo quien mueve con el saco sabe que pesa,"* I said.

This is an old Spanish maxim that translates, "Only he who carries the sack knows the weight of the burden.'' The Latino jurors nodded their heads in agreement, and I knew they shortly would explain the sentiment to their colleagues in the jury room. I continued in English:

''This girl, who showed you her wrists, who tried to kill herself because she didn't feel she could go on—she knows what that saying means better than anyone here. Understand what it is to be fifteen years old and living with this pain in your head for the rest of your life. You've got to do justice for her. Not ten percent justice. Not fifteen percent justice. Full one hundred percent justice.

''We owe her that. For you are the conscience of this community and your verdict will send a strong message to the City of Los Angeles.''

As I returned to my seat and sat down, I looked over at Eric. He just looked back and nodded. The jury was instructed and began its deliberations.

While they worked, I left for Italy, where I was to meet Dale and my best friend, Ron Sunderland, and his wife, Diane, at Villa d'Este in the lake country of northern Italy. We planned to celebrate Dale's birthday there before going on to the Barcelona Summer Olympics together. We were still in Italy a week later when, at 1:30 A.M., the phone in our hotel room rang. I answered—groggily. At the other end, I could make out Eric's excited voice, one word spilling out after another while in the background people seemed to be shouting in Spanish.

''Please speak slower, Eric,'' I mumbled, still trying to shake off a deep sleep.

''Nine million,'' he kept repeating like a mantra. ''Nine million. The jury just awarded Patty nine million dollars!''

I sat bolt upright in bed.

Actually, the full award was $9.4 million plus attorney's fees, and it remains the largest single award in a case resulting from the LAPD's chronic misconduct. My Philistine was still on his feet, but we were making him bleed badly.

Best of all, that money allowed Patty Díaz to obtain appropriate help and start life anew. She is now happily married and a young mother. That was a result worth working for. . . .

MARGARET WALKER

From *On Being Female, Black, and Free*

❧

MISSISSIPPI, 1980

MY BIRTH CERTIFICATE READS FEMALE, NEGRO, DATE of birth and place. Call it fate or circumstance, this is my human condition. I have no wish to change it from being female, black, and free. I like being a woman. I have a proud African American heritage, and I have learned from the difficult exigencies of life that freedom is a philosophical state of mind and existence. The mind is the only place where I can exist and feel free. In my mind, I am absolutely free.

My entire career of writing, teaching, lecturing, yes, and raising a family, is determined by these immutable facts of my human condition. As a daughter, a sister, a sweetheart, a wife, a mother, and now a grandmother, my sex or gender is preeminent, important, and almost entirely deterministic. Maybe my glands have something to do with my occupation as a creative person. About this, I am none too sure, but I think the cycle of life has much to do with the creative impulse, and the biorhythms of life must certainly affect everything we do. . . .

Ever since I was a little girl I have wanted to write, and I have been writing. My father told my mother it was only a puberty urge and would not last, but he encouraged my early attempts at rhyming verses just the same, and he gave me the notebook or daybook in which to keep my poems together. When I was eighteen and had ended my junior year in college, my father laughingly agreed it was probably more than a puberty urge. I had filled the 365 pages with poems.

Writing has always been a means of expression for me and for other African Americans who are just like me, who feel, too, the need for freedom in this "home of the brave, and land of the free." From the first, writing meant learning the craft and developing the art. Going to school had one major goal, to learn to be a writer. As early as my eighth year, I had the desire, at ten I was trying, at eleven and twelve I was learning, and at fourteen and fifteen I was seeing my first things printed in local school and community papers. I have a copy of a poem published in 1930 and an article with the caption, "What Is to Become of Us?" which appeared in 1931 or 1932. All of this happened before I went to Northwestern.

I spent fifteen years becoming a poet before my first book appeared in 1942. I was learning my craft, finding my voice, seeking discipline as life imposes and superimposes that discipline upon the artist. Perhaps my home environment was most important in the early stages—hearing my mother's music, my sister and brother playing the piano, reading my father's books, hearing his sermons, and trying every day to write a poem. Meanwhile, I found I would have to start all over again and learn how to write prose fiction in order to write the novel I was determined to create to the best of my ability, and thus fulfill my promise to my grandmother. A novel is not written exactly the same way as a poem, especially a long novel and a short poem. The creative process may be basically the same—that is, the thinking or conceptualization—but the techniques, elements, and form or craft are decidedly and distinctively different.

It has always been my feeling that writing must come out of living, and the writer is no more than his personality endures in the crucible of his times. As a woman, I have come through the fires of hell because I am a black woman, because I am poor, because I live in America, and because I am determined to be both a creative artist and maintain my inner integrity and my instinctive need to be free.

I don't think I noticed the extreme discrimination against women while I was growing up in the South. The economic struggle to exist and the racial dilemma occupied all my thinking until I was more than an adult woman. My mother had undergone all kinds of discrimination in academia because of her sex; so have my sisters. Only after I went back to school and earned a doctorate did I begin to notice discrimination against me as a woman. It seems the higher you try to climb, the more rarefied the air, the more obstacles appear. I realize I had been naive, that the issues had not been obvious and that as early as my first employment, I felt the sting of discrimination because I am female.

I think it took the women's movement to call my attention to cases of overt discrimination that hark back to my WPA days on the Writers' Project. It did not occur to me that Richard Wright as a supervisor on the project made $125 per month and that he claimed no formal education, but that I had just graduated from Northwestern University and I was a junior writer making $85 per month. I had no ambitions to be an administrator; I was too glad to have a job; I did not think about it. Now I remember the intense antagonism on the project toward the hiring of a black woman as a supervisor, none other than the famous Katherine Dunham, the dancer, but it never occurred to me then that she was undergoing double discrimination. . . .

I have read so many of those great women writers of the world—poets, novelists, and playwrights: Sigrid Undset and Selma Lagerlof, Jane Austen, George Sand, George Eliot, and Colette. All through the ages, women have been writing and publishing, black and white women in America and all over the world. A few women stand out as geniuses of their times, but those are all too few. Even the women who survive and are printed, published, taught and studied in the classroom, fall victim to negative male literary criticism. Black women suffer damages at the hands of every male literary critic, whether he is black or white. Occasionally, a man grudgingly admits that some woman writes well, but only rarely. . . .

There are additional barriers for the black woman in publishing, in literary criticism, and in promotion of her literary wares. It is an insidious fact of racism that the most highly intellectualized, sensitized white person is not always perceptive about the average black mind and feeling, much less the creativity of any black genius. Racism forces white humanity to underestimate the intelligence, emotion, and creativity of black humanity. Very few white Americans are conscious of the myth about race that includes the racial stigmas of inferiority and superiority. They do not understand its true economic and political meaning and therefore fail to understand its social purpose. A black, female person's life as a writer is fraught with conflict, competitive drives, professional rivalries, even danger, and deep frustrations. Only when she escapes to a spiritual world can she find peace, quiet, and hope of freedom. To choose the life of a writer, a black female must arm herself with a fool's courage, foolhardiness, and serious purpose and dedication to the art of writing, strength of will and integrity, because the odds are always against her. The cards are stacked. Once the die is cast, however, there is no turning back.

In the first place, the world of imagination in which the writer must live is constantly being invaded by the enemy, the mundane world. Even as the worker in the fires of imagination finds that the world around her is inimical to intellectual activity, to the creative impulse, and to the kind of world in which she must daily exist and also thrive and produce, so, too, she discovers that she must meet that mundane world head-on every day on its own terms. She must either conquer or be conquered.

A writer needs certain conditions in which to work and create art. She needs a piece of time; a peace of mind; a quiet place; and a private life.

Early in my life I discovered I had to earn my living and I would not be able to eke out the barest existence as a writer. Nobody writes while hungry, sick, tired, and worried. Maybe you can manage with one of these but not all four at one time. Keeping the wolf from the door has been my full-time job for more than forty years. Thirty-six of those years I have spent in the college classroom, and nobody writes to full capacity on a full-time teaching job. My life has been public, active, and busy to the point of constant turmoil, tumult, and trauma. Sometimes the only quiet and private place where I could write a sonnet was in the bathroom, because that was the only room where the door could be locked and no one would intrude. I have written mostly at night in my adult life and especially since I have been married, because I was determined not to neglect any members of my family; so I cooked every meal daily, washed dishes and dirty clothes, and nursed sick babies.

I have struggled against dirt and disease as much as I have against sin, which, with my Protestant and Calvinistic background, was always to be abhorred. Every day I have lived, however, I have discovered that the value system with which I was raised is of no value in the society in which I must live. This clash of my ideal with the real, of my dream world with the practical, and the mystical inner life with the sordid and ugly world outside—this clash keeps me on a battlefield, at war, and struggling, even tilting at windmills. Always I am determined to overcome adversity, determined to win, determined to be me, myself at my best, always female, always black, and everlastingly free. I think this is always what the woman writer wants to be, herself, inviolate, and whole. Shirley Chisholm, who is also black and female, says she is unbossed and unbought. So am I, and I intend to remain that way. Nobody can tell me what to write because nobody owns me and nobody pulls my strings. I have not been writing to make money or earn my living. I have taught school as my vocation. Writing is my life, but it is an avocation nobody can buy. In this respect I believe I am a free agent, stupid perhaps, but *me* and still free. . . .

For the past twenty years or longer I have constantly come into contact with women writers of many different races, classes, nationalities, and degrees. I look back on more than forty years of such associations. Whether at a cocktail party for Muriel Rukeyser at *Poetry* magazine or at Yaddo where Carson Mc-Cullers, Jean Stafford, Karen Blixen, Caroline Slade, and Katherine Anne Porter were guests; or meeting Adrienne Rich and Erica Jong in Massachusetts at Amherst; or having some twenty-five of my black sister-poets at a Phillis Wheatley poetry festival in Mississippi, including many of the young and brilliant geniuses of this generation; or in Mississippi where I have come to know Eudora Welty and Ellen Douglass; or having women from foreign countries journey to Jackson to see me, women like Rosey Poole from Amsterdam and Essim Erdim, a young woman writer from Turkey, or Bessie Head from South Africa—all these experiences have made me know and understand the problems of women writers and our search for freedom.

For the nonwhite woman writer, whether in Africa, Asia, Latin America, the islands of the Caribbean, or the United States, her destiny as a writer has always seemed bleak. Women in Africa and Asia speak of hunger and famine and lack of clean water at the same time that their countries are riddled with warfare. Arab women and Jewish women think of their children in a world that has no hope or peace. Irish women, Protestant and Catholic, speak of the constant threat of bombs and being blown to bits. The women of southern Africa talk of their lives apart from their husbands and their lives in exile from their homelands because of the racial strife in their countries. A Turkish woman speaks of the daily terrorism in her country, of combing the news each evening to see if there are names known on the list of the murdered.

I have read the works of scores of these women. I saw Zora Neale Hurston when I was a child and I know what a hard life she had. I read the works of a dozen black women in the Harlem Renaissance, who despite their genius received only a small success. Langston Hughes translated Gabriela Mistral, and I read her before she won the Nobel Prize for Literature. Hualing Hieh Engle tells of her native China, and my friends in Mexico speak of the unbelievable poverty of their people. Each of these internationally known women writers is my sister in search of an island of freedom. Each is part of me and I am part of her.

Writing is a singularly individual matter. At least it has historically been so. Only the creative, original individual working alone has been considered the artist working with the fire of imagination. Today, this appears no longer to be the case. In America, our affluent, electronic, and materialistic society does not respect the imaginative writer regardless of sex, race, color, or creed. It never thought highly of the female worker, whether an Emily Dickinson or Amy Lowell, Phillis Wheatley, or Ellen Glasgow. Our American society has no respect for the literary values of intellectual honesty nor for originality and creativity in the sensitive individual. Books today are managed, being written by a committee and promoted by the conglomerate, corporate structures. Best sellers are designed as commodities to sell in the marketplace before a single word is written. Plastic people who are phony writers pretending to take us into a more humanistic century are quickly designated the paper heroes who are promoted with super-HYPE. Do I sound bitter? A Black Woman Writer who is free? Free to do what? To publish? To be promoted? Of what value is freedom in a money-mad society? What does freedom mean to the racially biased and those bigots who have deep religious prejudices? What is my hope as a woman writer?

I am a black woman living in a male-oriented and male-dominated white world. Moreover, I live in an American Empire where the financial tentacles of the American Octopus in the business-banking world extend around the globe, with the multinationals and international conglomerates encircling everybody and impinging on the lives of every single soul. What then are my problems? They are the pressures of a sexist, racist, violent, and most materialistic society. In such a society, life is cheap and expendable; honor is a rag to be scorned; and justice is violated. Vice and money control business, the judicial system, government, sports, entertainment, publishing, education, and the church. Every other arm of this hydra-headed monster must render lip service and yeoman support to extend, uphold, and perpetuate the syndicated world-system. The entire world of the press, whether broadcast or print journalism, must acquiesce and render service or be eliminated. And what have I to do with this? How do I operate? How long can I live under fear before I too am blown to bits and must crumble into anonymous dust and nonentity?

Now I am sixty-three. I wish I could live the years all over. I am sure I would make the same mistakes and do all the things again exactly the same way. But perhaps I might succeed a little more; and wistfully I hope, too, I might have written more books.

What are the critical decisions I must make as a woman, as a writer? They are questions of compromise and of guilt. They are the answers to the meaning and purpose of all life; questions of the value of life lived half in fear and half in faith, cringing under the whip of tyranny or dying, too, for what one dares to believe, and dying with dignity and without fear. I must believe there is more wisdom in a righteous path that leads to death than an ignominious path of living shame; that the writer is still in the avant-garde for truth and justice, for freedom, peace, and human dignity. I must believe that women are still in that humanistic tradition, and I must cast my lot with them.

Across the world humanity seems in ferment, in war, fighting over land and the control of people's lives; people who are hungry, sick, and suffering, most of all fearful. The traditional and historic role of womankind is ever the role of the healing and annealing hand, whether the outworn modes of nurse, and mother, cook, and sweetheart. As a writer these are still her concerns. These are still the stuff about which she writes, the human condition, the human potential, the human destiny. Her place, let us be reminded, is anywhere she chooses to be, doing what she has to do, creating, healing, and always being herself. Female, Black, and Free, this is what I always want to be.

LEE STRINGER

From *Grand Central Winter*

❧

NEW YORK CITY, 1984

I'M KNOCKING BACK DOUBLES IN SOME OVERPRICED East Side bar. Eight hours and still I can't shake the feeling that I want to smash something. But by two a.m. I'm too blitzed to start any real trouble. There's nothing left for me but to go home and sleep it off.

Lucky for me my twenty-something bar buddy, Ed from New Jersey, has his Chevy and offers to drop me off. He deposits me at my apartment door and wheels back off into the night. I make a wobbly beeline for the bed, shedding clothing as I go.

I'm dead out when my door buzzer sounds. It's one of those annoying, tinny-voiced jobs that let out a shrill, petulant squeal that can't be ignored. It doesn't summon me so much as piss me off. For some reason I'm compelled to gather my discarded clothes from the floor as I make for the door.

I'm clutching them as I let Ed in.

"How're you feeling?" he wants to know.

"Like shit," I tell him.

"I've got something that will definitely make it better." He grins.

"Come on with it," I tell him.

He halts a few paces inside the door and requests a saucer and razor. But I'm already back on the bed, my body just waiting to extract swirling, nauseating revenge if I push the up-and-about act another second.

"Saucer's in the cabinet over your head," I tell him. "Razor's in the bathroom."

A little bustle and clatter and he has them.

He removes a small wad of tin foil from his pocket and unwraps a lima-bean-size nugget the color of cream. It makes a surprisingly sharp *click* when he drops it on the dish. A substantial sound. One that will forever after divide two different points in time in my life.

From the bed I watch Ed at work, bent over the counter, a chef whipping up some special delicacy. I'm transfixed. He carefully and precisely halves the rock, produces a Pyrex pipe—one with a bowl, not unlike those I once smoked hash in—drops a chunk into it, and walks over to me, pipe in one hand, lighter in the other.

"Age before beauty," he says.

I am no stranger to cocaine. It has fueled my after-hours wanderings on more than one occasion—and without morning-after agonies. A blessing, as far as I am concerned.

I have never smoked it before.

But what the hell.

"Pearls before swine," I retort.

I draw on the stem, and the bowl fills with a thick, swirling cloud. I cannot feel the heat of the smoke as it goes down. But I can taste it. It is a taste I know I am going to love. The taste of success, love, orgasm, omnipotence, immortality, and winning the lottery all rolled into one.

And then some.

My hangover evaporates like steam off a griddle. The dark corners of the room brighten, The predawn quietude explodes with bustle. Suddenly the room cannot contain my spirit.

I want to burst out the doors.

Careen into the last of the night.

Do things.

Go places.

I look up just as Ed's face reappears from behind the smoke, a hissing from his lips, his eyes glowing with exhilaration.

What a great feeling!

I love Ed!

I love the whole fucking free world!

"Where did you get this stuff?" I pant.

"There's a place a few blocks from here," he breathes back.

"You gotta go anywhere?" I ask.

"As a matter of fact," he says, "I wanted to ask if I could crash here a few days."

He tries to explain about an argument with his people in Jersey, about them asking him to leave. But I wave him off in mid sentence, walk over to him, hug him chest to chest.

"Brother," I coo, "me and you are going to par-TEE!"

A few minutes later the bottom starts to fall out of the high. Sadness and longing descend over me.

Utter desolation hovers moments away.

I am seized by a wave of panic.

I want that party feeling back.

"Listen, Ed," I say, "those guys still out? Can we get more—now?"

"Sure," he says.

I dig into my pocket and hand him the first fifty of the more than one hundred thousand dollars I will eventually smoke up before the party really ends.

SAM FULWOOD

From *Waking from the Dream*

§

SOUTH AFRICA, 1985

BY 1985, I HAD MADE A STRANGE sort of peace between myself and *The Sun*. My job was comfortable, even if I was uncomfortable in it. But I assumed everybody chafed in their jobs (that's the nature of work. I often said to myself) and I tried to make the best of it, which wasn't hard to do. I was a careerist who had a cushy life.

From time to time, I discussed my growing sense of racial frustration and isolation at work with Cynthia, but neither of us knew how to make any sense of these strange feelings. We had no mentors or reference points. Our parents had worked in segregated environments and could offer no guidance.

. . . The swirling confusion I felt at work pulled me all the closer to Cynthia at home. I held on to her as my link to the security and optimism I remembered feeling back when I lived in Charlotte, back when I believed anything was possible, when it all seemed so easy for me. I felt closer to her than anyone else I knew and assumed she shared the same feelings toward me. We drew strength from each other's fear, binding us in a mutually dependent and supportive way from the very start of our marriage. Alone at work, we protected ourselves as best we could during the day; together at home, we comforted each other through the night. Whatever the stresses, we offset them for each other because we were determined to advance in our careers.

In late April 1985, Richard O'Mara, foreign editor at *The Sun,* called me at home to ask if I would consider going to South Africa for a temporary assignment. I was shocked because I hardly knew O'Mara and had never worked with him. His call came totally out of the blue. I was elated because foreign jobs were about as high in the pecking order as a reporter could aspire. But until I answered O'Mara's phone call, I had taken little professional interest over events going on in South Africa.

So, I asked myself, why me? Why South Africa? Why now?

Of course I knew the answers to all the whys without putting them into words: the editors wanted a black reporter in Africa. Sending a black reporter there had been one of the demands of the NAACP protesters. Now, it seemed, the editors were asking me once again to be The All-Purpose Black.

The Sun had closed its Johannesburg bureau in 1983, shortly before I was hired at the paper, relocating its white correspondent to Moscow. The editors' thinking at the time was that the slow-moving story of black resistance to apartheid in South Africa failed to warrant the continuing expense of a full-time correspondent, one who in addition covered the entire fifty-four-country African continent.

Their opinion must have begun to change on November 21, 1984. On that Thanksgiving Day, the Free South Africa movement went public in the United States as a trio of civil rights leaders—Randall Robinson of TransAfrica, Mary Francis Berry of the U.S. Commission on Civil Rights and Delegate Walter Fauntroy, the Democratic congressional representative for the District of Columbia—launched a series of protests outside the South African embassy in Washington, D.C. Robinson, Berry and Fauntroy were mediagenic veterans of the 1960s. They knew their demonstrations would gain maximum coverage on Thanksgiving, a slow news day that offers newspaper readers and television viewers little but football games, parades, and banal features on do-good volunteers doing their once-a-year charity work of feeding the homeless turkey dinners.

It was a brilliant stroke of news manipulation—but by no means a spur-of-the-moment event. The antiapartheid movement had been organized and carefully choreographed to arouse public attention and focus opinion against South Africa and the Reagan Administration's wink-and-nod opposition to the apartheid regime. The protesters' well-covered arrests had been peaceful and were coordinated with the D.C. police, leading to further demonstrations at the embassy. A week later, some more protesters—mostly black leaders and celebrities—had been arrested in Washington, plus more than a dozen in New York City. All of them were released after being booked; the federal authorities refused to prosecute them because the Reagan Administration feared giving the activists a platform to further embarrass the government's relationship with South Africa. Meanwhile, a disinvestment movement swept the nation's college campuses and corporate board rooms; eventually, it made South Africa and its imprisoned martyr, Nelson Mandela, household words across the United States.

The Free South Africa movement captured my imagination, conjuring up the images and symbolism of the Civil Rights Movement that I knew only from old people's tales and televised news specials. For black folks of my generation, especially middle-class careerists like me, South Africa was our Civil Rights Movement. "Free South Africa" became our battle cry, complete with clenched and upraised fists. It had all the elements needed for our participation: white supremacist Boers as the oppressor bad guys and the too tolerant and long-suffering black majority population. But there was more to it than that. We could challenge South Africa's apartheid and not worry a whit about risking our station on the corporate treadmill in the United States. South Africa, for many buppies, was the safest and most comfortable means of protesting our pain and suffering in America.

Before the embassy protests, I knew next to nothing about what was happening in South Africa or, for that matter, how racist the country was. Steve Biko's death, the Soweto uprisings, Sharpeville—all occurred well before I began to pay attention. Few people I knew made an issue of these events, so South Africa easily escaped my notice. I was remotely aware of the horrors of apartheid, but in an academic and dispassionate way. That was way over there in Africa, someplace I had never imagined living or even visiting. As South African atrocities began to rule the daily newspapers, I began to pay more and more attention.

By the time O'Mara called, I could only regurgitate the skimpy facts I had gobbled up from the media. I knew the country was a sensational media story, but the finer details of who, why, how and what were missing.

No one in either my family or Cynthia's had ever been outside the United States. I was elated at being asked, but questioned whether I should accept the offer, since I knew so little about international politics—especially those on the African continent.

Cynthia was all for it from the start. "It will be a great career move," she said. "You can learn as you go. White people don't know much about Africa, but they go over there all the time. Why not you?"

Another of Cynthia's arguments carried the day. She said she would be willing to move in with a friend who had just had a baby and needed some help. "We can save money," she explained. "So by the time you get back, we will be able to afford to buy a house." That bit of logic settled it for me. I left the United States for South Africa thinking that when I returned our life as good, home-owning, middle-class buppies would be set. . . .

TYRONE POWERS

From *Eyes to My Soul*

QUANTICO, VIRGINIA, 1985

DECEMBER 1, 1985. I SUPPOSE THAT JUST LIKE every other new student, I was in awe when I entered the Federal Bureau of Investigation Academy in Quantico, Virginia. Its location was only about a two-and-a-half-hour drive south of Baltimore, but for me it seemed as if I were traveling to another world, another universe. The FBI was that world-renowned, secret and powerful organization that every other law enforcement agency envied. It was the organization that conjured up visions of "Big Brother," as described in George Orwell's book *1984*. It was the organization that was both feared and hated by the African American community. I was heading there. Driving to this place that I had heard and read so much about. . . .

I parked my 1983 blue Chevrolet Cavalier in the large parking lot, retrieved my suitcases from the trunk, and headed toward the seemingly infinitely tall flag poles, with their enormous waving flags, which stood in front of the FBI Training Academy administration building. When I entered the U-shaped driveway, I put my suitcases down and stared up at the building that stood before me. I took a deep breath and ran my hand over my head, as I had often seen Granddad and Nate do.

The sun shone brightly above the academy as if it were the North Star that I had learned so much about at Sunday school. Through squinted eyes I took it all in: the rippling flags, the academy campus, the tall dormitory buildings, the full parking lot. I smiled as I thought of the irony of my journey from the ghetto to the "sacrosanct" grounds of the FBI. I thought of the cold mean streets of Baltimore. I thought of the back porch and the little back-alley Negro League. I was proud of myself. Proud that I had done what many did not believe I could do. I had made an improbable journey. As Robert Frost stated in his poem "The Road Not Taken," I had certainly taken "the road less traveled by." What difference it would make, remained to be seen. I picked up my suitcases and packed my thoughts of Baltimore away in a small compartment of my glowing soul.

As I entered the lobby of the FBI administration building, I felt as if I had entered into the annals of history. I probably was making too much of the experience, attaching too much significance to my arrival at the academy, but my emotions were out of control. For I would be on the elite list of men who had served as FBI agents.

I looked around the lobby as if I were in some foreign land. Yet, strangely enough, I felt as if I belonged here, at this time in my life. I inhaled the atmosphere of the historic site that was to be my home for the next three months. My eyes moved slowly in their sockets, taking in all that was about me. A few other candidates stood around next to their luggage. They had the same look of pleasure and awe on their faces.

I moved toward the receptionist without consciously taking a step in her direction. It was as if I were a character in a Spike Lee movie—moving forward as though walking, yet standing perfectly still. I nervously uttered my name to her smiling face. An overwhelming feeling of anxiety and excitement engulfed my body. I didn't see all of her. I didn't hear the words, "Just one moment, please," uttered from her thin red lips. My attention on her pleasant smile was diverted by the movement of her slim white finger down the list of neatly typed names. Her finger nails were perfectly manicured. Her hair seemed to be combed perfectly. Her dress appeared to fit perfectly.

I shifted my attention and slowly looked about. I wanted to take in the rest of the room. I was determined not to miss a thing. I wanted to drink in and savor this special moment in my life. I looked down at the gleaming bright floor; it appeared to have been perfectly waxed. The pictures in the lobby were hung perfectly. The brass letters *FBI* on the wall behind the desk were perfectly affixed to the rich deep-brown wood panels and polished to a perfect shine. All of this perfection seemed to relay the message that the FBI was a perfect organization, and that it demanded perfection from all those who entered its academy doors. No imperfection or corruption of this image would be tolerated. . . .

Finally, the lady with the thin lips and fingers looked up and smiled a perfect smile. "Welcome to the FBI Academy!" I smiled back and the warm, stirring glow returned to my anxious soul. The beautiful friendly receptionist informed me of the room to which I had been assigned. She gently handed me a name tag inscribed with the words *FBI Academy Student*. She pointed in the direction of my assigned dormitory room and gave me specific instructions on how to reach it. I picked up my luggage and slowly walked through the glass hallways, which had been affectionately named gerbil tubes. I would be housed in this building for the next sixteen weeks.

I lugged my suitcases up a flight of stairs, through a corridor, and into an area where a group of people sat watching a big-screened television set. On the wall behind them was a large picture of a stony-faced, heroic-looking J. Edgar Hoover. No doubt about it, I was in his house now. This was his FBI. Even in death his presence could be felt roaming the halls, watching over the empire that he built. His picture was there to make sure that all who entered the academy understood that J. Edgar Hoover was still the owner of this property.

As I stood staring at the picture of Hoover, I thought of all the trouble that he and his FBI had caused Black people. I thought of his comments about Dr. Martin Luther King Jr. How Hoover had called King a "notorious liar." How he had had Dr. King followed. How his own sexual perversions had led Hoover to try to tape King's so-called sexual encounters. How he was hell-bent and determined, in his own words, to "neutralize" Dr. King.

It was J. Edgar Hoover and his suited henchmen who planned to disunite and ultimately divided the Black Panther Party. It was Hoover who orchestrated the murder of a young and energetic Fred Hampton. I thought of the infiltration of Black organizations by the FBI. I thought of the disinformation campaigns directed at Black leaders and especially at the feared "Black Messiah," Malcolm X.

I thought of the phone taps and phone traps. The counterfeit letters written by FBI handwriting specialists and sent out to various Black leaders, with the forged signatures of other Black leaders—to create a climate ripe for internal strife and murder. Hoover would forever be associated with the FBI. The FBI would forever be identified with J. Edgar Hoover. Now that I was becoming an FBI agent, Mr. Hoover would be associated with me.

I sighed deeply, walked to the elevator, and took it to the fifth floor. I stared straight ahead, never looking up at the lighted floor indicator. The elevator made several stops. People got on and off. I looked past them out into nothingness. My mind had latched on to the unpleasant thought that I was now an underling of the infamous J. Edgar Hoover. I couldn't free myself of this disturbing notion.

When the elevator reached the fifth floor, I instinctively exited. Still deep in my thoughts, I walked slowly, like a zombie, down the hallway toward my room. I noticed other new students smiling and greeting each other, introducing themselves to their elite colleagues. My mind was still with my new, historical associate, J. Edgar Hoover. I was in no mood for smiling. . . .

ɬ

BITTER THE

CHASTENING ROD

Apartheid continued to be a sensitive issue for African Americans throughout the eighties, and Audre Lorde would have been a potent resource for journalist Sam Fulwood. Praised for her searing, personal poetry, Lorde was deeply immersed in the antiapartheid struggle, as this moving testament reveals. She would demonstrate the same resolute fight against the cancer that would ravage her body and later take her life. Lorde's commitment to antiapartheid struggle was honed in her fight against the forces that daily ridiculed her lesbianism and her advocacy of feminist causes.

While Fulwood was preparing for his journey into the bowels of apartheid, Jill Nelson was packing her bags to discover life inside the Beltway, and more precisely, inside the *Washington Post*. A versatile and busy freelance writer, she was now on her way to a full-time gig, her lance sharpened to do battle with the corporate dragons at one of the nation's most powerful newspapers. Her assignments for the paper were never as engrossing as these confessions from the ramparts. Eventually, Nelson grew weary of the corporate snake pit, gathered her belongings and returned to the unpredictable world of the freelancer, where she currently thrives.

Much further to the South, Johnnetta Cole was making a debut, too, as the first "Sister President" of Spelman College. After years of struggling against inequity in society and in academic circles, she would be the head of an institution devoid of blatant racism and sexism. However, there were still challenges to surmount, ordeals to overcome, and money to raise. Bill and Camille Cosby provided her with a sizable cash relief in 1988 when they donated $20 million to Spelman. The contribution represented the largest individual gift in the 107-year history of the college and the largest such gift ever by African Americans.

Percussionist/composer Max Roach has also endowed black culture with his gifts. The last of the great progenitors of the so-called bebop revolution, Roach remains as active as ever, leading an assortment of ensembles at concert performances all over the world. Roach is a formidable musician who particularly since the 1960s has expressed a strong regard about the content, direction, and, most notably here, the often debilitating labels attached to African American music. While this essay was published in the late eighties, it is consistent with Roach's perspective prior to its appearance and it represents his current feelings about America's only indigenous art form.

Alvin Ailey waged a relentless fight to make the world of dance respect his blackness and his incomparable talent. Six years after he founded his American Dance Theater it dissolved because of a lack of funds. In 1967, the company was once again on the boards and on tour with Judith Jamison as the lead dancer. On a more personal level, Ailey suffered from a long drug addiction that perpetually undermined his efforts to triumph, and only a will of steel allowed him to accomplish as

much as he did, given the debilitating circumstances he routinely encountered. When Ailey died of a blood disorder in 1989, Jamison took over
the company, drawing new audiences with the revival of Ailey's best-
known works, *Revelations* and *Hidden Rites*.

A few weeks after Ailey's death, Gen. Colin Powell was cleaning out
his desk in the West Wing of the White House. His stint as the National
Security Adviser to President Reagan was over. An ultimate "insider,"
Powell was strategically placed to give a blow-by-blow account of the
transition from the Reagan to the Bush administration, a phase he relates
with typical nonchalance. No black man has ever achieved Powell's rank
and power in the military. He was chair of the Joint Chiefs of Staff in
1990 during the Operation Desert Shield and Operation Desert Storm, a
military offensive launched to free Kuwait from Iraq. There was great
hope that Powell would seek the presidency in 1996, but he disappointed
his supporters when he announced he would not be a candidate because
there was "no fire in his belly" for the office. It should be noted that
his wife also had counseled against his candidacy, fearing his life would
be in danger.

AUDRE LORDE

From *The Audre Lorde Compendium*

❧

NEW YORK CITY, 1985

NEW YORK CITY, 1985. THE HIGH SIGN that rules this summer is increasing fragmentation. I am filled with a sense of urgency and dread: dread at the apparently random waves of assaults against people and institutions closest to me; urgency to unearth the connections between these assaults. Those connections lurk beneath the newspaper reports of teargassed funeral processions in Tembisa and the charred remains of Baldwin Hills, California, a flourishing Black neighborhood leveled by arson.

I sit before the typewriter for days and nothing comes. It feels as if underlining these assaults, lining them up one after the other and looking at them squarely might give them an unbearable power. Yet I know exactly the opposite is true—no matter how difficult it may be to look at the realities of our lives, it is there that we will find the strength to change them. And to suppress any truth is to give it power beyond endurance.

As I write these words I am listening to the United Nations Special Session considering the 'state of emergency' in South Africa, their euphemism for the suspension of human rights for Blacks, which is the response of the Pretoria regime to the increasingly spontaneous eruptions in Black townships across that country. These outbursts against apartheid have greatly increased in the last eleven months since a new South African constitution further solidified the exclusion of the twenty-two million Black majority from the South African political process. These outbreaks, however severely curtailed by the South African police and military, are beginning to accomplish what Oliver Tambo, head of the African National Congress, hoped for in his call to make South Africa under apartheid 'ungovernable.'

So much Black blood has been shed upon that land, I thought, and so much more will fall. But blood will tell, and now the blood is speaking. Has it finally started? What some of us prayed and worked and believed would—must—happen, wondering when, because so few of us here in America even seemed to know what was going on in South Africa, nor cared to hear. The connections have not been made, and they must be if African-Americans are to articulate our power in the struggle against a worldwide escalation of forces aligned against people of Color the world over: institutionalized racism grown more and more aggressive in the service of shrinking profit-oriented economies. . . .

Every year over 500 million american dollars flow into the white South African death machine. How many of those dollars do you control as you sit reading this? Where do you bank? Buy your gas? What pressure can you bring to bear upon companies doing business in South Africa? Five hundred million dollars a year. Divestment. The withdrawal of american financial support from South Africa. Those who counter that divestment would mean additional suffering for Black South Africans are either cynical or misguided or unaware of the extent to which Black South Africans suffer every day of their lives. For any South African to even discuss divestment in South Africa is considered an act of treason against the state. . . .

We are Black Lesbians and Gays, fighting many battles for survival. We are also citizens of the most powerful country in the world, a country which stands upon the wrong side of every liberation struggle on earth. African-Americans control 200 billion dollars in buying power annually. As African-Americans we must learn to use our power, to establish the connections instantly between consistent patterns of slaughter of Black children and youth in the roads of Sebokeng and Soweto in the name of law and order in Johannesburg, and white america's not-so-silent applause for the smiling white vigilante who coolly guns down four Black youths in the New York City subway. Or the white policeman guarding the store of a Middle Eastern shopkeeper who had killed three Black children in Brooklyn in a dispute over one can of Coca-Cola. The multicorporate financial connections are a matter of record; it is the emotional ones which must become inescapable for each of us. We are members of an international community of people of Color, and must see our struggles as connected within that light.

How long will it take to escalate into our consciousness as Black people that this is *us*, that it is only a matter of location and progression of time and intensity from the molotov cocktails that were hurled into the brush in Los Angeles, starting the conflagration that burned out well-to-do Black Baldwin Hills—fifty-three homes gone, three lives lost—to government sanctioned segregation and violence. In California, U.S.A., the Aryan Brotherhood, the Posse Commitatus, and other white racist and anti-Semitic survivalist groups flourish rampant and poisonous, fertilized by a secretly sympathetic law enforcement team.

Eleanor Bumpurs, sixty-six, Black grandmother, evicted from her Bronx Housing Authority with two fatal shotgun blasts from New York City Housing police.

Allene Richardson, sixty-four, gunned down in her Detroit apartment house hallway by a policewoman after she was locked out of her apartment and a neighbor called the police to help her get back in.

It is ten years since a policeman shot ten-year-old Clifford Glover early one Saturday morning in front of his father in Queens, New York, eight years Thanksgiving Day since another white cop walked up to Randy Evans while he sat on his stoop talking with friends and blew his fifteen-year-old brains out. Temporary insanity, said the jury that acquitted that policeman.

Countless others since then—Seattle, New Orleans, Dallas. Yvonne Smallwood, a young Black woman arguing her husband's traffic ticket, kicked to death by police in Manhattan. Our dead line our dreams, their deaths becoming more and more commonplace.

How does a system bent upon our ultimate destruction make the unacceptable gradually tolerable? Observe closely, look around, read the Black press. How do you get a population to accept the denial of the most rudimentary freedoms this country is supposed to be about to over 12 percent of its population? And we know that Black americans are only the beginning, just as the moves against Black Lesbians and Gays are only the beginning within our communities.

In 1947, within my memory, apartheid was not the state policy of South Africa, but the supposedly far-out dream of the Afrikaner Broederbond. Living conditions of Black South Africans, although bad, were not yet governed by policies of institutional genocide. Blacks owned land, attended schools.

With the 1948 election of the Afrikaner white-supremacy advocate Malik, and the implementation of apartheid, the step-by-step attack upon Black existence was accelerated with the dismantling of any human rights as they pertained to Black people. Now, white South Africans who protest are being jailed and brutalized and blown up, also. Once liberal English-speaking white South Africans had to be conned into accepting this dismantling, lulled long enough for the apparatus which was to ensure all white privileged survival to be cemented into place by H. Verwoerd, its architect and later South African Prime Minister.

Now Johannesburg, city of gold, sits literally upon a mountain of gold and Black blood. . . .

How are we persuaded to participate in our own destruction by maintaining our silences? How is the american public persuaded to accept as natural the fact that at a time when prolonged negotiations can effect the release of hostages in the Middle East or terminate an armed confrontation with police outside a white survivalist encampment, a mayor of an american city can order an incendiary device dropped on a house with five children in it and police pin down the occupants until they perish? Yes, African-Americans can still walk the streets of america without passbooks—for the time being. . . .

How is the systematic erosion of freedoms gradually accomplished? What kind of gradual erosion of our status as United States citizens will Black people be persuaded first to ignore and then to accept?

In Louisville, Kentucky, a Workmen's Compensation ruling awards $231 weekly disability payments to a thirty-nine-year-old sanitation supervisor, white, for a mental breakdown he says he suffered as a result of having to work with Black people.

A peaceful, licensed march to the Haitian Embassy in New York to protest living conditions on that island, and the imprisonment of three priests, is set upon by New York City mounted police and trained attack dogs. Sixteen people are injured, including women and children, and one man, struck in the head by hooves, may lose his eye. The next day, no major newspaper or TV news station carries a report of the incident, except for Black media.

In New York, the self-confessed and convicted white ex-G.I. killer of at least six Black men in New York City and Buffalo is quietly released from jail after less than one year, on a technicality. He had been sentenced to life for three of the murders and never tried on the others. White men attack three Black transit workers in Brooklyn, stomping one to death. Of the three who are tried for murder, two are sentenced to less than one year in prison and one goes scot-free.

So the message is clear: stock in Black human life in the U.S.A., never high, is plunging rapidly in the sight of white american complacencies. But as African-Americans we cannot afford to play that market; it is our lives and the lives of our children that are at stake.

The political and social flavor of the African-American position in the 1980s feels in particular aspects to be analogous to occurrences in the Black South African communities of the 1950s, the period of the postwar construction of the apparati of apartheid, reaction, and suppression. . . .

No one in the U.S. government will say openly now that apartheid in South Africa is good, or that the advancing technocracy in this country is making a large underprivileged pool of cheap labor increasingly unnecessary. No one actually says that Black people are more frequently seen as expendable in this economy, but nonetheless the nation that plans to finance Star Wars in space and run shuttle flights to the moon cannot seem to remedy Black teenage unemployment. Because it does not wish to remedy it. Better to wipe them out, blow them away. African-Americans are increasingly superfluous to a shrinking economy. A different stage exists in South Africa where a cheap labor pool of Blacks is still pivotal to the economy. But the maintenance of the two systems is closely related, and they are both guided primarily by the needs of a white marketplace. Of course no one in the United States government will openly defend apartheid—they don't have to. Just support it by empty rhetorical slaps on the wrists and solid financial investments, all the time honoring South African orders for arms, nuclear technology, and sophisticated computerized riot-control mechanisms. The bully boys stick together.

I remember stories in the 1960s about the roving bands of homeless and predatory *tsotsis,* disenchanted and furious Black youths roaming the evening streets of Sharpeville and Soweto and other Black townships.

The fact that African-Americans can still move about relatively freely, do not yet have to carry passbooks or battle an officially named policy of apartheid, should not delude us for a minute about the disturbing similarities of the Black situation in each one of these profit-oriented economies. We examine these similarities so that we can more effectively devise mutually supportive strategies for action, at the same time as we remain acutely aware of our differences. Like the volcano, which is one form of extreme earth-change, in any revolutionary process there is a period of intensification and a period of explosion. We must become familiar with the requirements and symptoms of each period, and use the differences between them to our mutual advantage, learning and supporting each other's battles. African-Americans can wield the relative power of our dollars—for better or worse. We have the ability to affect South Africa where it lives, financially, through our support of divestment for companies doing business in South Africa. Black South Africans have the base of their own land upon which they operate. We lack that as African-Americans, suffer the rootlessness of a 'hyphenated' people. But within those differences, we can join together to effect a future the world has not yet conceived, let alone seen.

For no matter what liberal commitment to human rights is mouthed in international circles by the U.S. government, we know it will not move beyond its investments in South Africa unless we make it unprofitable to invest there. For it is economic divestment, not moral sanction, that South Africa fears most. No one will free us but ourselves, here nor there. So our survivals are not separate, even though the terms under which we struggle differ. African-Americans are bound to the Black struggle in South Africa by politics as well as blood. As Malcolm X observed more than twenty years ago, a militant, free Africa is a necessity to the dignity of African-American identity. . . .

JILL NELSON

From *Volunteer Slavery*

WASHINGTON, D.C., 1986

THE NEXT DAY I MOVE TO WASHINGTON, my promised land, my own private little *hajj,* only I am journeying to the nation's capital instead of Mecca. My motives are not very spiritual. If there is any religion involved at all, it is "spiritual materialism." I am coming in from the cold of activist journalism leftist politics, and poverty, and moving into the mainstream of so-called objective journalism, and more money than I've ever made before.

Not too long ago, when I showed up at my mother's house in a long skirt, she called me an "anachronism." Over time, I have come to suspect she was right. I've watched colleagues ascend the ladder of financial success and corporate irresponsibility. Meanwhile, I continued to write about black folks like Anthony Davis, work at home, and be poor.

While I was busy anguishing about how to reconcile my bourgeois background and tendencies with my commitment to being a "race woman," my black journalist colleagues were, by and large, unbothered by such dilemmas. They were busy getting over, making money, and trying to get as far away from their roots as politely possible.

I began to feel like a symbol, an icon, not a person. Colleagues could read my articles in the *Village Voice* about real-life black people being fucked and soothe their indifferent consciences. They could count on me standing up, in person and in print, to white folks, and then go back to their jobs and reap the benefits of my efforts. After all, Jill had it covered, for everyone. Why should it matter to them that I made next to no money, had a daughter to raise, zilch in the bank? My life was that way because I wanted it that way, wasn't it?

Well, not anymore. Freelancing gave me the freedom to be a full-time, at-home single parent to Misu. For thirteen years I'd been the parent able to chaperon class trips, host after-school dates, and "be there" for my daughter. Then she'd turned into an adolescent. Not only was she not dependent on me in the same ways, but now she didn't even want to be bothered.

Clearly, it was time for me to change, too. I was finally going to present myself to society, but instead of having the cotillion I'd rejected on political principle in 1970, when I was eighteen, I was going to work for the *Washington Post*.

It wasn't, I reasoned, really selling out, but more like buying in. Who said you had to be poor to understand poor people, to advocate for them? Both Martin Luther King Jr. and Malcolm X lived in houses, didn't they? Flo Kennedy kicked butt, but she always looked great. Even the Reverend Al Sharpton has his hair done religiously. I was tired of living in an apartment, cutting my own hair, wearing the same turquoise ultrasuede dress. I was sick of committing class suicide in the name of righteousness. I finally took to heart the words of evangelist Reverend Ike: "The only thing I have to say about poor people is don't be one of them."

I go to work at the *Post* not simply for the money, but for the power. Even though it is the mid-Eighties and I might be ten years too late, I am finally going to try to "change the system from within," what we all said back when the Sixties turned into the Seventies and got deadly. . . .

The streets here are named after states, presidents, letters of the alphabet, and flowers, all radiating out in circles. The man who designed the city, L'Enfant, was a Frenchman who wanted D.C. to look like Versailles. History tells us he had the city laid out in circles to keep the unruly mob from the houses of government. After L'Enfant's death, Washington was completed by its surveyor, Benjamin Banneker, a black man. Whatever L'Enfant's intentions, I suspect Banneker laid out the city so it goes round and round in circles just to mess with the white folks, his own brand of architectural revenge against racism.

At first, no matter where I am trying to go from my house in Northwest Washington, I wind up in Hyattsville, Maryland, or points east. Then, one day, the city clicks. Suddenly it makes its own senseless sense, and I can drive anywhere. The illogical becomes logical, lunacy becomes sanity, and I understand that this is a town where going in circles signals progress. It is a realization I am going to have many times in Washington.

It's pretty here, and coming from New York the livin' is easy. So easy that it's not difficult to get lulled into complacency.

D.C. is so neatly segregated that neither the classes nor the races need intermix after working hours. Divided into four virtually autonomous quadrants, after work there is no need to leave your neighborhood to get whatever you want.

If you are poor and black and live in Southeast Washington, there is no reason to leave your bantustan at all. They call where the black folks live "Far Southeast," and the distance is not just geographical. Across the Anacostia River, it might as well be the Red Sea before Moses. The people here are largely ignored by the mayor, the *Washington Post,* and everyone else, except regarding violent crimes, crack houses, and the obligatory "positive" lip service paid on Martin Luther King, Jr. Day. Unemployment is high, so there aren't that many people crossing the river to go to work. In 1986 the people of Southeast are last in line, still awaiting the arrival of D.C.'s subway, called the Metro. It is a long wait despite the presence of Marion Barry, homeboy mayor, for whom they overwhelmingly voted.

As for poor and working-class white folks, they don't live in Washington, but in the surrounding suburbs of Virginia and Maryland, where they also vote. The Metro has been out there for years.

The taxi passes a house with a supercan in the front yard. These multi-gallon green plastic trash cans, issued to every home by the city, are—besides racial solidarity—the single most frequent reason people in Northwest Washington, where I live, support the mayor.

"You gonna hear a lot of bullshit from these white folks," my neighbor across the alley tells me a few days later when we meet by our garbage cans. "But Barry's a good mayor."

Like one in twelve residents of Washington, he works for district government. Like more than half of D.C.'s residents, he owns his home. Like just about everyone, he keeps his lawn neatly mowed and plants azaleas.

"Why?" I am eager to learn, to live happily in Chocolate City, with a chocolate mayor, for everything to be sweet.

"Why? How the hell I'm gonna tell you why white folks act like they do? Don't quote me—" I am going to hear that a lot here "—but I believe it's racism. You know how they are. Just can't stand to see a black man in charge."

"Or black woman," I say. He ignores this.

"This is the nation's capitol, all that bull, and these ofays just can't deal with a black man . . ." He keeps on talking. I stand there, not really listening. I can tell by the cadence of his voice, its rise and fall, when to grunt or agree. It is a conversation I have nearly every day with at least one black person. It involves dissing white folks for always fucking with us, and celebrating the latest individual, and therefore collective, comeuppance. This is an authentic Negro experience.

He pauses. We chuckle.

"What specifically do you like about him?" After all, I'm a reporter. As Earl Caldwell told us when I was in journalism school, "If you ain't got it in your notes, you ain't got it."

"Supercans."

"Excuse me?"

"Supercans," my neighbor says, leaning toward me. There are beads of sweat on his forehead.

"Huh?"

"Right here!" He bangs closed the lid of the trash can into which I am stuffing crumpled cardboard boxes. Just in time, I snatch my fingers away. "Supercans," he says, stroking its dull green side.

"Oh. These are from the city. That's nice," I say, but I still don't get it. I guess it shows.

"You see, before we got these, we had a real problem . . ."

"Oh. What kind of problem?"

"Terrible," he says, drumming his fingers against the side of the supercan.

"With dogs?"

"No, with coons! Barry got us these supercans and got rid of the coons!" Depending on how you look at it, this is, I realize over time, an arguable assertion.

The taxi stops in front of the house I have rented. A walkway in the shape of an elongated "S" leads up to a wide, heavy front door. Azaleas, lilies, and peonies line the walkway, tumbling onto the path. A magnolia tree in flower stands on one side of the doorway, a pine on the other. The mingled scent of magnolias and peonies hangs in the air. Beside the door is a black wrought-iron dog with a flat blade across its back, a bootscraper. The nonracist equivalent of a black jockey holding a lantern, it signals that we have arrived.

"Look out Cosbys!" my daughter whoops and jumps out of the cab, laughing.

I watch her run into the house. As the taxi driver tries to compute the fare based on how many zones we've passed through, I sit there, feeling like Rod Serling.

JOHNNETTA B. COLE

From *Conversations*

§

ATLANTA, 1988

THERE IS A SENSE IN WHICH COMING to Spelman is more
. . . than a return to where I've come from. It is a reconnecting with my
beginnings and the most fundamental part of who I am. This reconnecting has
been expressed in simple things such as eating more collard greens (with, I
might add, the challenge of preparing them or having them prepared without
fatback) to matters far more significant such as rediscovering the importance of
the Black Church not only as our Town Hall, but also as the historical venue
where we African Americans express the deep and abiding spirituality our
forebears brought with them to America. Coming to Spelman has meant inter-
acting with women and men who remind me of the relatives, teachers, ministers, librarians, and YWCA directors in Jacksonville who played such positive
roles in my development.

As I was packing up to move to Atlanta, my middle son, Aaron, taunted
me with: "Twenty-one days until you move to the South! . . . Nineteen days
before you move to the South!" and so on. I would always respond, "I'm not
going to the *South*. I'm going to Atlanta."

To my mind, Atlanta represented the New South, a place far, far different
from the South in which I grew up. This is not to say that racist attitudes (not
to mention actions) no longer exist in Atlanta. For example, I am aware that in
the minds of many, Spelman is perceived as "that little colored girls' school
over there in the southwest part of town," and that I am seen yes, as a college
president, but as president of "one of those *Black* schools." Still in all, coming
to Atlanta has meant coming to a better, if not an ideal, South. Of course,

vestiges of the Old South are all the more muted in my life because I spend so much of my time in a place such as Spelman.

I would prefer not to describe an experience in terms of the absence of something else, but I cannot avoid it when it comes to describing what it is like to be at Spelman. The absence of persistent and blatant racism and sexism on our campus is not only joyous, it is exhilarating. Sometimes when I am not quite sure why it is that I am fundamentally so happy here, even when there are wrinkles in my day and setbacks that come with the territory of being a college president (and a human being), I realize that in large part the explanation lies in the fact that far more than at any other time in my life in the United States, I live without racism and sexism defining each and every one of my actions, thoughts, reflexes, and defenses. In some sense it is a model of what our nation might be like because the Spelman family is not without men, nor is it composed exclusively of African Americans; and Spelman is a place where African Americans and all others have the freedom, the encouragement, and the responsibility to reach their potential.

To acknowledge that Spelman is a gender- and racially mixed environment is not to minimize the fact that it is an historically Black college for women. When I was a student at Boylan-Haven had anyone asked me how I felt about going to an all girls' school, I don't know how I would have responded, other than, perhaps, with a shrug and a "It's okay, I guess." Over forty years later, however, I am very conscious and proud that I am at an African American women's institution and moreover one where two-thirds of the faculty are women and three-quarters are African Americans. And I see the positive effect it has on the students. A student does not enter a classroom braced to battle the assumption that she cannot and will not excel solely because she is an African American and a woman; nor when she does excel does she have to swallow or rail against the left-handed compliment that she is somehow different from other Black folk, an exception to the rule. Instead, she can devote her energies to the business of learning and achieving. Moreover, this student does not have to wonder about her possibilities for achieving because someone like her who has achieved is standing before her or not far away in the position of professor, department chair, dean, provost, and president. This is what role modeling is in its ultimate and most penetrating expression.

While coming to Spelman and Atlanta was much like coming home, it was certainly not a private affair. The prominence I knew in Jacksonville, Florida, and the recognition I received within academia for my work in the area of cross-cultural studies of race, gender, and class was nothing compared to what I would meet after my appointment to Spelman.

The media attention I received as Spelman's first "Sister President" was phenomenal. And I'll never forget the Saturday morning my youngest son,

Ethan Che, called me up while I was on a fundraising trip for Spelman to tell me excitedly that my name had appeared on the "Soul Train Scramble Board." He was impressed: his mom the educator and intellectual was being projected in a forum of popular culture.

On the heels of all the publicity came invitation after invitation for speaking engagements, numerous awards, and a host of honorary degrees. Much to my amazement, at various functions, and even at airports, people were asking for my autograph. Before long I was being projected as a national leader in American higher education. The attention was very satisfying because it helped bring Spelman and by extension all historically Black colleges and universities into the national consciousness as vital and significant institutions. At the same time the publicity was unsettling. For one, I knew that should something go awry, the media would in all likelihood be no less "on the case." Moreover, I could see at work the familiar scenario whereby the establishment singles out one or two individuals as the voice of all of Black America. Clearly, I and any other single individual should not be and could not be *the* spokesperson for historically Black colleges and universities or *the* spokesperson for African American women. Then, too, there are the little discomforts that come with being a public figure. For example, one evening I was at home in the President's house at Spelman in a pair of jeans and a sweatshirt that read: "Proud to be Black, Beautiful, and Brilliant." In a sudden dash to the supermarket I stopped inside my door and wondered, "Should the president of Spelman be seen in this particular sweatshirt? Should she even be seen in the local A & P in jeans and a sweatshirt at all?" Fortunately, I don't take myself so seriously as to think that Spelman or the state of American higher education will rise or fall based on what I wear. I kept on the sweatshirt and jeans, put on and zipped a jacket up all the way, and as we say, I try to "keep on steppin'."

One of the most positive consequences of being a public figure is that it has given me an opportunity to interact and talk with more African American women than ever before. It is not as if I go around "studying" you, my sisters, but there is a sense in which my sphere of inquiry into the conditions and concerns of African American women has dramatically expanded. At large functions and small gatherings, whether it is a speaking engagement at a church on Women's Day or a meeting of my Literary Club in Atlanta, the National Board of the Coalition of 100 Black Women in New York, or the Spelman College Corporate Women's Roundtable, I hear certain notes repeated over and over again.

On the one hand there is a note of fierce pride in the strides African American women have made in the arts, business, education, politics, science and technology, and other arenas. There is a yearning and an expectancy for still greater achievements. I also hear a very positive sense of self and a rejoicing in being an African American woman. One of the most visible signs of this spirit is in the growing number of African American women wearing naturals or braids, or who incorporate more and more African elements such as *kente* cloth into their wardrobes and into their work and home environments.

At the same time, I hear undertones of despair over aspects of the personal and professional lives of African American women, and the life of their community. One of the strains I hear is of a certain loneliness and a longing for an intimate and supportive relationship that will enhance as opposed to define and stifle their lives. Another is of profound frustration and anger over the persistence of racism and sexism in the workplace. I hear this from women in entry-level and middle-management positions, and particularly from those closest to the top of the corporate ladder—high-powered, superbly trained, top-level executives who are saying, "Because I am Black and a woman I *still* have to go to this highfalutin job day after day and prove that I am a person of value. . . . This is not the way I want to spend the rest of my life."

In social and professional settings alike, as I join in discussions with African American women on the crises that confront our people, one of the most painful admissions I hear is, as one woman put it, "I am afraid of my own people." This woman went on to recount an evening when she was walking down the street and saw an African American man headed in her direction and she panicked. With tears welling up in her eyes she went on to describe the agony and shame she felt the moment her eyes met his and she knew that he knew that she was afraid of him and he intended her no harm.

MAX ROACH

From *Jazz: A Four-Letter Word*

EVEN AS I REFLECT ON WHAT HAPPENED at Betty's house that Sunday afternoon, I still can't believe it. I was fifteen years old and full of myself. Betty was fifteen and the prettiest girl I had ever seen, and she really knew how to kiss. In those days we would kiss and hold each other real close. Betty's father was a preacher. He had a small storefront church in our Brooklyn neighborhood. Many people in those days were religious zealots. My family as well as Betty's had roots in the South but migrated north at the turn of the century. We brought religious fervor north with a dedication to the word that manifested itself in our music. My grandaunt was a gospel pianist. She lived and worked in Asbury Park, New Jersey. Whenever she visited, she insisted on teaching me and my brother the rudiments of music on a player piano we inherited from the house's previous occupant, who couldn't afford to move it. It was during this period that I met Betty. I must have been ten when I first saw Betty, and from that very moment I fell madly in love with her. During the five years that followed, my interest in instrumental music increased. The churches had bands and the same musicians who performed for the churches often worked the house-rent parties. Poor and destitute families often gave these parties to pay the rent and to raise money to buy other things needed to survive. I had access to a piano and drum set. I settled on the drum set. So on that fateful Sunday afternoon when Betty's father asked me what I wanted to do with my life, I told him that it was my ambition to be a "jazz," or a four-letter-word, musician. From that point forward I was persona non grata at Betty's house.

It didn't occur to me at the time, but now that I have realized my ambition as a four-letter-word musician, I have also come to realize just how sour a note that four-letter word can strike. For example, when the Black Achievement Awards are celebrated, I am persona non grata. When the American Music Awards are celebrated, I am persona non grata. When the Grammys are awarded, I am persona non grata.

For me, being a four-letter-word musician means years of hard work in mastering an extremely difficult and demanding art form—one in which creativity and individuality are the criteria. Finally, I have arrived and have been met with world acclaim for my genius (hard work) only to find that the rewards are poor working conditions in smoke-filled nightclubs without dressing rooms, impossible pianos and inadequate sound systems.

Let me define what I mean by four-letter-word music. This is the most advanced music of the twentieth century. It was created and performed by Louis Armstrong, Roy Eldridge, Charlie Parker, Lester Young, Billie Holiday, Dizzy Gillespie, Art Blakey, Ella Fitzgerald, Elvin Jones, Mary Lou Williams, Papa Jo Jones, Art Tatum, Charlie Mingus, Miles Davis, Thelonious Monk, Duke Ellington, Count Basie and Kenny Clarke to name a few. These and other great musicians are the cornerstones in the evolution of this great American art form. Whenever I am approached by entrepreneurs and producers about performing four-letter-word music, I am reminded that this four-letter-word music doesn't sell well and that they cannot afford to pay me much more than the union minimum.

To make matters worse, my royalty statements make it appear that the record companies are doing me a favor. And if I were to ask any four-letter-word musician (Wynton Marsalis, Herbie Hancock, Stanley Jordan) what he considered to be the minimum requirements to reach the heights of Charlie Parker, Dizzy Gillespie or Art Tatum, I am sure he would tell me that it takes many, many years of serious study and hard work. In fact, on the creative level the work never stops. For example, when I am approached by recording producers, I am always asked, "What have you got new?" It is either create new work or perish. Of all the important musical art forms to emerge in the twentieth century, this four-letter-word music is the most misunderstood and its practitioners the least appreciated. Fortunately, for the four-letter-word musicians the freedom of expression, the discipline that is constantly evolving, the challenges of unchartered new musical territories and knowing that you can be both creator and performer at the same time are reason enough to continue the pursuit.

This music has given me more than I ever imagined in terms of personal accomplishment. I have traveled extensively and learned many things about other people and their cultures. However, I am puzzled when the four-letter-word musicians are persona non grata. What is the problem, and why does this music and its practitioners turn people off?

Maybe a name change would solve the problem of not being accepted by the "establishment"—television, movies, theatre, Black Achievement Awards, American Music Awards, the Grammys and other talent barometers. What if I had said to Betty's father (when he asked me what I wanted to do with my life) that my ambition was to pursue a career as a CSA (creative sound architect)? And when he questioned whether this profession could support a family, I could have countered by citing its history of great success, for example: sold-out houses—Madison Square Garden, the Meadowlands, Radio City Music Hall—and going gold and platinum on record sales. Would I have been persona non grata with him or the "establishment" then?

This new music is both communal and democratic. One of its fortes is to learn how to create collectively. These four-letter-word musicians are indeed a very special breed. They are highly skilled in the art and science of organizing sounds to create structurally complete and profound musical compositions spontaneously. These very special people are also musically literate, meaning they can read and write music. Not only are they exploring new approaches to creating and performing this new music, but the language of the music world is being vastly expanded as a result of the efforts of these very special people from the realm of the four-letter word.

Betty's father did me a service when he declared me a persona non grata in his home. It freed up my time so that I could deal with four-letter-word music. Still I often wonder what happened to Betty.

ALVIN AILEY

From *Revelations*

NEW YORK CITY, 1988

OVER THE YEARS I HAVE BEEN OBSESSED with our dance company. During every waking minute, everything I do somehow revolves around the company; it's all-engrossing. I sacrificed everything to stay in dance—and dance requires enormous sacrifice. The touring, for example. Touring six months out of the year has a fatal effect on personal relations. I don't go all of the time anymore, but I'm a veteran of the tour, having done it for fifteen years.

There is also a physical sacrifice involved in my world. Dancing hurts. After doing a performance, you wake up with cramps at four o'clock in the morning. You don't make much money. You have to be obsessed with dance to do dance; it's not something you play with. The commitment must be there, and the involvement total. As a choreographer, I'm always thinking about the next dance. In my mind's eye I see these figures going across the stage. The creative process is not controlled by a switch you can simply turn on or off; it's with you all the time. For me, choreography is very difficult to do. It's both mentally and physically draining, and one wants to be physically drained by it. In the days when I was in terrific shape and we used to do intricate steps and hard falls on the floor during rehearsals, I felt terrific.

Choreography, as I have said, is also mentally draining, but there's a pleasure in getting into the studio with the dancers and the music and coming out with something that has passion and joy, that shows off the dancers and how they physically reflect the music. There's a kind of joy in creating something where before there was nothing. That keeps me going.

I am very fond of dancers. I like their personalities, I like who they are—

their spirit, their physicality, their creativity, their yearning to be perfect. I look for dancers who have something unusual about them physically—a special turn of the leg, a special stretch of the back. I look for dancers who have rubato in their bodies. I believe that dance is not what you do from one movement to the next, it's what happens in between those two movements with the body. I look for dancers who have an oozy quality in their movement. I like dancers who are temperamental, who are expressive, who show their feelings, who are open and out, not hidden, who want to show themselves to the audience. I like personalities, not cookie-cutter dancers—a row of this, a row of that. That's what I accuse Balanchine of: making everyone who dances for him blank-faced.

Dancers these days must also have technique—classical, modern, and jazz. My earlier dancers were not the world's greatest technicians. None of those girls were about to turn forty-two fouettés on a dime, but they had a funk; they had a stride; they had history; they had a menace about them that the young kids don't have today. Today's kids are very technical. They can do eighteen pirouettes on a dime and get their leg way above the head and hold it there. But the insight is not the same: It's not as giving, not as warm. They need to give themselves to the dance, to project themselves from the inside out. That's what we get after them about.

We coach and direct them to bring out their personalities. We want them to be capable of acting out various parts, to become the different individuals in each ballet. That's where personality comes in. . . .

The question of dance and race is an ever-present one. Look at the problem in England right now. There are black dancers in the Royal Ballet School, but the RBS doesn't want them, so as a result the really good black dancers with potential are sent to Arthur Mitchell's school. The Royal Ballet has an arrangement with Arthur to take them and nurture them so they don't have to deal with all those young black artists. You still don't see many black dancers in classical companies. The Europeans are more open than the Americans. (Maurice Béjart has three black dancers, for example.) In American companies, though, there is still an overlay of racism. I remember in 1966 when my company was going through one of its periodic dissolutions, some of our very top, fantastic dancers—Judith Jamison, Morton Winston, and Miguel Godreau—were invited to the Harkness Ballet. All had terrible times; when it came to utilizing their fantastic abilities, Harkness simply didn't have a clue.

Here, in short, is the big problem with white ballet companies: Does one really want to see a black swan among thirty-two swans in *Swan Lake* or a black peasant girl in *Giselle?* It's historically inaccurate, is the line taken by many of those in charge. Agnes de Mille used that argument with black dancers, and I'll never forgive her for it. When she was holding auditions for a Texas musical,

Ninety Degrees in the Shade, I believe, she told the black dancers who came to the audition that they were historically inappropriate and refused to hire them.

I give no credence to that position whatsoever. What we're talking about here is dance. We're talking about fantasy, not reality. We're in the theater, not in a history seminar. It's the same as saying that Japanese dancers can't dance the blues—well, they do in *my* company. Japanese dancers understand the blues as well as anybody. When I began using them and some white dancers in *Blues Suite* and *Revelations,* I got flack from some black groups who resented it. They felt anyone not black was out of place. I received many letters in protest. My answer was that their presence universalizes the material. . . .

I want to have a mixed company, but most of the white dancers who can dance at the level of my kids are off doing either television or films. At times, I've had superb white artists, such as Linda Kent, Jonathan Riseling, and Maxine Sherman. Maxine is with Martha Graham now; she left because she said she would never get to do *Cry,* and she was right. Even though she had every other leading part in the repertoire except *Cry,* she said, "I'm going back to Martha Graham." Other dancers in the company feel the same way. They're convinced that I favor the black dancers and that I'm never going to put an Asian or a Caucasian above the black women in my company. My response is they've danced the other leading parts, except for *Cry,* which is dedicated to my mother and black women everywhere. . . .

COLIN L. POWELL

From *My American Journey*

WASHINGTON, D.C., 1989

J ANUARY 20, 1989, A FRIDAY MORNING, INAUGURATION DAY. I was
sitting in my little office at home at Quarters 27A, Fort Myer, since I had
not been invited to the inaugural ceremonies. No reason why I should be, since
I was part of the departing old guard. The phone rang. It was Ken Duberstein,
who had succeeded Howard Baker as White House Chief of Staff.

"I'm coming over to pick you up," Ken said. "I think we should be with
the President in his office on his last day."

I had enjoyed working with Ken and was going to miss him. In the fourteen months that he had run the White House staff, he had achieved the
smoothest, most congenial operation I had seen during the Reagan years. I ran
the National Security Shop. Tom Griscom, as the public communications chief,
oversaw the speech, press, and other information activities. And Ken directed
the whole show. The three of us managed to do our jobs with few collisions
and a touch of fun. At one point, my staff kept pressing me to get approval for
a National Security Council seal for our stationery. Duberstein did not want
the NSC to be identified separately from the White House. Nevertheless, he
and his staff showed up one day at my office to present a seal. It was a little
stuffed seal with a bracelet dangling from its neck that read "National Security
Council staff." And that ended our ego trip. Unlike some personality combinations I had known running the White House, our group proved that you could
do a job without friction, even with pleasure, if you could get beyond the ego
game. And Ken Duberstein deserved most of the credit for that atmosphere.

On that last day of the administration, Ken picked me up and we arrived at
the White House a few minutes before 10:00 A.M. I stopped by my office first.

On the day before inauguration, the White House maintenance staff had come through the West Wing taking down every picture, cleaning out every desk, emptying all the files. With everything freshly painted and scrubbed and the sofa pillows fluffed, I felt like an intruder in my own office. I did not dare sit on anything. The room was now a neutral space suspended between me and my successor, Brent Scowcroft.

I went to the Oval Office and found the President sitting behind his desk, wearing a black suit with a striped tie, as impeccable as ever. With him were Duberstein, Marlin Fitzwater, Kathy Osborne, and Jim Kuhn, the President's personal assistant. The office was strangely naked, already stripped of any personal traces of Ronald Reagan. As we chatted, the President placed his last call. It was to Bonnie Nofziger, the wife of his political consultant Lyn Nofziger; the Nofziger's daughter, Sue Piland, was terminally ill, and the President was calling to express his concern to the family. He got off the phone, and started reminiscing about the Yellow Room, his favorite in the residential quarters of the White House. Someone suggested he carve his initials on his desk. He laughed and said he had already removed the "kickboard" as a souvenir. "I left a note for George in the desk drawer too," he said.

The President turned to me. "Oh, Colin," he said, "what should I do about this?" He pulled from his pocket the nuclear authentication code card he had carried all these years.

"Hold on to it, sir," Kuhn said. "You're still President. We'll turn it over after the swearing-in.

"Mr. President," he continued, "it's time." He let the press photographers in for the last photo op. They took several group shots of us standing behind the President, who was seated at his desk. The photographers then positioned themselves behind a sofa, cameras aimed at the door leading to the Rose Garden. "Now, Mr. President," Jim said. Action. Camera. Reagan got up and headed for the door, with that familiar athletic spring in his step. As he reached the doorway, he turned around and took one last look back. And that is the image the cameras captured and sent out to the world of the end of an era.

As the President left for the Capitol, I went back home to catch the inauguration on television. Just as the ceremony ended, I remembered that I had to call somebody at the office. I picked up my private White House line and it was already dead.

I had just completed the most crowded, momentous year of my life. I was leaving the White House with two problems nagging at me, the unsolved issue of Manuel Noriega in Panama, and the contras, still hanging by a thread, while a Marxist regime ruled in Nicaragua. Yet, I had also taken part in the historic turning point in the second half of this century, the seismic changes occurring in the Soviet Union. I had worked closely with major world figures. And I had helped shape the Reagan policies that reversed the race toward nuclear Armageddon. The best part for me had been working directly with Ronald Reagan. He may not have commanded every detail of every policy; but he had others to do that. The editor and author Michael Korda once wrote a perceptive definition: "Great leaders are almost always great simplifiers, who cut through argument, debate and doubt, to offer a solution everybody can understand. . . ." That description fit Ronald Reagan.

The man had been elected President twice by knowing what the American people wanted, and even rarer, by giving it to them. What he gave us was inspiration and pride, described best in, of all places, the *New York Times,* not ordinarily a bastion of Reagan support. In the lead editorial on the President's last day in office, the *Times* noted: ". . . he remains to the end, both amazing and comfortable." The editorial cited a key to the President's secret, sticking to his guns on a few fundamental themes—"strengthen defense and cut taxes." The piece also caught the essence of the man. "President Reagan," the *Times* noted, "has come across as something like Professor Harold Hill," from Meredith Willson's 1957 hit, *The Music Man,* about the dream merchant who comes to town and promises, "River City's gonna have her Boys' Band—as sure as the Lord made little green apples. . . ." Harold Hill, the *Times* said, made the children of River City "swell in pride in their will, unity and potential. Ronald Reagan has done that for America." The piece was entitled "Exit the Music Man." The show happens to be my favorite, and I thought the tribute was apt.

I was now leaving the service of this remarkable man, content with the job I had done, but eager to return to my first love, the uniform, the troops, the Army.

Part XVIII.

''NO JUSTICE, NO PEACE!''

Placing his activism within the tradition of Dr. Martin Luther King, Jr., and citing Adam Clayton Powell as one of his mentors, the Rev. Al Sharpton has rarely balked at taking on racists and abusive law enforcement officers. Practically every march in the New York metropolitan area from the 1970s to the 1990s has found the "people's preacher," as he is widely known, among the protesters at the front. It was this vanguard position that placed him in danger and almost cost him his life. The street minister survived the attack and later forgave the assailant. Today he continues to be on call for the people. When his critics called him an ambulance chaser, Sharpton replied, "I am the ambulance."

One of the demonstrations led by Rev. Sharpton took him to White Plains after he learned about a woman's claim of racist remarks among executives at Texaco. Bari-Ellen Roberts was one of the plaintiffs in the case against the giant oil company. Roberts knew from her first day at the company with its lily-white atmosphere that things were not going to be easy. She had stepped into a veritable caste society, and she was the untouchable. The events outlined in her case are examples of the racism and bigotry experienced by countless African Americans in the corporate world who have had to hold their tempers, bite their tongues, and otherwise endure endless slights before hitting the ultimate barrier: the "glass ceiling." When she and other plaintiffs were able to achieve financial retribution from the company, their victory was celebrated vicariously by many who knew firsthand of their humiliation.

Anita Hill knows something about humiliation herself. Her life became an open book after she and Clarence Thomas aired their differences on national television before the Senate Judiciary Committee. At the time she leveled her charge of sexual harassment against Thomas, he was being considered for a seat on the Supreme Court. The issue divided the black community, with her detractors asserting that Hill was the dupe of white feminists. On the other hand, black women saw her as a symbol, admiring her for standing up and forgoing the so-called "loyalty to race." The debacle was just a momentary setback for Thomas, who passed muster and replaced the retired Thurgood Marshall on the Supreme Court bench. Hill became the poster girl for the feminist movement, addressing workshops and seminars from Maine to California. When all the hoopla simmered down, she returned to the classroom as a law professor in her home state of Oklahoma.

As a black Republican, Congressman Gary Franks undoubtedly heard similar comments about race loyalty, and accusations of his being a sellout and an "Uncle Tom." The lone Republican in the Congressional Black Caucus (CBC), Franks was often the target of insults and denunciations from his colleagues, and here he remembers how perilously close he came to being dismissed from the CBC, which, after Franks's threats and remonstrations, decided not to pursue "a new form of bigotry." Once upon a time B.F.R. (Before Franklin Roosevelt), black Americans cast their votes for Republican candidates. This habit can be traced back to Abraham Lincoln and his Emancipation Proclamation. But black Americans turned Lincoln's picture to the wall or took it down during the Depression, hoping that Roosevelt's promise of a New Deal was not the same old raw deal. Since then the Democrats have taken the black vote for granted, much to the chagrin of Franks and the few black Republicans he can count on. Increasingly, a position of "no permanent friends, just permanent interests" is persuading black Americans to withhold putting all their votes in one basket.

It was not so much the question of race loyalty with James McBride, but race *itself*. The son of a black father and white mother, no matter what he did he could not escape the pressing synergy of black and white. Before he was thirty he had quit jobs at major publications, unable to reconcile his dilemma. Only when his mother decided to face her past was McBride able to put aside his constant embarrassment and fear.

No fear is as great as the fear of death. If he is afraid, Mumia Abu-Jamal has never mentioned it. Since 1982, he has been on death row in Pennsylvania after being convicted of killing a police officer. His supporters—and that army has grown to international proportions and includes such celebrities as Danny Glover, the Rev. Jesse Jackson, and actor Ed Asner—contend that Abu-Jamal is the victim of an unfair trial since he was poorly represented and was not judged by his peers. Their key demand is that he get a new trial. Meanwhile, Abu-Jamal does not sit and twiddle his thumbs. As an ex-journalist, he is a prolific writer, and not just about his fate but on the nature of the prison industrial complex and the criminal justice system.

Mumia Abu-Jamal's plight was one of several issues that occupied the minds of thousands of black men who trekked to Washington, D.C., in 1995. Kevin Powell, with some reluctance, was among that legion, and he allows us to look over his shoulder and into his mind as he muses over the question of power. He seems doubtful that the march will provide any concrete solutions to the black predicament, nor does he see power for black Americans emanating from the riches of Bill Cosby, Michael Jordan, or Tiger Woods. One of the stated aims of the Million Man March was the creation of local organizing committees to implement the ideas and strategies announced at the rally. Only in one or two instances has there been any meaningful action given to the agenda set forth in Washington, D.C. Nor were any of these proposals renewed at the Million Woman March in Philadelphia two years later or last year during the Million Youth March in Harlem. In short, we are still marching but have not stopped long enough to develop effective programs discussed at the massive demonstrations.

Much like Powell, Bernice King has little faith that black America's salvation is linked to any current icon, no matter how awesome or telegenic. But she does find sustenance in the past, believing we have a heritage to reclaim and a history to preserve. She asks us not to forget the courage of a Harriet Tubman, the vision of W. E. B. Du Bois, or the compassion of her father. Love, hope, faith, and convictions, she preaches, have not brought us this far to abandon us.

AL SHARPTON

From *Go and Tell Pharaoh*

NEW YORK CITY, 1990

I'D SPENT THE SUMMER OF 1990 PROTESTING out in Teaneck and defending the boys in the Central Park jogger rape case whom I thought were innocent—let me underscore, I didn't dispute the case or the facts, only that some of the accused were clearly uninvolved and that could be proved and I didn't want them railroaded in the fashion of the Scottsboro Boys—as well as monitoring the Bensonhurst trials in Brooklyn. Both Joey Fama and Keith Mondello, the gunman and one of the ringleaders, had been convicted, but Brooklyn D.A. Charles Hynes—my reluctant compatriot at Howard Beach, now celebrated as a crusader—had started losing some of the secondary Bensonhurst cases, which was unacceptable. There had been two dozen attackers out there the night Yusuf Hawkins was killed, and we wanted two dozen in jail, not three or four.

It was time to put some heat on Charles Hynes. There appeared to be a pattern developing that as each of the lesser cases fell apart it would be progressively more difficult to get any of the lesser convictions. Once one was cleared, he could say he was innocent and testify in ways beneficial to the others. We were very concerned about this, and late in 1990 I took more than two hundred people to Bensonhurst to encourage the neighborhood to work with us and help bring the killers to justice. The Bensonhurst people kept saying that everyone out there was not a racist, and we urged them to cooperate with us if in fact that was true. Tell the authorities what you know, we asked, hand over the guilty, support these trials that seem to be losing steam. We need your help to administer justice, don't forget about the dead boy. . . .

Then, in January 1991, I thought the most appropriate way to celebrate Martin Luther King's birthday, the fifteenth of that month, was to go back to Bensonhurst with a huge march, to remind the community there that lip service about empathy and doing the right thing was not going to be acceptable, and that we, their fellow Brooklynites and New Yorkers, were not going to let them forget. Some of the guilty were walking free, awaiting trial, some of them had not even been identified or apprehended. Dr. King was a man of action, not talk and ceremony, and we were going to remember him on his birthday by doing what he would have done, which is go out to Bensonhurst and speak up for justice, confront racial injustice in a very direct way.

On Saturday January 12, the weekend before the King holiday, about five hundred of us got on buses and headed out. This was to be the twenty-ninth march in Bensonhurst, counting from the week after Yusuf was killed. The police, as they always had, met us on Fulton Street where the various buses gathered from around the neighborhoods. We rode the half hour out to Bensonhurst and parked in a barricaded schoolyard—this was standard procedure—and I was sitting in my car, talking to Moses Stewart, waiting for everyone to line up and get ready for the march.

Finally, my assistant, Carl Redding, walked over and said it was time, they were ready for me, and I got out of the car and walked toward the front of the line. We were still, remember, inside the playground, which was supposed to be a secure area, and I turned my head to say something to Carl, and suddenly I felt someone punch me in the chest. Out of reflex I turned my head back toward the front and I saw this face, a white male, flash past me. He had this contorted look of hatred on his face, a real look of hate, I'll never forget that, and before I could get a clear look at him I looked down and saw a knife sticking out of my chest. "Oh my God, he stabbed me!" I thought, and out of reflex grabbed the handle and pulled it out. Until then I hadn't felt any pain, just that punch or brush to the chest, but when I grabbed the knife, the air hit the wound and I felt it, it really hurt. I fell down on my knees and saw that I had blood all over my hands. Then people started screaming.

This all happened so fast, in a matter of seconds, like boom-boom-boom! The assailant was running away, and though there were over two hundred policemen standing around in that playground, none of them made a move to grab him. Somehow he had known the color of the jackets the undercover cops were wearing to be able to recognize each other that day, and that was how he had gotten into the frozen zone. So Carl Redding—a former college and pro football player—with Henry Johnson, one of my security guards, and Moses Stewart tackled him and held him down and *then* the police started beating *them* on their heads and backs and ordering them to let this man go until finally someone ran up and convinced them that this man had just stabbed Reverend Sharpton. It was pandemonium.

Then, after all that, it turned out that with all those policemen, all those motorcycles, all those mobile command units, they didn't have an EMS truck or an ambulance. There was no way to get me to the hospital. I'm on my knees, bleeding, people screaming and running around, and the first thing that hit me was, *get that knife.*

In the corner of my eye I can see Carl and Henry and Moses scuffling with the perpetrator and the police, people are rushing back and forth and there's all this noise and things are starting to swirl, and I can see the knife about three feet in front of me. I started yelling, in all the confusion, "Get the knife, get the knife!" And somebody, one of my people, grabbed it.

Then I hear Moses Stewart in back of me screaming and crying, "Ambulance, ambulance! What's wrong with you guys!" He was cursing at the police, who didn't seem to know what to do, and finally one of the marchers ran over and said, "Let's take him in my car." They carried me over, put me in the backseat of a car, and at that point the police said, "We'll put a car in front of him and behind him so he can use our sirens." They put a rookie cop in the backseat with me, and we roared off to Coney Island Hospital.

I never, ever forget what happened as we came flying out of that playground, bumping over the curb with all those sirens blaring. The rookie cop riding with me says to the men in the front seat, "Damn, I hope there wasn't any poison on the knife." Now, I was delirious, in severe pain, but I hadn't, *truly,* felt any pain until that moment. The first thing I thought was, "Is this cop here especially to torment me?" . . .

Ten minutes later I was in the hospital. They run out a gurney to the parking lot and throw me on. They started wheeling me to the emergency room, and right away they start cutting my clothes, which is standard procedure, of course, because you're in an emergency situation and they don't have much time. I had on a jogging suit and a full-length leather coat that my wife had given me for Christmas, and when I realized what they were doing—I guess the Brownsville was still in me—in the midst of my pain and delirium I made them stop and hauled myself off the gurney and took my coat off. I had always wanted a leather coat and was not going to let them cut it under any circumstances. The doctors and nurses and I all had a good laugh about that later, and they teased me about it quite a bit.

After they got me back down, they took X rays and all that, and they realized that blood was filling my lungs. The wound was more than three inches deep, very close to my heart, and they decided to operate immediately and drain the lungs. I have a significant scar on my chest from the draining, and another from the stab wound, and every morning when I'm shaving and shuffling around, I look at those actual, real scars on my body from racism—which is academic and theoretical to most people—and I think about Howard Beach and Bensonhurst and what we've been through. People always accuse me of preaching hate, but I see it every morning in the mirror, and will continue to see it every morning as long as I live. . . .

BARI-ELLEN ROBERTS

From *Roberts vs. Texaco*

❦

HARRISON, NEW JERSEY, 1990

DECEMBER 17, 1990: MY FIRST DAY ON the Texaco payroll. I got up early after a sleepless night punctuated by alternating bouts of anxiety and anticipation. Office hours at Texaco began at 7:30 A.M. and I wanted to be there even earlier. I checked my appearance in the car's rearview mirror before pulling out of the driveway: dark blue business suit, single string of pearls, straightened, shoulder-length hair arranged in a conservative flip, the perfect invisible corporate uniform.

The drive to Texaco's headquarters in Harrison took exactly seventeen minutes. I drove past the unobtrusive Texaco sign, flashed my brand-new ID card at the guard and proceeded down the long curving driveway to the parking lot entrance at the rear of the building. The Texaco building was a blocky, three-story white stone monolith the size of three football fields, its blank immensity accentuated by the big artificial lake and exquisite landscaping that softened the rolling hills on the one-hundred-acre campus even in the bleak early morning. I had been here many times in the past, but this morning I looked at the building with new eyes. After nearly two decades of experience in corporate America, I was keenly aware of the nonverbal statements big companies send to their workers and customers through the design of their corporate buildings. In my heightened emotional state, this vast and inscrutable edifice struck me as a monument to a corporate colossus obsessed with its power and staggering wealth. It was blunt, expensive, and totally impersonal. It gave me the creeps.

Inside, I was soon to learn, was a corporate Calcutta, organized along caste lines as rigid and implacable as those of traditional Hindu society. The first division between Texaco's Brahmins and the lower castes came at a crossroads leading into the cavernous underground parking facility. Turn right, and you entered the regular lot, where thousands of workers parked their cars, then walked to elevators that rose to their floor. Turn left, and you came to a forbidding garage door that could only be opened with an electronic pass. This was the reserved parking area for a tiny elite of no more than fifteen or twenty top managers and members of the board of directors, complete with its own guarded entrance and private elevators that rose to the exalted Mahogany Suite on the third floor. It was a big change from what I was used to at Chase, where even David Rockefeller used the same entrance and rode the same crowded elevators as everyone else without complaint. At Texaco, the pecking order was evidently so inflexible that it even determined which elevator you rode on.

But maybe I'm reading too much into this, I thought as I made my way to Shelby's office in the finance department. He was in an expansive mood, but got straight down to business. "Let me introduce you to the rest of the team." He led me to a conference room where about a dozen people were waiting. Among them were two assistant managers of the pension and benefits division in the finance department where I would be working, John Dowling and Sigfrid Ciomek.

"This is Bari-Ellen Lewis, whom some of you already know," Shelby began, using the married name I was still known by at the time. "She's our new senior financial analyst and she's going to be overseeing our relationship with Chase Manhattan, working with the actuaries on forecasting, and serving on a task force on banking reform and how Texaco should manage all of its banking relationships. I'd like to officially welcome her aboard."

My new coworkers looked like they were in shock.

It turned out that Shelby had not told them until the close of business on the previous Friday that I would be joining their team. Though I had accepted Texaco's offer weeks before, he had given this close-knit, all-white group no time at all to prepare for the arrival of the first black woman to hold a professional position in Texaco's finance department. They'd not even been given an opportunity to ask such fundamental questions as what my duties would be. To me, the lack of preparation for my arrival was a serious mistake. Even in the 1990s, most white folks who hadn't worked with blacks needed some time to adjust to the idea. Having a black person among their peers—and a black woman at that—had evidently unnerved them.

After a brief exchange of pleasantries, Shelby turned me over to Sigfrid, who was going to be my direct supervisor. She was a small, fiftyish woman who still spoke in the accent of her native Norway. I had known Sigfrid for a while and admired her because she was one of the few women to have worked her way up into the virtually all-male ranks of Texaco management. In fact, I had even thought of her as a potential mentor. But as she led me to my new office, Sigfrid seemed fidgety and distracted. She was obviously uncomfortable.

"Gosh, Bari, I can't believe you're here and that you will be working under my supervision," she said as we walked along. "I mean, you've been a vice president at Chase, managing your own team, managing accounts worth billions of dollars. Gosh, under different circumstances, things could be the other way around: you would probably be managing me!" . . .

As she talked, I was startled by the sight of an odd machine that looked like a small refrigerator on wheels rolling silently down the corridor outside my office. "Oh, that's the robot mail cart," Sigfrid explained. "It's very efficient."

That's not the only robot working here, I thought, but didn't say it. I was in the early throes of a case of corporate culture shock.

It wasn't just the size of the building, or Sigfrid's obsession with what I regarded as meaningless perks. As I looked out into the corridor I could see only three other blacks—Brian Lewis, a junior analyst, and two female secretaries. There weren't many more among the scores of people Sigfrid introduced me to that morning as we went from division to division in the sprawling finance department. Texaco was the whitest place I had been in since lab school in Cincinnati. The hostile stares I evoked from many of my new white colleagues made it clear that they weren't prepared to accept me. It was as though I were a virus that had invaded Texaco's bloodstream and the corporate antibodies had to attack it. My mere presence was an offense against the nature of things.

For example, in the trading room, I was introduced to Silvanus Chambers, a cheerful extrovert who had been the highest ranking black in the finance department until my arrival. As we chatted, a sarcastic voice emanated from the other side of the trading room.

"Well, they say she was a vice president at Chase Manhattan's master trust department, but I never even heard of a master trust. What the heck is that?"

"Master what?" somebody else said, sounding like a school kid making a crude double entendre. There were a few muffled snickers.

I flinched and so did Sil, but Sigfrid did not seem to notice. This was like the hazing my sixth grade class had endured at that all-white elementary school in Cincinnati, and it called for the same dignified response. Like my teacher Mr. Gaston, I ignored the taunt, told Sil that I was glad to have met him, and resumed my tour with Sigfrid.

The reception was even frostier in the banking department, where a band of good old boys from the back room made no effort to conceal their contempt. They did not stand up to greet me or shake my hand. One of them actually got up and began to question me aggressively about my credentials. I kept my tone cordial as I ticked off some of the highlights of my résumé, including my experience managing accounts worth more than $11 billion at the time I left Chase. That seemed to silence him.

The worst was yet to come. As Sigrid escorted me to the office of Robert Ulrich, the deputy treasurer and second in command of the finance department, she admonished me about another aspect of the bizarre caste structure at Texaco. At this company, no employee could call on an executive who ranked two grades or higher above him or her unless accompanied by his or her direct supervisor. Since I was starting at level sixteen, that meant that any time I wanted to consult with someone grade eighteen or more—for instance, Shelby, the head of our department—Sigfrid had to come along. After my long years at Chase, where staff members had unceremoniously called on whomever they needed to see, regardless of rank, this regimented and inflexible rule struck me as archaic and insulting, almost like being in kindergarten. I couldn't imagine how it had survived into the 1990s.

I later came to realize that Bob Ulrich was a bitter man. Though he was a decade or so older and had been on the job longer, he had been passed over for the influential treasurer's job that had been given to David Crikelair. My first day at Texaco, he dove right into a belligerent, detailed grilling about my résumé, apparently trying to prove I had lied about my previous experiences to get the job. I was taken aback by his aggressiveness, but managed to answer every one of his probing queries as straightforwardly as I could. At the end of the interrogation, Ulrich grunted something unintelligible and waved me and Sigfrid out of his office.

I hadn't even had my lunch break yet and I felt as though I was being treated like a monkey in a cage.

After lunch, as I sat in my new office trying to collect my thoughts, someone knocked loudly on my door. Before I could say "come in," the door burst open and in strode a small, energetic black woman with her hand thrust out in greeting and the biggest and most genuine smile I had seen all day lighting up her pretty face.

"Hi, hi, hi, Bari," the human tornado prattled machine-gun style, as she breezed into my office. "I'm Florence Prawl, from human resources. Call me Flo, girlfriend. I knew you were coming and I want to welcome you to Texaco. If there's *anything* I can do to help you get settled, just let me know and it *will* be done! Do you need *anything*? Are they treating you right? What do you think of us?"

She hadn't been in my office for thirty seconds, but we had already clicked.

Florence walked over to my desk and lowered her voice to a conspiratorial whisper: "Girlfriend, we've got to talk. But we can't do it here. There are some things you need to know."

. . .

Florence and I didn't get a chance to speak candidly for several days. By then, word had spread throughout the company that a black woman was sitting in a two-pane office in the finance department, and people from all over the building were actually going out of their way to see this strange alien being for themselves. A steady stream of gawkers from other departments paraded along the corridor, trying to appear nonchalant as they gazed into my office. . . .

ANITA HILL

From *Speaking Truth to Power*

S

WASHINGTON, D.C., 1991

THE ACCUSATION THAT AFRICAN AMERICAN WOMEN bring
. . . down men is one that typically cuts deep to the quick of those
accused of such behavior. It was a clever and calculated use of the politics of
the African American community and our sensitivity to racism. The idea that I
was a woman used by liberal whites and in particular feminists to bring down
Clarence Thomas certainly had that very visceral effect upon community members.

The extreme to which this may be carried was tragically demonstrated in
the Mike Tyson rape trial. Desiree Washington, the eighteen-year-old black
beauty pageant contestant who accused Tyson of raping her in his hotel room,
hit the barrier of community politics late in 1991 when she made her claim.
Despite the fact that she, too, is African American, the community, led by a
group of ministers, threw its support to him. In his defense, even while the
facts of the incident were being discovered, they asserted that Mr. Tyson was a
victim of his own success. Accordingly, in combination with racism the Indiana
district attorney prosecuted him for rape because of his achievements and
popularity combined with his race. To believe this, Ms. Washington must be
cast as a liar or a pawn in the scheme to bring down Mike Tyson. Thus, the
community declared that the potential for racial bias in the prosecution was
more important than the possibility of sexual assault. More important, it played
into the hands of the stereotypical portrait of African American women as
untrustworthy attestants to sexual misconduct no matter who is the accused.
Unfortunately, the support Ms. Washington received from feminists hurt her in
the eyes of the community, fueling the community distrust of her claim. She

was seen as a pawn of the criminal justice system as well as the tool of white women. Since white women are the very individuals whose claims of rape, though often manipulated, lead to the lynching of black men, Ms. Washington by proxy became a party to Tyson's "lynching."

The picture of a lynching is as repugnant to the black community as any, and false rape charges have too often been the tool for advocating lynchings. Through rape some members of the white community manipulated racist fears of black sexuality. George Bush himself selected convicted rapist Willie Horton as a symbol of his tough stance on crime. And certainly, Mr. Tyson deserved the benefit of the doubt of his innocence, as does anyone accused of a criminal offense. Nevertheless, in denouncing Ms. Washington's claim as part of a conspiracy, the community played on another set of racist notions—those about the sexuality of African American women.

Race has been a determinant in the conviction rates for all crimes. Part of the present and the history against which the African American community reacts is that blacks are more likely to be convicted of rape than are whites and that for years in the South the rape of a white woman by a black man carried with it the death penalty. What the community does not react to is the fact that historically there was no criminal penalty in the South for the rape of a black woman by any man, black or white. Moreover, studies of rape today show that the likelihood of conviction in a rape trial depends more on the race of the alleged victim of the rape than on the race of the accused. The conviction is less likely to occur if the accuser is black regardless of whether the accused is black or white. Thus, there is evidence that society has bought into the stereotype of the dishonest and untrustworthy black woman more readily than it has the stereotype of the oversexed black man.

I accept that both may have been at work in Mike Tyson's conviction. The Tyson defense team played a dangerous card portraying him as a sexual aggressor whose behavior, no matter how bad, was part of a common knowledge Ms. Washington shared. Notwithstanding this obnoxious and offensive portrayal of Mike Tyson, many among the community leadership chose his perspective over hers. It was a predictable choice given the racial reality as they saw it—the reality of blackness as male and moreover as the successful male athlete role model, no matter how he treats African American women.

The same approach would be echoed by Ben Chavis in his reaction to his dismissal by the board of the NAACP. Chavis was accused of settling a sex discrimination suit that had shades of harassment with $300,000 of badly needed NAACP funds. In response, many said a woman caused his demise, and shamed the African American community for political reasons. Nevertheless, whether or not Chavis ever harassed his accuser, it was Chavis who used the money of the nation's leading civil rights organization to settle his personal claim, and ultimately it was Chavis whose behavior brought him down. In the same way it was Clarence Thomas' own behavior which led to his public scrutiny and embarrassment.

Thomas and Chavis as a pair of black men publicly accused of sex harassment certainly represent two sides of the political coin. Chavis, whose career had been in civil rights from the 1960s era of the movement, was everything Thomas had denounced politically. Yet their responses to the accusations of sexual misconduct are strikingly similar. Chavis claimed that the accusations and his resulting dismissal as director of the NAACP were motivated by those who objected to his change in the political direction of the organization. He challenged his dismissal, which was little more than suspension with pay until the matter was adjudicated in court, and sought a federal court order for his reinstatement. Chavis claimed that he had been "lynched," even "crucified." He railed against those whom he did not name who would seek to let outsiders dictate whom the organization would and would not communicate with.

Thomas, the other side of the political coin, has aligned himself with what is now called the Black Conservative and New Right Conservative movements. He openly denounced those who remained in the civil rights movements in the 1980s and 1990s as individuals who do nothing but "bitch and moan" about the inequalities in the world. When confronted with the accusations of sexual harassment, Thomas, like Chavis later, categorically denied any impropriety in his behavior. Thomas defiantly declared the proceeding a "high-tech lynching," refusing to take on the role of society's bogeyman, the sexually aggressive black male. Many commented that Thomas' use of the lynching metaphor to refer to accusations brought by a black woman was ahistorical. Yet the historical image of the lynched is so powerful that it defied the ill-fitting analogy. And one need only look to recent history to discover another irony in Thomas' defiance.

Thomas, who refused to be cast as the ominous carnal villain, was, after all, nominated by George Bush, who had taken that role to its lowest and most manipulative depths in the form of the Willie Horton political ad which used the image of the villainous black man as rapist to attack Bush's political opponent, Michael Dukakis. When it came to exploitation of racial fears, George Bush proved that he could indeed work both sides of the street. In the first instance he could exploit the racist fears held by society and in the later he could exploit the fear in society of being labeled racist. Both efforts represented brilliant and cynical rhetorical strategies and both worked.

Moreover, Thomas declared that the accusations were constructed by persons or groups who wanted to punish him for having the temerity to pursue his political agenda. In doing so he countered the response that the brutal lynchings of black men to which he referred do not stem from charges by black women. He pointed the finger at "someone who had put [me] up to this,"

perhaps "the feminists." Commentators Drs. Nathan and Julia Hare contributed to the perspective when they asserted, with no foundation at all, that I
was an instrument of white feminists—outsiders who were trying to destroy
the black community.

The willingness of African American intellectuals to embrace this theory
and point the finger at feminists as malevolent outsiders ignores a community
history as well a modern reality. It turns people like Senator Strom Thurmond, one of Judge Thomas' staunchest supporters, into community heroes,
and on no evidence, it turns people like Ms. Washington and me into traitors.
This is a product of racism that shows how deeply perverse gender bias is as
well.

If Thomas had been successful in painting such a picture, his analogy to
lynching might have made sense. Yet he named no groups or individuals who
were responsible for the accusations. There were none to be named because
none existed. He contrived the evidence to support his claim or acted on no
evidence at all, the very thing we fear from a judge. He angrily denounced the
process which called him to answer the charges, while all the time his chief
supporter, John Danforth, was manipulating it behind the scenes to assist him,
but declared that he would sooner die than give up his opportunity to serve on
the Supreme Court. In the end when Thomas was confirmed by the narrowest
of votes, he, according to the account by his friend John Danforth, felt that
"God's Will ha[d] been done."

The irony is that Thomas' philosophy of rejecting the use of racism as an
excuse was turned on its head as he used racism to escape responsibility for his
own behavior. Clearly, both Thomas and Chavis have political enemies. Anyone
who chooses to pursue the kinds of careers chosen by the two will undoubtedly
make political enemies in the process. Clearly, both Thomas' and Chavis'
enemies objected to positions each had taken. Some had done so on the record,
others off the record. Nevertheless, these enemies should not be used as the
scapegoats for gender subordination and illegal behavior engaged in by individuals.

In my effort to reconnect with the African American community I sought a
different community than the one that rejected the significance of the experience of half its population. I wanted a community that would look at gender
oppression as seriously as it looked for the political enemies behind a conspiracy to bring down a good man. I was not prepared to accept the fact that I
could not have such a community. Within the African American community
the discussion about gender-based exclusion and subordination is long overdue.
Reactions to charges of sexual impropriety such as those of Thomas and Chavis
threaten to postpone discussions of the subject indefinitely. Professor Emma
Coleman Jordan recognizes a "maxim of African-American participation in

public commentary: Never air your dirty linen in public." Its violation carries with it a heavy penalty—a community shunning.

I searched for others who sought the same. I found several outspoken women who have shared their concerns about sexism in the community. Elaine Brown came very close to violating the maxim when she discussed the misogyny and gender bias prominent in the Black Panther Party of the 1960s and 1970s. Dr. Billy Avery has long spoken against the abuse of black women in their home, starting her campaign against this abuse in the black church. Myrlie Evers, for years a member of the NAACP national board, later its president, has spoken to the issue and urged the organization to address sexism within it. I once engaged in a discussion of gender inequity with some local leadership in an African Canadian community. The discussion was enlightening, lively, and compelling but drenched in pain. Example followed example. Earnest attempts to understand followed pained recollection. The Canadians made most of the contributions; I sat listening and intrigued. At the end one woman in the group told me that this was the first time that they had an open forum to discuss their feelings with the men in their community. They announced it as if they were describing breathing air into a portion of their lungs previously unused. I can only hope that the dialogue has continued.

One discussion does not a revolution or revelation make. The powerful charges of bringing down good men and bringing shame to the community go a long way to silence those who speak out. African American women are thus forced into a position of choosing between race and gender. When forced, we are likely to identify with race. Consequently, except for individual efforts the problems get little attention and no community discussion. Once we give up for political reasons the right to claim gender bias; the male perspective, whether right or wrong, becomes the black community perspective.

Consequently, all claims of bias and oppression lose some of their validity inside and outside the community. By raising questions of racism, Thomas and his supporters capitalized on this reality, counting on the community supporting a black man over a black woman. Thomas himself had counted on it when he used the "welfare queen" image of his sister to gain political points with the conservatives back in 1981. Ten years later the Republican senators and even David Brock could count on the community identifying with Thomas, notwithstanding their own use of racially laden stereotypes of black women, to support their charges of racism.

I could not ignore these messages and the polls. I felt their sting. I read behind their open insult every plausible negative insinuation. Yet I longed for the community that was mine before partisanship and the politics of race and gender took it away from me. . . .

On October 10, 1991, as I prepared for my testimony, I spoke to my lawyers about my fear of this very rejection. "Whatever happens," I told them, "I do not want to destroy my ties with the community." I warned that the claim might be used to divide the community. Nevertheless, when I needed it most, it was not there. Nothing could have prepared me for the pain of what the rejection meant. Yet I could not bring myself to abandon it. . . .

GARY FRANKS

From *Searching for the Promised Land*

WASHINGTON, D.C., 1993

YOU SPOKE OUT OF ORDER," CHAIRMAN MFUME scolded me even before the caucus had reassembled for lunch.

"I asked to speak before going to the White House and you didn't answer," I reminded him. "I just assumed that, time permitting, I could make my comments to the president."

None of this soothed the nerves of caucus members. Mfume stared at me in silence.

"I think we should do what I felt should have been done a long time ago," Mel Reynolds stated matter-of-factly as the members settled into their chairs. "It's very clear, Gary, that we are not pleased with you. We do not feel comfortable with you in our presence and, quite frankly, you may not feel comfortable in our presence either. There are major differences between us. I personally believe it's time for a parting of the ways."

Louis Stokes, a senior member from Ohio, interrupted and warned Reynolds, "Before you say that, I think we should have a little dialogue on what we're getting ready to do because I think that this represents a significant step. We've never done anything like this before."

Eva Clayton of North Carolina added, "I'd like to hear from some of the more senior members on this subject."

I sat there listening as the members went back and forth over what they were prepared to do. I was seated between Floyd Flake of New York and Bobby Rush of Illinois, two of the more decent members who had always treated me with respect. They both looked very uncomfortable. Slowly it dawned on me that everyone was preparing to expel me this very afternoon.

After a few more people made points, Charles Rangel, the veteran from New York, spoke up. "We are about to make Mr. Franks much bigger than he is today," he warned. "We are going to make him into a martyr. You newer members may not realize it, but he's going to be much more famous outside the caucus than he ever was in it." You could hear a pin drop.

Louis Stokes turned to me. "Gary, I want to hear from you on this. Why do you want to be in this organization? You don't seem to fit our philosophical perspective."

"It's ironic to me," I began, "that the person who is making the motion to expel me here is somebody whom I've known since I was nineteen years old. I helped recruit Mel Reynolds to Yale University. I was asked by the basketball coach to take him in for the weekend and sell him on the school. Apparently I did a good job. I helped give him the opportunity to get a great education and you're the one leading the move to treat me in this manner." Reynolds refused to meet my gaze.

I began to get rather emotional. "During all my years as a college student I admired the Black Caucus. I still admire it. It has truly served as a conscience for this country. I may differ with you on many issues, but I don't think being different is wrong or bad. I have the same goals as you do, to improve the lives of African Americans and Americans in general. Yes, we differ on how to get there. But that doesn't make either of us any less desirous of reaching those goals."

Mfume went around the room asking each member to comment. Each one had a favorite Gary Franks story. They rehearsed things I had said on the floor of the House, votes I had cast, off-the-cuff comments I had made. When I tried to respond, Mfume cut me off. "You've already had your chance to talk," he snapped. On and on they went. I had consistently voted against the interests of the poor in general and African Americans in particular. They found my position on the Voting Rights Act indefensible. It went on endlessly.

Finally, I was given the opportunity to say a few more words. I replied to Eleanor Holmes Norton's charges that I never supported her legislative agenda.

"Eleanor, I've supported you on many issues, as you well know. I've been one of the strongest supporters in the Republican Party on District of Columbia funding." Looking at Louis Stokes, I said, "Lou, I can point to a number of votes on which you and I have agreed on things." (I had supported him on Veterans Administration, HUD, Department of Labor, and Health and Human Services appropriations bills.)

The others protested once again. The meeting dragged on and on. Eventually I left for a vote in the House chamber.

Late that afternoon, I ran into Kenneth Cooper of the *Washington Post* in the Speaker's press area just behind the House rostrum. "What's your response to the action the Black Caucus took against you today?" he asked.

"I have no idea what happened," I said.

After I left, he informed me, they had tabled Mel Reynolds's motion to expel me but had passed a motion by Alcee Hastings requiring me to leave each session after the thirty-minute lunch. Rather than having to vote on my departure at every meeting, it would become the rule.

"As long as I'm still a member of Congress, they'll be hearing from me," I told Cooper.

At our next meeting, Chairman Mfume began by announcing that every Wednesday the noon meeting would adjourn at 12:30 sharp. At that point, Mfume would turn the gavel over to CBC Vice Chairman Cardiss Collins (D-Ill.), who would preside over a meeting of the Democratic Congressional Black Caucus. When the DCBC dissolved, the gavel would return to Mfume and I would be allowed to return.

As the clock ticked closer to 12:30 P.M., I was still eating my lunch. Charles Rangel smiled and said, "Let him have his pie and ice cream before he leaves." Everyone chuckled.

"I bet he doesn't have chocolate ice cream on top of his apple pie," chortled Brooklyn's Major Owens. The laughter grew louder.

"I'll pass on both," I said and quickly departed. Outside a couple of reporters and a TV camera crew were waiting for me to emerge.

"What happened?" Alan McConagha of the *Washington Times* asked me.

"They told me to have my lunch and leave."

"What did you have for lunch?" he asked.

"Chicken."

"They told you to have your chicken and leave?"

"They told me to have my chicken and leave."

It had a nice ring to it. The quote appeared in several newspapers. . . .

The *Wall Street Journal* published three editorials supporting me. One chided the Black Caucus for treating me as "³/₅ of a member," a reference to the constitutional compromise that counted slaves as "three-fifths of all other Persons." The publicity could not have come at a worse time for them. The Congressional Black Caucus Foundation, the CBC's nonprofit educational organization, was preparing for its annual fund-raising dinner at which it regularly solicits millions of dollars from the business community. As a result of my ouster, many contributors were threatening to reduce their donations.

Money troubles aside, Charles Rangel's prediction was ringing loud and clear. Expelling me had given me much greater public attention than I had ever received while sitting in the caucus's meetings. A few days later, Mfume called my office. "Look, we've got to get this worked out," he said. "I don't know why these newer members have such a problem with you. The senior members may disagree with you, but we have no problem with you attending our meetings. I think these newer members now realize they have made a mistake. I hear you're preparing a lawsuit."

In fact, I was. "I've obtained a copy of the charter," I told him. "It says specifically that the CBC is a *bi*-partisan organization. There is no reference to anything called the Democratic Congressional Black Caucus. I think I've got a good case against you."

"Well, look, let's get this thing behind us," said Mfume. "What do we have to do?" . . .

I jotted down a few comments that captured my feelings about the issue. I also prepared a few words for Representative Mfume to tell the press. In a few moments, they were being faxed to his office in the Rayburn Building.

In order to hold a conference in the House Radio and TV Gallery, you must be sponsored by a broadcast media organization. I wanted the news conference to happen right away, so I called Phyllis Crockett of National Public Radio. Although NPR's slant is strictly liberal, Crockett had recently interviewed me and I thought she might be willing to help. Sure enough, she came through, and before you knew it, we were set for the next day.

Mfume was stunned that we were able to arrange a press conference so quickly. As Rick Genua said, he looked as if he were being led to the slaughter. I can't say I envied him. He was further startled by the crowd of journalists who showed up, especially since he had done nothing to arrange the gathering.

Before the glare of TV lights and the gallery's one microphone, Mfume promised that there would be no more Democrats-only meetings and that there would be no more overlap and confusion between the Congressional Black Caucus and the Democratic Congressional Black Caucus—not that such a thing existed anyway. Meetings would no longer be adjourned into "Democrats only" conferences and the Democrats could no longer use CBC facilities without paying. The Black Caucus would again become bipartisan. "Can the Congressional Black Caucus accommodate diversity and plurality?" Mfume concluded. "It must. And as long as I am chairman, it will." A reporter asked Mfume if the CBC had agreed to reverse itself because it feared losing money at the CBC Foundation dinner. He quickly brushed her suggestion aside.

My remarks were simple. "All I am asking is for a chance to have my views heard," I said. . . .

The African American community has grown best when we have had a variety of voices. We had the H. Rap Browns, the Stokely Carmichaels, the Black Panthers, the Nation of Islam, but we also had voices of moderation—the NAACP, the Urban League, the A. Philip Randolphs, the Roy Wilkinses, and even Dr. Martin Luther King. From the day Martin Luther King was shot until the nomination of Clarence Thomas, the country never heard one black leader criticize another black leader for offering a different approach to social issues.

This is suicidal. It opens us to the charge that all blacks think alike. By ostracizing people who express different ideas and branding them as "Uncle Toms," the black leadership creates a uniformity that makes us very vulnerable. It is an echo chamber that is void of ideas. There is no positive movement and very few tangible results.

By accepting me back, the Black Caucus renewed its bipartisan nature. When the political winds shifted and the Republicans gained control of both the House and Senate in 1994, black Republicans became important again. In fact, for a couple of meetings, I do not think that they started until I arrived (only a joke). At my encouragement, the caucus system itself was also revised so that taxpayers would no longer have to support the Black Caucus's annual budget of two hundred thousand dollars. Yet even as the Republicans have seized the agenda, the voices of the black members have remained spirited and relevant.

JAMES McBRIDE

From *The Color of Water*

❧

TRENTON, NEW JERSEY, 1993

DOCTORS FOUND SQUAMOUS CELL CANCER in a small
. . . mole they removed from Ma's face, a condition caused by too
much exposure to the sun. Ironically, it's a condition that affects mostly white
people. To the very end, Mommy is a flying compilation of competing interests
and conflicts, a black woman in white skin, with black children and a white
woman's physical problem. Fortunately the doctors got the mole off in time,
but the question of her own mortality is one she seems to be preoccupied with
of late, probably because she knows death is the one condition in life she can't
outrun. "Death is strange, isn't it?" she wonders. "It's so final. You know
time is not promised," she says, wagging a finger. "That's why you better get
to know Jesus."

If it takes as long to know Jesus as it took to know you, I think, *I'm in trouble.* It
took many years to find out who she was, partly because I never knew who I
was. It wasn't so much a question of searching for myself as it was my own
decision not to look. As a boy I was confused about issues of race but did not
consider myself deprived or unhappy. As a young man I had no time or money
or inclination to look beyond my own poverty to discover what identity was.
Once I got out of high school and found that I wasn't in jail, I thought I was in
the clear. Oberlin College was gravy—all you could eat and no one telling you
what to do and your own job to boot if you wanted one. Yet I laughed bitterly
at the white kids in ragged jeans who frolicked on the campus lawn tossing
Frisbees and went about campus caroling in German at Christmas. They
seemed free in ways I could not be. Most of my friends and the women I dated
were black, yet as time passed I developed relationships with white students as

well, two of whom—Leander Bien and Laurie Weisman—are close friends of mine today. During the rare, inopportune social moments when I found myself squeezed between black and white, I fled to the black side, just as my mother had done, and did not emerge unless driven out by smoke and fire. Being mixed is like that tingling feeling you have in your nose just before you sneeze—you're waiting for it to happen but it never does. Given my black face and upbringing it was easy for me to flee into the anonymity of blackness, yet I felt frustrated to live in a world that considers the color of your face an immediate political statement whether you like it or not. It took years before I began to accept the fact that the nebulous "white man's world" wasn't as free as it looked; that class, luck, religion all factored in as well; that many white individuals' problems surpassed my own, often by a lot; that all Jews are not like my grandfather and that part of me is Jewish too. Yet the color boundary in my mind was and still is the greatest hurdle. In order to clear it, my solution was to stay away from it and fly solo.

I ran for as long as I could. After I graduated from Oberlin College in 1979 and received my master's degree in journalism from Columbia University in 1980, I began a process of vacillating between music and writing that would take eight years to complete before I realized I could work successfully as a writer *and* musician. I quit every journalism job I ever had. I worked at the *Wilmington News Journal* and quit. The *Boston Globe*. Quit. *People* magazine, *Us* magazine, the *Washington Post*. Quit them all. This was before the age of thirty. I must've had some modicum of talent, because I kept getting hired, but I wore my shirt and tie like an imposter. I wandered around the cities by day, stumbling into the newsroom at night, exhausted, to write my stories. I loved an empty city room, just the blinking terminals and a few deadbeats like myself. It was the only time I could write, away from white reporters, black reporters, away from the synergy of black and white that was already simmering inside my soul, ready to burst out at the most inopportune moments. Being caught between black and white as a working adult was far more unpleasant than when I was a college student. I watched as the worlds of blacks and whites smashed together in newsrooms and threw off chunks of human carnage that landed at my feet. I'd hear black reporters speaking angrily about a sympathetic white editor and I'd disagree in silence. White men ruled the kingdom, sometimes ruthlessly, finding clever ways to gut the careers of fine black reporters who came into the business full of piss and vinegar, yet other white men were mere pawns like myself. Most of my immediate editors were white women, whom I found in general to be the most compassionate, humane, and often brightest in the newsroom, yet they rarely rose to the top—even when compared to their more conservative black male counterparts, some of whom marched around the newsroom as if they were the second coming of Martin Luther King, wielding their race like baseball bats. They were no closer to the black man in the ghetto than were their white counterparts. They spoke of their days of "growing up in Mississippi" or wherever it was, as proof of their knowledge of poverty and blackness, but in fact the closest most of them had come to an urban ghetto in twenty years was from behind the wheel of a locked Honda. Their claims of growing up poor were without merit in my mind. They grew up privileged, not deprived, because they had mothers, fathers, grandparents, neighbors, church, family, a system that protected, sheltered, and raised them. They did not grow up like the children of the eighties and nineties, stripped of any semblance of family other than the constant presence of drugs and violence. Their "I was raised with nuthin' and went to Harvard anyway" experience was the criterion that white editors used to hire them. But then again, that was partly how I got through too. The whole business made me want to scream.

I had no true personal life in those years. Few dates, few dinners, no power lunches. My college sweetheart, a mixed-race woman from Hyde Park, Chicago—her mother was black and her father Jewish—was the apple of my eye, but I was afraid of commitment then, afraid to have children because I didn't want them to be like me. I drifted away from her and let time and distance do the rest. Since I had no personal life outside of journalism other than music, I soared as a reporter, but I always parachuted out in the end, telling my white editors after a year or two that I had to leave to "find myself, write a book, play my sax," whatever the excuse was. Most black folks considered "finding myself" a luxury. White people seemed to think of it as a necessity—most white people that is, except for that all-important one.

Each time I quit a job, Mommy would do a war dance, complete with chants and dancing, usually beginning with, "Now what are you gonna do!? You had a second chance and you threw it out the window! You need a job!" Like most mothers, she wielded tremendous power and my staunch resolve would crumble like a sandcastle before her frontal assaults, which were like tidal waves. I'd stave her off and back out of her house, saying, "Don't worry, Ma. Don't worry," disappearing into the underworld labyrinth of the New York music scene for months, playing sax with this or that band, selling a piece of music here and there. I was always moderately successful, and later in life much more so, winning the Stephen Sondheim Award for musical theater composition, working with Anita Baker, Grover Washington, Jr., Jimmy Scott, Rachelle Ferrell, and many others, but the eighties were hard times for me as a composer, and each time I hit a dry spell I'd scurry back into journalism—until February 1988, when I was working for the *Washington Post* Style section and thinking of quitting to go back to music in New York. The *Post* Style section is the top of the line, the elite, the haute cuisine, the green, green grass of heaven for newspaper feature writers, and quitting there is not something you do lightly, not even for a seasoned quitter like me. As I pondered it, Ma called me out of the blue, smelling trouble. "I know you!" she snapped. "You're getting steady money now. And a lot of it. *Don't quit that job!*"

But I did quit, partly because I got tired of running, and partly because the little ache I had known as a boy was no longer a little ache when I reached thirty. It was a giant, roaring, musical riff, screaming through my soul like a distorted rock guitar with the sound turned all the way up, telling me, *Get on with your life:* Play sax, write books, compose music, do something, express yourself, who the hell are you anyway? There were two worlds bursting inside me trying to get out. I *had* to find out more about who I was, and in order to find out who I was, I had to find out who my mother was.

It was a devastating realization, coming to grips with the fact that all your life you had never really known the person you loved the most. Even as a young boy I was used to Mommy hiding her past, and I grew to accept it, and the details of her past got lost as my own life moved forward, which is probably how she wanted it anyway. I never even seriously broached the subject with her until 1977, when I was in college and had to fill out a form that for some reason or other required Ma's maiden name. I called her long-distance, in Philadelphia, to find out, and she was suddenly evasive. "What do you need that for?" she asked. "How come?" She hemmed and hawed awhile longer before finally coming out with it. "Shilsky," she said.

"Can you spell that, Ma?"

"Who's paying for this call? Am I paying for it? Did you call me collect?"

"No."

"You're in college," she snapped. "You can spell. Figure it out yourself." *Click.*

The subject was not broached again until I met Al Larkin, then *Sunday Magazine* editor at the *Boston Globe* in early 1982. Al talked me into writing a Mother's Day piece, which the *Philadelphia Inquirer* was kind enough to run simultaneously, since Ma was living in Philly at the time. The public response to the piece was so overwhelming I decided to delve further, partly to get out of working for a living and partly to expel some of my own demons regarding my brown skin, curly hair, and divided soul. I asked Mommy if she would be interested in doing a book and she said no. I told her it could make me a million bucks. She said, "Okay. If you're rich, I'm rich. Just don't quit your job." So I took a leave of absence from the *Boston Globe* in 1982 and *then* quit. "That was one of the stupidest things you've ever done," she snorted, when I announced I had quit.

MUMIA ABU-JAMAL

From *Live from Death Row*

PENNSYLVANIA, 1994

DON'T TELL ME ABOUT THE VALLEY OF the shadow of death. I live there. In south-central Pennsylvania's Huntingdon County, a one-hundred-year-old prison stands, its Gothic towers projecting an air of foreboding, evoking a gloomy mood of the Dark Ages. I and some seventy-eight other men spend about twenty-two hours a day in six- by ten-foot cells. The additional two hours may be spent outdoors, in a chain-link-fenced box, ringed by concertina razor wire, under the gaze of gun turrets.

Welcome to Pennsylvania's death row.

I'm a bit stunned. Several years ago the Pennsylvania Supreme Court affirmed my conviction and sentence of death, by a vote of four justices (three did not participate). As a black journalist who was a Black Panther way back in my yon teens, I've often studied America's long history of legal lynchings of Africans. I remember a front page of the *Black Panther* newspaper, bearing the quote "A black man has no rights that a white man is bound to respect," attributed to U.S. Supreme Court chief justice Roger Taney, of the infamous *Dred Scott* case, where America's highest court held that neither Africans nor their "free" descendants are entitled to the rights of the Constitution. Deep, huh? It's true.

Perhaps I'm naive, maybe I'm just stupid—but I thought the law would be followed in my case, and the conviction reversed. Really.

Even in the face of the brutal Philadelphia MOVE massacre of May 13, 1985, that led to Ramona Africa's frame-up, Eleanor Bumpurs, Michael Stewart, Clement Lloyd, Allan Blanchard, and countless other police slaughters of blacks from New York to Miami, with impunity, my faith remained. Even in the face of this relentless wave of antiblack state terror, *I thought my appeals would be successful.* I still harbored a belief in U.S. law, and the realization that my appeal had been denied was a shocker. I could understand intellectually that American courts are reservoirs of racist sentiment and have historically been hostile to black defendants, but a lifetime of propaganda about American "justice" is hard to shrug off.

I need but look across the nation, where, as of December 1994, blacks constituted some 40 percent of men on death row, or across Pennsylvania, where, as of December 1994, 111 of 184 men on death row—over 60%—are black, to see the truth, a truth hidden under black robes and promises of equal rights. Blacks constitute just over 9 percent of Pennsylvania's population and just under 11 percent of America's.

As I said, it's hard to shrug off, but maybe we can do it together. How? Try out this quote I saw in a 1982 law book, by a prominent Philadelphia lawyer named David Kairys: "Law is simply politics by other means." Such a line goes far to explain how courts really function, whether today, or 138 years ago in the *Scott* case. It ain't about "law," it's about "politics" by "other means." Now, ain't that the truth?

I continue to fight against this unjust sentence and conviction. Perhaps we can shrug off and shred some of the dangerous myths laid on our minds like a second skin—such as the "right" to a fair and impartial jury of our peers; the "right" to represent oneself; the "right" to a fair trial, even. They're *not* rights—they're privileges of the powerful and rich. For the powerless and the poor, they are chimera that vanish once one reaches out to claim them as something real or substantial. Don't expect the media networks to tell you, for they can't, because of the incestuousness between the media and the government, and big business, which they both serve.

I can.

Even if I must do so from the valley of the shadow of death, I will.

From death row, this is Mumia Abu-Jamal.

December 1994

KEVIN POWELL

From *Keepin' It Real*

§

WASHINGTON, D.C., 1995

WHEN I THINK BACK ON IT NOW, it was what I perceived
. . . to be the lack of a safe existence that led me to the Million Man
March on October 16, 1995. As I've said elsewhere, both publicly and privately, I had major problems with the leadership and the organization and much
of the archaic language surrounding the March. I mean, damn, it's 1997, and
things are mad hectic for male and female alike, so why would I want my
girlfriend or my wife to stay at home and take care of the children or prepare
my meals (as some not-so-bright "leaders" suggested either directly or indirectly) while I'm off saving the community? When in the history of African
Americans has that arrangement ever existed? And what kind of man would I
be for attempting to bring that arrangement into existence? However, I also
knew that such a gathering of black men might never occur again, at least not
in my lifetime. So I hopped an Amtrak and was on my way. Moreover, something, some spiritual force, was pulling me toward Washington, D.C., and I
knew that I could not ignore *that*.

On the nippy, overcast morning of the March, I arose from my hotel bed
and I felt, well, different. I wasn't going to work. I wasn't going to a church or
a mosque. Nor was I going to play basketball or to shake my ass at a club. I was
going to march—literally—to the Capitol to be with other black men, young
and old, rich and poor, from all over the country. And, I cannot lie, the whole
thing felt so surreal, so *un*real, to me. Nothing in my life had prepared me for
this: For the first time that I could recall, I didn't feel any pressure. No anger,
no fear, no pending humiliation. I just felt free. As I made my way outside to
the front of the hotel and spoke to other black men, complete strangers, and

they spoke to me, my eyes couldn't help but tear at the thought that there would be, for one day at least, some semblance of peace—and hope—engulfing people who looked like me. I walked down a long street—I can't remember which street it was—and solidly on both sides there were throngs of black men walking, marching, to the Million Man March. Seeing these men was, in a word, incredible: light-skinned, brown-skinned, dark-skinned. Fades, afros, jheri curls, baldies, and braids. Short, tall, skinny, fat. Southerners, northerners, West Indians, Africans born in Africa. Blue-collar, white-collar, students, and homeless. Muslims, Christians, Jews, Rastafarians, and atheists. Nationalists, Pan-Africanists, separatists, integrationists, reformists, pragmatists, and revolutionaries, straight, gay, and bisexual. Men, black men, whose stories overlapped with mine, and men, black men, whose stories were completely different from my own.

My pace picked up as the other men's pace accelerated. In fact, I wanted to run, because this walk was too slow for me—and too unbelievable. Black men—lots of black men!—marching down a major street in a major city with the police and the bystanders, black and white, male and female, simply watching. Tears streamed down my face, in spite of my promise to myself that this thing was not going to faze me like that. I could not help it. And no, I didn't think this March was going to save me or protect me or liberate me in any meaningful way. How could it? It was a one-day event with no particular game plan other than the day's assemblage—and a lot of rhetoric. But, as I neared the Mall area, it struck me, as it had never done before, just how much rage and pain and confusion and fear I had been traveling with my entire life. It was (and is) a rage, a pain, a confusion, a fear that no one can possibly understand if he or she hasn't had the life experiences I, and others thrown into similar circumstances, have had. They are circumstances that many Americans will never understand, nor would ever want to understand. I'm sure that much of what I have described in this letter sounds like an outrageous lie to some, or at best a stretch, an exaggeration of the truth. But it is my truth, and the truth of many others in this great nation. And the truth is, given what I have described here, and what I've actually experienced in my life, and what I continue to absorb and feel on a daily basis, that I often find it remarkable that I have made it out of childhood into adulthood—it's a miracle that I am not dead. And we know death takes on many forms. There is the physical dying, the death of one's psyche, and, perhaps most sinister of all, there is the death of one's soul. Soul death comes from believing that there is no hope at all for a happy and peaceful existence in this world. It comes from the soul asking matter-of-factly, "What is the point of living," or worse, "When is death going to come to end this nightmare?"

Many people of various hues and persuasions have suggested to me—and I thought about this on the day of the Million Man March—that because I managed to escape the ghetto, and because I've been to college, and because I've been on a hit MTV program, and because I'm a "successful" journalist and a published author, that I have, indeed, made it. I beg to differ. The diversity of black men at the Million Man March made it abundantly clear that status or material achievements did not, and cannot, eradicate—no matter how much we dupe ourselves into believing that it does—a very basic and spiritual need to be regarded *and* treated like a human being. Worldly success cannot heal the centuries-old pain of being regarded and treated like someone's scapegoat or source of entertainment or ridicule, or, ultimately, cease being seen as a "nigga" in the most despicable meaning of the word. Worse yet is being seen as a "nigga" with an attitude and no purpose or agenda whatever. That's how I've felt, off and on, for much of my life. That no matter what I do and no matter how well I "play the game," it finally comes down to whether I am seen as I see myself. And I see myself, minus all the glitz and glamor and accolades, as a first-generation northerner. The son of a southern-born mother who never made it out of elementary school and began working in cotton fields at age eight and still, to this day, works a menial job for meager wages. I am the grandson of grandparents who were illiterate and who lived in a weather-beaten, dilapidated shack in the low country of South Carolina with five children and no steady means of income, so they often starved. I am the great-grandson of a black man who was a chef and who for a short period of time did have land and a regular income. Until he was found dead, inexplicably, in a river, with food he had prepared stuffed in his mouth. And my great-great-grandparents were slaves.

That is the legacy, the tradition, the lineage, from which I come and which thrust me into this world. It is a world that most people do not want to acknowledge or see or believe actually exists. Ever. It is a world where I have not seen my father in twenty years, and my closest relative as a boy, my cousin Anthony, and I do not speak because we are both still grappling with the nightmare of our childhood experiences.

It is a world where, as an older black woman said to me recently, black mothers are forced to raise their black sons with a mixture of fear and hope. Fear because these mothers know, as my mother knew and still knows, what awaits the black boy who dares to be too aggressive or dares to speak too loudly. And hope because these mothers believe, as mothers, black or white, have always believed, that the birth of that child is a reaffirmation of life.

It is a world in which my childhood buddies are adult time bombs, their bodies or minds or both contaminated by the poison that is ghetto life. In fact, many of them are already dead—from AIDS, from drugs, from drink, from violence. And some of them dead because there is literally nothing to do except stand on a street corner and watch their lives slowly drift toward prison or death. Is there a difference? Again, the fanatical attraction many black men in the ghetto have for death stems from the fact that many of us have spent our entire lives living in a perpetual death zone.

If nothing else, it was the quest for life instead of death that made the Million Man March special. "Show me some love!" is how some of us greeted each other, and I knew exactly where folks were coming from. Because life and love go hand in hand—you cannot have the former, at least not in a very real and meaningful way, without the latter. I felt that love as I and some of my friends I met at the March pushed our way through the mighty crowd. Whatever brought each of these men to Washington did not matter in the end. What did matter was that we were looking for answers. And confirmation. And affirmation. And we were looking for life and love and a taste of power. That power, by and large, was not lost on me when, for example, Minister Louis Farrakhan and his escorts made their way down the Capitol steps late in the day for his speech. The image of proud, confident, and immaculately dressed black men walking boldly down the steps of a building that, heretofore, had meant very little to me was extraordinary. That image represented, in a word, "power." And I wasn't the only person in my immediate area who took note of that scene. Other men acknowledged it, sketched it in their minds, confirmed it, affirmed it. And really tasted it, too.

The walk down those steps seemed to me to answer the question so many white Americans were asking: "What do black people want now?" The question wouldn't be so patronizing, so shallow, so damn annoying, if we didn't see so clearly that beneath that question lay another more menacing and unbelievable one: "Haven't we done enough for them already?" And there, truly, lies the root of the most dysfunctional relationship in America's history, the relationship between white and black. This is not to say that other races and other ethnic or religious groups haven't had their share of problems in this nation, because they have—and still do. What I am saying is that the relationship, or lack thereof, between white Americans and black Americans has been one of the deepest issues in our national schizophrenia—inextricably linked since the founding of this nation, through slavery, through its great wars, through northern migration, through the Civil Rights Movement, and through its music. After all, how can you really talk about American music without talking about the kinship—and the music produced from the kinship—between black and white people? What is the blues if not a reaction to this astonishing relationship and the perverted conditions many blacks have lived under for generations in both the North and the South? It does not matter, as some whites say to me from time to time, whether their ancestors were in bondage in Europe while slavery existed or whether they are relatively new to this country. What matters, because race *does* matter, is whether you—if you happen to be of European descent or, should we say, white—have swallowed whole the beliefs and the behavioral patterns of the people who enslaved and oppressed my people.

That is precisely why President Bill Clinton, in his second inaugural address, said, "The divide of race has been America's constant curse."

Racism means, in effect, that a comfort zone exists in this country for those people who are racist. Or who, by virtue of their silence, condone racism. Or who think tokenism or shoddy symbolic gestures have or will eliminate the plague of racism once and for all. What far too many people in white America (and it is a tragedy that we must, at this late date, still declare which America we're referring to) don't realize is that most black Americans know the difference between symbolism and substance.

What does it matter that practically every inner city in this nation has a street named after Martin Luther King, Jr., when most of the streets in most of those inner cities have few, if any, black-owned businesses? What does it matter if I or any black young person can now attend a predominantly white college or university without the threat of someone blocking the doors or spitting in my face, when I am still forced, because of the entrenched attitudes of that college or university, to exist in a racially hostile environment in the classroom, in the dorms, and even in the school cafeteria? What does it matter if 80 to 90 percent of today's professional basketball players are black when the majority of head coaches, owners, announcers, and sportswriters are not? What does it matter if rap music has created a multimillion-dollar industry if the vast majority of people who propel the culture—namely, black people—have little or no control over the decision-making and moneymaking side of the business? It all comes down to the issue of power. Far too often in America we settle for the easy answers and the ready-made symbols. But I'm sorry to say that the success of a Michael Jordan or a Bill Cosby or a Tiger Woods does not translate into real power, not the kind of power that black America wants and desperately needs. They are, as I have been at various points in my life, tokens, symbols, of possibilities—possibilities that most of the black underclass rarely get to see up close and personal. . . .

REV. BERNICE KING

From Hard Questions, Heart Answers

ATLANTA, 1996

I STAND BEFORE YOU TODAY AS ONE WHO is tremendously proud. I am proud that I share in the rich history and heritage of a people who, in spite of the odds, have risen to the task and are still moving forward. I am proud that even though people have sought to rewrite history, and even to redefine a people, the truth has prevailed, and more and more those in authority are having to face the truth. I also realize that the truth can sometimes be very painful for people who have made it their life mission to seek to bend and even destroy the truth. But it is true that "Truth stands the test of time; lies are soon exposed." (Prov. 12:19)

We are now experiencing the dawning of a new day in America. It is a day of new possibilities and new challenges for African Americans. Even though many of the battles of the past are still with us, no one can deny that we have come a long way. In 1965, the year of the Voting Rights Act, we had less than six hundred black elected officials in the entire country. Today, there are more than six thousand African American elected officials. Let me hasten to add, however, that this is still less than 2 percent of the total number of elected officials in this nation.

I am encouraged and excited because great and notable gains have been made in the political arena. We have African Americans serving as speakers in state legislatures and as state court judges. We have African Americans whose names have appeared on U.S. currency. An African American has served as governor of one of the old confederate states.

On the other hand, I am sad because the U.S. Senate has only one African American among its ranks, and it is here that major decisions governing the lives of some forty million African Americans are being made. Something is seriously wrong when this injustice can continue, and the political process does not offer any resolution. When this is coupled with the fact that many African Americans have either forgotten where they come from, or simply don't want to remember, it makes the problem even more serious.

I do not have to tell you that the Civil Rights Commission has become the Civil Wrongs Commission, and Affirmative Action has become Affirmative Distractions, and that the battle is not over. Surely, there are many African Americans who have concluded that we have arrived. My question is, arrived where? Where are we as a people? Where is our culture, our history, our legacy?

It has been said, "He who does not know history is doomed to repeat it." We as African Americans must put forth a concerted effort to know and to write our own history. No longer can the FBI and ill-intentioned journalists and out-of-touch scholars be allowed to write our history. We have the knowledge, the know-how, the resources, and we were there. But when we allow others to define who we are and describe our experience, we invite distortion and half-truth.

It is not an accident that African American history has been left out of major textbooks in America. We must do something about this, and we must not wait for someone else to do for us what we ought to be doing ourselves. For too long, our people have been left in the dark about who we are and our rich and noble history. We must tell our story to give us the boost that we so desperately need.

Our history tells us that Christopher Columbus did not discover America. Hundreds of years before Columbus, African shipbuilders and sailors had journeyed to America many times. This has been verified by the remains of African skulls and artifacts found in several states and in Mexico. Our history also conveys that Africa is the birthplace of all of humanity and that the first university in the world was in Africa—it was called the Grand Lodge of Wa'at. The saying "Man, know thyself" did not come from Plato, or Socrates, but was inscribed on the wall at the Grand Lodge of Wa'at hundreds of years before Plato. This leads to the conclusion that the Greeks studied under the Egyptians, and we must constantly remind the world that Egypt is in Africa. Our history also reminds us that the Shrine of the Black Madonna is still viewed in Russia, Spain, and Poland and is frequented by Pope John Paul II. Furthermore, our history tells us that when King Herod ordered the young male children to be killed, Joseph and Mary took Jesus to Egypt, not to Europe, because they wanted to blend in with other dark-skinned people.

I've shared these facts to point out that history has been distorted and twisted to satisfy a few people in power who have wanted to remain in power. But it is our responsibility to stay informed so that we can keep our people informed. Information means power, and power is what the power structure wants us to believe we don't have, and yet nothing could be further from the truth. We have never been a powerless people. We have taken what others have discarded and turned them into things of value. We took scraps and made quilts and tables and art. We took discarded lives, mixed them with a little tender loving care, and created the Jesse Jacksons, Harriet Tubmans, Barbara Jordans, and the Nelson Mandelas.

We must continue to empower our people with knowledge. Education is still the key to our success, but we cannot teach that which we do not know ourselves. Therefore, we must first get all the knowledge we can. We must know that ours is a great tradition. We are the sons and daughters of great kings and queens, heroes and heroines. We come from a strong tradition of respect for family and the community where we live. We are created to be molders, builders, and founders of great civilizations. African Americans had talent that established the first mathematical system known to man; talent that was reading the heavens before there was ever a telescope; talent that founded the American Red Cross; talent that built institutions of higher learning from selling sweet potato pies and peanuts; talent that even invented ice cream and the golf tee. We are more than cotton pickers and ditch diggers and carriers of water. We are scholars, philosophers, teachers, inventors, doctors, lawyers, managers, manufacturers, and scientists.

We must teach our children that we cannot afford to waste this history on fast living, pump-up tennis shoes, Starter jackets, and arrow hairdos. We must insist that our children be educated about the truth, and we must be a part of the education process. We must go beyond traditional textbooks and make sure that good books about our history and heritage are readily available. This means that all of us must be conscientious about reading and getting away from the television where the images of who we are are often confusing, to say the least.

How do you think that the system was able to get us to start killing each other? They found every isolated case of a black-on-black crime and made sure that 100,000 people saw it on television, 50,000 read about it in the paper, and 150,000 heard about it on the radio. Our young people started believing this was who we are, and soon, the cases were not isolated but the norm, and black-on-black crime became a way of life.

We must dismiss the notion that the majority press is going to portray us in a positive manner. We must face the fact that it is not in their interest to do so. They know that if the truth got out it would reveal that the majority of our women are not on welfare, the majority of our men are not behind bars, the majority of our young men do not commit murder, the majority of our people do want a job, and the majority of our people do want to be self-sufficient and independent.

They tell us that, nationally, unemployment among black men is around 12.7 percent, and that is bad. That is twice as high as the unemployment rate of whites. But this also means that 88 percent of black men are working and want to work. True enough, almost 30 percent of black families nationally live below the poverty line, and that is terrible, but it also means that 70 percent live above the poverty line. It's all a matter of the glass being half full or half empty, and the system wants us to feel half empty. But too many people have fought, bled, and died so that I would feel good about myself rather than take on a defeatist attitude. We've come too far to let a few statistics beat us down and dictate the course of our future.

It is the intent of those in the power structure to portray average African Americans as weak, lazy, violent, uneducated, complacent, apathetic, and in some cases even uncivilized. And unless those of us who have made it are able, through our own means, to show and tell the positive side of our people, we will become part of the problem rather than part of the solution.

Admittedly, though, there are those who sit on the sideline (the apathetic people), those who don't know what's going on (the uninformed and in-the-dark people), and those who get involved (the enlightened and dedicated people). It is clear that the apathetic sideliners will not advance the struggle because they think that this is the way it is and always will be. The don't-know-what-happened, uninformed people can't take us anywhere because they don't know where to start, so they believe any road will get them there. But the enlightened and dedicated people will move us forward because they see what needs to be done and they do it.

If our history teaches us anything, it is that change takes place when people realize that if the struggle is to be advanced, then they are going to have to do it. We've got to start with ourselves. We can no longer wait for "somebody else" to do for us what we should do for ourselves because "somebody else" is dead. If you don't do it, then "somebody's" first cousin, Mr. Nobody, will.

In order to reclaim our African American heritage, we need those people who are not afraid to speak the truth and show the hypocrisies. We need people who value truth and honesty and who are willing to take a risk sometimes and bite the bullet rather than kowtow to corporate leaders. We need men and women who will challenge the double standards of one rule for whites and another rule for blacks. Certainly this is not an easy task, but as Frederick Douglass, noted black liberator, reminds us, "Where there is no struggle, there can be no progress." Certainly struggle has always been a part of our history. Somebody had to pay the price for us to be where we are. Somebody bled and somebody died. Somebody spent time in jail and we must never forget this. We must teach generations after us to value who we are and what we have achieved and how we overcame, or they will be born, raised, live, and die in ignorance of who they are. We must lay down our personality differences and lock our arms together, and use our minds creatively to build a more knowledgeable African American community. In order not to repeat mistakes of the past, we must realize where we are, and then act to make life better for all God's children.

We can no longer afford to be like Christopher Columbus. He didn't know where he was going when he got started. When he got there, he didn't know where he was. And when he got back, he couldn't tell anyone where he had been. We've got to know where we are, who we are, whose we are, and where we are going.

Someone once said that he who controls our children ultimately controls us. Our children, then, are the most important investments we can make in securing our African American heritage as well as the future. It's time that we stop giving our children things and start giving them ourselves, because every day our children are crying out for our love and attention. Drugs and gangs and fashions are mere substitutes for the lack of love and attention we give to our children. If you ask children why they join gangs, most will tell you that they find more love, attention, and acceptance in gangs than they've ever received at home. But this has not always been the story in the African American community. When the traditional nuclear family failed to sustain our children, there was always the extended family to back it up. But now that society has redefined family to include the corporation to the exclusion of the nuclear and extended family, too many of our African American brothers and sisters have become so caught up in pleasing the boss and making a living that we seldom leave time to teach our children how to live. Then we have the nerve to say that something is wrong with our children. No, nothing's wrong with them. They are just looking for what any child needs—love. Something is wrong with us because we're not giving it to them.

If ever there was a time to reclaim who we truly are as African Americans, now is that time. It's time to restore our sense of family and community. It's time to recapture the minds and imaginations of our young people, which means it's time to tell the true story of our history and our heritage. We must build from our proud and noble heritage.

African Americans are a great people, and we must keep holding our heads high because in our veins flows the courage of Harriet Tubman, the perseverance of Mary McLeod Bethune, the inspiration of Booker T. Washington, the vision of W. E. B. DuBois, the military genius of Hannibal, and the unconquerable beauty of Cleopatra and Queen Nefertiti. In our veins is the creativity of Paul Robeson, the bravery of Malcolm X, the hope of Whitney Young, and the challenge of the unforgettable Roy Wilkins. Tell our children that in their veins is the compassion of Martin L. King Jr., the intellectual astuteness of Dr. George Washington Carver, the business genius of Madame C. J. Walker, the political savvy of Jesse Jackson, and, yes, the convictions of Nelson Mandela. We have a heritage to reclaim and a history to preserve.

With hope above to inspire us, faith around us to encourage us, convictions beneath us to sustain us, love within us to guide us, and with God in front of us to direct us, we will overcome.

Selected Bibliography

Andrews, William. *Six Women's Slave Narratives* (Introduction). New York: Oxford University Press, 1988.

Aptheker, Herbert. *A Documentary History of the Negro People in the United States, 1960–1968,* vol. 7. New York: Carol Publishing Group, 1994.

Austin, Allan D. *African Muslims in Antebellum America.* New York: Routledge, 1977.

Berlin, Ira and Barbara Fields, et al. (editors). *Free At Last—A Documentary History of Slavery, Freedom, and the Civil War.* New York: The New Press, 1992.

Billington, Ray Allen. *The Journal of Charlotte Forten—A Free Negro in the Slave Era.* New York: W.W. Norton & Company, 1981.

Botkin, B. A. (editor). *Lay My Burden Down—A Folk History of Slavery.* New York: Dell Publishing, 1973.

Bracey, John, August Meier, and Elliott Rudwick (editors). *Black Nationalism in America.* New York: The Bobbs-Merrill Company, 1970.

Breitman, George. *Malcolm X Speaks.* New York: Grove Weidenfeld, 1966.

Busby, Margaret (editor). *Daughters of Africa.* New York: Pantheon Books, 1992.

Carretta, Vincent (editor). *Unchained Voices—An Anthology of Black Authors in the English-Speaking World of the Eighteenth Century.* Lexington: The University of Kentucky Press, 1996.

Clarke, John Henrik (editor). *The Second Crucifixion of Nat Turner.* Baltimore: Black Classic Press, 1997.

Etter-Lewis, Gwendolyn (editor). *My Soul Is My Own—Oral Narratives of African American Women in the Professions.* New York: Routledge, 1993.

Foner, Philip S. (editor). *The Voice of Black America—Major Speeches by Negroes in the United States, 1797–1971.* New York: Simon and Schuster, 1972.

———*Paul Robeson Speaks—Writings, Speeches and Interviews, 1918–1974.* New York: Brunner/Mazel, 1978.

Franklin, John Hope. *Three Negro Classics* (Introduction). New York: Avon Books, 1965.

Garvey, Amy Jacques (editor). *The Philosophy and Opinions of Marcus Garvey.* New York: Atheneum, 1969.

Hemenway, Robert (editor). *Zora Neale Hurston—Dust Tracks on the Road, An Autobiography.* Urbana and Chicago: University of Illinois Press, 1984.

Hunton, Addie W. and Kathryn M. Johnson. *Two Colored Women with the American Expeditionary Forces.* Brooklyn: Brooklyn Eagle Press, 1920.

Lerner, Gerda. *Black Women in White America—A Documentary History.* New York: Vintage Books, 1992.

Lomax, Alan (editor). *Mister Jelly Roll—The Fortunes of Jelly Roll Morton*. New York: Pantheon Books, 1993.

McPherson, James M. *The Negro's Civil War—How American Blacks Felt and Acted During the War for the Union*. New York: Ballantine Books, 1991.

Patterson, Haywood and Earl Conrad. *Scottsboro Boy*. New York: Doubleday & Company, Inc., 1950.

Potkay, Adam and Sandra Burr (editors). *Black Atlantic Writers of the Eighteenth Century*. New York: St. Martin's Press, 1995.

Prince, Nancy. *The Narrative of Nancy Prince: A Black Woman's Odyssey Through Russia and Jamaica,* Introduction by Ron Walters. New York: Markus Wiener Publishing, 1990.

Rosengarten, Theodore (editor). *All God's Dangers—the Life of Nate Shaw*. New York: Alfred A. Knopf, 1975.

Washington, Mary Helen. *A Voice from the South—Anna Julia Cooper* (Introduction). New York: Oxford University Press, 1988.

Wilson, Sondra Kathryn. *Along This Way—The Autobiography of James Weldon Johnson* (Introduction). New York: Penguin Books, 1990.

Woodson, Carter (editor). *The Mind of the Negro as Reflected in Letters Written During the Crisis 1800–1860*. Washington, D.C.: The Association for the Study of Negro Life and History, 1926.

HERB BOYD is the coeditor with Robert Allen of *Brotherman—The Odyssey of Black Men in America* and the author of *Down the Glory Road* and *Black Panthers for Beginners.* An award-winning journalist, his articles have appeared in *Amsterdam News, Black Scholar, Code, Down Beat, Emerge, Metro Times (Detroit),* and *The Source.* He is the national editor of *The Black World Today,* an online publication, and he teaches at the College of New Rochelle and New York University.